Family Therapy

Concepts and Methods   ### Sixth Edition

Michael P. Nichols

Virginia Consortium Program in Clinical Psychology
College of William and Mary

with
Richard C. Schwartz

Director, The Center for Self Leadership, Oak Park, IL

Foreword by
Salvador Minuchin

Boston ● New York ● San Francisco
Mexico City ● Montreal ● Toronto ● London ● Madrid ● Munich ● Paris
Hong Kong ● Singapore ● Tokyo ● Cape Town ● Sydney

Series Editor: *Patricia Quinlin*
Editorial Assistant: *Annemarie Kennedy*
Production Administrator: *Anna Socrates*
Marketing Manager: *Taryn Wahlquist*
Editorial-Production Service: *Omegatype Typography, Inc.*
Manufacturing Buyer: *JoAnne Sweeney*
Composition and Prepress Buyer: *Linda Cox*
Cover Administrator: *Linda Knowles*
Interior Design: *Glenna Collett*
Photo Researcher: *Laurie Frankenthaler, F & F Associates*
Electronic Composition: *Omegatype Typography, Inc.*

Copyright © 2004, 2001, 1998, 1995, 1991, 1984 Pearson Education, Inc.

All rights reserved. No part of the material protected by this copyright notice may be reproduced or utilized in any form or by any means, electronic or mechanical, including photocopying, recording, or by
any information storage and retrieval system, without written permission from the copyright owner.

To obtain permission(s) to use material from this work, please submit a written request to Allyn
and Bacon, Permissions Department, 75 Arlington Street, Boston, MA 02116 or fax your request to
617-848-7320.

Between the time Website information is gathered and then published, it is not unusual for some sites to
have closed. Also, the transcription of URLs can result in typographical errors. The publisher would appreciate notification where these errors occur so that they may be corrected in subsequent editions.

Library of Congress Cataloging-in-Publication Data

Nichols, Michael P.
    Family therapy : concepts and methods / Michael P. Nichols, Richard C. Schwartz ;
foreword by Salvador Minuchin.—6th ed.
      p.   cm.
    Includes bibliographical references and index.
    ISBN 0-205-35905-1
    1. Family psychotherapy.   I. Schwartz, Richard C.   II. Title.

RC488.5.N53 2004
616.89'156—dc21

                             2002043768

Printed in the United States of America

10 9 8 7 6 5 4   [RRD-IN] 08 07 06 05 04

Contents

PART ONE ● The Context of Family Therapy

3 Early Models and Basic Techniques: Group Process and Communications Analysis   51

PART TWO ● The Classic Schools of Family Therapy

9 Psychoanalytic Family Therapy   227

10 Cognitive-Behavioral Family Therapy   252

PART THREE ● Recent Developments in Family Therapy

11 Family Therapy in the Twenty-First Century   288

12 Solution-Focused Therapy   312

16   **Advances in Family Therapy Research**   **395**

Howard A. Liddle and Cindy L. Rowe

Major Events in the History of Family Therapy

	Social and Political Context	Development of Family Therapy
1945	F.D.R. dies, Truman becomes president World War II ends in Europe (May 8) and the Pacific (August 14)	Bertalanffy presents general systems theory
1946		Bowen at Menninger Clinic Whitaker at Emory
1947		
1948	Truman reelected U.S. president State of Israel established	Whitaker begins conferences on schizophrenia
1949	Communist People's Republic of China established	
1950		Bateson begins work at Palo Alto V.A.
1951		Ruesch & Bateson: *Communication: The Social Matrix of Society* Bowen residential treatment of mothers and children Lidz at Yale
1952	Eisenhower elected U.S. president	Bateson receives Rockefeller grant to study communication in Palo Alto Wynne at NIMH
1953		
1954	Supreme Court rules school segregation unconstitutional	Bateson project research on schizophrenic communication Bowen at NIMH

	Social and Political Context	Development of Family Therapy
1955		
1956		"Toward a Theory of Schizophrenia" Bateson, Jackson, Haley, & Weakland
1957		Jackson: "The Question of Family Homeostasis" Ackerman opens the Family Mental Health Clinic of Jewish Family Services in New York Boszormenyi-Nagy opens Family Therapy Department at EPPI in Philadelphia
1958		Ackerman: *The Psychodynamics of Family Life*
1959	Castro becomes premier of Cuba	MRI founded by Don Jackson
1960	Kennedy elected U.S. president	
1961	Berlin Wall erected	Bell: *Family Group Therapy* *Family Process* founded by Ackerman and Jackson
1962	Cuban Missile Crisis	
1963	Kennedy assassinated	Haley: *Strategies of Psychotherapy*
1964	Johnson elected U.S. president Nobel Peace Prize awarded to Martin Luther King, Jr.	Satir: *Conjoint Family Therapy*
1965	Passage of Medicare Malcolm X assassinated	Family Institute founded by Nathan Ackerman (renamed the Ackerman Institute in 1971) Minuchin becomes director of Philadelphia Child Guidance Clinic
1966	Red Guards demonstrate in China	Brief Therapy Center at MRI begun under directorship of Richard Fisch

	Social and Political Context	*Development of Family Therapy*
1967	Six-Day War between Israel and Arab states Urban riots in Cleveland, Newark, and Detroit	Watzlawick et al.: *Pragmatics of Human Communication* Dicks: *Marital Tensions* Brief Therapy Center founded at MRI
1968	Nixon elected U.S. president Robert Kennedy and Martin Luther King, Jr., assassinated	Don Jackson dies
1969	Widespread demonstrations against war in Vietnam	
1970	Student protests against Vietnam War result in killing of four students at Kent State	
1971	Twenty-Sixth Amendment grants right to vote to eighteen-year-olds	Nathan Ackerman dies
1972	Nixon reelected U.S. president	Bateson: *Steps to an Ecology of Mind*
1973	Supreme Court rules that states may not prohibit abortion Energy crisis created by oil shortages	Center for Family Learning founded by Phil Guerin
1974	Nixon resigns	Minuchin: *Families and Family Therapy* Watzlawick et al.: *Change*
1975	Vietnam War ends	
1976	Carter elected U.S. president	Haley: *Problem-Solving Therapy*
1977		Family Institute of Westchester founded by Betty Carter
1978	Camp David Accords between Egypt and Israel	Hare-Mustin: "A Feminist Approach to Family Therapy" Selvini Palazzoli et al.: *Paradox and Counterparadox*
1979		Haley: *Leaving Home* Founding of Brief Therapy Center in Milwaukee

	Social and Political Context	*Development of Family Therapy*
1980	Reagan elected U.S. president	Milton Erickson dies (b. 1901) Gregory Bateson dies (b. 1904)
1981		Hoffman: *The Foundations of Family Therapy*
1982		Gilligan: *In a Different Voice* Fisch, Weakland, & Segal: *Tactics of Change* *The Family Therapy Networker* founded by Richard Simon
1983		
1984	Reagan reelected U.S. president	
1985		de Shazer: *Keys to Solution in Brief Therapy*
1986		
1987		Tom Andersen: "The Reflecting Team"
1988	George Bush elected U.S. president	Kerr & Bowen: *Family Evaluation* Virginia Satir dies (b. 1916)
1989		
1990	The Berlin Wall comes down	Murray Bowen dies (b. 1913) White & Epston: *Narrative Means to Therapeutic Ends*
1991	Persian Gulf War against Iraq	Harold Goolishian dies (b. 1924)
1992	Clinton elected U.S. president	Family Institute of New Jersey founded by Monica McGoldrick
1993		

	Social and Political Context	*Development of Family Therapy*
1994	Republicans win majority in Congress	David and Jill Scharf leave Washington School of Psychiatry to begin the International Institute of Object Relations Therapy
1995	United Nations World Conference on Women, Beijing	Carl Whitaker dies John Weakland dies Salvador Minuchin retires Family Studies Inc. renamed The Minuchin Center
1996	Clinton reelected U.S. president	Edwin Friedman dies (b. 1932)
1997		Michael Goldstein dies (b. 1930)
1998	President Clinton impeached by House of Representatives	
1999		Neil Jacobson dies (b. 1949) John Elderkin Bell dies (b. 1913)
2000	George W. Bush elected U.S. president	Millennium Conference, Toronto, Canada
2001	September 11 terrorist attacks	James Framo dies (b. 1927)

Foreword

In this volume Mike Nichols and Dick Schwartz tell the story of family therapy—and tell it very well. It's hard to imagine a more readable and informative guide to the field.

Born in the late 1950s, family therapy seemed to spring fully formed out of the heads of a group of seminal thinkers and practitioners. Over four decades later both theory and practice show the uncertainties and doubts that define maturity. But in the beginning—as the storytellers say—there was Gregory Bateson on the West Coast, a tall, clean-shaven, angular intellectual, who saw families as systems, carriers of ideas. On the East Coast was Nathan Ackerman, short, bearded, portly, the quintessential charismatic healer, who saw families as collections of individuals struggling to balance feelings, irrationalities, and desires. Bateson, the man of ideas, and Ackerman, the man of passion, complemented each other perfectly, the Don Quixote and Sancho Panza of the family systems revolution.

For all the diversity of the 1960s and 1970s that saw the new clinical practice called family therapy take a variety of names—systemic, strategic, structural, Bowenian, experiential—there was also a remarkable solidarity in the shared beliefs that defined the field. The pioneers were united in their rejection of psychoanalysis and embrace of systems thinking, however much they might have differed in their therapeutic techniques.

From the mid-1970s on, as family therapy succeeded and expanded, it was extended to encompass different client populations, with specific interventions for various special groups; with drug addiction, hospitalized psychiatric patients, the welfare population, family violence. . . . All posed their own challenges. Practitioners responded to this expanded family therapy with an array of new approaches, some of which even challenged the fundamental allegiance to systems thinking.

The challenge to systems theory (the official science of the time) took two forms. One was purely theoretical: a challenge to the assumption that systemic thinking was a universal framework, applicable to the organization and functioning of all human collectives. A major broadside came from feminists who questioned the absence of concepts of gender and power in systems thinking, and pointed to the distorting consequences of genderless theory when focusing on family violence. The other concerned the connection between theory and practice: a challenge to the imposition of systems theory as the basis for therapeutic practice. The very techniques that once defined the field were called into question. Inevitably, the field began to recover specificity and to reopen for examination its old taboos: the individual, intrapsychic life, emotions, biology, the past, and the particular place of the family in culture and society.

As is always characteristic of an official science, the field tried to preserve established concepts while a pragmatic attention to specific cases was demanding new and specific responses. As a result, today we have an official family therapy that claims direct descendence from Bateson, and a multitude of excellent practitioners doing sensitive and effective work that is frequently quite different from what systems theory prescribes. The result has often produced conflict and controversy. One such controversy centers on the power of the therapist.

From the perspective of today, with its many challenges to the therapist's authority and responsibility, the early family therapists were all "conductors"—forceful advocates for change, with committed positions about how that change should occur. Therapy was always a joint endeavor, but the responsibility for leading the way was the therapist's.

A number of schools of family therapy now seek to protect the family from the intrusiveness of the therapist. They are concerned that a forceful therapist's interventions might dominate and disempower families. Starting with the Milan Associates' concern with neutrality, this stance has reappeared recently in the constructivists who propose that therapy can only be a dialogue between two coconstructors of a story that is not rooted in any testable reality. (Academic fashion being what it is, the story of family therapy is sometimes told in such a way that the contributions of Ackerman, Bowen, Boszormenyi-Nagy, Fleck, Haley, Lidz, Minuchin, Satir, Whitaker, and Wynne, among others, disappear in favor of a straight and narrow line from Bateson to the Milan group to the narrative constructivists.) The contemporary constructivists' emphasis on language and meaning and their caution to restrain the power of the therapist was presented as radically new. But in some way this concern that therapists not intrude on patients is a throwback to the Freudian concept of the therapist as a tabula rasa onto whom patients projected transferential fantasies.

Lurking between the lines in many recent family therapy articles and books is a straw man, a power-hungry therapist who measures patients against the procrustean bed of his or her own biases and then stretches or diminishes them to fit. It is to save families from the

misguided intrusiveness of this kind of expertise that many of the new modalities of therapy have been constructed. But equating expertise with domination is false mathematics. Besides, control doesn't disappear from family therapy by changing the language from "intervene" to "cocreate." All that happens is that the influence of the therapist goes underground. Made invisible, it may remain unexamined.

Narrative constructivism is an interesting way of looking at human experience—emphasizing as it does one important aspect of the thinking, feeling, and acting beings we all are. But such a philosophical point of view imported unmodified into an interventionist enterprise like family therapy (which is, after all, about reducing suffering) constructs a fairy tale ogre: a therapist unaware of the effect of his interventions, operating from a power base invisible to him. The only way to avoid wielding such a sledgehammer, many now believe, is to intervene only as a coconstructor of stories—as though people were not only influenced by but were nothing but the stories they tell about themselves.

But there is another way of thinking about families and their problems, one held by a group who believes that therapy is a field of human transactions and that it is impossible for the therapist not to influence that field. Therapists in this group tend to be proximal, inventive, committed, interventive, and optimistic that their involvement with families will help family members solve their problems. Positioned in this group, I think that only a clear recognition of the idiosyncrasies of the individual therapist and the partialities of any therapeutic approach offers the possibility of true respect for each family's unique and individual character. I see the therapeutic process as an encounter between distinct interpersonal cultures. Real respect for clients and their integrity can allow therapists to be other than fearfully cautious, can encourage them to be direct and authentic—respectful and compassionate—but also at times honest and challenging. Such a therapist accepts that family members have their own experience and their own integrity, and also that they project their own wishes and fantasies into the therapeutic area, which then becomes a field of forces in which all the participants pull each other in different directions.

The advantage of this position is that the therapist, as a repository of multiple "transferences," experiences varying pulls of behavior. As the therapist, a discrete self, his or her own person, experiences those pulls, he or she responds by creating contexts in which family members encounter themselves in new positions that foster the exploration of novelty and alternative choices.

This conception of the therapist as an active knower—of himself or herself *and* of the different family members—is very different from the neutral therapist of the constructivists. But, of course, these two prototypes are entirely too simplified. Most practitioners fall somewhere between these two poles of neutrality and decisiveness.

The choice between action and interventionism, on the one hand, and meaning and conversation, on the other, is but one of the questions the field is grappling with today; there are many others. Are there useful models of human nature and of functional families, or must every situation be responded to de novo? Are the norms of human behavior and family function universal, or are they culturally constructed products of political and ideological constraint? How do we become experts? How do we know what we know? If we become ex-perts, are we creating the fields that we then discover? Can we influence people? Can we not influence them? How do we know that we are not simply agents of social control? How do we know that we are accomplishing anything at all? What right do we have to constrain diversity, imposing ways of being on others? Are questions better than statements?

These questions and the rich history and contemporary practice of family therapy are explored magnificently in *Family Therapy: Concepts and Methods*. It is a thorough and thoughtful, fair and balanced guide to the ideas and techniques that make family therapy such an exciting enterprise. Nichols and Schwartz have managed to be comprehensive without becoming tedious. Perhaps the secret is the engaging style of their writing, or perhaps it is how they avoid getting lost in abstraction while keeping a clear focus on clinical practice. In any case, this superb book has long set the standard of excellence as the best introduction and guide to the practice of family therapy.

Much has changed in the field, and this new edition brings readers right up-to-date, describing the latest approaches and continuing to offer insightful and balanced commentary. Without a doubt the definitive textbook of family therapy, this volume offers a wealth of information presented with refreshing clarity and a total absence of cant. It all adds up to an exciting, highly readable book. It is a fascinating journey. Enjoy it.

Salvador Minuchin, M.D.
Boston, Massachusetts

Preface

One thing that tends to get lost in academic discussions of family therapy is the feeling of accomplishment that comes from sitting down with an unhappy family and being able to help them. Beginning therapists are understandably anxious about how to proceed, and not sure they'll know how to be helpful. ("How do you get *all of them* to come in?") Veterans often speak in abstractions. They have opinions and discuss big issues—social constructionism, postmodernism, managed care, second-order cybernetics. While it's tempting to use this space to say Important Things, I prefer to be a little more personal. Treating troubled families has given me the deepest satisfaction imaginable, and I hope that the same is, or will be, true for you.

In this sixth edition of *Family Therapy: Concepts and Methods* we've tried to describe the full scope of family therapy—its rich history, the classic schools, the latest developments—but with increasing emphasis on practical issues. There are lots of changes in this edition: quite a few more case studies, new sections on home-based therapy, ethical issues in treating families, working with violent couples, community family therapy, spirituality, more up-to-date descriptions of the latest models, an expanded treatment of the cognitive-behavioral approach, a richer description of the research literature, an improved chapter on the dos and don'ts of integrating across models, and a more consistent emphasis on clinical technique throughout.

When you read about therapy it can be hard to see past the jargon and political packaging to the essential ideas and practices. So, in preparing this edition, we've traveled widely to visit and observe actual sessions of the leading practitioners. The result is a more pragmatic, clinical focus. We hope you like it.

So many people have contributed to my development as a family therapist and to the writing of this book that it is impossible to thank them all. But I would like to single out a few. To the people who taught me family therapy—Lyman Wynne, Murray Bowen, and Salvador Minuchin—thank you.

Some of the people who went out of their way to help us prepare this sixth edition were Frank Dattilio, David Greenan, Denise Miles, Melody Nichols, Eve Lipchik, Bill Pinsof, Kathy Weingarten, Vicki Dickerson, Jeff Zimmerman, Cloe Madanes, Jay Haley, and Salvador Minuchin. To paraphrase John, Paul, George, and Ringo, we get by with *a lot* of help from our friends—and we thank them one and all. We are especially grateful to Janice Wiggins, Patricia Quinlin, Annemarie Kennedy, and Allyn and Bacon for making a hard job easier.

I wish to express my gratitude to the reviewers of this text, whose comments have greatly enriched our work: Jerome Adams, University of Rhode Island; Chrystal C. Barranti, California State University, Sacramento; Maria Napoli, Arizona State University; and Judith A. Stang, Springfield College–Wilmington Campus.

Finally, I would like to thank my postgraduate instructors in family life: my wife, Melody, and my children, Sandy and Paul. In the brief span of thirty-six years Melody has seen me grow from a shy young man, totally ignorant of how to be a husband and father, to a shy middle-aged man, still bewildered and still trying. Sandy and Paul never cease to amaze me. My little red-haired girl (who can bench-press like a football player) is about to finish law school and embark on a career in environmental conservation. Proud of her? You bet I am! And my son Paul, to whom (masculine reticence being what it is) maybe I haven't always shown the depth of my love, has grown to young manhood true to himself, true to his friends, and true to his mother and me. If in my wildest dreams I had imagined children to love and be proud of, I wouldn't even have come close to anyone as fine as Sandy and Paul.

M. P. N.

●

Each of my three daughters graduates this spring—from college, high school, and junior high. The jolt of these transitions has my head spinning. My thoroughly mixed emotions include being proud of their growth but nostalgic for earlier days, concerned about their futures, and excited to watch them unfold.

Much as with my daughters, I have passionate and protective feelings for family therapy. The family therapy I grew up with is a distant memory. A very different field greets the new millennium and I feel the way my parents must have felt in the 1960s when they kept telling me that not everything had to be reinvented. Yet, no doubt like my parents, I am also intrigued by the new ideas and live vicariously through the adventures of those pursuing them.

I'll confess to still another parental emotion. I feel sorry for the beginning family therapy student. When I was smitten by the field in the early 1970s, things were simpler and students had fewer choices. There were a handful of models, and all you had to do was pick one and then idolize and impersonate its creator. Now there is so much more detail about different kinds of families, so many different, rapidly evolving approaches and perspectives, and few charismatic leaders to impersonate or clear-cut models to follow. The novice facing all these choices may, understandably, be daunted.

Yet, while all this diversity and change has increased the challenges we face, it also represents a welcome new approach to learning. There's less of the chauvinism of those earlier days and more openness both within the field and toward other disciplines. Perhaps it's good that we all have to work harder to grasp the complexity of the human condition.

As with previous editions, Mike and I have tried to provide a fair representation of the concepts and methods of the approaches we cover, but also to openly discuss our opinions of them, rather than pretending to be totally objective. This book therefore is a perspective on family therapy, not the truth about family therapy.

Like Mike, I've been blessed with more teachers than space allows me to mention. Special thanks are due, however, to Doug Sprenkle, Howard Liddle, Doug Breunlin, Betty Mac Kune-Karrer, Rich Simon, and Mary Jo Barrett. Finally, I thank my wife, Nancy, and my three graduating daughters—Jessie, Sarah, and Hali—for their sacrifice and support. Each time I step back and look at them, my heart fills with joy.

R. C. S.

The Foundations of Family Therapy

Leaving Home

There wasn't much information on the intake sheet. Just a name, Holly Roberts, the fact that she was a senior in college, and her presenting complaint: "trouble making decisions."

The first thing Holly said when she sat down was, "I'm not sure I need to be here. You probably have a lot of people who need help more than I do." Then she started to cry.

It was springtime. The tulips were up; the trees were turning light, leafy green; and purple clumps of lilacs perfumed the air. Life and all its possibilities stretched out before her, but Holly was naggingly, unaccountably depressed.

The decision Holly was having trouble making was what to do after graduation. The more she tried to figure it out, the less able she was to concentrate. She started sleeping late, missing classes. Finally, her roommate talked her into going to the Health Service. "I wouldn't have come," Holly said. "I can take care of my own problems."

I was into cathartic therapy back then. Most people have stories to tell and tears to shed. Some of the stories, I suspected, were drama-tized for sympathy and attention. We seem to give ourselves permission to cry only with some very acceptable excuse. Of all the human emotions we're ashamed of, feeling sorry for ourselves tops the list.

I didn't know what was behind Holly's depression, but I was sure I could help. I felt comfortable with depressed people. Ever since my senior year in high school, when my friend Alex died, I'd been a little depressed myself.

●

After Alex died, the rest of the summer was a dark blur. I cried a lot. And I got mad whenever anybody suggested that life goes on. Alex's minister said that his death wasn't a real tragedy, because now "Alex was with God in heaven." I wanted to scream, but I numbed myself instead. In the fall I went off to college, and, even though it seemed somehow disloyal to Alex, life did go on. I still cried from time to time, but with the tears came a painful discovery. My grief wasn't all for Alex. Yes, I loved him. Yes, I missed him. But his death also provided me the justification to cry about the everyday sorrows in my own life. Maybe grief is always like that. At the time it struck me as a betrayal. I was using Alex's death to feel sorry for myself.

●

What, I wondered, was making Holly so sad? In fact, Holly didn't have a dramatic story. Her feelings weren't focused. After those first moments in my office, she rarely cried. When she did, it was more an involuntary leakage than a sobbing release. She talked about the future and not knowing what she wanted to do with her life. She talked about not having a boyfriend—in fact, she rarely ever had any dates. She never said much about her family. If the truth be told, I wasn't much interested. Back then I thought home was the place you have to leave in order to grow up.

Holly was vulnerable and needed someone to lean on, but something made her hold back, as though she didn't feel safe, didn't quite trust me. It was frustrating. I wanted very badly to help her.

A month went by and Holly's depression got worse. I started seeing her three times a week, but we weren't getting anywhere. One Friday afternoon Holly was feeling so despondent that I didn't think she should go back to her dorm alone. I asked her instead to lie down on the couch in my office and, with her permission, I called her parents.

Mrs. Roberts answered the phone. I told her that I thought she and her husband should come to Rochester and meet with me and Holly to discuss the advisability of Holly taking a medical leave of absence and going home. Unsure as I was of my authority back then, I steeled myself for an argument. Mrs. Roberts surprised me by agreeing to come at once.

The first thing that struck me about Holly's parents was the disparity in their ages. Lena Roberts looked like a slightly older version of Holly; she couldn't have been much over thirty-five. Her husband looked sixty. It turned out

that he was Holly's stepfather. They had gotten married when Holly was sixteen.

Looking back, I don't remember much being said in that first meeting. Both parents were very concerned about Holly. "We'll do whatever you think best," Mrs. Roberts said. Mr. Morgan (Holly's stepfather) said they could arrange for a good psychiatrist "to help Holly over this crisis." But Holly said she didn't want to go home, and she said this with more energy than I'd heard from her in a long time. That was on Saturday. I suggested that there was no need to rush into a decision, so we arranged to meet again on Monday.

When Holly and her parents sat down in my office on Monday morning it was obvious that something had happened. Mrs. Roberts's eyes were red from crying. Holly glowered at her and looked away, her mouth tight and grim. Mr. Morgan turned to me. "We've been fighting all weekend. Holly heaps abuse on me, and when I try to respond, Lena takes her side. That's the way it's been since day one of this marriage."

The story that came out was one of those sad histories of jealousy and resentment that turn ordinary love into bitter, injured feelings and, all too often, tear families apart. Lena Roberts was thirty-four when she met Tom Morgan. He was a robust fifty-six. Apart from their ages, the second obvious difference between them was money. He was a successful stockbroker who'd retired to run a horse farm. She was waitressing to support herself and her daughter. It was a second marriage for both of them.

Lena looked to Tom to be the missing role model and source of discipline in Holly's life. Unfortunately, Lena couldn't accept the strict rules Tom felt invited to enforce. And so Tom became the wicked stepfather. He made the mistake of trying to take over and, when the predictable arguments ensued, Lena sided with her child. There were tears and midnight shouting matches. Twice Holly ran away to a friend's house for a few days. This triangle nearly proved Lena and Tom's undoing, but things calmed down when Holly left for college.

Holly expected to leave home and not look back. She would make new friends. She would study hard and choose a career. She would *never* depend on a man to support her. Unfortunately, she left home with a lot of unfinished business. She hated Tom for the way he picked on her and for the way he treated her mother. He was always demanding to know where her mother was going, who she was going with, and when she would be back. If her mother was the least little bit late, there would be a scene. Why did her mother put up with it?

Blaming Tom was simple and satisfying. But another set of feelings, harder to face, was eating at Holly. She hated her mother for marrying Tom and for letting him be so mean to her. What had her mother seen in him in the first place? Had she sold out for a big house and a fancy car? Holly didn't have an answer to these questions; she didn't even dare allow them into full awareness. Unfortunately, repression doesn't work like locking something away in a closet and forgetting about it. It takes a lot of energy to keep unwelcome emotions at bay.

Holly found excuses not to go home much during college. It didn't feel like her home anymore. She buried herself in her studies. But rage and bitterness gnawed at her, slowly sapping her strength until, in her senior year, facing an uncertain future, knowing only that she couldn't go home again, she gave in to hopelessness. No wonder she was depressed.

I found the whole story sad. Not knowing about family dynamics and never having lived in a stepfamily, I wondered why they couldn't just get along better. They had so little sympathy for each other. Why couldn't Holly accept her mother's right to find love a second time around? Why couldn't Tom respect the priority of his wife's relationship with her daughter? And why couldn't Holly's mother listen to her daughter's adolescent anger without getting so defensive?

That session with Holly and her parents was my first lesson in family therapy. Family members in therapy talk, not about actual experiences, but about reconstructed memories that resemble the original experiences only in certain ways. Holly's memories resembled her mother's memories very little, and her stepfather's not at all. In the gaps between their truths there was little room for reason and no desire to pursue it.

Although that meeting may not have been terribly productive, it certainly put Holly's unhappiness in perspective. No longer did I think of her as a tragic young woman, all alone in the world. She was that, of course, but she was also a daughter torn between running as far away as possible from a home she no longer felt part of and being afraid to leave her mother alone with a man she didn't trust. I think that's when I became a family therapist. To say that I didn't know much about families, much less about techniques for helping them reason together, would be an understatement. But family therapy isn't just a new set of techniques; it's a whole new approach to understanding human behavior—as fundamentally shaped by its social context.

The Myth of the Hero

Ours is a culture that celebrates the uniqueness of the individual and the search for an autonomous self. Holly's story could be told as a coming-of-age drama: a young person's struggle to break away from childhood and provincialism, to take hold of adulthood and promise and the future. If she fails, we're tempted to look inside the young adult, the failed hero.

While the unbounded individualism of the "hero" may be encouraged more for men than women, as a cultural ideal it casts its shadow on us all. Even if Holly cares about connection as much as autonomy, she may be judged by the prevailing image of accomplishment.

We were raised on the myth of the hero: the Lone Ranger, Robin Hood, Wonder Woman. When we got older we searched out real-life heroes: Eleanor Roosevelt, Martin Luther King, Jr., Nelson Mandela. These men and women stood for something. If only we could be a little more like these larger-than-life individuals who seem to rise above their circumstances.

Only later did some of us realize that the "circumstances" we wanted to rise above were part of the human condition—our inescapable connection to our families. The romantic image of the hero is based on the illusion that authentic selfhood can be achieved as a proud, autonomous individual. We do many things alone, including some of our most heroic acts, but we are defined and sustained by a network of human relationships. Our need to worship heroes is partly a need to rise above littleness and self-doubt, but perhaps equally a product of imagining a life unfettered by all those pesky relationships that somehow never quite go as we would wish.

When we do think about families, we often think of them in negative terms—as forces of dependency holding us back or as destructive elements in the lives of our patients. What catches our attention in families are differences and discord. The harmonies of family life—loyalty, tolerance, mutual aid and assistance—often slide by unnoticed, part of the taken-for-granted background of life. If we would be heroes, then we must have villains.

These days there's a lot of talk about "dysfunctional families." Unfortunately, some of this amounts to little more than parent bashing. We suffer because of what *they* did: Our mother's drinking, our father's brutishness or cold ways—these are the cause of our unhappiness. Perhaps this is an advance on stewing in guilt and shame, but it's a long way from understanding what really goes on in families.

One reason for blaming family sorrows on the personal failings of parents is that it's hard for the average person to see past individual personalities to the structural patterns that make them a family—a system of interconnected lives governed by strict but unspoken rules.

People feel controlled and helpless not because they are victims of parental folly and deceit, but because they don't understand the forces that hurl husbands and wives and parents and children together. Plagued by anxiety and depression, or merely troubled and uncertain, some people turn to psychotherapy for help and consolation. In the process, they turn away from the irritants that propel them into therapy. Chief among these aggravations are unhappy relationships—with friends and lovers *and* with the family. Our disorders are private ailments. When we retreat to the safety of a synthetic relationship, the last thing we want is to take our families with us. Is it any wonder, then, that when Freud ventured to explore the dark forces of the mind, he locked the family outside the consulting room?

Psychotherapeutic Sanctuary

Psychotherapy was once a private enterprise. The consulting room was a place of healing, yes, but it was equally a sanctuary, a refuge from a troubled and troubling world.

Buffeted about in love and work, unable to find comfort and solace elsewhere, adults came to therapy to find lost satisfaction and meaning. Parents, worried about their children's misbehavior, shyness, or lack of achievement, sent them for guidance and direction. In many ways psychotherapy displaced the family's role in solving the problems of everyday life.

It's tempting to look back on the days before family therapy and see those who insisted on segregating patients from their families as naive and wrongheaded, exponents of a fossilized view of mental disorder, according to which psychiatric maladies were firmly embedded in the heads of individuals. Considering that clinicians didn't begin treating whole families together until the mid 1950s, it's tempting to ask, "What took them so long?" In fact, there were good reasons for conducting psychotherapy in private.

The two most influential approaches to psychotherapy in the twentieth century, Freud's psychoanalysis and Rogers's client-centered therapy, were both predicated on the assumption that psychological problems arose from unhealthy interactions with others, and could best be alleviated in a private relationship between therapist and patient.

Freud's discoveries indicted the family, first as a breeding ground of childhood seduction and later as the agent of cultural repression. If people grow up a little bit neurotic—afraid of their own natural instincts—who should we blame but their parents?

Given that neurotic conflicts were spawned in the family, it seemed only natural to assume that the best way to undo the family's influence was to isolate relatives from treatment, to bar their contaminating influence from the psychoanalytic operating room.

Freud discovered that the less he revealed of himself, the more his patients reacted toward him as though he were a significant figure from their families. At first these *transference* reactions seemed a hindrance, but Freud soon realized that they provided an invaluable glimpse into the past. Thereafter, analyzing transference became the cornerstone of psychoanalytic treatment. This meant that since the analyst was interested in the patient's memories and fantasies, the family's presence would only obscure the subjective truth of the past. Freud wasn't interested in the living family; he was interested in the family-as-remembered, locked away in the unconscious.

By conducting treatment in private, Freud safeguarded patients' trust in the sanctity of the therapeutic relationship and thus maximized the likelihood that the patients would repeat, in relation to the analyst, the understandings and misunderstandings of early childhood.

●

Carl Rogers also believed that psychological problems stemmed from destructive early interactions. Each of us, Rogers said, is born with an innate tendency toward *self-actualization,* an idea that became the premise of all humanistic psychotherapies. Left to our own devices, we tend to follow our own best interests. Because we are curious and intelligent, we explore and learn; because we have strong bodies, we play and exercise; and because being with others brings us joy, we are outgoing, loving, and affectionate.

Unhappily, said Rogers, our healthy instinct toward actualization gets subverted by our craving for approval. We learn to do what we think others want, even though it may not be what's best for us.

Gradually, this conflict between self-fulfillment and need for approval leads to denial and distortion of our inner promptings—and even of the feelings that signal them. We swallow our anger, stifle our exuberance, and bury our lives under a mountain of expectations.

The therapy Rogers developed was designed to help patients uncover their real feelings and honest impulses. His image of the therapist was that of a midwife—passive, but supportive. The

*F*reud excluded the family from psychoanalysis to help patients feel safe to explore the full range of their thoughts and feelings.

Rogerian therapist didn't *do* anything for patients, but offered support to help them discover what needed to be done, primarily by providing *unconditional positive regard.* The therapist listened carefully and sympathetically, offering understanding, warmth, and respect. In the presence of such an accepting listener, patients gradually got in touch with their own feelings and inner promptings.

Like the psychoanalyst, the client-centered therapist maintained absolute privacy in the therapeutic relationship to avoid any possibility that patients' real feelings might be subverted to win approval. Only an objective outsider could be counted on to provide the unconditional acceptance to help patients rediscover their real selves. That's why family members had no place in the work of client-centered therapy.

Family versus Individual Therapy

As you can see, there were, and continue to be, valid reasons for conducting psychotherapy in a private and confidential relationship. But although a strong claim can be made for individual psychotherapy, equally strong claims can be made for family therapy.

Individual psychotherapy and family therapy each offer two things: an approach to treatment and a way of understanding human behavior. As approaches to treatment, both have their virtues. Individual therapy can provide the concentrated focus to help people face their fears and learn to become more fully themselves. Individual therapists have always recognized the importance of family life in shaping personality, but they assumed that these influences were internalized and that intrapsychic dynamics became the dominant forces controlling behavior. Treatment could and should, therefore, be directed at the person and his or her personal makeup. Family thera-

pists, on the other hand, believe that the dominant forces in our lives are located externally, in the family. Therapy based on this framework is directed at changing the organization of the family. When family organization is transformed, the life of every family member is altered accordingly.

This last point—that changing a family changes the life of each of its members—is important enough to elaborate. Family therapy isn't predicated merely on changing the individual patient in context. Family therapy exerts change on the entire family; therefore, improvement can be lasting because each family member is changed *and* continues to exert synchronous change on each other.

Almost any human difficulty can be treated with either individual or family therapy. But certain problems are especially suited to the family approach, among them problems with children (who must, regardless of what happens in therapy, return home to their parents), complaints about a marriage or other intimate relationship, family feuds, and symptoms that develop in an individual around the time of a major family transition.

If problems that arise around family transitions make a therapist think first about the role of the family, individual therapy may be especially useful when people identify something about themselves that they've tried in vain to change *and* their social environment seems to be stable. Thus, if a woman gets depressed during her first year at college, the therapist might wonder if her sadness is related to leaving home, and leaving her parents alone with each other. But if the same woman were to get depressed in her forties, during a long period of stability in her life, we might wonder if there's something about her approach to life that hasn't fulfilled her and is responsible for her unhappiness. Examining her life in private—away from troubled relationships—doesn't mean that she should believe she can fulfill herself in isolation from other people in her life.

The view of persons as separate entities, with families acting on them, is consistent with the way we experience ourselves. We recognize the influence of intimates—especially as obligation and constraint—but it's hard to see that we are embedded in a network of relationships, that we are part of something larger than ourselves.

Psychology and Social Context

Family therapy has flourished not only because of its proven clinical effectiveness, but also because we are rediscovering the interconnectedness that characterizes our human community. Ordinarily, the question of individual versus family therapy is posed as a technical one: Which approach works best with a given problem? But the choice also reflects a philosophical understanding of human nature. Although psychotherapy can succeed by focusing on either the psychology of the individual or the organization of the family, both perspectives—psychology and social context—are indispensable for a full understanding of people and their problems.

Family therapists teach us that the family is more than a collection of separate individuals; it is a system, an organic whole whose parts function in a way that transcends their separate characteristics. But even as members of family systems, we don't cease being individuals, with hearts, minds, and wills of our own. Although it isn't possible to understand people without taking into account their social context, notably the family, it is misleading to limit the focus to the surface of interactions—to social behavior divorced from inner experience.

Working with the whole system means not only considering all the members of the family but also the personal dimensions of their experience. Consider a father who smiles despite himself during a discussion of his son's delinquent behavior. Perhaps the smile reveals the father's secret pleasure at the boy's rebelling in a way the father is afraid to. Or take the case of a husband who complains that his wife won't let him do anything with his friends. The wife may indeed restrict him, but the fact that the husband surrenders without a fight suggests that he may be conflicted about having fun. Will negotiating with his wife clear up this man's inner anxieties about doing things on his own? Probably not. If he resolves his own inner constraints, will his wife suddenly start encouraging him to go out and have a good time? Not likely. These impasses, like most human problems, exist in the psychology of individuals *and* are played out in their interactions. The point is this: To provide effective and lasting psychological help, a therapist needs to understand and motivate individuals *and* influence their interactions.

The Power of Family Therapy

Family therapy was born in the 1950s, grew up in the 1960s, and came of age in the 1970s. The initial wave of enthusiasm for treating the family as a unit was followed by an increasing diversification of schools, each vying for a corner of the truth, and of the market for services.

Someday we may look back on the years from 1975 to 1985 as family therapy's golden age. Those years saw the full flowering of the most imaginative and vital approaches to treatment. It was a time full of enthusiasm and confidence. Family therapists may have had their differences about technique, but they shared a sense of optimism and common purpose. Since then several upheavals have shaken the field out of its zealousness and overconfidence. The pioneering models were challenged (on both clinical and sociocultural grounds) and their boundaries blurred; today fewer family therapists identify themselves exclusively with any one particular school. Even the distinction between individual and family therapy is less clear-cut, as more and more therapists practice both forms of treatment.

The dominating trends of the past decade were social constructionism (the idea that our experience is a function of the way we think about it), narrative therapy, integrative approaches, and a growing concern with social and political issues. The chapters that follow explore these and other developments. Here, we simply suggest that as you read about them you consider the possibility that, like all new developments, they have pluses and minuses.

Thinking in Lines, Thinking in Circles

Mental illness has traditionally been explained in linear terms, either medical or psychoanalytic. Both paradigms treat emotional distress as a symptom of an internal dysfunction with historical causes. The medical model assumes that clustering symptoms into syndromes will lead to biological solutions for psychological problems. In psychoanalytic explanations, symptoms are said to arise from conflict that originated in the patient's past. In both models, treatment focuses on the individual.

Linear explanations take the form of *A* causes *B*. This type of thinking works fine in some situations. If you're driving along and your car suddenly sputters to a stop, go ahead and look for a simple explanation. Maybe you're out of gas. If so, there's a simple solution. Human problems are usually a bit more complicated.

When things go wrong in relationships, most people generously give credit to the other person. Since we look out at the world from inside our own skins, we see other people's contributions to our mutual problems most clearly. Blaming is only natural. The illusion of unilateral influence tempts therapists too, especially when they hear only one side of a story. But

once they understand that reciprocity is the governing principle of relationship, therapists can help people get past thinking in terms of villains and victims.

Suppose, for example, that a father complains about his teenage son's behavior.

Father: It's my son. He's rude and defiant.
Therapist: Who taught him that?

Instead of accepting the father's perspective that he's a victim of his son's villainy, the therapist's provocative question invites him to look for patterns of mutual influence. The point isn't to shift blame from one person to another but to get away from blame altogether. As long as he sees the problem as his son's doing, the father has little choice but to hope that the boy will change. (Waiting for other people to change is like planning your future around winning the lottery.) Learning to think in circles rather than lines empowers the father to look at the half of the equation he can control.

The power of family therapy derives from bringing parents and children together to transform their interactions. Instead of isolating individuals from the emotional origins of their conflict, problems are addressed at their source.

What keeps people stuck is their great difficulty in seeing their own participation in the problems that plague them. With eyes fixed firmly on what those recalcitrant others are doing, it's hard for most people to see the patterns that bind them together. Part of a family therapist's job is to give them a wake-up call. When a husband complains that his wife nags, and the therapist asks him how he contributes to her doing that, the therapist is challenging the husband to see the hyphenated him-and-her that is the product of their interactions.

When Bob and Shirley came for help with marital problems, her complaint was that he never shared his feelings; his was that she always criticized him. This is the classic trading of complaints that keeps couples stuck as long as they fail to see the reciprocal pattern in which each partner provokes in the other precisely the behavior he or she cannot stand. So the therapist said to Bob, "If you were a frog, what would you be like if Shirley changed you into a prince?" When Bob countered that he doesn't talk with her more because she's so critical, it seemed to the couple like the same old argument. But the therapist saw this as the beginning of a change—Bob starting to speak up. One way to create an opening for change in rigid families is to support the blamed person and help bring him back into the fray.

When Shirley criticized Bob for complaining, he tried to retreat, but the therapist said, "No. Continue. You are still a frog."

Bob tried to shift responsibility back to Shirley. "Doesn't she have to kiss me first?" But the therapist said, "No, in real life that comes afterwards. You have to earn it."

In the opening of *Anna Karenina*, Tolstoy wrote: "All happy families resemble one another; each unhappy family is unhappy in its own way." Each unhappy family may be unhappy in its own way, but they all stumble over the same familiar challenges of family life. It's no secret what these challenges are—learning to live together, dealing with difficult relatives, chasing after children, coping with adolescence, and so on. What not everyone realizes, however, is that, once understood, a relatively small number of systems dynamics illuminate these challenges and enable families to move successfully through the predictable dilemmas of life. Like all healers, family therapists sometimes deal with bizarre and baffling cases, but much of their work is with ordinary human beings learning life's painful lessons. Their stories, and the stories of the men and women of family therapy who have undertaken to help them, make up the theme of this book.

—Recommended Readings

Nichols, M. P. 1987. *The self in the system.* New York: Brunner/Mazel.

Nichols, M. P. 1999. *Inside family therapy.* Boston: Allyn & Bacon.

—References

Minuchin, S. 1974. *Families and family therapy.* Cambridge, MA: Harvard University Press.
Selvini Palazzoli, M., Boscolo, L., Cecchin, G., and Prata, G. 1978. *Paradox and counterparadox.* New York: Jason Aronson.

Watzlawick, P., Beavin, J., and Jackson, D. 1967. *Pragmatics of human communication.* New York: Norton.

The Evolution of Family Therapy

A Revolutionary Shift in Perspective

In this chapter we will explore the antecedents and early years of family therapy. There are two fascinating stories here, one of personalities, one of ideas. You will read about the pioneers—iconoclasts and great originals who somehow broke the mold of seeing life and its problems as a function of individuals and their psychology. Make no mistake: The shift from an individual to a systemic perspective was a revolutionary one, providing those who grasped it with a powerful tool for understanding and resolving human problems.

The second story in the evolution of family therapy is one of ideas. The restless curiosity of the first family therapists led them to a variety of ingenious new ways to conceptualize the joys and sorrows of family life.

As you read this history, stay open to surprises. Be ready to reexamine easy assumptions—including the assumption that family therapy started out as a benevolent effort to support the institution of the family. The truth is, therapists first encountered the family system as an adversary.

The Undeclared War

Although we came to think of asylums as places of cruelty and detention, they were originally built to rescue the insane from persecution by their relatives, from being locked away and tortured in the family attic. Accordingly, except for purposes of footing the bill, hospital psychiatrists have long kept families at arm's length. In the 1950s, however, two puzzling developments forced therapists to recognize the family's power to influence the course of treatment.

Therapists began to notice that often when a patient got better, someone else in the family got worse, almost as though the family *needed* a symptomatic member. As in the game of hide-and-seek, it didn't seem to matter who was "It" as long as someone played the part. In one case, Don Jackson (1954) was treating a woman for depression. When she began to improve, her husband complained that her condition was getting worse. When she continued to improve, her husband lost his job. Eventually, when the woman was completely well, her husband killed himself. Apparently this man's stability was predicated on having a sick wife.

In another of Jackson's cases, a husband urged his wife to seek treatment for "frigidity." When, after several months of therapy, she grew sexually responsive, he became impotent.

—Case Study—

The other strange story of shifting disturbance was that patients frequently improved in the hospital only to get worse when they went home. In a bizarre case of Oedipus revisited, Salvador Minuchin treated a young man hospitalized multiple times for trying to scratch out his own eyes. The man functioned normally in Bellevue but returned to self-mutilation each time he went home. He could be sane, it seemed, only in an insane world.

It turned out that the young man was extremely close to his mother, a bond that grew even tighter during the seven years of his father's mysterious absence. The father was a compulsive gambler who disappeared shortly after being declared legally incompetent. The rumor was that the Mafia kidnapped him. When, just as mysteriously, the father returned, his son began his bizarre attempts at self-mutilation. Perhaps he wanted to blind himself so as not to see his obsession with his mother and hatred of his father.

But this family was neither ancient nor Greek, and Minuchin was more pragmatist than poet. So he challenged the father to protect his son by beginning to deal directly with his wife, and then challenged the man's demeaning attitude toward her, which made her feel all the more need of her son's proximity and protection. The therapy was a challenge to the family's structure and, in Bellevue, working with the psychiatric staff toward easing the young man back into the family, into harm's way.

Minuchin confronted the father, saying, "As a father of a child in danger, what you're doing isn't enough."

"What should I do?" asked the man.

"I don't know," Minuchin replied. "Ask your son." Then, for the first time in years, father and son began talking to each other. Just as they were about to run out of things to say, Dr. Minuchin commented to both parents: "In a strange way, he's telling you that he prefers to be treated like a young child. When he was in the hospital he was twenty-three. Now that he's returned home again, he's six."

What this case dramatized was how parents sometimes use their children—as a buffer to protect them from intimacy they can't handle—*and* how some children accept that role.

To the would-be Oedipus, Minuchin said, "You're scratching your eyes for your mother, so that she'll have something to worry about. You're a good boy. Good children sacrifice themselves for their parents."

What these and other cases like them demonstrated was that families are made of strange glue—they stretch but they never let go. Few blamed the family for outright malevolence, yet there was an invidious undercurrent to these observations. The official story of family therapy is one of respect for the institution of the family, but maybe none of us ever quite gets over the adolescent idea that families are the enemy of freedom.

The impact of a patient's improvement on the family isn't always negative. Fisher and Mendell (1958) reported a spread of positive changes from patients to other family members. However, whether the influence patients and their families have on each other is benign or malignant isn't the point. The point is, change in one person changes the system.

Small Group Dynamics

Those who first sought to understand and treat families found a ready parallel in small groups. Group dynamics are relevant to family therapy because group life is a complex blend of individual personalities and superordinate properties of the group.

During the 1920s social scientists began studying natural groups in society in the hope of learning to solve political problems by understanding social interaction in organized

The first people to practice family therapy turned to group therapy for a model.

groups. In 1920 the pioneering social psychologist William McDougall published *The Group Mind,* in which he described how a group's continuity depends on the group being an important idea in the minds of its members; on the need for boundaries and structures in which differentiation of function could occur; and on the importance of customs and habits, so that relationships could be fixed and defined. A more scientific approach to group dynamics was ushered in during the 1940s by Kurt Lewin, whose *field theory* (Lewin, 1951) guided a generation of researchers, industrial psychologists, group therapists, and agents of social change.

Drawing on the Gestalt school of perceptual psychology, Lewin developed the notion that the group is more than the sum of its parts. This transcendent property of groups has obvious relevance to family therapists, who must work not only with individuals but also with family systems—and with their famous resistance to change.

Analyzing what he called *quasi-stationary social equilibrium,* Lewin pointed out that change in group behavior requires "unfreezing." Only after something shakes up a group's beliefs will

its members be prepared to accept change. In individual therapy this process is initiated by the disquieting experiences that lead a person to seek help. Once an individual accepts the status of patient and meets with a therapist, that person has already begun to unfreeze old habits. When families come for treatment, it's a different matter.

Many family members aren't sufficiently unsettled by the symptomatic member's predicament to be prepared to change their own ways. Furthermore, family members bring their primary reference group with them, with all its traditions, mores, and habits. Consequently, more effort is required to unfreeze, or shake up, families before real change can take place. The need for unfreezing foreshadowed early family therapists' concern about disrupting family *homeostasis,* a notion that dominated family therapy for decades.

Wilfred Bion was another major figure in the study of group dynamics who emphasized the group as a whole, with its own dynamics and structure. According to Bion (1948), most groups become diverted from their primary tasks by engaging in patterns of *fight–flight, dependency,* or *pairing.* Bion's "basic assumptions" are easily extrapolated to family therapy: Some families are so afraid of conflict that they skirt around hot issues like a cat circling a snake. Others use therapy just to vent their spleen, preferring to fight endlessly rather than contemplate compromise, much less change. Dependency masquerades as therapy when overly active therapists subvert families' autonomy in the name of problem solving. Pairing is seen in families when one parent colludes with the children to mock and undermine the other parent.

The **process/content** distinction in group dynamics had a major impact on family treatment. Experienced therapists learn to attend as much to *how* families talk as to the content of their discussions. For example, a mother might tell her daughter that she shouldn't play with Barbie dolls because she shouldn't aspire to an image of bubble-headed beauty. The *content* of the mother's message is: Respect yourself as a person, not as an ornament. But if the mother expresses her point of view by disparaging the daughter's feelings, then the *process* of her message would be: Your feelings don't count.

Unfortunately, the content of some discussions is so compelling that therapists get sidetracked from the process. Suppose, for example, that a therapist invites a teenager to talk with his mother about wanting to drop out of school. Say that the boy mumbles something about school being stupid, and his mother responds with a lecture about the need for an education. A therapist who gets drawn in to support the mother's position may be making a serious mistake. In terms of content, the mother might be right, a high school diploma does come in handy. But maybe it's more important at the moment to help the boy learn to speak up for himself—and to help his mother learn to listen.

Role theory, explored in the literatures of psychoanalysis and group dynamics, had particularly important applications to the study of families. The expectations that roles provide bring regularity to complex social situations.

We often describe family members in terms of a single role (wife or husband), but we need to remember that a wife may also be a mother, a friend, a daughter, and a career person. Even roles that aren't currently being performed are potential and therefore important. When members of unhappy families get bogged down in few and rigid roles, they develop interpersonal arthritis, a disease that leads to family rigidity and the atrophy of unused life.

While a narrowing of roles shrinks the possibilities of group (and family) life, group members required to play too many roles are subject to overload (Sherif, 1948). Among the potential roles in a family, for example, are parent, housekeeper, breadwinner, cook, and chauffeur. These roles can be divided—one partner is the breadwinner, the other cooks and cleans—or shared—both work outside the home and divide the other chores. But one partner can be caught in a role conflict if she's forced to choose between staying late for a staff meeting and going home to cook dinner and drive the kids to soccer practice—because, even though she has a partner, he doesn't play those roles.

Roles tend to be stereotyped in most groups and so there are characteristic behavior patterns of group members. Virginia Satir (1972) described family roles such as "the placator" or "the disagreeable one" in her book *Peoplemaking.* You may realize that you played a fairly predictable role growing up in your family. Perhaps you were "the helpful child," "the quiet one," "the comedian," "the counselor," "the rebel," or "the successful child." The trouble is, such roles, once learned, can be hard to put aside. Dutifully doing what you're told and patiently waiting for recognition may work for "the helpful child," but it may not work in a professional career, where more assertive action is sometimes called for.

One thing that makes role theory so useful in understanding families is that roles tend to be reciprocal and complementary. Say, for example, that a woman is slightly more anxious to spend time with her boyfriend than he is. Maybe, left to his own devices, he'd call twice a week. But if she calls three times a week, he may never get around to picking up the phone. If their relationship progresses and this pattern is played out, she may always be the pursuer and he the distancer. Or take the case of two parents, both of whom like their children to behave at the dinner table. The father has a slightly shorter fuse—he tells them to quiet down ten seconds after they start getting rowdy, whereas his wife would wait half a minute. But if he always speaks up first, she'll never get a chance. Eventually these parents may become polarized into complementary roles of strictness and leniency. What makes such reciprocity resistant to change is that the roles reinforce each other—and each person waits for the other to change.

Psychoanalytic group therapists regarded the group as a re-creation of the family, with the therapist as a parent figure and group members as siblings. Thus, ironically, analytic group therapy, which became one of the prototypes for family treatment, began by treating the group as an ersatz family. Analytic groups were designed to be frustratingly unstructured to arouse latent unconscious conflicts and revive problems from the original family group. Group members' basic motives were considered to be conflicting combinations of love and hate, pain and pleasure, and strictures of the superego versus demands of primitive impulses. Notice that the emphasis was on the individual, rather than on the group as a whole.

In the group dynamics approach, developed by Foulkes, Bion, Ezriel, and Anthony in Great Britain, the focus shifted from individuals to the group itself, seen as a transcendent entity with its own inherent laws. These therapists studied group interactions not only for what they revealed about individual personalities, but also to discover themes or dynamics common to all group members. This *group process* was consid-

ered a fundamental characteristic of social interaction and a major vehicle for change.

Another departure from psychoanalytic group therapy was the experiential model. Experiential group therapy, stimulated by existential psychiatrists Ludwig Binswanger, Medard Boss, and Rollo May in Europe and by Carl Rogers, Carl Whitaker, and Thomas Malone in the United States, emphasized deep personal involvement with patients as opposed to dissection of people as objects. Phenomenology took the place of analysis, and immediate experience, especially emotional experience, was seen as the royal road to personal growth.

Moreno's psychodrama, in which patients act out their conflicts instead of discussing them, was one of the earliest approaches to group treatment (Moreno, 1945). Psychodramas are dramatic enactments from the lives of participants, using techniques to stimulate emotional expression and clarify conflicts. Because the focus is on interpersonal action, psychodrama is a direct and powerful means of exploring relationships and resolving family problems. Although psychodrama remained tangential to the mainstream of group therapy, Moreno's role-playing techniques were widely adopted by group leaders and family therapists.

Fritz Perls's Gestalt therapy aims to enhance awareness to increase spontaneity, creativity, and personal responsibility. Although frequently used in groups, Gestalt therapy discourages group members from interacting while one person at a time works with the therapist. Although more widely used in individual than in group or family treatment, Gestalt techniques have been borrowed by encounter group leaders and some family therapists to stimulate emotional interaction (e.g., Kempler, 1974; Schwartz, 1995).

Given the extensive and diverse procedures for exploring interpersonal relationships developed by group therapists, it was natural that some family therapists would apply group treatment models to working with families. It was a short step from observing a patient's re-actions to other members of a group—some of whom might be similar to siblings or parents—to observing interactions in real families. What are families, after all, but collective groups with various subgroups?

From a technical viewpoint, group and family therapies are similar: Both involve several people. Both are complex and amorphous, more like everyday social reality than individual therapy. In groups and families each patient must react to a number of people, not just to the therapist, and therapeutic use of this interaction is the definitive mechanism of change in both settings. Consequently, many group and family therapists endeavor to remain relatively inactive and decentralized so that patients in the room will relate to each other.

In individual treatment the therapist is a safe but artificial confidant. Patients expect therapists to be understanding and accepting, an audience of one friendly person. Not so with groups and families. In both, the situation is more natural, more threatening perhaps, but also more like everyday experience. Transfer to life outside the consulting room is therefore more direct.

On closer examination, however, we can see that the differences between families and groups are so significant that the group therapy model has only limited applicability to family treatment. Family members have a long history and—more important—a future together. Revealing yourself to strangers is safer than exposing yourself to members of your own family. In fact serious harm can be done by therapists who are so naive as to push family members to always be "completely honest and open" with each other. Once blurted out, there's no taking back rash disclosures that might better have remained private—the affair, long since over, or the admission that a woman *does* care more about her career than about her children. Continuity, commitment, and shared distortions all mean that treatment for families has to differ from therapy for groups.

In one of the few small group studies using families, Strodtbeck (1954) tested a variety of propositions derived from groups of strangers and found major differences, which he ascribed to the enduring relationship of family members. Strodtbeck (1958) later substantiated the opinion that family interactions, unlike those in ad hoc groups, can be understood only in terms of the history of the family group.

Therapy groups are designed to provide an atmosphere of warmth and support. This feeling of safety among sympathetic strangers cannot be part of family therapy, for instead of separating treatment from a stressful environment, the stressful environment is brought into treatment. Furthermore, in group therapy, patients can have equal power and status, whereas democratic equality isn't appropriate in families. Someone has to be in charge. Furthermore, the official patient in the family is likely to feel isolated and stigmatized. After all, he or she is "the problem." The sense of protection in being part of a therapeutic group of strangers, who won't have to be faced across the dinner table, doesn't exist in family therapy, where it *isn't* always safe to speak openly.

Although group therapy was used as a model for family therapy by some early practitioners, only the process/content distinction and role theory had any lasting impact on the mainstream of family therapy. One application of group methods that has persisted in family therapy are couples groups, and we will examine this form of treatment in later chapters.

The Child Guidance Movement

It was Freud who introduced the idea that psychological disorders were the consequence of unsolved problems of childhood. Alfred Adler was the first of Freud's followers to pursue the implication that treating the growing child might be the most effective way to prevent adult neuroses. To that end Adler organized child guidance clinics in Vienna, where children, families, and teachers were counseled. Adler offered encouragement and support in an atmosphere of optimism and confidence. His technique helped alleviate children's feelings of *inferiority* so they could work out a healthy *lifestyle*, achieving competence and success through *social usefulness*.

In 1909 the psychiatrist William Healy founded the Juvenile Psychopathic Institute (now known as the Institute for Juvenile Research) in Chicago, a forerunner among child guidance clinics. In 1917 Healy moved to Boston and there established the Judge Baker Guidance Center, devoted to evaluation and treatment of delinquent children.

When the child guidance movement expanded in the 1920s, under a grant from the Commonwealth Fund (Ginsburg, 1955), Rudolph Dreikurs, one of Adler's students, was one of its most effective proponents. In 1924 the American Orthopsychiatric Association was organized to work toward the prevention of emotional disorders in children. Although child guidance clinics remained few in number until after World War II, they now exist in every city in the United States, providing a setting for the treatment of childhood psychological problems and of the complex social and family forces contributing to these problems. Treatment was carried out by psychiatrist–psychologist–social worker teams, who focused much of their attention on the child's family environment.

Gradually, child guidance workers concluded that the real problem wasn't the obvious one, the child's symptoms, but rather the tensions in the family that were the source of those symptoms. At first there was a tendency to blame the parents, especially mothers.

The chief cause of childhood psychological problems, according to David Levy (1943), was *maternal overprotectiveness*. Mothers who had themselves been deprived of love while growing up became overprotective of their children. Some were domineering, others overindulgent. Children of domineering mothers were submissive at home but had difficulty making friends; children with indulgent mothers were disobedient at home but well-behaved at school.

During this period, Frieda Fromm-Reichmann (1948) coined one of the most damning phrases in the history of psychiatry, the **schizophrenogenic mother**. These domineering, aggressive, rejecting, and insecure women, especially when they were married to inadequate, passive, and indifferent men, were thought to provide the pathological parenting that produces schizophrenia. Adelaide Johnson's description of the transmission of *superego lacunae* was another example of how parents were blamed for causing their children's problems (Johnson & Szurek, 1954). According to Johnson, antisocial behavior in delinquents and psychopaths was due to defects in their superegos passed on to them by their parents.

The tendency to blame parents, especially mothers, for problems in the family was an evolutionary misdirection that continues to haunt the field. Nevertheless, by paying attention to what went on between parents and children, Levy, Fromm-Reichmann, and Johnson helped pave the way for family therapy.

Although the importance of the family was recognized, mothers and children were still treated separately, and discussion between therapists was discouraged on the grounds that it might compromise the individual therapeutic relationships. The usual arrangement was for a psychiatrist to treat the child while a social worker saw the mother. Counseling the mother was secondary to the primary goal of treating the child. In this model, the family was viewed as an extension of the child, rather than the other way around.

Eventually, the emphasis in the child guidance movement changed from seeing parents as noxious agents to the view that pathology was inherent in the relationships among patients, parents, and significant others. This shift had profound consequences. No longer was psychopathology located within individuals; no longer were parents villains and patients victims. Now their interaction was seen as the problem.

John Bowlby's work at the Tavistock Clinic exemplified the transition from an individual to a family approach. Bowlby (1949) was treating a child and making slow progress. Feeling frustrated, he decided to see the child and his parents together for one session. During the first half of this two-hour session, the child and parents took turns complaining, each blaming the other. During the second half of the session, Bowlby interpreted to each of them what he thought their contributions to the problem were. Eventually, by working together, all three members of the family developed some sympathy for each other's point of view.

Although he was intrigued by the possibilities of these conjoint interviews, Bowlby remained wedded to the one-to-one format. Family meetings might be a useful catalyst, Bowlby believed, but only as an adjunct to the *real* treatment, individual psychoanalytic therapy.

What Bowlby began as an experiment, Nathan Ackerman saw to fruition—family therapy as the primary form of treatment in child guidance clinics. As early as 1938, Ackerman suggested the value of viewing the family as a whole entity when dealing with disturbance in any of its members (Ackerman, 1938). Subsequently he recommended studying the family as a means of understanding the child—instead of the other way around (Ackerman & Sobel, 1950). Once he saw the need to understand the family in order to diagnose problems, Ackerman soon took the next step—family treatment. Before we get to that, however, let us examine parallel developments in social work and research on schizophrenia that led to the birth of family therapy.

The Influence of Social Work

No history of family therapy would be complete without mentioning the enormous contribution of social workers and their tradition of public service. Since the beginning of the profession social workers have been concerned with the family, both as the critical social unit and as the focus of intervention (Ackerman, Beatman, & Sherman, 1961). Indeed, the core paradigm of social work—treating the person-in-the-environment—anticipated family therapy's ecological approach long before systems theory was introduced.

The field of social work grew out of the charity movements in Great Britain and the United States in the late nineteenth century. Then, as now, social workers were dedicated to improving the condition of society's poor and underprivileged. In addition to ministering to basic needs for food, clothing, and shelter, social workers tried to relieve emotional distress in their client families and to redress the social forces responsible for extremes of poverty and privilege.

The *friendly visitor* was a caseworker who visited clients in their homes to assess their needs and offer help. By bringing helpers out of their offices and into the homes of their clients, these visits broke down the artificiality of the doctor–patient model that prevailed for so long. (Family therapists these days are relearning the value of getting out of the office and meeting clients where they live.)

Family casework was the most important focus of early social work training. In fact, the first course taught by the original school of social work in the United States was "The Treatment of Needy Families in Their Own Homes" (Siporin, 1980). Friendly visitors were taught the importance of interviewing both parents at the same time to get a complete and accurate picture of a family's problems—long before traditional mental health workers began experimenting with conjoint family sessions.

These turn-of-the-century caseworkers were well aware of something it took psychiatry fifty more years to discover—that families must be considered as units. Mary Richmond (1917), in her classic text, *Social Diagnosis,* prescribed treatment of "the whole family" and warned against isolating family members from their natural context. Richmond's concept of *family cohesion* had a strikingly modern ring, anticipating as it did later work on role theory, group dynamics, and, of course, structural family theory. According to Richmond, the degree of emotional bonding between family members was critical to their ability to survive and flourish.

Richmond anticipated developments that family therapy became concerned with in the 1980s by viewing families as systems within systems. As Bardhill and Saunders (1988) pointed out,

> She recognized that families are not isolated wholes (closed systems), but exist in a particular social context, which interactively influences and is influenced by their functioning (i.e., they are open). She graphically depicted this situation using a set of concentric circles to represent various systemic levels from the individual to the cultural. Her approach to practice was to consider the potential effect of all interventions on every systemic level, and to understand and to use the reciprocal interaction of the systemic hierarchy for therapeutic purposes. She truly took a systemic view of human distress. (p. 319)

When the family therapy movement was launched, social workers were among the most numerous and important contributors. Among the leaders who came into family therapy through social work training are Virginia Satir, Ray Bardhill, Peggy Papp, Lynn Hoffman, Froma Walsh, Insoo Berg, Jay Lappin, Richard Stuart, Harry Aponte, Michael White, Doug Breunlin, Olga Silverstein, Lois Braverman, Steve de Shazer, Peggy Penn, Betty Carter, Braulio Montalvo, and Monica McGoldrick. (In-cidentally, even starting such a list is difficult because unless it went on for pages it would have to omit a host of important names.)

Research on Family Dynamics and the Etiology of Schizophrenia

Families with schizophrenic members proved to be an especially fertile area for research because their strange patterns of interaction were so dramatic. However, the fact that family therapy emerged from research on schizophrenia led to an overly optimistic hope that family therapy might be the way to cure this baffling form of madness. Moreover, because abnormal families are so resistant to change, early family therapists tended to exaggerate the homeostatic properties of family life.

Family therapists didn't discover the role of the family in schizophrenia but, by actually observing families interacting, they witnessed patterns that their predecessors had only speculated about. Family influences on schizophrenia had been recognized at least as early as Freud's famous account (1911) of Dr. Schreber. In this first psychoanalytic formulation of psychosis, Freud discussed psychological factors in paranoia and schizophrenia, and also suggested how the patient's bizarre relationship with his father played a role in his fantastic delusions.

Harry Stack Sullivan focused on interpersonal relations in his brilliant work with schizophrenics. Beginning in 1927, he emphasized the importance of the "hospital family"—physicians, nurses, and aides—as a benevolent substitute for the patient's real family. Sullivan did not, however, take his ideas a step further and directly involve families in treatment. Frieda Fromm-Reichmann also believed that the family played a part in the dynamics of schizophrenia and considered the hospital family crucial in the resolution of schizophrenic episodes. Although these interpersonal psychiatrists recognized the importance of family life in schizophrenia, they continued to treat the family as a pathogenic environment from which patients must be removed.

In the 1940s and 1950s, research on the link between family life and schizophrenia led to the pioneering work of the first family therapists.

Gregory Bateson—Palo Alto

One of the groups with the strongest claim to originating family therapy was Gregory Bateson's schizophrenia project in Palo Alto, California. A scientist in the classic mold, Bateson did research on animal behavior, learning theory, evolution, and ecology, as well as in hospital psychiatry. He worked with Margaret Mead in Bali and New Guinea; then, becoming interested in cybernetics, he wrote *Naven* and worked on synthesizing cybernetic ideas with anthropological data.[1] He entered the psychiatric field when, together with Jurgen Ruesch at the Langley Porter Clinic, he wrote *Communication: The Social Matrix of Psychiatry.* In 1962 Bateson shifted to studying communication among animals and from 1963 until his death in 1980 worked at the Oceanographic Institute in Hawaii.

The Palo Alto project began in the fall of 1952 when Bateson received a grant from the Rockefeller Foundation to study the nature of communication in terms of levels. All communications, Bateson (1951) had written, have two different levels or functions—*report* and *command.* Every message has a stated content, as, for instance, "Wash your hands, it's time for dinner"; but in addition, the message carries

how it is to be taken. In this case the second message is that the speaker is in charge. This second message—*metacommunication*—is covert and often goes unnoticed. If a wife scolds her husband for running the dishwasher when it's only half full, and he says OK but turns around and does exactly the same thing two days later, she may be annoyed that he doesn't listen to her. She means the message. But maybe he didn't like the metamessage. Maybe he doesn't like her telling him what to do as though she were his mother.

Bateson was joined in 1953 by Jay Haley and John Weakland. Haley was primarily interested in social and psychological analysis of fantasy; Weakland was a chemical engineer who'd become interested in cultural anthropology. Later that same year a psychiatrist, William Fry, joined them; his major interest was the study of humor. This group of eclectic talents and catholic interests studied otters at play, the training of guide dogs, the meaning and uses of humor, the social and psychological significance of popular movies, and the utterances of schizophrenic patients. Bateson gave the project members free rein; but although they investigated many kinds of complex human and animal behaviors, all their studies dealt with possible conflicts between messages and qualifying messages.

In 1954 Bateson received a two-year grant from the Macy Foundation to study schizophrenic communication. Shortly thereafter the group was joined by Don Jackson, a brilliant psychiatrist who served as clinical consultant and supervisor of psychotherapy.

The group's interests turned to developing a communication theory that might explain the origin and nature of schizophrenic behavior, particularly in the context of families. Worth noting, however, is that in the early days of the project none of them thought of actually observing schizophrenics and their families.

Bateson and his colleagues hypothesized that family stability is achieved by feedback that

---

1. Norbert Wiener (1948) coined the term *cybernetics* for the emerging body of knowledge about how feedback controls information-processing systems. Applied to families, the cybernetic metaphor focused attention on how families become stuck in repetitive loops of unproductive behavior.

regulates the behavior of the family and its members. Whenever the family system is threatened—that is, disturbed—it endeavors to maintain stability or **homeostasis.** Thus, apparently puzzling behavior might become understandable if it were perceived as a homeostatic mechanism. For example, if whenever two parents argue one of the children exhibits symptomatic behavior, the symptoms may be a way to interrupt the fighting by uniting the parents in concern. Thus symptomatic behavior serves the cybernetic function of preserving the family's equilibrium. Unhappily, in the process, one of the family members may have to assume the role of "identified patient."

Speculating that schizophrenia might be a result of family interaction, Bateson's group tried to identify sequences of exchange that might induce symptomatology. Once they agreed that schizophrenic communication must be a product of what was learned inside the family, the group looked for circumstances that could lead to such confused and confusing patterns of speech.

In 1956 Bateson and his colleagues published their famous report, "Toward a Theory of Schizophrenia," in which they introduced the concept of the **double bind.** They assumed that psychotic behavior might make sense in the context of pathological family communication. Patients weren't crazy in some autonomous way; they were an understandable extension of a crazy family environment. Consider someone in an important relationship where escape isn't feasible and response is necessary; if he or she receives two related but contradictory messages on different levels, but finds it difficult to detect or comment on the inconsistency (Bateson, Jackson, Haley, & Weakland, 1956), then that person is in a double bind.

Because this difficult concept is often misused as a synonym for paradox or simply contradictory messages, it's worth reviewing each feature of the double bind as the authors listed them. The double bind has six characteristics:

1. Two or more persons in an important relationship.
2. Repeated experience.
3. A primary negative injunction, such as "Don't do X or I will punish you."
4. A second injunction at a more abstract level conflicting with the first, also enforced by punishment or perceived threat.
5. A tertiary negative injunction prohibiting escape and demanding a response. Without this restriction the "victim" won't feel bound.
6. Finally, the complete set of ingredients is no longer necessary once the victim is conditioned to perceive the world in terms of double binds; any part of the sequence becomes sufficient to trigger panic or rage.

Most examples of double binds in the literature are inadequate because they don't include all the critical features. Robin Skynner, for instance, cited (1976): "Boys must stand up for themselves and not be sissies"; but "Don't be rough . . . don't be rude to your mother." Confusing? Yes. Conflict? Maybe. But these two messages don't constitute a double bind; they're merely a contradiction. Faced with two such statements, a child is free to obey either one, alternate, or even complain about the contradiction. This and many similar examples neglect the specification that the two messages are conveyed on different levels.

A better example is the one given in the original article by Bateson, Jackson, Haley, and Weakland (1956). A young man recovering in the hospital from a schizophrenic episode was visited by his mother. When he put his arm around her, she stiffened. But when he withdrew, she asked, "Don't you love me anymore?" He blushed, and she said, "Dear, you must not be so easily embarrassed and afraid of your feelings." Following this exchange, the patient became upset; after the visit was over he assaulted an aide and had to be put in seclusion.

Notice that all six features of the double bind were present in this exchange, and also that the young man was obviously caught. There is no bind if the subject is not bound. The concept is interactional.

Another example of a double bind would be a teacher who urges his students to participate in class but gets impatient if one of them actually interrupts with a question or comment. Then a baffling thing happens. For some strange reason that scientists have yet to decipher, students tend not to speak up in classes where their comments are dismissed or ridiculed. When the professor finally does get around to asking for questions and no one responds, he gets angry. ("Students are so passive!") If any of the students has the temerity to comment on the professor's lack of receptivity, he'll probably get even angrier. Thus the students will be punished for accurately perceiving that the teacher really wants only his own ideas to be heard and admired. (This example is, of course, purely fictitious.)

We're all caught in occasional double binds, but the schizophrenic has to deal with them continually—and the effect is maddening. Unable to comment on the dilemma, the schizophrenic responds defensively, perhaps by being concrete and literal, perhaps by speaking in disguised answers or metaphors. Eventually the schizophrenic, like the paranoid, may come to assume that behind every statement is a concealed meaning.

The discovery that schizophrenic symptoms made sense in the context of some families may have been a scientific advance, but it had moral and political overtones. Not only did these investigators see themselves as avenging knights bent on rescuing "identified patients" by slaying family dragons, they were also crusaders in a holy war against the psychiatric establishment. Outnumbered and surrounded by hostile critics, the champions of family therapy challenged the orthodox assumption that schizophrenia was a biological disease. Psychological

healers everywhere cheered. Unfortunately, they were wrong.

The observation that schizophrenic behavior seems to *fit* in some families doesn't mean that families *cause* schizophrenia. In logic, this kind of inference is called "Jumping to Conclusions." Sadly, families of schizophrenic members suffered for years under the assumption that they were to blame for the tragedy of their children's psychoses.

After the publication of the double-bind paper, members of the project began interviewing parents together with their schizophrenic offspring. These meetings were exploratory rather than therapeutic, but they did represent a major advance: actually observing family interactions rather than merely speculating about them. These conjoint family sessions helped launch the family therapy movement, and we'll see what they revealed in the next section.

All the discoveries of the Bateson group were united on one point, the centrality of communication to the organization of families. What makes families pathological, they concluded, was pathological communication. What they disagreed about was the underlying motivation for the obscurant messages they observed. Haley believed that a covert struggle for interpersonal control was the motivating force for double binding; Bateson and Weakland thought it was the urge to conceal unacceptable feelings. But they all agreed that even unhealthy behavior may be adaptive in the family context. The two great discoveries of this talented team's output were: (1) multiple levels of communication, and (2) that destructive patterns of relationship are maintained by self-regulating interactions of the family group.

Theodore Lidz—Yale

Theodore Lidz's investigations of the family dynamics of schizophrenia focused on two traditional psychoanalytic concerns: rigid family roles and faulty parental models of identification.

Lidz challenged the then current belief that maternal rejection was the major distinguishing feature of schizophrenic families and, in one of his most notable findings, observed that frequently the more destructive influence was that of the fathers. In a landmark paper entitled "Intrafamilial Environment of the Schizophrenic Patient, I: The Father" (Lidz, Cornelison, Fleck, & Terry, 1957a), Lidz and his colleagues described five patterns of pathological fathering in families of schizophrenics.

The first group was domineering and rigidly authoritarian, constantly in conflict with their wives. The second group was hostile toward their children rather than toward their wives. These men rivaled their children for the mother's attention and affection, behaving more like a jealous sibling than a parent. The third group of fathers exhibited frankly paranoid grandiosity. They were aloof and distant. The fourth group of fathers were failures in life and nonentities in their homes. Children in these families grew up as though fatherless. The fifth group of fathers were passive and submissive men who acted more like children than parents. They were pleasant, almost motherly, but offered weak models of identification. These submissive fathers failed to counterbalance the domineering influence of their wives. Lidz concluded that it might be better to grow up without a father than with one who is too aloof or weak to serve as a healthy model for identification.

After describing some of the pathological characteristics of fathers in schizophrenic families, Lidz turned his attention to defects in the marital relationships. The theme underlying his findings was an absence of *role reciprocity.* In a successful relationship, it's not enough to fulfill your own role—to be an effective person; it's also necessary to balance your role with your partner's—to be an effective pair. In the schizophrenic families Lidz studied, the spouses were inadequate to fulfill their own role and disinclined to support that of their mate.

Lidz found disturbed marital relationships in all the cases he studied (Lidz, Cornelison, Fleck, & Terry, 1957b). In focusing on the failure to arrive at reciprocal, cooperative roles, Lidz identified two general types of discord. In the first, **marital schism,** there was a chronic failure to accommodate to each other or to achieve role reciprocity. These husbands and wives chronically undercut each other's worth and compete openly for their children's loyalty and affection. Their marriages were combat zones. The second pattern, **marital skew,** involves serious psychopathology in one partner who dominates the other. Thus one parent becomes extremely dependent while the other appears to be a strong parent figure, but is, in fact, a pathological bully. The weaker spouse, in Lidz's cases usually the father, goes along with the pathological distortions of the dominant one. In all these families, unhappy children are torn by conflicting loyalties and weighted down with the pressure to balance their parents' precarious marriages.

Lyman Wynne—National Institute of Mental Health

None of the leaders of family therapy has had as long and distinguished a career as Lyman Wynne. His impeccable scholarship and passionate concern for the unfortunate have been guiding inspirations for forty years of hardnosed and enormously productive research. Like others before him, Wynne examined the effects of communication and family roles. What distinguished his work was his focus on how pathological thinking is transmitted in families.

After completing his medical training at Harvard in 1948, Wynne went on to earn a Ph.D. in the Department of Social Relations. There he encountered the work of leading figures in sociology, psychology, and social systems, including Talcott Parsons, from whom he came to see personality as a subsystem within a larger family system. For Wynne, the notion

*L*yman Wynne's studies linked communication deviance in families to thought disorder in schizophrenic patients.

that we are part of something larger than ourselves has been the hallmark of his professional approach to troubled individuals and of his personal commitment to the problems of society. In these twin concerns, Lyman Wynne stands as a model for the entire field.

In 1952 Wynne joined John Clauson's Laboratory of Socioenvironmental Studies at the National Institute of Mental Health (NIMH), where he first began working intensively with the families of mental patients (Broderick & Schrader, 1991). In 1954, when Murray Bowen came to NIMH as head of a research project on schizophrenics and their families, Wynne found a colleague who shared his belief that the family should be the unit of treatment (even if the two didn't quite agree about the nature of that treatment). When Bowen left NIMH in 1959, Wynne took over as chief of family research, where he remained until the early 1970s.

During his tenure at NIMH, Wynne studied at the Washington Psychoanalytic Institute and was on the faculty of the Washington School of Psychiatry. From the 1950s through the 1970s, Wynne published many research reports and trained several talented researcher clinicians, including Shapiro, Beels, and Reiss. In 1972 Wynne left NIMH to become Professor and Chair of the Department of Psychiatry at the University of Rochester. He retired in 1997.

Wynne's studies of schizophrenic families began in 1954 when he started seeing the parents of his hospitalized patients in twice-weekly therapy sessions. What struck Wynne most forcefully about disturbed families were the strangely unreal qualities of both positive and negative emotions, which he labeled pseudomutuality and pseudohostility, and the nature of the boundaries around them—rubber fences—apparently yielding, but actually impervious to outside influence (especially from therapists).

Pseudomutuality (Wynne, Ryckoff, Day, & Hirsch, 1958) is a facade of togetherness that masks conflict and blocks intimacy. Pseudomutual families have an unnatural dread of separateness. They are so preoccupied with fitting together that there's no room for separate identities or divergent self-interests. These families cannot tolerate either deeper, more honest relationships or independence. This surface togetherness submerges deep affectionate and sexual feelings and keeps both conflict and greater intimacy from emerging.

Pseudohostility is a different guise for a similar collusion to obscure *alignments* and *splits* (Wynne, 1961). Pseudohostility is a self-rescuing operation. Although noisy and intense, it signals only a superficial split. Pseudohostility is more like the bickering and sparring of situation-comedy families than it is real animosity. Like pseudomutuality, it blurs intimacy and affection as well as deeper hostility; pseudohostility distorts communication and impairs realistic perception of and rational thinking about relationships.

The **rubber fence** is an invisible barrier that stretches to permit obligatory extrafamilial involvement, such as going to school, but springs back tightly if that involvement goes too far. The family's rigid role structure persists, protected by the family's isolation. The most damaging feature of the rubber fence is that precisely those who most need outside contact to correct family distortions of reality are the ones allowed it least. Instead of being a subsystem of society (Parsons & Bales, 1955), the schizophrenic family becomes a sick little society unto itself.

Wynne linked the new concept of *communication deviance* with the older notion of *thought disorder.* He saw communication as the vehicle for transmitting thought disorder, which is the defining characteristic of schizophrenia. Communication deviance is a more interactional concept than thought disorder, and more readily observable than double binds. By 1978 Wynne had studied over 600 families and gathered incontrovertible evidence that disordered styles of communication are a distinguishing feature of families with young adult schizophrenics. Similar disorders also appear in families of borderlines, neurotics, and normals, but are progressively less severe (Singer, Wynne, & Toohey, 1978). This observation—that communication deviance isn't confined solely to schizophrenic families, but exists on a continuum (greater deviance with more severe pathology)—is consistent with other studies that describe a "spectrum of schizophrenic disorders."

Role Theorists

The founders of family therapy gained momentum for their fledgling discipline by concentrating narrowly on verbal communication. Doing so may have been adaptive at the time, but focusing exclusively on this one aspect of family life neglected both individual intersubjectivity and broader social influences.

Role theorists, like John Spiegel, described how individuals were differentiated into social roles within family systems. This important fact was obscured by oversimplified versions of systems theory, according to which individuals were treated like cogs in a machine. As early as 1954, Spiegel pointed out that the system in therapy includes the therapist as well as the family (an idea reintroduced later as "second-order cybernetics"). He also made a valuable

distinction between "interactions" and "transactions." Billiard balls *interact*—they collide and alter each other's course, but remain essentially unchanged. People *transact*—they come together in ways that not only alter each other's course, but also effect internal changes.

Ironically for a field in which circular causality was to become a favorite concept, the unfortunate evolutionary misdirection of describing negative influences in families as linear—blaming parents for rejecting or overprotecting or double binding their children—was not only unfair, but also did lasting damage to the reputation of family therapy. Families of mentally ill persons had reason to be on guard against being blamed for the misfortunes of their children.

In 1951 the Group for the Advancement of Psychiatry (GAP) decided that families had been neglected in psychiatry and therefore appointed a committee, chaired by John Spiegel, to survey the field and report their findings. The GAP committee's report (Kluckhohn & Spiegel, 1954) emphasized roles as the primary structural components of families. They concluded that healthy families contained relatively few and stable roles, and that this pattern was essential to teach children a sense of status and identity. There were norms for every role, and children learned these norms by imitation and identification.

Family roles don't exist independently of each other; every role is circumscribed by other, reciprocal roles. You can't have a domineering spouse, for example, without a submissive partner. Role behavior of two or more people involved in a reciprocal transaction defines and regulates their interchange. A common example is that in many families one parent is stricter than the other. Their differences may be slight at first, but the stricter one parent is, the more lenient the other is likely to become. The GAP committee explained roles as a function both of external social influences and of inner needs and drives. Thus role theory served as a link between *intra*personal and *inter*personal structures.

Spiegel went on to Harvard Medical School in 1953, where he pursued his interests in role theory and family pathology. He observed that symptomatic children tend to be involved in their parents' conflicts; nonsymptomatic children may also have parents in conflict, but these children don't get directly involved. Spiegel (1957) described his observations in psychoanalytic terms: The child identifies with the unconscious wishes of the parents and acts out their emotional conflict. The child's acting out serves as a defense for the parents, who are thereby able to avoid facing their own conflicts—and each other.

R. D. Laing's analysis of family dynamics was often more polemical than scholarly, but his observations helped popularize the family's role in psychopathology. Laing (1965) borrowed Marx's concept of **mystification** (class exploitation) and applied it to the "politics of families." Mystification refers to the process of distorting children's experience by denying or relabeling it. One example of this is a parent telling a child who's feeling sad, "You must be tired" (*Go to bed and leave me alone*). Similarly, the idea that "good" children are always quiet breeds compliant, but spiritless, children.

The prime function of mystification is to maintain the status quo. Mystification contradicts perceptions and feelings and, more ominously, reality. When parents continually mystify a child's experience, the child's existence becomes inauthentic. Because their feelings aren't accepted, these children project a *false self* while keeping the *real self* private. In mild instances, this produces a lack of authenticity, but if the real self/false self split is carried to extremes, the result is madness (Laing, 1960).

Marriage Counseling

The history of professional marriage counseling is a less well-known contributor to family therapy because much of it took place outside the mainstream of psychiatry. For many years

there was no apparent need for a separate profession of marriage counselors. People with marital problems were—and still are—more likely to discuss them with their doctors, clergy, lawyers, or teachers than to seek out mental health professionals. The first professional centers for marriage counseling were established around 1930. Paul Popenoe opened the American Institute of Family Relations in Los Angeles, and Abraham and Hannah Stone opened a similar clinic in New York. A third center was the Marriage Council of Philadelphia, begun in 1932 by Emily Hartshorne Mudd (Broderick & Schrader, 1981). Members of this new profession started meeting annually in 1942 and formed the American Association of Marriage Counselors in 1945.

While these developments were taking place, a parallel trend among some psychoanalysts led to conjoint marital therapy. Although the majority of psychoanalysts have always followed Freud's prohibition against contact with the patient's family, a few have broken the rules and experimented with **concurrent** and **conjoint therapy** for married partners.

The first report on the psychoanalysis of married couples was made by Clarence Oberndorf at the American Psychiatric Association's 1931 convention (Oberndorf, 1938). Oberndorf advanced the theory that married couples have interlocking neuroses and that they are best treated in concert. This view was to be the underlying point of agreement among those in the analytic community who became interested in treating couples. "Because of the continuous and intimate nature of marriage, every neurosis in a married person is strongly anchored in the marital relationship. It is a useful and at times indispensable therapeutic measure to concentrate the analytic discussions on the complementary patterns and, if necessary, to have both mates treated" (Mittleman, 1944, p. 491).

In 1948 Bela Mittleman of the New York Psychoanalytic Institute published the first account of concurrent marital therapy in the

United States. Previously, Rene LaForgue had reported in 1937 on his experience analyzing several members of the same family concurrently. Mittleman suggested that husbands and wives could be treated by the same analyst, and that by seeing both it was possible to reexamine their irrational perceptions of each other (Mittleman, 1948). This was truly a revolutionary point of view from an analyst: that the reality of object relationships may be at least as important as their intrapsychic representations. Nathan Ackerman (1954) agreed that the concomitant treatment of married partners was a good idea and also suggested that mothers and children could profit from being treated together.

Meanwhile in Great Britain, where **object relations** were the central concern of psychoanalysts, Henry Dicks and his associates at the Tavistock Clinic established a Family Psychiatric Unit. Here couples referred by the divorce courts were helped to reconcile their differences (Dicks, 1964). Subsequently, the Balints affiliated their Family Discussion Bureau with the Tavistock Clinic, adding the clinic's prestige to their marital casework agency and, indirectly, to the entire field of marriage counseling.

In 1956 Victor Eisenstein, Director of the New Jersey Neuropsychiatric Institute, published an edited volume, entitled *Neurotic Interaction in Marriage*. In it were several articles describing the state of the art in marital therapy. Frances Beatman, Associate Director of Jewish Family Services in New York, described a casework treatment approach to marital problems (Beatman, 1956); Lawrence Kubie wrote a psychoanalytic analysis of the dynamics of marriage (Kubie, 1956); Margaret Mahler described the effects of marital conflict on child development (Mahler & Rabinovitch, 1956); and Ashley Montague added a cultural perspective to the dynamic influences on marriage (Montague, 1956).

In the same volume, Mittleman (1956) wrote a more extensive description of his views on marital disorders and their treatment. He described a number of complementary marital patterns, including aggressive/submissive and detached/demanding. These odd matches are made, according to Mittleman, because courting couples distort each other's personalities through the eyes of their illusions: She sees his independence as strength; he sees her dependency as adoration. Mittleman also pointed out that the couple's reactions to each other may be shaped by their relationships with their parents. Without insight, unconscious motivation may dominate marital behavior, leading to reciprocal neurotic actions and reactions. For treatment, Mittleman believed that 20 percent of the time one therapist could handle all members of the family, but in other cases separate therapists for each member may be better.

At about this time Don Jackson and Jay Haley were also writing about marital therapy within the framework of communications analysis. As their ideas gained prominence among marital therapists, the field of marital therapy was absorbed into the larger family therapy movement.

Many writers don't distinguish between marital and family therapy. Therapy for couples, according to this way of thinking, is just family therapy applied to a particular family subsystem. We tend to agree with this way of thinking and, therefore, you will find our description of various approaches to couples and their problems embedded in the discussions of the various models considered in this book. There is, however, a case to be made for considering couples therapy a distinct enterprise (Gurman & Jacobson, 2002).

Historically, many of the influential approaches to couples therapy came before their family therapy counterparts. Among these are cognitive-behavioral marital therapy, object relations marital therapy, emotionally focused couples therapy, and many of the integrative approaches considered in Chapter 14. Beyond the question of which came first, couples therapy differs in practice from family therapy in allowing for more in-depth focus on the psychology and experience of individuals. Sessions with the whole family tend to be noisy affairs. While it is possible in this context to spend time talking with family members about their feelings, wishes, and fears, it isn't possible to spend much time exploring the psychology of any one individual—much less two. Doing therapy with couples, on the other hand, permits a much closer focus on both dyadic exchanges and on the underlying experience of intimate relationships.

From Research to Treatment: The Pioneers of Family Therapy

We have seen how family therapy was anticipated by developments in hospital psychiatry, group dynamics, interpersonal psychiatry, the child guidance movement, research on schizophrenia, and marriage counseling. But who actually started family therapy? Although there are rival claims to this honor, the distinction should probably be shared by John Elderkin Bell, Don Jackson, Nathan Ackerman, and Murray Bowen. In addition to these founders of family therapy, Jay Haley, Virginia Satir, Carl Whitaker, Lyman Wynne, Ivan Boszormenyi-Nagy, Christian Midelfort, and Salvador Minuchin were also significant pioneers.

John Bell

John Elderkin Bell, a psychologist at Clark University in Worcester, Massachusetts, who began treating families in 1951, occupies a unique position in the history of family therapy. He may have been the first family therapist, but is mentioned only tangentially in two of the most important historical accounts of the movement (Guerin, 1976; Kaslow, 1980), because although he began seeing families in the 1950s, he didn't publish his ideas until a decade later. Moreover, unlike the other parents

of family therapy, he had few offspring. He didn't establish an important clinical center, develop a training program, or train well-known students.

Bell's approach (Bell, 1961, 1962) was taken directly from group therapy. "Family group therapy" relied primarily on stimulating an open discussion to help families solve their problems. Like a group therapist, Bell intervened to encourage silent participants to speak up, and he interpreted the reasons for their defensiveness.

Bell believed that family group therapy goes through predictable phases just as do groups of strangers. In his early work (Bell, 1961), he carefully structured treatment in a series of stages, each of which concentrated on a particular segment of the family. Later, he became less directive and allowed families to evolve through a naturally unfolding sequence. For a more complete description of family group therapy, see Chapter 3.

Palo Alto

The Bateson group stumbled onto family therapy more or less by accident. Once the group began to meet with schizophrenic families in 1954, hoping to decipher their patterns of communication, project members found themselves drawn into helping roles by the pain of these unhappy people (Jackson & Weakland, 1961). While Bateson was the undisputed scientific leader of the group, Don Jackson and Jay Haley were most influential in developing family therapy.

Jackson rejected the psychoanalytic concepts he learned in training and focused instead on the dynamics of interchange between persons. Analysis of communication was his primary instrument.

By 1954 Jackson had developed a rudimentary family interactional therapy, which he reported in "The Question of Family Homeostasis," a paper delivered to the American

Don Jackson described problematic patterns of communication in ways that are still useful today.

Psychiatric Association convention in St. Louis. Borrowing from biology and systems theory, Jackson described families as homeostatic units that maintain relative constancy of internal functioning.

Jackson's concept of **family homeostasis**—families as units that resist change—was to become the defining metaphor of family therapy's first three decades. In hindsight, we can say that the emphasis on homeostasis overestimated the conservative properties of families and underestimated their flexibility. But at the time the recognition that families resist change and act as a constraining influence was enormously productive for understanding what keeps people stuck.

Although in practice Jackson and his colleagues probably oversimplified the homeostatic nature of families, their theoretical papers became increasingly sophisticated. Consistency, they realized, doesn't necessarily mean rigidity. (As far back as 1939, the physiologist Walter Cannon said that, like the physiological systems of the body, "even social and industrial organizations maintain a relatively steady state in the face of external perturbations.") Family homeostasis is a dynamic state of, as Cannon said, *relative* stability. Families seek to maintain or restore the status quo; family members function as governors, and the family is said to act in error-activated ways (Haley, 1963). The result is not invariance, but stability in variance of behavior.

In "Schizophrenic Symptoms and Family Interaction" (Jackson & Weakland, 1959), Jackson illustrated how patients' symptoms preserve stability in their families. In one such case a young woman diagnosed as a catatonic schizophrenic had as her most prominent symptom a profound indecisiveness. However, when she did behave decisively, her parents fell apart. Her mother became helpless and dependent; her father became, literally, impotent. In one family meeting her parents failed to notice when the patient made a simple decision. Only after listening to a taped replay of the session *three* times did the parents finally hear their daughter's statement. The patient's indecision was neither crazy nor senseless; rather it protected her parents from facing their own difficulties. This case is one of the earliest published examples of how even psychotic symptoms can be meaningful in the family context. This paper also contains the shrewd observation that children's symptoms are often an exaggerated version of their parents' problems.

In moving away from mentalistic inference to behavioral observation of sequences of communication, Jackson found that he needed a new language of interaction. His basic assumption was that all people in continuing relationships develop set patterns of interaction. He called this patterning "behavioral redundancy" (Jackson, 1965).

The term *redundancy* not only captures an important feature of family behavior, but also reflects Jackson's phenomenological stance. Traditional psychiatric terms like *projection, defense,* and *regression* imply far more about inner states of motivation than the simple descriptive language of early family therapists. Even when using concepts that imply prescription, Jackson remained committed to description. Thus, his *rules hypothesis* was simply a means of summarizing the observation that within any committed unit (dyad, triad, or larger group) there were redundant behavior patterns. Rules (as any student of philosophy learns when studying determinism) can describe regularity, rather than regulation. A second part of the rules hypothesis was that family members use only some of the full range of behavior available to them. This seemingly innocent fact is precisely what makes family therapy possible.

Families who come to therapy can be seen as stuck in a narrow range of options, or unnecessarily rigid rules. Since the rules in most families aren't spelled out, no one ratifies them, and they're hard to change. The therapist, however, as an outsider can help families see—and re-examine—the rules they live by.

Jackson's therapeutic strategies were based on the premise that psychiatric problems resulted from the way people behave with each other in a given context. He saw human problems as interactional *and* situational. Problem resolution involves shifting the context in which problems occur. Although Jackson wrote more about understanding families than about treating them, many of his explanatory concepts (*homeostatic mechanisms, quid pro quo, double bind, symmetry,* and *complementarity*) informed his strategies and became the early language of systems-oriented family therapists. He sought first to distinguish interactions (*redundant behavior patterns*) that were functional from those that were dysfunctional (*problem-maintaining*). To do so, he observed when problems occurred and in what context, who was present, and how people responded to the problem. Given the assumption that symptoms are homeostatic mechanisms, Jackson often inquired how a family might be worse off if the problem got better. The individual might want to get better, but the family may need someone to play the sick role. Improvement can be a threat to the defensive order of things.

Jackson's model of the family as a homeostatic system emphasized the equilibrium-maintaining qualities of symptomatic behavior. This led to the idea that deviation or deviance, including symptomatic and irrational behavior, wasn't necessarily negative, at least not from the point of view of those who learned to live with it. A father's drinking, for example, might keep him from making demands on his wife or from enforcing discipline on his children. Unfortunately, following Jackson, some family therapists jumped from the observation that symptoms may serve a purpose to the assumption that some families *need* a sick member, which, in turn, often led to a view of parents victimizing *scapegoated* children. Despite the fancy language, this was part of the time-honored tradition of blaming parents for the failings of their children. If a six-year-old boy misbehaves around the house, perhaps we should look to his parents. But a husband's drinking isn't necessarily his family's fault, and certainly it wasn't fair to imply that families were responsible for the psychotic behavior of their schizophrenic members.

Looking back, we can see how the early emphasis on homeostasis, as well as the cybernetic metaphor of family as machine, led to a view of the therapist as more mechanic than healer. In their zeal to rescue "family scapegoats" from the clutches of their "pathological" families, early family therapists provoked some of the resistance they complained of. Therapists who see themselves as rescuing innocent victims from their families and who take up an adversarial stance are not unlike the person who whacks a turtle on the back and then notices that the creature doesn't want to come out of its shell.

Among Jackson's most trenchant and influential papers was "Family Rules: Marital Quid Pro Quo" (Jackson, 1965). The role divisions in a marriage are not, according to Jackson, simply a matter of gender differences; instead they result from a series of **quid pro quos,** worked out in any long-term relationship. The traditional view that marital roles stem from sex-role differences ascribes behavior to individual personalities, instead of recognizing the extent to which relationships depend on the interactions and the rules for interaction worked out between people. Jackson's view wasn't that sexual differences don't exist, but that they were relatively unimportant. The major differences in a marriage, as in any other relationship, are worked out, not given.[2] The fact that many marital quid pro quos aren't conscious or overt means that family therapists can play a useful role in ferreting out those arrangements that don't work or aren't fair.

Another construct important to Jackson's thinking was the dichotomy between *complementary* relationships and *symmetrical* ones. (Like so many of the seminal ideas of family therapy, this one was first articulated by Bateson.) In **complementary relationships** people are different in ways that fit together: If one is logical, the other is emotional; if one is weak, the other is strong. **Symmetrical relationships** are based on equality and similarity. Marriages between two people who both have careers and share housekeeping chores are symmetrical.

Most of Jackson's concepts (*complementary/ symmetrical, quid pro quo, double bind*) describe relationships between two people. Although his intent was to develop a descriptive language of family interactions, Jackson's major success was in describing relationships between husbands and wives. This narrow focus on the marital dyad has always been one of the limits of the Palo Alto group. Their interest in communication led to an adult-centered bias, and they tended to neglect children as well as the various triads that make up families.

●

The great discovery of the Bateson group was that there's no such thing as a simple communication; every message is qualified by another message on a higher level. In *Strategies of Psychotherapy*, Jay Haley (1963) explored how covert messages are used in the struggle for control that

characterizes many relationships. Symptoms, he argued, represent an incongruence between levels of communication. The symptomatic person does something, such as touching a doorknob six times before turning it, while at the same time denying that he's *really* doing it. He can't help it; it's just his condition. Meanwhile, the person's symptoms—over which he has no control—have consequences. A person who "has a compulsion" of such proportions can hardly be expected to get himself out of the house in the morning, can he?

Since symptomatic behavior wasn't "reasonable," Haley didn't rely on reasoning with patients to help them. Instead, therapy became a strategic game of cat and mouse.

Haley (1963) defined his therapy as a directive form of treatment and acknowledged his debt to Milton Erickson, with whom he studied hypnosis from 1954 to 1960. Indeed, in Haley's early writings it's difficult to know where Erickson leaves off and Haley begins. In what he called "brief therapy," Haley zeroed in on the context and possible function of the patient's symptoms. His first moves were often designed to gain control of the therapeutic relationship. Haley cited Erickson's device of advising patients that in the first interview there will be things they may be willing to say and other things they'll want to withhold, and that these, of course, should be withheld. Here, of course, the therapist is directing patients to do precisely what they would do anyway, and thus the therapist is subtly gaining the upper hand.

The decisive technique in brief therapy has always been the use of *directives*. As Haley put it, it isn't enough to explain problems to patients; what counts is getting them to *do* something about them.

One of Haley's patients was a freelance photographer who compulsively made silly blunders that ruined every picture. Eventually the patient became so preoccupied with avoiding mistakes that he was too nervous to take pic-

---

2. In their enthusiasm for newly discovered interactional forces, early family therapists may have underestimated the importance of gender and the effect of gender bias on families.

tures at all. Haley instructed the man to go out and take three pictures, making one deliberate error in each. The paradox here is that you can't make a mistake accidentally if you're doing so deliberately.

In another famous case, Haley told an insomniac that if he woke up in the middle of the night he should get out of bed and wax the kitchen floor. Instant cure! The cybernetic principle illustrated here is: People will do anything to get out of housework.

Most of the ideas that came out of the Palo Alto group—double bind, complementarity, quid pro quo—focused on dyads, but Haley also became interested in triads or, as he called them, **coalitions.** Coalitions are distinct from alliances, cooperative arrangements between two parties, not formed at the expense of a third. In symptomatic families Haley observed, most coalitions were "cross-generational," one parent ganging up with a child against the other parent. For example, a mother might speak for a child in a way that discredited the father. In other cases, a child might insinuate himself between bickering parents by being "helpful" or getting "sick."

In "Toward a Theory of Pathological Systems," Haley described what he called "perverse triangles," which often lead to violence, psychopathology, or the breakup of a system. A perverse triangle is a hidden coalition that undermines generational hierarchies. Examples include a child running for comfort to his grandmother every time his mother tries to punish him, or one parent complaining about the other to the children. Perverse triangles also occur in organizations when, for example, a supervisor joins with one subordinate against another, or when a professor complains to his students about the department chair. In looking beyond cybernetics and dyads to triads and hierarchies, Haley was to become an important bridging figure between strategic and structural approaches to family therapy.

Another member of the Palo Alto group who played a leading role in family therapy's

first decade was Virginia Satir, one of the great charismatic originals. Known more for her clinical artistry than for theoretical contributions, Satir's impact was most vivid to those lucky enough to see her in action. Like her confreres, Satir was interested in communication, but she added a dimension of feeling that helped counterbalance what was otherwise a relatively cool and cerebral approach.

Satir saw troubled family members as trapped in narrow family roles, like *victim, placator, defiant one,* or *rescuer,* that constrained relationships and sapped self-esteem. Her concern with identifying such life-constricting roles and freeing family members from their grip was consistent with her major focus, which was always on the individual. Thus, Satir was a humanizing force in the early days of family therapy, when many were so enamored of the systems metaphor that they neglected the emotional life of families.

Satir concentrated on clarifying communication, expressing feelings, and fostering a climate of mutual acceptance and warmth. Her great strength was to connect with families not in terms of anger and resentment, but in terms of hopes and fears, yearnings and disappointments. A therapist who can bring out the loneliness and longing behind an angry outburst is a therapist who can bring people together.

Satir was justly famous for her ability to turn negatives into positives. What makes this such an important skill for a family therapist is that most families have at least one member whose faults or failings have cast him in the role of outsider. Unless these less favored ones can be brought into the family circle, neither healing nor cooperation is very likely.

In one case, cited by Lynn Hoffman (1981), Satir interviewed the family of an adolescent boy, son of the local minister, who had gotten two of his classmates pregnant. On one side of the room sat the boy's parents and siblings. The boy sat in the opposite corner with his head down. Satir introduced herself and said to the boy, "Well, your father has told me a lot about the situation on the phone, and I just want to say before we begin that we know one thing for sure: We know you have good seed." The boy looked up in amazement as Satir turned to the boy's mother and asked brightly, "Could you start by telling us your perception?"

The 1964 publication of Satir's book *Conjoint Family Therapy* did much to popularize the family therapy movement. This book, along with *Pragmatics of Human Communication* (Watzlawick, Beavin, & Jackson, 1967), helped spread the influence of the Palo Alto group's brand of systemic thinking. Eventually, Satir went on to become a leader in the human potential movement, and we will consider her work more fully in Chapter 8.

Murray Bowen

Like many of the founders of family therapy, Murray Bowen was a psychiatrist who specialized in schizophrenia. Unlike others, however, he emphasized theory in his work, and to this day Bowen's theory is the most fertile system of ideas family therapy has produced.

Bowen began his clinical work at the Menninger Clinic in 1946, where he studied mothers and their schizophrenic children who lived together in small cottages. His major interest at the time was mother–child symbiosis, which led to the formation of his concept of **differentiation of self** (autonomy from others and separation of thought from feeling). From Menninger, Bowen moved to NIMH, where he developed a project to hospitalize whole families with schizophrenic members. This project expanded the concept of mother–child symbiosis to include the role of fathers, and led to the concept of *triangles* (diverting conflict between two people by involving a third). In 1959 Bowen left NIMH for Georgetown Medical School where he was a professor of psychiatry and director of his own training program until his death in 1990.

In the first year of the NIMH project (1954), Bowen provided separate therapists for individual family members. He discovered, however, that these efforts tended to fractionate families. Instead of trying to work out their mutual problems together, family members had a tendency to think, "I'll take up my problems with *my* therapist" (Bowen, 1976). (Of course this never happens when nice people like you and me go to *our* individual therapists.) After a year, concluding that the family was the unit of disorder, Bowen began treating the families together. Thus, in 1955, Bowen became one of the first to invent family therapy.

Beginning in 1955 Bowen began holding large group therapy sessions for the entire project staff and all the families. In this early form of network therapy, Bowen assumed that togetherness and open communication would be therapeutic—for problems within families and between families and staff.

At first Bowen employed four therapists to manage these multifamily meetings, but he became dissatisfied when he noticed that the therapists tended to pull in different directions. So he put one therapist in charge and consigned the others to supporting roles. However, just as multiple therapists tended to pull in different directions, so did multiple families. As soon as a hot topic was broached in one family, someone from another family would become anxious and change the subject. Finally, Bowen decided that families had to take turns—one family became the focus for each session, with the others as silent auditors.

At first Bowen's approach to single families was the same one he used in the large meetings. He did what most new family therapists do: brought family members together and just tried to get them talking. He reasoned that families would improve simply by coming together and discussing mutual concerns. He soon rejected this idea. Unstructured family chats are about as productive for therapy as an unrefereed boxing match between several combatants of various sizes.

When Bowen brought family members together to discuss their problems, he was struck by their intense **emotional reactivity.** Feelings overwhelmed thinking and drowned out individuality in the chaos of the group. Bowen felt the family's tendency to pull him into the center of this **undifferentiated family ego mass,** and he had to make a concerted effort to remain neutral and objective (Bowen, 1961). The ability to remain neutral and attentive to the process, rather than the content, of family discussions is what distinguishes a therapist from a participant in a family's drama.

To control the level of emotion, Bowen encouraged family members to talk to him, not to each other. He found that it was easier for people to listen without becoming reactive when their partners spoke to the therapist instead of directly to them.

Bowen also discovered that therapists weren't immune from being sucked into family conflicts. This awareness led to his greatest insight: Whenever two people are struggling with a conflict they can't resolve, there is an automatic tendency to draw in a third party. In fact, as Bowen came to believe, the **triangle** is the smallest stable unit of relationship.

Any two-person emotional system will form a three-person system under stress. A husband who can't stand his wife's habitual lateness, but who also can't stand up and tell her so, may start complaining about her to one of his children. His complaining may relieve some of his tension, but the very process of complaining to a third party makes him less likely to address the original problem at its source. We all complain about other people from time to time, but Bowen realized that this "triangling" process is destructive when it becomes a regular feature of a system.

Another thing Bowen discovered about triangles is that they spread out: If relationship tension doesn't remain localized in the original

pair, it's likely to activate more and more triangles. In the following case, a family had become entangled in a whole labyrinth of triangles.

One Sunday morning "Mrs. McNeil," who was anxious to get the family to church on time, yelled at her nine-year-old son to hurry up. When he told her to "quit bitching," she slapped him. At that point her fourteen-year-old daughter, Megan, grabbed her, and the two of them started wrestling. Then Megan ran next door to her friend's house. When the friend's parents noticed that Megan had a cut lip and she told them what had happened, they called the police. By the time the family came to therapy, the following triangles were in place: Mrs. McNeil, who'd been ordered out of the house by the family court judge, was allied with her lawyer against the judge; she also had an individual therapist who joined her in thinking she was being hounded unfairly by the child protective workers. The nine-year-old was still mad at his mother, and his father supported him in blaming her for flying off the handle. Mr. McNeil, who was a recovering alcoholic, formed an alliance with his sponsor, who felt that Mr. McNeil was on his way to a breakdown unless his wife started being more supportive. Meanwhile Megan had formed a triangle with the neighbors, who thought her parents were awful and shouldn't be allowed to have children. In short, everyone had an advocate—everyone, that is, except the family unit.

In 1966 an emotional crisis in Bowen's family led him to initiate a personal voyage of discovery that turned out to be as significant for Bowen's theory as Freud's self-analysis was for psychoanalysis.

As an adult, Bowen, the oldest of five children from a tightly knit rural family, kept his distance from his parents and the rest of his extended family. Like many of us, he mistook avoidance for emancipation. But as he later realized, unfinished emotional business stays with us, making us vulnerable to repeat conflicts we never got around to working out with our families.

Bowen's most important achievement was detriangling himself from his parents, who'd been accustomed to complaining to him about each other. Most of us are flattered to receive these confidences, but Bowen came to recognize this triangulation for what it was, and when his mother complained about his father, he told his father: "Your wife told me a story about you; I wonder why she told me instead of you." Naturally, his father discussed this with his mother and, naturally, she was annoyed.

Although his efforts generated the kind of emotional upheaval that comes of breaking family rules, Bowen's maneuver was effective in keeping his parents from trying to get him to take sides—and made it harder for them to avoid discussing things between themselves. Repeating what someone says to you about someone else is one way to stop triangling in its tracks.

Through his efforts in his own family Bowen discovered that *differentiation of self* is best accomplished by developing an individual, person-to-person relationship with each parent and with as many members of the extended family as possible. If visiting is difficult, letters and phone calls can help reestablish relationships, particularly if they're personal and intimate. Differentiating one's self from the family is completed when these relationships are maintained without emotional fusion or triangulation. The details of Bowen's personal work on his family relationships are complex but make rewarding reading for the serious student (Anonymous, 1972).

Thus, beginning in 1971, studying one's own family became one of the cornerstones of Bowen's approach to training. The goal is to return to your family of origin, make contact, develop an honest personal relationship with every member of the family, and learn to discuss family issues without becoming emotionally reactive or taking part in triangles.

Nathan Ackerman

Nathan Ackerman was a child psychiatrist whose pioneering work with families remained faithful to his psychoanalytic roots. Although his focus on intrapsychic conflict may have seemed less innovative than the Palo Alto group's attention to communication as feedback, he had a keen sense of the overall organization of families. Families, Ackerman said, may give the appearance of unity, but underneath they are emotionally split into competing factions. This you may recognize as similar to the psychoanalytic model of individuals who, despite apparent unity of personality, are actually minds in conflict, driven by warring drives and defenses.

Ackerman joined the staff at the Menninger Clinic and in 1937 became chief psychiatrist of the Child Guidance Clinic. At first he followed the child guidance model of having a psychiatrist treat the child and a social worker see the mother. But by the mid-1940s he began to experiment with having the same therapist see both. Unlike Bowlby, Ackerman did more than use these conjoint sessions as a temporary expedient; instead, he began to see the family as the basic unit for diagnosis and treatment.

In 1955 Ackerman organized the first session on family diagnosis at a meeting of the American Orthopsychiatric Association. There Jackson, Bowen, Wynne, and Ackerman learned about each other's existence and joined in a sense of common purpose. Two years later Ackerman opened the Family Mental Health Clinic of Jewish Family Services in New York City and began teaching at Columbia University. In 1960 he founded the Family Institute, which was renamed the Ackerman Institute following his death in 1971.

In addition to his clinical innovations, Ackerman also published several important articles and books. As early as 1938, he wrote "The Unity of the Family," and some consider his article "Family Diagnosis: An Approach to the

Preschool Child" (Ackerman & Sobel, 1950) as the beginning of the family therapy movement (Kaslow, 1980). In 1962 Ackerman, with Don Jackson, cofounded the field's first journal, *Family Process.*

While other family therapists downplayed the psychology of individuals, Ackerman was always concerned with what goes on inside people, as well as between them. He never lost sight of feelings, hopes, and desires. In fact, Ackerman's model of the family was like the psychoanalytic model of an individual writ large; instead of conscious and unconscious issues, Ackerman talked about how families confront some issues while avoiding and denying others, particularly those involving sex and aggression. He saw his job as a therapist as one of stirring things up, bringing family secrets into the open.

In *Treating the Troubled Family,* Ackerman (1966a) illustrated his irreverence for politeness and pretense with a clinical vignette. A family of four came for treatment when the fighting between the eleven-year-old daughter and sixteen-year-old son started getting out of hand. The girl had recently threatened her brother with a butcher knife. The father sighed as he sat down. Ackerman asked him why he was sighing and refused to be put off by the father's excuse that he was tired, suggesting that perhaps he had another reason to sigh. Then his wife broke in to announce that she'd been keeping a journal of everyone's misdeeds during the week. Her stridency perfectly complemented her husband's mild-mannered evasiveness. Ackerman's bemused response was: "You come armed with a notebook. Fire away!"

As the mother began to read out her bill of particulars, Ackerman, who sensed that this was just business as usual, commented on the father's nonverbal behavior. "You're picking your fingers." This triggered a discussion about who does what, which the mother gradually took over and turned into an indictment of the father's many nervous habits. At this point the

son broke in with an accusation. Pointing to his mother, he said, "She belches!" The mother acknowledged this little embarrassment, then tried to change the subject. But Ackerman wasn't about to let her off the hook.

It turned out that the mother's belching occurred mostly when she was lying down. The father said he was upset by her belching in his face, but he was interrupted by the children, who started bickering. Ackerman said, "Isn't it interesting that this interruption occurs just as you two are about to talk about your love life?" The father then described how it felt when he wanted to kiss his wife and she belched in his face. "You need a gas mask," he said. The daughter tried to interrupt, but Ackerman asked her to move her seat so that her parents could talk.

A few minutes later the children left the session and Ackerman reopened the door to the parents' bedroom. At first the couple played out their familiar pattern: She complained and he withdrew. They were a perfectly matched pair: She was up, he was down. But Ackerman unbalanced them by playfully teasing the wife and provoking the husband to stand up for himself.

Although there's always room in after-the-fact descriptions to accuse a therapist of taking sides, it's worth noting that in this instance the wife didn't seem to feel criticized or put down by Ackerman. Nor did the husband seem to get the idea that Ackerman was trying to elevate him over his wife. Rather, by the end of the session, this grim, angry couple were beginning to laugh and appreciate each other. They saw how they'd drifted apart and allowed the children to distract them. Thus, although Ackerman's work has been described as essentially psychoanalytic, we see here beginning efforts to reorganize the structure of families.

Ackerman recommended that everyone living under the same roof be present in family interviews. As he put it, "It is very important at the outset to establish a meaningful emotional contact with all members of the family, to create a climate in which one really touches them and they feel they touch back" (Ackerman, 1961, p. 242). Once contact was made, Ackerman encouraged open and honest expression of feeling. He was an *agent provocateur,* prompting revelations and confrontations with his wit and willingness to stick his nose into personal family issues.

Ackerman pointed out that each person's identity has various aspects: as an individual, as a member of family subsystems, and as a member of the family as a whole. In order to pinpoint these components of identity, he was alert to the coalitions revealed in family interviews. One clue was found in the seating arrangement. When family members enter the consulting room they tend to pair off in ways that reveal alignments. To show these alliances more clearly, Ackerman recommended mobilizing conversations among family members. Once family members start talking among themselves, it's easier to see how they are emotionally divided and what problems and prohibitions are present. Ackerman also paid close attention to nonverbal cues, because he believed that disguised feelings were conveyed in body language far more eloquently than in words.

To promote honest emotional interchange, Ackerman "tickled the defenses" of family members—his phrase for provoking people to open up and say what's really on their minds.

To encourage families to relax their emotional restraint, Ackerman himself was unrestrained. He freely sided first with one part of the family and later with another. He didn't think it was necessary—or possible—to always be neutral; instead, he believed that an impartial balance was achieved in the long run by moving back and forth, giving support now to one, later to another family member. At times he was unabashedly blunt. If he thought someone was lying, he said so. To critics who suggested this directness might generate too much anxiety, Ackerman replied that people get more reassurance from honesty than from pious politeness.

Ackerman saw family problems as the product of conflict. He said that conflicts within individuals, among family members, and between families and the larger community must be identified and resolved if psychological hurts are to be mended. Conflicts between and within family members are related in a circular feedback system; that is, intrapsychic conflict promotes interpersonal conflict and vice versa (Ackerman, 1961). To reverse symptomatic disturbances, the therapist must bring conflicts into the open, into the field of family interaction, where new solutions can be found. As long as conflicts remain locked within individuals, Ackerman believed, psychopathology remains fixed.

While it's impossible to neatly summarize Ackerman's freewheeling approach, there were consistent themes. One was the necessity for depth of therapeutic commitment and involvement. Ackerman himself became deeply emotionally involved with families, in contrast, for example, to Murray Bowen, who cautioned therapists to remain somewhat distant to avoid being triangulated. Depth also characterized the issues on which Ackerman focused—family analogues of the kinds of conflicts, feelings, and fantasies that lie buried in the individual unconscious. His psychoanalytic orientation sensitized him to hidden themes in the interpersonal unconscious of the family, and his provocative style enabled him to help families bring these themes into the light of day.

Ackerman's contributions to family therapy were extensive and important: He was one of the first to envision whole family treatment *and* he had the inventiveness and energy to actually carry it out. As far back as the late 1940s, he pointed out that treating family members individually without considering the configuration of the family was often futile.

Ackerman's second major impact was as a peerless artist of therapeutic technique. He was one of the great geniuses of the movement. Those who studied with him all attest to his clinical wizardry. He was a dynamic catalyst— active, open, and forthright, never rigid or shy. He was passionate *and* effective. Nor was he always content to remain in the office, for he recommended and made frequent home visits (Ackerman, 1966b).

Finally, Ackerman's contributions as a teacher may be his most important legacy. On the East Coast his name was synonymous with family therapy throughout the 1960s. Among those fortunate enough to study with him was Salvador Minuchin, who openly acknowledges his debt to Ackerman's genius.

Ackerman consistently urged therapists to become emotionally engaged with families and to use confrontation to transform dormant conflicts into open discussion. How does a therapist provoke candid disclosures? Ackerman did it by challenging avoidance and emotional dishonesty ("tickling the defenses"). Perhaps his most enduring contribution was his consistent stress on individual persons *and* whole families; he never lost sight of the self in the system.

Carl Whitaker

Even among the strong-willed founders of family therapy, Carl Whitaker stands out as the most irreverent. His view of psychologically troubled people was that they are alienated from feeling and frozen into devitalized routines (Whitaker & Malone, 1953). Whitaker turned up the emotional temperature. His "Psychotherapy of the Absurd" (Whitaker, 1975) was a blend of warm support and unpredictable emotional goading, designed to loosen people up and help them get in touch with their experience in a deeper, more personal way.

Given his innovative approach to individual therapy, it wasn't surprising that Whitaker became one of the first who broke with psychiatric tradition to experiment with family treatment. In 1943 he and John Warkentin, working in Oak Ridge, Tennessee, began including spouses and children in their patients' treatment. Whitaker also pioneered the use of cotherapy, in the belief that a supportive partner helped free therapists to react spontaneously without fear of unchecked countertransference.

In 1946 Whitaker became Chairman of the Department of Psychiatry at Emory University, where he continued to experiment with family treatment with a special interest in schizophrenics and their families. During this period Whitaker organized a series of conferences that eventually led to the first meeting of the family therapy movement. Beginning in 1946, Whitaker and his colleagues began twice-yearly conferences during which they observed and discussed each other's work with families. The group found these sessions enormously helpful, and mutual observation, using one-way vision screens, has since become one of the hallmarks of family therapy.

Whitaker resigned from Emory in 1955 and entered private practice with Warkentin, Malone, and Richard Felder. He and his partners at the Atlanta Psychiatric Clinic developed an "experiential" form of psychotherapy, using a number of provocative techniques, combined with the force of their own personalities, in the treatment of families, individuals, groups, and couples (Whitaker, 1958).

In 1965 Whitaker left Atlanta to become a Professor of Psychiatry at the University of Wisconsin, where he worked until his retirement in 1982. After that he devoted himself to treating families and traveling all over the world conducting workshops. During the late 1970s Whitaker seemed to mellow and added a greater understanding of family dynamics to his shoot-from-the-hip interventions. In the process, the former wild man of family therapy became one of its elder statesmen. Whitaker's death in April 1995 left the field with a piece of its heart missing.

At the beginning of the family therapy movement, Whitaker was less well known than many of the other first-generation family therapists. Perhaps this was due to his atheoretical position. Whereas Jackson, Haley, and Bowen developed theoretical concepts that were intriguing and easy to grasp, Whitaker eschewed theory in favor of creative spontaneity. His work has therefore been less accessible to students than that of his colleagues. Nevertheless, he always had the respect of his peers. Those who really understood what went on in families could see that there was always method to his madness.

Whitaker created tension by teasing and confronting families because he believed that stress is necessary for change. He never seemed to have an obvious strategy, nor did he use predictable techniques, preferring, as he said, to let his unconscious run the therapy (Whitaker, 1976). Although his work seemed totally spontaneous, even outrageous at times, there was a consistent theme. All of his interventions promoted flexibility. He didn't so much push families to change in a particular direction as he challenged and cajoled them to open up—to become more fully themselves and more fully together.

Ivan Boszormenyi-Nagy

Ivan Boszormenyi-Nagy, who came to family therapy from psychoanalysis, has been one of the seminal thinkers in the movement since its earliest days. In 1957 he founded the Eastern Pennsylvania Psychiatric Institute (EPPI) in Philadelphia, where he was able to attract a host of highly talented colleagues and students. Among these were James Framo, one of the few psychologists in the early family therapy movement; David Rubenstein, a psychiatrist who later launched a separate family therapy training program; and Geraldine Spark, a social worker who worked with Boszormenyi-Nagy as cotherapist and coauthor of *Invisible Loyalties* (Boszormenyi-Nagy & Spark, 1973).

In 1960 Albert Scheflen moved from Temple University to EPPI and joined with Ray Birdwhistell to study body language in psychotherapy. Ross Speck, who did his psychiatric residency in the early 1960s, developed, along with Carolyn Attneave, "network therapy," which broadened the context of treatment far beyond the nuclear family. In this approach, as many people as possible who are connected to the patient are invited to attend therapy sessions. Often as many as fifty people, including extended family, friends, neighbors, and teachers, are brought together for approximately three four-hour sessions led by a minimum of three therapists to discuss ways to support and help the patient change (Speck & Attneave, 1973).

In addition to his sponsorship of students and associates, Boszormenyi-Nagy himself has made major contributions to the study of schizophrenia (Boszormenyi-Nagy, 1962) and family therapy (Boszormenyi-Nagy, 1966, 1972; Boszormenyi-Nagy & Spark, 1973). Boszormenyi-Nagy describes himself as a therapist who went from being an analyst, prizing secrecy and confidentiality, to a family therapist, fighting the forces of pathology on an open battlefield. One of his most important contributions was to add ethical accountability to therapeutic goals and techniques. According to Boszormenyi-Nagy, neither the pleasure–pain principle nor transactional expediency is a sufficient guide to human behavior. Instead, he believes that family members have to base their relationships on trust and loyalty, and that they must balance the ledger of entitlement and indebtedness.

Salvador Minuchin

When Minuchin first burst onto the scene, it was the drama of his brilliant clinical demonstrations that people found so captivating. This compelling man with the elegant Latin accent would seduce, provoke, bully, or bewilder families into changing—as the situation required. But even Minuchin's legendary flair didn't have the same galvanizing impact of the elegant simplicity of his structural model.

Minuchin began his career as a family therapist in the early 1960s when he discovered two patterns common to troubled families: Some are "enmeshed"—chaotic and tightly interconnected; others are "disengaged"—isolated and seemingly unrelated. Both types lack clear lines of authority. Enmeshed parents are too entangled with their children to exercise leadership and control; disengaged parents are too distant to provide effective support and guidance.

Family problems are tenacious and resistant to change because they're embedded in powerful but unseen structures. Take, for example, a mother futilely remonstrating with a willful child. The mother can scold, punish, reward with gold stars, or try leniency; but as long as she's "enmeshed" (overly involved) with the child, her efforts will lack force because she lacks authority. Moreover, because the behavior of one family member is always related to that of others, the mother will have trouble stepping back as long as her husband is disengaged.

Once a social system such as a family becomes structured, attempts to change the rules constitute what family therapists call "first-order change"—change within a system that itself remains invariant. For the mother in the previous example to start practicing stricter discipline would be first-order change. The enmeshed mother is caught in an illusion of alternatives. She can be strict or lenient; the result is the same because she remains trapped in a triangle. What's needed is "second-order change"—a change in the system itself.

Minuchin first worked out his ideas while struggling with the problems of juvenile delinquency at the Wiltwyck School for Boys in New York. Family therapy with urban slum families was a new development, and publication of his ideas (Minuchin, Montalvo, Guerney, Rosman, & Schumer, 1967) led to his being invited to become the director of the Philadelphia Child Guidance Clinic in 1965. Minuchin brought Braulio Montalvo and Bernice Rosman with him, and they were joined in 1967 by Jay Haley. Together they transformed a traditional child guidance clinic into one of the great centers of the family therapy movement.

Minuchin's first notable achievement at the Philadelphia Child Guidance Clinic was a unique program for training members of the local black community as paraprofessional family therapists. In 1969 Minuchin received a training grant to launch an intensive two-year program in which Minuchin, Haley, Montalvo, and Rosman developed a highly successful approach to training as well as one of the most important systems of family therapy. According to Haley, one of the advantages to training people with no previous experience as clinicians is that they have less to unlearn and therefore are less resistant to thinking in terms of systems. Minuchin and Haley sought to capitalize on this by developing an approach with the least possible number of theoretical concepts. Conceptual elegance became one of the hallmarks of "structural family therapy."

The techniques of structural family therapy fall into two general strategies. First the therapist must accommodate to the family in order to "join" them. To begin by challenging a family's preferred mode of relating is almost guaranteed to provoke resistance. If, instead, the therapist starts by trying to understand and accept the family, they'll be more likely to accept treatment. (No one is eager to accept advice from someone they feel doesn't really understand them.) Once this initial *joining* is accomplished, the structural family therapist begins to use *restructuring* techniques. These are active maneuvers designed to disrupt dysfunctional structures by strengthening diffuse boundaries and loosening rigid ones (Minuchin & Fishman, 1981).

In 1981 Minuchin moved to New York and established what is now known as the Minuchin Center for the Family, where he pursued his dedication to teaching family therapists from all over the world and his commitment to social justice by working with the foster care system. He also continued to turn out a steady stream of the most influential books in the field. His 1974 *Families and Family Therapy* is deservedly the most popular book in the history of family therapy, and his 1993 *Family Healing* contains some of the most moving descriptions of family therapy ever written. In 1996 Dr. Minuchin retired and now lives in Boston with his wife Patricia.

Other Early Centers of Family Therapy

In New York, Israel Zwerling (who had been analyzed by Nathan Ackerman) and Marilyn Mendelsohn (who was analyzed by Don Jackson) organized the Family Studies Section at Albert Einstein College of Medicine and Bronx State Hospital. Andrew Ferber was named Director in 1964, and later Philip Guerin, a protégé of Murray Bowen's, joined the section. Nathan Ackerman served as a consultant, and the group assembled an impressive array of family therapists with diverse orientations. These included Chris Beels, Betty Carter, Monica Orfanidis (now McGoldrick), Peggy Papp, and Thomas Fogarty.

Philip Guerin became Director of Training of the Family Studies Section in 1970 and in 1972 established an extramural training program in Westchester. Shortly thereafter, in 1973, he founded the Center for Family Learning, where he developed one of the finest family therapy training programs in the nation.

In Galveston, Texas, Robert MacGregor and his colleagues developed "multiple impact therapy" (MacGregor, 1967). It was a case of necessity being the mother of invention. MacGregor's clinic served a large population scattered widely over southeastern Texas, and many of his clients had to travel hundreds of miles. Because they had to come such distances, most of these people were unable to return for weekly sessions. Therefore, to have maximum impact in a short time, MacGregor assembled a large team of professionals who worked intensively with the families for two full days. Although few family therapists have used such marathon sessions, the team approach continues to be one of the hallmarks of the field.

In Boston the two most significant early contributions to family therapy were both in the existential–experiential wing of the movement. Norman Paul developed an "operational mourning" approach designed to uncover and express unresolved grief. According to Paul, this cathartic approach is useful in almost all families, not just those who've suffered an obvious recent loss.

Also in Boston, Fred and Bunny Duhl set up the Boston Family Institute, where they developed "integrative family therapy." Along with David Kantor and Sandy Watanabe, the Duhls combined ideas from several family theories and added a number of expressive techniques, including *family sculpting.*

In Chicago, the Family Institute of Chicago and the Institute for Juvenile Research were important centers of the early scene in family therapy. At the Family Institute, Charles and Jan Kramer developed a clinical training program, which was later affiliated with Northwestern University Medical School. The Institute for Juvenile Research also mounted a training program under the leadership of Irv Borstein, with the consultation of Carl Whitaker.

The work of Nathan Epstein and his colleagues, first formulated in the department of psychiatry at McMaster University in Hamilton, Ontario, was a problem-centered approach (Epstein, Bishop, & Baldarin, 1981). The "McMaster Model of Family Functioning" goes step by step—

elucidating the problem, gathering data, considering alternatives for resolution, and assessing the learning process—to help families understand their own interaction and build on their newly acquired coping skills. Epstein later relocated to Brown University in Providence, Rhode Island.

●

Important early developments in family therapy outside the United States included Robin Skynner's (1976) use of psychodynamic family therapy at the Institute of Family Therapy in London; British psychiatrist John Howells's (1971) system of family diagnosis as a necessary step for planning therapeutic intervention; West German Helm Stierlin's (1972) integrative efforts, bringing together psychodynamic and systemic ideas to bear on understanding and treating troubled adolescents; in Rome, Maurizio Andolfi's work with families early in the 1970s, and his founding, in 1974, of the Italian Society for Family Therapy; and the work of Mara Selvini Palazzoli and her colleagues, who founded the Institute for Family Studies in Milan in 1967.

We conclude this section by mentioning the contributions of Christian Midelfort. Even more than was the case with John Bell, Midelfort's pioneering work in family therapy was slow to gain recognition. He began treating families of hospitalized patients in the early 1950s, delivered what was probably the first paper on family therapy at a professional meeting in 1952 at the American Psychiatric Association Convention, and published one of the first complete books on family therapy in 1957. Nevertheless, as a staff psychiatrist in LaCrosse, Wisconsin, he remained isolated from the rest of the family therapy movement. Midelfort's method of treating families was based on the group therapy model, and it combined psychoanalytic insights with techniques of support and encouragement. At first his concern was to counsel family members on the best ways to help the identified patient,

but gradually he evolved a systems viewpoint and conceived of the family as the patient. His technique was to encourage family members to give each other the love and support that was initially provided by the therapist.

●

Now that you've seen how family therapy emerged in several different places at once, we hope you haven't lost sight of one thing: There is a tremendous excitement to seeing how people's behavior makes sense in the context of their families. Meeting with a family for the first time is like turning on a light in a dark room.

The Golden Age of Family Therapy

In their first decade family therapists had all the enthusiasm and bravado of new kids on the block. "Look at this!" Haley and Jackson and Bowen seemed to say when they discovered the extent to which the whole family was implicated in the symptoms of individual patients. These new-style healers were pioneers, busy opening up new territory and staking their claim against unfriendly elements in the psychiatric establishment.

While they were struggling for legitimacy, family clinicians emphasized their common beliefs and downplayed their differences. Troubles, they agreed, came in families. But if the watchword of the 1960s had been "Look at this!"—emphasizing the leap of understanding made possible by seeing whole families together—the rallying cry of the 1970s was "Look what I can do!" as the new kids flexed their muscles and carved out their own turf.

The period from 1970 to 1985 saw the flowering of the famous schools of family therapy as the pioneers established training centers and worked out the implications of their models. The leading approach to family therapy in the

1960s was the communications model developed in Palo Alto. The book of the decade was *Pragmatics of Human Communication*, the text that introduced the systemic version of family therapy (and led some to believe that reading it would make them family therapists). The model of the 1980s was strategic therapy, and the books of the decade described its three most vital approaches: *Change* by Watzlawick, Weakland, and Fisch[3]; *Problem-Solving Therapy* by Jay Haley; and *Paradox and Counterparadox* by Mara Selvini Palazzoli and her Milan associates. The 1970s belonged to Salvador Minuchin. His *Families and Family Therapy* and the simple yet compelling model of family structure it described dominated the decade.

Structural theory seemed to offer just what the would-be family therapist was looking for: a simple, yet meaningful way of describing family organization, and a set of easy-to-follow steps to treatment. So compelling were the ideas described in *Families and Family Therapy* that it seemed all you had to do to transform families was join them, map their structure—and then do what Salvador Minuchin did to unbalance them. That was the rub.

In hindsight we might ask whether the impressive power of Minuchin's approach was a product of the method or the man? (The answer is, probably a little of both.) But in the 1970s the widely shared belief that structural family therapy could be easily learned drew people from all over the world to study at what for a decade was the mecca of family therapy: the Philadelphia Child Guidance Clinic.

The strategic therapy that flourished in the 1980s was centered in three unique and creative groups: MRI's brief therapy group, including John Weakland, Paul Watzlawick, and Richard Fisch; Jay Haley and Cloe Madanes, codirectors of the Family Therapy Institute of Washington, DC; and Mara Selvini Palazzoli and her colleagues in Milan. But the leading influence on the decade of strategic therapy was exerted by Milton Erickson, albeit from beyond the grave.

Erickson's genius was much admired and much imitated. Family therapists came to idolize Erickson the way we as children idolized Captain Marvel. We may have been little and the world big, but we could dream of being heroes—strong enough to overpower or clever enough to outwit all that we were afraid of. We'd come home from Saturday matinees all pumped up, get out our toy swords, put on our magic capes—and presto! *We* were superheroes. We were just kids and so we didn't bother translating our heroes' mythic powers into our own terms. Unfortunately, many of those who were starstruck by Erickson's legendary therapeutic tales did the same thing. Instead of grasping the principles on which they were predicated, too many therapists just tried to imitate his "uncommon techniques." To be any kind of competent therapist you must keep your psychological distance from the supreme artists—the Minuchins, the Milton Ericksons, the Michael Whites. Otherwise you end up aping the magic of their style, rather than grasping the substance of their ideas.

Erickson's emphasis on common, even unconscious, natural abilities is illustrated in his *utilization principle*—using clients' language and preferred ways of seeing themselves to minimize resistance. Instead of analyzing and interpreting dysfunctional dynamics, the idea was to get clients active and moving. Erickson believed that the movement that counted occurred outside the consulting room, so he made great use of assignments to be carried out between sessions. Such assignments, or "directives," were to become the hallmark of Jay Haley's strategic approach.

Part of what made Haley's strategic directives so attractive was that they were a wonderful way to gain power and control over people—for their

---

3. Although actually published in 1974, this book and its sequel, *The Tactics of Change*, were most widely read and taught in the 1980s.

own good—without the usual frustration of trying to convince them to do the right thing. (Most people already know what's good for them. The hard part is getting them to *do* it.) So, for example, in the case of a bulimic, a strategic directive might be for the bulimic's family to set out a mess of fried chicken, french fries, cookies, and ice cream. Then, with the family watching, the bulimic would mash up all the food with her hands, symbolizing what goes on in her stomach. After the food was reduced to a soggy mess, she would stuff it in the toilet. Then when the toilet clogged, she would have to ask the family member she resented most to unclog it. This task would symbolize not only what the bulimic does to herself, but also what she puts the family through (Madanes, 1981).

So compelling were such clever interventions that they were much imitated, unfortunately often with little appreciation of the basic principles underlying them. People were so taken by the creative directives that they often lost sight of Haley's developmental framework and emphasis on hierarchical structure.

What the strategic camp added to Erickson's creative approach to problem solving was a simple framework for understanding how families get stuck in their problems. According to the MRI model, problems develop from mismanagement of ordinary life difficulties, not necessarily by dysfunctional persons or systems. The original difficulty becomes a problem when mishandling leads people to get stuck in more-of-the-same solutions. It was a perverse twist on the old adage, "If at first you don't succeed, try, try again."

The interventions that attracted the most attention were symptom prescriptions, or *paradoxical injunctions.* Why not? They were fun (and their undercurrent of condescension wasn't immediately obvious). The point wasn't really to enact the symptom, but to reverse the attempted solution. If an overweight man tried unsuccessfully to diet, the idea behind telling him to stop denying himself the foods he craved would be just to do something different; it's making a 180-degree shift in the attempted solution. Whether or not the intervention is a paradox was irrelevant. The idea was to change the attempted solution. Keeping the underlying principle in mind, rather than being captured by the alleged novelty of what was after all only reverse psychology, one might come up with a more effective alternative. Instead of trying to stop eating, perhaps the man could be encouraged to start exercising. (It's always harder to *stop* doing something than it is to *start* doing something else.)

The Milan group built on the ideas pioneered at MRI, especially the use of the therapeutic double bind, or what they referred to as "counterparadox." Here's an example from *Paradox and Counterparadox* (Selvini Palazzoli, Boscolo, Cecchin, & Prata, 1978). The authors describe using a counterparadoxical approach with a six-year-old boy and his family. At the end of the session a letter from the observing team was read to the family. Young Bruno was praised for acting crazy to protect his father. By preoccupying his mother's time with fights and tantrums, the boy generously allowed his father more time for work and relaxation. Bruno was encouraged to continue doing what he was already doing, lest this comfortable arrangement be disrupted.

The appeal of the strategic approach was pragmatism. Complaints that brought people to therapy were treated as *the* problem, not symptoms of some underlying disorder. Making good use of the cybernetic metaphor, strategic therapists zeroed in on how family systems were regulated by negative feedback. They achieved remarkable results simply by disrupting the interactions that surrounded and maintained symptoms. What eventually turned therapists off to these approaches was their gamesmanship. Reframing was often transparently manipulative. The result was like watching a clumsy magician—you could see him stacking the deck.

Meanwhile, as structural and strategic approaches rose and fell in popularity, four other models of family therapy flourished quietly. Though they never really took center stage, experiential, psychoanalytic, behavioral, and Bowenian models grew and prospered. Although these schools never achieved the cachet of family therapy's latest fads, each of them produced powerful clinical advances, which will be examined at length in subsequent chapters.

Looking back, it's difficult to convey the excitement and optimism that energized family therapy in its golden age. Training centers sprouted up all over the country, workshops were packed, and the leaders of the movement were celebrated like rock stars. Active and forceful interveners, their self-assurance was infectious. Minuchin, Whitaker, Haley, Madanes, Selvini Palazzoli—they seemed to rise above the limitations of ordinary forms of talk therapy. Young therapists needed inspiration, and they found it. They learned from the masters, and they legendized them.

Somewhere in the mid 1980s a reaction set in. Despite optimistic assumptions, these activist approaches didn't always work. And so the field took revenge on those they'd idealized by cutting them down to size. Maybe it was Haley's manipulativeness that turned them off, or that Minuchin sometimes seemed more bossy than brilliant. Family therapists had marveled at their creativity and tried to copy it, but creativity can't be copied.

By the end of the decade the leaders of the major schools were growing older, their influence waning. What once seemed heroic now seemed aggressive and overbearing. A series of challenges—feminist and postmodern critiques, the reemergence of analytic and biological models, the magic bullet Prozac, the success of recovery programs like Alcoholics Anonymous, the ugly facts of wife beating and child abuse that challenged the notion that domestic problems were always a product of relationship—all shook our confidence in the models we knew to be true, knew would work. We'll take a close look at these challenges in subsequent chapters.

—Summary

Family therapy has a short history but a long past. For many years therapists resisted the idea of seeing members of a patient's family, to safeguard the privacy of the patient–therapist relationship. Freudians excluded the real family to uncover the unconscious, introjected family; Rogerians kept the family away to provide unconditional positive regard; and hospital psychiatrists discouraged family visits because they might disrupt the benign milieu of the hospital.

Several converging developments in the 1950s led to a new view of the family as a living system, an organic whole. Hospital psychiatrists noticed that often when patients improved, someone else in the family got worse. Thus it be-

came clear that change in any one person changes the whole system. Eventually it became apparent that changing the family might be the most effective way to change the individual.

Although practicing clinicians in hospitals and child guidance clinics prepared the way for family therapy, the most important breakthroughs were achieved in the 1950s by workers who were scientists first, healers second. In Palo Alto, Gregory Bateson, Jay Haley, Don Jackson, and John Weakland, studying communication, discovered that schizophrenia made sense in the context of pathological family communication. Schizophrenics weren't crazy in some meaningless way; their apparently senseless behavior made sense in the context of their families. At Yale, Theodore Lidz found a striking pattern of instability and conflict in the families of schizophrenics. *Marital schism* (open conflict) and *marital skew* (pathological balance) had profound effects on the development of children. Murray Bowen's observation of how mothers and their schizophrenic offspring go through cycles of closeness and distances was the forerunner of the *pursuer–distancer* dynamic. By hospitalizing whole families for observation and treatment, Bowen implicitly located the problem of schizophrenia in an *undifferentiated family ego mass* and even extended it beyond the nuclear family to three generations. Lyman Wynne linked schizophrenia to the family by demonstrating how communication deviance contributes to thought disorder.

These observations launched the family therapy movement, but the excitement they generated blurred the distinction between what the research teams observed and what they concluded. What they observed was that the behavior of schizophrenics *fit* with their families; what they concluded was far more momentous. First it was implied that since schizophrenia fit (made sense) in the context of the family, then the family must be the *cause* of schizophrenia. A second conclusion was even more influential. Family dynamics—double binds, pseudomutuality, undifferentiated family ego mass—began to be seen as products of a "system," rather than features of persons who share certain qualities because they live together. Thus was born a new creature, "the family system."

Once the family became the patient, there was a need for new ways to think about human problems. The systems metaphor was pivotal in this endeavor. And, although neither could be considered the founder of family therapy, no one had greater influence on how we think about families than Gregory Bateson and Milton Erickson, the anthropologist and the alienist.

Erickson's legacy was the pragmatic, problem-solving approach. He helped us to figure out what keeps families stuck, how to get them unstuck—using creative, sometimes counterintuitive ideas—and then get out, letting families get on about their business. But Erickson's mesmerizing artistry also promoted a tradition of the quick fix, done *to* rather than *with* families.

Bateson was the patron saint of the intellectual wing of family therapy. His ideas were so profound that they're still being mined by the most sophisticated thinkers in the field. Bateson also set an example of abstract theorizing and importing ideas from other—"more scientific"—disciplines. In the early days of family therapy, perhaps we needed models from fields like cybernetics to help us get started. But when so many family therapists continue to lean on the intellectual underpinnings of physics and biology, one wonders, why this physics envy? Perhaps, after all this time, we are still insecure about the legitimacy of psychology and about our ability to observe human behavior in human terms, without losing our objectivity.

Another reason family therapists gravitated to theories from mechanics and the natural sciences is that they rejected the major body of literature about human psychology: psychoanalysis. The psychoanalytic establishment was none too enthusiastic about this new challenge to their way of thinking, and in many quarters family therapists had to fight to win a place for their beliefs. Perhaps it was this resistance that pushed family therapists into a reactive position. The animosity between family therapists and psychodynamic therapists cooled off in the 1970s after family therapy won a place for itself in the mental health establishment. One reason family therapy gained acceptance was that it carved out its domain in areas traditionally neglected by the psychiatric establishment: services to children and the poor. An unfortunate legacy of this early antagonism, however, was a prolonged period of ignorance and neglect. In the 1990s the pendulum began to shift. Family therapists started to discover that, while trying to understand hidden forces in the family, it may also be useful to pay attention to the hidden forces in the individuals who make up the family. Perhaps the fullest appreciation of human nature lies in the fullest understanding of self *and* system.

Obvious parallels between small groups and families led some therapists to treat families as though they were just another form of group. They were well served in this endeavor by a volume of literature on group dynamics and group therapy. Some even saw therapy groups as models of family functioning, with the therapist as father, group members as siblings, and the group collectively as mother (Schindler, 1951). While group therapists experimented with married couples in groups, some family therapists began to conduct group therapy with individual families. John Bell was preeminent among these; his family group therapy was one of the most widely imitated of the early models (see Chapter 3).

As therapists gained experience with families, they discovered that the group therapy model wasn't entirely appropriate. Therapy groups are made up of unrelated individuals, strangers with no past or future outside the group. Families, on the other hand, consist of intimates who share the same myths, defenses, and points of view. Moreover, family members aren't peers who relate democratically as equals; generational differences create hierarchical structures that should not be ignored. For these reasons family therapists eventually abandoned the group therapy model, replacing it with a variety of systemic models.

The child guidance movement contributed the team approach to family therapy. At first members of interdisciplinary teams were assigned to different family members but, gradually, as they came to appreciate the interlocking behavior patterns of their separate clients, they started integrating and later combining their efforts. The child guidance movement began in this country in 1909 as a creation of the juvenile courts to treat delinquent children who were considered disturbed. Soon these clinics

broadened their scope to include a wide range of disorders, and at the same time they broadened the unit of treatment from the child to include the family. At first family therapy was seen as a better means of helping the patient; later it was conceived as a way to serve the needs of the entire family.

Who was the first to practice family therapy? This is a difficult question. As in every field, there were visionaries who anticipated the recognized development of family therapy. Freud, for example, treated "Little Hans" by working with his father as early as 1909. However, such experiments weren't sufficient to challenge the hegemony of individual therapy until the climate of the times was receptive. In the early 1950s family therapy was begun independently in four different places: by John Bell at Clark University, by Murray Bowen at the Menninger Clinic and later at NIMH, by Nathan Ackerman in New York, and by Don Jackson and Jay Haley in Palo Alto.

These pioneers had distinctly different backgrounds and clinical orientations. Not surprisingly, the approaches they developed were also quite different. This diversity still characterizes the field today. Had family therapy been started by a single person, as was psychoanalysis, it's unlikely that there would have been so much creative competition so soon.

In addition to those just mentioned, others who made significant contributions to the founding of family therapy include Lyman Wynne, Theodore Lidz, Virginia Satir, Carl Whitaker, Ivan Boszormenyi-Nagy, Christian Midelfort, Robert MacGregor, and Salvador Minuchin.

What we've called family therapy's golden age—the flowering of the schools in the 1970s and 1980s—was the high-water mark of our self-confidence. Armed with Haley's or Minuchin's latest text, therapists pledged allegiance to one school or another and set off with a sense of mission. What drew them to activist approaches was certainty and charisma. What soured them was hubris. To some, structural family therapy—at least as they had seen it demonstrated at workshops—began to seem like bullying. Others saw the shrewdness of the strategic approach as calculated, distant, manipulative. The tactics were clever but cold. Families were described as stubborn, they couldn't be reasoned with. You don't tell a cybernetic machine what you really believe. Therapists got tired of that way of thinking.

In the early years family therapists were animated by a tremendous sense of enthusiasm and conviction. Today, in the wake of postmodern critiques, managed care, and a resurgence of biological psychiatry, we're less sure of ourselves. In subsequent chapters we'll see how today's family therapists have managed to synthesize creative new ideas with some of the best of the earlier models. But as we explore each of the famous models in depth, we'll also see some good ideas that have been unwisely neglected.

All the complexity of the family field should not, however, obscure its basic premise: The family is the context of human problems. Like all human groups, the family has emergent properties—the whole is greater than the sum of its parts. Moreover, no matter how many and varied the explanations of these emergent properties, they all fall into two categories: structure and process. The structure of families includes triangles, subsystems, and boundaries. Among the processes that describe family interaction— emotional reactivity, dysfunctional communication, and so on—the central concept is *circularity*. Rather than worrying about who started what, family therapists understand and treat human problems as a series of moves and countermoves, in repeating cycles.

—Recommended Readings

Ackerman, N. W. 1958. *The psychodynamics of family life.* New York: Basic Books.

Bowen, M. 1960. A family concept of schizophrenia. In *The etiology of schizophrenia,* D. D. Jackson, ed. New York: Basic Books.

Greenberg, G. S. 1977. The family interactional perspective: A study and examination of the work of Don D. Jackson. *Family Process. 16:*385–412.

Haley, J., and Hoffman, L., eds. 1968. *Techniques of family therapy.* New York: Basic Books.

Jackson, D. D. 1957. The question of family homeostasis. *The Psychiatric Quarterly Supplement. 31:* 79–90.

Jackson, D. D. 1965. Family rules: Marital quid pro quo. *Archives of General Psychiatry. 12:*589–594.

Lidz, T., Cornelison, A., Fleck, S., and Terry, D. 1957. Intrafamilial environment of schizophrenic patients. II: Marital schism and marital skew. *American Journal of Psychiatry. 114:*241–248.

Vogel, E. F., and Bell, N. W. 1960. The emotionally disturbed child as the family scapegoat. In *The family,* N. W. Bell and E. F. Vogel, eds. Glencoe, IL: Free Press.

Weakland, J. H. 1960. The "double-bind" hypothesis of schizophrenia and three-party interaction. In *The etiology of schizophrenia,* D. D. Jackson, ed. New York: Basic Books.

Wynne, L. C., Ryckoff, I., Day, J., and Hirsch, S. I. 1958. Pseudo-mutuality in the family relationships of schizophrenics. *Psychiatry. 21:*205–220.

—References

Ackerman, N. W. 1938. The unity of the family. *Archives of Pediatrics. 55:*51–62.

Ackerman, N. W. 1954. Interpersonal disturbances in the family: Some unsolved problems in psychotherapy. *Psychiatry. 17:*359–368.

Ackerman, N. W. 1961. A dynamic frame for the clinical approach to family conflict. In *Exploring the base for family therapy,* N. W. Ackerman, F. L. Beatman, and S. N. Sherman, eds. New York: Family Services Association.

Ackerman, N. W. 1966a. *Treating the troubled family.* New York: Basic Books.

Ackerman, N. W. 1966b. Family psychotherapy—theory and practice. *American Journal of Psychotherapy.* 20:405–414.

Ackerman, N. W., Beatman, F., and Sherman, S. N., eds. 1961. *Exploring the base for family therapy.* New York: Family Service Assn. of America.

Ackerman, N. W., and Sobel, R. 1950. Family diagnosis: An approach to the preschool child. *American Journal of Orthopsychiatry.* 20:744–753.

Anonymous. 1972. Differentiation of self in one's family. In *Family interaction,* J. L. Framo, ed. New York: Springer.

Bardhill, D. R., and Saunders, B. E. 1988. In *Handbook of family therapy training and supervision,* H. A. Liddle, D. C. Breunlin, and R. C. Schwartz, eds. New York: Guilford Press.

Bateson, G. 1951. Information and codification: A philosophical approach. In *Communication: The social matrix of psychiatry,* J. Ruesch and G. Bateson, eds. New York: Norton.

Bateson, G., Jackson, D. D., Haley, J., and Weakland, J. 1956. Toward a theory of schizophrenia. *Behavioral Sciences.* 1:251–264.

Beatman, F. L. 1956. In *Neurotic interaction in marriage,* V. W. Eisenstein, ed. New York: Basic Books.

Bell, J. E. 1961. *Family group therapy.* Public Health Monograph No. 64. Washington, DC: U.S. Government Printing Office.

Bell, J. E. 1962. Recent advances in family group therapy. *Journal of Child Psychology and Psychiatry.* 3:1–15.

Bion, W. R. 1948. Experience in groups. *Human Relations.* 1:314–329.

Boszormenyi-Nagy, I. 1962. The concept of schizophrenia from the point of view of family treatment. *Family Process.* 1:103–113.

Boszormenyi-Nagy, I. 1966. From family therapy to a psychology of relationships; fictions of the individual and fictions of the family. *Comprehensive Psychiatry.* 7:408–423.

Boszormenyi-Nagy, I. 1972. Loyalty implications of the transference model in psychotherapy. *Archives of General Psychiatry.* 27:374–380.

Boszormenyi-Nagy, I., and Spark, G. L. 1973. *Invisible loyalties: Reciprocity in intergenerational family therapy.* New York: Harper & Row.

Bowen, M. 1961. Family psychotherapy. *American Journal of Orthopsychiatry.* 31:40–60.

Bowen, M. 1976. Principles and techniques of multiple family therapy. In *Family therapy: Theory and practice,* P. J. Guerin, ed. New York: Gardner Press.

Bowlby, J. P. 1949. The study and reduction of group tensions in the family. *Human Relations.* 2:123–138.

Broderick, C. B., and Schrader, S. S. 1981. The history of professional marriage and family therapy. In *Handbook of family therapy,* A. S. Gurman and D. P. Kniskern, eds. New York: Brunner/Mazel.

Broderick, C. B., and Schrader, S. S. 1991. The history of professional marriage and family therapy. In *Handbook of family therapy,* Vol. II, A. S. Gurman and D. P. Kniskern, eds. New York: Brunner/Mazel.

Brown, G. W. 1959. Experiences of discharged chronic schizophrenia patients in various types of living groups. *Milbank Memorial Fund Quarterly.* 37:105–131.

Dicks, H. V. 1964. Concepts of marital diagnosis and therapy as developed at the Tavistock Family Psychiatric Clinic, London, England. In *Marriage counseling in medical practice,* E. M. Nash, L. Jessner, and D. W. Abse, eds. Chapel Hill: University of North Carolina Press.

Elizur, J., and Minuchin, S. 1989. *Institutionalizing madness: Families, therapy, and society.* New York: Basic Books.

Epstein, N. B., Bishop, D. S., and Baldarin, L. M. 1981. McMaster Model of Family Functioning. In *Normal family problems,* F. Walsh, ed. New York: Guilford Press.

Fisher, S., and Mendell, D. 1958. The spread of psychotherapeutic effects from the patient to his family group. *Psychiatry.* 21:133–140.

Freud, S. 1911. Psycho-analytical notes on an autobiographical case of paranoia. *Standard Edition.* 12:3–84. London: Hogarth Press.

Fromm-Reichmann, F. 1948. Notes on the development of treatment of schizophrenics by psychoanalytic psychotherapy. *Psychiatry.* 11:263–274.

Ginsburg, S. W. 1955. The mental health movement and its theoretical assumptions. In *Community programs for mental health,* R. Kotinsky and H. Witmer, eds. Cambridge: Harvard University Press.

Guerin, P. J. 1976. Family therapy: The first twenty-five years. In *Family therapy: Theory and practice,* P. J. Guerin, ed. New York: Gardner Press.

Gurman, A. S., and Jacobson, N. S. 2002. *Clinical handbook of couple therapy*, 3rd ed. New York: Guilford Press.

Haley, J. 1961. Control in brief psychotherapy. *Archives of General Psychiatry.* 4:139–153.

Haley, J. 1963. *Strategies of psychotherapy.* New York: Grune & Stratton.

Hoffman, L. 1981. *Foundations of family therapy.* New York: Basic Books.

Howells, J. G. 1971. *Theory and practice of family psychiatry.* New York: Brunner/Mazel.

Jackson, D. D. 1954. Suicide. *Scientific American.* 191:88–96.

Jackson, D. D. 1965. Family rules: Marital quid pro quo. *Archives of General Psychiatry.* 12:589–594.

Jackson, D. D., and Weakland, J. H. 1959. Schizophrenic symptoms and family interaction. *Archives of General Psychiatry.* 1:618–621.

Jackson, D. D., and Weakland, J. H. 1961. Conjoint family therapy, some considerations on theory, technique, and results. *Psychiatry.* 24:30–45.

Johnson, A. M., and Szurek, S. A. 1954. Etiology of anti-social behavior in delinquents and psychopaths. *Journal of the American Medical Association.* 154:814–817.

Kaslow, F. W. 1980. History of family therapy in the United States: A kaleidoscopic overview. *Marriage and Family Review.* 3:77–111.

Kempler, W. 1974. *Principles of Gestalt family therapy.* Salt Lake City: Desert Press.

Kluckhohn, F. R., and Spiegel, J. P. 1954. *Integration and conflict in family behavior.* Group for the Advancement of Psychiatry, Report No. 27. Topeka, Kansas.

Kubie, L. S. 1956. Psychoanalysis and marriage. In *Neurotic interaction in marriage,* V. W. Eisenstein, ed. New York: Basic Books.

Laing, R. D. 1960. *The divided self.* London: Tavistock.

Laing, R. D. 1965. Mystification, confusion and conflict. In *Intensive family therapy,* I. Boszormenyi-Nagy and J. L. Framo, eds. New York: Harper & Row.

Levy, D. 1943. *Maternal Overprotection.* New York: Columbia University Press.

Lewin, K. 1951. *Field theory in social science.* New York: Harper.

Lidz, T., Cornelison, A., Fleck, S., and Terry, D. 1957a. Intrafamilial environment of the schizophrenic patient. I: The father. *Psychiatry.* 20:329–342.

Lidz, T., Cornelison, A., Fleck, S., and Terry, D. 1957b. Intrafamilial environment of the schizophrenic patient. II: Marital schism and marital skew. *American Journal of Psychiatry.* 114: 241–248.

Lidz, T., Parker, B., and Cornelison, A. R. 1956. The role of the father in the family environment of the schizophrenic patient. *American Journal of Psychiatry.* 113:126–132.

MacGregor, R. 1967. Progress in multiple impact theory. In *Expanding theory and practice in family therapy,* N. W. Ackerman, F. L. Bateman, and S. N. Sherman, eds. New York: Family Services Association.

Madanes, C. 1981. *Strategic family therapy.* San Francisco: Jossey-Bass.

Mahler, M. S., and Rabinovitch, R. 1956. The effects of marital conflict on child development. In *Neurotic interaction in marriage,* V. W. Eisenstein, ed. New York: Basic Books.

Minuchin, S. 1974. *Families and family therapy.* Cambridge, MA: Harvard University Press.

Minuchin, S., and Fishman, H. C. 1981. *Family therapy techniques.* Cambridge, MA: Harvard University Press.

Minuchin, S., Montalvo, B., Guerney, B. G., Rosman, B. L., and Schumer, F. 1967. *Families of the slums.* New York: Basic Books.

Minuchin, S., and Nichols, M. P. 1993. *Family healing.* New York: Free Press.

Mittleman, B. 1944. Complementary neurotic reactions in intimate relationships. *Psychoanalytic Quarterly.* 13:474–491.

Mittleman, B. 1948. The concurrent analysis of married couples. *Psychoanalytic Quarterly.* 17: 182–197.

Mittleman, B. 1956. Analysis of reciprocal neurotic patterns in family relationships. In *Neurotic interaction in marriage,* V. W. Eisenstein, ed. New York: Basic Books.

Montague, A. 1956. Marriage—A cultural perspective. In *Neurotic interaction in marriage,* V. W. Eisenstein, ed. New York: Basic Books.

Moreno, J. L. 1945. *Psychodrama.* New York: Beacon House.

Oberndorf, C. P. 1938. Psychoanalysis of married people. *Psychoanalytic Review.* 25:453–475.

Parsons, T., and Bales, R. F. 1955. *Family, socialization and interaction process.* Glencoe, IL: Free Press.

Richmond, M. E. 1917. *Social diagnosis.* New York: Russell Sage.

Satir, V. 1964. *Conjoint family therapy.* Palo Alto, CA: Science and Behavior Books.

Satir, V. 1972. *Peoplemaking.* Palo Alto, CA: Science and Behavior Books.

Schindler, W. 1951. Counter-transference in family-pattern group psychotherapy. *International Journal of Group Psychotherapy. 1:*100–105.

Schwartz, R. 1995. *Internal family systems therapy.* New York: Guilford Press.

Selvini Palazzoli, M., Boscolo, L., Cecchin, G., and Prata, G. 1978. *Paradox and counterparadox.* New York: Jason Aronson.

Sherif, M. 1948. *An outline of social psychology.* New York: Harper & Brothers.

Singer, M. T., Wynne, L. C., and Toohey, M. L. 1978. Communication disorders and the families of schizophrenics. In *The nature of schizophrenia,* L. C. Wynne, R. L. Cromwell, and S. Matthysse, eds. New York: Wiley.

Siporin, M. 1980. Marriage and family therapy in social work. *Social Casework. 61:*11–21.

Skynner, A. C. R. 1976. *Systems of family and marital psychotherapy.* New York: Brunner/Mazel.

Speck, R., and Attneave, C. 1973. *Family networks: Rehabilitation and healing.* New York: Pantheon.

Spiegel, J. P. 1957. The resolution of role conflict within the family. *Psychiatry. 20:*1–16.

Stierlin, H. 1972. *Separating parents and adolescents.* New York: Quadrangle/New York Times Books.

Strodtbeck, F. L. 1954. The family as a three-person group. *American Sociological Review. 19:*23–29.

Strodtbeck, F. L. 1958. Family interaction, values, and achievement. In *Talent and society,* D. C. McClelland, A. L. Baldwin, A. Bronfenbrenner, and F. L. Strodtbeck, eds. Princeton, NJ: Van Nostrand.

Watzlawick, P. A., Beavin, J. H., and Jackson, D. D. 1967. *Pragmatics of human communication.* New York: Norton.

Whitaker, C. A. 1958. Psychotherapy with couples. *American Journal of Psychotherapy. 12:*18–23.

Whitaker, C. A. 1975. Psychotherapy of the absurd: With a special emphasis on the psychotherapy of aggression. *Family Process. 14:*1–16.

Whitaker, C. A. 1976. A family is a four-dimensional relationship. In *Family therapy: Theory and practice,* P. J. Guerin, ed. New York: Gardner Press.

Whitaker, C. A., and Malone, T. P. 1953. *The roots of psychotherapy.* New York: Balkiston.

Wiener, N. 1948. *Cybernetics, or control and communication in the animal and the machine.* New York: Wiley.

Wynne, L. C. 1961. The study of intrafamilial alignments and splits in exploratory family therapy. In *Exploring the base for family therapy,* N. W. Ackerman, F. L. Beatman, and S. N. Sherman, eds. New York: Family Services Association.

Wynne, L. C., Ryckoff, I., Day, J., and Hirsch, S. I. 1958. Pseudomutuality in the family relationships of schizophrenics. *Psychiatry. 21:*205–220.

Early Models and Basic Techniques

Group Process and Communications Analysis

A Very Special Kind of Group

Most people who practiced family therapy in the early years used some combination of a group therapy approach and the communications model that came out of Bateson's schizophrenia project. In this chapter, we will explore those two models and see how they had to be modified to fit the unique challenges of treating troubled families. We will conclude with a section on the basic techniques of family therapy.

•

Those of us who practiced family therapy in the 1960s could often be seen engaged in a strange ritual. When a family filed in for their first session, all anxious and uncertain, the therapist, all smiles, would kneel in front of one of the children. "Hi! What's your name?" Then, "Do you know why you're here?" meanwhile ignoring the parents. The most common answers to this question were: "Mommy said we were going to the doctor's," in a frightened

voice, or, confused, "Daddy said we were going for a ride." Then the therapist, trying not to sound scornful, would turn to the parents and say, "Perhaps you could explain to Johnny why you *are* here."

The reason for this little charade was that before they understood how families were structured, many therapists treated the family as a group, in which the youngest members were presumed to be the most vulnerable and, therefore, in need of "expert" help to express themselves—as though the parents weren't in charge, as though everybody's opinion were equal.

Another common scene was therapists making solemn comments about patterns of communication: "I notice that when I ask Suzie a question, she first turns to Mom to see if it's okay to answer." Very clever. Not only did we expect families to be impressed by such bright remarks, we imagined that they'd somehow instantly start communicating according to some

51

ideal model in *our* heads—"I-statements" and all the rest.

Are we being a little condescending here? Absolutely. The first family therapists turned to models from group therapy and communications analysis because there were no other models available.

Sketches of Leading Figures

Not only did many of the early family therapists turn to the group therapy literature for guidance in treating families, many of the pioneers of family therapy were themselves products of group therapy training. By far the most influential of these was John Elderkin Bell.

Bell (1975) credited his start as a family therapist to a fortunate misunderstanding. When he was in London in 1951, Bell heard that Dr. John Bowlby of the Tavistock Clinic was experimenting with group therapy for families. This caught Bell's interest and inspired him to try this approach as a means of dealing with behavior problems in children. As Bell later put it, if so eminent an authority as John Bowlby was using family therapy, it must be a good idea. It turned out that Bowlby had only interviewed one family as an adjunct to treating a troubled child, but Bell didn't learn this until years later.

Communications therapy was one of the earliest and certainly the most influential approaches to family therapy. The leading characters who developed the communications model were the members of Bateson's schizophrenia project and the Mental Research Institute in Palo Alto, most notably Don Jackson and Jay Haley.

Virginia Satir was also a prominent member of the Mental Research Institute group, but because her emphasis shifted to emotional experiencing, we will consider her in Chapter 8.

Theoretical Formulations

Although he's better known for studying the psychology of individuals, Freud was also interested in interpersonal relations, and many would consider his *Group Psychology and the Analysis of the Ego* (Freud, 1921) the first major text on the psychology of the group. According to Freud, the major requirement for transforming a collection of individuals into a group is the emergence of a leader. In addition to manifest tasks of organization and direction, the leader serves as a parent figure on whom the members become more or less dependent. Members *identify* with the leader as a parent surrogate and with other group members as siblings. *Transference* occurs in groups when members repeat unconscious attitudes formed in the process of growing up. Freud's concept of *resistance* in individual therapy also applies to groups, because group members, seeking to ward off anxiety, may oppose the progress of treatment by being silent or hostile, missing sessions, and avoiding painful topics. Family groups resist treatment by scapegoating, superficial chatting, prolonged dependency on the therapist, refusing to follow therapeutic suggestions, and allowing difficult family members to stay home.

Like Freud, Wilfred Bion (1961) attempted to develop a group psychology of the unconscious and described groups as functioning on *manifest* and *latent* levels. The group's official task is on the manifest level, but people also join groups to fulfill powerful, but unconscious, primal needs. At the latent level, groups seek a leader who will permit them to gratify their needs for *dependence, pairing,* and *fight–flight*.

According to Kurt Lewin's (1951) *field theory,* conflict is an inevitable feature of group life, as members vie with one another for adequate *life space*. Just as animals need their own territory, people seem to need their own "space" (or turf), and for this reason there is an inherent tension between the needs of the individual and those of the group. The amount of conflict generated by this tension depends on the amount of restriction imposed by the group, compared with the amount of support it gives in exchange. (People who give up a lot for their families expect a lot in return.)

What distinguished Lewin's model of group tensions from earlier theories is that it was *ahistorical*. Instead of worrying about who did what to whom in the past, Lewin concentrated on what was going on in the *here and now*. This focus on *process* (how people talk), rather than *content* (what they talk about), is one of the keys to understanding the way a group (or family) functions.

Communications therapists adopted the **black box** concept from telecommunications and applied it to the individuals within the family. This model disregards the internal complexities of individuals and concentrates on their input and output—that is, communication. It isn't that these clinicians denied the phenomena of mind—thinking and feeling—they just found it useful to ignore them. By limiting their focus to what goes on between, rather than within, family members, communications theorists qualify as "systems purists" (Beels & Ferber, 1969).

Communications theorists also disregarded the past, leaving that to psychoanalysts, while they searched for patterns with which to understand behavior in the present. They considered it unimportant to figure out what's cause and what's effect, preferring to use a model of circular causality in which chains of behavior are seen as effect-effect-effect.

Communications theorists found in *general systems theory* (von Bertalanffy, 1950) a number of ideas useful in explaining how families work. But while they (Watzlawick, Beavin, & Jackson, 1967) described families as *open systems* in their theoretical statements, they tended to treat them as *closed systems* in their clinical work. Thus they concentrated their therapeutic efforts on the nuclear family, with little or no consideration of inputs from the community or extended family.

Relationships between communicants can also be described as either complementary or symmetrical. *Complementary* relationships are based on differences that fit together. A common complementary pattern is where one person is assertive and the other submissive, with each reinforcing the other's position. It's important to understand that these are descriptive, not evaluative, terms. Moreover, it's a mistake to assume that one person's position *causes* the other's, or that one is weaker than the other. As Sartre (1964) pointed out, it is the masochist as well as the sadist who creates a sadomasochistic relationship.

Symmetrical relationships are based on equality; the behavior of one mirrors that of the other. Symmetrical relationships between husbands and wives, where both are free to pursue careers and share housekeeping and childrearing, are often thought of as ideal by today's standards. However, from a communications analysis, there's no reason to assume that such a relationship would be any more stable or functional for the system than a traditional, complementary one.

Another aspect of communication is that it can be *punctuated* in various ways (Bateson & Jackson, 1964). An outside observer may hear a dialogue as an uninterrupted flow of communication, but each of the participants may believe that what he or she says is caused by what the other says. Couples therapists are familiar with the impasse created by the wife who says she only nags because her husband withdraws, while he says he only withdraws because she nags. Another example is the wife who says she'd be in the mood for sex more often if her husband was more affectionate; to which he counters that he'd be more affectionate if she'd have sex more often.

As long as couples punctuate their interactions in this fashion, there is little likelihood of change. Each insists that the other causes the stalemate, and each waits for the other to change. The impasse is created by the universal tendency for people to punctuate a sequence of interactions so that it appears the other one has control—in other words, power. Children illustrate this when they have a fight and run to a parent, both crying, "He started it!" Their mutual illusion is based on the mistaken notion that such sequences have a discrete beginning, that one person's behavior is caused by another's, in linear fashion.

Communications theory doesn't accept linear causality or look for underlying motives; instead, this model assumes circular causality and analyzes interactions occurring at the present time. Considerations of underlying causality are treated as conceptual noise, with no practical therapeutic value. The behavior that communications theorists observe is a pattern of communication linked in additive chains of stimulus and response. This model of sequential causality enables therapists to treat behavioral chains as *feedback loops.* When the response to one family member's problematic behavior exacerbates the problem, that chain is seen to be a *positive feedback loop.* The advantage of this formulation is that it focuses on interactions that perpetuate problems, which can be changed, instead of inferring underlying causes, which aren't observable and often not subject to change.

Normal Family Development

Now that we have rich literatures on child development and the family life cycle, it doesn't seem worthwhile to turn to the group dynamics literature to help us understand normal family development. Nevertheless, in the early days of family therapy, therapists borrowed concepts of group development and applied them to families. Among the most notorious of these was Talcott Parsons's idea (1950) that

groups need an **instrumental** leader and an **expressive** leader to look after the *social-emotional* needs of the group. Guess who was elected to which roles—and consider how that helped to legitimize an artificial and unfair division of labor.

●

As "systems purists," communications therapists treated behavior as ahistorical. Whether describing or treating family interactions, their attention was on the here and now, with very little interest in development. Normal families were described as functional systems, which like all living systems depend on two important processes (Maruyama, 1968). First, they must maintain integrity in the face of environmental disturbances. This is accomplished through *negative feedback,* often illustrated by the example of the thermostat in a home heating unit. When the heat drops below a set point, the thermostat activates the furnace until the room returns to the desired temperature.

No living system can survive without a regular structure, but too rigid a structure leaves a system ill-equipped to adapt to changing circumstances. This is why normal families also have mechanisms of *positive feedback.* Negative feedback minimizes change to maintain a steady state; positive feedback alters the system to accommodate to novel inputs. For example, as children grow older, they change the nature of their input to the family system. The most obvious instance of this is adolescence, at which time children demand more independence. A family system limited to negative feedback can only resist such changes. Normal families, on the other hand, also have positive feedback mechanisms and can respond to new information by modifying their structure.

Normal families become periodically unbalanced (Hoffman, 1971) during transition points in the family life cycle. No family passes through these changes unperturbed; all experience stress, resist change, and develop vicious cycles. But flexible families aren't trapped in these cycles; they're able to engage in positive feedback to modify themselves. Symptomatic families remain stuck, using the symptomatic member to avoid change.

Concepts from general systems theory, such as positive feedback, have the virtues of wide applicability and theoretical elegance, but often seem a little abstract. When we recognize that the channel for positive feedback is communication, it's possible to state the case more plainly. Healthy families are able to change because they communicate clearly and are flexible. When their children say they want to grow up, healthy parents listen.

Development of Behavior Disorders

From a group theory perspective, symptoms were considered products of disturbed and disturbing group processes. But groups weren't thought to *cause* disturbance in their members; rather, the behavior of the members was part of the disturbance of the group. Thus group researchers and therapists rejected linear causality in favor of a form of circular causality they called "group dynamics." Family group therapists were less concerned with the origins of psychopathology than with the conditions that perpetuate it. These include stereotyped roles, breakdowns in communication, and blocked channels for giving and receiving support.

Rigidity of roles forces group interactions to occur within a narrow, stereotyped range. When options are reduced for individuals, the flexibility of the group is constrained. Groups stuck with inflexible roles and unvarying structures tend to malfunction when called upon to handle changed circumstances. Moreover, if flexibility is threatening, such groups don't risk communicating about unmet needs; the result is often frustration and sometimes symptomatic disturbance in one of the group's members. If the needs that generate acute disturbance continue to go unmet, symptoms may be perpetuated as a role, and the group organizes itself around a "sick" member.

●

According to communications therapists, the function of symptoms is to maintain the homeostatic equilibrium of family systems. (As we shall see, the notion that symptoms are functional—implying that families *need* their problems—was to become controversial.) Pathological families were seen as trapped in dysfunctional, but tenacious, homeostatic patterns of communication (Jackson & Weakland, 1961). These families cling to their rigid structures and respond to signs of change as negative feedback. That is, change is treated not as an opportunity for growth but as a threat and a signal to change back.

In their theoretical papers, communications theorists maintained the position that pathology inheres in the system as a whole (Hoffman, 1971; Jackson, 1967; Watzlawick, Beavin, & Jackson, 1967). The *identified patient* was considered a role with complementary counterroles, all of which contributed to the maintenance of the system. The identified patient might be the victim, but in this framework "victim" and "victimizer" were seen as mutually determined roles—neither is good or bad, and neither causes the other. However, although this circular causality was a consistent feature of their theorizing, communications therapists often lapsed into demonizing parents.

It's difficult to judge a single communication as normal or pathological. Instead the judgment must be made on a series or sequence of communications. One can look at syntax and semantics, that is, the content of speech, for clarity or confusion. This approach is exemplified by Lyman Wynne's studies in which he found that schizophrenics' speech could be differentiated from that of normals or delinquents (Wynne & Singer, 1963). Alternatively one can look at the pragmatics of communication, as did the members of the Palo Alto group. Here the emphasis wasn't on clarity or content, but on the *metacommunication* or command aspects of language.

Goals of Therapy

The goal of treating family groups was the same as treating stranger groups: individuation of group members and improved relationships. Individual growth is promoted when unmet needs are verbalized and when overly confining roles are explored and expanded. When family members are released from their inhibitions, it was assumed that they would develop greater family cohesiveness. Notice the difference in emphasis between this—considering families as groups of individuals, each of whom must be helped to develop—and the systemic view of the family as a unit. Treating families as though they were like any other group failed to appreciate the need for hierarchy and structure.

Improved communication was seen as the primary way to meet the goal of improved group functioning. The aims of this approach reflected the fairly simple view of families and their problems that was prevalent among practitioners before they learned to think systemically. While Bateson and his colleagues were laboring with their complex systems analyses, the average therapist still thought that the way to help troubled families was simply to have them sit down and talk to one another.

●

The goal of communications family therapy was to take "deliberate action to alter poorly functioning patterns of interaction . . ." (Watzlawick, Beavin, & Jackson, 1967, p. 145). Because "patterns of interaction" are synonymous with communication, this meant changing patterns of communication. In the early days of communications family therapy, especially in Virginia Satir's work, this translated into a generic goal of improving communication in the family. Later the goal was narrowed to altering specific patterns of communication that maintained problems. By 1974 Weakland wrote that the goal of therapy was resolving symptoms, not reorganizing families: "We see the resolution of problems as primarily requiring a substitution of behavior patterns so as to interrupt the vicious, positive feedback circles" (Weakland, Fisch, Watzlawick, & Bodin, 1974, p. 149).

The goal of the communications therapist was, like that of the behavior therapist, to interdict behavior that stimulated and reinforced symptoms. These two models also shared the assumption that once pathological behavior was blocked, it would be replaced by constructive alternatives, instead of by other symptoms. The limitation of the behavioral model was that it treated the symptomatic person as the problem, and conceived of the symptom as a response rather than as both a response and a stimulus in a chain of interaction. The limitation of the communications model was that it isolated sequences of behavior that maintained symptoms and focused on two-person interactions without considering triangles or other structural problems. If, for example, a child is fearful because her overinvolved father yells at her, and her father yells at her because his wife isn't emotionally involved, then changing the father's behavior might result in a different form of a symptomatic behavior in the child, unless the relationship with the wife is addressed.

Conditions for Behavior Change

Group family therapists thought the way to bring about change was to help family members open up and talk to each other. The therapist encourages them to talk openly, supports those who seem reticent, and then critiques the process of their interaction. It is the power of the therapist's support that helps family members open up where they once held back, and this, in turn, often shows them in a new light, which enables others in the family to relate to them in new ways. For example, children who aren't accustomed to being listened to by grown-ups tend to make themselves "heard" by disruptive behavior. But if a therapist demonstrates willingness to listen, the children may learn to express their feelings in words rather than actions.

Group-oriented therapists promoted communication by concentrating on *process* rather than *content* (Bion, 1961; Bell, 1975; Yalom, 1985). This is an important point. The minute a therapist gets caught up in the details of a family's problems or thinks about solving them, he or she loses the opportunity to discover the process of what family members are doing that prevents them from working out their own solutions.

●

According to the communications theorists, all actions have communicative properties: Symptoms can be considered as covert messages, commenting on relationships (Jackson, 1961). Even a headache that develops from prolonged tension in the occipital muscles is a message, since it is a report on how the person feels and also a command to be responded to. If a symptom is seen as a covert message, then by implication making the message overt eliminates the need for the symptom. Therefore one of the important ways to change behavior is to bring hidden messages out into the open.

As we have pointed out, an essential ingredient of the double bind is that it is impossible to escape or look at the binding situation from the outside. But no change can be generated from within: it can only come from outside the pattern. So, according to communications theorists (Watzlawick, Beavin, & Jackson, 1967), the paradigm for psychotherapy is an intervention from the outside to resolve relational dilemmas. The therapist is an outsider who supplies what the relationship cannot: a change in the rules.

A therapist can either point out problematic sequences or simply manipulate them to produce therapeutic change. The first strategy relies on the power of insight and depends on a willingness to change; the second does not. It's an attempt to beat families at their own games, with or without their cooperation. Included in the second strategy are many of the most clever and interesting tactics of communications therapy, and much more was written about these than about simple interpretation. Nevertheless, early family therapists relied more on pointing out communication problems than on any other technique.

The first strategy, simply pointing out communicational problems, was represented in Virginia Satir's work and widely practiced by those new to family therapy. The second, less direct, approach was characteristic of Haley and Jackson and eventually became the predominant strategy.

Jackson and Haley's early work with families was influenced by the hypnotherapy they learned from Milton Erickson. The hypnotherapist works by giving explicit instructions whose purpose is often obscure. However, before patients will follow directions, the therapist must gain control of the relationship. Jackson sometimes began by advising patients about their symptoms. He did so to point up the problem area, just as interpretation would do; but at the same time his comments made the patient focus on the relationship with the therapist—regardless of whether the patient accepted or rejected the advice. Haley (1961) recommended asking certain kinds of patients to do something in order to provoke a rebellious response, which served to make them concede that they were relating to the therapist. He mentions, as an example, directing a schizophrenic patient to hear voices. If the patient hears voices, then he is complying with the therapist's request; if he doesn't hear voices, then he can no longer claim to be crazy.

Techniques

The techniques of family group therapy were similar to those of analytic and supportive group therapy. The role of the therapist was that of a *process leader.* The model of the family was a democratic group, and the therapist related to the family members democratically, just as the members were expected to do with each other. The therapist saw them as people with something to say, often in need of help saying it. There was little concern with structure or reinforcing the parents' hierarchical position. If anything, there was a tendency to give extra support to children and encourage them to assume a more equal role in family interactions.

John Bell's original approach (1961) was orchestrated in a series of stages. First was a *child-centered phase,* in which children were helped to express their wishes and concerns. Bell was so anxious to help children participate that he held preliminary meetings with parents to encourage them not only to listen but also to go along with some of the children's requests as a means of gaining their cooperation.

After the children spoke up and were rewarded with some additional privileges, it was the parents' turn. In the *parent-centered stage,* parents usually began by complaining about their children's behavior. During this phase, Bell was careful to soften the harshest parental criticisms and to focus on problem solving. In the final, or *family-centered,* stage, the therapist equalized support for the entire family while they continued to improve their communication and work out solutions to their problems. The following vignette illustrates Bell's (1975) directive style of intervening.

> After remaining silent for a few sessions, one father came in with a great tirade against his son,

daughter, and wife. I noticed how each individual in his own way, within a few minutes, was withdrawing from the conference. Then I said, "Now I think we should hear what Jim has to say about this, and Nancy should have her say, and perhaps we should also hear what your wife feels about it." This restored family participation without closing out the father. (p. 136)

Three specialized applications of group methods to family treatment were *multiple family group therapy, multiple impact therapy,* and *network therapy.*

Peter Laqueur began **multiple family group therapy** in 1950 at Creedmore State Hospital in New York and refined this approach at Vermont State Hospital (Laqueur, 1966, 1976). Multiple family group therapy involved treating four to six families together for weekly sessions of ninety minutes. Laqueur and his cotherapists conducted multiple family groups like traditional therapy groups with the addition of encounter-group and psychodrama techniques. Structured exercises were used to increase the level of interaction and intensity of feeling; families were used as "cotherapists" to help confront members of other families from a more personal position than therapists could take.

Although multiple family therapy lost its most creative force with Peter Laqueur's untimely death, it is still occasionally used, especially in hospital settings, both inpatient (McFarlane, 1982) and outpatient (Gritzer & Okum, 1983).

Robert MacGregor and his colleagues at the University of Texas Medical Branch in Galveston developed **multiple impact therapy** as a way to have maximum impact on families who came from all over Texas to spend several days with a large team of professionals (MacGregor, Richie, Serrano, Schuster, McDonald, & Goolishian, 1964; MacGregor, 1967, 1972). Team members met with various combinations of family members and then assembled in a large group to make recommendations. Although multiple impact therapy is no longer practiced, its intense but infrequent meetings were a powerful stimulus for change and prefigured later developments in experiential therapy (Chapter 8) and the Milan model (Chapter 6).

Network therapy was an approach developed by Ross Speck and Carolyn Attneave for assisting families in crisis by assembling their entire social network—family, friends, neighbors—in gatherings of as many as fifty people. Teams of therapists were used, and their emphasis was on breaking destructive patterns of relationship and mobilizing support for new options (Speck & Attneave, 1973; Ruevini, 1975).

Therapeutic teams meet with networks in meetings lasting from two to four hours; groups typically meet three to six times. Encounter group techniques are used to alleviate defensiveness and foster a climate of warm involvement. After five or ten minutes of shaking hands, jumping up and down, shouting, huddling together, and swaying back and forth, the group experiences a release of tension and a sense of cohesiveness.

The *polarization phase* begins when the leader activates conflicting points of view in the network. These may be dramatized by arranging people into concentric circles and inviting them to confront their differences. Under the guidance of the leaders, confrontation is moved toward compromise and synthesis. During the *mobilization phase,* tasks are presented, and subgroups are asked to develop plans for solving concrete problems. If the identified patient needs a job, a committee might be formed to help; if young parents are stuck at home fighting over who's going to take care of the baby, a group might be asked to develop baby-sitting resources and allow the couple to get out together.

After the initial enthusiasm wears off, network groups often fall into exhaustion and despair as members realize just how entrenched certain problems are. Uri Ruevini (1975) described one case in which a period of depression set in and the problem family felt isolated and abandoned by the network. Ruevini broke

through this impasse by prescribing a cathartic group exercise, "the death ceremony." Family members were asked to close their eyes and imagine themselves dead. The rest of the network were asked to share their feelings about the family: their strengths, their weaknesses, and what each of them meant to their friends. This dramatic device produced an outpouring of feeling that roused the network out of depression.

Speck and Attneave (1973) described breaking the network into problem-solving subgroups, using action instead of affect to move beyond despair. In one case they assigned a group of friends to watch over an adolescent who was abusing drugs and another group to arrange for him to move out of his parents' house. Breakthrough is achieved when the network's energies are unleashed and directed toward active resolution of problems. Network sessions often produce what Speck and Attneave called "the network effect"—a feeling of euphoric connectedness and the satisfaction of solving problems once thought to be overwhelming. Once a network has been activated, there's always someone to call when the need arises.

●

Most of the techniques of communications family therapy consisted of teaching rules of clear communication, analyzing and interpreting communication patterns, and manipulating interactions through a variety of strategic maneuvers. The progression of these strategies from straightforward to strategic reflected the growing awareness of how families resist change.

In their early work (Jackson & Weakland, 1961), communications therapists opened by indicating their belief that the whole family was involved in the presenting problem. Then they explained that all families develop habitual patterns of communication, including some that are problematical. This attempt to convert families from seeing the identified patient as the problem to accepting mutual responsibility underestimated families' resistance to change. Later these therapists were more likely to begin by accepting a family's own definition of their problems (Haley, 1976).

After the therapists made their opening remarks, they asked family members, usually one at a time, to discuss their problems. The therapist listened but concentrated on the process of communication, rather than the content. When someone in the family spoke in a confused or confusing way, the therapist would point this out and insist on certain rules of clear communication. Satir (1964) was the most straightforward teacher. When someone said something that was unclear, she would question and clarify the message, offering guidelines for clear speaking.

When he began treating families of schizophrenics, Don Jackson thought he needed to protect patients from their families (Jackson & Weakland, 1961) but came to realize that parents and children were bound together in mutually destructive ways. Even now those who are new to family therapy, especially if they haven't yet become parents themselves, tend to identify with children and see parents as the bad guys. Not only is this wrong, as Jackson later realized, it alienates parents and drives them out of treatment. Young therapists often begin "knowing" that parents are to blame for their children's problems. Only later, when they become parents themselves, do they achieve a more balanced perspective—namely, that family problems are all the children's fault.

Jackson emphasized the need for structure and control in family meetings. He began first sessions by saying, "We are here to work together on better understanding one another so that you all can get more out of your family life" (Jackson & Weakland, 1961, p. 37). Not only does this remark structure the meeting, it also conveys the idea that all members of the family are to become the focus of discussion.

Furthermore it reveals the therapist's intentions and may, therefore, precipitate a struggle with parents who may resent the implication that they are part of the problem. Thus we see that Jackson was an active therapist who set the rules at the outset and explained openly what he was doing, to anticipate and disarm resistance. Today most family therapists find it more effective to be subtler, meeting families' resistance not with psychological karate but with jujitsu—using their own momentum for leverage, instead of opposing them head on.

Jackson may have found it so difficult to deal with schizophrenic families that he became active and intrusive to avoid being caught up in their craziness. In any case, there is a suggestion of combativeness in his writings, as though he saw himself beating families at their own game (Jackson & Weakland, 1961), using double messages, provoking them to do something in defiance of therapeutic directives whose real purpose may be concealed (therapeutic double binds).

If Jackson was subtly combative with families, Jay Haley wasn't subtle about it. He was clear and explicit in defining therapy as a battle for control.[1] Haley believed that therapists need to maneuver into a position of power over their patients to manipulate them into changing. Although the notion of manipulation may have unpleasant connotations, moral criticism should be reserved for those who use patients covertly for their own ends, rather than against those who seek the most effective means of helping patients achieve their goals.

Although Haley's analysis of human relations was highly rational, he believed that family members can't be rational about their own problems. He probably exaggerated people's inability to understand their own behavior. His

---

1.   Haley has continued to develop and revise his thinking and, today, he is far from this blunt and provocative. See Chapter 6 on strategic family therapy for a description of Haley's contemporary work.

therapy therefore tended to be done *to* patients rather than *with* them. Although Haley ridiculed the idea that insight is curative, he put a lot of faith in simple, open communication as a way of dealing with family problems.

According to Haley the mere presence of a third person, the therapist, helps couples solve their problems. By dealing fairly with each partner and not taking sides, the therapist disarms the usual blaming maneuvers; in other words, the therapist acts as a referee. In addition to being a referee, the communications therapist relabeled the activity of family members with each other. One strategy was to redefine what family members say, stressing the positive aspects of their relationship. "For example," Haley (1963) said, "if a husband is protesting his wife's constant nagging, the therapist might comment that the wife seems to be trying to reach her husband and achieve more closeness with him. If the wife protests that her husband constantly withdraws from her, the husband might be defined as one who wants to avoid discord and seeks an amiable relationship" (p. 139). This technique, later called *reframing*, became a central feature of strategic therapy.

One of Haley's strategies was to make explicit the rules that govern family relationships. Dysfunctional rules made explicit become more difficult to follow. For example, some partners berate their mates for not expressing themselves, but the partners talk so much and criticize so loudly that the mates hardly have a chance. If the therapist points this out, it becomes more difficult to follow the implicit rule that the mate should not talk. Haley believed that disagreements about what rules to follow are relatively easily solved through discussion and compromise. Conflicts about who is to set rules are stickier. Because the issue of control is too explosive to be dealt with openly, Haley recommended subtle directives.

Haley's directives were of two sorts: suggestions to behave differently and suggestions to continue to behave the same. Haley's suggestion that family members continue to behave in the same way was a therapeutic paradox. When a rebellious teenager is instructed to "continue to rebel," he is caught in a paradoxical position. Continuing to rebel means following the direction of an authority figure (and admitting that what you're doing is rebellious). Only by giving up this behavior can the teenager maintain the illusion of freedom. Sometimes it's effective to have one partner suggest that the other continue symptomatic behavior. This may produce a major shift because it alters who defines the nature of the relationship.

Lessons from the Early Models

The most important contribution from group studies to family therapy was the idea that all groups, including families, have emergent properties. When people join together in a group, relational processes emerge that reflect the individuals involved *and* their collective patterns of interaction. Family therapists used systems theory to elaborate the nature of these interpersonal forces. Among the **group dynamics** that family therapists deal with are triangulation, scapegoating, alignments, coalitions, and splits.

Group theorists also taught us the importance of *roles*, official and unofficial, and how *roles* organize behavior in groups. Family therapists draw on role theory when they support parents in their role as leaders or point out how covert roles can detract from group functioning, such as how a father who constantly plays the role of jokester undermines his wife and distracts the family from discussing and solving problems. Family therapists also help family members realize how rigid roles trap them in narrow and inflexible performances, such as when teenagers are so busy *not* being their parents that they never figure out how to be themselves.

The **process/content** distinction was also profoundly important to family therapists. When families seek help, they expect help solving their problems. They might want to know how to help a shy youngster make friends or how to get a defiant teenager to show more respect. But what the family therapist tries to figure out is: Why hasn't the family been able to solve their own problems? What about the way they've been going about it isn't working? Therefore, when a family discusses their problems, the therapist listens as much to the process of the discussion—who speaks to whom and in what way—as to the content of what they're saying.

The shift from attending to what people say to how they say it—openly or defensively, cooperatively or competitively—is one of the critical strategies of all forms of therapy. Stated another way, most family therapists focus on the here and now, bringing problems into the consulting room in the form of the way family members relate to one another.

The primary group therapy technique—promoting free and open discussion—helped family therapists encourage dialogue and mutual understanding in families. But although helping families talk over their problems may enable them to resolve a minor crisis, conversation alone is rarely sufficient to solve more difficult problems. Moreover, the model of a democratic group on which this technique is predicated overlooked the unique structural properties of families. Unlike therapy groups, families are *not* made up of equals. Every member of a family may have an equal right to his or her feelings, but someone has to be in charge. Therapists who invite everyone in the family to have an equal say fail to respect the family's need for leadership and hierarchy.

The other major technique used by group therapists is the process interpretation, of which Bell (1961) delineated four varieties: *Re-flective interpretations* describe what's going on at the moment: "I notice that when your wife says something critical, you just hang your head, as if to say 'Poor me.' " *Connective interpretations* point out unrecognized links between various actions among family members: "Have you noticed that Jenny starts to misbehave the minute you two start to argue?" *Reconstructive interpretations* explain how events in the family's history provide the context for current experience. *Normative interpretations* are remarks designed to support or challenge a family member by comparing that person to what most people do: "Most teenagers are sassy with their parents. It's part of growing up."

The most obvious comment we can make about process interpretations is that simply pointing out what family members are doing may not help them to see that their behavior isn't productive, or to change it. The reason people don't usually change when something is pointed out to them isn't that they are mindless puppets of a family system, but that even well-intended criticism often feels more critical than constructive.

Group family therapists were directive to the extent of encouraging people to speak up when they appeared to have something to say; otherwise they were relatively passive and confined themselves to describing the interactional motifs they saw in families. In therapy groups of strangers, with contrasting defenses and personality styles, therapists can act as catalysts to prompt members to confront and challenge each other. Families, however, often share defenses and unproductive attitudes, and therapists can't rely on other group members to challenge family norms. That's why contemporary family therapists, who treat families more actively, confront family patterns of interaction (rather than individual reticence) and look for ways to circumvent defenses that are more powerful in families than in groups of strangers.

The three specialized applications of group methods considered in this chapter—multiple family group therapy, multiple impact therapy, and network therapy—were experiments of the 1960s. Treating more than one family at the same time allows members of one family to see how others deal with similar problems. However, when other families are present to serve as distractions, it's hard to focus on entrenched or anxiety-arousing problems for any length of time. What works in group therapy may not work with families.

Both multiple impact therapy and network therapy brought tremendous resources to bear on families in crisis. Although family therapists in clinics often work in teams, today we usually rely on one therapist to treat a family. Perhaps there are times when it makes sense to launch the all-out effort that multiple impact therapy represented. The additional advantage of network therapy was that it mobilized the natural resources of a family's community. Perhaps this model is still useful: It uses community resources that remain available after treatment is over, and it's a useful antidote to the isolation of many families.

●

Communications therapy was one of the first and most influential forms of family treatment. Its theoretical development was closely tied to general systems theory, and the therapy that emerged was a systems approach par excellence. Communication was the detectable input and output therapists used to analyze the black box of interpersonal systems. Communication was described as *feedback,* as a tactic in interpersonal power struggles, and as symptoms. In fact, all behavior was considered communication. The trouble is, when all actions are treated as communication, communications analysis may be taken to mean everything, and therefore nothing. Human relations aren't all a matter of communication; communication may be the matrix in which interactions are embedded, but human interactions have other attributes as well—love, hate, fear, cognition, conflict.

The Bateson group may be best remembered for the concept of the double bind, but their enduring contribution was that of applying communications analysis to a wide range of behavior, including family dynamics. In fact, the idea of metacommunication is a more useful concept than that of the double bind, and it has been incorporated not only by family therapists but also by the general public. Whether they are familiar with the term *metacommunication,* most people understand that all messages have both report and command functions.

Another of the most significant ideas of communications therapy is that families are rule-governed systems, maintained by homeostatic, *negative feedback* mechanisms. Negative feedback accounts for the stability of normal families and the inflexibility of dysfunctional ones. Because such families don't have adequate positive feedback mechanisms, they're unable to adjust to changing circumstances.

Communications theorists borrowed the *open systems* model from general systems theory, but their clinical interventions were based on the *closed systems* paradigm of cybernetics. Relationships were portrayed as struggles for control. Haley emphasized the power struggle between spouses; Watzlawick said that the major problem of control in families is cognitive. Therapy was conceived as a power struggle in which the therapist takes control to outwit the forces of symptom maintenance.

When communication takes place in a closed system—an individual's fantasies or a family's private conversations—there's little opportunity for adjusting the system. Only when someone outside the system provides input can correction occur. This is the premise on which communications family therapy was based. Because the rules of family functioning are largely unknown to the family, the best way to examine and correct them is to consult an expert.

While there were major differences among the therapeutic strategies of Haley, Jackson,

Satir, and Watzlawick, they were all committed to altering dysfunctional patterns of communication. They pursued this goal by direct and indirect means. The direct approach, favored by Satir, sought change by making family rules explicit and by teaching clear communication. This approach could be described as establishing ground rules, or metacommunicational principles, and included such tactics as telling people to speak for themselves and pointing out nonverbal and multileveled channels of communication.

The trouble is, as Haley noted, "One of the difficulties involved in telling patients to do something is the fact that psychiatric patients are noted for their hesitation about doing what they are told." For this reason, communications therapists began to rely on more indirect strategies, designed to provoke change rather than foster awareness. Telling family members to speak for themselves, for example, may challenge a family rule and therefore meet with resistance. With this realization, communications therapy became a treatment of resistance.

Resistance and symptoms were treated with a variety of paradoxical directives, known loosely as "therapeutic double binds." Milton Erickson's technique of prescribing resistance was used as a lever to gain control; for example, as when a therapist tells family members not to reveal everything in the first session. The same ploy was used to prescribe symptoms, an action that made unrecognized rules explicit, implied that such behavior was voluntary, and put the therapist in control.

Eventually communications therapy became symptom-focused, brief, and directive. The focus on symptoms is consistent with the general systems concept of **equifinality,** which means that no matter where systems change begins, the final result is the same.

Today the theories of communications therapy have been absorbed into the mainstream of family therapy and the symptom-focused interventions became the basis of the strategic and solution-focused models. Unfortunately, when group and communications therapists were confounded by the inflexibility of families, they may have exaggerated the irrational power of the family system.

Systems Anxiety

Therapists first encountered the family as an adversary. Freud's discoveries indicted families as seducers of innocent children and, later, as agents of cultural repression, the source of all guilt and anxiety. Hospital psychiatrists saw patients as victims of their families and, except for purposes of footing the bill, kept the family at arm's length. Child guidance workers approached domestic life with a built-in prejudice. Their vision that flawed relations in the family held the key to psychopathology was blurred by their loyalty to their child patients, with whom they identified. Bent on saving the child, they saw mothers as enemies to be overcome and fathers as peripheral figures to be ignored.

Communications family therapists rescued schizophrenics from psychiatric invalidation by demonstrating that their crazy conversation made sense as a desperate solution to desperate family situations. It wasn't the patient but the **family system** that was deranged. Family therapy aimed to humanize mental illness, but it created a nonhuman, mechanistic entity—the system—to do so.

In their efforts to make individual family members unrepressed agents in their own right, practicing therapists ran smack into powerful family opposition to personal autonomy. The individual may want to get better, but the family may need someone to play the sick role. Some families apparently require a "scapegoat" to maintain their equilibrium.

The Bateson group's observations were meant to be scientific, yet their language for describing family systems was combative, often suggesting not just resistance, but willful opposition to change. The idea that families were oppositional put family therapists in an adversarial stance. Because families were seen as mindless systems, at once rigid (holding fast to their own ways) and slippery (hard to pin down), interviewing them became a struggle.

Even when family therapists got past the idea that patients were innocent victims of malevolent kinfolk, they felt themselves in opposition to families who stubbornly resisted efforts to change them.

The shift from working with individuals to families was discontinuous and required new ways of thinking. Therapists, unused to seeing whole families interacting, eagerly imported nonclinical models to help them conceptualize patterned interactions.

Cybernetics and general systems theory provided useful metaphors to help clinicians organize the patterned interactions of family life. Describing the family as a system helped them see that a group of interacting personalities can function like a single entity, a unit. Families were said to be like systems in that the behavior of every member is dependent on the behavior of all the others.

The great advance of systemic thinking was the recognition that people's lives are linked together such that behavior in families becomes a product of mutual influence. The danger of forgetting that systems metaphors are just that is the danger of overestimating their influence— and of dehumanizing individual family members. One myth of the system is that it is determinative rather than influential. Thus, for example, an overinvolved mother who steps back, makes room for her husband to become more involved; but this shift in the system doesn't *make* him get involved. By the same token, while it may be difficult for a disengaged parent to spend more time with children enmeshed with the other parent, it isn't impossible.

The systems metaphor was thought to have the advantage of removing blame from individuals who were seen as caught up in the structure of their families. Avoiding blame and fault-finding is all to the good, but denying the possibility of self-determination may not be so good. The danger here is the danger of mechanism.

Much of what we do may be automatic and channeled by patterns of interaction. But although we don't always reflect and act rationally, we sometimes do. We aren't just links in a circular chain of events; we are people with names who experience ourselves as centers of initiative. Certainly we are linked to others. Much of what we do is with other people in mind, some of what we do is with others, and once in a while for others. But the "we" who are the authors of the doing are individuals, with hearts and minds and bodies.

Family therapists taught us that our behavior is controlled in unseen but powerful ways by the actions of those around us. The idea that people behave as they do because they are induced to live out defined roles can have a liberating effect; if one is playing a role, it's possible to play a new one. For example, modifying roles of manhood and womanhood that were based on sexual stereotypes permits a broader and more authentic definition of self. If overextended, however, this kind of thinking implies that the role is everything.

Systems thinking in the extreme dismisses selfhood as an illusion. The problem is when roles become reified as prescribed determinants of behavior *and* as independent of personal agency. Systems thinkers unfortunately implied that the role plays the person, rather than the other way around.

Early family therapists treated the family as a *cybernetic system* that governs itself through feedback. Perhaps they overemphasized negative feedback, which makes families resist change, in part because they were studying schizophrenic families, who tend to be particularly rigid. Nevertheless, as we came to realize, although systems thinking alerts us to our interconnections, the metaphor of an inanimate system is not an adequate model for human

systems. When we think systemically, we realize that individuals are systems within systems,
and that although they respond to forces outside themselves, they are also initiators, with
imagination, memory, reason, and desire.

The Stages of Family Therapy

The Initial Telephone Call

The goal of the initial contact is to get an
overview of the presenting problem and arrange
for the entire family to come for a consultation.
Listen to the caller's description of the problem
and then identify all members of the household
as well as others who might be involved (including the referral source and other agencies). Then
arrange for the first interview, specifying who
will attend (usually everyone in the household)
and the time and place.

While there are things you can learn to say
to convert requests for individual therapy into
family cases, the most important consideration

is attitudinal. First, understand and respect
that the parent who wants you to treat her
child individually or the partner who wants to
talk to you alone has a perfectly legitimate
point of view, even if it doesn't happen to coin-
cide with your own. Second, if you expect to
meet with the whole family, a matter-of-fact
statement that that's how you work, at least for
the initial assessment, will get most families to
agree to a consultation.

When the caller presents the problem as limited to one person, a useful way to broaden the
focus is to ask how the problem is affecting
other members of the family. If the caller balks
at the idea of bringing in the whole family or
says that a particular member won't attend,
say that you'll need to hear from everyone, at
least initially, in order to get as much information as possible. Most people accept the need to
give their point of view; what they resist is the
implication that they're to blame.

When a child is the identified patient, parents may be willing to attend but reluctant to

The initial phone contact should be relatively brief to avoid developing an alliance with just one family member.

bring siblings whom they don't see as part of the problem. Like the uninvolved husband who is "too busy" to attend, nonsymptomatic brothers and sisters may be important to help broaden the focus from the identified patient's failings to relationship issues in the family.

Broadening the focus does not, however, mean broadening the blame. Family members can often acknowledge a role in problematic family patterns if they sense that the therapist isn't looking to assign criticism. It isn't necessary to suggest that everyone is involved in the problem. What is important is getting everyone to work together toward a solution.[2]

Finally, because *most* families are reluctant to sit down together and face their conflicts, a reminder call before the first session helps cut down on the no-show rate. Another alternative, which puts a little more responsibility on the family, is to ask them to call the day before the appointment to confirm that everyone will be able to attend.

The First Interview

The goal of the first interview is to build an alliance with the family and develop a hypothesis about what's maintaining the presenting problem. It's a good idea to come up with a tentative hypothesis (in technical terms, a "hunch") after the initial phone call, and then test it in the first interview. (In order to avoid imposing pet theories on patient families, re-creating them in the

_____
2. Not all therapists routinely meet with the entire family. Some find they have more room to maneuver by meeting first with individuals or subgroups and then gradually involving others. Others attempt to work with the "problem-determined system," only those people directly involved. Still others try to determine who are the "customers"—namely, those who seem most concerned. If a therapist suspects violence or abuse, confidential individual sessions may enable family members to reveal what they might not discuss in front of the whole family. The point to remember is that family therapy is more a way of looking at things than a technique based on always seeing the whole family together.

image of one's own bias, it's important to remain open to refuting, not just confirming, your initial hypothesis.) The point isn't to jump to conclusions, but to start actively thinking.

The primary objectives of a consultation are to establish rapport and gather information. Introduce yourself to the contact person and then to other adults in the household. Ask parents to introduce their children. Shake hands and greet everyone. Orient the family to the room (e.g., observation mirrors, videotaping, toys for children) and to the format of the session (length and purpose). Repeat briefly what the caller told you over the phone (so as not to leave others wondering), and then ask for elaboration. Once you've heard and acknowledged that person's point of view ("So what you're saying is . . . ?"), ask each succeeding member of the family for their viewpoint.

While most of the session should be taken up with a discussion of the presenting problem, this problem-centered focus can have a disheartening effect. Therefore, spending some time exploring family members' interests and accomplishments is never wasted and sometimes changes the emotional energy of sessions dramatically.

In gathering information, some therapists find it useful to take a family history, and many use **genograms** to diagram the extended family network (see Chapter 5 for a complete description). Others believe that whatever history is essential will emerge in the natural course of events and prefer to concentrate on the family's presenting concerns and the circumstances surrounding them.

Family therapists develop hypotheses about how family members might be involved in the presenting problem by asking *what* they've done to try to solve it, and by watching *how* they interact. Ideas are as important as actions; so it's useful to notice unhelpful explanations of problems as well as unproductive interactions.

Two kinds of information (content) that are particularly important are *solutions that don't*

The challenge of first interviews is to develop an alliance without accepting at face value the family's description of one person as the problem.

work and *transitions in the life cycle.* If whatever the family has been doing to resolve their difficulties hasn't worked, then it may be that those attempts are part of the problem. A typical example would be overinvolved parents trying to help a shy child make friends by spending a lot of time coaxing and criticizing him. Sometimes family members will say they've "tried everything" to solve their problems. In such cases, the problem may be inconsistency. They try everything but give up too quickly in the face of opposition.

Despite the natural tendency to focus on problems and what causes them, it is a family's strengths, not their weaknesses, that will be most important in successful therapy. Therefore the therapist should search for resilience (Walsh, 1998). What have these people been doing well? How have they successfully handled difficulties in the past? What would a hopeful future look like? Even the most discouraged families have had times when they were suc-

cessful, even though those positive episodes may be obscured by the frustration they feel over their current difficulties.

Although it isn't always immediately apparent (especially to them), most families seek treatment because they have failed to adjust to changing circumstances. If a husband or a wife develops problems within the first few months after a baby's birth, it may be because they haven't shifted effectively from being a unit of two to being a unit of three. A young mother may be depressed because she doesn't have enough support to meet the consuming demands of a new baby. A young father may be jealous of the attention his wife now lavishes on the infant.

Although the strain of having a new baby seems obvious, you'd be amazed at how often depressed young mothers are treated as though there were something wrong with them—"unresolved dependency needs," perhaps, or maybe a Prozac deficiency. The same is true when families develop problems around the time a child enters school or reaches adolescence, or any other developmental shift: The transitional demands on the family are obvious, *if* you think about them.

Young therapists may have no experience with some of the transitions with which their clients are struggling. When this is the case, it underscores the need for the therapist to remain curious and respectful of a family's predicament rather than jump to uninformed conclusions. For example, as a single man one of us couldn't understand why so many clients with young children rarely went out together as a couple any more. He assumed that they were overly focused on their children or afraid of being alone together. Subsequent events in his own life taught him differently. With small children of his own, he began to wonder how those couples got out so often!

Family therapists explore the process of family interaction by asking questions about how family members relate to each other and by inviting them to discuss their problems with one another in the session. The first strategy, asking "process" or "circular" questions, is favored by Bowenians and systemic therapists; the second, by structural therapists. In either case, the key question for the therapist is: What's keeping the family stuck? What forces are keeping them from adapting to the pressures of development and change?

Once they've met with the family, learned about the problem that brings them to treatment, made an effort to understand the family's context, and formulated a conjecture about what needs to be done to resolve the problem, therapists should make a recommendation to the family. This may include consulting another professional (a learning disability expert, a physician, a lawyer) or even suggesting that the family doesn't need—or doesn't seem ready for—treatment. Most often, however, the recommendation will be for a course of family therapy. Although many therapists try to make

their recommendation at the end of the first interview, doing so may be hasty. If it takes two sessions to form a bond with the family, understand their situation, and find out if you can work with them, then take two sessions.

If you think you can help the family resolve their problem, offer them a treatment contract. Acknowledge why they came in, say that it was a good idea, and say that you think you can help. Then negotiate a regular meeting time, the frequency and length of sessions, who will attend, the presence of observers or use of videotape, the fee, and how insurance is handled. Remember that family resistance doesn't magically disappear after the first (or fourteenth) session: So stress the importance of keeping appointments and the need for everyone to attend. Finally, don't forget to emphasize the family's goals and the strengths you have observed in people to meet them.

First Session Checklist

1. Make contact with each member of the family and acknowledge his or her point of view about the problem and feelings about coming to therapy.
2. Establish leadership by controlling the structure and pace of the interview.
3. Develop a working alliance with the family by balancing warmth and professionalism.
4. Compliment family members on positive actions and family strengths.
5. Maintain empathy with individuals and respect for the family's way of doing things.
6. Focus on specific problems and attempted solutions.
7. Develop hypotheses about unhelpful interactions around the presenting problem. Be curious about why these have persisted.
8. Don't overlook the possible involvement of family members, friends, or helpers who aren't present.

9. Negotiate a treatment contract that acknowledges the family's goals and specifies the therapist's framework for structuring treatment.
10. Invite questions.

The Early Phase of Treatment

The early phase of treatment is devoted to refining the therapist's hypothesis into a formulation about what's maintaining the problem and beginning to work on resolving it. Now the strategy shifts from building an alliance to challenging actions and assumptions. Most therapists are able to figure out *what* needs to change. What sets good therapists apart is their willingness to push for those changes.

"Pushing for change" may suggest a confrontational style, like that of, say, Salvador Minuchin. But what is required to help people risk change isn't any one particular way of working; rather, it is a relentless commitment to helping make things better. This commitment is evident in Michael White's dogged questioning of problem-saturated stories, Phil Guerin's calm insistence that family members stop blaming each other and start looking at their own reactions, and Virginia Goldner's determined insistence that violent men take responsibility for their behavior.

Regardless of what model they follow, effective therapists share a willingness to be persistent in their pursuit of change. This doesn't just mean devotion, commitment, or sticking with families. It means being willing to intervene, at times energetically. Some therapists prefer to avoid confrontation and find it more effective to use gentle but dogged encouragement. However, regardless of whether they work directly (and at times use confrontation) or indirectly (and avoid it), good therapists are finishers. Strategies and techniques may vary, but what sets the best therapists apart is their personal commitment to do what it takes to see

families through to successful resolution of their problems.

Effective family therapy addresses interpersonal conflict, and the first step (especially in structural family therapy) is to bring it into the consulting room and put it between family members. Often this is not a problem. Couples in conflict or parents feuding with their children will usually speak right up about their disagreements. If the family has only come because someone sent them (the court, the school, the Department of Protective Services), the therapist begins by addressing the family's problem with these outside agencies. How must the family change so as to resolve their conflict with these authorities? How must the family change so that members won't be in trouble?

When one person is presented as the problem, the therapist challenges linearity by asking others how they are involved (or affected). What was their role in creating (or managing) the problem? How have they responded to it?

For example: "The problem is Malik. He's disobedient." "How does he get away with that?" Or, "How do you respond when he's disobedient?"

Less confrontive therapists might ask: "When do you notice this?" "What does he do that seems disobedient?" "How does this disobedience affect you?"

Or, "It's me, I'm depressed." "Who in the family is contributing to your depression?" "No one." "Then who's helping you get over being depressed?"

Challenges can be blunt or gentle, depending on the therapist's preferred style and assessment of the family. The point, incidentally, is not to switch from blaming one person (a disobedient child, say) to another (a parent who doesn't discipline effectively), but to broaden the problem to an interactional one. Maybe mother is too lenient with Malik because she finds father too strict, and moreover she may be overinvested in the boy because of emotional distance in the marriage.

The best way to challenge unhelpful interactions is to point out patterns that seem to be keeping people stuck. A useful formula for this is: "The more you do X, the more he does Y—and the more you do Y, the more she does X." (For X and Y, try substituting *nag* and *withdraw*, or *control* and *rebel*.) Incidentally, when therapists point out what people are doing that isn't working, it's a tactical error to then tell them what they *should* be doing. Once a therapist shifts from pointing something out to giving advice, the client's attention shifts from their own behavior to the therapist and his or her advice.

> *Therapist:* When you ignore your wife's complaints, she feels hurt and angry. You may have trouble accepting the anger, but she doesn't feel supported.
> *Client:* What should I do?
> *Therapist:* I don't know, ask your wife.

Refusing to make suggestions, especially when asked, creates tension that is designed to encourage family members to discover their own resources. A solution-focused alternative to challenging unhelpful actions is to ask about successful efforts and then to encourage more of these.

Even though family therapists sometimes challenge assumptions or actions, they continue to listen to family members' feelings and points of view. Listening is a silent activity, rare at times, even among therapists. Family members often don't listen to each other for long without becoming defensive and reactive. Unfortunately, therapists don't always listen, either—especially when they're too eager to jump in to disagree or give advice. But remember that people aren't likely to reconsider their assumptions until they've been heard and understood.

Homework assignments can be used to test flexibility (simply seeing if they are carried out measures willingness to change), make family members more aware of their role in problems (telling people just to notice something, without necessarily trying to change it, is very instructive), and to suggest new ways of relating. Typical homework assignments include: Suggesting that overinvolved parents hire a baby-sitter and go out together, having argumentative partners take turns talking about their feelings while the other one listens without saying anything (but noticing tendencies to become reactive), and having dependent family members practice spending time alone (or with someone outside the family) and doing more things for themselves. Homework assignments that are likely to generate conflict, such as negotiating house rules with teenagers, should be avoided. Difficult discussions should be saved for when the therapist can act as referee.

Early Phase Checklist

1. Identify major conflicts and bring them into the consulting room.
2. Develop a hypothesis and refine it into a formulation about what the family is doing to perpetuate or fail to resolve their presenting problem. Formulations should consider process and structure, family rules, triangles, and boundaries.
3. Keep the focus on primary problems and the interpersonal conditions supporting them.
4. Assign homework that addresses both problems and the underlying structure and dynamics perpetuating them.
5. Challenge family members to see their own role in the problems that plague them.
6. Push for change, during the session and between sessions at home.
7. Make effective use of supervision to test the validity of formulations and effectiveness of interventions.

The Middle Phase of Treatment

When therapy is anything other than brief and problem-focused, much of the middle phase is devoted to helping family members express themselves and achieve mutual understanding. If the therapist plays too active a role in this process—filtering all conversation through himself or herself—family members won't learn how to deal with each other, and will continue to manage only as long as they remain in therapy. For this reason, in the middle phase, the therapist takes a less active role and encourages family members to interact more with each other. As they do so, the therapist steps back and observes the process. When dialogue bogs down, the therapist either points out what went wrong, or simply encourages them to keep talking—but with less interruption and criticism.

When family members address their conflicts directly, they tend to become anxious and reactive. Anxiety is the enemy of listening. Some therapists (Bowenians, for example) attempt to control anxiety by having family members talk only to the therapist. Others prefer to let family members deal with their own anxiety by helping them learn to talk with each other less defensively (by saying how they feel, and listening to and acknowledging what others say). However, even therapists who work primarily with family dialogue need to interrupt when anxiety escalates and conversations become defensive and destructive.

Thus in the middle phase of treatment the therapist takes a less directive role and encourages family members to begin to rely on their own resources. The level of anxiety is regulated by alternating between having family members talk among themselves or with the therapist. In either case, the therapist encourages family members to get beyond criticism and blaming to talking directly about what they feel and what they want—and to learn to see their own part in unproductive patterns of interaction.

Middle Phase Checklist

1. Use intensity to challenge family members (or ingenuity to get around resistance, or empathy to get underneath defensiveness).
2. Avoid being so directive and controlling that the family doesn't learn to rely on and improve their own ways of relating to each other.
3. Foster individual responsibility and mutual understanding.
4. Make certain that efforts to improve relationships are having a positive effect on the presenting complaint.
5. Even if you meet with subgroups, don't lose sight of the whole family picture, and don't neglect any individuals or relationships—*especially* those "difficult" ones that are so tempting to avoid.
6. Is therapy stuck on a plateau? Have sessions taken on a sameness and predictability? Does the therapist assume too active a role in choosing what to talk about? Have therapist and family developed a social relationship that has become more important than addressing conflicts? Has the therapist assumed a regular role in the family (an empathic listener to the spouses or a firm parent figure to the children), substituting for a missing function in the family (the spouses aren't listening to each other, the parents aren't nurturing or controlling their own children)? When therapists find themselves drawn to taking an active response to family members' needs, they should ask themselves who in the family should be taking that role, and then encourage that person to do so.

Termination

Termination comes for brief therapists as soon as the presenting problem is resolved. For psychoanalytic therapists, therapy is a long-term learning process and may continue for a year or two, or longer. For most therapists termination comes somewhere between these two extremes and has to do both with the family feeling that they've gotten what they came for and the therapist's sense that treatment has reached the point of diminishing returns. One clue that it may be time to terminate is when the family comes in with nothing to say but small talk (assuming, of course, that they aren't avoiding conflict).

In individual therapy, where the relationship to the therapist is often the primary vehicle of change, termination focuses on reviewing the relationship and saying good-bye. In family therapy, the focus is more on what the family has been doing. Termination is therefore a good time to review and consolidate what they've learned. Although some strategic therapists are content to manipulate change without being concerned that the family understands it, most family therapy has a kind of teaching function, and termination is the time to make sure the family has learned something about how to get along.

It can be helpful to ask clients to anticipate upcoming challenges that might cause setbacks and to discuss how they will handle those difficulties. The question, "How will you know when things are heading backwards and what will you do?" is useful in this regard. Families can also be reminded that their present harmony can't be maintained indefinitely and that people have a tendency to overreact to the first sign of relapse, which can trigger a vicious cycle. To paraphrase Zorba the Greek, life *is* trouble. To be alive is to confront difficulties. The real test is how you handle them.

Finally, although in the business of therapy no news is usually good news, it might be a good idea to check in a few weeks after termination with the family to see how they're doing. This can be done with a letter, phone call, or brief follow-up session. The family will appreciate the therapist's interest, and the therapist will feel a sense of closure. A therapeutic relationship is, of necessity, somewhat artificial or at least constrained. But there's no reason to make it less than human—or to forget about families once you've terminated with them.

Termination Checklist

1. Has the presenting problem improved?
2. Is the family satisfied that they have gotten what they came for, or are they interested in continuing to learn about themselves and improve their relationships?
3. Does the family have an understanding of what they were doing that wasn't working, and how to avoid the recurrence of similar problems in the future?
4. Do minor recurrences of problems reflect lack of resolution of some underlying dynamic or merely that the family has to readjust to function without the therapist?
5. Have family members developed and improved relationships outside the immediate family context as well as within it?

Family Assessment

Family therapists vary widely in the extent to which they make formal assessments. Bowen systems therapists complete elaborate three-generational genograms before beginning treatment, psychoanalysts take thorough personal histories, and behavioral therapists routinely employ a variety of questionnaires and checklists. At the other extreme, structural, solution-focused, and narrative therapists do very little in the way of formal evaluation. But regardless of their model's official posture on assessment, most therapists spend too little time making careful evaluations before launching into treatment.

Rather than attempt an exhaustive comparison of various assessment procedures, we will instead describe some of the dimensions of family functioning that therapists should consider before embarking on a course of treatment. This summary is designed to be illustrative rather than exhaustive, and therefore you are quite likely to think of at least one or two important issues we've neglected to mention.

The Presenting Problem

It may seem obvious that the first consideration should be the presenting complaint. Nevertheless it's worth emphasizing that inquiry into the presenting problem should be both detailed and empathic. The minute some therapists hear that a family's problem is, say, misbehavior or poor communication, they're ready to jump into action. Their training has prepared them to deal with misbehaving children or communication problems, and they're raring to go. They know what needs to be done. But before they get started they should realize that they're *not* dealing with "misbehaving children" or "communication problems," they're dealing with a unique instance of one of these difficulties.

Exploring the presenting problem begins with simply hearing the family's account. All members of the family should have a chance to express their perspective—and both their description and their feelings should be acknowledged. This open-ended inquiry should be followed by detailed questions to find out more about the precise nature of the problem. If a child misbehaves, what exactly does he do? How often? Under what circumstances? Does he misbehave at school or at home, or both?

The next thing to explore are the family's attempts to deal with the problem. What have they tried? What's been helpful? What hasn't? Has anyone other than those present been involved in trying to help (or hinder) dealing with these difficulties?

Understanding the Referral Route

Beginning with the initial phone call and following through in the first session, it's important to understand who referred your clients

and why. What were their expectations? What expectations did they communicate to the family?

In many cases the referral process is routine and of no major import. However, it is important to know whether a family's participation is voluntary or coerced, whether all or only some of them recognize the need for treatment, and whether other agencies will have continuing involvement with the case.

When individual therapists make a family referral, they often have a particular agenda in mind. A college student's counselor once referred him and his family for treatment. It turned out that the young man had uncovered a repressed memory of sexual abuse and assumed that it must have been his father. The family therapist was somehow supposed to mediate between the young man, who couldn't imagine who else might have been responsible for this vaguely remembered incident, and his parents, who absolutely denied that any such thing ever happened. Did the individual therapist expect confrontation, confession, atonement? Some sort of negotiated agreement? It's best to find out.

It's also important to find out if clients have been in treatment elsewhere. If so, what happened? What expectations or concerns did previous therapy generate? It's even more important to find out if anyone in the family is currently in treatment. Few things are more likely to stalemate progress than two therapists pulling in opposite directions.

Identifying the Systemic Context

Regardless of who the therapist elects to work with, it's imperative to have a clear understanding of the interpersonal context of the problem. Who all is in the family? Are there important figures in the life of the problem who aren't present? A live-in boyfriend? A grandparent who lives next door? Are other social agencies involved with the family? What is the nature of their input? Does the family see them as helpful?

Remember that family therapy is an approach to people in context. The most relevant context may be the immediate family, but families don't exist in a vacuum. It may be important to meet with the teachers and counselors of a child who misbehaves at school to find out what's going on. There are even times when the nuclear family may not be the most important context of a person's problems. Sometimes, for example, a college student's depression has more to do with what's going on in the classroom or dormitory than with what's happening back home.

Stage of the Life Cycle

A family's context has temporal as well as interpersonal dimensions. Most families come to treatment not because there's something inherently wrong with them, but because they've gotten stuck in life-cycle transitions (Chapter 4). Sometimes this will be immediately apparent. Parents may complain, for example, that they don't know what's gotten into Janey. She used to be such a good girl. But now that she's fourteen she's become sullen and argumentative. (One reason parenting remains an amateur sport is that just when parents think they've got the hang of it, the kids get a little older and throw them a whole new set of curves.) Adolescence is that stage in the life cycle when young parents have to grow up and relax their grip on their children.

Sometimes it isn't so obvious that a family is having trouble adjusting to a new stage in the life cycle. Couples who marry after living together for years may not anticipate that matrimony can stir up a number of unconscious expectations related to what it means to be part of a family. More than one couple has been surprised to discover a sharp falling off in their love life after formally tying the knot. At other times significant life-cycle changes occur in the grandparents' generation, and you won't always learn of these influences unless you ask.

Family Structure

The simplest systemic context for a problem is an interactional process between two parties. She nags and he withdraws; one parent is lenient to make up for the other one's strictness, and vice versa. But sometimes, a dyadic perspective doesn't take in the whole picture.

Family problems become entrenched because they're embedded in powerful but unseen structures. Regardless of what approach a therapist takes, it's wise to understand something about the family's **structure.** What are the actual functioning **subsystems** and what is the nature of the **boundaries** between them? What is the nature of the boundary around the couple or the family? What triangles are present?

Who plays what roles in the family? Are these individuals and subsystems protected by boundaries that allow them to operate without undue interference—but with access to needed support? Here, too, there is a temporal dimension. If a wife goes back to work after years of staying home with the children, the parental subsystem is challenged to shift from a complementary to a symmetrical form. Whether or not family members complain directly about these strains, they're likely to be relevant to wherever their distress happens to be focused.

Communication

Although some couples still come to therapy saying they have "communication problems" (usually meaning that one partner won't do what the other one says), working on communication has become a cliché in family therapy. Because communication is the vehicle of relationship, all therapists deal with communication. But clarifying communication is rarely sufficient to solve family problems.

However, although conflict doesn't magically disappear when family members start to listen to each other, it's unlikely that conflicts will get solved *before* people start to listen to each other (Nichols, 1995). If, after a session or two—and the therapist's "encouragement"—family members still seem unable to listen to each other, talking therapy is going to be an uphill battle.

One other point to be made about listening falls under the category of What's Good for the Goose is Good for the Gander. Therapists who encourage family members to listen to each other don't always practice what they preach. A family member will start to protest or explain and the therapist cuts that person off to direct him or her to listen to someone else's point of view. The person who gets cut off may listen grudgingly, but most people aren't really interested in hearing what anyone else has to say until they first feel heard and understood themselves.

Family members who learn to listen to each other with understanding often discover that they don't need to change each other (Jacobson & Christensen, 1996). Many problems can be solved, but the problem of living with other people who don't always see things the way you do isn't one of them.

Drug and Alcohol Abuse

Although it may not be necessary to ask every client about drug and alcohol consumption, it's critical to inquire carefully if there is any suspicion that this may be a problem. Don't be too polite. Ask straightforward and specific questions. If a member of a family who's seeking couples or family therapy seems to be abusing drugs or alcohol, think twice about assuming that talk therapy will be the answer to the family's problems.

Domestic Violence and Sexual Abuse

If there is any hint of domestic violence or sexual abuse, the clinician should look into it. The process of questioning can start with the whole family present, but when there is a suspicion of abuse or neglect, it may be wise to meet with family members individually to allow them to talk more openly. While there's room for disagreement about the advisability of a conjoint approach in cases of mild domestic violence, such as slapping or pushing, it's imperative to consider whether the inevitable stress of seeing a couple together will expose a woman to greater danger from her abusive partner.

As you know, most states require professionals to report any suspicion of child abuse. Any clinician who considers not reporting suspected child abuse should also consider the consequences of this failure to report becoming known if someone else does report it. It's called losing your license.

Extramarital Involvements

The discovery of an affair is a crisis that will strike many couples some time in their relationship. Infidelity is common, but it's still a crisis. It can destroy a marriage. Extramarital involvements that don't involve sexual intimacy, although less obvious, can sabotage treatment if one or both partners regularly turn to third parties to deal with issues that should be worked out by the couple. (One clue that an outside relationship is part of a triangle is that it isn't openly talked about.) Would-be helpful third parties may include family members, friends, and therapists.

A couple once came to therapy complaining that the intimacy had gone out of their relationship. It wasn't so much a matter of conflict, it was just that they never seemed to spend any time together. After a few weeks of slow progress, the wife revealed that she'd been seeing an individual therapist. When the couples therapist asked why, she replied that she needed to have someone to talk to.

Gender

Unrecognized gender inequalities contribute to family problems in a variety of ways. A wife's dissatisfaction may have deeper roots than the family's current problems. A husband's reluctance to become more involved in the family may be as much a product of cultural expectations and rewards for career achievement as of anything missing in his personality.

Every therapist must work out for himself or herself how to balance between the extremes of naively ignoring gender inequality and imposing one's personal point of view on clients. However, it's not reasonable to assume that both partners enter marriage with equal power, or that complementarity between spouses is the only dynamic operating on their relationship.

Conflict over gender expectations, whether it's directly talked about or not, is epidemic given the enormous shifts in cultural expectations over the last few years. Is it still considered a woman's duty to follow her husband's career, moving whenever and wherever necessary for his advancement, regardless of how this affects her (and the children's) interests? Is it still true that women are expected to be the primary (which often turns out to be a euphemism for only) caregivers for infants and young children?

Regardless of the therapist's values, do the gender roles established in a couple seem to work for them? Or do unresolved differences, conflict, or confusion appear to be sources of stress? Perhaps the single most useful question to ask about gender inequality is, "How does each of the partners experience the fairness of give-and-take in their relationship?"

Cultural Factors[3]

In assessing families for treatment a therapist should consider and respect the unique subculture a family is from (McGoldrick, Giordano, & Pearce, 1996) as well as the effect of unquestioned assumptions from the larger culture that

may have an impact on their problems (Doherty, 1991).

In working with minority families, it may be more important to develop **cultural competence** than to have cultural syntonicity. That is, families may come to trust a therapist who has taken the time to learn about their cultural context as much as one who happens to be of the same race or nationality. One way to develop cultural competence is to make connections after working hours—for example, if you happen to be white, by attending black church services in the community where your clients live or by attending a Latino dance or hanging out in an Asian community center. Such experiences certainly don't make one an expert, but they may help client families feel that you care enough to respect their ways. It's also important to take a one-down position in regard to cultural and ethnic diversity—that is, to ask your clients to teach you about their experience and traditions.

The challenge for the practitioner is twofold: learning to respect diversity and developing sensitivity to the issues faced by members of other cultures and ethnic groups. There are now a host of books describing the characteristics and values of various ethnic groups, many of which are listed in the section on multiculturalism in Chapter 11 of this volume. In addition to these academic books, novels—such as *Love in the Time of Cholera, Beloved, The Scent of Green Papaya, The Mambo Kings Play Songs of Love,* and so on—often bring other cultures more vividly to life.

In working with clients from other cultures it's probably more important to be respectful of differences and curious about other ways of doing things than to attempt to become an expert on ethnicity. However, while it is important to respect other people's differences, it can be a problem to accept uncritically statements to the effect that "We do these (counterproductive) things because of our culture." Unfortunately, it's difficult for a therapist from another culture to assess the validity of such claims. Perhaps

---

3. Issues of culture, as well as race, ethnicity, and social class, will be examined throughout this book. Here we merely wish to offer some preliminary considerations to help beginning therapists get through their first few family sessions.

the best advice is to be curious; stay open, but ask questions.

Even when working with clients from your own culture, it's important to consider the impact of cultural assumptions. How do cultural expectations and aspirations affect the family you're working with? One patient recently complained that his wife expected family life to be like *The Brady Bunch*. His wife's reply was: "It doesn't always have to be *The Jerry Springer Show*, either."

Among the cultural assumptions you may want to be alert for are that getting married means living happily ever after, that sexual satisfaction is something which just comes naturally, that adolescence is necessarily a time of turmoil, and that teenagers only want freedom and no longer need their parents' love and understanding.

The Ethical Dimension

Most therapists are aware of the ethical responsibilities of their profession: Therapy should be for the client's benefit, not to work out unresolved issues for the therapist. Clients are entitled to confidentiality, and so limits on privacy imposed by requirements to report to probation officers, parents, or managed care companies should be made clear from the outset. Therapists avoid exploiting the trust and dependency of their clients (and students) and therefore must make every effort to avoid dual relationships. Professionals are obligated to provide the best possible treatment, and if they aren't qualified by training or experience to meet the needs of a particular client, they should refer the case to someone else.

Although most therapists are aware of their own responsibilities, many think less than they might about the ethical dimensions of their clients' behavior. This is another area where there are no hard and fast rules. However, a complete and conscientious assessment of every family should include some consideration of family members' entitlements and obligations. What loyalty obligations do members of the family have? Are invisible loyalties (Boszormenyi-Nagy & Spark, 1973) constraining their behavior? If so, are these just and equitable? What is the nature of the partners' commitment to each other? Are these commitments clear? Balanced? What obligations do family members have with regard to fidelity and trustworthiness? Are these obligations being met?

A good place to start understanding the ethical responsibilities of clinical practice is by studying the guidelines of your profession. The Ethics Code of the American Psychological Association, for example, outlines such principles as:

- Psychologists offer services only within the areas of their competence, based on education, training, supervision, or professional experience.
- Where there is evidence that an understanding of age, gender, race, ethnicity culture, national origin, religion, sexual orientation, disability, language, or socioeconomic status is essential for effective implementation of services, psychologists have or seek out training and supervision in these areas—or they make appropriate referrals.
- When psychologists become aware of personal problems that might interfere with their professional duties, they take appropriate measures, such as obtaining professional assistance, and determining whether they should limit, suspend, or terminate their work-related duties.

The Code of Ethics for the National Association of Social Workers mandates that:

- Social workers should not engage in dual relationships with clients or former clients.
- Social workers should not solicit private information from clients unless it is essential to providing services.

- Social workers should not disclose confidential information to third-party payers unless clients have authorized such disclosure.
- Social workers should terminate services to clients when such services are no longer required.

While some of these principles may seem obvious, they provide fairly strict guidelines within which practitioners should operate. When it comes to working with couples and families, however, complications arise that create a host of unique ethical dilemmas. When, for example, should a family therapist share with parents information learned in separate sessions with a child? If a teenage son has joined a gang, should the therapist tell his mom? If a twelve-year-old starts drinking, does the therapist tell her parents?

Recently, professional codes of conduct have added guidelines to address issues involved in treating couples and families. For example, the American Psychological Association specifies that:

- When psychologists provide services to several people who have a relationship (such as spouses or parents and children), they clarify at the outset which individuals are clients and the relationship the psychologist will have with each person.
- If it becomes apparent that psychologists may be called on to perform potentially conflicting roles (such as family therapist and then witness for one party in divorce proceedings), they attempt to clarify and modify, or withdraw from roles appropriately.

The National Association of Social Workers states that:

- When social workers provide services to couples or family members, they should clarify with all parties the nature of their professional obligations to the various individuals receiving services.
- When social workers provide counseling to families, they should seek agreement among the parties concerning each individual's right to confidentiality.

The American Association for Marriage and Family Therapy (AAMFT, 1991) publishes its own code of ethics, which covers much of the same ground as those of the APA and NASW. The AAMFT does, however, directly address complications with respect to confidentiality when a therapist sees more than one person in a family:

- Without a written waiver, a family therapist should not disclose information received from any family member—including, presumably, to other family members.

Still, as with many things, it may be easier to expound ethical principles in the classroom than to apply them in the crucible of clinical practice, especially in situations that engage powerful emotions.

—Case Study—

It's clear that therapists must protect their clients' right to confidentiality. But what if a woman reveals that she's having an extramarital affair and isn't sure whether to end it? When she goes on to say that her marriage has been stale for years, the therapist suggests a course of couples therapy to see if the marriage can be improved. The woman agrees. But when the therapist then suggests that she either break off the affair or tell her husband about it, the woman adamantly refuses. What should the therapist do?

Can a therapist offer effective couples treatment while one of the partners is carrying on an extramarital relationship? How much pressure should a therapist exert on a client to do something she or he doesn't want to do? How much pressure should a therapist apply to urge a family member to reveal a secret that might have dangerous consequences? When does a therapist have the right to discontinue treatment of a client who wants to continue, because the client refuses to accept the therapist's recommendation?

One way to resolve ambiguous ethical dilemmas is to use your own best judgment. In the case of the woman who wanted to work on her marriage but wasn't willing to end her affair or inform her husband, a therapist might decline to offer therapy under circumstances that would make it unlikely to be effective. In that case, the therapist is obligated to refer the client to another therapist.

Subprinciple 1.6 of the *AAMFT Code of Ethical Principles* states:

- Marriage and family therapists assist persons in obtaining other therapeutic services if a marriage and family therapist is unable or unwilling, for appropriate reasons, to see a person who has requested professional help.

And Subprinciple 1.7 states:

- Marriage and family therapists do not abandon or neglect clients in treatment without making reasonable arrangements for the continuation of such treatment.

Given the same set of circumstances, another therapist might decide that treating the married couple even though the woman refused to end her affair would mean that improvements in the couple's relationship might make it possible for the woman to either break off the affair or talk to her husband about it. In this scenario the therapist would be bound by the principle of confidentiality not to reveal—directly or indirectly—what the woman talked about in private.

While the outlines of ethical professional conduct are clear, the pressures on the practitioner are often powerful, and subtle. When dealing with clients who are having affairs, or considering divorce—or marriage, for that matter—therapists may be influenced by their own unconscious feelings as well as the client's projections. What would you assume, for example, about a therapist whose depressed, married clients all tended to get divorced after their individual therapy? What might you speculate about the level of satisfaction in that therapist's own marriage?

The risk of trusting your own judgment in ambiguous ethical situations is imposing your own values on what should be a professional decision. The principles of sound ethical practice are wider, and may be stricter, than our own private morality and good intentions. When in doubt, we recommend that clinicians ask themselves two questions: First, what would happen if the client or important others found out about your actions? Thus, for example, "strategically" telling two siblings in separate conversations that only he or she is mature enough to end the fighting between them, violates the "what if" principle, because it's entirely possible that one or both of them might brag to the other about what the therapist said. (Trust us!)

The second question to ask in order to do the right thing is, can you talk to someone you respect about what you're doing (or considering)? If you're afraid to discuss with a supervisor or a colleague that you are treating two married couples in which the wife of one is having an affair with the husband of the other, or that you're considering lending a client money, you may be guilty of the arrogance of assuming that you are above the rules that govern others in your profession. Feeling compelled to keep something secret strongly suggests that it may be wrong. Otherwise, why not talk about it? The road to hell is paved with the assumption that this situation is special, this client is special, or that you are special.

The following red flags may signal potential unethical practices:

- Specialness—something about this situation is special and the ordinary rules don't apply.
- Attraction—intense attraction of any kind, not only romantic but also being impressed with the stature of the client.
- Alterations in the therapeutic frame—longer or more frequent sessions, excessive self-disclosure, being unable to say no to the client, and so on may signal a potential violation of professional boundaries.
- Violating clinical norms—not referring someone in a troubled marriage for couples therapy, accepting personal counseling from a supervisor, and so on.
- Professional isolation—not being willing to discuss your decisions with professional colleagues.

●

In reading over our topics for family assessment, you may have noticed that there is no section on individual dynamics. This is deliberate. The distinction between individual and systemic levels of experience is useful but artificial. Regardless of whether you're treating individuals or family groups, competent therapists should keep in mind that there are both interactional and personal dimensions to all human experience (Nichols, 1987).

An individual therapist who fails to consider the impact of the therapeutic relationship (as well as relationships outside the office) on a patient's material is missing a most important contribution. Therapists are never blank screens. By the same token, a family therapist who fails to consider the psychology of a family member's behavior is dealing with only half a deck. Families were never black boxes. Sometimes when family interactions get stuck, it's important to consider the contributions of individual psychopathology, psychodynamics, or just plain failures of nerve.

Family Therapy with Specific Presenting Problems

Once it was common for family therapists to assume that their approach could usefully be applied to almost any problem. Today, this one-size-fits-all notion is no longer valid, and it has become increasingly necessary to develop specific techniques for particular populations and problems.

The following discussions are a sample of special treatment considerations for two commonly encountered clinical problems: marital violence and sexual abuse of children. While we hope that these suggestions will provide some ideas for dealing with these difficult situations, remember that responsible therapists recognize the limits of their expertise and refer cases they aren't equipped to deal with to more experienced practitioners.

Marital Violence

The question of how best to treat marital violence polarizes the field like no other. Currently the dominant paradigm is to separate the couple and assign the offender to an anger-management program while his partner is treated in a battered women's group (Edleson & Tolman, 1992; Gondolf, 1995). Traditional couples therapy is seen as potentially dangerous because placing a violent man and his abused partner in close quarters and inviting them to address heated issues in their relationship has the potential to put the woman in danger and to provide the offender with a platform for self-justification (Avis, 1992; Bograd, 1984, 1992; Hansen, 1993). Treating the partners together implies that both share responsibility for the violence and

In cases of domestic violence, couples therapy may be inadvisable unless the man's violence is infrequent, not physically injurious, not psychologically intimidating, and not fear-producing for his partner.

confers a sense of legitimacy on a relationship that may be malignant.

The argument for seeing violent couples together is that violence is the outcome of mutual provocation—an escalation, albeit unacceptable, of the emotionally destructive behavior that characterizes many relationships (Goldner, 1992; Minuchin & Nichols, 1993). When both partners are treated together, violent men can learn to recognize the emotional triggers that set them off and to take responsibility for controlling their actions. Their partners can learn to recognize the same danger signals—and to take responsibility for ensuring their own safety.

Because many systemic therapists who are willing to do couples therapy when there have been minor episodes of violence will not treat couples when the violence has gone beyond pushing and shoving, some of the debate between advocates of a systemic versus an offender-and-victim model is between apples and oranges. Nevertheless, many feminist thinkers remain opposed to couples therapy when any form of domestic violence is present (Avis, 1992; Bograd, 1984; Hansen, 1993).

In the absence of empirical evidence showing gender-specific group treatment to be safer or more effective than couples therapy (Brown & O'Leary, 1995; Feldman & Ridley, 1995), most clinicians remain split into two camps when it comes to the treatment of marital violence. However, rather than choose between attempting to resolve the relationship issues that lead to violence or concentrating on providing safety and protection for the victims of violence, it is possible to combine elements of both approaches; not, however, by attempting to do traditional couples therapy.[4]

---

4.   The following guidelines draw heavily from the work of Virginia Goldner and Gillian Walker, codirectors of the Gender and Violence Project at the Ackerman Institute.

In working with violent couples there must be no compromise or ambiguity on the issue of safety. Rather than choosing between therapeutic neutrality—and focusing on relationship issues—or advocating on behalf of the victim—and focusing on safety—it's possible to pursue both agendas. Relationship issues can properly be construed as mutual, but for the crime of violence the perpetrator must be held responsible.

In the initial consultation with couples in which there is a suspicion of violence, it's useful to meet with the partners together and then with each of them separately. Seeing the couple together permits you to see them in action, while speaking with the woman privately allows you to inquire whether out of fear she has left out important information about the level of violence or other forms of intimidation to which she has been subjected. These separate meetings help foster a therapeutic alliance with both partners.

Violent men and battered women trigger strong reactions in anyone who tries to help them. When such couples seek therapy they are often polarized between love and hate, blaming and feeling ashamed, wanting to escape and remaining obsessed with each other. Thus it's not surprising that professional helpers tend to react to them in extremes: siding with one partner against the other, refusing ever to take sides, exaggerating or minimizing danger, treating the partners like children, or like monsters. In order to form an alliance with both partners, it's important to convey respect for them as persons, even if you cannot condone all of their actions.

To assess the level and frequency of violence, it's necessary to ask direct questions. "How often do conflicts between the two of you end in some kind of violence?" "When did this happen most recently?" "What's the worst thing that's ever happened?" It's important to find out if any of the incidents have resulted in injuries, if weapons have been used, and if the woman is currently afraid of her partner.

If the woman has been violent as well as the man, the therapist can make it clear that violence in any form is unacceptable. But it is also useful to point out that unless a woman uses a weapon, her aggression is not as dangerous, because she is not as physically powerful. This point can be emphasized by asking the man if he actually feels physically afraid of his partner during an argument (which is her experience of him).

The more that violence is used to intimidate and the more there is a pattern of violence, the more dangerous the man. This is especially true of violence outside the home. A man who gets into fights with other men is far more explosive than a man who is only violent toward someone who can't really fight back. It's also important to inquire about drinking and drug use, because they loosen inhibitions, and therapy must emphasize restraint.

In addition to assessing the level of violence, the therapist must also evaluate the partners' ability to work constructively in therapy. Is the man willing to accept responsibility for his behavior? Is he argumentative or defensive toward his partner? Toward the therapist? Is the woman willing to take responsibility for her own protection, making her physical safety the first priority? Is the couple able to talk together and to take turns, or are they so emotionally reactive that the therapist must constantly interrupt and control them?

If a therapist decides to risk treating the couple together, it's important to establish zero tolerance for violence. One way of doing this is to make therapy contingent on no further episodes of physical aggression. Virginia Goldner and Gillian Walker define the first couple of sessions as a "consultation" to determine whether it's possible to create a "therapeutic safety zone" where issues can be confronted without putting the woman in harm's way. They use these initial sessions to focus intensively on the risk of violence and the question of safety, while reserving the right to terminate the consultation and propose other treatment alternatives if they feel the case is too dangerous for couples therapy (Goldner, 1998).

With most couples it's useful to encourage dialogue as a way of exploring how the partners communicate. But violent couples tend to be emotionally reactive and, when that is the case, it's better to have them take turns talking to the therapist. In the early stages of work with such couples, therapists should do everything possible to slow them down and make them think.

One of the best antidotes to emotionality is to ask for specific, concrete details. A good place to start is with the most recent violent incident. Ask each of them for a detailed, moment-to-moment description of exactly what happened. Be alert for linguistic evasions. A violent man may describe his actions as the result of his partner's "provocation" or of "built-up pressures." Thus it is not he who hits his wife, it's the pressures that are the culprit. A subtler form of evasion is for the violent partner to describe the problem as his impulsivity. When arguments escalate, he starts to "lose it." In this formulation, the man's impulsive actions are not a choice he makes but an unavoidable consequence of emotions welling up inside of him.

Once both partners have begun to own responsibility for their actions—he for choosing to control his violent impulses, she for taking steps to ensure her safety—it becomes possible to explore the relationship issues that lead to escalating emotional reactivity. This does *not*, however, mean that at a certain point violent couples can be treated just like any other couple. Exploring the interactional processes that both partners participate in, should never be allowed to imply that both are mutually *responsible* for acts of violence.

When the couple is ready to explore relationship issues, it should be possible to encourage dialogue, so that the therapist and couple can learn to understand what transpires when they try to talk with each other. This brings the relationship into the consulting room. It's one thing to tell a man that he should leave before he gets too angry. It's another thing to actually observe the beginnings of emotional escalation and ask him if he's aware that he's started to get upset and interrupt his partner. It then becomes possible to say, "*This* is the moment when you should leave." At this same point his partner can be asked if she has begun to feel the first signs of tension and fear.

Taking a time-out is an almost universally employed strategy in marital violence programs. Recognizing the cues of escalating anger (racing heart, growing agitation, standing up, pacing) and removing oneself from the situation before violence occurs is encouraged as a way to head off destructive actions that the partners will later regret. Saying that "I'm feeling angry (or scared), and I'm going to take a time-out" helps distinguish this safety device from simply refusing to talk. It must be emphasized that each person is responsible for his or her own time-outs. Telling the other person to take a time-out is not allowed, nor is trying to stop the other from leaving.

Although eliminating escalating aggressive interactions must be the first priority, couples must also learn more constructive methods of addressing their differences. Here there is a paradox. Violent men must learn to control their behavior, but it is counterproductive to control their feelings when this amounts to stifling their resentments and complaints. In fact, it is precisely this kind of suppression that leads to the emotional buildups that result in violent explosions. Moreover, a man who resorts to violence with his partner is often a weak man—weak in the sense of not knowing how to articulate his feelings in a way that his partner can hear. Thus in helping couples learn to negotiate their differences it is essential to ensure that both partners learn to speak up, and to listen to each other.

Sexual Abuse of Children

When treating families in which a child has been sexually abused, the primary goals are, first, ensuring that the abuse does not recur, and, second, reducing the long-term effects of the trauma (Trepper & Barrett, 1989). As with marital violence, treatment of sexual abuse tends to fall into one of two categories: a child protective approach, which can undermine the integrity of the family, or a family systems approach, which can fail to protect the child victims. We recommend trying to nurture the family while at the same time trying to protect the child. When these goals seem incompatible—for example, when a father has raped his daughter—protection of the child takes precedence.

Assessment of sexual abuse is often complicated by divergent points of view about what happened (Herman, 1992). A father may say that touching his daughter's labia was an accidental occurrence, whereas the daughter reports that this has happened more than once and that she experiences it as abusive. A grandfather may claim that his caressing of his grandson is perfectly innocent, while the district attorney is filing charges of indecent assault. A child protective worker may believe that a mother is tacitly supporting her husband's abuse of her child, while a family therapist may see a mother who is doing her best to save her marriage. Such discrepancies must be resolved by social and legal control agencies.

The first priority is restricting unsupervised access to children for the offender. Next a careful assessment should be made to uncover other possible incidents of abuse or patterns of inappropriate sexual expression (Furniss, 1991). The offender must take responsibility for his behavior and receive appropriate treatment for his actions (which may include legal punishment). Often these measures will have already been taken by a child protective agency before the family is referred for therapy.

One of the goals of therapy should be to establish a support system to break through the isolation that facilitates sexual abuse and inhibits disclosure. For this reason, many programs favor a multimodal approach that includes individual, group, and family sessions (Bentovim, Elton, Hildebrand, Tranter, & Vizard, 1988; Trepper & Barrett, 1989). Family sessions should be geared toward increasing support for the victimized child, which may entail strengthening the parental unit.

When a child is the victim of sexual abuse, social control agents may have to step in to protect the child, which can involve taking over what might be considered parental responsibilities. In the long run, however, it is the parents and the family who will be responsible for the child. Therefore supporting the parents, rather than taking over for them, is usually in the best interests of the child.

In cases where a father or stepfather is sent to jail for sexual crimes against his children, part of a therapist's job is to help the family draw and adjust to a boundary that excludes the guilty person. The same is true if the children are taken out of the home and sent to live with relatives or foster parents. Subsequently, however, if reunion is planned, therapy involves gradually reopening this boundary through visits and phone calls, which gives the family and therapist the opportunity to work together to improve the family's functioning.

One of the keys to helping resolve the trauma of abuse is to give the child a safe forum to express and explore her complex and often ambivalent feelings about what happened. In addition to feeling violated and angry, she may feel guilty about having gotten an adult in trouble. Often a child will secretly blame the nonoffending parent, usually the mother, for not preventing the abuse. And, finally, the child may also fear that the mother's dependence on the abuser may result in his return, making the child again vulnerable to abuse.

A combination of individual and conjoint sessions helps make it safe to talk about feelings, and then to share them. Meeting first with the nonoffending parent (or parents) allows the mother (or parents) to describe what happened and to express feelings about the abuse without having to edit what she says because the child is present.[5] Among the mother's complex feelings will surely be rage and a sense of betrayal. But a part of her may still love the abuser and miss him if he's been sentenced. She may also feel guilty for not having protected her child. It's important to make it safe for her to share all of these feelings.

When first meeting with the mother and abused daughter, it's reassuring to say that although they would eventually probably want to talk about the abuse, it's up to them to choose where to start. It's also helpful to give parents and children the choice of how much to talk about the abuse and whether to do so first in an individual session or conjointly. If children opt to discuss their feelings privately, they can be reassured that it's up to them to decide what they subsequently want to share with their parents.

When meeting with abused children privately, it's helpful to explain that the more they talk about what happened, the less troubling their feelings are likely to be. However, it's essential to let them decide when and how much to open up. Remember that abused children very badly need to recover a sense of control over their own lives (Sheinberg, True, & Fraenkel, 1994). When family members begin to talk about their feelings, it's wise to keep in mind that feelings don't come in either–or categories. One way to help make it safe for them to talk about complex or even contradictory emotions is to use the metaphor of parts of the self (Schwartz, 1995). Thus an abused child might be asked, "So does part of you think your mother should have figured out what was happening?" Likewise, the mother might be asked, "Does part of you miss him?"

One problem with meeting privately with a child is that doing so creates secrets between

the child and therapist. At the end of such sessions, it's helpful to ask the child what she wants to share with her family and how she wants to do so. Some children will ask the therapist to take the lead in opening up some of what they want their mothers to understand but find it hard to talk about. Finally, although it's important to help children voice any feelings they may have about feeling guilty for what happened, after exploring these feelings, abused children need to hear over and over that what happened was not their fault.

Working with Managed Care

Rarely has a profession undergone such upheaval as mental health providers have experienced with the advent of **managed care.** Practitioners, used to making decisions based on their own clinical judgment, are now told by the managed care industry which patients they can see, which treatments are preferred, what they can charge, and how many sessions they should offer. Professionals taught to maintain absolute confidentiality in their dealings with patients now find themselves negotiating treatment arrangements with anonymous strangers over the telephone.

The managed care industry itself has been slow to get its act together. Some of the horror stories we've all heard about treatment being disallowed or abruptly terminated stem from the early days of managed care when the industry tended to manage by refusal rather than mediation. Given the mandate to stem the flow of hemorrhaging health care costs, when asked to approve any but the most limited forms of treatment, the industry's first impulse was to just say no.

Now fifteen years into its existence the managed care industry is coming to terms with two important facts: first, that although their mandate is still to contain costs, their ultimate responsibility is to see that patients receive effec-

---

5.   For the sake of simplicity, the following discussion will assume the common instance of a stepfather as abuser and a mother and her abused daughter as clients.

tive treatment; and second, although there seems to be an almost built-in adversarial relationship to practitioners, industry case managers are discovering something that clinicians should also come to terms with—that both sides profit when they begin to work in partnership.[6]

That's why we titled this section Working *with* Managed Care, rather than something that might better describe how many therapists feel, such as Surviving Managed Care. The key to succeeding in a managed care environment is learning to work within the system and getting over the sense that the case manager at the other end of the line is your enemy. Actually, for those who learn to collaborate effectively with managed care, case managers can be the best source of referrals.

For students, learning to work with managed care should begin as early as planning their education. Most managed care companies accept licensed practitioners with graduate degrees in nursing, social work, psychology, and psychiatry. Some, but by no means most, accept other degrees—though not usually on their preferred provider lists. So, just as it's prudent to take state licensing requirements into account when planning a postgraduate education, it's also wise to consider the requirements of the major managed care companies. Moreover, because most companies require at least three years of postdegree experience, it's a good idea to plan on beginning your career in a supervised agency.

In areas with a high concentration of mental health providers it may be necessary to market your skills in order to be selected as a managed care provider. Even where managed care panels are already crowded, case managers are always looking for competent professionals who can make their jobs easier. The willingness to accept crisis referrals and to work with difficult cases

(e.g., borderlines, chronic and multiproblem clients), accessibility, and having specialized expertise help make therapists attractive to managed care companies.

Once you have the opportunity to become a provider, remember to work *with* case managers, not against them. The regulations and paper work can be frustrating, but keep in mind that case managers have feelings, too—and they have memories. They're just trying to do the job they were hired to do. The biggest mistake practitioners make is to allow themselves to become oppositional when talking to case managers.

Case managers appreciate succinct and informative verbal and written reports. When challenged, many therapists eventually fall back on justifying their requests by saying, "It's my clinical opinion." Being asked to justify their conclusions makes some established practitioners angry. We *are* doing the best we can for patients. We *are* practicing efficiently. But we're not used to being held accountable. We're not used to someone looking over our shoulder, checking up on us. Get used to it. If you use sound clinical judgment, you should be able to provide reasons for your recommendations.

If you can't reach agreement with a case manager, don't lose your temper. If you can't be friendly, don't be hostile. Follow the grievance procedure. Do the required paper work and submit it on time. Write concise, well-defined treatment plans. Be available and accessible. Return phone calls promptly. Make arrangements with a colleague to provide backup if you're out of town or unable to accept a referral.

In addition to maintaining a positive, constructive attitude, being successful in the current health care climate means developing a results-oriented mindset. If you're trained in solution-focused therapy, by all means say so, but don't try to pass yourself off as something you're not. Calling yourself "eclectic" is more likely to sound fuzzy than flexible. The important point is to get a reputation for working within established time limits—and getting results.

---

6. Increased competition among managed care companies has increased pressure to build trust and loyalty among providers and to reduce internal costs by spending less administrative time managing providers.

—Recommended Readings

Anderson, C., and Stewart, S. 1983. *Mastering resistance: A practical guide to family therapy.* New York: Guilford Press.

Bell, J. E. 1961. *Family group therapy.* Public Health Monograph No. 64, Washington, DC: U.S. Government Printing Office.

Bell, J. E. 1975. *Family therapy.* New York: Jason Aronson.

Haley, J. 1963. *Strategies of psychotherapy.* New York: Grune & Stratton.

Hoffman, L. 1971. Deviation-amplifying processes in natural groups. In *Changing families,* J. Haley, ed. New York: Grune & Stratton.

Jackson, D. D. 1961. Interactional psychotherapy. In *Contemporary psychotherapies,* M. T. Stein, ed. New York: Free Press of Glencoe.

Jackson, D. D. 1967. *Therapy, communication and change.* Palo Alto, CA: Science and Behavior Books.

Lederer, W., and Jackson, D. D. 1968. *Mirages of marriage.* New York: Norton.

MacGregor, R., Richie, A. M., Serrano, A. C., Schuster, F. P., McDonald, E. C., and Goolishian, H. A. 1964. *Multiple impact therapy with families.* New York: McGraw-Hill.

Minuchin, S., and Fishman, H. C. 1981. *Family therapy techniques.* Cambridge, MA: Harvard University Press.

Patterson, J. E., Williams, L., Grauf-Grounds, C., and Chamow, L. 1998. *Essential skills in family therapy.* New York: Guilford Press.

Satir, V. 1964. *Conjoint family therapy.* Palo Alto, CA: Science and Behavior Books.

Sheinberg, M., True, F., and Fraenkel, P. 1994. Treating the sexually abused child: A recursive, multimodel program. *Family Process.* 33:263–276.

Sluzki, C. E. 1978. Marital therapy from a systems theory perspective. In *Marriage and marital therapy,* T. J. Paolino and B. S. McCrady, eds. New York: Brunner/Mazel.

Speck, R. V., and Attneave, C. A. 1971. Social network intervention. In *Changing families,* J. Haley, ed. New York: Grune & Stratton.

Taibbi, R. 1996. *Doing family therapy: Craft and creativity in clinical practice.* New York: Guilford Press.

Trepper, T. S., and Barrett, M. J. 1989. *Systemic treatment of incest: A therapeutic handbook.* New York: Brunner/Mazel.

Walsh, F. 1998. *Strengthening family resilience.* New York: Guilford Press.

Watzlawick, P., Beavin, J. H., and Jackson, D. D. 1967. *Pragmatics of human communication.* New York: Norton.

—References

AAMFT Code of Ethics. (1991). Washington, DC: American Association for Marriage and Family Therapy.

Avis, J. M. 1992. Where are all the family therapists? Abuse and violence within families and family therapy's response. *Journal of Marital and Family Therapy.* 18:223–233.

Bateson, G., and Jackson, D. D. 1964. Some varieties of pathogenic organization. *Disorders of Communication.* 42:270–283.

Beels, C. C., and Ferber, A. 1969. Family therapy: A view. *Family Process.* 8:280–318.

Bell, J. E. 1961. *Family group therapy.* Public Health Monograph No. 64. Washington, DC: U.S. Government Printing Office.

Bell, J. E. 1975. *Family group therapy.* New York: Jason Aronson.

Bentovim, A., Elton, A., Hildebrand, J., Tranter, M., and Vizard, E. eds. 1988. *Child sexual abuse within the family.* London: Wright.

Bion, W. R. 1961. *Experiences in groups.* New York: Tavistock Publications.

Bograd, M. 1984. Family systems approaches to wife battering: A feminist critique. *American Journal of Orthopsychiatry.* 54:558–568.

Bograd, M. 1992. Values in conflict: Challenges to family therapists' thinking. *Journal of Marital and Family Therapy.* 18:243–257.

Boszormenyi-Nagy, I., and Spark, G. 1973. *Invisible loyalties: Reciprocity in intergenerational family therapy.* New York: Harper & Row.

Brown, P. D., and O'Leary, K. D. July, 1995. Marital treatment for wife abuse: A review and evaluation. Paper presented at the 4th International Family Violence Research Conference, Durham, NC.

Doherty, W. 1991. Family therapy goes postmodern. *Family Therapy Networker.* 15(5):36–42.

Edelson, E., and Tolman, R. 1992. *Intervention for men who batter.* Newbury Park, CA: Sage Publications.

Feldman, C. M., and Ridley, C. A. 1995. The etiology and treatment of domestic violence between adult partners. *Clinical Psychology: Science and Practice.* 2:317–348.

Freud, S. 1921. *Group psychology and the analysis of the ego.* Standard Edition. Vol. 18. London: Hogarth Press, 1955.

Furniss, T. 1991. *The multiprofessional handbook of child sexual abuse: Integrated management, therapy, and legal intervention.* London: Routledge.

Goldner, V. 1992. Making room for both/and. *The Family Therapy Networker.* 16(2): 55–61.

Goldner, V. 1998. The treatment of violence and victimization in intimate relationships. *Family Process.* 37:263–286.

Gondolf, E. W. 1995. Gains and process in state batterer programs and standards. *Family Violence and Sexual Assault Bulletin.* 11:27–28.

Gritzer, P. H., and Okum, H. S. 1983. Multiple family group therapy: A model for all families. In *Handbook of family and marital therapy,* B. B. Wolman and G. Stricker, eds. New York: Plenum Press.

Haley, J. 1961. Control in psychotherapy with schizophrenics. *Archives of General Psychiatry.* 5:340–353.

Haley, J. 1963. *Strategies of psychotherapy.* New York: Grune & Stratton.

Haley, J. 1976. *Problem-solving therapy.* San Francisco: Jossey-Bass.

Hansen, M. 1993. Feminism and family therapy: A review of feminist critiques of approaches to family violence (pp. 69–82). In *Battering and family therapy: A feminist perspective,* M. Hansen and M. Harway, eds. Newbury Park, CA: Sage Publications.

Herman, J. L. 1992. *Trauma and recovery.* New York: Basic Books.

Hoffman, L. 1971. Deviation-amplifying processes in natural groups. In *Changing families,* J. Haley, ed. New York: Grune & Stratton.

Jackson, D. D. 1961. Interactional psychotherapy. In *Contemporary psychotherapies,* M. T. Stein, ed. New York: Free Press of Glencoe.

Jackson, D. D. 1965. Family rules: The marital quid pro quo. *Archives of General Psychiatry.* 12:589–594.

Jackson, D. D. 1967. Aspects of conjoint family therapy. In *Family therapy and disturbed families,* G. H. Zuk and I. Boszormenyi-Nagy, eds. Palo Alto: Science and Behavior Books.

Jackson, D. D., and Weakland, J. H. 1961. Conjoint family therapy: Some considerations on theory, technique, and results. *Psychiatry.* 24:30–45.

Jacobson, N. S., and Christensen, A. 1996. *Integrative couple therapy.* New York: Guilford Press.

Laqueur, H. P. 1966. General systems theory and multiple family therapy. In *Handbook of psychiatric therapies,* J. Masserman, ed. New York: Grune & Stratton.

Laqueur, H. P. 1972a. Mechanisms of change in multiple family therapy. In *Progress in group and family therapy,* C. J. Sager and H. S. Kaplan, eds. New York: Brunner/Mazel.

Laqueur, H. P. 1972b. Multiple family therapy. In *The book of family therapy,* A. Ferber, M. Mendelsohn, and A. Napier, eds. Boston: Houghton Mifflin.

Laqueur, H. P. 1976. Multiple family therapy. In *Family therapy: Theory and practice,* P. J. Guerin, ed. New York: Gardner Press.

Lewin, K. 1951. *Field theory in social science.* New York: Harper.

MacGregor, R. 1967. Progress in multiple impact theory. In *Expanding theory and practice in family therapy,* N. W. Ackerman, F. L. Beatman, and S. N. Sherman, eds. New York: Family Service Association.

MacGregor, R. 1972. Multiple impact psychotherapy with families. In *Family therapy: An introduction to theory and technique,* G. D. Erickson and T. P. Hogan, eds. Monterey, CA: Brooks/Cole.

MacGregor, R., Richie, A. M., Serrano, A. C., Schuster, F. P., McDonald, E. C., and Goolishian, H. A. 1964. *Multiple impact therapy with families.* New York: McGraw-Hill.

Marayuma, M. 1968. The second cybernetics: Deviation-amplifying mutual causal processes. In *Modern systems research for the behavioral scientist,* W. Buckley, ed. Chicago: Aldine.

McFarlane, W. R. 1982. Multiple-family therapy in the psychiatric hospital. In *The psychiatric hospital and the family,* H. T. Harbin, ed. New York: Spectrum.

McGoldrick, M., Giordano, J., and Pearce, J. 1996. *Ethnicity and family therapy,* 2nd ed. New York: Guilford Press.

Meyer, J. P., and Pepper, S. 1977. Need compatibility and marital adjustment among young married couples. *Journal of Personality and Social Psychology.* 35:331–342.

Minuchin, S., and Nichols, M. P. 1993. *Family healing: Tales of hope and renewal from family therapy.* New York: Free Press.

Morris, C. W. 1938. Foundations on the theory of signs. In *International encyclopedia of united science,* O. Neurath, R. Carnap, and C. O. Morris, eds. Chicago: University of Chicago Press.

Nichols, M. P. 1987. *The self in the system.* New York: Brunner/Mazel.

Nichols, M. P. 1995. *The lost art of listening.* New York: Guilford Press.

Parsons, T. 1950. Psychoanalysis and the social structure. *Psychoanalytic Quarterly.* 19:371–380.

Ruesch, J., and Bateson, G. 1951. *Communication: The social matrix of psychiatry.* New York: Norton.

Ruevini, U. 1975. Network intervention with a family in crisis. *Family Process.* 14:193–203.

Ruevini, U. 1979. *Networking families in crisis.* New York: Human Sciences Press.

Sartre, J. P. 1964. *Being and nothingness.* New York: Citadel Press.

Satir, V. 1964. *Conjoint family therapy.* Palo Alto, CA: Science and Behavior Books.

Schutz, W. C. 1958. *FIRO: A three-dimensional theory of interpersonal behavior.* New York: Holt, Rinehart and Winston.

Schwartz, R. C. 1995. *Internal family systems therapy.* New York: Guilford Press.

Shaw, M. E. 1981. *Group dynamics: The psychology of small group behavior.* New York: McGraw-Hill.

Sheinberg, M., True, F., and Fraenkel, P. 1994. Treating the sexually abused child: A recursive, mulitmodal program. *Family Process.* 33:263–276.

Speck, R. V., and Attneave, C. A. 1973. *Family networks.* New York: Pantheon.

Trepper, T. S., and Barrett, M. J. 1989. *Systemic treatment of incest: A therapeutic handbook.* New York: Brunner/Mazel.

Walsh, F. 1998. *Strengthening family resilience.* New York: Guilford Press.

Watzlawick, P., Beavin, J. H., and Jackson, D. D. 1967. *Pragmatics of human communication.* New York: Norton.

Weakland, J., Fisch, R., Watzlawick, P., and Bodin, A. M. 1974, Brief therapy focused problem resolution. *Family Process.* 13:141–168.

Winch, R. F. 1955. The theory of complementary needs in mate selection: A test of one kind of complementariness. *American Sociological Review.* 20: 52–56.

Wynne, L., and Singer, M. 1963. Thought disorder and family relationships of schizophrenics: I. Research strategy. *Archives of General Psychiatry.* 9:191–198.

Yalom, I. D. 1985. *The theory and practice of group psychotherapy,* 3rd ed. New York: Basic Books.

The Fundamental Concepts
of Family Therapy

A Whole New Way of Thinking about Human Behavior

Family therapy is often misunderstood as just another variation of psychotherapy, one in which the whole family is brought into treatment. It is that, of course, but more importantly it involves a whole new way of thinking about human behavior—that is, as fundamentally organized by interpersonal context.

Prior to the advent of family therapy, the individual was regarded as the locus of psychological problems and the obvious target for treatment. If a mother called to complain that her fifteen-year-old son was depressed, a clinician would meet with the boy to find out what was wrong with him. A Rogerian might look for low self-esteem, a Freudian for repressed anger, a behaviorist for a lack of reinforcing activities; but all would assume that the primary forces shaping the boy's mood were located within him, and that therapy, therefore, required only the presence of the patient and a therapist.

Family therapy changed all that. Today, if a mother were to seek help for a depressed teenager, most therapists would meet with the boy and his parents together. If a fifteen-year-old is depressed, it's not unreasonable to assume that something might be going on in the family. Perhaps the boy's parents don't get along and he's worried that they might get divorced. Or maybe he's having a hard time living up to the expectations created by a successful older sister.

Suppose further that you are the therapist. You meet with the boy and his family and discover that he's not worried about his parents or jealous of his sister. In fact, "everything is fine" at home. The boy is just depressed. Now what?

That *now-what* feeling is a common experience when you start seeing families. Even when there *is* something obviously wrong—the boy is worried about his parents, or everybody seems to be shouting and no one is listening—it's often hard to know where to start. You could start by trying to solve the family's problems for them. But then you wouldn't be helping them deal with *why* they're having problems.

To address what's making it hard for a family to cope with their problems, you have to know where to look. For that, you need some way of understanding what makes families tick. You need some kind of theory.

When they first began to observe whole families discussing their problems, therapists could see immediately that everyone was involved. In the clamor of noisy quarrels, however, it's hard to see beyond personalities—the sullen adolescent, the controlling mother, the distant father—to notice the patterns that connect them. Instead of concentrating on individuals and their personalities, family therapists consider how problems may be, at least in part, a product of the relationships surrounding them. How to understand those relationships is the subject of this chapter.

Cybernetics

The first and perhaps most influential model of how families operate was **cybernetics,** the study of feedback mechanisms in self-regulating systems. What the family shares with other cybernetic systems is a tendency to maintain stability by using information about its performance as feedback.

At the core of cybernetics is the **feedback loop,** the process by which a system gets the information necessary to maintain a steady course. This feedback includes information about the system's performance relative to its external environment as well as the relationship among the system's parts. Feedback loops can be negative or positive. This distinction refers to the effect they have on deviations from a homeostatic state, not to whether they are beneficial. **Negative feedback** indicates a change that threatens the integrity of the system; it signals the system to restore the status

quo. **Positive feedback** signals the need to modify the system.

A familiar example of negative feedback occurs in a home heating system. When the temperature drops below a certain point, the thermostat triggers the furnace to heat the house back to the pre-established range. It is this self-correcting feedback loop that makes the system cybernetic, and it is the system's response to change as a signal to restore its previous state that illustrates negative feedback.

Figure 4.1 shows the basic circularity involved in a feedback loop. Each element has an effect on the next, until the last element "feeds back" the cumulative effect into the first part of the cycle. Thus A affects B, which in turn affects C, which feeds back to affect A, and so on.

In the example of a home heating system, A might be the room temperature; B the thermostat; and C the furnace. Figure 4.2 shows a similar, cybernetic feedback loop for a couple. In this case, Jan's housecleaning efforts (output) affect how much housework gets done, which subsequently affects how much housecleaning Billie has to do, which then feeds back (input) to how much housecleaning Jan thinks still needs to be done, and so on.

The cybernetic system turned out to be a particularly useful metaphor for describing how families maintain their stability (Jackson, 1959). Sometimes this is a good thing, as for example when a family continues to function as a cohesive unit despite being threatened by conflict or stress. Sometimes, however, resisting change is not such a good thing, as when a family fails to readjust to accommodate to the

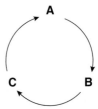

FIGURE 4.1   Circular Causality of a Feedback Loop

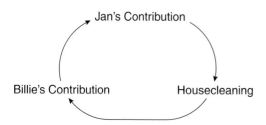

FIGURE 4.2   Feedback Loop in a Couple's Housecleaning Efforts

growth or change of one of its members. More about this later.

Remember that while negative feedback reduces change, positive feedback amplifies it. Like negative feedback, positive feedback can have desirable or undesirable consequences. If a young woman falls in love and marries someone of a different race, her parents can readjust to accept her married status and allow her new husband into their hearts, or they can stop speaking to their daughter and cut her out of their lives. To maintain stability *and* flexibility,

families need to respond to both negative and positive feedback. As we shall see, however, early family therapists had a tendency to overemphasize negative feedback and resistance to change.

As applied to families, cybernetics focused attention on several phenomena: (1) **family rules,** which govern the range of behavior a family system can tolerate (the family's homeostatic range); (2) *negative feedback* mechanisms that families use to enforce those rules (guilt, punishment, symptoms); (3) *sequences of family interaction* around a problem that characterize a system's reaction to it (the feedback loops around a deviation); and (4) what happens when a system's accustomed negative feedback is ineffective, triggering *positive feedback loops.*

Examples of positive feedback loops are those pesky "vicious cycles," in which the actions taken only make things worse. The well-known "self-fulfilling prophecy" is one such positive feedback loop; one's apprehensions lead to actions that precipitate the feared situation, which in turn justifies one's fears, and so on.

Cybernetics was the brainchild of MIT mathematician Norbert Wiener (1948), who developed what was to become the first model of family dynamics in a very unlikely setting. During World War II, Wiener was asked to work on the problem of how to get antiaircraft guns to hit German planes moving so fast that it was impossible to calibrate settings rapidly enough for gunnery batteries to hit their targets. His solution was to incorporate a system of internal feedback rather than to rely on observers to readjust the guns after every miss.

Gregory Bateson came into contact with cybernetics at a remarkable series of interdisciplinary meetings called the Macy conferences, beginning in 1946 (Heims, 1991). Bateson and Wiener immediately hit it off at these meetings, and their dialogues were to have a profound impact on Bateson's application of systems theory to family therapy.

Because cybernetics emerged from the study of machines, where positive feedback loops led to destructive "runaways," causing the machinery to break down, the emphasis was on negative feedback and the maintenance of homeostasis. The system's environment would change—the temperature would go up or down—and this change would trigger negative feedback mechanisms to bring the system back to homeostasis—the heat would go on or off. Negative feedback loops control everything from endocrine systems to ecosystems. Animal species are balanced by starvation and predators when they overpopulate and by increases in birthrates when their numbers are depleted. Blood sugar levels are balanced by increases in insulin output when they get too high and increases in appetite when they get too low.

Another example of positive feedback is the "bandwagon effect"—the tendency of a cause to gain support simply because of its growing number of adherents. You can probably think of some fads and more than a few pop music groups that owe much of their popularity to the bandwagon effect.

As an example of a self-fulfilling prophecy, let's consider Jerry. He wants to find a girlfriend, but he sees himself as boring. Consequently, he's convinced that women will reject him. Each time he summons up the courage to talk to a girl, he looks for evidence that she's not interested in what he's saying. At the first look of distraction, he becomes self-consciously anxious and starts making wisecracks. Her ensuing annoyance becomes more evidence (positive feedback) for his belief that he's basically unlikable.

To shift to a family example, in a family with a low threshold for the expression of anger, Marcus, the adolescent son, blows up at his parents over their insistence that he not stay out past midnight. Mother is shocked by his outburst and begins to cry. Father responds by grounding Marcus for a month. Rather than reducing Marcus's deviation—bringing his anger back within homeostatic limits—this negative feedback produces the opposite effect: Marcus explodes and challenges their authority. The parents respond with more crying and punishing, which further increases Marcus's anger, and so on. In this way, the intended negative feedback (crying and punishing) becomes positive feedback. It amplifies rather than diminishes Marcus's deviation. The family is caught in a positive-feedback "runaway," otherwise known as a vicious cycle, which escalates until Marcus runs away from home.

Later, cyberneticians like Walter Buckley and Ross Ashby recognized that positive feedback loops aren't always bad; if they don't get out of hand, they can help systems adjust to changed circumstances. Marcus's family might need to recalibrate their rules for anger to accommodate an adolescent's increased assertiveness.

The crisis that this positive feedback loop produced could lead to a reexamination of the family's rules, if the family could step out of the loop long enough to get some perspective. In so doing they would be **metacommunicating,** communicating about their ways of communicating, a process that can lead to a change in a system's rules (Bateson, 1956).

As should now be clear, family cyberneticians focused on the feedback loops within families, otherwise known as patterns of communication, as the fundamental source of family dysfunction. Hence the family theorists most influenced by cybernetics came to be known as the *communications school* (see Chapters 3 and 6). Faulty or unclear communication results in inaccurate or incomplete feedback, so the system cannot self-correct (change its rules) and, consequently, overreacts or underreacts to change.

Systems Theory

The greatest challenge facing anyone who treats families is finding a way to see past personalities to the patterns of influence that shape family members' behavior. We're so used to seeing what happens in families as a product of individual qualities, like selfishness, generosity, rebelliousness, passivity, tolerance, submissiveness, and so on, that learning to see patterns of relationship requires a radical shift in perspective.

Experience teaches that what shows up as one person's behavior may be a product of relationship. The same individual may be submissive in one relationship, dominant in another. Like so many qualities we attribute to individuals, submissiveness is only half of a two-part equation. In fact, family therapists use a host of concepts to describe how two people in a relationship contribute to what goes on between them, including *pursuer–distancer, overfunctioning-underfunctioning, control-and-rebel cycles,* and so on. The obvious advantage of such concepts is that either party to the relationship can change their part in the pattern. But while it's relatively easy to discover themes in two-person relationships, it's more difficult to see patterns of interaction in larger groups like whole families. That's why family therapists have found systems theory so useful.

Systems theory had its origins in mathematics, physics, and engineering in the 1940s, when theoreticians began to construct models of the structure and functioning of organized mechanical and biological units. What these theorists discovered was that things as diverse as simple machines, jet engines, amoebas, and the human brain share the attributes of a system—that is, an organized assemblage of parts forming a complex whole. Bateson and his colleagues found systems theory to be the perfect vehicle for illuminating the ways in which families functioned as organized units rather than merely as a collection of individuals.

According to systems theory, the essential properties of an organism, or living system, are properties of the whole, which none of the parts have. They arise from the interactions and relationships among the parts. These properties are destroyed when the system is reduced to isolated elements. The whole is always greater than the sum of its parts. Thus, from a systems perspective, it would make little sense to try to understand a child's behavior by interviewing him without the rest of his family.

While some people use terms like *systemic* and *systems theory* to mean little more than considering families as units, systems actually have a number of more specific and interesting properties. To begin with, the shift from looking at the individual to considering the family as a system means shifting the focus from individuals to the patterns of their relationship. From a systemic perspective, the family is more than a collection of individuals; it is a network of relationships.

Let's take a simple example. If a mother scolds her son, and her husband tells her not to

be so harsh, and the boy continues to misbehave, a systemic analysis would concentrate on this sequence. For it is this *observable interaction* that reveals how the system functions. In order to focus on inputs and outputs, a systems analysis avoids speculating about individuals or asking *why* they do what they do. The most radical expression of this systemic perspective was the "black box" metaphor:

> The impossibility of seeing the mind "at work" has in recent years led to the adoption of the Black Box concept from telecommunication . . . applied to the fact that electronic hardware is by now so complex that it is sometimes more expedient to disregard the internal structure of a device and concentrate on the study of its specific input-output relations. . . . This concept, if applied to psychological and psychiatric problems, has the heuristic advantage that no ultimately unverifiable intrapsychic hypotheses need be invoked, and that one can limit oneself to observable input-output relations, that is, to communication. (Watzlawick, Beavin, & Jackson, 1967, pp. 43–44)

Viewing people as black boxes may seem like the ultimate expression of mechanistic thinking; but this metaphor had the advantage of simplifying the field of study by eliminating speculation about the mind and emotions in order to concentrate on people's input and output (communication, behavior).

Among the features of systems functioning seized on by the early family therapists, few were more influential—or later more controversial—than **homeostasis,** the self-regulation that keeps systems in a state of dynamic balance. Don Jackson's notion of **family homeostasis** emphasized that dysfunctional families' tendency to resist change went a long way toward explaining why, despite heroic efforts to improve, so many patients remain stuck (Jackson, 1959). Today we look back on this emphasis on homeostasis as shortchanging families by exaggerating their conservative properties and underestimating their flexibility and resourcefulness.

Thus, although many of the cybernetic concepts used to describe machines could be extended by analogy to human systems like the family, living systems, it turns out, cannot be adequately described by the same principles as mechanical systems.

General Systems Theory

During the 1940s an Austrian biologist, Ludwig von Bertalanffy, attempted to combine various concepts from systems thinking and biology into a universal theory of living systems—from the human mind to the global ecosphere. Starting with his investigations of the endocrine system, he began extrapolating to more complex social systems, and he developed a model that came to be called **general systems theory.**

Mark Davidson (1983), in his fascinating biography *Uncommon Sense,* summarized Bertalanffy's definition of a system as:

> any entity maintained by the mutual interaction of its parts, from atom to cosmos, and including such mundane examples as telephone, postal, and rapid transit systems. A Bertalanffian system can be physical like a television set, biological like a cocker spaniel, psychological like a personality, sociological like a labor union, or symbolic like a set of laws. . . . A system can be composed of smaller systems and can also be part of a larger system, just as a state or province is composed of smaller jurisdictions and also is part of a nation. Consequently, the same organized entity can be regarded as either a system or a subsystem, depending on the observer's focus of interest. (p. 26)

The last point is important. Every system is a subsystem of larger systems. But when they adopted the systems perspective, family therapists tended to forget this spreading network of influence. They regarded the family as a system while largely ignoring the larger systems of community, culture, and politics in which families are embedded.

Bertalanffy pioneered the idea that a system is more than the sum of its parts, in the same sense that a watch is more than a collection of cogs and springs. There's nothing mystical about this, just that when things are organized into a system, something new emerges, the way water comes from the interaction of hydrogen and oxygen. Applied to family therapy, these ideas—that a family system should be seen as more than just a collection of individuals and that therapists should focus on interactions rather than on personalities—became central tenets of the field.

Bertalanffy used the metaphor of an organism for social groups, but an organism that was an **open system,** continuously interacting with its environment. Open systems, as opposed to closed systems (e.g., machines), sustain themselves by continuously exchanging resources with their environment—for example, taking in oxygen and expelling carbon dioxide. Another property of living systems that mechanists forgot was that they don't just react to stimuli, they actively initiate efforts to flourish. Thus, in healthy families, parents appreciate the new ideas children bring home as a source of enrichment, and such families often seek out ways to benefit and enjoy each other.

Bertalanffy was a life-long crusader against the mechanistic view of living systems, particularly those living systems called people. He believed that, unlike machines, living organisms demonstrate **equifinality,** the ability to reach a given final goal in a variety of ways. (In mechanical systems, the final state and the means to that state are fixed.) He and other biologists used that term to identify the organism's inner-directed ability to protect or restore its wholeness, as in the human body's mobilization of antibodies and its ability to repair skin and bone (von Bertalanffy, 1950).

Thus living organisms are active and creative. They work to sustain their organization, but they aren't motivated solely to preserve the status quo. Family therapists picked up on the concept of homeostasis but, according to Bertalanffy, an overemphasis on this conservative aspect of the organism reduced it to the level of a machine: "If [this] principle of homeostatic maintenance is taken as a rule of behavior, the so-called well-adjusted individual will be [defined as] a well-oiled robot. . . ." (quoted in Davidson, 1983, p. 104).

While homeostasis remains an important concept in family therapy, its limited ability to account for the wide variety of human behavior has been repeatedly acknowledged by family therapists in ways that echo Bertalanffy's concerns (Hoffman, 1981; Speer, 1970; Dell, 1982). Cyberneticians had to propose new concepts like **morphogenesis** (Speer, 1970) to account for what Bertalanffy believed was simply a natural property of organisms—to seek, in addition to resisting, change.

Bertalanffy also recognized that the act of observation has an effect on the observed. This awareness strengthened his conviction that we should be humble about our assumptions. A Bertalanffian therapist would be careful to not impose his or her perspective on clients and would try to understand their perspectives on their own problems. Unlike some postmodernists, who take the position that since we can't know absolute reality then we can't have strong values because nothing is better than anything else, Bertalanffy believed that we should be more, rather than less, concerned with our values and assumptions, because some perspectives are ecologically destructive. Thus therapists should scrutinize their assumptions and those implicit in their theories in terms of their impact on families and society.

To summarize, Bertalanffy brought up many of the issues that have shaped and still are shaping family therapy:

- A system as more than the sum of its parts
- Emphasis on interaction within and among systems versus reductionism
- Human systems as ecological organisms versus mechanism
- Concept of equifinality
- Homeostatic reactivity versus spontaneous activity
- Importance of ecologically sound beliefs and values versus valuelessness

Many of these issues will reappear in the ensuing discussion and throughout the book.

Social Constructionism

Family therapy was born at a time when the prevailing psychoanalytic paradigm emphasized unconscious conflicts as the source of human unhappiness. To be effective, therapy had to delve deep to uncover those conflicts—and that was a long, slow process. In rejecting this mentalistic model, family therapists turned to systems metaphors that focused on behavior, interaction, and feedback. As we have seen, systems theory taught us to see how people's lives are shaped by their interchanges with those around them. But, in focusing on patterns of family interactions, systems theory left something out. Actually, two things: how family members' beliefs affected their actions, and how cultural forces shaped those beliefs.

Constructivism

Constructivism captured the imagination of family therapists in the 1980s when studies of the way the brain works showed that we can never know the world as it exists "out there"; all we can know is our subjective experience of it. Research on neural nets (von Foerster, 1981) and experiments on the vision of the frog (Maturana & Varela, 1980) indicated that the brain doesn't process images of the world literally, like a camera, but rather registers experience in patterns organized by the nervous system of the observer.[1] Nothing is perceived directly. Everything is filtered through the mind of the observer.

When this new perspective on knowing was reported to the family field by Paul Watzlawick (1984), Paul Dell (1985), and Lynn Hoffman (1988), the effect was a wake-up call—alerting us to the importance of cognition in family life, and jolting therapists out of the assumption that they could be objective experts.

Constructivism is the modern expression of a philosophical tradition that goes back at least as far as the eighteenth century. Immanuel Kant (1724–1804), one of the pillars of Western intellectual tradition, regarded knowledge as a product of the way our imaginations are organized. The outside world doesn't simply impress itself onto the tabula rasa (blank slate) of our minds, as British Empiricist John Locke (1632–1704) believed. In fact, Kant argued, our minds are anything but blank. They are active filters through which we process, categorize, and interpret the world.

Constructivism first found its way into psychotherapy in the **personal construct theory** of George Kelly (1955). According to Kelly, we make sense of the world by creating our own unique constructs of the environment. We interpret and organize events, and we make predictions that guide our actions on the basis of these constructs. You might compare this subjective way of interpreting experience to seeing the world through a pair of eyeglasses. Because we may need to alter or discard constructs, therapy became a matter of revising old constructs and developing new ones—trying on different lenses to see which ones enabled a person to navigate the world in more satisfying and more functional ways.

The first example of constructivism in family therapy was the strategic technique of **reframing**—relabeling behavior to shift how family members respond to it. Clients will respond very differently to a child who is seen as "hyperactive" than to one perceived as "misbehaving." Likewise, the dispirited parents of a rebellious ten-year-old will feel better about themselves if they become convinced that, rather than being "ineffectual disciplinarians," they have an "oppositional child." The first diagnosis suggests that the parents should get tough, but also that they probably won't succeed. The second suggests that coping with a difficult child may require strategizing. The point isn't that one description is inherently better than the other, but rather that if whatever label a family applies to its problems leads to ineffective coping strategies, then perhaps a new label will alter their viewpoint sufficiently to trigger a more effective response.

When constructivism took hold of family therapy in the mid-1980s, it triggered a fundamental shift in emphasis. Systems metaphors focused on action; constructivism emphasized cognitive meaning and personal interpretation. Instead of concentrating on patterns of interaction, constructivism shifted the focus toward exploring the assumptions that people have about their problems.

Constructivism is, of course, a theory of knowledge, not a set of techniques. However, the constructivist viewpoint was conducive to a model of therapy as a conversational search for meaning. Meaning itself became the primary target. The goal of therapy shifted from interrupting problematic patterns of behavior to helping clients find new perspectives in their lives through the liberating process of dialogue.

In the vanguard of this movement were Harry Goolishian and Harlene Anderson, whose "collaborative language-based systems approach" was defined less by what therapists do than by what they don't do. In this model therapists *don't* assume the role of expert, *don't*

---

1.   The eye of the frog, for example, doesn't register much but lateral movement, which may be all you really need to know if your main interest in life is catching flies with your tongue.

assume that they know how families should change, and *don't* push them in any particular direction. The role of the therapist isn't to try to change people but to open doors for them to explore new meanings in their lives.

> The therapist does not control the interview by influencing the conversation toward a particular direction in the sense of content or outcome, nor is the therapist responsible for the direction of change. The therapist is only responsible for creating a space in which dialogical conversation can occur. (Anderson & Goolishian, 1988, p. 385)

Constructivism teaches us to look beyond behavior to the ways we perceive, interpret, and construct our experience in order to make sense of it and thereby guide our lives. Constructivism boils down to this: There is more than one way of looking at things; and that is hard to argue with. Moreover, in a world where all truth is relative, the perspective of the therapist began to be seen as having no more claim to objectivity than that of the clients. Thus constructivism undermined the status of the therapist as an objective authority with privileged knowledge of cause and cure.

Acknowledging that how we perceive and understand reality is a construction does not mean, of course, that there is nothing real out there to perceive and understand. Sticks and stones *can* break your bones. Moreover, even the most ardent constructivists (e.g., Efran, Lukens, & Lukens, 1990) remind us that some constructions are more useful than others. Constructivism is not a license to fabricate indiscriminantly for the sake of therapeutic leverage.

Others have challenged the opposite implication of constructivism—namely, that a therapist without the status of expert is a therapist without influence. In her thoughtful analysis of postmodern therapy *Back to Reality*, Barbara Held (1995) points out that: ". . . surely there is a contradiction to be faced by these authors when they attempt to deny or minimize the expertise that they also apparently want themselves to have—that therapists must indeed have to legitimate their activity as a profession/discipline" (p. 244).

One of us felt strongly enough about what he perceived as the abdication of leadership to remind therapists:

> Are therapists and clients partners in a joint undertaking? Are they equals? No. Clients are, to paraphrase George Orwell, "more equal" when it comes to whose point of view ultimately counts. Therapists are, or should be, more equal when it comes to training, expertise, and objectivity—*and* taking the lead in what happens during the therapy hour. It's fine to criticize power—if what's meant by that is domination and control: it's not so fine to abdicate leadership. (Nichols, 1993, p. 165)

And further:

> If arranging and hosting conversations were all that a therapist did, that person should be called a mediator, or the opposite of a talk-show host (whose aim is to arrange conversations that are nasty and abusive). The therapist as host neglects the role of teacher—a much maligned but essential aspect of any transformative therapy. Therapists teach not by telling people how to run their lives, but by helping them learn something about themselves. (p. 164)

But "telling people how to run their lives" is exactly what Anderson and Goolishian (1988) were concerned about. Constructivism was a revolt against an authoritarian model of therapy, against the image of the therapist as bully. You don't have to agree that interventionist therapists like Salvador Minuchin or Jay Haley were authoritarian in order to respect the constructivist's admonition to avoid aggressive intrusiveness. A therapist who is too anxious to change people is a little like a cat waiting to pounce. (It's not a very good way to get to know people.)

Anderson and Goolishian favored what they called an attitude of "not-knowing" in which they subsume their expertise and make room for the clients' ideas to come forward. Instead of approaching families with preconceived notions about structure and functioning, they brought only curiosity. It is probably well to remember that even our most cherished metaphors for family life—"system," "enmeshment," "dirty games," "triangles," and so on—are just that: metaphors. They don't exist in some objective reality; they are constructions, some more useful than others.

The construction favored by Anderson and Goolishian was that language makes rather than reflects reality. There is, of course, nothing new in describing therapy—"the talking cure"—as dialogue. What was new was the elevation of personal narrative to the pinnacle of interest in family therapy—a field born of the discovery of how the personal is shaped by the interpersonal context.

In emphasizing the idiosyncratic perspective of the individual, constructivists were accused by some (e.g., Minuchin, 1991) of ignoring the social context. While there is nothing inherently insensitive to social consciousness in constructivism, it was true that many of the writers in this tradition focused more on how individuals perceived their situation than on the actual social conditions of their lives. Once that solipsistic streak was pointed out, leading constructivists clarified their position: When they said that reality is constructed, they meant *socially* constructed.

The Social Construction of Reality

Social constructionism expands on constructivism much as family therapy expanded on individual psychology. Constructivism says that we perceive and relate to the world on the basis of our own interpretations. **Social constructionism** points out that those interpretations are shaped by the social context in which we live.

If a fourteen-year-old consistently disobeys his parents, a constructivist might point out

that the boy may not think they deserve his respect. In other words, the boy's actions are not simply a product of the parents' disciplinary efforts but also of the boy's construction of their authority. A social constructionist would add that an adolescent's attitudes about such things as parental authority are shaped not only by what goes on in the family but also by messages transmitted from the culture at large.

At school or work, at lunch, in phone conversations, at the movies and from television, we absorb attitudes and opinions that we carry into our families. Television, to pick one very potent influence on the average fourteen-year-old, has made today's children more sophisticated, and more cynical. As communications scholar Joshua Meyrowitz (1985) argues in *No Sense of Place*, today's children are exposed to the "back stage" of the adult world, to otherwise hidden doubts and conflicts, foolishness and failures of adult types they see on TV. This demystification undermines adolescent trust and confidence in traditional authority structures. It's hard to maintain an ideal of adult wisdom when your image of a parent figure is Homer Simpson.

Both constructivism and social constructionism focus on interpretation of experience as a mediator of behavior. But while constructivists emphasized the subjective mind of the individual, social constructionists place more emphasis on social interpretation and the intersubjective influence of language and culture. According to constructivism, people have problems not merely because of the objective conditions of their lives but also because of their interpretation of those conditions. What social constructionism adds is a recognition of how such meanings emerge and change in the process of talking with other people.

Therapy then becomes a process of deconstruction and reconstruction—of freeing clients from the tyranny of entrenched beliefs and helping them develop new and more promising perspectives. How this plays out in practice is illustrated in the two most influential new versions of family therapy: the solution-focused model and narrative therapy.

Inherent in most forms of therapy is the idea that before a problem can be solved, client and therapist must figure out what's wrong. This notion seems almost self-evident, but it is a construction—only one way of looking at things. **Solution-focused therapy** turns this assumption on its head, using a totally different construction—namely, that the best way to solve problems is to discover what people do when they're *not* having the problem, and then building on that.

Suppose, for example, that a woman's complaint is that her husband never talks to her. Instead of trying to figure out what's wrong, a solution-focused therapist might ask the woman if she can remember **exceptions** to this complaint. Perhaps she and her husband do have reasonably good conversations when they go for walks or out to dinner together. In that case, the therapist might simply suggest that they do more of that. We'll see how solution-focused therapy builds on the basic insights of constructivism in Chapter 12.

Like their solution-focused colleagues, **narrative** therapists help create a shift in their clients' experience by helping them reexamine how they look at things. But whereas solution-focused therapy shifts attention from current failures to past successes in order to mobilize behavioral solutions, narrative therapy's aim is broader and more attitudinal. The decisive technique in this approach—**externalization**—involves the truly radical reconstruction of defining problems, not as properties of the persons who suffer them, but as alien oppressors. Thus, for example, while the parents of a boy who doesn't keep up with his homework might define him as lazy or as a procrastinator, a narrative therapist would talk instead about times when "Procrastination" gets the better of him—*and* times when "it" doesn't.

Notice how the former construction—the boy is a procrastinator—is relatively deterministic, while the latter—Procrastination sometimes gets the better of him—frees the boy from a negative identity, and turns therapy into a struggle for liberation. We'll talk more about narrative therapy and the process of externalization in Chapter 13.

Both solution-focused and narrative therapists take an active role in helping clients question self-defeating constructions. Both are founded on the premise that we develop our ideas about the world in conversation with other people (Gergen, 1985). Moreover, if some of those ideas bog us down in our problems, then new and more productive perspectives can usefully evolve within a cradle of narrative reconstruction. If problems are stories that people have learned to tell themselves, then deconstructing these stories can be an effective way to help people master their problems.

Critics, ourselves among them (Nichols & Schwartz, 2001), have pointed out that by emphasizing the cognitive dimension of individuals and their experience, social constructionists have turned their backs on some of the defining insights of family therapy—namely, that families operate as complex units and that psychological symptoms are often the result of conflicts within the family. Our experience and our identities are partly linguistic constructions, but only partly. But if social constructionists have thus far tended to ignore the insights of systems theory and to downplay family conflict, there is nothing inherent in social constructionism that makes this necessary. The kinds of polarized interactions that Bateson, Jackson, and Haley first described forty years ago—in terms like *complementary* and *symmetrical*—can be understood as reflecting both behavioral interactions *and* social constructions, rather than either one or the other.

Italian psychiatrist Valeria Ugazio (1999) describes how family members differentiate themselves not merely by their actions but by the way they talk about themselves in "semantic polarities." Thus, for example, in a family whose talk about themselves and others can be characterized by the polarity dependence/independence, conversations will tend to be organized around fear and courage, the need for protection and the desire for exploration. As a result of these conversations, members of such a family will grow to define themselves as shy and cautious or bold and adventurous.

Attachment Theory

As the field has matured, family therapists have shown a renewed interest in the inner life of the individuals who make up the family. Now, in addition to theories that help us understand the broad, systemic influences on family members' behavior, *attachment theory* has emerged as a leading tool for describing the deeper roots of the dynamics of close relationships.

Attachment theory has been especially fruitful in couples therapy (e.g., Johnson, 2002) where it helps explain how even healthy adults need to depend on each other. In the early years of family therapy, couples treatment was a therapy without a theory. With few exceptions, most therapists treated couples with the same models designed for families (e.g., Bowen, 1978; Haley, 1976; Minuchin, 1974). The exceptions were behaviorists, who implied that intimacy was a product of reinforcement, and cognitive psychologists, who suggested that if we changed the way couples thought and communicated, their emotions would follow. Nobody talked much about love or longing, or trust. Dependency might be okay for children, but in adults, we were told, it was a sign of "enmeshment."

In emotionally focused couples therapy, Susan Johnson uses attachment theory to deconstruct the familiar dance in which one partner criticizes and complains while the other becomes defensive and withdraws. What attachment theory suggests is that the criticism and complaining are a protest against the disruption of the attachment bond—in other words, the nagging partner may be more insecure than angry. Once the insecure partner's feelings are softened and he or she can show vulnerability, the other partner is less likely to feel threatened and more likely to come forward to offer comfort and reassurance.

The notion that how couples deal with each other reflects their attachment history can be traced back to the pioneering studies of John Bowlby and Mary Ainsworth. When Bowlby graduated from Cambridge in the 1940s, it was assumed that infants become attached to their mothers as a consequence of being fed. But Konrad Lorenz (1935) showed that baby geese become attached to parents who don't feed them, and Harry Harlow (1958) observed that, under stress, infant monkeys prefer not the wire-mesh "mothers" that provided food but the cloth-covered "mothers" who provided contact comfort. It turns out that human babies, too, become attached to people who do not feed them (Ainsworth, 1967).

In the 1940s and 1950s, a number of studies found that young children who were separated from their mothers go through a series of reactions that can be described as "protest," "despair," and, finally, "detachment" (e.g., Burlingham & Freud, 1944; Robertson, 1953). In attempting to understand these reactions, Bowlby (1958) concluded that the intense bond formed between infants and their parents was based on a biologically based drive for proximity that arose through the process of natural selection. When danger threatens, infants who stay close to their parents are less likely to be killed by predators.

Attachment means seeking proximity in the face of stress. (You can hug your blankie, but it doesn't hug back.) Attachment can be seen in cuddling up to mother's soft, warm body and being cuddled in return; looking into her eyes and being looked at fondly; and holding on to her and being held. These experiences are profoundly comforting and reassuring.

Attachment is regulated by strong emotion. "The formation of a bond is described as falling in love, maintaining a bond as loving someone, and losing a partner as grieving over someone. Similarly, threat of loss arouses anxiety and actual loss gives rise to sorrow; whilst each of these situations is likely to arouse anger. The unchallenged maintenance of a bond is experienced as a source of joy" (Bowlby, 1979, p. 130). Cognitive components are also involved in attachment in the form of what Bowlby referred to as "representational models" or "internal working models."

According to Mary Ainsworth (1967), infants use their attachment figure (usually the mother) as a *secure base* for exploration. When an infant feels threatened, he or she will turn to the caregiver for protection and comfort. Variations in this pattern are evident in two different insecure strategies of attachment. In the "avoidant" strategy, the infant tends to inhibit attachment behavior; in the "resistant" strategy, the infant tends to cling to mother and avoid exploration.

Security in the relationship with an attachment figure indicates that an infant is able to rely on that caregiver as an available source of protection and comfort if the need arises. When threats arise, infants in secure relationships are able to direct "attachment behavior" (approaching, crying, reaching out) to their caregivers and take comfort in the reassurance offered by them. Infants with secure attachments are confident in the availability of their caregivers and, consequently, confident in their own interactions in the world.

This confidence is not evident in infants who have anxious attachment relationships with their caregivers. Bids for attention may have been met with indifference or rebuff (Ainsworth, et al., 1978; Bowlby, 1973). As a result, such infants remain anxious about the availability of caregivers. Moreover, Bowlby argued

that because attachment relationships are internalized, these early experiences shape expectations for later relationships of friendship, parenting, and romantic love.

One of the things that distinguishes attachment theory is that it has been extensively studied. What is clear is that it is a stable and influential trait throughout childhood. The type of attachment shown at twelve months predicts: (1) type of attachment at eighteen months (Waters, 1978; Main & Weston, 1981); (2) frustratability, persistence, cooperativeness, and task enthusiasm at eighteen months (Main, 1977; Matas, Arend, & Sroufe, 1978); (3) social competence of preschoolers (Lieberman, 1977; Easterbrook & Lamb, 1979; Waters, Wippman, & Sroufe, 1979); and (4) self-esteem, empathy, and classroom deportment (Sroufe, 1979). Indeed the quality of relationship at one year is an excellent predictor of quality of relating in various other ways up through five years, with the advantage to the securely attached infant compared with the resistantly or avoidantly attached infant.

What is less clearly supported by research is the proposition that styles of attachment in childhood are correlated with attachment styles in intimate adult relationships. Nevertheless, the idea that romantic love can be conceptualized as an attachment process (Hazan & Shaver, 1987) remains a compelling, if not yet proven, proposition. What the research has established is that individuals who are anxious over relationships report more relationship conflict, suggesting that some of this conflict is driven by basic insecurities over love, loss, and abandonment. Those who are anxious about their relationships often engage in coercive and distrusting ways of dealing with conflict, which are likely to bring about the very outcomes they fear most (Feeney, 1995).

Lyman Wynne (1984) was among the first family therapists to refer to attachment theory when he described attachment as the first priority in the development of relationships.

Attachment theory is applied to clinical treatment by linking symptomatic expressions of fear and anger to disturbances in attachment relationships. Parents can be helped to understand some of their children's disruptive behavior as stemming from the child's anxiety about the parents' availability and responsiveness. Couples can be helped to understand the attachment fears and vulnerabilities behind angry and defensive interactions (Gottman, 1994; Johnson, 1996).

Bowlby (1988) outlined five tasks for therapists to perform in relation to attachment: (1) providing a secure therapeutic base; (2) exploring contemporary relationships; (3) exploring the relationship with the therapist; (4) reviewing how current patterns of relating may reflect past experiences; and (5) recognizing that the images from past relationships may or may not be appropriate for contemporary relationships.

To be experienced as a secure base, a therapist must be able to protect family members from attack at the same time that they explore their most worrying situations. The therapist who comes across as helpfully in charge helps make a family feel secure enough to face their conflicts and experiment with new ways of interacting. Therapists can use attachment theory to illuminate current relationships by showing how a child's misbehavior might reflect an insecure attachment, or how a husband's avoidance may be due to ambivalent attachment, or a wife's animosity may be an expression of anxious attachment. When family therapists feel drawn in to play a role in the family's script, they can not only avoid being inducted into playing a role that's missing in the family but they can also use attachment theory to point out family members' needs for being securely cared for. Instead of being recruited to soothe an anxious child or comfort a distressed spouse, the therapist can hand back responsibility to the parents or the partner and encourage them to become less defensive and more sympathetic and supportive.

Conclusions

After reading this chronology of how the dominant theories in family therapy have evolved, the reader may feel overwhelmed at the number of paradigm shifts the field has undergone in the few decades of its existence. It may help to point out a pattern in this apparent discontinuity. The focus of therapy has continually expanded toward ever wider levels of context. This process started when therapists looked beyond individuals to their families. Suddenly, unexplainable behavior began to make sense. Early family therapists concentrated on assessing and altering the sequences of behavioral interaction surrounding problems. Next, it was recognized that those sequences were manifestations of a family's underlying structure, and structure became the target of change. Then a family's structure was seen to be a product of a long-term, multigenerational process that was governed by belief systems, and therapists aimed their interventions at these underlying beliefs. More recently it dawned on therapists that these belief systems did not arise in a vacuum, hence the current interest in cultural influences.

Another reason for the discontinuous shifts in the field's history is that, beginning with their rebellion against the psychoanalytic and medical models, family therapists have tended to be mavericks. Whenever family therapy begins to coalesce around a certain paradigm such that it becomes the dominant narrative, the field reinvents itself. A new metaphor is proposed and the old one is rejected as passé. A new minority of therapists become the progressives on the cutting edge, relegating the leaders of the former revolution to the status of has-beens.

Currently, many therapists are rejecting systems thinking, referring to it as modernist, mechanistic, and consequently less useful than the new narrative metaphor. Decades of study, conceptual refinement, and technical development are blithely discarded for the new, improved way of thinking. While we believe that it's important to try on new metaphors and practices and to continuously reexamine the old, it may not be necessary for each advance to be accompanied by a rejection of the past. Our goal is to capture the exciting spirit of the new but maintain respect for the contributions of the giants on whose shoulders we stand.

●

Family therapists, naturalists on the human scene, discovered how individual behavior is shaped by transactions we don't always see. Systems concepts—feedback, circularity, and so on—were useful devices that helped make complex interactions predictable. In keeping with our emphasis on how ideas are actually applied in clinical practice, we will now consider the fundamental working concepts of family therapy.

The Working Concepts of Family Therapy

Interpersonal Context

The fundamental premise of family therapy is that people are products of their **context.** Because few people are closer to us than our parents and partners, this notion can be translated into saying that a person's behavior is powerfully influenced by interactions with other family members. Thus the importance of context can be reduced to the importance of family. It can be, but it shouldn't be.

While it's true that the immediate family is often the most relevant context for understanding behavior, it isn't always. A depressed college student, for example, might be more unhappy about what's going on in the dormitory than about what's happening at home. Furthermore, although the context that family therapists first focused on was behavioral, the interpersonal environment also includes cognitive dimensions like expectations and assumptions, as well as influences from outside the family, at school, at work, with friends, and from the surrounding culture.

The clinical significance of context is that attempts to treat individuals by talking to them once a week for fifty minutes may have less influence than the interactions they have with other people during the remaining 167 hours of the week. Or to put this positively: Often the most effective way to help people resolve their problems is to meet with them *and* important others in their lives to help them reorganize their interactions.

Complementarity

Complementarity refers to the reciprocity that is the defining feature of any relationship. In every relationship one person's behavior is yoked to the other's. Remember the symbol for yin and yang, the masculine and feminine forces in the universe? Notice how together they are complementary and occupy one space. Relationships are like that. If one person changes, the relationship changes—and the other person will automatically be influenced. If John starts doing more grocery shopping, Mary will likely do less.

Family therapists should think of complementarity whenever they hear one person complaining about another. Take, for example, a husband who complains that his wife nags. "She's always after me about something, she's always complaining." From the perspective of complementarity, a family therapist would assume that the wife's complaining is only half of a pattern of mutual influence. Whenever a person is perceived as nagging, it probably means that she hasn't received a fair hearing for her concerns in a long while. Not being listened to makes her feel angry and unsupported. No wonder she comes across as nagging.

If, instead of waiting for her to complain, John starts asking her how she feels, Mary will feel like he cares about her enough to be concerned about her feelings. Or at least she is likely to feel that way. Complementarity doesn't mean that people in relationships control each other; it means they influence each other.

A therapist can help family members get past blaming—and the powerlessness that goes with it—by pointing out the complementarity of their actions. "The more you nag, the more he ignores you. *And* the more you ignore her, the more she nags."

Circular Causality

Before the advent of family therapy, explanations of psychopathology were based on linear models: medical, psychodynamic, or behavioral. Etiology was conceived in terms of prior events—disease, emotional conflict, or learning history—that caused symptoms in the present. Using the concept of *circularity*, Bateson helped change the way we think about psychopathology, from something caused by events in the past to something that is part of ongoing, circular feedback loops.

The notion of **linear causality** is based on the Newtonian model, in which the universe is like a billiard table where the balls act unidirectionally on each other. Bateson believed that while linear causality is useful for describing the world of forces and objects, it is a poor model for the world of living things, because it neglects to account for communication and relationships.

To illustrate this difference, Bateson (1979) used the example of a man kicking a stone. The effect of kicking a stone can be precisely predicted by measuring the force and angle of the kick and the weight of the stone. If the man kicked a dog, on the other hand, the effect would be less predictable. The dog might respond to a kick in any number of ways—cringing, running away, biting the man, or trying to play—depending on the temperament of the dog and how it interpreted the kick. In response to the dog's reaction, the man might modify his behavior, and so on, so that the number of possible outcomes is unlimited.

The dog's actions (biting, for example) loop back and affect the man's next moves (taking the Lord's name in vain, for example), which in turn affects the dog, and so on. The original action prompts a circular sequence in which each subsequent action recursively affects the other. Linear cause and effect is lost in a circle of mutual influence. This idea of mutual or **circular causality** is enormously useful for therapists because so many families come in looking to find "the cause" of their problems and to determine who is responsible. Instead of joining the family in a logical but unproductive search for who started what, circular causality suggests that problems are sustained by an ongoing series of actions and reactions. Who started it? It rarely matters. You don't have to get back to first causes to alter a cycle of interaction.

Triangles

Most clients express their concerns in linear terms. It might be a four-year-old who is "unmanageable," or perhaps an ex-wife who "refuses to cooperate" about visitation rights. Even though such complaints suggest that the problem resides in a single individual, most therapists would think to look for relationship issues. "Unmanageable" four-year-olds often turn out to have parents who are ineffective disciplinarians, and ex-wives who are "unreasonable" probably have their own sides of those stories. And so a therapist, certainly a family therapist, would probably want to see the four-year-old together with her parents and to meet with both the angry father and his ex-wife.

Let's suppose that the therapist who meets with the four-year-old and her parents sees that indeed the real problem is a lack of discipline. The mother complains that the girl never does what she's told, the father nods in agreement, and the child runs around the room ignoring her mother's commands to sit still. The parents look as if they could use some advice about setting limits. Perhaps. But experience teaches that a child who misbehaves is often standing on one parent's shoulders. When young children are consistently disobedient, it usually means that their parents have some conflict about what the rules should be and how to enforce them.

Perhaps the father is a strict disciplinarian. If so, his wife might feel that she needs to protect her daughter against her husband's harshness, and so she becomes more of a friend and ally to her child than a parent-in-charge. Some parents are so angry with each other that their disagreements are plain to see. But many are not so open. Their conflicts are painful, so they keep them private. Maybe they think that their personal relationship is none of the therapist's business, or perhaps the father has decided that if his wife doesn't like how he does things, "Then she can damn well do them herself!" The point is this: Relationship problems often turn out to be triangular (Bowen, 1978), even though it may not always be immediately apparent.

A less obvious example of triangular complications often occurs in the case of divorced parents who fight over visitation rights. Most divorces generate enough hurt and anger to make a certain amount of animosity between the exes inevitable. Add to that a healthy dose of parental guilt (felt and projected), and you would seem to have a formula for arguments about who gets the kids for the holidays, whose turn it is to buy a new pair of sneakers, and who was late picking them up or dropping them off last weekend. Meeting with the embattled exes is likely to do little to disconfirm the assumption that the problem is between the two of them. And yet even two people who are very angry at each other will eventually find a way to work things out—unless third parties mix in.

What do you suppose happens when a divorced father complains to his new girlfriend about his ex's "unreasonableness"? The same thing that usually happens when one person complains about another. The girlfriend sympathizes with him and, often as not, urges him to get tough with his ex. Meanwhile the children's mother is equally likely to have a friend encouraging her to become more aggressive. Thus instead of two people left to work things out between them, one or both of them is egged on to escalate their conflict.

Triangulation tends to stabilize relationships—but also to freeze conflict in place. Do all relationship problems involve third parties? No, but most do.

Family Structure

Family patterns of interaction are predictable—some might say stubborn—because they are embedded in powerful but unseen structures. Dynamic patterns, like pursuer/distancer, describe the **process** of interaction; **structure** defines the organization within which those interactions take place. Initially, interactions shape structure; but once established, structure shapes interactions.

Families, like other groups, have many options for relating. Very quickly, however, interactions that were once free to vary become regular and predictable. Once these patterns are established, family members use only a small fraction of the full range of behavior available to them (Minuchin & Nichols, 1993). Families are structured in **subsystems**—determined by generation, gender, and function—which are demarcated by interpersonal **boundaries,** invisible barriers that regulate the amount of contact with others (Minuchin, 1974). Boundaries safeguard the separateness and autonomy of the family and its subsystems. For example, a rule forbidding phone calls at dinnertime establishes a boundary that shields the family from intrusion. Subsystems that aren't adequately protected by boundaries limit the development of relationship skills. If children are permitted to freely interrupt their parents' conversations, the boundary separating the generations is eroded, and the couple's relationship is subverted to parenting. If parents always step in to settle arguments between their children, the children won't learn to fight their own battles.

Rigid boundaries are overly restrictive and permit only limited contact, resulting in **disengagement.** Disengaged subsystems are independent but isolated. On the plus side, this fosters autonomy. On the negative side, disengagement limits warmth and affection. **Enmeshed** subsystems offer a heightened sense of support but at the expense of independence and competence. Enmeshed parents offer their kids closeness, but too much closeness cripples initiative.

It should not go unnoticed that these arrangements are gendered. That they are doesn't make them any more right or wrong. But it should make us cautious about blaming mothers for cultural expectations and arrangements that perpetuate their role as primary caretakers of children (Luepnitz, 1988). A therapist who recognizes the normative nature of the enmeshed-mother/disengaged-father syndrome but puts the burden on the mother to let go, should ask himself why it

doesn't occur to him to challenge the father to take hold.

Process/Content

Focusing on the **process** of communication, or *how* people talk, rather than on its **content,** or *what* they talk about, may be the single most productive shift a family therapist can make. Imagine, for example, that a therapist encourages a moody freshman to talk to her parents. Imagine further that the young woman rarely expresses herself in words but rather in passive-aggressive protest, and that her worried parents are, in contrast, all too good at putting their opinions into words. Suppose that the young woman finally begins to express her feeling that college is a waste of time, and her parents counter with a forceful argument about the importance of staying in school. A therapist made anxious by the idea that the young woman might actually drop out of college who intervenes to support the *content* of the parents' position will miss an important opportunity to support the *process* whereby the young woman learns to put her feelings into words rather than into self-destructive actions.

Families who come for treatment are usually focused on content. A husband wants a divorce, a child refuses to go to school, a wife is depressed, and so on. The family therapist talks with the family about the content of their problems but thinks about the process by which they try to resolve issues. While the family discusses what to do about the child's refusal to go to school, the therapist notices whether the parents seem to be in charge and whether they support each other. A therapist who tells the parents how to solve the problem (by making the child go to school) is working with content, not process. The child may start going to school, but the parents won't have improved their decision-making process.

Sometimes, of course, content is important. If a wife is drinking to drown her worries or a husband is molesting his daughter, the therapist needs to know and do something about it. But to the extent that therapists focus exclusively on content, they're unlikely to help families become better functioning systems.

The Meaning (Function) of Symptoms

When family therapists discovered that an identified patient's symptoms often had a stabilizing influence on the family, they spoke of this homeostatic influence as the **function of the symptom** (Jackson, 1957). In a seminal paper, "The Emotionally Disturbed Child as a Family Scapegoat," Ezra Vogel and Norman Bell (1960) observed that emotionally disturbed children are almost invariably involved in the tensions between their parents. By detouring their conflicts onto one of their children, the parents are able to maintain a reasonably stable relationship, though the cost to the child may be great.

According to Vogel and Bell, some chance characteristic of a child may be singled out for anxious attention in a process that typecasts the child as the family's deviant member. Meanwhile, as long as the parents focus their concern on the child, their own conflicts can be ignored.

The idea that a family member's symptoms may serve a homeostatic function alerted therapists to look beyond presenting complaints for latent conflicts that might lie behind them. If a child is a behavior problem, for example, it is often the case that his parents will be in conflict about how to deal with him. However, this is not the same thing as saying that the child's misbehavior *benefits* the family. The parents' conflict may be a result rather than the cause of the child's problems. Notice, incidentally, that the term *scapegoat* is one-sided and judgmental.

One consequence of assuming that symptoms serve the family's purposes was setting up an adversarial relationship between families and therapists. This antagonism is often fueled by a tendency to sympathize with children and to see parents as oppressors. (Isn't that how a lot of us felt growing up?) It's hard being a parent. In fact, it may be the most difficult job in the world. Having a difficult child doesn't make it any easier. If, on top of that, parents have to deal with a therapist who assumes that they somehow profit from their children's problems, who could blame them for resisting?

Today the idea that symptoms serve a function in families has been discredited, and most schools of therapy now call for a collaborative relationship with clients. However, while it is a mistake to assume that symptoms necessarily serve a homeostatic function for the family, it is worth considering the possibility that in some cases a mother's depression or a child's refusal to attend school *might* turn out to serve a protective function for the family.

Family Life Cycle

When we think of the life cycle, we tend to think of individuals moving through time, mastering the challenges of one period, then moving on to the next. The cycle of human life may be orderly, but it's not a steady, continuous process. We progress in stages with plateaus and developmental hurdles that demand change. Periods of growth and change are followed by periods of relative stability during which changes are consolidated.

The idea of a **family life cycle** adds two things to our understanding of individual development: First, families must reorganize to accommodate to the growth and change of their members; second, developments in any of the family's generations may have an impact on one or all of the family's members. When a son or daughter heads off to kindergarten or reaches puberty, not only must the child learn to cope with a new set of circumstances, but the whole family must readjust. Moreover, the developmental transitions that affect children aren't merely their own but their parents' as

TABLE 4.1   The Stages of the Family Life Cycle

Family Life-Cycle Stage	Emotional Process of Transition: Key Principles	Second-Order Changes in Family Status Required to Proceed Developmentally
Leaving home: single young adults	Accepting emotional and financial responsibility for self	a. Differentiation of self in relation to family of origin b. Development of intimate peer relationships c. Establishment of self in respect to work and financial independence
The joining of families through marriage: the new couple	Commitment to new system	a. Formation of marital system b. Realignment of relationships with extended families and friends to include spouse
Families with young children	Accepting new members into the system	a. Adjusting marital system to make space for children b. Joining in child rearing, financial and household tasks c. Realignment of relationships with extended family to include parenting and grandparenting roles
Families with adolescents	Increasing flexibility of family boundaries to permit children's independence and grandparents' frailties	a. Shifting of parent–child relationships to permit adolescent to move into and out of system b. Refocus on midlife marital and career issues c. Beginning shift toward caring for older generation
Launching children and moving on	Accepting a multitude of exits from and entries into the family system	a. Renegotiation of marital system as a dyad b. Development of adult-to-adult relationships c. Realignment of relationships to include in-laws and grandchildren d. Dealing with disabilities and death of parents (grandparents)
Families in later life	Accepting the shifting generational roles	a. Maintaining own and/or couple functioning and interests in face of physiological decline: exploration of new familial and social role options b. Support for more central role of middle generation

TABLE 4.1   Continued

Family Life-Cycle Stage	Emotional Process of Transition: Key Principles	Second-Order Changes in Family Status Required to Proceed Developmentally
Families in later life	Accepting the shifting generational roles	c. Making room in the system for the wisdom and experience of the elderly, supporting the older generation without overfunctioning for them d. Dealing with loss of spouse, siblings, and other peers and preparation for death

well. In some cases, even their grandparents'. The strain on a fourteen-year-old's relationship with his parents may be due as much to his father's midlife crisis or his mother's worrying about her own father's retirement as anything the boy himself is going through.

Changes in one generation complicate adjustments in another. A middle-aged father may become disenchanted with his career and decide to become more involved with his family just as his children are growing up and pulling away. His wish to get closer may frustrate their need to be on their own. Or to cite another example becoming more and more familiar, just as a man and woman begin to do more for themselves after launching their children, they may find the children back in the house (after dropping out of school, being unable to afford housing, or recovering from an early divorce), and are therefore faced with an awkward version of second parenthood.

One property that families share with other complex systems is that they don't change in a smooth, gradual process of evolution, but rather in discontinuous leaps. Falling in love and political revolutions are examples of such leaps. Having a baby is like falling in love and undergoing a revolution at the same time.

Sociologists Evelyn Duvall and Reuben Hill began applying a developmental framework to families in the 1940s by dividing family development into discrete stages with tasks to be performed at each stage (Duvall, 1957; Hill & Rodgers, 1964). Family therapists Betty Carter and Monica McGoldrick (1980, 1999) enriched this framework by adding a *multigenerational* point of view, recognizing culturally diverse patterns, and considering stages of divorce and remarriage (Table 4.1).

It is important to recognize that there is no one fixed and standard version of the family life cycle. Not only do families come in a variety of forms—single-parent families, same-sexed couples, stepfamilies—but various religious, cultural, and ethnic groups may have vastly different norms for various stages. The real clinical value of the life-cycle concept isn't so much learning what's normal or expected at particular stages but recognizing that families often

*M*onica McGoldrick's work reminds therapists that families often have trouble coping with changes in the family life cycle.

develop problems at transitions in the life cycle because of inability or fear of making the transition.

Problems develop when a family encounters a challenge—environmental or developmental—and is unable to accommodate its structure to the changed circumstances. Thus problems are usually assumed to be a sign not of a "dysfunctional family" but simply of one that's failed to readjust at one of life's turning points. Whenever someone develops psychological symptoms, the family life-cycle concept teaches us to consider the possibility that the family may simply be stuck in transition from one developmental stage to another.

Resistance

Because families often fear what might happen if their conflicts were brought into the open, they may resist focusing on their most sensitive problems. Early family therapists misinterpreted resistance—fear might be a better word—as stubbornness or opposition to change (homeostasis). More recently, therapists have recognized that all human systems are reluctant to make changes they perceive as risky. Families *should* resist change—even change that to outsiders may seem beneficial—until it's clear that the consequences of those changes are safe and the therapist is trustworthy. Thus it's possible to see resistance as prudent, rather than bullheaded. Therapists who recognize the protective function of resistance realize that it's better to make families feel secure enough to lower their walls than to sneak around them or batter them down. They try to create a warm, nonblaming therapeutic environment that engenders the hope that healing of even the most threatening issues is possible.

—Case Study—

Emily was a single mother whose attempts to discipline her son were undermined by his grandmother's protectiveness. Emily avoided taking on her mother because she didn't believe it would do any good. She was afraid

that if challenged, her mother would become even more critical of her and make her feel more depressed. These fears weren't unrealistic. In the past when Emily had said anything critical of her mother that's just what had happened. Other people's defenses look unreasonable only because we can't see their memories.

For Emily to be convinced to try again to let her mother know about her feelings, the therapist needed to build up her trust that working with him would improve things with her mother. To achieve this credibility, the therapist had to respect Emily's pace and recognize her fears, rather than confront or manipulate her resistance. Therapists encounter far less resistance when they approach families as partners, trying to help them identify what constrains them from relating the way they want, rather than as experts who give advice and point out their flaws.

As you imagine doing family therapy, you may wonder how, as a nice, respectful therapist, you can keep angry family members from screaming at one another or glaring in stony silence as the minutes tick by. Creating a safe atmosphere involves more than just establishing credibility and hope. A therapist must also show that he or she can prevent family members from hurting each other so they know that they can drop their protective armor without fear of attack. In family therapy's early years, it was thought that pushing family members into emotional crises was necessary to unfreeze their homeostatic patterns. Over time, however, therapists learned that while conflict is real and shouldn't be feared—as the saying goes, "You can't make an omelet without breaking eggs"—change is still possible when family members interact in respectful and compassionate ways. It's in those moments that they feel safe enough to be real with each other.

One of family therapy's distinguishing features is its optimistic view of people. A number of family therapy models subscribe to the assumption that behind people's protective fortresses of anger or anxiety lies a healthy core self that can be reasonable, respectful, empathic, tolerant, and willing to change. When family members interact in this state, they often find that they can solve their problems themselves. It's their protective emotions that produce impasses.

Regardless of the therapist's technique, the key to generating productive interactions even in acrimonious sessions is the belief that such constructive potential exists in everyone. With that belief, therapists are able to take a collaborative role because they trust that clients have the resources they need. Without that trust, therapists are pushed into the role of the expert who supplies the missing ingredients—advice, insight, reparenting, education, or medication. This isn't to suggest that family therapists who hold this respectful view of people never offer any of those ingredients; they just don't assume that they always know what's best.

Family Narratives

The first family therapists looked beyond individuals to their family relationships to explain how problems developed and were perpetuated. Actions, it turned out, were embedded in interactions—and, of course, the most obvious interactions are behavioral. Double binds, problem-maintaining sequences, aversive control, triangles, enmeshment, and disengagement—these and other classic concepts in family therapy all focused on behavior. But in addition to being actors in each other's lives, family members are also storytellers.

By reconstructing the events of their lives in coherent narratives, family members are able to make sense of their experience (White & Epston, 1990). Thus it is not only actions and interactions that shape a family's life but also the stories members construct and tell. The parents of a two-year-old who tell themselves that he's "oppositional" will respond very differently than parents who tell themselves that their little one is "spunky."

Family narratives organize and make sense out of experience. They emphasize certain events that reinforce the plot line and screen out or distort other events that don't fit. The parents who see their two-year-old as oppositional are more likely to remember the times she said no than the times she said yes. The family's interactions and their narrative of events are related in circular fashion: Behavioral events are perceived and organized in narrative form; this narrative in turn shapes expectations that influence future behavior, and so on.

Interest in family narrative has become identified with one particular school, Michael White's narrative therapy, which emphasizes the fact that families with problems come to therapy with pessimistic narratives that tend to keep them from acting effectively. But a sensitivity to the importance of personal narrative is a useful part of any therapist's work. Therapy is conducted as a dialogue. However much a family therapist may be interested in the process of interaction or the structure of family relationships, he or she must also learn to respect the influence of how they experience events—including the therapist's input.

Gender

When the early family therapists first applied the systems metaphor—an organization of parts plus the way they function together—they paid more attention to the way families functioned than to their parts. Families were understood in terms of abstractions like "boundaries," "triangles," and "parental subsystems," while family members were sometimes treated as cogs in a machine. The "parts" of the family system never ceased being individual human beings; but the preoccupation with the way families were organized tended to obscure the personhood of the individuals who made up the family, including their psychodynamics, psychopathology, personal responsibility—and gender.

Common sense tells us that gender is a fact of life. (Though no one should underestimate social scientists' ability to transcend common sense.) As long as society expects the primary parenting to be done by mothers, girls will shape their identities in relation to someone they expect to be like, while boys will respond to their difference as a motive for separating from their mothers. The result is what Nancy Chodorow (1978) aptly called "the reproduction of mothering." Traditionally, women have been raised to have more permeable psychological boundaries, to develop their identities in terms of connection, to cultivate their capacity for empathy, and to be at greater risk for losing themselves in relationships. Men, on the other hand, tend to emerge with more rigid psychological boundaries, disown their dependency needs and fear being engulfed, and often have relatively greater difficulty empathizing with others. We all know men who are nurturing and women who are not, but these are exceptions that prove the rule.

Awareness of gender and gender inequity have long since penetrated not only family therapy but our entire culture. Translating this awareness into concrete clinical practice, however, is complicated, and controversial.

There is room for disagreement between those who strive to maintain clinical neutrality and those who believe that failing to raise gender issues in treatment—money, power, child care, fairness, and so on—runs the risk of reinforcing traditional roles and social arrangements (Walters, Carter, Papp, & Silverstein, 1988). However, it is not possible to be a fair and effective therapist without being sensitive to how gender issues pervade the life of the family. A therapist who ignores gender may inadvertently show less interest in and sensitivity to a woman's career, assume that a child's problems, and child rearing in general, are primarily the mother's responsibility, have a double standard for extramarital affairs, and expect—or at least tolerate—fathers' nonparticipation in the family's treatment.

If patriarchy begins in the home, a gender-sensitive therapist must recognize the enduring significance of early experience and of unconscious fantasies. How children respond to their parents has significance not only for how they get along but also for the men and women they will become. When a girl speaks derisively about her "bitchy" mother she may unknowingly be disparaging the female in herself. In addition to identification with the same-sex parent, the child's relationship with the other parent is part of what programs future experience with the opposite sex.

A gender-sensitive therapist must also avoid potential inequities in some of the basic assumptions of family therapy. The notion of *circular causality*, for example, which points to repetitive patterns of mutually reinforcing behavior, when applied to problems such as battering, incest, or alcoholism, tends to bypass questions of responsibility and makes it hard to consider influences external to the interaction, such as cultural beliefs about appropriate gender behavior. The concept of *neutrality* suggests that all parts of the system contribute equally to its problems and thus renders invisible the differences between family members in power and influence. The same is true of *complementarity*, which suggests that in traditional relationships between men and women the roles are equal though different. Reconciling these contradictions is not always easy, but ignoring them isn't the answer.

Culture

Among the influences shaping family behavior few are more powerful than the cultural context. A family from Puerto Rico, for example, may have very different expectations of loyalty and obligation from their adult children than, say, a white middle-class family from Minnesota. One reason for therapists to be sensitive to cultural diversity is to avoid imposing majority values and assumptions on minority groups. There are now a host of excellent books and articles designed to familiarize therapists with families from a variety of backgrounds, including African American (Boyd-Franklin, 1989), Latino (Falicov, 1998), Haitian (Bibb &

Casimir, 1996), Asian American (Lee, 1996), and urban poverty (Minuchin, Colapinto, & Minuchin, 1998), to mention just a few. These texts and others like them serve as guides for therapists who are about to venture into relatively unknown territory. Although the best way to develop an understanding of people from other cultures may be to spend time with them.

Some students are unsure of the difference between culture and ethnicity. **Culture** refers to common patterns of behavior and experience derived from the settings in which people live. **Ethnicity** refers to the common ancestry through which individuals have evolved shared values and customs—especially among groups that are not white Anglo-Saxon Protestants. Culture is the more generic term, and we have chosen it here to emphasize that cultural context is *always* an issue, even with families who come from backgrounds similar to the therapist's.

Although cultural influences may be most obvious with families from distinctly foreign backgrounds, it is a mistake to assume that members of the same culture necessarily share values and assumptions. A young Jewish therapist might, for example, be surprised at the unsympathetic attitudes of a middle-aged Jewish

couple about their children's decision to adopt a black baby. Just because a therapist is African American or Italian or Irish doesn't mean that he or she shares the same experience or attitudes of families from a similar background. Every family is unique.

Appreciating the cultural context of families is complicated by the fact that most families are influenced by multiple contexts, which makes generalization difficult. For example, as noted by Nancy Boyd-Franklin (1989), middle-class African American families stand astride three cultures. There are cultural elements that may be traced to African roots, those that are part of the dominant American culture, and finally the adaptations that people of color have to make to racism in the dominant culture. Moreover, the cultural context may vary among family members. In immigrant families, for example, it's not uncommon to see conflicts between parents who retain a strong sense of ethnic identity and children who are more eager to adopt the ways of the host country. First-generation parents may blame their children for abandoning the old ways and dishonoring the family, while the children may accuse their parents of being stubborn and stuck in the past. Later, the children's

*A*mong Latino families, family loyalty is often a paramount virtue.

children may develop a renewed appreciation for their cultural roots and traditions.

The first mistake many therapists make in working with clients from different backgrounds is to pathologize cultural differences. Although a lack of boundaries between a family and their neighbors and kin might seem problematic to a middle-class white therapist, more inclusive family networks are not atypical for African American families. The second mistake is to think that a therapist's job is to become an expert on the various cultures with which he or she works. While it may be useful for therapists to familiarize themselves with the language, customs, and values of the major groups in their catchment area, an attitude of respect and curiosity about other people's cultures may be more useful than imposing ethnic stereotypes or assuming an understanding of other people. It's important to acknowledge what we do not know.

The third mistake therapists make in working with families from other cultures is to accept everything assumed to be a cultural norm as functional. An effective therapist must be respectful of other people's ways of doing things without giving up the right to question patterns that appear to be counterproductive. Although fluid boundaries may be typical among urban poor families, that doesn't mean that it's inevitable for poor families to be dependent on various social services or for agency staff to presume that a family's need entitles workers to enter, unannounced and uninvited, into the family's space, physically and psychologically (Minuchin, Lee, & Simon, 1996).

—Recommended Readings

Bateson, G. 1971. *Steps to an ecology of mind.* New York: Ballantine.

Bateson, G. 1979. *Mind and nature.* New York: Dutton.

Bertalanffy, L. von. 1950. An outline of General System Theory. *British Journal of the Philosophy of Science.* 1:134–165.

Bertalanffy, L. von. 1967. *Robots, men and minds.* New York: Braziller.

Bowlby, J. 1988. *A secure base: Clinical application of attachment theory.* London: Routledge.

Carter, E., and McGoldrick, M., eds. 1999. *The expanded family life cycle: A framework for family therapy,* 3rd ed. Boston: Allyn & Bacon.

Davidson, M. 1983. *Uncommon sense: The life and thought of Ludwig von Bertalanffy.* Los Angeles: Tarcher.

Dell, P. F. 1982. Beyond homeostasis: Toward a concept of coherence. *Family Process.* 21:21–42.

Haley, J. 1985. Conversations with Erickson. *Family Therapy Networker.* 9(2):30–43.

Hoffman, L. 1981. *Foundations of family therapy.* New York: Basic Books.

Weiner, N. 1948. *Cybernetics or control and communication in the animal and the machine.* Cambridge, MA: Technology Press.

—References

Ainsworth, M. D. S. 1967. *Infancy in Uganda: Infant care and the growth of attachment.* Baltimore: Johns Hopkins University Press.

Ainsworth, M. D. S., Blehar, M. C., Walters, E., and Wall, S. 1978. *Patterns of attachment: A psychological study of the strange situation.* Hillsdale, NJ: Erlbaum.

Anderson, H., and Goolishian, H. A. 1988. Human systems as linguistic systems: Evolving ideas about the implications of theory and practice. *Family Process.* 27:371–393.

Bateson, G. 1956. *Naven.* Stanford, CA: Stanford University Press.

Bateson, G. 1972. *Steps to an ecology of mind.* New York: Ballantine.

Bateson, G. 1979. *Mind and nature.* New York: Dutton.

Bernard, C. 1859. *Lecons sur les proprietes physi-ologiques et les alterations pathologiques des liquides de l'organsime.* Paris: Balliere.

Bertalanffy, L. von. 1950. An outline of general systems theory. *British Journal of Philosophy of Science.* 1:139–164.

Bertalanffy, L. von. 1968. *General systems theory.* New York: Braziller.

Bibb, A., and Casimir, G. J. 1996. Hatian families. In *Ethnicity and family therapy,* M. McGoldrick, J. Giordano, and J. K. Pearce, eds. New York: Guilford Press.

Bowen, M. 1978. *Family therapy in clinical practice.* New York: Jason Aronson.

Bowlby, J. 1958. The nature of the child's tie to his mother. *International Journal of Psycho-Analysis.* 41:350–373.

Bowlby, J. 1973. *Attachment and loss: Vol. 2. Separation.* New York: Basic Books.

Bowlby, J. 1979. *The making and breaking of affectional bonds.* London: Tavistock.

Bowlby, J. 1988. *A secure base: Parent-child attachment and healthy human development.* New York: Basic Books.

Boyd-Franklin, N. 1989. *Black families in therapy: A multisystems approach.* New York: Guilford Press.

Burlingham, D., and Freud, A. 1944. *Infants without families.* London: Allen & Unwin.

Cannon, W. B. 1939. *The wisdom of the body.* New York: Norton.

Carter, E., and McGoldrick, M., eds. 1980. *The family life cycle: A framework for family therapy.* New York: Gardner Press.

Carter, E., and McGoldrick, M., eds. 1999. *The expanded family life cycle.* 3rd ed. Boston: Allyn & Bacon.

Chodorow, N. 1978. *The reproduction of mothering.* Berkeley, CA: University of California Press.

Davidson, M. 1983. *Uncommon sense.* Los Angeles: Tarcher.

Dell, P. F. 1982. Beyond homeostasis: Toward a concept of coherence. *Family Process.* 21(1):21–42.

Dell, P. F. 1985. Understanding Bateson and Maturana: Toward a biological foundation for the social sciences. *Journal of Marital and Family Therapy.* 11:1–20.

Duvall, E. 1957. *Family development.* Philadelphia: Lippincott.

Easterbrook, M. A., and Lamb, M. E. 1979. The relationship between quality of infant-mother attachment and infant competence in initial encounters with peers. *Child Development.* 50:380–387.

Efran, J. S., Lukens, M. D., and Lukens, R. J. 1990. *Language, structure and change: Frameworks of meaning in psychotherapy.* New York: Norton.

Falicov, C. J. 1998. *Latino families in therapy.* New York: Guilford Press.

Feeney, 1995. Adult attachment and emotional control. *Personal Relationships.* 2:143–159.

Foerster, H. von. 1981. *Observing systems.* Seaside, CA: Intersystems.

Gergen, K. J. 1985. The social constructionist movement in modern psychology. *American Psychologist.* 40:266–275.

Gottman, J. 1994. *What predicts divorce.* Hillsdale, NJ: Erlbaum.

Haley, J. 1976. *Problem-solving therapy.* San Francisco: Jossey-Bass.

Harlow, H. 1958. The nature of love. *American Psychologist.* 13:673–685.

Hazan, C., and Shaver, P. R. 1987. Romantic love conceptualized as an attachment process. *Journal of Personality and Social Psychology.* 52:511–524.

Heims, S. 1991. *The cybernetics group.* Cambridge, MA: MIT Press.

Held, B. S. 1995. *Back to reality: A critique of postmodern theory in psychotherapy.* New York: Norton.

Hill, R., and Rodgers, R. 1964. The developmental approach. In *Handbook of marriage and the family,* H. T. Christiansen, ed. Chicago: Rand McNally.

Hoffman, L. 1981. *Foundations of family therapy.* New York: Basic Books.

Hoffman, L. 1988. A constructivist position for family therapy. *The Irish Journal of Psychology.* 9:110–129.

Hoffman, L. 1990. Constructing realities: An art of lenses. *Family Process.* 29:1–12.

Jackson, D. D. 1957. The question of family homeostasis. *Psychiatric Quarterly Supplement.* 31:79–90.

Jackson, D. D. 1959. Family interaction, family homeostasis, and some implications for conjoint family therapy. In *Individual and family dynamics,* J. Masserman, ed. New York: Grune & Stratton.

Johnson, S. 1996. *Creating connection: The practice of emotionally focused marital therapy.* New York: Brunner/Mazel.

Johnson, S. 2002. *Emotionally focused couple therapy with trauma survivors: Strengthening attachment bonds.* New York: Guilford Press.

Kelly, G. A. 1955. *The psychology of personal constructs.* New York: Norton.

Lee, E. 1996. Asian American families: An overview. In *Ethnicity and family therapy,* M. McGoldrick, J. Giordano, and J. K. Pearce, eds. New York: Guilford Press.

Lieberman, A. F. 1977. Preschoolers' competence with a peer: Relations with attachment and peer experience. *Child Development. 48:*1277–1287.

Lorenz, K. E. 1935. Der Kumpan in der Umvelt des Vogels. In *Instinctive behavior,* C. H. Schiller, ed. New York: International Universities Press.

Luepnitz, D. A. 1988. *The family interpreted: Feminist theory in clinical practice.* New York: Basic Books.

Main, M. 1977. Sicherheit und wissen. In *Entwicklung der Lernfahigkeit in der sozialen umwelt,* K. E. Grossman, ed. Munich: Kinder Verlag.

Main, M., and Weston, D. 1981. The quality of the toddler's relationships to mother and father: Related to conflict behavior and readiness to establish new relationships. *Child Development. 52:*932–940.

Matas, L. Arend, R. and Sroufe, L. A. 1978. Continuity of adaptation in the second year: The relationship between quality of attachment and later competence. *Child Development. 49:*547–556.

Maturana, H. R., and Varela, F. J. eds. 1980. *Autopoiesis and cognition: The realization of the living.* Boston: Reidel.

Meyrowitz, J. 1985. *No sense of place.* New York: Oxford University Press.

Minuchin, S. 1974. *Families and family therapy.* Cambridge, MA: Harvard University Press.

Minuchin, S. 1991. The seductions of constructivism. *Family Therapy Networker. 1*5(5):47–50.

Minuchin, P., Colapinto, J., and Minuchin, S. 1998. *Working with families of the poor.* New York: Guilford Press.

Minuchin, S., Lee, W-Y., and Simon, G. M. 1996. *Mastering family therapy: Journeys of growth and transformation.* New York: Wiley.

Minuchin, S., and Nichols, M. P. 1993. *Family healing: Tales of hope and renewal from family therapy.* New York: Free Press.

Neimeyer, R. A. 1993. An appraisal of constructivist psychotherapies. *Journal of Consulting and Clinical Psychology. 61:*221–234.

Nichols, M. P. 1993. The therapist as authority figure. *Family Process. 32:*163–165.

Nichols, M. P., and Schwartz, R. C. 2001. *Family therapy: Concepts and methods,* 5th ed. Boston: Allyn & Bacon.

Robertson, J. 1953. *A two-year-old goes to hospital.* [Film]. London: Tavistock Child Development Research Unit.

Simon, G. M. 1993. Revisiting the notion of hierarchy. *Family Process. 32:*147–155.

Speer, D. C. 1970. Family systems: Morphostasis and morphogenesis, or "Is homeostasis enough?" *Family Process. 9*(3):259–278.

Sroufe, L. A. 1979. The coherence of individual development: Early care, attachment and subsequent developmental issues. *American Psychologist. 34:*834–841.

Ugazio, V. 1999. *Storie permesses, storie proibite: Polarita semantiche familiari e psicopatologie.* Turin: Bollati Boringhieri.

Vogel, E. F., and Bell, N. W. 1960. The emotionally disturbed child as a family scapegoat. In *The family,* N. W. Bell and E. F. Vogel, eds. Glencoe, IL: Free Press.

Walters, M., Carter, B., Papp, P., and Silverstein, O. 1988. *The invisible web: Gender patterns in family relationships.* New York: Guilford Press.

Waters, E. 1978. The reliability and stability of individual differences in infant-mother attachment. *Child Development. 49:*483–494.

Waters, E., Wippman, J., and Sroufe, L. A. 1979. Attachment, positive affect and competence in the peer group: Two studies of construct validation. *Child Development. 51:*208–216.

Watzlawick, P., ed. 1984. *The invented reality.* New York: Norton.

Watzlawick, P., Beavin, J. H., and Jackson, D. D. 1967. *Pragmatics of human communication.* New York: Norton.

White, M., and Epston, D. 1990. *Narrative means to therapeutic ends.* New York: Norton.

Wiener, N. 1948. *Cybernetics or control and communication in the animal and the machine.* Cambridge, MA: MIT Press.

Wynne, L. 1984. The epigenesis or relational systems: A model for understanding family development. *Family Process. 23:*297–318.

5

Bowen Family Systems Therapy

An Intergenerational Approach to Family Therapy

The pioneers of family therapy recognized that people are products of their social context but limited the focus to the nuclear family. Yes, our actions are influenced by what goes on in our families. But what are the forces, past and present, that mold those influences? What makes a husband distance himself from the demands of family life? What makes a wife neglect her own development to manage her children's lives? Murray Bowen sought answers to such questions in the larger network of family relationships.

According to Bowen, human relationships are driven by two counterbalancing life forces: *individuality* and *togetherness.* Each of us needs companionship, and a degree of independence. What makes life interesting—and frustrating— is the tendency for these needs to polarize each other. When one partner presses for more connection, the other may feel crowded and pull away. As time goes by, the pursuit of one and withdrawal of the other drives the pair through cycles of closeness and distance.

How successfully people reconcile these two polarities of human nature depends on the ex-

tent to which they have learned to manage emotionality, or to use Bowen's term, on their *differentiation of self.* More about this later.

While no one doubts the formative influence of the family in molding personality, many people imagine that once they leave home they are grown-up, independent adults, free at last of their parents' influence. Some people prize individuality and take it as a sign of growth to separate from their parents. Others wish they could be closer to their families but find visits home too painful, and so they stay away to protect themselves from disappointment and hurt. Once out of range of the immediate conflict, they forget and deny the discord. But as Bowen discovered, the family remains with us wherever we go. As we shall see, unresolved emotional reactivity to our parents is the most important unfinished business of our lives.

Sketches of Leading Figures

Murray Bowen's professional interest in the family began when he was a psychiatrist at the

Menninger Clinic in the late 1940s. Turning his attention to the enigma of schizophrenia, Bowen was struck by the exquisite emotional sensitivity between patients and their mothers. Others who had observed this reactivity called it *symbiosis,* as though it were some kind of parasitic mutation. Bowen saw it simply as an exaggeration of a natural process, a more intense and prolonged version of the tendency to react emotionally to one another that exists in all relationships.

In 1954 Bowen moved east to the National Institute of Mental Health (NIMH), where he initiated a project of hospitalizing entire families containing a schizophrenic member. What he found was that the intense emotional tie between mothers and their emotionally disturbed offspring inevitably involved the whole family. At the heart of the problem was "anxious attachment," a pathological form of closeness driven by anxiety. In these troubled families, people were emotional prisoners of the way the others behaved. The hallmark of these emotionally stuck-together, or *fused,* relationships was a lack of personal autonomy.

Another of the discoveries to come out of Bowen's research on "mother–child symbiosis" was the observation of a repetitive pattern: alternating cycles of closeness and distance, exquisitely sensitive to shifts in emotional tension within either mother or child, or the relationship between them. Separation anxiety coupled with incorporation anxiety was believed to be the underlying dynamic.

When the NIMH project ended in 1959 and Bowen moved to Georgetown University, he began working with families whose problems were less severe. What he discovered, to his surprise, were many of the same mechanisms he had observed in psychotic families. This convinced him that there is no discontinuity between normal and pathological families, but that all families vary along a continuum from emotional fusion to differentiation.

During his thirty-one years at Georgetown, Bowen developed a comprehensive theory of family therapy, inspired an entire generation of students, and became an internationally renowned leader of the family therapy movement. He died after a long illness in October 1990.

Among the most prominent of Bowen's students are Philip Guerin and Thomas Fogarty, who joined together in 1973 to form the Center for Family Learning in New Rochelle, New York. Under Guerin's leadership, the Center for Family Learning became one of the major centers of family therapy training and practice. Guerin is a laid-back, virtuoso therapist and teacher, and two of his books, *The Evaluation and Treatment of Marital Conflict* and *Working with Relationship Triangles,* are among the most clinically useful in all the family therapy literature.

Murray Bowen's extended family systems model is the most comprehensive theory in family therapy.

Philip Guerin's applications of Bowen theory have produced some of the most useful books in family therapy.

Betty Carter and Monica McGoldrick are best known for their excellent book on the family life cycle (Carter & McGoldrick, 1999) and for championing feminism in family therapy. Michael Kerr, M.D., was a long-time student and colleague of Bowen's, and since 1977 has been the director of training at the Georgetown Family Center. Kerr is perhaps the most faithful advocate of all Bowen's students, as his brilliant account of Bowenian theory in the book *Family Evaluation* (Kerr & Bowen, 1988) richly demonstrates.

Theoretical Formulations

Most of family therapy's pioneers were pragmatists, more concerned with action than insight, more interested in technique than theory. Bowen was the exception. He was always more committed to systems theory as a way of thinking than as a set of interventions.

According to Bowen, we have less autonomy in our emotional lives than we assume. Most of us are more dependent and reactive to one another than we like to think. Bowen's systems theory describes how the family, as a multigenerational network of relationships, shapes the interplay of individuality and togetherness using six interlocking concepts (Bowen, 1966): differentiation of self, triangles, nuclear family emotional process, family projection process, multigenerational transmission process, and sibling position. In the 1970s Bowen (1976) added two additional concepts: *emotional cutoff* and *societal emotional process.*

Differentiation of Self

Differentiation of self, the cornerstone of Bowen's theory, is both an intrapsychic and an interpersonal concept. Roughly analogous to *ego strength*, differentiation is the capacity to think and reflect, to not respond automatically to emotional pressures, internal or external

(Kerr & Bowen, 1988). It is the ability to be flexible and act wisely, even in the face of anxiety.

Undifferentiated people are easily moved to emotionality that subverts self-control. Their lives are driven by reactivity to those around them. The differentiated person is able to balance thinking and feeling: capable of strong emotion and spontaneity, but also possessing the self-restraint that comes with the ability to resist the pull of emotional impulses.

In contrast, undifferentiated people tend to react emotionally—with submissiveness or defiance—toward other people. They have little autonomous identity; instead they have a tendency toward emotional **fusion** with others. They find it difficult to maintain their own autonomy, especially around anxious issues. Asked what they think, they say what they feel; asked what they believe, they echo what they've heard. They either agree with everything you say or argue with everything. In contrast, differentiated people are able to take definite stands on issues because they're able to think things through, decide what they believe, and then act on those beliefs.

Guerin defines differentiation as the process of partially freeing oneself from the emotional chaos of one's family. Getting free takes analyzing one's own role as an active participant in relationships systems, instead of blaming problems on everyone but oneself (Guerin, Fay, Burden, & Kautto, 1987). Guerin uses the concept of *adaptive level of functioning* to define and evaluate the ability to continue functioning in the face of stress. Adaptive level of functioning is the capacity to make the conscious effort to be objective and behave rationally in the face of pressures of emotionality.

Emotional Triangles

Take a minute to think about the most troublesome relationship in your life right now. Actually, that relationship almost certainly involves one or more third persons. Virtually all emotionally significant relationships are shadowed by third parties—relatives, friends, even memories.

The major influence on the activity of triangles is *anxiety* (Guerin, Fogarty, Fay, & Kautto, 1996). As anxiety increases, people experience a greater need for emotional closeness—or, in reaction to pressures from others, a greater need for distance. The more people respond based on anxiety, the less tolerant they are of one another and the more they are polarized by differences.

When two people have problems that they've been unable to work out, they usually get to the point where it's hard to talk about certain things. Why go through all that aggravation when it only leads to hurt feelings and angry silence? Eventually one or both partners will turn to someone else for sympathy. Or the conflict will draw in a third person to try to fix it or take sides. If the third party's involvement is only temporary or pushes the two people to work out their differences, the triangle doesn't become fixed. But if the third person stays involved, as more often happens, the triangle become a regular part of the relationship.

The involvement of a third person decreases anxiety in the twosome by spreading it through three relationships. Thus, for example, a wife upset with her husband's distance may increase her involvement with one of the children. What makes this a triangle is diverting energy that might otherwise go into the marriage. Spending time with her daughter may take pressure off the wife's husband to do things he doesn't care to. However, it also decreases the likelihood that husband and wife will learn to develop interests they can share—and it undermines the child's independence.

Guerin distinguished between "triangles" as a stable relationship structure and "triangulation" as a reactive process (Guerin & Guerin, 2002). In the process of **triangulation,** a third person, who is sensitized to the anxiety in a couple, moves in to offer reassurance or calm

things down. "For example, an older daughter may attempt to reduce intense marital conflict by talking individually to each parent or to the parent with whom she has the most influence. Meanwhile, her younger brother may absorb the tension of his parents or handle it by acting in an antisocial way. The acting-out behavior also serves the function of pulling the parents together to try to solve the common problem of the son's acting out" (Guerin et al., 1987, p. 62).

Some triangles seem so innocent that we hardly notice their destructiveness. Most parents can't resist complaining to their children once in a while about their mates. "Your mother's *always* late!" "Your father *never* lets anyone else drive!" These interchanges seem harmless enough. What makes triangles problematic is that they have a tendency to become habitual and to corrupt the original relationship.

Triangulation lets off steam but freezes conflict in place. It isn't so much that complaining or seeking solace is wrong, but rather that triangles become chronic diversions that undermine relationships.

Most family problems are triangular, which is why working only on a twosome may have limited results. Teaching a mother better techniques for disciplining her son won't resolve the problem if she is overinvolved with the boy as a result of her husband's emotional distance.

Nuclear Family Emotional Process

This concept deals with the emotional forces in families that operate over the years in recurrent patterns. Bowen originally used the term *undifferentiated family ego mass* to describe an excess of emotional reactivity or *fusion* in families. Lack of differentiation in the family of origin leads to an *emotional cutoff* from parents, which in turn leads to fusion in marriage—because people with limited emotional resources typically project all their needs onto each other.

Since this new fusion is unstable, it tends to produce one or more of the following: (1) reactive emotional distance between the partners; (2) physical or emotional dysfunction in one partner; (3) marital conflict; or (4) projection of the problem onto one or more children. The intensity of these problems is related to the degree of undifferentiation, extent of emotional cutoff from families of origin, and level of stress in the system.

Family Projection Process

This is the process by which parents transmit their lack of differentiation to their children. Emotional fusion in a couple creates tension which leads to conflict, emotional distance, or reciprocal over- and underfunctioning. A common case is when a husband, who is cut off from his parents and siblings, relates in a very distant way to his wife. This predisposes her to focus on the kids. Kept at arm's length by her husband, she becomes anxiously attached to the children, usually with greatest intensity toward one particular child. This may be the oldest son or daughter, the youngest, or perhaps the child who possesses traits most like one of the parents. This attachment is different from caring concern; it's anxious, enmeshed concern. Since it relieves his own anxiety, the husband accepts his wife's overinvolvement with the children which, in turn, reinforces their entanglement and his distance.

The object of this projection process—the child the mother lives through most—achieves the least differentiation of self and becomes the most vulnerable to problems. This doesn't mean that patterns of emotional functioning *cause* physical or emotional dysfunction; it means that these emotional processes in the family are a major influence on an individual's ability to adapt to other factors that precipitate dysfunction.

The more the mother focuses her anxiety on a child, the more that child's functioning is stunted. This underdevelopment encourages the mother to hover over the child, distracting her from her own anxieties but crippling the child emotionally.

Multigenerational Transmission Process

This concept describes the transmission of chronic anxiety from generation to generation. In every generation the child most involved in the family's fusion moves toward a lower level of differentiation of self (and chronic anxiety), while the least involved child moves toward a higher level of differentiation (and less anxiety).

When a person (second generation) who has less differentiation than his parents marries, he will, like his parents, select a mate who has about the same level of differentiation. These two people then establish the emotional atmosphere in their new family and incorporate their children into that atmosphere. If a spouse has less differentiation than his parents, the level of anxiety in the new family is likely to be higher. Because there is more anxiety, the mechanisms for binding it (marital conflict, spouse dysfunction, or child dysfunction) will be more active in this generation than in the previous one. The specific ways in which anxiety is bound determine the degree of emotional separation of each child in the third generation. The more anxiety that's focused on one of the children, the less that child will be able to regulate his or her own emotionality and grow up a mature and happy person. The less anxiety is focused on the children, the more likely they are to grow up with greater differentiation than their parents. Thus Bowen's theory goes beyond saying that the past influences the present; it specifies the pathways along which emotional processes are passed down through the generations.

Parents who anxiously intrude their concerns on their children leave them little choice but to conform or rebel. Instead of learning to think for themselves, such children function in reaction to others. When these children leave home, they expect to become authors of their own lives. They're not going to turn out like their parents! Unfortunately, although many people fight against their inheritance, it usually catches up with them.

Sibling Position

Bowen agreed with the notion that children develop personality characteristics based on their position in the family (Toman, 1969). So many variables are involved that prediction is complex, but knowledge of general characteristics plus specific knowledge of a particular family is helpful in predicting what part a child will play in the family emotional process.

Bowen's theory offers an interesting perspective with which to reconsider the familiar notion of sibling rivalry. Say that a mother is anxious that her children never get jealous and takes responsibility for ensuring that they feel equally loved. (As though the truth might be otherwise.) Her anxiety is translated into action by making a show of treating them exactly alike—an attempt at perfect fairness that betrays the anxiety behind it. Each child then becomes highly sensitive to the amount of attention he or she receives in relation to siblings. This can result in fighting and resentment—just what the mother sought to prevent. Moreover, since the mother is anxious to control how the children feel, she may step in to settle their fights, thus depriving them of the opportunity to do so themselves— and giving them additional reason to feel unequally treated. ("How come *I* have to go to my room? *He* started it!")

Thus sibling conflict, often explained as an outcome of inevitable rivalry (as though rivalrousness were the only natural relationship between brothers and sisters), may be just one side of a triangle. (Of course the intensity of a mother's preoccupation with her children is re-lated to other triangles—including her relationships with friends, career, her husband.)

The importance of birth order was documented in the compelling book *Born to Rebel* by Frank Sulloway (1996). Culling biographical data from five hundred years of history, Sulloway's conclusions were supported by a multivariate analysis of more than a million biographical data points. Personality, he argues, is the repertoire of strategies that siblings use to compete with one another to secure a place in the family.

Firstborns have a tendency to identify with power and authority: They employ their size and strength to defend their status and try to minimize the cost of having siblings by dominating them. (Alfred Adler suggested that firstborns become "power-hungry conservatives" as they struggle to restore their lost primacy within the family.) Winston Churchill, George Washington, Ayn Rand, and Rush Limbaugh are illustrative examples.

As underdogs in the family, laterborns are more inclined to identify with the oppressed and to question the status quo. They're more open to experience because this openness aids them, as latecomers to the family, in finding an unoccupied niche. From their ranks have come the bold explorers, iconoclasts, and heretics of history. Joan of Arc, Marx, Lenin, Jefferson, Rousseau, Virginia Wolf, Mary Wollstonecraft, and Bill Gates are representative laterborns.

What developmentalists once thought of as a shared family context turns out not to be shared at all. Every family is actually a multiplicity of microenvironments, a collection of niches, consisting of distinct vantage points from which siblings experience the same events in very different ways.

Emotional Cutoff

Emotional cutoff describes the way people manage undifferentiation (and the associated anxiety) between generations. The greater the emotional fusion between parents and children, the greater the likelihood of cutoff. Some people seek distance by moving away; others do so emotionally, by avoiding personal conversations or insulating themselves with the presence of third parties.

Michael Nichols (1986) describes how some people mistake emotional cutoff for maturity:

> We take it as a sign of growth to separate from our parents, and we measure our maturity by independence of family ties. Yet many of us still respond to our families as though they were radioactive and capable of inflicting great pain. Only one thing robs Superman of his extraordinary power: kryptonite, a piece of his home planet. A surprising number of adult men and women are similarly rendered helpless by even a brief visit to or from their parents. (p. 190)

Societal Emotional Process

Bowen anticipated the contemporary concern about social influence on how families function. Kerr and Bowen (1988) cite the example of the high crime rate that results in communities with great social pressure. Bowen acknowledged that sexism and class and ethnic prejudice are examples of unhappy social emotional processes, but he believed that individuals and families with higher levels of differentiation were better able to resist these negative social influences.

●

To the theoretical concerns of Bowenian therapists, Monica McGoldrick and Betty Carter added gender and ethnicity. These feminist Bowenians believe that it isn't possible to ignore gender inequalities without ignoring some of the primary forces that keep men and women trapped in inflexible roles. Moreover, they might point out that the previous sentence is inaccurate in implying that men and women alike are victims of gender bias. Women live with constraining social conditions *and* with

*B*etty Carter is a
highly respected
Bowenian therapist
and a forceful advocate
for gender equality.

men who perpetuate them—men who may not notice their advantage or feel powerful with their wives and mothers, but who live with, and take for granted, social conditions that make it easier for men to get ahead in the world.

McGoldrick has also been a leader in calling attention to ethnic differences among families. Her book *Ethnicity and Family Therapy* (McGoldrick, Pearce, & Giordano, 1982) was a landmark in family therapy's developing sensitivity to this issue. Without understanding how cultural norms and values differ from one ethnic group to the next, the danger is of therapists imposing their own ways of looking at things on families whose perspectives aren't "dysfunctional" but legitimately different.

Normal Family Development

Optimal family development is thought to take place when family members are well differentiated, anxiety is low, and partners are in good emotional contact with their own families. Most people leave home in the midst of transforming relationships with their parents from an adolescent to an adult basis. Thus the transformation is usually incomplete, and most of us, even as adults, continue to react with adolescent sensitivity to our parents—or anyone else who pushes the same buttons.

Normally, but not optimally, people reduce contact with their parents and siblings to avoid the anxiety of dealing with them. Once out of the house and on their own, people tend to assume that they've put the old difficulties behind them. However, we all carry with us unfinished business in the form of unresolved sensitivities that flare up in intense relationships wherever we go. Having learned to ignore their role in family conflicts, most people are unable to prevent recurrences in new relationships.

Another heritage from the past is that the emotional attachment between intimate partners comes to resemble that which each had in their families of origin. People from undifferentiated families will continue to be undifferentiated when they form new families. Those who handled anxiety by distance and withdrawal will tend to do the same in their marriages. Therefore Bowen was convinced that differentiation of autonomous personalities, accomplished primarily in the family of origin, was both a description of normal development and a prescription for therapeutic improvement.

Carter and McGoldrick (1999) have described the **family life cycle** as a process of expansion, contraction, and realignment of the relationship system to support the entry, exit, and development of family members. In the *leaving home stage* the primary task for young adults is to separate from their families without cutting off or fleeing to an emotional substitute. This is the time to develop an autonomous self before pairing off to form a new union. In the *joining of families through marriage stage* the primary task is commitment to the new couple. But this is not simply a joining of two individuals; it is a transformation of two entire systems. While problems in this stage may seem to be primarily between the partners, they may also reflect a failure to separate from families of origin or cutoffs that put too much pressure on a couple.

Families with young children must adjust to make space for the new additions, cooperate in the tasks of childrearing, keep the marriage from being submerged in parenting, and realign relationships with the extended family. Young mothers and fathers are challenged to fulfill their children's needs for nurture and control—and to work together as a team. This is an extremely stressful stage, especially for new mothers, and it is the life-cycle phase with the highest divorce rate.

The reward for parents who survive the preceding stages is to have their children turn into adolescents. *Adolescence* is a time when children no longer want to be like mommy and daddy; they want to be themselves. They struggle to become autonomous individuals and to open family boundaries—and they struggle however hard they must. Parents with satisfying lives of their own welcome (or at least tolerate) the fresh air (pun intended) that blows through the house at this time. Those who insist on controlling their teenagers as though they were still little ones, provoke the painful escalations of the rebelliousness that's normal for this period.

In the *launching of children and moving on stage*, parents must let their children go and take hold of their own lives. This can be a liberating time of fulfillment, but it can also be a time of *midlife crisis* (Nichols, 1986). Parents must not only deal with changes in their children's and their own lives, but also with changes in their relationships with aging parents, who may need increasing support—or at least don't want to act like parents anymore.

Families in later life must adjust to retirement, which not only means a sudden loss of vocation but also a sudden increase in proximity for the couple. With both partners home all day, the house may suddenly seem a lot smaller. Later in life families must cope with declining health, illness, and then death, the great equalizer.

One variation in the life cycle, that can no longer be considered a deviation, is *divorce.* With the divorce rate at 50 percent and the rate of redivorce at 61 percent (Glick, 1984), divorce now strikes the majority of American families. The primary tasks of a divorcing couple are to end the marriage but maintain cooperation as parents. Some post-divorce families become single-parent families—consisting in the main of mothers and children, and in the vast majority of those cases staggering under the weight of financial strain. The alternative is remarriage and the formation of stepfamilies, in which, often, loneliness is swapped for conflict.

Development of Behavior Disorders

Symptoms result from stress that exceeds a person's ability to manage it. The ability to handle stress is a function of differentiation: The more well-differentiated the person, the more resilient he or she will be and the more flexible and sustaining his or her relationships. The less well-differentiated the person, the less stress it takes to produce symptoms.

If "differentiation" were reduced to "maturity," the Bowenian formula wouldn't add much to the familiar diathesis–stress model, which says that illness develops when an individual's vulnerability is taxed. The difference is that differentiation isn't just a quality of individuals but also of relationships. A person's basic level of differentiation is largely determined by the degree of autonomy achieved in his or her family, but the *functional level of differentiation* is influenced by the quality of current relationships. Thus a somewhat immature person who manages to develop healthy relationships will be at less risk than an equally immature person who's alone or in unhealthy relationships. Symptoms develop when the level of anxiety exceeds the *system's* ability to handle it.

The most vulnerable individual (in terms of isolation and lack of differentiation) is most likely to absorb the anxiety in the system and

develop symptoms. For example, a child of ten with a conduct disorder is likely to be the most triangled child in the family and, thereby, the one most emotionally caught up in the conflict between the parents or most affected by one of the parent's tensions.

According to Bowen, the underlying factor in the genesis of psychological problems is *emotional fusion*, passed down from one generation to the next. The greater the fusion, the more one is programmed by primitive emotional forces, and the more vulnerable to the emotionality of others. Although it isn't always apparent, people tend to choose mates with equivalent levels of undifferentiation.

Emotional fusion is based on anxious attachment, which may be manifest either as dependency or isolation. Both the overly dependent and the emotionally isolated person respond with a high level of emotional reactivity to stress. The following clinical vignette illustrates how emotional fusion in the family of origin is transmitted.

—Case Study—

Janet and Warren Langdon requested help for their fifteen-year-old son Martin after Mrs. Langdon found marijuana in a plastic bag at the bottom of his underwear drawer. Mr. and Mrs. Langdon didn't object when the therapist said she'd like to meet with the three of them together in order to get as much information as possible. It turned out that the discovery of marijuana was just the latest incident in a long series of battles between Mrs. Langdon and her son. Lots of fifteen-year-olds experiment with marijuana, but not all of them leave the evidence around for their mothers to find.

After meeting with the family and then talking with the boy and his parents separately, the therapist concluded that Martin did not appear to have a serious drug problem. Of greater concern, however, were the intensity of his shouting matches with his mother and his poor social adjustment at school and with friends. What she told the family was that she was concerned not only about the marijuana but also about these other signs of unhappy adjustment and that she'd like to extend the evaluation by having a couple of additional meetings with Martin and his parents separately. Mr. and Mrs. Langdon agreed, though without much enthusiasm. Martin didn't protest as much as might have been expected.

After his father died, Mr. Langdon and his older sister were raised by their mother. They were all she had left, and she increasingly devoted all her energy to shaping their lives. She was demanding and critical, and resentful of anything they wanted to do outside the family. By late adolescence Warren could no longer tolerate his domineering mother. His sister was never able to break free; she remained single and lived at home with her mother. Warren, however, was determined to become independent. Finally, in his mid-twenties, he left home and turned his back on his mother.

Janet Langdon came from a large, close-knit family. She and her four sisters were very much attached to each other and remained best friends. After graduating from high school, Janet announced that she wanted to go to college. This was contrary to the family norm that daughters remain at home and prepare themselves to be wives and mothers. Hence a major battle ensued between Janet and her parents; they were struggling to hold on, and she was struggling to break free. Finally she left for college, but she was ever after estranged from her parents.

When Janet met Warren, they were immediately drawn to one another. Both were lonely and cut off from their families. After a brief, passionate courtship, they married. The honeymoon didn't last long. Never having really differentiated himself from his dictatorial mother, Warren was exquisitely sensitive to criticism and control. He became furious at Janet's slightest attempt to change his habits. Janet, on the other hand, sought to reestablish in her marriage the closeness she'd had in her family. In order to be close, she and Warren would have to share interests and activities. But when she moved toward him, suggesting that they do something together, Warren got angry and resentful, feeling that Janet was impinging on his individuality. After several months of conflict, the two settled into a period of relative equilibrium. Warren put most of his energy into his work, leaving Janet to adjust to the distance between them. A year later Martin was born.

Both parents were delighted to have a baby, but what was for Warren a pleasant addition to the family was for Janet a way to fulfill a desperate need for closeness. The baby meant everything to her. While he was an infant she was the perfect mother, loving him tenderly and caring for his every need. When Warren tried to become involved with his infant son, Janet hovered about making sure he didn't do anything "wrong." This infuriated Warren, and after a few bitter blowups he left Martin more and more to his wife's care.

As he learned to walk and talk, Martin got into mischief, as all children do. He grabbed things, refused to stay in his playpen, and fussed whenever he didn't get his way. His crying was unbearable to Janet, and she found herself unable to set limits on her precious child.

Martin grew up with a doting mother, thinking he was the center of the universe. Whenever he didn't get what he wanted, he threw a tantrum. Bad as things got, at least the family existed in a kind of equilibrium. Warren was cut off from his wife and son, but he had his work. Janet was alienated from her husband, but she had her baby. Martin's difficulties began when he went off to school. Used to getting his own way, he found it impossible to get along with other children or to abide by the rules. His tantrums did nothing to endear him to his schoolmates or teachers. Other children avoided him, and he grew up having few friends. With teachers he acted out his father's battle against any efforts to control him. When Janet heard complaints about Martin's behavior, she sided with her son. "Those people just don't know how to deal with a creative child!"

Martin grew up with a terrible pattern of adjustment to school and friends, but retained his extremely close relationship with his mother. The crisis came with adolescence. Like his father before him, Martin tried to develop independent interests outside the home. However, he was far less capable of separating than his father had been, and his mother was incapable of letting go. The result was the beginning of chronic conflicts between Martin and his mother. Even as they argued and fought, they remained centered on each other. Martin spent more time battling his mother than doing anything else with his life.

Martin's history illustrates Bowen's theory of behavior disorder. As Betty Carter explains (personal communication), symptoms break out when the "vertical" problems of anxiety and toxic family issues that come down through the generations intersect with the "horizontal" stresses that come at transition points in the life cycle. Thus Martin's time of greatest vulnerability came when the unresolved fusion he inherited from his mother intersected with the stress of his adolescent urge for independence.

Even emotionally fused children reach a point when they try to break away. But breaking away in such instances tends to be accomplished by emotional cutoff rather than mature resolution of family ties. In childhood we relate as children to our parents. We depend on them to take care of us, we uncritically accept most of their attitudes and beliefs, and we behave in ways that are generally effective in getting our way with them. This usually means some combination of being good, patiently waiting to be rewarded, and being upset and demanding. Most of this childish behavior just doesn't work in the adult world. However, most of us leave home before changing to an adult-to-adult pattern with our parents. We—and they—only begin to change before it's time to leave.

A meek, patient child may become a bit more assertive and demanding in adolescence. Predictably, parents react with disappointment and anger. But instead of weathering the storm, most people get hurt and withdraw. This is the emotional cutoff. Instead of persisting long enough to transform the relationship to an adult basis, most people decide that the only way to deal with their parents is to move away. Unhappily, this only gives the illusion of independence.

The daughter who didn't get past the good-little-girl stage with her parents will probably adopt a similar stance outside the home. When it doesn't work, she may react with temper—which also won't work. Those who cut themselves off from their parents to minimize tension, carry their childish ways with them.

According to Bowen, people tend to choose mates with equivalent levels of undifferentiation. When conflict develops, each partner will be aware of the contribution of emotional immaturity—in the other one. Each will be prepared for change—in the other one. He will discover that her treating him like a father entails not only clinging dependence but also tirades and temper tantrums. She will discover that he withdraws the closeness she found so attractive in courtship as soon as she makes any demands. He fled from his parents because he needs closeness but can't handle it. Faced with conflict, he again withdraws. Sadly, what turned them on to each other carries the switch that turns them off.

What follows is marital conflict, dysfunction in one of the spouses, debilitating overconcern with one of the children, or various combinations of all three. When families come for help, they may present with any one of these problems. Whatever the presenting problem, however, the dynamics are similar; undifferentiation in families of origin is transmitted to marital problems, which are in turn projected onto a symptomatic spouse or child. Thus the problems of the past are visited on the future.

Goals of Therapy

Bowenians don't try to change people; nor are they much interested in solving problems. Instead they see therapy as an opportunity for people to learn more about themselves and their relationships, so that they can assume responsibility for their own problems. This is not to say, however, that therapists sit back and allow families to sort out their own issues. On the contrary, Bowenian therapy is a process of active inquiry, in which the therapist, guided by the most comprehensive theory in family therapy, helps family members get past blaming and fault finding in order to face and explore their own roles in family problems.

Tracing the pattern of family problems means paying attention to two things: **process** and **structure.** Process refers to patterns of emotional reactivity; structure, to the interlocking network of triangles.

In order to change the system, modification must take place in the most important triangle in the family—the one that involves the marital couple. To accomplish this the therapist creates a new triangle, a therapeutic one. If the therapist stays in contact with the partners, while remaining emotionally neutral, they can begin the process of **detriangulation** and differentiation that will profoundly and permanently change the entire family system.

The clinical methodology tied to this formulation calls for: (1) increasing the parents' ability to manage their own anxiety, and thereby becoming better able to handle their children's behavior; and (2) fortifying the couple's level of emotional functioning by increasing their ability to operate with less anxiety in their families of origin.

In the modification of these goals taken by Guerin and Fogarty, more emphasis is put on establishing a relationship with the symptomatic child, and working with the dysfunctional struggle and reactive emotional process in the nuclear family triangles. Extended family work is put off unless it's directly and explicitly linked to symptom formation and maintenance. In other words, where Bowen generally went straight for the **family of origin,** second-generation Bowenians pay more attention to the **nuclear family,** and are likely to wait to institute work on the family of origin as a way to reinforce gains and to enhance individual and family functioning. Behavior disorders in adults—such as repeated job loss, uncontrollable anger, and compulsions of substance, sex, or acquisition—are viewed in the context of either dysfunctional spouse– or adult–child triangles, and clinical interventions are planned accordingly.

The goal of marital therapy is to improve self-focus, decrease emotional reactivity, and modify dysfunctional patterns. If this can be accomplished, the spouses can become better partners, lovers, and friends. As part of this process, they will learn to recognize what they believe in, not just what they are against, appreciate their idiosyncracies and those of their partners, and become better able to accept their own assets and limitations as well as those of their partners.

Monica McGoldrick, speaking from a feminist perspective, argues that it isn't enough to approach marital relationships with neutrality—to help couples negotiate compromises with each other in their own terms. As long as marital relationships are based on inherent imbalances, conscientious therapists must be aware of inequality and actively work to redress it.

> Most men have trouble with intimacy. It's part of how they were socialized. We've got to admit it to ourselves, and help men change. We need to help them see the detrimental impact of the dominant value system that makes it difficult for them to relate effectively to their families. At the same time we need to help women to become effective in the areas where they are lacking: dealing with money, anger, and effective participation in the world of paid work and success. (McGoldrick, 1990)

McGoldrick believes that economic inequality between men and women is a powerful and neglected context of marriage, making it harder for women to insist on change because it's harder for them to be financially self-sufficient. Money means options.

> If the wife is not in an economically viable position, marital therapy may be impossible. If she does not have the power to negotiate the relationship from a position of equality, the pretense of negotiation may be a farce. Beware of urging her to leave before having some awareness of the limitations and her options.
>
> HIS therapy may involve attention to his dreams, keeping a journal, learning to be intimate with his children or his friends.

HER therapy may involve focusing on her resumé, a Dale Carnegie course, or a consultation with a financial planner, and taking a vacation from family responsibilities. (McGoldrick, 1990)

Betty Carter puts the case for gender sensitivity this way: "Marital therapy that ignores sexism is like rearranging the deck chairs on the Titanic."

Conditions for Behavior Change

Increasing the ability to distinguish between thinking and feeling and learning to use that ability to resolve relationship problems is the guiding principle of Bowenian therapy. Lowering anxiety and increasing self-focus—the ability to see one's own role in interpersonal processes—is the primary mechanism of change.

Understanding, not action, is the vehicle of cure. Therefore two of the most important elements in Bowenian therapy may not be apparent to anyone who thinks primarily about techniques. The atmosphere of sessions and the therapist's stance are both designed to minimize emotionality. Therapists ask questions to foster self-reflection and direct them at individuals one at a time, rather than encourage family dialogues—which have an unfortunate tendency to get overheated. Because clients aren't the only ones to respond emotionally to family dramas, Bowenian therapists strive to control their own reactivity and to avoid triangulation. This, of course, is easier said than done. The keys to staying detriangled are to never take sides, and to nudge each party toward accepting more responsibility for making things better.

Being triangled means taking sides. Whenever motives are imputed to the behavior of any one person ("the husband is domineering"), awareness of processes that transcend individuals is lost. Instead of becoming partisan (overtly or otherwise), therapists resist triangu-

lation by urging people to work out their differences between them. And since blaming each other is what makes it hard to solve problems in the first place, individuals are encouraged to look to their own roles in the process.

Bowen differed from most systems therapists in believing that meaningful change does not require the presence of the entire family.[1] Instead he believed that change is initiated by individuals or couples who are capable of affecting the rest of the family. Therapy can be described as proceeding from inside out. Differentiation of self, which begins as a personal and individual process, is the vehicle for transforming relationships and the entire family system.

Therapy may not require the presence of the entire family, but it *does* require an awareness of the entire family. "A family therapist may treat two parents and their schizophrenic son, but not attach much importance to the fact that the parents are emotionally cut off from their families of origin. The parents' cutoff from the past undermines their ability to stop focusing on their son's problems; once again, the therapy will be ineffective" (Kerr & Bowen, 1988, p. vii).

Part of the process of differentiating a self is to develop a personal relationship with everyone in the **extended family.** The power of these connections may seem mysterious—particularly for people who don't think of their well-being as dependent on family ties. A little reflection reveals that increasing the number of important relationships will enable an individual to spread out his or her emotional energy. Instead of concentrating one's investment in one or two family relationships, it's diffused into several. Freud had a similar notion on an intrapsychic level. In "The Project for a Scientific Psychology," Freud described his neurological model of the mind. The immature mind has few outlets ("cathexes") for

---

1. Although willingness to see individuals has become commonplace among solution-focused and narrative therapists, these therapists don't always take a systemic perspective.

channeling psychic energy, and hence little flexibility or capacity to delay responding. The mature mind, on the other hand, has many channels of response, which permits greater flexibility. Bowen's notion of increasing the emotional family network is like Freud's model, writ large.

Therapy with couples is based on the premise that tension in the dyad will dissipate if they remain in contact with a third person (in a stable triangle)—*if* that person remains neutral and objective rather than emotionally entangled. Thus a therapeutic triangle can reverse the insidious process of problem-maintaining triangulation. Furthermore, change in any one triangle will change the entire family system.

Family therapy with individuals is based on the premise that if one person in the family achieves a higher level of differentiation, this will enable other members of the family to do the same. Bowenians teach individuals about triangles and then coach them to return to their families, where they work to detriangle themselves, develop greater objectivity, and thus achieve a permanent reduction in emotional reactiveness. This in turn has a therapeutic impact on all systems of which these individuals are a part.

Therapy

The major techniques in Bowenian therapy include genograms, process questions, relationship experiments, detriangling, coaching, taking "I-positions," and displacement stories. Because seeing one's own role in family problems as well as how those problems are embedded in the history of the extended family are so important in Bowenian therapy, assessment is more critical in this approach than in almost any other.

Assessment

An extended family systems assessment begins with a description and history of the presenting problem. Exact dates are noted and later checked for their relationship to events in the extended family life cycle. Next comes a history of the nuclear family, including information about when the parents met, their courtship, their marriage, and childrearing. Particular attention is paid to where the family lived and when they moved, especially in relation to the location of the extended families. The next part of the evaluation is devoted to the history of both spouses' births, sibling positions, significant facts about their childhoods, and about the past and current functioning of their parents. All of this information is recorded on a "genogram," covering at least three generations.

Genograms are schematic diagrams listing family members and their relationships to one another. Included are ages, dates of marriage, deaths, and geographical locations. Men are represented by squares and women by circles, with their ages inside the figures. Horizontal lines indicate marriages, with the date of the marriage written on the line; vertical lines connect parents and children (Figure 5.1).[2]

What makes the genogram more than a static portrait of a family's history is the inclusion of relationship conflicts, cutoffs, and triangles. The fact that uncle Fred was an alcoholic or that great grandmother Sophie migrated from

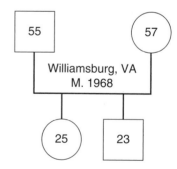

FIGURE 5.1   Basic Symbols Used in Genograms

---

2.   For more detailed suggestions, see McGoldrick & Gerson, 1985.

Russia is relatively meaningless without some understanding of the patterns of emotional reactivity passed down through the generations.

Dates of important events, such as deaths, marriages, and divorces, deserve careful study. These events send emotional shock waves throughout the family, which may open lines of communication and foster contact, or these issues may get buried and family members progressively more cut off. Another significant piece of information on the genogram is the location of various segments of the family. Dates, relationships, and localities provide the framework to explore emotional boundaries, fusion, cutoffs, critical conflicts, amount of openness, and the number of current and potential relationships in the family. Figure 5.2 shows symbols that can be used to describe the relationship dynamics among family members.

If three parallel lines are used to indicate very close (or fused) relationships, a zigzag line to indicate conflict, a dotted line to indicate emotional distance, and a broken line to indicate estrangement (or cutoff), triangular patterns across three generations often become vividly clear—as shown in an abbreviated diagram of Sigmund Freud's family (Figure 5.3).

A Bowenian family evaluation begins, as do most approaches, with a history of the presenting complaint. The therapist lets the family tell its story and listens carefully to each family member's perception of the problem.

History taking expands the focus from the symptomatic person to the relationship network of which that person is a part. In the case

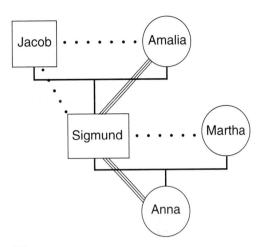

FIGURE 5.3   Genogram of Sigmund Freud's Family

of the Langdons (see page 127), this meant talking with Martin about his relationships at school and with friends as well as those with his parents. With his parents, it meant putting their current problems with Martin in the context of the story of their relationship.

The history of the nuclear family begins with the meeting and courtship of the parents: "What attracted them to each other?" "What was the early period of their relationship like?" "Were there any serious problems during that period?" "When were the children born, and how did each of the partners adapt to the new additions?"

If a therapist fails to take a careful history, associations that can help people gain perspective on their problems may be overlooked. Things like moves and important events, such as a husband's cancer surgery two years earlier, may not even be mentioned, unless a therapist asks. One woman who had been seeing an individual therapist didn't consider it important enough to mention. "What does my seeing a therapist have to do with my daughter's problems?" she said.

Of particular interest are what stresses the family has endured and how they have adapted. This information helps determine the intensity of chronic anxiety in the family and

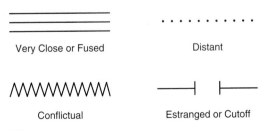

FIGURE 5.2   Genogram Symbols for Relationship Dynamics

whether it is linked more to an overload of difficult life events or to a low degree of adaptiveness in the family.

As Figure 5.4 shows, the bare facts of the nuclear family genogram only provide the skeleton upon which to flesh out information about the Langdon family.

The decision to extend the assessment beyond the nuclear family depends on the extent of crisis and degree of anxiety the immediate family is in. In the case of the Langdons, both parents seemed eager to discuss their family backgrounds.

In gathering information about extended families, a therapist should ascertain which members of the clan are most involved with the family being evaluated, for it is the nature of ongoing ties to the extended family that has a great impact on both parents and their role in the nuclear family. Of equal importance, however, is finding out who is *not* involved, because people with whom contact has been cut off can be an even greater source of anxiety than the people with whom contact has been maintained.

Therapeutic Techniques

Bowenian therapists believe that understanding how family systems operate is more important than this or that technique. Bowen himself spoke of "technique" with disdain, and he was distressed to see anyone relying on formulaic interventions.

If there were a magic bullet in Bowenian therapy—one essential technique—it would be the "process question." Process questions are designed to slow people down, diminish reactive anxiety, and start them thinking—not just about how others are upsetting them, but about how they participate in interpersonal problems.

—Case Study——————

In interviewing a couple in which the husband was a recovering alcoholic with a history of abuse, the therapist asked: "Where are you with the thoughts about the damage you've done to your wife and kids with your alcoholism?"

When the man acknowledged responsibility for his abusive behavior and seemed genuinely remorseful, the therapist asked about his progress toward recovery, again using process questions to focus on rational planning and personal responsibility. For example:

"What makes that step so hard?"
"Pride."
"How does that manifest itself?"
"I get nasty."

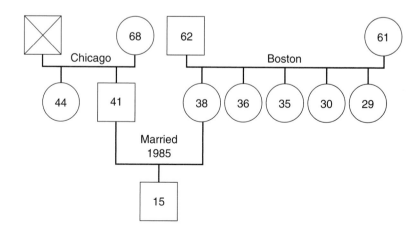

FIGURE 5.4   Langdon
Family Genogram

Notice how this line of questioning explores not only the man's personal progress, but also how his problems affect others in the family. Relationships take place in a systemic web of connections, but individuals are responsible for their own behavior.

Then the therapist shifted to open a discussion of the wife's role in the couple's difficulties. "So, you're getting better at taking responsibility for the drinking and the behavior connected with it? Do you think your wife appreciates what you're doing and the progress you're making?" And then a few minutes later: "Has your wife ever been able to talk to you about the things she's contributed to the relationship going sour?"

When the therapist asked the wife about her thinking, she switched back to talking about all the annoying things her husband was doing–pressuring her to forgive him and get back together. Although he would eventually like her to consider her own role in the process, the therapist tried to empathize with her upset. "So, he's just bugging you by trying to get you to change your mind?" Then after a few minutes, the therapist tried to shift the wife to thinking more and feeling less. "Can you give me a summary of your thinking–how you came to that conclusion?" And when the wife again got angry and blamed her husband, the therapist just listened. A moment later he asked, "What do you do in the face of that abuse?"

"I get upset."

"Do you understand what it is about you that sets him off?"

"No."

"Has he ever been able to tell you?"

Notice how in this series of questions the therapist attempts to explore the process of the couple's relationship, asking both partners to think about what's going on between them, increase their awareness of their own contributions, and consider what they're planning to do to take responsibility to make things better.

Those who followed Bowen also ask questions, but move in occasionally to challenge, confront, and explain. Betty Carter, for example, asks questions designed to help couples understand their situation, but she then tries to intensify the process and speed it up by explaining what works or doesn't work, and by assigning tasks calculated to move people out of triangles. She might, for example, encourage a wife to visit her mother-in-law, or a husband to begin calling his mother on the phone. Another favorite device of Carter's is to encourage people to write letters, addressing unresolved issues in the family. One way to prevent such letter writing from degenerating into telling people off is to have clients bring in the letters and help them edit out the anger and emotional reactivity.

Guerin, perhaps more than any other Bowenian, has developed clinical models that feature specific techniques for specific situations. His categorizing marital conflict into four stages of severity with detailed suggestions for treating each stage (Guerin et al., 1987) is the most elaborate demonstration of his well worked out technique.

Bowen advocated a variety of methods all aimed at the same goals. Whether treatment involves nuclear families, couples, individuals, or multiple family groups, the effort is directed at modifying the whole family system.

Bowenian Therapy with Couples. Whenever possible, Bowenians prefer to work with both parents or partners. When a therapist joins a couple, a therapeutic triangle is formed. If the therapist avoids taking sides, the couple will be forced to deal with each other. The emotional tone of sessions should be lively enough to be meaningful but cool enough to be objective. This is accomplished by asking more, and less, provocative questions, and by regulating the amount of interaction between the partners. When things are calm, conflicting feelings can be dealt with more objectively and partners can talk rationally with each other. But when feeling outruns thinking, it's best to ask questions that get couples to think more and feel less, and to talk to the therapist rather

*B*owenian couples
therapy is designed
to reduce anxiety and
foster self-focus.

than to each other. Couples who've argued for years about the same old bugaboos are often amazed to discover that the first time they ever really hear each other is when they listen as their partners talk to the therapist. It's easier to hear when you aren't busy planning your own response. If all else fails to cool things down, Fogarty (1976b) recommends seeing spouses in separate sessions.

Contrary to popular belief, couples don't solve problems just by talking about them. Left to their own devices they tend to argue unproductively, project responsibility onto each other, and complain instead of negotiate. Change requires talking *and* listening. Because of the universal tendency to see only others' contributions to problems, special techniques are required to help family members see the process, not just the content, of their interactions; to see their own part in the process, instead of just blaming others; and finally to change.

Guerin (1971) recommends the "displacement story" as a device for helping family members achieve sufficient distance to see their own roles in the family system. The displacement story is about other families with similar problems. For example, a couple too busy attacking

each other to listen might be told: "It must be terribly frustrating not getting through to each other. Last year I saw a couple who just couldn't stop arguing long enough to listen to each other. Only after I split them up and they blew off steam for a few sessions individually did they seem to have any capacity to listen to what the other was saying."

Displacement can also be used to frame process questions to avoid provoking angry or defensive responses. Instead of asking someone in the throes of upset and anger when they think they might get over those feelings in order to start working to change things—which might provoke them to think that their feelings are being denied—a therapist might ask, "Do you think anyone ever gets over all that anger and upset?" Or, if asking why someone hasn't been able to accomplish something might make him or her defensive, a therapist might ask, "What do you think makes that step so hard for people?"

Guerin also uses films as displacement materials. If the proper aesthetic distance is maintained, people can become emotionally involved with a movie so that it has an impact but at the same time remain sufficiently removed to be objective. Underdistancing, in a therapy session or a highly provocative movie, results in an emotional experience devoid of reflection. Overdistancing, such as may occur in a lecture or preachy film, leads to a lack of involvement and impact. Guerin selects films like *Kramer* vs. *Kramer, The War of the Roses, I Never Sang for My Father, Scenes from a Marriage,* and *Breaking Away* to use as displacement materials for teaching family dynamics to trainees and to families in therapy.

Armed with a knowledge of triangles, the therapist endeavors to remain neutral and objective. This requires an optimal level of emotional distance, which Bowen (1975) said is the point where a therapist can see both the tragic and comic aspects of a couple's interactions. Although other people's problems are nothing to laugh at, a sense of irony may be preferable to the unctuous earnestness so popular in some quarters.

Staying detriangled requires a calm tone of voice and talking about facts more than about feelings. This calm objectivity on the part of Bowen systems therapists is expressed and enhanced by the use of process questions—questions aimed to cut through emotional reactivity and make contact with family members' reasonableness.

As partners talk, the therapist concentrates on the *process* of their interaction, not on the details under discussion. Concentrating on the content of a discussion is a sign that the therapist is emotionally entangled in a couple's problems. It may be hard to avoid being drawn in by hot topics like money, sex, or discipline, but a therapist's job isn't to settle disputes, it's to help couples do so. The aim is to get clients to express ideas, thoughts, and opinions to the therapist in the presence of their partners. Should one break down in tears, the therapist remains calm and inquires about the thoughts that touched off the tears. If a couple begins arguing, the therapist becomes more active, calmly questioning one, then the other, focusing on their respective thoughts. Asking for minutely detailed descriptions of events is one of the best ways to subdue overheated emotion and make room for reason.

Although Bowen considered strict neutrality essential, those of his followers with feminist convictions believe that it's important to address issues of inequality, even if couples don't bring them up. Betty Carter raises the issue of gender by asking questions about who does what in the family and how much time each parent spends with the kids. She asks partners how much money each makes. When the usual discrepancy emerges, she asks, "What role do you think this plays in the decision-making process?"

Metaphors of complementarity are helpful for highlighting the process underlying the content of family interactions. Fogarty (1976b), for example, described the "pursuer–distancer" dynamic among couples. The more one pursues—presses for more communication and togetherness—the more the other distances—watches TV, works late, or goes off with the kids. Frequently, partners pursue and distance in different areas. Husbands commonly distance themselves emotionally but pursue sexually. The trick, according to Fogarty, is, "Never pursue a distancer." Instead, help the pursuer explore his or her own inner emptiness. "What's in your life other than the other person?" It's also important for therapists not to pursue distancers. If no one is chasing, the distancer is more likely to move toward the family.

To underscore the need for objectivity, Bowen spoke of the therapist as a "coach" or "consultant." He didn't mean to imply coldness or indifference, but rather to emphasize the neutrality required to avoid triangulation. In traditional terms this is known as "managing transference and countertransference." And just as analysts are analyzed themselves so they can recognize their own countertransference, so Bowen considered differentiating a self in one's own family the best way to avoid being emotionally triangled by couples. Guerin suggests that the best way to develop a genuine understanding of family concepts is to try them out in your own family (Guerin & Fogarty, 1972).

To help partners define positions as differentiated selves, it's useful for a therapist to establish an "I-position" (Guerin, 1971). The more a therapist defines an autonomous position in relation to the family, the easier it is for family members to define themselves to each other. Gradually family members learn to calmly state their own beliefs and convictions and to act on them without attacking others or becoming overly upset by their responses.

When one partner begins differentiating, the other may be thrown off balance and press for a return to the status quo (Carter & Orfanidis, 1976). If this emotional counterreaction is weathered calmly, without giving in or becoming hostile, both partners can move toward a higher level of differentiation. The process takes place in small steps, with couples alternating between separateness and togetherness. Eventually, when each has achieved a sufficiently well-articulated self, they can come together in mutual caring and respect, rather than continuing to try to remake each other in their own image and likeness.

After sufficient harmony had been won with progress toward self-differentiation, Bowen taught couples how emotional systems operate and encouraged them to explore those webs of relationship in their own families (Bowen, 1971). He prepared them for this by first making occasional references to their respective families. Once couples recognize the relevance of their prior family experience to their current problems, transition to the focus on families of origin will be smoother.

For example, a woman locked into the role of emotional pursuer might be asked to describe her relationship with her father and then compare it to her current relationships with men. If lessening her preoccupation with her husband

and children seems advisable, the therapist might encourage her to connect with the most emotionally distant member of her family of origin, usually her father. The idea wouldn't be to shift her attachment from one set of relationships to another, but to help her understand that the intensity of her need is due in part to unfinished business. Understanding and beginning to address unsatisfied longings at their source can help a person achieve more balanced relationships in the present—and begin to start focusing more on herself and her own needs.

Kerr (1971) suggests that when relationship problems in the nuclear family are being discussed, therapists should occasionally ask questions about similar patterns in the family of origin. If family members can see that they're repeating earlier patterns, they are more likely to recognize their own emotional reactivity. Recently, Nichols saw a couple unable to decide what to do with their mentally ill teenage daughter. Although the daughter was seriously disturbed and virtually uncontrollable, her mother found it very difficult to consider hospitalization. When asked what her own mother would have done, without hesitating she replied that her long-suffering mother would have been too guilt-ridden even to consider placement—"no matter how much she and the rest of the family might suffer." Little more needed to be said.

More didactic teaching occurs in the transition from brief to long-term therapy. Knowledge of family systems theory helps people trace the patterns that have a hold on them, so they can unlock themselves. Such information is useful when tensions have abated, but trying to impart it can be risky during periods of conflict and anxiety. At such times, battling couples are liable to distort any statements about how families function as support for one or the other of their opposing positions. So primed are warring mates to make the other "wrong" in order for themselves to be "right," that they "hear" much of what a therapist says as either for or against them. But when calm, they get past the idea that for one to be right the other must be wrong, and they can profit from didactic sessions. As they learn about systems theory, both partners are sent home for visits to continue the process of differentiation in their extended families. During this phase of treatment—coaching—Bowen believed that infrequent meetings aren't only possible, but desirable (1976). Having sessions less often forces people to become more resourceful.

Bowenian Therapy with One Person. Bowen's personal success at differentiating from his family convinced him that a single highly motivated person can be the fulcrum for changing an entire family system (Anonymous, 1972). Subsequently he made family therapy with one person a major part of his practice. He used this method with one spouse when the other refused to participate, or with single adults who lived far from their parents or whose parents wouldn't come for treatment. Aside from these cases in which Bowen made a virtue of necessity, he used this approach extensively with mental health professionals. Extended family work with partners is also the focus of couples treatment after the presenting anxiety and symptoms subside.

The goal of working with individuals is the same as when working with larger units: differentiation. With individuals the focus is on resolving neurotic patterns in the extended family. This means developing person-to-person relationships, seeing family members as people rather than emotionally charged images, learning to observe one's self in triangles, and, finally, detriangling oneself (Bowen, 1974).

The extent of unresolved emotional attachment to parents defines the level of undifferentiation. More intense levels of undifferentiation go hand in hand with more extreme efforts to achieve emotional distance, either through de-

fense mechanisms or physical distance. A person may handle mild anxiety with parents by remaining silent or avoiding personal discussions; but when anxiety rises he or she might find it necessary to walk out of the room or even leave town. However, the person who runs away is as emotionally attached as the one who stays home and uses psychological distancing mechanisms to control the attachment. People who shrink from contact need closeness but can't handle it. When tension mounts in other intimate relationships, they will again withdraw.

Two sure signs of emotional cutoff are denial of the importance of the family and an exaggerated facade of independence. Cut-off people boast of their emancipation and infrequent contact with their parents. The opposite of emotional cutoff is an open relationship system, in which family members have genuine, but not confining, emotional contact. Bowenian therapy is designed to increase the extent and intimacy of connections with the extended family. In fact, Bowen found the results of extended family work superior to working directly on the nuclear family (Bowen, 1974).

Two prerequisites to differentiating a self in the extended family are some knowledge of how family systems function and strong motivation to change. It's difficult to sustain the effort to work on family relationships in the absence of distress, and many people work only in spurts from one crisis to the next (Carter & Orfanidis, 1976). When things are calm, they relax; when problems arise again, they renew efforts to make changes.

The person who embarks on a quest of learning more about his or her family usually knows where to look. Most families have one or two members who know who's who and what's what—perhaps a maiden aunt, a patriarch, or a cousin who's very family-centered. Phone calls, letters, or, better yet, visits to these family archivists will yield much information, some of which may produce surprises.

Gathering information about the family is also an excellent vehicle for the second step toward differentiation, establishing person-to-person relationships with as many family members as possible. This means getting in touch and speaking personally with them, not about other people or impersonal topics. If this sounds easy, try it. Few of us can spend more than a few minutes talking personally with certain family members without getting a bit anxious. When this happens, we're tempted to withdraw, physically or emotionally, or triangle in another person. Gradually extending the time of real personal conversation will improve the relationship and help differentiate a self.

There are profound benefits to be derived from developing person-to-person relationships with members of the extended family, but they have to be experienced to be appreciated. In the process of opening and deepening personal relationships, you will learn about the emotional forces in the family. Some family triangles will immediately become apparent; others will emerge only after careful examination. Usually we notice only the most obvious triangles because we're too emotionally engaged to be good observers. Few people can be objective about their parents. They're either comfortably fused or uncomfortably reactive. Making frequent short visits helps control emotional reactiveness so that you can become a better observer.

Many of our habitual emotional responses to the family impede our ability to understand and accept others; worse, they make it impossible for us to understand and govern ourselves. It's natural to get angry and blame people when things go wrong. The differentiated person, however, is capable of stepping back, controlling emotional responsiveness, and reflecting on how to improve things. Bowen (1974) called this "getting beyond blaming and anger," and said that, once learned in the family, this ability is useful for handling emotional snarls throughout life.

Ultimately, differentiating a self requires that you identify interpersonal triangles you participate in, and detriangle from them. The goal is to relate to people without gossiping or taking sides and without counterattacking or defending yourself. Bowen suggested that the best time to do this is during a family crisis, but it can be begun at any time.

A common triangle starts with one parent and a child. Suppose that every time you visit your folks your mother takes you aside and starts complaining about your father. Maybe it feels good to be confided in. Maybe you'll have fantasies about rescuing your parents—or at least your mother. In fact, this triangle is destructive to all three relationships: you and Dad, Dad and Mom, and, yes, you and Mom. In triangles, one pair will be close and two will be distant (Figure 5.5). Sympathizing with Mom alienates Dad. It also makes it less likely that she'll do anything about working out her complaints with him.

Finally, although this triangle may give you the illusion of being close to your mother, it's an ersatz intimacy. Nor is defending your father a solution. That only moves you away from Mom towards Dad, and widens the gulf between them. As long as the triangulation continues, personal and open one-to-one relationships cannot develop.

Once you recognize a triangle for what it is, you can make a plan of action so you stop participating in it. The basic idea is to do something, anything, to get the other two people to work out their own relationship. The simplest and most direct approach is to suggest that they

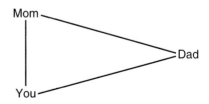

FIGURE 5.5   Cross-Generational Triangle

do so. In the example just given you might suggest that your mother discuss her concerns with your father, *and* you can refuse to listen to more of her complaints. Less direct, but more powerful, is to tell Dad that his wife has been complaining about him, and you don't know why she doesn't tell him about it. She'll be annoyed, but not forever. A more devious ploy is to overagree with Mom's complaints. When she says he's messy, you say he's a complete slob; when she says he's not very thoughtful, you say he's totally uncaring. Pretty soon she'll begin to defend him. Maybe she'll decide to work out her complaints with him, or maybe she won't. But either way you'll have removed yourself from the triangle.

Once you become aware of them, you'll find that triangles are ubiquitous. Some common examples include griping with colleagues about the boss; telling someone that your partner doesn't understand you; undercutting your spouse with the kids; and watching television to avoid talking to your family. Breaking free of triangles may not be easy, but the rewards are great. Bowen believed that differentiating an autonomous self requires opening relationships in the extended family, and then ceasing to participate in triangles. The payoff comes not only from enriching these relationships, but also from enhancing your ability to relate to anyone—friends, fellow workers, patients, and your spouse and kids. Furthermore, if you can remain in emotional contact, but change the part you play in your family—and maintain the change in spite of family pressure to change back—your family will have to adjust to accommodate to your change.

Some degree of rejection is expectable when one embarks on a direction for oneself that isn't approved of by partners, parents, colleagues, or others. The rejection, which is triggered by the threat to the relationship balance, is designed to restore the balance (Kerr & Bowen, 1988).

Some useful guidelines to resisting the family's attempts to get you to change back to un-productive but familiar patterns of the past have been enumerated by Carter and Orfanidis (1976), by Guerin and Fogarty (1972), and by Herz (1991). You can read about how to work on family tensions by resolving your own emotional sensitivities in two marvelous books by Harriet Lerner: *The Dance of Anger* (Lerner, 1985) and *The Dance of Intimacy* (Lerner, 1989).

Reentry into your family of origin is necessary to open the closed system. Sometimes all that's required is visiting. Other times, buried issues must be raised, activating dormant triangles by stirring up emotions in the system. If you can't move directly toward your father without his withdrawing, move toward other people with whom he is close, thus activating a triangle. If your father is tense about being alone with you, spend some time alone with your mother. This is likely to make him want to have equal time.

In reentry, it's advisable to begin by opening closed relationships before trying to change conflictual ones. Don't start by trying to resolve the warfare between yourself and your mother. Begin by looking up a sibling or cousin with whom you've been out of touch. Deal with personal issues, but avoid stalemated conflicts. If your contacts with some sections of the family are routine and predictable, make them more creative. Those who continue working on their family relationships beyond the resolution of a crisis, or beyond the first flush of enthusiasm for a new academic interest, can achieve profound changes in themselves, in their family systems, and in their own clinical work.

Evaluating Therapy Theory and Results

What makes Bowen's theory so useful is that it describes and explains the emotional forces within us that regulate how we relate to other people. The single greatest impediment to understanding one another is our tendency to become emotionally reactive and respond defensively instead of listening and hearing each other. Like all things about relationships, this emotionality is a two-way street: Some speakers express themselves with such emotional pressure that listeners inevitably react to that pressure rather than hear what the speaker is trying to say. Bowenian theory describes this reactivity, locates its origins in the lack of differentiation of self, and explains how to reduce emotionalism and move toward mature self-control—by cultivating relationships widely in the family and learning to listen without becoming defensive or untrue to one's own beliefs.

In Bowenian theory, anxiety is the all-purpose explanation (for why people are dependent or avoidant and why they become emotionally reactive), reminiscent of Freudian conflict theory (which explains all symptoms as the result of anxiety stemming from conflicts over sex and aggression). The second all-purpose concept in the Bowenian system is differentiation. Since differentiation is roughly synonymous with maturity, students might ask, to what extent is the proposition that more differentiated people function better in a circular argument? In respect to the Bowenian tradition of asking questions rather than imposing opinions, we'll let this stand as an open question for your consideration.

The major shortcoming of the Bowenian approach is that in concentrating on individuals and their extended family relationships, it neglects the power of working directly with the nuclear family. In many cases the most direct way to resolve family problems is to bring together everyone in the same household and encourage them to face each other and talk about their conflicts. These discussions may turn noisy and unproductive, but a skilled therapist can help family members realize what they're doing and guide them toward understanding. There are times when couples or families are so hostile and defensive that their dialogues must be interrupted to help individuals get beyond

defensiveness to the hurt feelings underneath. At such times, it is useful, perhaps imperative, to block family members from arguing with each other. But an approach, such as Bowen's, that encourages therapists to speak to individual family members one at a time underutilizes the power of working directly with nuclear families in action.

The status of extended family systems therapy and theory rests not on empirical research but on the elegance of Murray Bowen's theory, clinical reports of successful treatment, and the personal profit experienced by those who have worked at differentiating a self in their families of origin. Bowen's original research with schizophrenic families was more clinical observation than controlled experimentation. In fact, Bowen was decidedly cool to empirical research (Bowen, 1976), preferring instead to refine and integrate theory and practice. The little empirical work done in the field is reported at the annual Georgetown Family Symposia. There, evaluations of various programs and occasional research reports have been presented. One of these, a study by Winer, was of sufficient interest to be published in *Family Process* (Winer, 1971). Winer reported on observations of four families in multiple family therapy led by Murray Bowen. Over the course of treatment, the experimenter tracked the ratio of self references to other references, and the number of differentiated-self references. Statements considered as differentiated-self references included speaking for self without blaming, dealing with change or desired change in self rather than in others, distinguishing thoughts from feelings, and showing awareness and goal-directedness. There were two significant findings, both of which supported Bowen's position. First, in early sessions there were fewer self statements; the greatest number referred to "we" and "us," indicating that the spouses did not differentiate separate positions. Second, there was an evolution toward more differentiated I-statements over the course of treatment. Initially these occurred less than half the time, but after a few sessions differentiated statements predominated.

Although it does support the effectiveness of Bowen's therapy in increasing differentiation, the Winer study didn't test the premise that differentiation of self is synonymous with positive therapeutic outcome. In fact that is an article of faith with Bowen, and it points to a certain circularity in this theory: Symptoms indicate emotional fusion, and fusion is demonstrated by the presence of symptoms (Bowen, 1966).

Bowen repeatedly stressed the importance of theory in clinical practice (Bowen, 1976), and so invites judgment on the basis of his theory. Therefore, it should be noted that although his theory is thorough, consistent, and useful, it's largely a series of constructs based on clinical observation. The basic tenets aren't supported by empirical research and, in fact, are probably not amenable to confirmation or disconfirmation in controlled experimentation. Bowen's theory, like psychoanalysis, is probably best judged not as true or false, but as useful or not useful. On balance, it seems eminently useful.

Evidence for the effectiveness of extended family systems therapy rests largely on personal experience and clinical reports. Bowenian therapists apparently do at least as well as the standard figures; that is, one-third of the patients get worse or no better; one-third of the patients get somewhat better; and one-third get significantly better.

People who develop systems of therapy are influenced by their personal and emotional experiences, and Bowen was more aware and candid than most about this (Anonymous, 1972). His family was middle-class, symptom-free, and relatively enmeshed; and his techniques seem most relevant for this sort of family. Like Bowen, most of the other therapists considered in this chapter also work in private practice with primarily middle-class patients.

Phil Guerin and Tom Fogarty have made notable contributions, not only in keeping alive and teaching Bowenian theory, but also in refining techniques of therapy. Both are master therapists. Betty Carter and Monica McGoldrick have made more of a contribution in studying how families work: the normal family life cycle, ethnic diversity, and the pervasive role of gender inequality. Because they are students of the family as well as therapists, some of their interventions have a decidedly educational flavor. In working with stepfamilies, for example, Betty Carter takes the stance of an expert and teaches the stepparent not to try to assume an equal position with the biological parent. Stepparents have to earn moral authority; meanwhile what works best is supporting the role of the biological parent. Just as Bowen's approach is influenced by his personal experience, it seems that both Carter and McGoldrick infuse their work as family therapists with their experience as career women and their convictions about the price of inequality.

All these therapists are fine clinicians; and they and their students have the advantage of working with theories that are sufficiently specific to provide clear strategies for treatment. Particularly now when family therapy is so fashionable, most people who see families use an eclectic hodgepodge of unrelated concepts and techniques; they're not apt to have a coherent theory or a consistent strategy. The unhappy result is that most family therapists are drawn into families' emotional processes and absorbed in content issues. The treatment that results tends to be supportive and directive.

Second-generation family therapists, like Guerin and Fogarty, are well-grounded enough in a theoretical system (for them, Bowen's) that they are able to diverge from it and add to it without losing focus. However, third-generation family therapists (students of students) are often left with no clear theoretical underpinning, and their work suffers for it. Interestingly, students of the pioneer family therapists haven't been particularly innovative. None of them has surpassed their teachers. These observations underscore the plight of graduate students who are exposed to a variety of approaches, often presented with more criticism than sympathetic understanding. Consequently they're left with no single coherent approach. Probably the best way to become an effective clinician is to begin as a disciple of one particular school. Appren- tice yourself to an expert—the best you can find—and immerse yourself in one system. After you have mastered that approach and practiced it for a few years, then you can begin to modify it, without losing focus and direction.

—Summary

Bowen's conceptual lens was wider than that of most family therapists, but his actual unit of treatment was smaller. His concern was al- ways with the multigenerational family system, even though he usually met with individuals or couples. Since he first introduced the **three- generational hypothesis of schizophrenia,** he was aware of how interlocking triangles con- nect one generation to the next—like threads interwoven in a total family fabric. Although Bowenian therapists are unique in sending pa- tients home to repair their relationships with parents, the idea of intergenerational connec- tions has been very influential in the field.

According to Bowen, the major problem in families is emotional fusion; the major goal is differentiation. Emotional fusion grows out of an instinctual need for others, but is an un- healthy exaggeration of this need. Some people manifest fusion directly as a need for together- ness; others mask it with a pseudo-independent facade. The person with a differentiated self need not be isolated, but can stay in contact with others and maintain his or her own in- tegrity. Similarly, the healthy family is one that remains in viable emotional contact from one generation to another.

In Bowenian theory the triangle is the uni- versal unit of analysis—in principle and in practice. Like Freud, Bowen stressed the pivotal importance of early family relations. The rela- tionship between the self and parents is de- scribed as a triangle and considered the most important in life. Bowen's understanding of tri- angles is one of his most important contribu- tions and one of the seminal ideas in family therapy.

For Bowen, therapy was a logical extension of theory. Before you can make significant in-roads into family problems, you must have a thorough understanding of how family systems operate. The cure is to go backwards, to visit your own parents, grandparents, aunts, and uncles, and to learn to get along with them.

Bowen's theory espouses a balance between togetherness and independence, but the prac- tice has a distinctly intellectual character. He saw anxiety as a threat to psychic equilibrium, consequently his approach to treatment often seems dispassionate. Bowen moved away from the heat of family confrontations to contem- plate the history of family relationships. Like moving from the playing field into the stands, patterns become more visible, but it may be more difficult to have an immediate impact.

Bowen's model defocuses on symptoms in favor of systems dynamics. The treatment dis- courages therapists from trying to "fix" rela- tionships and instead encourages clients to begin a lifelong effort at self-discovery. This isn't, however, merely a matter of introspec- tion, but of actually making contact with the family. Clients are equipped for these journeys of self-discovery with tools for understanding their own patterns of emotional attachment and disengagement.

Seven techniques are most prominent in the practice of Bowenian family systems therapy:

1. *Genogram.* From his earliest NIMH days, Bowen used what he termed a "family diagram" to collect and organize important data concerning the multigenerational family system. In a 1972 publication Guerin renamed the family diagram the "genogram," a name that stuck. The main function of the genogram is to organize data during the evaluation phase and to track relationship processes and key triangles over the course of therapy. The most comprehensive guide to working with genograms is Monica McGoldrick and Randy Gerson's book, *Genograms in Family Assessment* (McGoldrick & Gerson, 1985).

2. *The Therapy Triangle.* This technique is based on the theoretical assumption that conflictual relationship processes within the family have activated key symptom-related triangles in an attempt to reestablish stability; and the family will automatically attempt to include the therapist in the triangling process. If they succeed, therapy will be stalemated. On the other hand, if the therapist can remain free of reactive emotional entanglements—in other words, stay detriangled—the family system and its members will calm down to the point where they can begin to work out solutions to their dilemmas.

In the treatment of couples, each spouse is asked a series of process questions aimed at toning down emotion and fostering objective observation and thought. Some effort is made to slow down the overfunctioner in the dyad, while engaging and making it safe for more distant underfunctioners to open up and get involved. This same technique can be used with child-centered families by having the therapist place himself or herself at the point of a potential triangle with the symptomatic child and each parent, as well as between the parents. (Notice how similar this is to structural family therapists' attempts to get enmeshed mothers to pull back, and disengaged fathers involved. See Chapter 7.)

3. *Relationship Experiments.* Relationship experiments are carried out around structural alterations in key triangles. The goal is to help family members become aware of systems processes—and learn to recognize their own role in them. Perhaps the best such experiments are those developed by Fogarty for use with emotional pursuers and distancers. Pursuers are encouraged to restrain their pursuit, stop making demands, and decrease pressure for emotional connection—and see what happens, in themselves and in the relationship. This exercise isn't designed to be a magic cure (as some people have hoped), but to help clarify the emotional processes involved. Distancers are encouraged to move toward the other person and communicate personal thoughts and feelings—in other words, to find an alternative to either avoiding or capitulating to the other's demands.

4. *Coaching.* Coaching is the Bowenian alternative to a more personal and emotionally involved role common to most other forms of therapy. By acting as coach, the Bowenian therapist hopes to avoid taking over for patients or becoming embroiled in family triangles. Coaching doesn't mean telling people what to do. It means asking process questions designed to help clients figure out family emotional processes and their role in them. The goal is increased understanding, increased self-focus, and more functional attachments to key family members.

5. *The I-Position.* Taking a personal stance—saying what you feel, instead of what others are "doing"—is one of the most direct ways to break cycles of emotional reactivity. It's the difference between saying "You're lazy" and "I wish you would help me more"; or between "You're always spoiling the children" and "I think we should be stricter with them." It's a big difference.

Bowenian therapists not only encourage clients to take I-positions, they also do so themselves. An example would be when after a family session the mother pulls the therapist aside and confides that her husband has terminal cancer, but she doesn't want the children to know. What to do? Take an I-position: Say to the mother: "I believe your children have a right to know about this." What she does, of course, is still up to her.

Another assumption in Bowenian therapy is that confrontation increases anxiety and decreases the ability to think clearly and see options. Therefore, displacing the focus, making it less personal and less threatening, is an excellent way to increase objectivity. This forms the basis for two related techniques, multiple family therapy and displacement stories.

6. *Multiple Family Therapy.*   In his version of multiple family therapy, Bowen worked with couples, taking turns focusing on first one, then another, and minimizing interaction. The idea is that one couple may learn more about emotional process by observing others—others in whom they are not so invested as to have their

vision clouded by feelings. James Framo uses a similar approach.

7. *Displacement Stories.*   This is Guerin's technique, showing films and videotapes and telling stories, to teach family members about systems functioning in a way that minimizes their defensiveness.

Finally, although students of family therapy are likely to evaluate different approaches according to how much sense they make and how useful they promise to be, Bowen himself considered his most important contribution to be showing the way to make human behavior a science. Far more important than methods and techniques of family therapy, Murray Bowen made profound contributions to our understanding of how we function as individuals, how we get along with our families, and how these are related.

—Recommended Readings

Anonymous. 1972. Differentiation of self in one's family. In *Family interaction,* J. Framo, ed. New York: Springer.

Bowen, M. 1978. *Family therapy in clinical practice.* New York: Jason Aronson.

Carter, E., and Orfanidis, M. M. 1976. Family therapy with one person and the family therapist's own family. In *Family therapy: Theory and practice,* P. J. Guerin, ed. New York: Gardner Press.

Fogarty, T. F. 1976. Systems concepts and dimensions of self. In *Family therapy: Theory and practice,* P. J. Guerin, ed. New York: Gardner Press.

Fogarty, T. F. 1976. Marital crisis. In *Family therapy: Theory and practice,* P. J. Guerin, ed. New York: Gardner Press.

Guerin, P. J., Fay, L., Burden, S., and Kautto, J. 1987. *The evaluation and treatment of marital conflict: A four-stage approach.* New York: Basic Books.

Guerin, P. J., Fogarty, T. F., Fay, L. F., and Kautto, J. G. 1996. *Working with relationship triangles: The one-two-three of psychotherapy.* New York: Guilford Press.

Guerin, P. J., and Pendagast, E. G. 1976. Evaluation of family system and geogram. In *Family therapy: Theory and practice,* P. J. Guerin, ed. New York: Gardner Press.

Kerr, M. E., and Bowen, M. 1988. *Family evaluation.* New York: Norton.

—References

Anonymous. 1972. Differentiation of self in one's family. In *Family interaction,* J. Framo, ed. New York: Springer.

Boer, F. 1990. *Sibling relationships in middle childhood.* Leiden, the Netherlands: DSWO Press.

Bowen, M. 1966. The use of family theory in clinical practice. *Comprehensive Psychiatry.* 7:345–374.

Bowen, M. 1971. Family therapy and family group therapy. In *Comprehensive group psychotherapy,* H. Kaplan and B. Sadock, eds. Baltimore: Williams & Wilkins.

Bowen, M. 1974. Toward the differentiation of self in one's family of origin. In *Georgetown Family Symposium,* Vol. 1, F. Andres and J. Lorio, eds. Washington, DC: Department of Psychiatry, Georgetown University Medical Center.

Bowen, M. 1975. Family therapy after twenty years. In *American handbook of psychiatry,* vol. 5, S. Arieti, ed. New York: Basic Books.

Bowen, M. 1976. Theory in the practice of psychotherapy. In *Family therapy: Theory and practice,* P. J. Guerin, ed. New York: Gardner Press.

Carter, B., and McGoldrick, M. 1980. *The family life cycle.* New York: Gardner Press.

Carter, B., and McGoldrick, M. 1988. *The changing family life cycle: A framework for family therapy.* 3rd ed. Boston: Allyn & Bacon.

Carter, E., and Orfanidis, M. M. 1976. Family therapy with one person and the family therapist's own family. In *Family therapy: Theory and practice,* P. J. Guerin, ed. New York: Gardner Press.

Fogarty, T. F. 1976a. Systems concepts and dimensions of self. In *Family therapy: Theory and practice,* P. J. Guerin, ed. New York: Gardner Press.

Fogarty, T. F. 1976b. Marital crisis. In *Family therapy: Theory and practice,* P. J. Guerin, ed. New York: Gardner Press.

Ford, D. H., and Urban, H. B. 1963. *Systems of psychotherapy.* New York: Wiley.

Glick, P. 1984. Marriage, divorce and living arrangements. *Journal of Family Issues.* 5(1):7–26.

Guerin, K., and Guerin, P. 2002. Bowenian family therapy. In *Theories and strategies of family therapy,* J. Carlson and D. Kjos, eds. Boston: Allyn & Bacon.

Guerin, P. J. 1971. A family affair. *Georgetown Family Symposium,* Vol. 1, Washington, DC.

Guerin, P. J. 1972. We became family therapists. In *The book of family therapy,* A. Ferber, M. Mendelsohn, and A. Napier, eds. New York: Science House.

Guerin, P. J., ed. 1976. *Family therapy: Theory and practice.* New York: Gardner Press.

Guerin, P. G., Fay, L., Burden, S., and Kautto, J. 1987. *The evaluation and treatment of marital conflict: A four-stage approach.* New York: Basic Books.

Guerin, P. J., and Fogarty, T. F. 1972. Study your own family. In *The book of family therapy,* A. Ferber, M. Mendelsohn, and A. Napier, eds. New York: Science House.

Guerin, P. J., Fogarty, T. F., Fay, L. F., and Kautto, J. G. 1996. *Working with relationship triangles: The one-two-three of psychotherapy.* New York: Guilford Press.

Herz, F., ed. 1991. *Reweaving the family tapestry.* New York: Norton.

Hill, R. 1970. *Family development in three generations.* Cambridge, MA: Schenkman.

Kerr, M. 1971. The importance of the extended family. *Georgetown Family Symposium,* Vol. 1, Washington, DC.

Kerr, M., and Bowen, M. 1988. *Family evaluation.* New York: Norton.

Lerner, H. G. 1985. *The dance of anger: A woman's guide to changing patterns of intimate relationships.* New York: Harper & Row.

Lerner, H. G. 1989. *The dance of intimacy: A woman's guide to courageous acts of change in key relationships.* New York: Harper & Row.

McGoldrick, M. 1990. Gender presentation. Article in progress.

McGoldrick, M., and Gerson, R. 1985. *Genograms in family assessment.* New York: Norton.

McGoldrick, M., Pearce, J., and Giordano, J. 1982. *Ethnicity in family therapy.* New York: Guilford Press.

McGoldrick, M., Preto, N., Hines, P., and Lee, E. 1990. Ethnicity in family therapy. In *The handbook of family therapy.* 2nd ed. A. S. Gurman and D. P. Kniskern, eds. New York: Brunner/ Mazel.

Nichols, M. P. 1986. *Turning forty in the eighties.* New York: Norton.

Nichols, M. P., and Zax, M. 1977. *Catharsis in psychotherapy.* New York: Gardner Press.

Nisbett, R. E., and Wilson, T. D. 1977. The halo effect: Evidence for unconscious alteration of judgments. *Journal of Personality and Social Psychology.* 35:250–256.

Rodgers, R. 1960. Proposed modification of Duvall's family life cycle stages. Paper presented at the American Sociological Association Meeting, New York.

Solomon, M. 1973. A developmental conceptual premise for family therapy. *Family Process. 12:* 179–188.

Sulloway, F. 1996. *Born to rebel.* New York: Pantheon.

Toman, W. 1969. *Family constellation.* New York: Springer.

Winer, L. R. 1971. The qualified pronoun count as a measure of change in family psychotherapy. *Family Process. 10:*243–247.

6

Strategic Family Therapy

Problem-Solving Therapy

With their compelling application of cybernetics and systems theory, strategic approaches captivated family therapy from the mid-1970s to the mid-1980s. Part of the appeal was their pragmatic, problem-solving focus; but there was also a fascination with strategies that could be designed to outwit resistance and provoke families into changing, with or without their cooperation. It was this second, more manipulative aspect that eventually turned family therapists against strategic therapy.

The dominant approaches of the 1990s elevated cognition over behavior and encouraged therapists to be collaborative rather than manipulative. Instead of trying to solve problems and provoke change, therapists began to reinforce solutions and inspire change. And so the once celebrated voices of strategic therapy—Jay Haley, John Weakland, Mara Selvini Palazzoli—have been virtually forgotten. Too bad, because their strategic approaches introduced two of the most powerful insights in all of family therapy: that family members often perpetuate problems by their own actions; and that directives tailored to the needs of a particular family can sometimes bring about sudden and decisive change.

Sketches of Leading Figures

Strategic therapy grew out of the **communications theory** developed in Bateson's schizophrenia project, which evolved into three distinct models: *MRI's brief therapy model, Haley and Madanes's strategic therapy,* and the *Milan systemic model.* The birthplace of all three was the Mental Research Institute (MRI), where strategic therapy was inspired by Gregory Bateson and Milton Erickson, the anthropologist and the alienist.

In 1952, funded by a Rockefeller Foundation grant to study paradox in communication, Bateson invited Jay Haley, John Weakland, Don Jackson, and William Fry to join him in Palo Alto. Their seminal project, which can be considered the intellectual birthplace of family therapy, led to the conclusion that the interchange of multilayered messages between people defined their relationships.

149

Under Bateson's influence the orientation was anthropological. Their goal was to observe, not change, families, and they stumbled into family therapy more or less by accident. Given Bateson's disinclination to change people, it's ironic that it was he who introduced project members to Milton Erickson. At a time when therapy was considered a laborious, long-term proposition, Erickson's experience as a hypnotherapist convinced him that people could change quickly, and he made therapy as brief as possible.

Many of what have been called *paradoxical techniques* came out of Erickson's application of hypnotherapeutic principles to turn resistance to advantage (Haley, 1981). For example, to induce trance a hypnotist learns not to point out that a person is fighting going under but, instead, might tell the person to keep his or her eyes open, "until they became unbearably heavy."

Don Jackson founded the Mental Research Institute in 1959 and assembled an energetic and creative staff including Jules Riskin, Virginia Satir, Jay Haley, John Weakland, Paul Watzlawick, Arthur Bodin, and Janet Beavin. After a few years, several of the staff members became fascinated with the pragmatic, problem-solving approach of Milton Erickson. This led Jackson to establish the Brief Therapy Project under the direction of Richard Fisch. The origi-

nal group included Arthur Bodin, Jay Haley, Paul Watzlawick, and John Weakland. What emerged was an active approach, focused on the presenting symptom and limited to ten sessions. This approach, known as the MRI model, was described by Watzlawick, Weakland, and Fisch (1974) in *Change: Principles of Problem Formation and Problem Resolution,* and later in a follow-up volume *The Tactics of Change: Doing Therapy Briefly* (Fisch, Weakland, & Segal, 1982), which remains the most comprehensive statement to date of the MRI model.

When Jackson died tragically in 1968 at the age of 48, he left a legacy of seminal papers, the leading journal in the field, *Family Process* (which he cofounded with Nathan Ackerman in 1962), and a great sadness at the passing of such a creative talent. The MRI group and the whole field suffered another painful loss in 1995 when John Weakland died of Lou Gehrig's disease.

Jay Haley was always something of an outsider. He entered the field without clinical credentials and established his reputation as a gadfly and critic. His initial impact came from his writing, in which he infused sarcasm with incisive analysis. In "The Art of Psychoanalysis" (Haley, 1963), Haley redefined psychoanalysis as a game of one-upmanship:

*M*ilton Erickson is the guiding genius behind the strategic approach to therapy.

> By placing the patient on a couch, the analyst gives the patient the feeling of having his feet up in the air and the knowledge that the analyst has both feet on the ground. Not only is the patient disconcerted by having to lie down while talking, but he finds himself literally below the analyst and so his one-down position is geographically emphasized. In addition, the analyst seats himself behind the couch where he can watch the patient but the patient cannot watch him. This gives the patient the kind of disconcerted feeling a person has when sparring with an opponent while blindfolded. Unable to see what response his ploys provoke, he is unsure when he is one-up and when one-down. Some patients try to solve this problem by saying

something like, "I slept with my sister last night," and then whirling around to see how the analyst is responding. These "shocker" ploys usually fail in their effect. The analyst may twitch, but he has time to recover before the patient can whirl fully around and see him. Most analysts have developed ways of handling the whirling patient. As the patient turns, they are gazing off into space, or doodling with a pencil, or braiding belts, or staring at tropical fish. It is essential that the rare patient who gets an opportunity to observe the analyst see only an impassive demeanor. (pp. 193–194)

After the Bateson project disbanded in 1962, Haley moved to MRI until 1967 when he joined Salvador Minuchin at the Philadelphia Child Guidance Clinic. It was there that Haley became interested in training and supervision, areas in which he made his greatest contribution (Haley, 1996). In 1976 Haley moved to Washington, DC, where he founded the Family Therapy Institute with Cloe Madanes. Madanes, known as one of the most creative therapists in the field, had previously worked at both MRI and the Philadelphia Child Guidance Clinic. In 1995 Haley moved back to California.

Haley and Madanes are such towering figures that their names often overshadow those who follow in their footsteps. James Keim in Colorado, who developed an innovative way of working with oppositional children, is ably carrying on the Haley–Madanes tradition. Other prominent practitioners of this model include Jerome Price in Michigan, who specializes in difficult adolescents, and Pat Dorgan, who combines strategic therapy with a community mental health model in Gloucester, Virginia.

The MRI model had a major impact on the Milan Associates, Mara Selvini Palazzoli, Luigi Boscolo, Gianfranco Cecchin, and Guiliana Prata. Selvini Palazzoli was a prominent Italian psychoanalyst, specializing in eating disorders, when, out of frustration with her psychoanalytic orientation (Selvini Palazzoli, 1981), she began to develop her own approach

to families. In 1967 she led a group of eight psychiatrists who turned to the ideas of Bateson, Haley, and Watzlawick, which led them to form the Center for the Study of the Family in Milan, where they developed the Milan systemic model.

When the Milan Associates came together in 1971, they invited Paul Watzlawick to serve as their consultant, but although the group followed the basic MRI model, they always insisted on seeing the whole family. The fundamental question they asked was "What kind of game is the family playing that maintains their symptoms?" Once they figured out the family's game, they disarmed resistance by offering a positive connotation to the game and then prescribed some kind of ritual to disarm it. What evolved was a clever, though somewhat formulaic set of procedures to reverse the family's problem-maintaining pattern.

In 1980 the Milan Associates underwent another split, with Boscolo and Cecchin moving toward training and Selvini Palazzoli and Prata remaining more interested in research. Each group formed separate centers with new staffs, and their approaches also diverged: the women pursued their interest in the destructive games in which they believed severely disturbed families were caught up, and the men grew increasingly less strategic and more interested in changing family belief systems through a process of asking questions. This shift away from interaction patterns and toward belief systems paved the way for the solution-focused and narrative approaches that dominated the 1990s.

Lynn Hoffman's evolution as a therapist parallels that of the strategic-systemic branch of family therapy. In the 1960s she collaborated with Haley, and in 1977 she joined the Ackerman Institute where she experimented with strategic approaches and later became a proponent of the Milan model (Hoffman, 1981). Subsequently, she left Ackerman for Amherst, Massachusetts, and left the Milan model for a "collaborative" approach based on social constructionist, narrative principles (see Chapter 13).

The Ackerman Institute has been an incubator for both the strategic and Milan models. Prominent contributors from the Ackerman faculty include Peggy Papp (1980, 1983), a creative force in the strategic school; Joel Bergman (1985), who developed many original strategies for dealing with difficult families; Peggy Penn (1982, 1985), who elaborated on the Milan innovation of circular questioning; and Olga Silverstein, known for her clinical artistry.

Karl Tomm (1984a, 1984b, 1987a, 1987b), a Canadian psychiatrist in Calgary, Alberta, had been the most prominent interpreter of the Milan model in North America. Recently, with the influence of Michael White's work (see Chapter 13), Tomm has been developing his own ideas about the impact of the therapist on families. Joseph Eron and Thomas Lund (1993, 1996), in Kingston, New York, have tried to bring strategic therapy up to date by integrating it with narrative approaches, based on constructionist principles. Finally, Richard Rabkin (1977), a literate and eclectic social psychiatrist practicing in New York City, was influenced by all the developers of strategic therapy, and in turn influenced them.

Theoretical Formulations

In *Pragmatics of Human Communication,* Watzlawick, Beavin, and Jackson (1967) sought to develop a calculus of human communication, which they stated in a series of axioms about the interpersonal implications of conversation. The first of these axioms is that *people are always communicating.* Since all behavior is communicative, and since one cannot *not* behave, then it follows that one cannot *not* communicate. Consider the following example.

Mrs. Rodriguez began by saying, "I just don't know what to do with Ramon anymore. He's not

doing well in school and he doesn't help out around the house. All he wants to do is hang with those awful friends of his. But the worst thing is that he refuses to communicate with us."

At this point, the therapist turned to Ramon and said, "Well, what do you have to say about all of this?" Ramon said nothing. Instead he continued to sit slouched in the far corner of the room, with an angry, sullen look on his face.

Ramon isn't "*not* communicating." He's communicating that he's angry and refuses to talk about it. Communication also takes place when it isn't intentional, conscious, or successful—that is, in the absence of mutual understanding.

The second axiom is that all messages have *report* and *command* functions (Ruesch & Bateson, 1951). The report (or content) of a message conveys information, while the command is a statement about the definition of the relationship. For example, the message, "Mommy, Sandy hit me!" conveys information but also implies a command—*Do something about it.* Notice, however, that the implicit command is ambiguous. The reason for this is that the printed word omits facial and contextual clues. This statement shrieked by a child in tears would have very different implications than if it were uttered by a giggling child.

In families, command messages are patterned as *rules* (Jackson, 1965), which can be deduced from observed redundancies in interaction. Jackson used the term **family rules** as a description of regularity, not regulation. Nobody "lays down the rules." In fact, families are generally unaware of them.

The rules, or regularities, of family interaction operate to preserve **family homeostasis** (Jackson, 1965, 1967). Homeostatic mechanisms bring families back to a previous equilibrium in the face of any disruption, and thus serve to resist change. Jackson's notion of family homeostasis describes the conservative aspect of family systems and is similar to the cybernetic concept of **negative feedback.** Thus, according to communications analysis, families operate as goal-directed, rule-governed systems.

Communications theorists didn't look for underlying motives; instead, they assumed circular causality and analyzed patterns of communications linked together in additive chains of stimulus and response as *feedback loops.* When the response to a family member's problematic behavior exacerbates the problem, that chain is seen as a *positive feedback loop.* The advantage of this formulation is that it focuses on interactions that perpetuate problems, which can be changed, instead of inferring underlying causes, which are often not subject to change.

●

Strategic therapists took the concept of the positive feedback loop and made it the centerpiece of their models. For the MRI group, this translated into a simple yet powerful principle of problem formation: Families encounter many difficulties over the course of their lives, but whether a difficulty becomes a "problem" (needing intervention) depends on how family members respond to it (Watzlawick, Weakland, & Fisch, 1974). That is, families often make commonsensical but misguided attempts to solve their difficulties and, on finding that the problem persists or gets worse, apply more-of-the-same attempted solutions. This only produces an escalation of the problem, which provokes more of the same, and so on—in a vicious cycle.

For example, if Jamal feels threatened by the arrival of a baby sister, he may become temperamental. If so, his father might think he's being defiant and try to get him to act his age by punishing him. But his father's harshness only confirms Jamal's belief that his parents love his sister more than him, and so he acts even younger. Father, in turn, becomes more critical and punitive, and Jamal becomes increasingly sullen and alienated. This is an es-

calating positive feedback loop: The family system is reacting to a deviation in the behavior of one of its members with feedback designed to dampen that deviation (*negative feedback*), but it has the effect of amplifying the deviation (*positive feedback*).

What's needed is to get father to reverse his solution. If he could comfort rather than criticize Jamal and help him see that he isn't being displaced, then Jamal might calm down. The system is governed, however, by unspoken rules that allow only one interpretation of Jamal's behavior—as disrespectful. For father to alter his solution, this rule would have to change.

In most families, there are unspoken rules governing all sorts of behavior. Where a rule promotes the kind of rigid attempted solutions described above, it isn't just the behavior but the rule that must change. When only a specific behavior within a system changes, this is **first-order change,** as opposed to **second-order change,** which occurs when the rules of the system change (Watzlawick et al., 1974). How does one change the rules? One way is through the technique of **reframing**—that is, changing father's interpretation of Jamal's behavior from disrespect to fear of displacement, from bad to sad.

Thus, the MRI approach to problems is elegantly simple: first, identify the positive feedback loops that maintain problems; second, determine the rules (or frames) that support those interactions; and third, find a way to change the rules.

Jay Haley added a functionalist emphasis to the cybernetic interpretation, with his interest in the interpersonal payoff of behavior. Later, he added many structural concepts picked up in the years he spent working with Minuchin in Philadelphia. For example, Haley might notice that whenever Jamal and his father quarrel, Jamal's mother protects him by criticizing father for being so harsh. Haley might also see Jamal becoming more agitated when mother criticizes father, trying to get his parents' attention off their conflicts and onto him.

Haley believes that the rules around the **hierarchy** in the family are crucial and finds inadequate parental hierarchies lurking behind most problems. Indeed, Haley (1976) suggests that, "an individual is more disturbed in direct proportion to the number of malfunctioning hierarchies in which he is embedded" (p. 117).

To counter a problem's payoff, Haley borrowed Erickson's technique of prescribing **ordeals,** so that the price for keeping a symptom outweighed that of giving it up. To illustrate, consider Erickson's famous maneuver of prescribing that an insomniac set his alarm every night to wake up and wax the kitchen floor. Haley tried to explain all therapy as based on ordeals, suggesting people will change to avoid the many ordeals inherent in being a client (Haley, 1984).

Cloe Madanes (1981, 1984) also emphasized the functional aspect of problems, particularly the rescuing operations involved when children use their symptoms to engage their parents. For example, when a daughter sees her mother looking depressed, the daughter can provoke a fight which prods the mother into taking charge. Much of Madanes's approach involves finding ways for symptomatic children to help their parents openly, so that they won't have to resort to symptoms as sacrificial offerings.

Like Haley, Mara Selvini Palazzoli and her associates (1978b) focused on the power-game aspect of family interactions and, similarly, on the protective function symptoms served for the whole family. They interviewed families about their history, sometimes over several generations, searching for evidence to confirm their hypotheses about how the children's symptoms came to be necessary. These hypotheses often involved elaborate networks of family alliances and coalitions. They usually concluded that the patient developed symptoms to protect one or more other family members so as to maintain the delicate network of extended family alliances.

Normal Family Development

According to **general systems theory,** normal families, like all living systems depend on two important processes (Maruyama, 1968). First, they must maintain integrity in the face of environmental challenges through *negative feedback.* No living system can survive without a coherent structure. On the other hand, too rigid a structure leaves systems ill equipped to adapt to changing circumstances. That's why normal families must also have mechanisms of *positive feedback.* Negative feedback resists disruptions to maintain a steady state; positive feedback amplifies innovations to accommodate to altered circumstances. Recognizing that the channel for positive feedback is communication, makes it possible to state the case more plainly: Healthy families are able to change because they communicate clearly and are adaptable.

The MRI group conscientiously opposed standards of normality: "As therapists, we do not regard any particular way of functioning, relating, or living as a problem if the client is not expressing discontent with it" (Fisch, 1978). Thus, by limiting their task to eliminating problems presented to them, the MRI group avoided taking any position regarding how families *should* behave.

The Milan Associates strove to maintain an attitude of "neutrality" (Selvini Palazzoli, Boscolo, Cecchin, & Prata, 1980). They didn't apply preconceived goals or normative models to their client families. Instead, by raising questions that helped families examine themselves and that exposed hidden power games, they trusted that families would reorganize in better ways on their own.

In contrast to the relativism of these two approaches, Haley's assessments *were* based on assumptions about sound family functioning. His therapy was designed to help families reorganize into more functional structures, with clear boundaries and generational hierarchy (Haley, 1976).

Development of Behavior Disorders

According to communications theory, the essential function of symptoms is to maintain the homeostatic equilibrium of family systems.[1] Symptomatic families were considered to be trapped in dysfunctional, homeostatic patterns of communication (Jackson & Weakland, 1961). These families cling to their rigid ways and respond to signs of change as negative feedback. That is, change is treated not as an opportunity for growth but as a threat, as the following example illustrates.

—Case Study—

Laban was a quiet boy, the only child of Orthodox Jewish parents from Eastern Europe. His parents left their small farming community to come to the United States where they both found factory work in a large city. Although they were now safe from religious persecution, the couple felt alien and out of synch with their new neighbors. They kept to themselves and took pleasure in raising Laban.

Laban was a frail child with a number of peculiar mannerisms, but to his parents he was perfect. Then he started school. Laban began to make friends with other children and, eager to be accepted, picked up a number of American habits. He chewed gum, watched cartoons, and rode his bicycle all over the neighborhood. His parents were annoyed by the gum chewing and by Laban's fondness for television, but they were genuinely distressed by his eagerness to play with gentile children. They may have come to

America to escape persecution, but not to embrace pluralism, much less assimilation. As far as they were concerned, Laban was rejecting their values—"Something must be wrong with him." By the time they called the child guidance clinic, they were convinced that Laban was disturbed, and they asked for help to "make Laban normal again."

Symptoms were seen as messages: "It is not I who does not (or does) want to do this, it is something outside my control—my nerves, my illness, my anxiety, my bad eyes, alcohol, my upbringing, the Communists, or my wife" (Watzlawick, Beavin, & Jackson, 1967, p. 80). As the Palo Alto group became more sophisticated, they tried to get past blaming parents for victimizing their children. Symptoms were no longer considered *caused* by communication problems in the family; they were seen as embedded in a pathological context, within which they might be the only available option. Among the forms of pathological communication identified were denying that one is communicating, disqualifying the other person's message, confusing levels of communication, discrepant punctuation of communication sequences, symmetrical escalation to competitiveness, rigid complementarity, and paradoxical messages.

A **paradox** is a contradiction that follows correct deduction from logical premises. In family communications, paradoxes usually take the form of *paradoxical injunctions*. A common example is to demand some behavior that by its very nature can only be spontaneous— "You should have more self-confidence." "Tell me you love me." "Be spontaneous!" A person exposed to such paradoxical injunctions is caught in an untenable position. To comply— to act spontaneous or self-confident—means to be self-consciously deliberate or eager to please. The only way to escape the dilemma is to step outside the context and comment on it, but such metacommunication rarely occurs in

---

1. The notion that symptoms are functional—implying that families *need* their problems—was to become controversial.

families. (It's hard to communicate about communication.)

Paradoxical communications are harmless in small doses, but when they take the form of **double binds** the consequences are malignant. In a double bind the two contradictory messages are on different levels of abstraction, and there is an implicit injunction against commenting on the discrepancy. A familiar example is the person who critizes others for not expressing their feelings but then attacks them when they do.

Continual exposure to paradoxical communication is like the dilemma of a dreamer caught in a nightmare. Nothing the dreamer tries to do in the dream works. The only solution is to step outside the context by waking up. Unfortunately, for people who live in a nightmare, it isn't always easy to wake up.

●

In strategic models there are three basic explanations of how problems develop. The first is cybernetic: Difficulties are turned into chronic problems by the persistence of misguided solutions, forming *positive-feedback escalations.* The second is structural: Problems are the result of *incongruous hierarchies.* The third is functional: Problems result when people try to protect or control one another covertly, so that their *symptoms serve a function for the system.* The MRI group limited itself to the first explanation, while Haley and the Milan associates embraced all three.

To clarify these differences, consider the following example: Sixteen-year-old Juwan recently began refusing to leave the house. An MRI therapist might ask his parents how they had tried to get him to venture out. The focus would be on the parents' attempted solution, on the assumption that this was likely to be maintaining Juwan's refusal, and on their explanation or "frame" for Juwan's behavior, believing that their framing of the problem might be driving their false solution.

A Haley-style therapist might be interested in the parents' attempted solutions but would also inquire about their marriage, the ways in which Juwan was involved in struggles between them or other family members, and the possible protective nature of Juwan's problem. This therapist would be acting on the assumption that Juwan's behavior might be part of a dysfunctional triangle. The therapist might further assume that this triangular pattern was fueled by unresolved conflicts between the parents. Madanes would also be interested in this triangle but, in addition, would be curious about how Juwan's behavior might be protecting his parents from having to face some threatening issue.

A Milan systemic therapist wouldn't focus so much on attempted solutions but, instead, would ask about past and present relationships in the family. In so doing, the therapist would be trying to uncover a network of power alliances, often running across generations, that constituted the family's "game." Some such game left Juwan in the position of having to use his symptoms to protect other family members. The family might reveal, for example, that if Juwan were to grow up and leave home, his mother would be sucked back into a power struggle between her parents, which she had avoided by having a symptomatic child. Also, by not succeeding in life, Juwan might be protecting his father from the shame of having a child who exceeded him in accomplishment, just as he had done with his father.

The essential insight of the strategic model is that problems are often maintained by self-defeating patterns of behavior. By adding a structural perspective to this largely behavioral position, Haley pointed out that such self-defeating patterns may be imbedded in dysfunctional family organizations. Not only must families have an effective hierarchal organization—with the parents firmly in charge—but families must also modify their organization to accommodate changes in the lives of family members.

Problems, according to Haley (1976, 1980), are often maintained by a faulty hierarchy within the family. Thus, when dealing with problems in children, Haley will align with and support the parents. Haley (1986) also believes that the presenting problem is often a metaphor for the actual problem. A man who is neurotically worried about his heart may be covertly expressing unhappiness with his marriage; a woman's agoraphobia may be both a symptom of and an attempt to deal with problems in her relationship with her adult children.

Haley also pointed out that symptoms often develop when a family becomes stuck at a transition in the life cycle (Haley, 1973). The problem, then, is not the identified patient but rather that the family has somehow failed to reorganize in order to move on to the next stage of the life cycle. Haley (1980) eventually focused on the *leaving home stage* as often the most problematical one for families.

Goals of Therapy

The MRI group is proudly minimalistic. Once the presenting problem is resolved, therapy is concluded. Even where other problems are apparent to the therapist, if the family doesn't ask for help with those problems, they aren't targeted. MRI therapists justify this minimalist position by asserting that, because they view people who have problems as stuck rather than sick, their job is simply to help them get moving again, not to overhaul their family structures.

MRI therapists pride themselves on helping families define clear and reachable goals so that everyone knows when and how successfully treatment has concluded. They often find that much of the therapy takes place simply in the process of pushing clients to set clear behavioral goals, because in doing so clients are forced to clarify vague dissatisfactions. Also, in getting clients to define achievable goals, MRI therapists

help people let go of utopian aspirations, which are bound to lead to disappointment.

The MRI model is behavioral, both in its goals and its focus on observable patterns of interaction, while scrupulously avoiding speculation about intrapsychic intentions. In trying to achieve the larger goal of problem-resolution, the immediate goal is to change the behavioral responses of people to their problems. More specifically, as described earlier, MRI therapists try to interrupt (often to reverse) more-of-the-same vicious feedback loops. To achieve this behavioral change they may try to "reframe the problem," and, in that sense, introduce a cognitive element. But any cognitive change still is in the service of the primary goal of behavior change.

Haley's approach is also behavioral and, even more than the MRI group, downplays the importance of insight. He was always scornful of therapies that helped clients understand why they did things but did little to get them to do something different. Haley's ultimate goal is often a structural reorganization of the family, particularly its hierarchy and generational boundaries. Unlike with structural family therapy, however, these structural goals are always directly connected to the presenting problem. For example, to improve the relationship between the polarized parents of a rebellious teenager, a structural therapist might get the parents to talk about their marital problems, where Haley would have them talk instead about their difficulty working together to deal with their rebellious son. Only after the problems with their son had improved would Haley allow their discussion to shift to the marriage.

Haley's inclination to divide therapy into stages extended to specific sessions. He recommended a first-session format that included several stages: a social stage in which the goal is to make the family feel comfortable; a stage in which the problem is defined and family members' opinions about it are solicited; and a stage in which family members talk with each other about the problem (1976).

Haley's interest in stages and his systematic approach reflects the strategic therapist's ethic that responsibility for change rests with the therapist. Strategic therapists believe that therapists shouldn't blame treatment failures on their clients' lack of motivation, but instead should find ways to motivate them. With this conviction comes the responsibility to develop specialized techniques for all kinds of problems.

Madanes (1990) expanded the goals of strategic therapy beyond problem-focused or even structural goals to include growth-oriented objectives like balance, harmony, and love. She stated that, "A goal of therapy is to bring harmony and balance into people's lives. To love and to be loved, to find fulfillment in work, to play and enjoy: All are part of a necessary balance" (p. 13). While her practice is still strategic, this is a big departure from the standard goals of strategic therapy and brings Madanes closer to Satir and other experientialists. Indeed, the name of her therapy has shifted to "strategic humanism" to emphasize its softer aspects.

It's in the area of goals of and responsibility for therapy that strategic and Milan therapies eventually diverged. The early work of the Milan group (Selvini Palazzoli, Boscolo, Cecchin, & Prata, 1978b) was heavily influenced by the MRI and Haley models. The Milan associates expanded the network of people involved in maintaining the problem, but were still primarily interested in finding ways to interrupt family games. The techniques they developed differed from those of the strategic schools in that they were less behavioral and instead were designed to expose games and reframe motives for strange behavior. Thus, while being less problem-focused and more interested in changing a family's awareness or beliefs than strategic therapists, the original Milan approach was no less manipulative: the responsibility for change rested

on the therapist whose job it was to outwit resistance.

When the Milan associates split into two groups in the early 1980s, this strategic emphasis remained with Selvini Palazzoli and the groups she subsequently formed. She, however, took a low profile during the 1980s while she researched her hypotheses and developed a new strategic approach (Selvini Palazzoli, 1986). The goal of that therapy was to disrupt and expose the "dirty games" that severely disturbed family members play with each other. Later, she abandoned brief, strategic models altogether and now does long-term therapy with more focus on insight for the individual patient (Selvini, 1993).

After the break up of the Milan group, Luigi Boscolo and Gianfranco Cecchin moved away from strategically manipulating families and toward collaborating with them to form systemic hypotheses about their problems. Therapy became more of a research expedition that the therapist entered without specific goals or strategies, trusting that the process of self-examination would allow families to choose to change rather than continuing their unproductive patterns. The therapist was released from responsibility for any certain outcome and adopted an attitude of "curiosity" (Cecchin, 1987) toward families, rather than the interventive attitude of strategic therapists.

By moving in this direction, Boscolo and Cecchin took a position relative to therapist goals and attitudes directly opposite to that of their strategic predecessors. This collaborative philosophy became the bridge over which many other strategic and Milan therapists crossed into the narrative approaches of the 1990s.

Conditions for Behavior Change

In the early days of family therapy the goal was simply to improve communication. Later the goal was refined to altering specific patterns of communication that maintained problems: "We see the resolution of problems as primarily requiring a substitution of behavior patterns so as to interrupt the vicious, positive feedback circles" (Weakland, Fisch, Watzlawick, & Bodin, 1974, p. 149).

A therapist can either point out problematic sequences or simply manipulate them to effect therapeutic change. The first strategy relies on the power of insight and depends on a willingness to change. The second does not; it is an attempt to beat families at their own games, with or without their cooperation.

Jackson and Haley's work was influenced by the hypnotherapy they learned from Milton Erickson. The hypnotist works by giving instructions whose purpose is often obscure. Haley (1961) recommended asking uncooperative patients to do something in order to provoke a rebellious response, which served to make them concede that they were relating to the therapist. He mentions, as an example, directing a schizophrenic patient to hear voices. If the patient hears voices, then he is complying with the therapist's request; if he doesn't hear voices, he can no longer claim to be crazy.

Haley's (1961) direction to hear voices illustrates the technique of *prescribing the symptom.* By instructing a patient to enact symptomatic behavior the therapist is demanding that something "involuntary" be done voluntarily. This **paradoxical injunction** forces one of two outcomes. Either the patient performs the symptom and thus admits it isn't involuntary, or the patient gives up the symptom.

●

For the MRI school the primary condition for resolving problems is to change the behavior associated with them. It's believed that through seeing the results of altering rigid behavioral responses, clients will become more flexible in their problem-solving strategies. When this happens, clients achieve a second-order change—a change in the rules governing their response to problems.

For example, Lateesha argues with her father about her curfew and her father grounds her. She then runs away and stays with a friend. A first-order intervention at this point might be to help Lateesha's father find a more effective punishment to tame this out-of-control child. A second-order strategic intervention might be to direct the father to act distracted and sad around his daughter, implying that he has given up trying to control her. This shifts Lateesha from feeling trapped by father to feeling concerned about him, and she becomes more reasonable. Her father learns that when attempted solutions aren't working, try something different. This change is second-order in that it is a change in the rules governing the way father and daughter interact.

Haley (1976) believed that telling people what they're doing wrong only mobilizes resistance. He believed that changes in behavior alter perceptions, rather than the other way around. Madanes (1980) said "if a problem can be solved without the family's knowing how or why, that is satisfactory" (p. 79).

The Milan group turned this behaviorism on its head. They were more interested in getting families to *see* things differently (through a reframing technique called "positive connotation," to be discussed later) than in getting family members to *behave* differently. This shift from behavior to meaning set the stage for the constructivist and narrative movements (see Chapters 4 and 13).

Therapy

Assessment

Formal assessment was typically not a part of communications therapy, although Watzlawick (1966) did introduce a *structured family interview.* In this procedure, families were given five tasks to complete, including:

1. Deciding their main problem
2. Planning a family outing
3. Parents discussing how they met
4. Discussing the meaning of a proverb
5. Identifying faults and placing the blame on the correct person

While the family worked on these tasks, the therapist observed the family's patterns of communication, methods of decision making, and scapegoating. Although useful for research, the structured family interview never gained acceptance as a clinical tool.

Remember that the MRI model is based on two interlocking assumptions:

1. [T]he problems people bring to psychotherapists persist only if they are maintained by ongoing current behavior of the client and others with whom he interacts.
2. Correspondingly, if such problem-maintaining behavior is appropriately changed or eliminated, the problem will be resolved. (Weakland, Fisch, Watzlawick, & Bodin, 1974, p. 144)

Thus the MRI assessment consists of defining the problem and finding out what people have done to try to resolve it.

The first step is to get a very specific, behavioral picture of the complaint, who sees it as a problem, and why it's a problem now. When a therapist asks, "What is the problem that brings you here today," many clients reply ambiguously: "We don't communicate," "We think our fourteen-year-old is depressed," or "Clarence seems to be hyperactive." The MRI therapist then inquires about exactly what these complaints mean. "We don't communicate" might mean "My son argues with everything I say," or "My husband hides behind the newspaper and never talks to me." "Depressed" might mean sad and withdrawn or sullen and disagreeable; "hyperactive" might mean disobediant or unable to concentrate. A useful de-

vice is to ask, "If we had a videotape of this, what would it look like?"

Once the problem has been defined, the therapist tries to determine who has tried to solve it and how. Sometimes the attempted solution seems obviously to have made things worse. For example, the wife who nags her husband to spend more time with her is likely to succeed only in driving him further away. Likewise the parents who punish their son for fighting with his sister may convince him that they do like her better. Or the husband who does everything his wife asks in order to keep the peace may become so resentful that he starts to hate her.

Haley's assessment begins with a careful definition of the problem, expressed from the point of view of every member of the family. But, unlike the MRI group, Haley also observes how family members interact in the session to explore the possibility that structural arrangements in the family may be contributing to their problems—especially pathological triangles or "cross-generational coalitions." As Haley has said, "Problem children tend to determine what happens in families, which makes for hierarchical difficulties" (Haley, 1996, p. 96).

In addition to structural problems, Haley and Madanes also consider the possible interpersonal payoff of problem behavior. According to Haley the apparent helplessness of a patient often turns out to be a significant source of power in relation to others whose lives are often dominated by the demands and fears of the symptomatic person. A schizophrenic who refuses to take his medication might, for example, be seen as trying to avoid having to go to work. While it's not necessary to decide what is or isn't a real illness, Haley tends to assume that all symptomatic behavior is voluntary. Sometimes this is a crucial distinction—as, for example, in cases of drug addiction or "losing one's temper."

In the Milan model, assessment begins with a preliminary hypothesis, which is then explored and confirmed or disconfirmed in the initial session. These hypotheses are generally based on the assumption that the identified patient's problems were serving a homeostatic or protective function for the family. Therefore assessment of the presenting problem and the family's response to it, is based on questions designed to explore the family as a set of interconnected relationships. For example, the reply to a question like, "Who has been more worried about this problem, you or your wife?" will suggest a hypothesis about the closeness and distance of family members. The ultimate goal of assessment is to achieve a systemic perspective on the problem.

Therapeutic Techniques

Most of the actual techniques of communications therapy consisted of teaching rules of communication and manipulating interactions through a variety of strategic maneuvers. The progression of these approaches from straightforward to strategic reflected the growing awareness of how families resist change.

After their opening remarks, therapists asked family members, usually one at a time, to discuss their problems. The therapist listened but concentrated on the process, rather than content, of communication. When someone spoke in a confused or confusing way, the therapist would point this out and insist on certain rules of clear communication. Satir (1964) was the most straightforward teacher. When someone said something that was unclear, she would question and clarify the message, and as she did she impressed on the family basic guidelines for clear speaking.

One rule is that people should always speak in the first person singular when saying what they think or feel. For example:

Husband: We always liked Celia's boyfriends.

Therapist: I'd like you to speak for yourself; later your wife can say what she thinks.

Husband: Yes, but we've always agreed on these things.

Therapist: Perhaps, but you are the expert on how you feel. Speak for yourself, and let your wife speak for herself.

A similar rule is that opinions and value judgments should be acknowledged as that, not passed off as facts or general principles. Owning personal perspectives, as such, is a necessary step to discussing them in a way that permits legitimate differences of opinion.

Wife: People shouldn't want to do things without their children.

Therapist: So you like to bring the kids along when you and your husband go out?

Wife: Well yes, doesn't everybody?

Husband: I don't. I'd like to go out, just the two of us, once in a while.

Another rule is that people should speak directly to, not about, each other. This avoids ignoring or disqualifying family members and prevents the establishment of destructive coalitions. For example:

Teenager: (To therapist) My mother always has to be right. Isn't that so, Dad?

Therapist: Would you say that to her?

Teenager: I have, but she doesn't listen.

Therapist: Tell her again.

Teenager: (To therapist) Oh, okay. (To mother) Sometimes I get the feeling . . . (Shifts back to therapist) Oh, what's the use!

Therapist: I can see how hard it is, and I guess you've decided that it's no use trying to talk to your mom if she isn't going to listen. But in here, I hope we can learn to speak more directly to each other, so that no one will give up on having his or her say.

As this exchange illustrates, it's difficult to teach people to communicate clearly just by telling them how. It seemed like a good idea, but it didn't work very well. In recognizing that families frequently don't respond to direct advice, Jay Haley began to focus more on the family patterns underlying communication problems and to use more indirect means of influence.

In *Strategies of Psychotherapy*, Haley (1963) described the marital relationship in terms of conflicting levels of communication. Conflicts occur not only over what rules a couple will follow in dealing with each other, but also over who sets the rules.[2] One of Haley's strategies was to make explicit the implicit rules that govern family relationships. Dysfunctional rules made explicit become more difficult to follow. For example, some people berate their partners for not expressing themselves, but they talk so much and criticize so loudly that the partners hardly have a chance to speak. If the therapist points this out, it becomes more difficult to follow the implicit rule that one person should only say what the other one wants to hear.

Some of Haley's directives were for changes that seemed so small that the full ramifications weren't immediately apparent. For one couple, for example, in which the husband seemed to have his own way most of the time, the wife was asked to say "no" on some minor issue once during the week. This may seem trivial, but it accomplished two things: It made the wife practice speaking up, and it made the husband aware that he'd been domineering.

Haley's use of directives to manipulate changes in the way families were organized was the pivotal step in the evolution of communications therapy into strategic therapy. Although strategic therapists shared a belief in the need for indirect methods to induce change in families, they developed distinctly different techniques for doing so, which we will therefore examine separately.

---

2.   Recognizing the cybernetic principle in a home heating system may be easier than agreeing on who gets to set the temperature.

The MRI Approach.   The MRI model follows a six-step treatment procedure:

1. Introduction to the treatment setup
2. Inquiry and definition of the problem
3. Estimation of the behavior maintaining the problem
4. Setting goals for treatment
5. Selecting and making behavioral interventions
6. Termination

Once the preliminaries are concluded, the therapist asks for a clear definition of the major problem. If a problem is stated in vague terms, such as "We just don't seem to get along," or in terms of presumptive causes, such as "Dad's job is making him depressed," the therapist helps translate it into a clear and concrete goal, asking questions like "What will be the first small sign that things are getting better?"

Once the problem and goals are defined, MRI therapists inquire about attempted solutions, which might be maintaining the problem. In general, the solutions that tend to perpetuate problems fall into one of three categories:

1. The solution is simply to deny that a problem exists; action is necessary, but not taken. For instance, parents do nothing despite growing evidence that their teenage son is heavily involved with drugs.

2. The solution is an effort to solve something that isn't really a problem; action is taken when it shouldn't be. For example, parents punish a child for masturbating.

3. The solution is an effort to solve a problem within a framework that makes a solution impossible; action is taken, but at the wrong level. For instance, a husband buys increasingly expensive gifts for his unhappy wife, when what she wants is affection.

These three classes of problem-maintaining solutions imply therapeutic strategies. In the first, clients need to act; in the second, to stop acting; and in the third, to act in a different way. Once the therapist conceives of a strategy for changing the problem-maintaining sequence, clients must be convinced of the value of following this strategy. To sell their directives, MRI therapists *reframe* the problem to increase the likelihood of compliance. Thus a therapist might tell an angry teenager that when his father punishes him, it's the only way his father knows how to show his love.

As described earlier, to interrupt problem-maintaining sequences, strategic therapists may try to get family members to do something that runs counter to common sense. Such counterintuitive techniques have been called *paradoxical interventions* because it seems paradoxical that people must sometimes do things in apparent opposition to their goals in order to reach those goals (Haley, 1973; Watzlawick, Weakland, & Fisch, 1974).

For example, Watzlawick and his colleagues (1974) described a young couple who were bothered by their parents' tendency to treat them like children by doing everything for them. Despite the husband's adequate salary, the parents continued to send money and lavish gifts on them, refused to let them pay even part of a restaurant check, and so on. The strategic team helped the couple solve their difficulty with their doting parents by having them become *less* rather than more competent. Instead of trying to show the parents that they didn't need help, the couple was told to act helpless and dependent, so much so that the parents got disgusted and finally backed off.

The techniques most commonly thought of as paradoxical are symptom prescriptions in which a family is told to continue or embellish the behavior they complain about. In some contexts, such a prescription might be made with the hope that the family will try to comply with it, and thereby be forced to reverse their attempted solutions. If Jorge, who is sad, is told to try to become depressed several times a day and his family is asked to encourage him to be sad,

then they will no longer try ineffectively to cheer him up, and he won't feel guilty for not being happy.

At other times, a therapist might prescribe the symptom while secretly hoping that the clients will rebel against this directive. The therapist might encourage Jorge to continue to be depressed because, in doing so, he's helping his brother (with whom Jorge is competitive) feel superior.

At still other times, the therapist might prescribe the symptom with the hope that in doing so the network of family relationships that maintain the problem will be exposed. The therapist says that Jorge should remain depressed because that way he can continue to keep his mother's attention, which will keep her from looking to father for affection, since father is still emotionally involved with his own mother, and so on.

To preclude power struggles, MRI therapists avoid assuming an authoritarian position. Their *one-down stance* implies equality and invites clients to reduce anxiety and resistance. Although some strategists adopt a one-down position disingenuously, this modest stance was consistent with the late John Weakland's own unassuming character. While sitting clouded in the smoke of his pipe, Weakland discouraged families from trying to change too fast, warning them to go slowly and worrying out loud about the possibility of relapse when improvements did occur. This **restraining** technique reinforced the therapist's one-down position.

The Haley and Madanes Approach. Jay Haley's approach is harder to describe because it's tailored to address the unique requirements of each case. If "strategic" implies systematic, as in the MRI approach, it also implies artful, which is especially true of Haley's strategies. As with other strategic approaches, the definitive technique is the use of **directives.** But Haley's directives aren't simply ploys to outwit families or reverse what they're doing. Rather, they are thoughtful suggestions targeted to the specific requirements of the case.

Haley (1976) believes that if therapy is to end well, it must begin properly. Therefore, he devotes a good deal of attention to the opening moves of treatment. Regardless of who is presented as the official patient, Haley begins by interviewing the entire family, or as much of it as can be assembled. His approach to this initial interview follows four stages: a social stage, a problem stage, an interaction stage, and finally a goal-setting stage.

Families are often defensive when they come to therapy for the first time. Family members may not know why they're there or what to expect, and they may be afraid that the therapist will blame them for the problem. Therefore, Haley uses the initial minutes of a first session to help everyone relax. He makes a point of greeting each family member and trying to make sure they're comfortable. He acts as a host, making sure that his guests feel welcome.

After the *social stage,* Haley gets down to business in the *problem stage,* asking each person to give his or her perspective on the problem. Since mothers are usually more central than fathers, Haley recommends speaking first to the father in order to increase his involvement. This suggestion nicely illustrates Haley's strategic maneuvering, which begins with the first contact and characterizes all subsequent meetings.

Haley listens carefully to the way each family member describes the problem and his or her involvement in it, making sure that no one interrupts until each has had a turn. During this phase, Haley looks for clues about triangles and hierarchy, but he discourages therapists from making any comments about these observations because this might make the family defensive.

Once everyone has had a chance to speak, Haley encourages them to discuss their points of view among themselves. In this, the *interactional stage,* the therapist can observe, rather

than just hear about, the interchanges that surround the problem. As they talk, Haley looks for coalitions between family members against others. How functional is the hierarchy? Do the parents work well together, or do they undercut each other? During this stage, the therapist is like an anthropologist, trying to discover patterns in the family's actions.

Sometimes Haley ends the first session by giving the family a task. In subsequent sessions, directives play a central role. Effective directives don't usually take the form of simple advice, which is rarely helpful because problems usually persist for a reason.

The following two tasks are taken from Haley's *Problem-Solving Therapy.* One couple, who were out of the habit of being affectionate with each other, were told to behave affectionately "to teach their child how to show affection." In another case, a mother who was unable to control her twelve-year-old son had decided to send him away to military school. Haley suggested that since the boy had no idea how tough life would be at military school, it would be a good idea for the mother to help prepare him. They both agreed. Haley directed her to teach the boy how to stand at attention, be polite, and wake up early every morning to make his bed. The two of them followed these instructions as if playing a game, with mother as sergeant and son as private. After two weeks

*J*ay Haley tailors directives to fit the needs of specific clients and their problems.

Cloe Madanes's "pretend techniques" are a clever way to help break control-and-rebel cycles.

the son was behaving so well that his mother no longer felt it necessary to send him away.

Madanes (1981) used the observation that people will often do something they wouldn't ordinarily do if it's framed as play, to develop a whole range of **pretend techniques.** One such strategy is to ask a symptomatic child to pretend to have the symptom and encourage the parents to pretend to help. The child can give up the actual symptom now that pretending to have it is serving the same family function. The following two cases summarized from Madanes (1981) illustrate the pretend technique.

—Case Study—

In the first case, a mother sought therapy because her ten-year-old son had night terrors. Madanes suspected that the boy was concerned about his mother, who was poor, spoke little English, and had lost two husbands. Since the boy had night terrors, the therapist asked all the members of the family to describe their dreams. Only the mother and the son had nightmares. In the mother's nightmare someone was breaking into the house. In the boy's, he was being attacked by a witch. When Madanes asked what the mother did when the boy had nightmares, she said that she took him into her bed and told him to pray to God. She explained that she thought his nightmares were the work of the devil.

Madanes's conjecture was that the boy's night terrors were both a metaphorical expression of the mother's fears and an attempt to help her. As long as the boy was afraid,

his mother had to be strong. Unfortunately, while trying to protect him, she frightened him further by talking about God and the devil. Thus, both mother and child were helping each other in unproductive ways.

The family members were told to pretend that they were home and mother was afraid that someone might break in. The son was asked to protect his mother. In this way the mother had to pretend to need the child's help instead of really needing it. At first the family had difficulty playing the scene because the mother would attack the make-believe thief before the son could help. Thus she communicated that she was capable of taking care of herself and didn't need the son's protection. After the scene was performed correctly, with the son attacking the thief, they all discussed the performance. The mother explained that it was difficult to play her part because she was a competent person who could defend herself. Madanes sent the family home with the task of repeating this dramatization every evening for a week. If the son started screaming during his sleep, his mother was to wake him up and replay the scene. They were told that this was important to do no matter how late it was or how tired they were. The son's night terrors soon disappeared.

—Case Study—

In the second case, a mother sought psychiatric treatment for her five-year-old because he had uncontrollable temper tantrums. After talking with the family for a few minutes Madanes asked the boy to show her what his tantrums were like by pretending to have one. "Okay," he said, "I'm the Incredible Hulk!" He puffed out his chest, flexed his muscles, made a monster face, and started screaming and kicking the furniture. Madanes asked the mother to do what she usually did in such circumstances. The mother responded by telling her son, in a weak and ineffective way, to calm down. She pretended to send him to another room as she tried to do at home. Next, Madanes asked the mother if the boy was doing a good job of pretending. She said that he was.

Madanes asked the boy to repeat the scene. This time he was Frankenstein and his tantrum was performed with a rigid posture and a grimacing face. Then Madanes talked with the boy about the Incredible Hulk and Frankenstein and congratulated the mother for raising such an imaginative child.

Following this discussion, mother and son were told to pretend that he was having a tantrum while she was walking him to his room. The boy was told to act like the Incredible Hulk and to make lots of noise. Then they were told to pretend to close the door and hug and kiss. Next Madanes instructed the mother to pretend that *she* was having a tantrum, and the boy was to hug and kiss her. Madanes instructed mother and son to perform both scenes every morning before school and every afternoon when the boy came home. After every performance the mother was to give the boy milk and cookies, if he did a good job. Thus the mother was moved from a helpless position to one of authority in which she was in charge of rewarding her son's make-believe performance. The next week the mother called to say that they didn't need to come for therapy because the boy was behaving very well and his tantrums had ceased.

Haley (1984) returned to his Ericksonian roots in a book called *Ordeal Therapy*, a collection of case studies in which **ordeals** were prescribed to make symptoms more trouble than they're worth. "If one makes it more difficult for a person to have a symptom than to give it up, the person will give up the symptom" (p. 5). For example, a standard ordeal is for a client to have to get up in the middle of the night and exercise strenuously whenever he or she had symptoms during that day. Another example might be for the client to have to give a present to someone with whom he or she has a poor relationship—for example, a mother-in-law or ex-spouse—each time the symptoms occur.

Haley also used ordeals to restructure families. For example, a sixteen-year-old boy put a variety of items up his behind and then expelled them, leaving his stepmother to clean up the mess. Haley (1984) arranged that, after each such episode, the father had to take his son to their backyard and have the boy dig a hole three feet deep and three feet wide, in which he was to bury all the things he was putting up his rear end. After a few weeks of this, Haley reported that the symptom stopped, the father became more involved with his son, and the stepmother became closer to the father.

The current form of Haley/Madanes therapy, called *strategic humanism*, still involves giving directives based on hypotheses the therapist generates. In this, strategic humanism isn't in step with the contemporary trend in family therapy toward collaborative approaches. The directives they deliver, however, are more oriented toward increasing family members' abilities to soothe and love than to gain control over one another. This represents a major shift and *is* in synch with family therapy's shift away from the power elements of hierarchy and toward finding ways to increase harmony. The expression of emotions such as repentance, sorrow, love, and empathy is a larger part of this new form of strategic therapy than existed in former versions. The strategic therapist, too, has been humanized. The expression of empathy for clients is given as much weight as the ability to design effective directives.

An excellent example of strategic humanism's combination of compassion and technology is James Keim's work with oppositional children (Keim, 1998). Keim begins by reassuring anxious parents that they aren't to blame for their children's oppositionalism. Next he explains that there are two sides of parental authority—discipline and nurture. To reinforce the parents' authority while avoiding power struggles, Keim encourages them to concentrate on being sympathetic and supportive for a while. The parent who soothes a child with the forgotten language of understanding is every bit as much in charge as one who tries to tell the child what to do. After progress has been made in calming the child down—especially in breaking the pattern by which oppositional children control the mood in the family by arguing with anything their parents say—Keim coaches the parents to post rules and enforce consequences. This strategy puts parents back in charge of unruly children without the kind of high-intensity melodrama that usually attends work with this population.

The Milan Model. The original Milan model was ultra-strategic and formulaic. Families were treated by male-female cotherapists and observed by other members of a therapy team. The standard format had five parts: the *presession*, the *session*, the *intersession*, the *intervention*, and the *postsession discussion*. As Boscolo, Cecchin, Hoffman, and Penn (1987) describe:

> During the presession the team came up with an initial hypothesis about the family's presenting problem. . . . During the session itself, the team members would validate, modify, or change the hypothesis. After about forty minutes, the entire team would meet alone to discuss the hypothesis and arrive at an intervention. The treating therapists would then go back to deliver the intervention to the family, either by positively connoting the problem situation or by a ritual to be done by the family that commented on the problem situation and was designed to introduce change. . . . Finally, the team would meet for a postsession discussion to analyze the family's reactions and to plan for the next session. (p. 4)

As indicated in this description, the primary intervention was either a ritual or a positive connotation. The **positive connotation** was the most distinctive innovation to emerge from the Milan model. Derived from the MRI technique of reframing the symptom as serving a protective function—for example, Carlo needs to continue to be depressed to distract his parents from their marital issues—the positive connotation avoided the implication that family members benefited from the patient's symptoms. This implication made for resistance that the Milan team found could be circumvented if the patient's behavior was construed not as protecting specific people but as preserving the family's overall harmony. Indeed, every family

member's behavior was often connoted in this system-serving way.

The treatment team would hypothesize about how the patient's symptom fit into the family system and, after a mid-session break, the therapists would deliver this hypothesis to the family, along with the injunction that they should not try to change. Carlo should continue to sacrifice himself by remaining depressed as a way to reassure the family that he will not become an abusive man like his grandfather. Mother should maintain her overinvolvement with Carlo as a way to make him feel valued while he sacrifices himself. Father should continue to criticize mother and Carlo's relationship so that mother will not be tempted to abandon Carlo and become a wife to her husband.

Rituals were used to engage the whole family in a series of actions that ran counter to, or exaggerated, rigid family rules and myths. For example, one family, which was enmeshed with their large extended family, was told to hold family discussions behind locked doors every other night after dinner during which each family member was to speak for fifteen minutes about the family. Meanwhile they were to redouble their allegiance and courtesy to the other members of the clan. By exaggerating the family's loyalty to the extended family while simultaneously breaking that loyalty's rule by meeting apart from the clan and talking about it, the family could examine and break the rule that perpetuated their dysfunctional system.

Rituals were also used to dramatize the positive connotation. For example, each family member might have to express his or her gratitude each night to the patient for having the problem (Boscolo et al., 1987). The Milan group also devised a set of rituals based on an "odd and even days" format (Selvini Palazzoli et al., 1978a). For example, a family in which the parents were deadlocked over parental control might be told that on even days of the week father should be in charge of the patient's behavior and mother should act as if she wasn't there. On odd days, mother's in charge and father is to stay out of the way. Here, again, the family's rigid sequences are interrupted and they must react differently to each other.

These positive connotations and rituals were powerful and provocative interventions. To keep families engaged while using such methods, the therapist–family relationship became crucial. Unfortunately, the Milan team originally portrayed therapy as a power struggle between therapists and families. Their main advice to therapists was to remain neutral in the sense of avoiding the appearance of taking sides with one family member or another. This **neutrality** was often manifest as distance, so that therapists delivered these dramatic interventions while acting aloof; not surprisingly, families often became angry and didn't return.

In the late 1970s and early 1980s, the original Milan team began to split around the nature of therapy. Selvini Palazzoli maintained the model's strategic and adversarial bent, although she stopped using paradoxical interventions. Instead she and Guiliana Prata experimented with a specific ritual called the **invariant prescription,** which they assigned to every family they treated.

Selvini Palazzoli (1986) believed that psychotic and anorexic patients are caught up in a "dirty game," a power struggle originally between their parents that these patients are pulled into and, ultimately, wind up using their symptoms in an attempt to defeat one parent for the sake of the other. In the invariant prescription, parents were directed to tell their children they had a secret. They were to go out together for varying periods of time and to do so mysteriously, without warning other family members. Therapy continued this way until the patient's symptoms abated.

In the early 1990s Selvini Palazzoli reinvented her therapy once more, this time abandoning short-term, strategic therapy (invariant prescription included) for long-term therapy with patients and their families (Selvini, 1993).

Thus, she came full circle, beginning with psychodynamic roots, then focusing on family patterns, and finally returning to a long-term therapy that emphasizes insight and focuses again on the individual. This new therapy revolves around understanding the denial of family secrets and suffering over generations. In this way it is linked conceptually, if not technically, to her former models.

Boscolo and Cecchin also moved away from strategic intervening, but they moved toward a collaborative style of therapy. This therapy grew from their increasing impression that the value in the Milan model wasn't so much in the directives (positive connotations or rituals), which had been the model's centerpiece, but in the interview process itself. Their therapy came to center around **circular questioning,** a clinical translation of Bateson's notion of double description. Circular questions are designed to decenter clients by orienting them toward seeing themselves in a relational context and seeing that context from the perspectives of other family members. For example, a therapist might ask, "How might your father have characterized your mother's relationship with your sister, if he had felt free to speak with you about it?" Such questions are structured so that one has to give a relational description in answer.

By asking about relationship patterns like this, the circular nature of problems becomes apparent as family members are lifted out of their limited and linear perspectives. Circular questions have been further refined and cataloged by Peggy Penn (1982, 1985) and Karl Tomm (1987a, 1987b). Boscolo (Boscolo & Bertrando, 1992) remains intrigued with their potential. As an example, let's return to Carlo's family and imagine the following conversation (adapted from Hoffman, 1983):

Q: Who is most upset by Carlo's depression?

A: Mother.

Q: How does mother try to help Carlo?

A: She talks to him for hours and tries to do things for him.

Q: Who agrees most with mother's way of trying to help Carlo?

A: The psychiatrist who prescribes his medication.

Q: Who disagrees?

A: Father. He thinks Carlo shouldn't be allowed to do what he wants.

Q: Who agrees with father?

A: We all think Carlo is babied too much. And grandma too. Grandpa would probably agree with mother but he died.

Q: Did Carlo start to get depressed before or after grandfather's death?

A: Not long after, I guess.

Q: If grandfather hadn't died, how would the family be different now?

A: Well, mother and grandma probably wouldn't fight so much because grandma wouldn't be living with us. And mother wouldn't be so sad all the time.

Q: If mother and grandma didn't fight so much and mother wasn't so sad, how do you think Carlo would be?

A: Well, I guess he might be happier too. But then he'd probably be fighting with father again.

Just by asking questions, the frame for Carlo's problem gradually shifts from a psychiatric one to being symptomatic of difficult changes in the family structure.

Boscolo and Cecchin became aware that the spirit in which these questions were asked determined their usefulness. If a therapist maintains a strategic mind-set—uses the questioning process to strive for a particular outcome—the responses of family members will be constrained by their sense that the therapist is after something. If, on the other hand, the therapist asks circular questions out of genuine curiosity (Cecchin, 1987), as if joining the

family in a research expedition regarding their problem, an atmosphere can be created in which the family can arrive at new understandings of their predicament.

Other Contributions. Strategic therapists pioneered the *team approach* to therapy. Originally, the MRI group used teams behind one-way mirrors to help brainstorm strategies, as did the Milan group. Peggy Papp (1980) and her colleagues at the Ackerman Institute brought the team more directly into the therapy process by turning the observers into a "Greek chorus" who reacted to events in the therapy session. For example, the team might, for strategic purposes, disagree with the therapist. In witnessing the staged debates between the team and their therapist over whether a family should change, family members might feel that both sides of their ambivalence were being represented. Having the team interact openly with the therapist or even with the family during sessions paved the way for later approaches in which the team might enter the treatment room and discuss the family while the family watched (Andersen, 1987).

Jim Alexander was a behaviorist who, out of frustration with the limits of his exclusively behavioral orientation, incorporated strategic ideas. The result was *functional family therapy* (Alexander & Parsons, 1982), which, as the name implies, is concerned with the function that family behavior is designed to achieve (see also Chapter 10). Functional family therapists assume that most family behaviors are attempts to become more or less intimate and, through "relabeling" (another word for reframing), help family members see each other's behavior in that benign light. They also help family members set up contingency management programs to help them get the kind of intimacy they want more directly. Functional family therapy represents an interesting blend of strategic and behavioral therapies and, unlike other strategic models, retains the be-haviorist ethic of basing interventions on sound research.

Evaluating Therapy Theory and Results

Communications family therapy was no mere application of individual psychotherapy to families; it was a radical new conceptualization that altered the very nature of imagination. What was new was the focus on the *process,* the form and impact of communication, rather than its *content.* Communication was described as feedback, as a tactic in interpersonal power struggles, and as symptoms. In fact, all behavior was communicative.

When communication takes place in a closed system—an individual's fantasies or a family's private conversations—there's little opportunity for adjusting the system. Only when someone outside the system provides input can correction occur. Because the rules of family functioning are largely unknown to the family, the best way to examine and correct them is to consult an expert in communications. Today the theories of communications therapy have been absorbed into the mainstream of family therapy, while its symptom-focused interventions became the basis of the strategic and solution-focused models.

The strategic therapies reached the height of their popularity in the early 1980s. They were clever, prescriptive, and systematic—qualities appreciated by therapists who often felt overwhelmed by the emotionality of families in treatment. Then in the mid-1980s a backlash occurred, and people began criticizing strategic therapy's manipulative aspects. Unfortunately, when communications and strategic therapists were confounded by the anxious inflexibility of some families, they may have exaggerated the irrational power of the family system.

In the 1990s the strategic and systemic approaches described in this chapter were replaced on family therapy's center stage by more collaborative approaches. But even as the field moves away from an overreliance on technique and manipulation, we shouldn't lose sight of valuable aspects of strategic therapy. These include having a clear therapeutic goal, anticipating ways that families will react to interventions, understanding and tracking sequences of interaction, and creatively using directives.

Most of the meager research on the effectiveness of strategic therapy isn't rigorous. More than any other model in this book, information about strategic therapy is exchanged through the case report format. Nearly all of the hundreds of articles and books on strategic therapy include at least one description of a successful technique or therapy outcome. Thus strategic therapy appears to have a great deal of anecdotal support for its efficacy (although people tend not to write about their failed cases).

Some strategic groups have tracked their outcomes a little more systematically. In the book *Change,* which launched the MRI model, Watzlawick and colleagues (1974) conducted follow-up phone interviews with ninety-seven consecutive cases three months after treatment and found that 40 percent reported complete relief, 32 percent reported considerable but not complete relief, and 28 percent reported no change. Haley (1980) reported on the outcome of his "leaving home" model with schizophrenic young adults and found that, between two and four years after terminating, three of the fourteen had been rehospitalized, while another patient had committed suicide.

Some early studies of the outcome of family therapies based on strategic therapy helped fuel its popularity. In their classic study, Langsley, Machotka, and Flomenhaft (1971) found that family crisis therapy, with similarities to both the MRI and Haley models, drastically reduced the need for hospitalization. Alexander and Parsons found their functional family therapy to be more effective in treating a group of delinquents than a client-centered family approach, an eclectic-dynamic approach, or a no-treatment control group (Parsons & Alexander, 1973). Stanton and Todd (1982) demonstrated the effectiveness of combining structural and strategic family therapies for treating heroin addicts. The results were impressive because family therapy resulted in twice as many days of abstinence from heroin than a methadone maintenance program.

In the early 1980s the Milan associates offered anecdotal case reports of amazing outcomes with anorexia nervosa, schizophrenia, and delinquency (Selvini Palazzoli, Boscolo, Cecchin, & Prata, 1978b, 1980). Later, however, members of the original team expressed reservations about the model and implied that it wasn't as effective as they originally suggested (Selvini Palazzoli, 1986; Selvini Palazzoli & Viaro, 1988; Boscolo, 1983). Some who have studied the Milan model more systematically concur with these less enthusiastic impressions (Machal, Feldman, & Sigal, 1989). In discussing their disappointing results with the Milan model, the authors cited clients' negative reactions to the therapist or team. Families frequently felt that the therapists were distant and the team was impersonal. Apparently the attitude of adversarial strategizing recommended in *Paradox and Counterparadox* showed through the therapists' attempts to positively connote family members. It seems that people have trouble changing if they don't feel cared about. While the original Milan model appears to have gone the way of the dinosaurs, there currently exist two thriving strategic camps: the MRI group on the West Coast, and the Washington School started by Haley and Madanes on the East Coast.

What people came to rebel against was the gimmickry of formulaic techniques. But gimmickry was never inherent in the strategic models. For example, the MRI's emphasis on reversing attempted solutions that don't work is a sound idea. People *do* stay stuck in ruts as long as they pursue self-defeating strategies. If, in some hands, blocking more-of-the-same solutions resulted in a rote application of reverse psychology, that's not the fault of the cybernetic metaphor, but of the way it was applied.

Strategic therapists are also integrating other ideas and keeping up with the postmodern spirit of the twenty-first century. Haley published a book in which the evolution of his thinking is apparent (Haley, 1996), and a new book on the influence of the MRI on the field was released (Weakland & Ray, 1995). In addition, some authors have integrated MRI strategic concepts with narrative approaches (Eron & Lund, 1993, 1996). It's good to see that strategic thinking is evolving because even in this era of the nonexpert therapist, there is still room for thoughtful problem-solving strategies and therapeutic direction.

—Summary

Communications family therapy was one of the first and most influential forms of family treatment. Its theoretical development was based on general systems theory, and the therapy that emerged was a systems approach par excellence. Communication was the detectable input and output therapists used to analyze the black box of interpersonal systems.

Another of the significant ideas of communications therapy was that families are rule-governed systems, maintained by homeostatic, negative feedback mechanisms. Negative feedback accounts for the stability of normal families and the inflexibility of dysfunctional ones. Because such families don't have adequate positive feedback mechanisms, they're unable to adjust to changing circumstances.

While there were major differences among the therapeutic strategies of Haley, Jackson, Satir, and Watzlawick, they were all committed to altering destructive patterns of communication. They pursued this goal by direct and indirect means. The direct approach, favored by Satir, sought change by making family rules explicit and by teaching clear communication. This approach could be described as establishing ground rules, or metacommunicational principles, and included such tactics as telling people to speak for themselves and pointing out nonverbal and multilevel channels of communication.

The trouble is, as Haley noted, "One of the difficulties involved in telling patients to do something is the fact that psychiatric patients are noted for their hesitation about doing what they are told." For this reason, communications therapists began to rely on more indirect strategies, designed to provoke change rather than to foster awareness. Telling family members to speak for themselves, for example, may challenge a family rule and therefore meet with resistance. With this realization, communications therapy became a treatment of resistance.

Resistance and symptoms were treated with a variety of paradoxical directives, known loosely as "therapeutic double binds." Milton Erickson's technique of prescribing resistance was used as a lever to gain control, as, for example, when a therapist tells family members not to reveal everything in the first session. The same ploy was used to prescribe symptoms, an action that made unrecognized rules explicit,

implied that such behavior was voluntary, and put the therapist in control.

Strategic therapy, derived from Ericksonian hypnotherapy and Batesonian cybernetics, developed a body of powerful procedures for treating psychological problems. Strategic approaches vary in the specifics of theory and technique, but share a problem-centered, pragmatic focus on changing behavioral sequences, in which therapists take responsibility for the outcome of therapy. Insight and understanding are eschewed in favor of directives designed to change the way family members interact.

The MRI model tries to remain strictly interactional—observing and intervening into sequences of interaction surrounding a problem rather than speculating about the feelings or intentions of the interactants. Haley and Madanes are interested in motives, Haley mainly in the desire to control others and Madanes in the desire to love and be loved. In addition, unlike the MRI group, Haley and Madanes incorporate structural goals in their models and don't limit their efforts to simple problem resolution. They believe successful treatment often requires structural change, with an emphasis on improving family hierarchy.

Like Haley, the Milan Associates originally saw power in the motives of family members. They tried to understand the elaborate multigenerational games that surrounded symptoms. They designed powerful interventions—positive connotation and rituals—to expose these games and change the meaning of the problem. Later the original group split, with Selvini Palazzoli going through several transformations until her current long-term approach based on family secrets. Cecchin and Boscolo moved away from formulaic interventions, became more interested in the questioning process as a way to help families to new understandings, and in so doing paved the way for family therapy's current interest in conversation and narrative.

—Recommended Readings

Cecchin, G. 1987. Hypothesizing, circularity and neutrality revisited: An invitation to curiosity. *Family Process. 26:* 405–413.

Fisch, R., Weakland, J. H., and Segal, L. 1982. *The tactics of change: Doing therapy briefly.* San Francisco: Jossey-Bass.

Haley, J. 1976. *Problem-solving therapy.* San Francisco: Jossey-Bass.

Haley, J. 1980. *Leaving home.* New York: McGraw-Hill.

Jackson, D. D. 1961. Interactional psychotherapy. In *Contemporary psychotherapies,* M. T. Stein, ed. New York: Free Press of Glencoe.

Jackson, D. D. 1967. *Therapy, communication and change.* Palo Alto, CA: Science and Behavior Books.

Keim, J. 1998. Strategic therapy. In *Case studies in couple and family therapy,* F. Dattilio, ed. New York: Guilford Press.

Lederer, W., and Jackson, D. D. 1968. *Mirages of marriage.* New York: Norton.

Madanes, C. 1981. *Strategic family therapy.* San Francisco: Jossey-Bass.

Madanes, C. 1984. *Behind the one-way mirror.* San Francisco: Jossey-Bass.

Price, J. 1996. *Power and compassion: Working with difficult adolescents and abused parents.* New York: Guilford Press.

Rabkin, R. 1972. *Strategic psychotherapy.* New York: Basic Books.

Selvini Palazzoli, M., Boscolo, L., Cecchin, G., and Prata, G. 1978. *Paradox and counterparadox.* New York: Jason Aronson.

Tomm, K. 1987. Interventive interviewing: Part 1. Strategizing as a fourth guideline for the therapists. *Family Process. 26:*3–14.

Watzlawick, P., Beavin, J. H., and Jackson, D. D. 1967. *Pragmatics of human communication.* New York: Norton.

Watzlawick, P., Weakland, J., and Fisch, R. 1974. *Change: Principles of problem formation and problem resolution.* New York: Norton.

—References

Alexander, J., and Parsons, B. 1973. Short-term behavioral intervention with delinquent families: Impact on family process and recidivism. *Journal of Abnormal Psychology. 81:* 219–225.

Alexander, J., and Parsons, B. 1982. *Functional family therapy.* Monterey, CA: Brooks Cole.

Andersen, T. 1987. The reflecting team: Dialogue and meta-dialogue in clinical work. *Family Process. 26:* 415–417.

Bergman, J. 1985. *Fishing for barracuda: Pragmatics of brief systems therapy.* New York: Norton.

Boscolo, L. 1983. Final discussion. In *Psychosocial intervention in schizophrenia: An international view,* H. Stierlin, L. Wynne, and M. Wirsching, eds. Berlin: Springer-Verlag.

Boscolo, L., and Bertrando, P. 1992. The reflexive loop of past, present, and future in systemic therapy and consultation. *Family Process. 31:* 119–133.

Boscolo, L., Cecchin, G., Hoffman, L., and Penn, P. 1987. *Milan systemic family therapy.* New York: Basic Books.

Cecchin, G. 1987. Hypothesizing, circularity and neutrality revisited: An invitation to curiosity. *Family Process. 26:* 405–413.

Eron, J., and Lund, T. 1993. An approach to how problems evolve and dissolve: Integrating narrative and strategic concepts. *Family Process. 32:* 291–309.

Eron, J., and Lund, T. 1996. *Narrative solutions in brief therapy.* New York: Guilford Press.

Fisch, R. 1978. Review of problem-solving therapy, by Jay Haley. *Family Process. 17:* 107–110.

Fisch, R., Weakland, J., and Segal, L. 1982. *The tactics of change.* San Francisco: Jossey-Bass.

Haley, J. 1961. Control in psychotherapy with schizophrenics. *Archives of General Psychiatry. 5:* 340–353.

Haley, J. 1963. *Strategies of psychotherapy.* New York: Grune & Stratton.

Haley, J. 1973. *Uncommon therapy.* New York: Norton.

Haley, J. 1976. *Problem-solving therapy.* San Francisco: Jossey-Bass.

Haley, J. 1980. *Leaving home: The therapy of disturbed young people.* New York: McGraw-Hill.

Haley, J. 1981. *Reflections on therapy.* Chevy Chase, MD: Family Therapy Institute of Washington, DC.

Haley, J. 1984. *Ordeal therapy.* San Francisco: Jossey-Bass.

Haley, J. 1986. *The power tactics of Jesus Christ,* 2nd ed. Rockville, MD: Triangle Press.

Haley, J. 1996. *Learning and teaching therapy.* New York: Guilford Press.

Hoffman, L. 1981. *Foundations of family therapy.* New York: Basic Books.

Hoffman, L. 1983. A co-evolutionary framework for systemic family therapy. In *Diagnosis and assessment in family therapy,* J. Hansen and B. Keeney, eds. Rockville, MD: Aspen Systems.

Jackson, D. D. 1961. Interactional psychotherapy. In *Contemporary psychotherapies,* M. T. Stein, ed. New York: Free Press of Glencoe.

Jackson, D. D. 1965. Family rules: The marital quid pro quo. *Archives of General Psychiatry. 12:* 589–594.

Jackson, D. D. 1967. Aspects of conjoint family therapy. In *Family therapy and disturbed families,* G. H. Zuk and I. Boszormenyi-Nagy, eds. Palo Alto, CA: Science and Behavior Books.

Jackson, D. D., and Weakland, J. H. 1961. Conjoint family therapy: Some consideration on theory, technique, and results. *Psychiatry. 24:* 30–45.

Keim, J. 1998. Strategic family therapy. In *Case studies in couple and family therapy,* F. Dattilio, ed. New York: Guilford Press.

Langsley, D., Machotka, P., and Flomenhaft, K. 1971. Avoiding mental hospital admission: A follow-up study. *American Journal of Psychiatry. 127:* 1391–1394.

Machal, M., Feldman, R., and Sigal, J., 1989. The unraveling of a treatment program: A follow-up study of the Milan approach to family therapy. *Family Process. 28:* 457–470.

Madanes, C. 1980. Protection, paradox and pretending. *Family Process. 19:* 73–85.

Madanes, C. 1981. *Strategic family therapy.* San Francisco: Jossey-Bass.

Madanes, C. 1984. *Behind the one-way mirror.* San Francisco: Jossey-Bass.

Madanes, C. 1990. *Sex, love, and violence: Strategies for transformation.* New York: Norton.

Madanes, C. 1991. Strategic family therapy. In *Handbook of family therapy, Vol. II,* A. S. Gurman and D. P. Kniskern, eds. New York: Brunner/Mazel.

Marayuma, M. 1968. The second cybernetics: Deviation-amplifying mutual causal processes. In *Modern systems research for the behavioral scientist,* W. Buckley, ed. Chicago: Aldine.

Papp, P. 1980. The Greek chorus and other techniques of paradoxical therapy. *Family Process. 19:* 45–57.

Papp, P. 1983. *The process of change.* New York: Guilford Press.

Parsons, B., and Alexander, J. 1973. Short-term family intervention: A therapy outcome study. *Journal of Consulting and Clinical Psychology. 41:* 195–201.

Penn, P. 1982. Circular questioning. *Family Process. 21:* 267–280.

Penn, P. 1985. Feed-forward: Further questioning, future maps. *Family Process. 24:* 299–310.

Rabkin, R. 1977. *Inner and outer space.* New York: Basic Books.

Ruesch, J., and Bateson, G. 1951. *Communication: The social matrix of psychiatry.* New York: Norton.

Satir, V. 1964. *Conjoint family therapy.* Palo Alto, CA: Science and Behavior Books.

Selvini, M. 1993. Major mental disorders, distorted reality and family secrets. Unpublished manuscript.

Selvini Palazzoli, M. 1981. *Self-starvation: From the intrapsychic to the transpersonal approach to anorexia nervosa.* New York: Jason Aronson.

Selvini Palazzoli, M. 1986. Towards a general model of psychotic games. *Journal of Marital and Family Therapy. 12:* 339–349.

Selvini Palazzoli, M., Boscolo, L., Cecchin, G., and Prata, G. 1978a. A ritualized prescription in family therapy: Odd days and even days. *Journal of Marriage and Family Counseling. 4:* 3–9.

Selvini Palazzoli, M., Boscolo, L., Cecchin, G., and Prata, G. 1978b. *Paradox and counterparadox.* New York: Jason Aronson.

Selvini Palazzoli, M., Boscolo, L., Cecchin, G., and Prata, G. 1980. Hypothesizing—circularity—neutrality: Three guidelines for the conductor of the session. *Family Process. 19:* 3–12.

Selvini Palazzoli, M., and Prata, G. 1983. A new method for therapy and research in the treatment of schizophrenic families. In *Psychosocial intervention in schizophrenia: An international view,* H. Stierlin, L. Wynne, and M. Wirsching, eds. Berlin: Springer-Verlag.

Selvini Palazzoli, M., and Viaro, M. 1988. The anorectic process in the family: A six-stage model as a guide for individual therapy. *Family Process.* 27: 129–148.

Stanton, D., Todd, T., and Associates. 1982. *The family therapy of drug abuse and addiction.* New York: Guilford Press.

Tomm, K. 1984a. One perspective on the Milan systemic approach: Part I. Overview of development, theory and practice. *Journal of Martial and Family Therapy. 10:* 113–125.

Tomm, K. 1984b. One perspective on the Milan systemic approach: Part II. Description of session format, interviewing style and interventions. *Journal of Marital and Family Therapy. 10:* 253–271.

Tomm, K. 1987a. Interventive interviewing: Part I. Strategizing as a fourth guideline for the therapist. *Family Process. 26:* 3–13.

Tomm, K. 1987b. Interventive interviewing: Part II. Reflexive questioning as a means to enable self-healing. *Family Process. 26:* 167–184.

Watzlawick, P. A. 1966. A structured family interview. *Family Process. 5:* 256–271.

Watzlawick, P., Beavin, J., and Jackson, D. 1967. *Pragmatics of human communication.* New York: Norton.

Watzlawick, P., Weakland, J., and Fisch, R. 1974. *Change: Principles of problem formation and problem resolution.* New York: Norton.

Weakland, J., Fisch, R., Watzlawick, P., and Bodin, A. 1974. Brief therapy: Focused problem resolution. *Family Process. 13:* 141–168.

Weakland, J., and Ray, W., eds. 1995. *Propagations: Thirty years of influence from the Mental Research Institute.* Binghamton, NY: Haworth Press.

Structural Family Therapy

The Underlying Organization of Family Life

One of the reasons family therapy can be difficult is that families often appear as collections of individuals who affect each other in powerful but unpredictable ways. Structural family therapy offers a framework that brings order and meaning to those transactions. The consistent patterns of family behavior are what allow us to consider that they have a structure, although, of course, only in a functional sense. The boundaries and coalitions that make up a family's structure are abstractions; nevertheless, using the concept of family structure enables therapists to intervene in a systematic and organized way.

Families who seek help are usually concerned about a particular problem. It might be a child who misbehaves or a couple who don't get along. Family therapists typically look beyond the specifics of those problems to the family's attempts to solve them. This leads them to the dynamics of interaction. The misbehaving child might have parents who scold but never reward him. The couple may be caught up in a pursuer–distancer dynamic, or they might be unable to talk without arguing.

What structural family therapy adds to the equation is a recognition of the overall organization that supports and maintains those interactions. The "parents who scold" might turn out to be two partners who undermine each other because one is wrapped up in the child while the other is an angry outsider. If so, attempts to encourage effective discipline are likely to fail unless the structural problem is addressed and the parents develop a real partnership. Similarly a couple who don't get along may not be able to improve their relationship until they create a boundary between themselves and intrusive children or in-laws.

The discovery that families are organized into **subsystems** with **boundaries** regulating the contact family members have with each other turned out to be one of the defining insights of family therapy. Perhaps equally important, though, was the introduction of the technique of **enactment,** in which family members are encouraged to deal directly with each other in sessions, permitting the therapist to observe and modify their interactions.

When he first burst onto the scene, Salvador Minuchin's galvanizing impact was as an incomparable master of technique. His most lasting contribution, however, was a theory of family structure and a set of guidelines to organize therapeutic techniques. This structural approach was so successful that it captivated the field in the 1970s, and Minuchin built the Philadelphia Child Guidance Clinic into a world-famous complex, where thousands of family therapists have been trained in structural family therapy.

Sketches of Leading Figures

Minuchin was born and raised in Argentina. He served as a physician in the Israeli army, then came to the United States, where he trained in child psychiatry with Nathan Ackerman in New York. After completing his studies Minuchin returned to Israel in 1952 to work with displaced children—and became absolutely committed to the importance of families. He moved back to the United States in 1954 to begin psychoanalytic training at the William Alanson White Institute, where he studied the interpersonal psychiatry of Harry Stack Sullivan. After leaving the White Institute, Minuchin took a job at the Wiltwyck School for delinquent boys, where he suggested to his colleagues that they start seeing families.

Salvador Minuchin's structural model is the most influential approach to family therapy throughout the world.

At Wiltwyck, Minuchin and his colleagues—Dick Auerswald, Charlie King, Braulio Montalvo, and Clara Rabinowitz—taught themselves to do family therapy, inventing it as they went along. To do so, they built a one-way mirror and took turns observing each other work. In 1962 Minuchin made a hajj to what was then the mecca of family therapy, Palo Alto. There he met Jay Haley and began a friendship that was to bear fruit in an extraordinarily fertile collaboration.

The success of Minuchin's work with families at Wiltwyck led to a groundbreaking book, *Families of the Slums*, written with Montalvo, Guerney, Rosman, and Schumer. Minuchin's reputation as a practitioner of family therapy grew, and he became the Director of the Philadelphia Child Guidance Clinic in 1965. The clinic then consisted of less than a dozen staff members. From this modest beginning Minuchin created one of the largest and most prestigious child guidance clinics in the world.

Among Minuchin's colleagues in Philadelphia were Braulio Montalvo, Jay Haley, Bernice Rosman, Harry Aponte, Carter Umbarger, Marianne Walters, Charles Fishman, Cloe Madanes, and Stephen Greenstein, all of whom had a role in shaping structural family therapy. By the 1970s structural family therapy had become the most influential and widely practiced of all systems of family therapy.

In 1976 Minuchin stepped down as Director of the Philadelphia Child Guidance Clinic, but stayed on as head of training until 1981. After leaving Philadelphia, Minuchin started his own center in New York, where he continued to practice and teach family therapy until 1996, when he retired and moved to Boston. Long committed to addressing problems of poverty and social justice, Minuchin is now consulting with the Massachusetts Department of Mental Health on home-based therapy programs. In 1996 he completed his ninth book, *Mastering Family Therapy: Journeys of Growth and Transformation*, coauthored with nine of his supervisees, which explains his views on the state of the art in family therapy and training.

Like good players on the same team with a superstar, some of Minuchin's colleagues are not as well known as they might be. Foremost among these is Braulio Montalvo, one of the underrated geniuses of family therapy. Born and raised in Puerto Rico, Montalvo, like Minuchin, has always been committed to treating minority families. Like Minuchin, he is also a brilliant therapist, though he favors a gentler, more supportive approach. Montalvo was instrumental in building the Philadelphia Child Guidance Clinic, but his contributions are less well-known because he is a quiet man who prefers to work behind the scenes.

Following Minuchin's retirement the center in New York was renamed the Minuchin Center for the Family in his honor, and the torch has been passed to a new generation. The staff of leading teachers at the Minuchin Center now includes Ema Genijovich, David Greenan, George Simon, and Wai-Yung Lee. Their task is to keep the leading center of structural family therapy in the forefront of the field without the charismatic leadership of its progenitor.

Among Minuchin's other prominent students are Jorge Colapinto, now at the Ackerman Institute in New York; Michael Nichols, who teaches at the College of William and Mary; Jay Lappin who works with child welfare for the state of Delaware; and Charles Fishman, in private practice in Philadelphia.

Theoretical Formulations

Beginners tend to get bogged down in the content of family problems because they don't have a theory to help them see the patterns of family dynamics. Structural family therapy offers a blueprint for analyzing the process of family interactions. As such, it provides a basis for consistent strategies of treatment, which obviates the need to have a specific technique—usually someone else's—for every occasion. Three constructs are the essential components of structural family theory: structure, subsystems, and boundaries.

Family structure, the organized pattern in which family members interact, is a deterministic concept, but it doesn't prescribe or legislate behavior; it *describes* sequences that are predictable. As family transactions are repeated they foster expectations that establish enduring patterns. Once patterns are established, family members use only a small fraction of the full range of behavior available to them. The first time the baby cries, or a teenager misses the school bus, it's not clear who will do what. Will the load be shared? Will there be a quarrel? Will one person get stuck with most of the work? Soon, however, patterns are set, roles assigned, and things take on a sameness and predictability. "Who's going to . . . ?" becomes "She'll probably . . . " and then "She always."

Family structure is reinforced by the expectations that establish rules in the family. For example, a rule such as "family members should always protect one another" will be manifest in various ways depending on the context and who is involved. If a boy gets into a fight with another boy in the neighborhood, his mother will go to the neighbors to complain. If a teenager has to wake up early for school, mother wakes her. If a husband is too hung over to get to work in the morning, his wife calls in to say he has the flu. If the parents have an argument, their kids interrupt. The parents are so preoccupied with the doings of their children that it keeps them from spending time alone together. These sequences are *isomorphic*: They're structured. Changing any of them may not affect the basic structure, but altering the underlying structure will have ripple effects on all family transactions.

Family structure is shaped partly by universal and partly by idiosyncratic constraints. For example, all families have some kind of hierarchical structure, with adults and children having different amounts of authority. Family members also tend to have reciprocal and complementary functions. Often these become so ingrained that their origin is forgotten and they are presumed necessary rather than optional. If a young mother, burdened by the demands of her infant, gets upset and complains to her husband, he may respond in various ways. Perhaps he'll move closer and share the demands of childrearing. This creates a united parental team. On the other hand, if he decides that his wife is "depressed," she may end up in psychotherapy to get the emotional support she needs. This creates a structure where the mother remains distant from her husband, and learns to turn outside the family for sympathy. Whatever the chosen pattern, it tends to be self-perpetuating. Although alternatives are available, families are unlikely to consider them until changing circumstances produce stress in the system.

Families don't walk in and hand you their structural patterns as if they were bringing an apple to the teacher. What they bring is chaos and confusion. You have to discover the subtext—and you have to be careful that it's accurate—not imposed but discovered. Two things are necessary: a theoretical system that explains structure, and seeing the family in action. Knowing that a family is a single-parent family with three children, or that two parents are having trouble with a middle child doesn't tell you what their structure is. Structure becomes evident only when you observe the actual interactions among family members.

Consider the following. A mother calls to complain of misbehavior in her seventeen-year-old son. She is asked to bring her husband, son, and their three other children to the first session. When they arrive, the mother begins to describe a series of minor ways in which the son is disobedient. He interrupts to say that she's always on his case, he never gets a break

from his mother. This spontaneous bickering between mother and son reveals an intense involvement between them—a mutual preoccupation no less intense simply because it's conflictual. This sequence doesn't tell the whole story, however, because it doesn't include the father or the other children. They must be engaged to observe their role in the family structure. If the father sides with his wife but seems unconcerned, then it may be that the mother's preoccupation with her son is related to her husband's lack of involvement. If the younger children tend to agree with their mother and describe their brother as bad, then it becomes clear that all the children are close to the mother—close and obedient up to a point, then close and disobedient.

Families are differentiated into *subsystems* based on generation, gender, and common interests. Obvious groupings such as the parents or the teenagers are sometimes less significant than covert coalitions. A mother and her youngest child may form such a tightly bonded subsystem that others are excluded. Another family may be split into two camps, with mom and the boys on one side, and dad and the girls on the other. Though certain patterns are common, the possibilities for subgrouping are endless.

Every family member plays many roles in several subgroups. Mary may be a wife, a mother, a daughter, and a niece. In each of these roles she will be required to behave differently and exercise a variety of interpersonal options. If she's mature and flexible, she will be able to vary her behavior to fit different subgroups. Scolding may be okay from a mother, but it can cause problems from a wife or a daughter.

Individuals, subsystems, and whole families are demarcated by interpersonal *boundaries*, invisible barriers that regulate contact with others. A rule forbidding phone calls at dinner establishes a boundary that protects the family from outside intrusion. When small children are permitted to freely interrupt their parents' conversations, the boundary separating the generations is eroded. Subsystems that aren't adequately protected by boundaries limit the development of interpersonal skills achievable in these subsystems. If parents always step in to settle arguments between their children, the children won't learn to fight their own battles.

Interpersonal boundaries vary from rigid to diffuse (see Figure 7.1). Rigid boundaries are overly restrictive and permit little contact with outside subsystems, resulting in *disengagement.* Disengaged individuals or subsystems are independent but isolated. On the positive side, this fosters autonomy. On the other hand, disengagement limits affection and assistance. Disengaged families must come under extreme stress before they mobilize mutual support.

Enmeshed subsystems offer a heightened sense of mutual support, but at the expense of independence and autonomy. Enmeshed parents are loving and considerate; they spend a lot of time with their kids and do a lot for them. However, children enmeshed with their parents become dependent. They're less comfortable by themselves and may have trouble relating to people outside the family.

Minuchin described some of the features of family subsystems in his most accessible work, *Families and Family Therapy* (Minuchin, 1974). Families begin when two people join together to form a spouse subsystem. Two people in love agree to share their lives and futures and expectations; but a period of often difficult adjustment is required before they can complete the transition from courtship to a functional spouse subsystem. They must learn to *accommodate* each other's needs and preferred styles of interaction. In a healthy couple, each gives

and gets. He learns to accommodate her wish to be kissed hello and goodbye. She learns to leave him alone with his paper and morning coffee. These little arrangements, multiplied a thousand times, may be accomplished easily or only after intense struggle. Whatever the case, this process of accommodation cements the couple into a unit.

The couple must also develop complementary patterns of mutual support. Some patterns are transitory and may later be reversed—perhaps, for instance, one works while the other completes school. Other patterns are more stable and lasting. Exaggerated complementary roles can detract from individual growth; moderate complementarity enables spouses to divide functions, to support and enrich each other. When one has the flu and feels lousy, the other takes over. One's permissiveness with children may be balanced by the other's strictness. One's fiery disposition may help to melt the other's reserve. Complementary patterns exist in most couples. They become problematic when they are so exaggerated that they create a dysfunctional subsystem. Therapists must learn to accept those structural patterns that work and challenge only those that do not.

The spouse subsystem must also develop a boundary that separates it from parents, children, and other outsiders. All too often, husband and wife give up the space they need for supporting each other when children are born. Too rigid a boundary around the couple can deprive the children of the care they need; but in our child-centered culture, the boundary between parents and children is often ambiguous at best.

The birth of a child instantly transforms the family structure; the pattern of interaction between the parental and child subsystems must

	Rigid Boundary		Clear Boundary		Diffuse Boundary
FIGURE 7.1 **Boundaries**	Disengagement		Normal Range		Enmeshment

be worked out and then modified to fit changing circumstances. A clear boundary enables children to interact with their parents but excludes them from the spouse subsystem. Parents and children eat together, play together, and share much of each others' lives. But there are some spouse functions that need not be shared. Husband and wife are sustained as a loving couple, and enhanced as parents, if they have time to be alone together—to talk, to go out to dinner occasionally, to fight, and to make love. Unhappily, the clamorous demands of small children often make parents lose sight of their need to maintain a boundary around their relationship.

In addition to maintaining privacy for the couple, a clear boundary establishes a **hierarchical structure** in which parents exercise a position of leadership. All too often this hierarchy is disrupted by a child-centered ethos, which influences helping professionals as well as parents. Parents enmeshed with their children tend to argue with them about who's in charge, and misguidedly share—or shirk—the responsibility for making parental decisions.

In *Institutionalizing Madness* (Elizur & Minuchin, 1989), Minuchin makes a compelling case for a systems view of family problems that extends beyond the family to encompass the entire community. As Minuchin points out, unless therapists learn to look beyond the limited slice of ecology where they work to the larger social structures within which their work is embedded, their efforts may amount to little more than spinning wheels.

Normal Family Development

What distinguishes a normal family isn't the absence of problems, but a functional structure for dealing with them. All couples must learn to adjust to each other; rear their children, if they choose to have any; deal with their parents; cope with their jobs; and fit into their communities. The nature of these struggles changes with developmental stages and situational crises.

When two people join to form a couple, the structural requirements for the new union are *accommodation* and *boundary making.* The first priority is mutual **accommodation** to manage the myriad details of everyday living. Each partner tries to organize the relationship along familiar lines and pressures the other to comply. Each must adjust to the other's expectations and wants. They must agree on major issues, such as where to live and if and when to have children; less obvious, but equally important, they must coordinate daily rituals, like what to watch on television, what to eat for supper, when to go to bed, and what to do there.

In accommodating to each other, a couple must also negotiate the nature of the boundary between them, as well as the boundary separating them from the outside. A diffuse boundary exists between the couple if they call each other at work frequently, if neither has their own friends or independent activities, and if they come to view themselves only as a pair rather than as two separate personalities. On the other hand, they've established a rigid boundary if they spend little time together, have separate bedrooms, take separate vacations, have different checking accounts, and each is considerably more invested in careers or outside relationships than in the marriage.

Each partner tends to be more comfortable with the sort of proximity that existed in their own family. Since these expectations differ, a struggle ensues that may be the most difficult aspect of a new union. He wants to play golf with the boys; she feels deserted. She wants to talk; he wants to watch ESPN. His focus is on his career; her focus is on the relationship. Each thinks the other is unreasonable.

Couples must also define a boundary separating them from their original families. Rather suddenly the families that each grew up in must take second place to the new marriage. This, too, is a difficult adjustment, both for newlyweds and for their parents. Families vary in the ease with which they accept and support these new unions.

The addition of children transforms the structure of the new family into a *parental subsystem* and a *child subsystem*. It's typical for spouses to have different patterns of commitment to the babies. A woman's commitment to a unit of three is likely to begin with pregnancy, since the child inside her womb is an unavoidable reality. Her husband, on the other hand, may only begin to feel like a father when the child is born. Many men don't accept the role of father until their infants are old enough to respond to them. Thus, even in normal families, children bring with them great potential for stress and conflict. A mother's life is usually more radically transformed than a father's. She sacrifices a great deal and typically needs more support from her husband. The husband, meanwhile, continues his job, and the new baby is far less of a disruption. Though he may try to support his wife, he's likely to resent some of her demands as inordinate.

Children require different styles of parenting at different ages. Infants primarily need nurture and support. Children need guidance and control; and adolescents need independence and responsibility. Good parenting for a two-year-old may be totally inadequate for a five-year-old or a fourteen-year-old. Normal parents adjust to these developmental challenges. The family modifies its structure to adapt to new additions, to the children's growth and development, and to changes in the external environment.

Minuchin (1974) warns family therapists not to mistake growing pains for pathology. The normal family experiences anxiety and disruption as its members adapt to growth and change. Many families seek help at transitional stages, and therapists should keep in mind that they may simply be in the process of modifying their structure to accommodate to new circumstances.

All families face situations that stress the system. Although no clear dividing line exists between healthy and unhealthy families, we can say that healthy families modify their structure to accommodate to changed circumstances; dysfunctional families increase the rigidity of structures that are no longer effective.

Development of Behavior Disorders

Family systems must be stable enough to ensure continuity, but flexible enough to accommodate to changing circumstances. Problems arise when inflexible family structures cannot adjust adequately to maturational or situational challenges. Adaptive changes in structure are required when the family or one of its members faces external stress and when transitional points of growth are reached.

Family dysfunction results from a combination of stress and failure to realign themselves to cope with it (Colapinto, 1991). Stressors may be environmental (a parent is laid off, the family moves) or developmental (a child reaches adolescence, parents retire). The family's failure to handle adversity may be due to flaws in their structure or merely to their inability to adjust to changed circumstances.

In disengaged families, boundaries are rigid and the family fails to mobilize support when it's needed. Disengaged parents may be unaware that a child is depressed or experiencing difficulties at school until the problem is far advanced. In enmeshed families, on the other hand, boundaries are diffuse and family members overreact and become intrusively involved with one another. Enmeshed parents create difficulties by hindering the development of more mature forms of behavior in their children and by interfering with their ability to solve their own problems.

In their book of case studies, *Family Healing*, Minuchin and Nichols (1993) describe a common example of enmeshment as a father jumps in to settle minor arguments between his two boys—"as though the siblings were Cain and Abel, and fraternal jealousy might lead to murder" (p. 149). The problem, of course, is that if parents always interrupt their children's quarrels, the children won't learn to fight their own battles.

Although we may speak of enmeshed and disengaged families, it is more accurate to speak of particular subsystems as being enmeshed or disengaged. In fact, enmeshment and disengagement tend to be reciprocal, so that, for example, a father who's overly involved with his work is likely to be less involved with his family. A frequently encountered pattern is the enmeshed mother/disengaged father syndrome— "the signature arrangement of the troubled middle-class family: a mother's closeness to her children substituting for closeness in the marriage" (Minuchin & Nichols, 1993, p. 121).

Feminists have criticized the notion of an enmeshed mother/disengaged father syndrome because they reject the stereotypical division of labor (instrumental role for the father, expressive role for the mother) that they think Minuchin's belief in hierarchy implies, and because they worry about blaming mothers for an arrangement that is culturally sanctioned. Both concerns are valid. But prejudice and blaming are due to insensitive application of these ideas, not inherent in the ideas themselves. Skewed relationships, whatever the reason for them, can be problematic, though no single family member should be blamed or expected to unilaterally redress imbalances. Likewise, the need for hierarchy doesn't imply any particular division of roles; it only implies that families need *some* kind of structure, *some* parental teamwork, and *some* degree of differentiation between subsystems.

Hierarchies can be weak and ineffective, or rigid and arbitrary. In the first case, younger members of the family may find themselves unprotected because of a lack of guidance; in the second, their growth as autonomous individuals may be impaired, or power struggles may

ensue. Just as a functional hierarchy is necessary for a healthy family's stability, flexibility is necessary for them to adapt to change.

The most common expression of fear of change is *conflict avoidance*, when family members shy away from addressing their disagreements to protect themselves from the pain of facing each other with hard truths. Disengaged families avert conflict by avoiding contact; enmeshed families avoid conflict by denying differences or by constant bickering, which allows them to vent feelings without pressing for change or resolving conflict.

Structural family therapists use a few simple symbols to diagram structural problems and these diagrams usually make it clear what changes are required. Figure 7.2 shows some of the symbols used to diagram family structure.

One problem often seen by family therapists arises when parents who are unable to resolve conflicts between them divert the focus of concern onto a child. Instead of worrying about

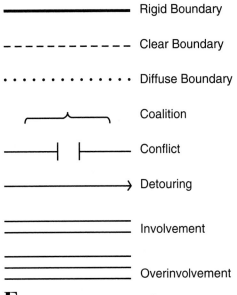

FIGURE 7.2   Symbols of Family Structure

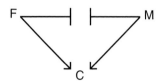

FIGURE 7.3   Scapegoating as a Means of Detouring Conflict

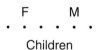

Children

FIGURE 7.5   Parents Enmeshed with Children

each other, they worry about the child (see Figure 7.3). Although this reduces the strain on father (F) and mother (M), it victimizes the child (C) and is therefore dysfunctional.

An alternate but equally common pattern is for the parents to continue to argue through the children. Father says mother is too permissive; she says he's too strict. He may withdraw, causing her to criticize his lack of concern, which in turn causes further withdrawal. The enmeshed mother responds to the child's needs with excessive concern. The disengaged father tends not to respond even when a response is necessary. Both may be critical of the other's way, but both perpetuate the other's behavior with their own. The result is a **cross-generational coalition** between mother and child, which excludes the father (Figure 7.4).

Some families function well when the children are small but are unable to adjust to a growing child's need for discipline and control. Young children in enmeshed families (Figure 7.5) receive wonderful care: Their parents hug them, love them, and give them lots of attention. Although such parents may be too tired from caring for the children to have much time for each other, the system may be moderately successful. How-

ever, if these doting parents don't teach their children to obey rules and respect authority, the children may be unprepared to negotiate their entrance into school. Used to getting their own way, they may be unruly and disruptive. Several possible consequences of this situation may bring the family into treatment. The children may be reluctant to go to school, and their fears may be covertly reinforced by "understanding" parents who permit them to remain at home (Figure 7.6). Such a case may be labeled as school phobia, and may become entrenched if the parents permit the children to remain at home for more than a few days.

Alternatively, the children of such a family may go to school, but since they haven't learned to accommodate to others, they may be rejected by their schoolmates. Such children often become depressed and withdrawn. In other cases, children enmeshed with their parents become discipline problems at school, and the school authorities may initiate counseling.

A major change in family composition that requires structural adjustment occurs when divorced or widowed spouses remarry. Such "blended families" either readjust their boundaries or soon experience transitional conflicts. When a woman divorces, she and the children

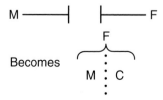

Becomes

FIGURE 7.4   Mother–Child Coalition

FIGURE 7.6   School Phobia

must first learn to readjust to a structure that establishes a clear boundary separating the divorced spouses but still permits contact between father and children; then if she remarries, the family must readjust to functioning with a new husband and stepfather (Figure 7.7). Sometimes it's hard for a mother and children to allow a stepfather to participate as a partner in the new parental subsystem. Mother and children have long since established transactional rules and learned to accommodate to each other. The new parent may be treated as an outsider who's supposed to learn the "right" (accustomed) way of doing things, rather than as a new partner who will give as well as receive ideas about childrearing (Figure 7.8). The more mother and children insist on maintaining their familiar patterns without modifications required to absorb the stepfather, the more frustrated and angry he'll become. The result may lead to child abuse or chronic arguing between the parents. The sooner such families enter treatment, the easier it is to help them adjust to the transition. The longer they wait, the more entrenched structural problems become.

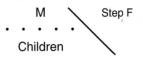

FIGURE 7.8 Failure to Accept a Stepparent

An important aspect of structural family problems is that symptoms in one member reflect not only that person's relationships with others, but also the fact that those relationships are a function of still other relationships in the family. If Johnny, aged sixteen, is depressed, it's helpful to know that he's enmeshed with his mother. Discovering that she demands absolute obedience from him and refuses to let him develop his own thinking or outside relationships helps to explain his depression (Figure 7.9). But that's only a partial view of the family system.

Why is the mother enmeshed with her son? Perhaps she's disengaged from her husband. Perhaps she's a widow who hasn't found new friends, a job, or other interests. Helping Johnny resolve his depression may best be accomplished by helping his mother satisfy her need for closeness with her husband or friends.

Because problems are a function of the entire family structure, it's important to include the whole group for assessment. For example, if a father complains of a child's misbehavior, seeing the child alone won't help the father to state

M   F
– – – – – – – –
   Children

Becomes

       M | F
– – – | – – –
     Children

Becomes

     M | Step F
– – – ⌐– –
    Children \
            F

FIGURE 7.7 Divorce and Remarriage

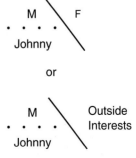

FIGURE 7.9 Johnny's Enmeshment with His Mother and Disengagement with Outside Interests

rules clearly or enforce them effectively. Nor will seeing the father and child together do anything to stop the mother from undercutting the father's authority. Only by seeing the whole family interacting is it possible to get a complete picture of their structure.

Sometimes even seeing the whole family isn't enough. Structural family therapy is based on recognition of the importance of the context of the social system. The family may not always be the complete or most relevant context. If one of the parents is having an affair, that relationship is a crucial part of the family's context. It may not be advisable to invite the lover to family sessions, but it is crucial to recognize the structural implications of the extramarital relationship.

In some cases, the family may not be the context most relevant to the presenting problem. A mother's depression might be due more to her relationships at work than at home. A son's problems at school might be due more to the structural context at school than to the one in the family. In such instances, structural family therapists work with the most relevant context to alleviate the presenting problems.

Finally, some problems may be treated as problems of the individual. As Minuchin (1974) has written, "Pathology may be inside the patient, in his social context, or in the feedback between them" (p. 9). Elsewhere Minuchin (Minuchin, Rosman, & Baker, 1978) referred to the danger of "denying the individual while enthroning the system" (p. 91). Family therapists shouldn't overlook the possibility that some problems may be most appropriately dealt with on an individual basis. The therapist must not neglect the experience of individuals, although this is easy to do, especially with young children. While interviewing a family to see how the parents deal with their children, a careful clinician may notice that one child has a neurological problem or a learning disability. These problems need to be identified and appropriate referrals made. Usually when a child

has trouble in school, there's a problem in the family or school context. Usually, but not always.

Goals of Therapy

Structural family therapists believe that problems are maintained by dysfunctional family organization. Therefore therapy is directed at altering family structure so that the family can solve its problems. The goal of therapy is structural change; problem-solving is a by-product of this systemic goal.

The idea that family problems are embedded in dysfunctional family structures has led to the criticism of structural family therapy as pathologizing. Critics see structural maps of dysfunctional organization as portraying a pathological core in client families. This isn't true. Structural problems are generally viewed as a simple failure to adjust to changing circumstances. Far from seeing families as inherently flawed, structural therapists see their work as activating latent adaptive structures that are already in client families' repertoires (Simon, 1995).

The structural family therapist joins the family system to help its members change their structure. By altering boundaries and realigning subsystems, the therapist changes the behavior and experience of each family member. The therapist doesn't solve problems; that's the family's job. The therapist helps modify the family's functioning so that family members can solve their own problems. In this way, structural family therapy is like dynamic psychotherapy—symptom resolution is sought not as an end in itself, but as a result of lasting structural change. The analyst modifies the structure of the patient's mind; the structural family therapist modifies the structure of the patient's family.

The most effective way to change symptoms is to change the family patterns that maintain them. The goal of structural family therapy is to facilitate the growth of the system to resolve symptoms and encourage growth in individuals, while also preserving the mutual support of the family.

Short-range goals may be to alleviate acute problems, especially life-threatening symptoms such as anorexia nervosa (Minuchin, Rosman, & Baker, 1978). At times, behavioral techniques, suggestion, or manipulation may be used to achieve an immediate effect. However, unless structural change in the family system is achieved, short-term symptom resolution may collapse.

The goals for each family are dictated by the problems they present and by the nature of their structural dysfunction. Although every family is unique, there are common problems and typical structural goals. Most important of the general goals for families is the creation of an effective hierarchical structure. Parents are expected to be in charge, not to relate as equals to their children. Another common goal is to help parents function together as a cohesive executive subsystem. When there is only one parent, or when there are several children, one or more of the oldest children may be encouraged

to become a parental assistant. But this child's needs must not be neglected, either.

With enmeshed families the goal is to differentiate individuals and subsystems by strengthening the boundaries around them. With disengaged families the goal is to increase interaction by making boundaries more permeable.

Conditions for Behavior Change

Structural therapy changes behavior by opening alternative patterns of interaction that can modify family structure. It's not a matter of creating new structures, but of activating dormant ones. When new transactional patterns become regularly repeated and predictably effective, they will stabilize the new and more functional structure.

The therapist produces change by **joining** the family, probing for areas of flexibility, and then activating dormant structural alternatives. Joining gets the therapist into the family; *accommodating* to their style gives him or her leverage; and *restructuring* maneuvers transform the family structure. If the therapist

Structural therapists use enactments to observe and modify problematic family patterns.

remains an outsider or uses interventions that are too dystonic, the family will reject him or her. If the therapist becomes too much a part of the family or uses interventions that are too syntonic, the family will assimilate the interventions into previous transactional patterns. In either case there will be no structural change.

Joining and accommodating are considered prerequisite to restructuring. To join the family the therapist must convey acceptance of family members and respect for their way of doing things. Minuchin (1974) likened the family therapist to an anthropologist who must first join a culture before being able to study it.

To join a family's culture the therapist makes accommodating overtures—the sort of thing we usually do unthinkingly, although not always successfully. If parents come for help with a child's problems, the therapist doesn't begin by asking for the child's views. This conveys a lack of respect for the parents and may lead them to reject the therapist. Only after the therapist has successfully joined with a family is it fruitful to attempt restructuring—the often dramatic confrontations that challenge families and force them to change.

The first task is to understand the family's view of their problems. The therapist does this by tracking their formulation in the content they use to explain it and in the sequences with which they demonstrate it. Then the family therapist *reframes* their formulation into one based on an understanding of family structure.

In fact, all psychotherapies use reframing. Patients, whether individuals or families, come with their own views as to the cause of their problems—views that usually haven't helped them solve the problems—and the therapist offers them a new and potentially more constructive view of these same problems. What makes structural family therapy unique is that it uses **enactments** within therapy sessions to make the reframing happen. This is the sine qua non of structural family therapy: observ-

ing and modifying the structure of family transactions in the immediate context of the session. Structural therapists work with what they see going on in the session, not what family members describe. Action in the session, family dynamics in process, is what structural family therapists deal with.

There are two types of live, in-session material on which structural family therapy focuses—*enactments* and *spontaneous behavior sequences.* An enactment occurs when the therapist stimulates the family to demonstrate how they handle a particular type of problem. Enactments commonly begin when the therapist suggests that specific subgroups begin to discuss a particular problem. As they do so, the therapist observes the family process. Working with enactments requires three operations. First, the therapist defines or recognizes a sequence. For example, the therapist observes that when mother talks to her daughter they talk as peers, and little brother gets left out. Second, the therapist directs an enactment. For example, the therapist might say to the mother, "Talk this over with your kids." Third, and most important, the therapist must guide the family to modify the enactment. If mother talks to her children in such a way that she doesn't take responsibility for major decisions, the therapist must guide her to do so as the family continues the enactment. All the therapist's moves should create new options for the family, options for more productive interactions.

Once an enactment breaks down, the therapist intervenes in one of two ways: commenting on what went wrong, or simply pushing them to keep going. For example, if a father responds to the suggestion to talk with his twelve-year-old daughter about how she's feeling by berating her, the therapist could say to the father: "Congratulations." Father: "What do you mean?" Therapist: "Congratulations; you win, she loses." Or the therapist could simply nudge the transaction by saying to the father: "Good, keep talking, but help her express her feelings more. She's still a little girl; she needs your help."

In addition to working with enacted sequences, structural therapists are alert to spontaneous sequences that illustrate family structure. Creating enactments is like directing plays; working with spontaneous sequences is like focusing a spotlight on action that occurs without direction. By observing and modifying such sequences early in therapy the therapist avoids getting bogged down in a family's usual nonproductive ways of doing business. Dealing with problematic behavior as soon as it occurs enables the therapist to organize the session, to underscore the process, and to modify it.

An experienced therapist develops hunches about family structure even before the first interview. For example, if a family is coming to the clinic because of a "hyperactive" child, it's possible to guess something about the family structure and something about sequences that may occur as the session begins, since "hyperactive" behavior is often a function of a child's enmeshment with the mother. Mother's relationship with the child may be a product of a lack of hierarchical differentiation within the family; that is, parents and children relate to each other as peers, not as members of different generations. Furthermore, mother's overinvolvement with the "hyperactive" child is likely to be both a result and a cause of emotional distance from her husband. Knowing that this is a common pattern, the therapist can anticipate that early in the first session the "hyperactive" child will begin to misbehave, and that the mother will be ineffective in dealing with this misbehavior. Armed with this informed guess the therapist can spotlight (rather than enact) such a sequence as soon as it occurs. If the "hyperactive" child begins to run around the room, and the mother protests but does nothing effective, the therapist might say, "I see that your child feels free to ignore you." This challenge may push the mother to behave in a more competent manner.

Therapy

Assessment

Diagnosis implies knowledge: You describe something and give it a name. Assessment deals with assumptions. A structural assessment is based on the assumption that a family's difficulties often reflect problems in the way the family is organized. It is assumed that if the organization shifts, the problem will shift. Perhaps it's important to add, that difficulties often reflect problems in the way the *whole* family is organized. Thus, it is assumed that if change occurs between mother and daughter, things will also change between husband and wife.

Structural therapists make assessments first by joining with the family to build an alliance, and then by setting the family system in motion through the use of enactments, in-session dialogues that permit the therapist to observe how family members actually interact.

Suppose, for example, a young woman complains of obsessional indecisiveness. In responding to the therapist's questions during an initial meeting with the family, the young woman becomes indecisive and glances at her father. He speaks up to clarify what she was having trouble explaining. Now the daughter's indecisiveness could be linked to the father's helpfulness, suggesting a pattern of enmeshment. When the therapist asks the parents to discuss their opinions about their daughter's problems, they have trouble talking without becoming reactive and the discussion doesn't last long. This suggests disengagement between the parents, which may be related (as cause and effect) to enmeshment between parent and child.

Notice how the structural assessment extends beyond the presenting problem to include the whole family, and—let's be frank—to the assumption that families with problems often have some kind of underlying structural problem. However, it is important to note that structural therapists make no assumptions about how families *should be* organized. Single-parent families can be perfectly functional, as can families with two mommies (or daddies), or indeed any other family variation. It is the fact that a family seeks therapy for a problem they have been unable to solve that gives a therapist license to assume that something about the way this particular family is organized may not be working for them.

Although structural assessments are fairly global—that is, they involve the basic organization of the whole family—making an assessment is best done by focusing on the presenting problem and then exploring the family's response to it. Consider the case of a thirteen-year-old girl whose parents complain that she lies. The first question might be, "Who is she lying to?" Let's say the answer is both parents. The next question would be, "How good are the parents at detecting when the daughter is lying?" And then, less innocently, "Which parent is better at detecting the daughter's lies?" Perhaps it turns out to be the mother. In fact, let's say the mother is obsessed with detecting the daughter's lies—most of which have to do with seeking independence in ways that raise the mother's anxiety. Thus a worried mother and a disobedient daughter are locked in struggle over growing up that excludes the father.

To carry this assessment further, a structural therapist would explore the relationship between the parents. The assumption would not, however, be that the child's problems are the result of marital problems, but simply that the mother–daughter relationship might be related to the relationship between the parents. Perhaps the parents got along famously until their first child approached adolescence, and then the mother began to worry much more than the father. Whatever the case, the assessment would also involve talking with the parents about growing up in their own families in order to explore how their pasts helped make them the way that they are.

Therapeutic Techniques

In *Families and Family Therapy,* Minuchin (1974) taught family therapists to see what they were looking at. Through the lens of structural family theory, previously puzzling family interactions suddenly swam into focus. Where others saw only chaos and cruelty, Minuchin saw structure: families organized into subsystems with boundaries. This enormously successful book (over 200,000 copies in print) not only taught us to see *enmeshment* and *disengagement,* but also let us hope that changing them was just a matter of *joining, enactment,* and *unbalancing.* Minuchin made changing families look simple. It isn't.

Anyone who watched Minuchin at work ten or twenty years after the publication of *Families and Family Therapy* would see a creative therapist still evolving, not someone frozen in time back in 1974. There would still be the patented confrontations ("Who's the sheriff in this family?") but there would be fewer enactments, less stage-directed dialogue. We would also hear bits and pieces borrowed from Carl Whitaker ("When did you divorce your wife and marry your job?"), Maurizio Andolfi ("Why don't you piss on the rug, too?"), and others. Minuchin combines many things in his work. To those familiar with his earlier work, all of this raises the question: Is Minuchin still a structural family therapist? The question is, of course, absurd; we raise it to make one point: Structural family therapy isn't a set of techniques; it's a way of looking at families.

In the remainder of this section, we will present the classic outlines of structural family technique, with the caveat that once therapists master the basics of structural theory, they must learn to translate the approach in a way that suits their own personal style. Implementing interventions is an art; therapists must discover and create techniques that fit each family's transactional style and the therapist's personality. Because every therapeutic session has idiosyncratic features, there can be no immediacy if the context is ignored. Imitating someone else's technique is stifling and ineffective—stifling because it doesn't fit the therapist, ineffective because it doesn't fit the family.

In *Families and Family Therapy*, Minuchin (1974) listed three overlapping phases in the process of structural family therapy. The therapist (1) joins the family in a position of leadership; (2) maps their underlying structure; and (3) intervenes to transform this structure. This program is simple, in the sense that it follows a clear plan, but immensely complicated because there are an endless variety of family patterns.

Observed in practice, structural family therapy is an organic whole, created out of the very real human interaction of therapist and family. To be genuine and effective, a therapist's moves cannot be preplanned or rehearsed. Good therapists are more than technicians. The strategy of therapy, on the other hand, must be thoughtfully planned. In general, the strategy of structural family therapy follows these seven steps:

1. Joining and accommodating
2. Working with interaction
3. Structural mapping
4. Highlighting and modifying interactions
5. Boundary making
6. Unbalancing
7. Challenging unproductive assumptions

Joining and Accommodating. Because most families have firmly established homeostatic patterns, effective family therapy requires challenge and confrontation. But assaults on a family's habitual style will be dismissed unless they're made from a position of acceptance and understanding. Families, like you and me, resist efforts to change them by people they feel don't understand and accept them.

Individual patients generally enter treatment already predisposed to accept the therapist's authority. By seeking therapy, an individual tacitly acknowledges a need for help and a willingness to trust the therapist. Not so with families.

The family therapist is an unwelcome outsider. After all, why did she insist on seeing the whole family rather than just the official patient? Family members expect to be told that they're doing something wrong, and they're prepared to defend themselves. The family is thus a group of nonpatients who feel anxious and exposed; they're set to resist, not to cooperate.

First the therapist must disarm defenses and ease anxiety. This is done by building an alliance of understanding with every single member of the family. The therapist greets each person by name and makes some kind of friendly contact.

These initial greetings convey respect, not only for the individuals in the family, but also for their hierarchical structure and organization. The therapist shows respect for parents by taking their authority for granted. They, not their children, are asked first to describe the problems. If a family elects one person to speak for the others, the therapist notes this but does not initially challenge it.

Children also have special concerns and capacities. They should be greeted gently and asked simple, concrete questions, "Hi, I'm so-and-so; what's your name? Oh, Shelly, that's a nice name. Where do you go to school, Shelly?" With older children, try to avoid the usual sanctimonious grown-up questions ("And what do *you* want to be when you grow up?"). Try something a little fresher (like "What do you hate most about school?"). Those who wish to remain silent should be "allowed" to do so. They will anyway, but the therapist who accepts their reticence will have made a valuable step toward keeping them involved. "And what's your view of the problem?" (Grim silence.) "I see, you don't feel like saying anything right now? That's fine; perhaps you'll have something to say later."

Failure to join and accommodate produces resistance, which is often blamed on the family. It may be comforting to blame others when things don't go well, but it doesn't improve matters. Family members can be called "negative," "rebellious," "resistant," or "defiant," and seen as "unmotivated"; but it's more useful to make an extra effort to connect with them.

It's particularly important to join powerful family members, as well as angry ones. Special pains must be taken to accept the point of view of the father who thinks therapy is hooey or the angry teenager who feels like an accused criminal. It's also important to reconnect with such people at frequent intervals, particularly as things begin to heat up.

A useful beginning is to greet the family and then ask for each person's view of the problems. Listen carefully and acknowledge each person's position by reflecting what you hear. "I see, Mrs. Jones, you think Sally must be depressed about something that happened at school." "So Mr. Jones, you see some of the same things your wife sees, but you're not convinced it's that serious a problem. Is that right?"

Working with Interaction. Family structure is manifest in the way family members interact. It can't always be inferred from their descriptions. Therefore, asking questions such as "Who's in charge?" or "Do you two agree?" tends to be unproductive. Families generally describe themselves more as they think they should be than as they are.

Getting family members to talk among themselves runs counter to their expectations. They expect to present their case to an expert and then be told what to do. If asked to discuss something in the session, they'll say: "We've talked about this many times"; or "It won't do

any good, he (or she) doesn't listen"; or "But *you're* supposed to be the expert."

If the therapist begins by giving each person a chance to speak, usually one will say something about another that can be a springboard for an enactment. When, for example, one parent says that the other is too strict, the therapist can develop an enactment by saying: "She says you're too strict; can you answer her?" Picking a specific point for response is more effective than a vague request, such as "Why don't you two talk this over?"

Once an enactment is begun, the therapist can discover many things about a family's structure. How long can two people talk without being interrupted—that is, how clear is the boundary? Does one attack, the other defend? Who is central, who peripheral? Do parents bring children into their discussions—that is, are they enmeshed?

Families demonstrate enmeshment by frequently interrupting each other, speaking for other family members, doing things for children that they can do for themselves, or by constantly arguing. In disengaged families one may see a husband sitting impassively while his wife cries; a total absence of conflict; a surprising ignorance of important information about the children; a lack of concern for each other's interests.

If, as soon as the first session starts, the kids begin running around the room while the parents protest ineffectually, the therapist doesn't need to hear descriptions of what goes on at home to see the executive incompetence. If a mother and daughter rant and rave at each other while the father sits silently in the corner, it isn't necessary to ask how involved he is at home. In fact, asking may yield a less accurate picture than the one revealed spontaneously.

Structural Mapping. Families usually conceive of problems as located in the identified patient and as determined by events from the past. They hope the therapist will change the identified patient—with as little disruption to the family as possible. Family therapists regard the identified patient's symptoms as an expression of dysfunctional patterns affecting the whole family. A structural assessment broadens the problem beyond individuals to the family system, and moves the focus from discrete events in the past to ongoing transactions in the present.

Even family therapists often categorize families with constructs that apply more to individuals than to systems. "The problem in this family is that the mother is smothering the kids," or "These kids are defiant," or "He's uninvolved." Structural family therapists diagnose so as to describe the interrelationship of all family members. Using the concepts of boundaries and subsystems, the structure of the whole system is described in a way that points to desired changes.

Preliminary assessments are based on observed interactions in the first session. In later sessions these formulations are refined and revised. Although there is some danger of bending families to fit categories when they're applied early, the greater danger is waiting too long. We see people with the greatest clarity and freshness during the initial contact. Later, as we come to know them better, we get used to their idiosyncrasies and soon no longer notice them.

Families quickly *induct* therapists into their culture. A family that initially appears to be chaotic and enmeshed soon comes to be just the familiar Jones family. For this reason, it's critical to develop structural hypotheses as quickly as possible.

In fact, it's helpful to make some guesses about family structure even before the first session. This starts a process of active thinking and sets the stage for observing the family. For example, suppose you're about to see a family consisting of a mother, a sixteen-year-old daughter, and a stepfather. The mother called to complain of her daughter's misbehavior.

What do you imagine the structure might be, and how would you test your hypothesis? A good guess might be that mother and daughter are enmeshed, excluding the stepfather. This can be tested by seeing if mother and daughter tend to talk mostly about each other in the session—whether positively or negatively. The stepfather's disengagement would be confirmed if he and his wife were unable to converse without the daughter's intrusion.

Structural assessments take into account both the problem the family presents and the structural dynamics they display. And they include all family members. In this instance, knowing that the mother and daughter are enmeshed isn't enough; you also have to know what role the stepfather plays. If he's reasonably close with his wife but distant from the daughter, finding mutually enjoyable activities for stepfather and stepdaughter will help increase the girl's independence from her mother. On the other hand, if the mother's proximity to her daughter appears to be a function of her distance from her husband, then the marital pair may be the most productive focus.

Without a structural formulation and a plan, a therapist is defensive and passive. Instead of knowing where to go and moving deliberately, the therapist lays back and tries to cope with the family, to put out brush fires, and to help them through a succession of incidents. Consistent awareness of the family's structure and focus on one or two structural changes helps the therapist see behind the various content issues that family members bring up.

Highlighting and Modifying Interactions.
Once families begin to interact, problematic transactions emerge. Recognizing their structural implications demands focus on process, not content. Nothing about structure is revealed by hearing who is in favor of punishment or who says nice things about whom. Family structure is revealed by who says what to whom, and in what way.

Perhaps a wife complains, "We have a communication problem. My husband won't talk to me; he never expresses his feelings." The therapist then stimulates an interaction to see what actually does happen. "Your wife says you have a communication problem; can you respond to that? Talk with her." If, when they talk, the wife becomes domineering and critical while the husband grows increasingly silent, then the therapist sees what's wrong: The problem isn't that he doesn't talk, which is a linear explanation. Nor is the problem that she nags, also a linear explanation. The problem is that the more she nags, the more he withdraws, and the more he withdraws, the more she nags.

The trick is to modify this pattern. This may require forceful intervening, or what structural therapists call **intensity.**

Minuchin speaks to families with dramatic and forceful impact. He regulates the intensity of his messages to exceed the threshold family members have for not hearing challenges to the way they perceive reality. When Minuchin speaks, families listen.

Minuchin is forceful, but intensity isn't merely a function of personality; it reflects clarity of purpose. Knowledge of family structure and a commitment to help families change makes powerful interventions possible.

Structural therapists achieve intensity by selective regulation of affect, repetition, and duration. Tone, volume, pacing, and choice of words can be used to raise the affective intensity of statements. It helps if you know what you want to say. Here's an example of a limp statement: "People are always concerned with themselves, kind of seeing themselves as the center of attention and just looking for whatever they can get. Wouldn't it be nice, for a change, if everybody started thinking about what they could do for others?" Compare that with, "Ask not what your country can do for you—ask what you can do for your country." John Kennedy's words had impact because they were carefully chosen and clearly put. Family

therapists don't need to make speeches, but they do occasionally have to speak forcefully to get their points across.

Affective intensity isn't simply a matter of crisp phrasing. You have to know how and when to be provocative. For example, Mike Nichols worked with a family in which a twenty-nine-year-old woman with anorexia nervosa was the identified patient. Although the family maintained a facade of togetherness, it was rigidly structured; the mother and her anorexic daughter were enmeshed, while the father was excluded. In this family, the father was the only one to express anger openly, and this was part of the official rationale for why he was excluded. His daughter was afraid of his anger, which she freely admitted. What was less clear, however, was that the mother had covertly taught the daughter to avoid him, because she, the mother, couldn't deal with his anger. Consequently, the daughter grew up afraid of her father, and of men in general.

At one point the father described how isolated he felt from his daughter; he said he thought it was because she feared his anger. The daughter agreed, "It's his fault, all right." The therapist asked the mother what she thought, and she replied, "It isn't *his* fault." The therapist said, "You're right." She went on, denying her real feelings to avoid conflict, "It's no one's fault." The therapist answered in a way that got her attention, "That's not true." Startled, she asked what he meant. "It's *your* fault," he said.

This level of intensity was necessary to interrupt a rigid pattern of conflict avoidance that sustained a destructive alliance between mother and daughter. The content—who really is afraid of anger—is less important than the structural goal: freeing the daughter from her position of overinvolvement with her mother.

Therapists too often dilute their interventions by overqualifying, apologizing, or rambling. This is less of a problem in individual therapy, where it's often best to elicit interpretations from the patient. Families are more like the farmer's proverbial mule—you sometimes have to hit them over the head to get their attention.

Intensity can also be achieved by extending the duration of a sequence beyond the point where the dysfunctional homeostasis is reinstated. A common example is the management of temper tantrums. Temper tantrums are maintained by parents who give in. Most parents *try* not to give in; they just don't try long enough. Recently a four-year-old girl began to scream bloody murder when her sister left the room. She wanted to go with her sister. Her screaming was almost unbearable, and the parents were soon ready to back down. However, the therapist urged that they not allow themselves to be defeated, and suggested that they hold her "to show her who's in charge" until she calmed down. She screamed for thirty minutes! Everyone in the room was frazzled. But the little girl finally realized that this time she was not going to get her way, and so she calmed down. Subsequently, the parents were able to use the same intensity of duration to break her of this highly destructive habit.

Sometimes intensity requires repetition of one theme in a variety of contexts. Infantilizing parents may have to be told not to hang up their child's coat, not to speak for her, not to take her to the bathroom, and not to do many other things that she's able to do for herself.

Shaping competence is another method of modifying interactions, and it's a hallmark of structural family therapy. Intensity is generally used to block the stream of interactions. Shaping competence is like nudging the direction of the flow. By highlighting and shaping the positive, structural therapists help family members use functional alternatives that are already in their repertoire.

A common mistake made by beginning therapists is to attempt to foster competent performance by pointing out mistakes. This focuses on content without regard for process. Telling parents that they're doing something wrong or

suggesting they do something different has the effect of criticizing their competence. However well-intentioned, it's still a put-down. While this kind of intervention cannot be completely avoided, a more effective approach is to point out what they're doing right.

Even when people do most things ineffectively, it's usually possible to pick out something that they're doing successfully. A sense of timing helps. For example, in a large chaotic family the parents were extremely ineffective at controlling the children. At one point the therapist turned to the mother and said, "It's too noisy in here; would you quiet the kids?" Knowing how much difficulty the woman had controlling her children, the therapist was poised to comment immediately on any step in the direction of effective management. The mother had to yell "Quiet!" a couple of times before the children momentarily stopped what they were doing. Quickly—before the children resumed their misbehavior—the therapist complimented the mother for "loving her kids enough to be firm with them." Thus the message delivered was "You're a competent person, you know how to be firm." If the therapist had waited until the chaos resumed before telling the mother she should be firm, the message would be "You're incompetent."

Wherever possible, structural therapists avoid doing things for family members that they're capable of doing themselves. Here, too, the message is "You are competent, you can do it." Some therapists justify taking over family functions by calling it "modeling." Whatever it's called it has the impact of telling family members that they're inadequate. Recently a young mother confessed she hadn't known how to tell her children that they were coming to see a family therapist and so had simply said she was taking them for a ride. Thinking to be helpful, the therapist then explained to the children that "Mommy told me there were some problems in the family, so we're all here to talk things over to see if we can improve things." This lovely explanation tells the kids why they came, but confirms the mother as incompetent to do so. If instead the therapist had suggested to the mother, "Would you like to tell them now?" Then the mother, not the therapist, would have had to perform as an effective parent.

Boundary Making. Dysfunctional family dynamics are a product of overly rigid or diffuse boundaries. Structural therapists intervene to realign boundaries, increasing either proximity or distance between family subsystems.

In enmeshed families the therapist's interventions are designed to strengthen boundaries between subsystems and increase the independence of individuals. Family members are urged to speak for themselves, interruptions are blocked, and dyads are helped to finish conversations without intrusion from others. A therapist who wishes to support the sibling system and protect it from unnecessary parental intrusion may say, "Susie and Sean, talk this over, and everyone else will listen carefully." If children frequently interrupt their parents, a therapist might challenge the parents to strengthen the hierarchical boundary by saying, "Why don't you get them to butt out so that you two grown-ups can settle this."

Although structural family therapy is begun with the total family group, subsequent sessions may be held with individuals or subgroups to strengthen the boundaries surrounding them. A teenager who is overprotected by her mother is supported as a separate person by participating in some individual sessions. Parents so enmeshed with their children that they never have private conversations may begin to learn how if they meet separately with the therapist.

When a forty-year-old woman called the clinic for help with depression, she was asked to come in with the rest of the family. It soon became apparent that this woman was overburdened by her four children and received little support from her husband. The therapist's strategy was to strengthen the boundary between the mother and children and help the parents move closer toward each other. This was done in stages. First the therapist joined the oldest child, a sixteen-year-old girl, and supported her competence as a potential helper for her mother. Once this was done, the girl was able to assume a good deal of responsibility for her younger siblings, both in sessions and at home.

Freed from preoccupation with the children, the parents now had the opportunity to talk more with each other. They had little to say, however. This wasn't the result of hidden conflict but instead reflected the marriage of two relatively nonverbal people. After several sessions of trying to get the pair talking, the therapist realized that while talking may be fun for some people, it might not be for others. So to support the bond between the couple the therapist asked them to plan a special trip together. They chose a boat ride on a nearby lake. When they returned for the next session, they were beaming. They had a wonderful time, being apart from the kids and enjoying each other's company. Subsequently they decided to spend a little time out together each week.

Disengaged families tend to avoid conflict, and thus minimize interaction. The structural therapist intervenes to challenge conflict avoidance, and to block detouring in order to help disengaged members increase contact with each other. Without acting as judge or referee, the structural therapist encourages family members to face each other squarely and struggle with the difficulties between them. When beginners see disengagement, they tend to think of ways to increase positive interaction. In fact, disengagement is usually a way of avoiding arguments. Therefore, spouses isolated from each other typically need to fight before they can become more loving.

Most people underestimate the degree to which their own behavior influences the behavior of those around them. This is particularly true in disengaged families. Problems are usually seen as the result of what someone else is doing, and solutions are thought to require that the others change. The following complaints are typical: "We have a communication problem; he won't tell me what he's feeling." "He just doesn't care about us. All he cares about is that damn job of his." "Our sex life is lousy—my wife's frigid." "Who can talk to her? All she does is complain about the kids." Each of these statements suggests that the power to change rests solely with the other person. This is the almost universally perceived view of linear causality.

Whereas most people see things this way, family therapists see the inherent circularity in systems interaction. He doesn't tell his wife what he's feeling, because she nags and criticizes; *and* she nags and criticizes because he doesn't tell her what he's feeling.

Structural therapists move family discussions from linear to circular perspectives by stressing complementarity. The mother who complains that her son is naughty is taught to consider what she's doing to trigger or maintain his behavior. The one who asks for change must learn to change his or her way of trying to get it. The wife who nags her husband to spend more time with her must learn to make increased involvement more attractive. The husband who complains that his wife never listens to him may have to listen to *her* more, before she's willing to reciprocate.

Minuchin emphasizes complementarity by asking family members to help each other change. When positive changes are reported, he's liable to congratulate others, underscoring family interrelatedness.

Unbalancing. In boundary making the therapist aims to realign relationships between subsystems. In unbalancing, the goal is to change the relationship of members *within* a subsystem. What often keeps families stuck in stalemate is that members in conflict check and balance each other and, as a result, remain frozen in inaction. In unbalancing, the therapist joins and supports one individual or subsystem at the expense of others.

Taking sides—let's call it what it is—seems like a violation of therapy's sacred canon of neutrality. However, the therapist takes sides to unbalance and realign the system, not because she is the judge of who's right and wrong. Ultimately, balance and fairness are achieved because the therapist sides in turn with various members of the family.

—**Case Study**——————

When the MacLean family sought help for an "unmanageable" child, a terror who'd been expelled from two schools, Dr. Minuchin uncovered a covert split between the parents, held in balance by not being talked about. The ten-year-old boy's misbehavior was dramatically visible; his father had to drag him kicking and screaming into the consulting room. Meanwhile, his seven-year-old brother sat quietly, smiling engagingly. The good boy.

To broaden the focus from an "impossible child" to issues of parental control and cooperation, Minuchin asked about seven-year-old Kevin, who misbehaved invisibly. He peed on the floor in the bathroom. According to his father, Kevin's peeing on the floor was due to "inattentiveness." The mother laughed when Minuchin said "Nobody could have such poor aim."

Minuchin talked with the boy about how wolves mark their territory, and suggested that he expand his territory by peeing in all four corners of the family room.

Minuchin: Do you have a dog?
Kevin: No.
Minuchin: Oh, so you are the family dog.

In the process of discussing the boy who peed—and his parents' response—Minuchin dramatized how the parents polarized each other.

Minuchin: Why would he do such a thing?
Father: I don't know if he did it on purpose.
Minuchin: Maybe he was in a trance?
Father: No, I think it was carelessness.
Minuchin: His aim must be terrible.

The father described the boy's behavior as accidental; the mother considered it defiance. One of the reasons parents fall under the control of their young children is that they avoid confronting their differences. Differences are normal, but they become toxic when one parent undercuts the other's handling of the children. (It's cowardly revenge for unaddressed grievances.)

Minuchin's gentle but insistent pressure on the couple to talk about how they respond, without switching to focus on how the children behave, led to their bringing up long-held but seldom-voiced resentments.

> *Mother:* Bob makes excuses for the children's behavior–because he doesn't want to get in there and help me find a solution for the problem.
> *Father:* Yes, but when I did try to help, you'd always criticize me. So after a while I gave up.

Like a photographic print in a developing tray, the spouses' conflict had become visible. Minuchin protected the parents from embarrassment (and the children from being burdened) by asking the children to leave the room. Without the preoccupation of parenting, the spouses could face each other, man and woman–and talk about their hurts and grievances. It turned out to be a sad story of lonely disengagement.

> *Minuchin:* Do you two have areas of agreement?

He said yes; she said no. He was a minimizer; she was a critic.

> *Minuchin:* When did you divorce Bob and marry the children?

She turned quiet; he looked off into space. She said, softly: "Probably ten years ago."

What followed was a painful but familiar story of how a marriage can drown in parenting and its conflicts. The conflict was never resolved because it never surfaced. And so the rift never healed; it just expanded.

With Minuchin's help, the couple took turns talking about their pain–and learning to listen. By unbalancing, Minuchin brought enormous pressure to bear to help this couple break through their differences, open up to each other, fight for what they want, and, finally, begin to come together–as husband and wife, and as parents.

Unbalancing is part of a struggle for change that sometimes takes on the appearance of combat. When a therapist says to a father that he's not doing enough or to a mother that she's unwittingly excluding her husband, it may seem that the combat is between the therapist and the family, that he or she is attacking them. But the real combat is between them and fear—fear of change.

Challenging Unproductive Assumptions. Although structural family therapy is not primarily a cognitive approach, its practitioners sometimes challenge the way family members see things. Changing the way family members relate to each other offers alternative views of their situation. The converse is also true: Changing the way family members view their situation enables them to change the way they relate to each other.

When six-year-old Cassie's parents complain about her behavior, they say she's "hyper," "sensitive," a "nervous child." Such labels convey how parents respond to their children and have a tremendous controlling power. Is a child's behavior "misbehavior," or is it a symptom of "nervousness?" Is it "naughty," or is it a "cry for help?" Is the child mad or bad, and who is in charge? What's in a name? Plenty.

Sometimes the structural family therapist acts as teacher, offering information and advice, often about structural matters. Doing so is likely to be a restructuring maneuver and must be done in a way that minimizes resistance. A therapist does this by delivering first a "stroke," then a "kick." If the therapist were dealing with a family in which the mother speaks for her children, he might say to her, "You are very helpful" (stroke). But to the child, "Mommy takes away your voice. You can speak for yourself" (kick). Thus mother is defined as helpful but intrusive (a stroke and a kick).

Structural therapists also use pragmatic fictions to provide family members with a different frame for experiencing. The aim isn't to educate or deceive, but to offer a pronouncement that will help the family change. For instance, telling children that they're behaving younger than they are is a very effective means of getting them to change. "How old are you?" "Seven." "Oh, I thought you were younger; most seven-year-olds don't need Mommy to take them to school anymore."

Paradoxes are cognitive constructions that frustrate or confuse family members into a search for alternatives. Minuchin makes little use of paradox, but sometimes it's helpful to express skepticism about people changing. Although this can have the paradoxical effect of challenging them to prove you wrong, it isn't so much a clever stratagem as it is a benign statement of the truth. Most people *don't* change— they wait for others to do so.

Evaluating Therapy Theory and Results

While he was Director of the Philadelphia Child Guidance Clinic, Minuchin developed a highly pragmatic commitment to research. As an administrator he learned that research demonstrating effective outcomes is the best argument for the legitimacy of family therapy. Both his studies of psychosomatic children and Stanton's studies of drug addicts show very clearly how effective structural family therapy can be.

In *Families of the Slums,* Minuchin and his colleagues (1967) described the structural characteristics of low socioeconomic families and demonstrated the effectiveness of family therapy with this population. Prior to treatment, mothers in patient families were found to be either over- or undercontrolling; either way their children were more disruptive than those in control families. After treatment mothers used less coercive control, yet were clearer and more firm. In this study, seven of eleven families were judged to be improved after six months to a year of family therapy. Although no control group was used, the authors compared

their results favorably to the usual 50 percent rate of successful treatment at Wiltwyck. The authors also noted that none of the families rated as disengaged improved.

By far the strongest empirical support for structural family therapy comes from a series of studies with psychosomatic children and adult drug addicts. Studies demonstrating the effectiveness of therapy with severely ill psychosomatic children are convincing because of the physiological measures employed, and dramatic because of the life-threatening nature of the problems. Minuchin, Rosman, and Baker (1978) reported one study that clearly demonstrated how family conflict can precipitate ketoacidosis crises in psychosomatic-type diabetic children. In baseline interviews parents discussed family problems with their children absent. Normal spouses showed the highest levels of confrontation, while psychosomatic spouses exhibited a wide range of conflict-avoidance maneuvers. Next, a therapist pressed the parents to increase the level of their conflict, while their children observed behind a one-way mirror. As the parents argued, only the psychosomatic children seemed really upset. Moreover, these children's manifest distress was accompanied by dramatic increases in free fatty acid levels of the blood, a measure related to ketoacidosis. In the third stage of these interviews, the patients joined their parents. Normal and behavior-disorder parents continued as before, but the psychosomatic parents detoured their conflict, either by drawing their children into their discussions or by switching the subject from themselves to the children. When this happened, the free fatty acid levels of the parents fell, while the children's levels continued to rise. This study provided strong confirmation of the clinical observations that psychosomatic children are used (and let themselves be used) to regulate the stress between their parents.

Minuchin, Rosman, and Baker (1978) summarized the results of treating fifty-three cases of anorexia nervosa with structural family therapy. After a course of treatment that included hospitalization followed by family therapy on an outpatient basis, forty-three anorexic children were "greatly improved," two were "improved," three showed "no change," two were "worse," and three had dropped out. Although ethical considerations precluded a control treatment with these seriously ill children, the 90 percent improvement rate is impressive, especially compared with the 30 percent mortality rate for this disorder. Moreover, the positive results at termination were maintained at follow-up intervals of several years. Structural family therapy has also been shown to be effective in treating psychosomatic asthmatics and psychosomatically complicated cases of diabetes (Minuchin, Baker, Rosman, Liebman, Milman, & Todd, 1975).

While no body of empirical evidence has established that any one psychotherapeutic approach is consistently better than the others, structural family therapy has proven to be effective in a variety of studies, including many that involved what are usually considered very difficult cases. Duke Stanton showed that structural family therapy can be effective for drug addicts and their families. In a well-controlled study, Stanton and Todd (1979) compared family therapy with a family placebo condition and individual therapy. Symptom reduction was significant with structural family therapy; the level of positive change was more than double that achieved in the other conditions, and these positive effects persisted at follow-up of six and twelve months.

More recently, structural family therapy has been successfully applied to establish more adaptive parenting roles in heroin addicts (Grief & Dreschler, 1993) and as a means to reduce the likelihood that African American and Latino youths would initiate drug use (Santisteban, Coatsworth, Perez-Vidal, Mitrani, Jean-Gilles, & Szapocznik, 1997). Other studies indicate that structural family therapy is equal in effectiveness to communication training and behavioral management training in reducing negative communication, conflicts, and expressed anger between adolescents diagnosed with attention deficit hyperactivity disorder (ADHD) and their parents (Barkley, Guevremont, Anastopoulos, & Fletcher, 1992). Structural family therapy has also been effective for treating adolescent disorders, such as conduct disorders (Szapocznik et al., 1989; Chamberlain & Rosicky, 1995), and anorexia nervosa (Campbell & Patterson, 1995).

—Summary—

Minuchin may be best known for the artistry of his clinical technique, yet his structural family theory has become one of the most widely used conceptual models in the field. The reason structural theory is so popular is that it's simple, inclusive, and practical. The basic concepts—boundaries, subsystems, alignments, and complementarity—are easily grasped and applied. They take into account the individual, family, and social context, and they provide a clear organizing framework for understanding and treating families.

The single most important tenet of this approach is that every family has a structure, and that this structure is revealed only when the family is in action. According to this view, therapists who fail to consider the entire family's structure, and intervene in only one subsystem, are unlikely to effect lasting change. If a mother's overinvolvement with her son is part of a structure that includes distance from her husband, no amount of therapy for the mother and son is likely to bring about basic change in the family.

Subsystems are units of the family based on function. If the leadership of a family is taken over by a father and daughter, then they, not the husband and wife, are the executive subsystem. Subsystems are circumscribed and regulated by interpersonal boundaries. In healthy families boundaries are clear enough to protect independence and autonomy, and permeable enough to allow mutual support and affection. Enmeshed families are characterized by diffuse boundaries; disengaged families by rigid boundaries.

Structural family therapy is designed to resolve presenting problems by reorganizing family structure. Assessment, therefore, requires the presence of the whole family, so that the therapist can observe the structure underlying the family's interactions. In the process, therapists should distinguish between dysfunctional and functional structures. Families with growing pains shouldn't be treated as pathological. Where structural problems do exist, the goal is to create an effective hierarchical structure. This means activating dormant structures, not creating new ones.

Structural family therapists work quickly to avoid being *inducted* as members of the families they work with. They begin by making concerted efforts to accommodate to the family's accustomed ways of behaving, in order to circumvent resistance. Once they've gained a family's trust, therapists promote family interaction, while they assume a decentralized role. From this position they can watch what goes on in the family and make a structural assessment, which includes the problem and the organization that supports it. These assessments are framed in terms of boundaries and subsystems, easily conceptualized as two-dimensional maps used to suggest avenues for change.

Once they have successfully joined and assessed a family, structural therapists proceed to activate dormant structures using techniques that alter alignments and shift power within and between subsystems. These restructuring techniques are concrete, forceful, and sometimes dramatic. However, their success depends as much on the joining and assessment as on the power of the techniques themselves.

Structural family therapy's popularity is based on its theory and techniques of treatment; its central position in the field has been augmented by its research and training programs. There is now a substantial body of research that lends considerable empirical support to this school's approach. Moreover, the training programs at the Philadelphia Child Guidance Clinic and Minuchin Center in New York have influenced an enormous number of family therapy practitioners throughout the world.

Although structural family therapy is so closely identified with Salvador Minuchin that they once were synonymous, it may be a good idea to differentiate the man from the method. When we think of structural family therapy, we tend to remember the approach as described in *Families and Family Therapy*, published in 1974. That book adequately represents structural theory, but emphasizes only the techniques Minuchin favored at the time. Minuchin, the thinker, has always thought of families in organizational terms. He read Talcott Parsons and Robert Bales and George Herbert Mead; and in Israel he saw how children from unstructured Moroccan families often became delinquents, while those from organized Yemenite families did not. Minuchin the therapist has always been an opportunist, using whatever works. Today you can see Carl Whitaker and constructivism in Minuchin's work. From Whitaker, he took the idea of challenging families' myths and engaging with them from a position of passionate involvement. The young Minuchin followed families and watched them in action; that's why he made such use of enactments. The older

Minuchin, who has seen thousands of families, now sees things faster; he uses enactment less and is likely to confront one family on the basis of what he has seen in hundreds of similar cases. Should we follow him in this? Yes, as soon as we have the same experience.

Minuchin has always been a constructivist, though he comes by it intuitively, not from reading books. He challenges families, telling them, essentially, that they are wrong; their stories are too narrow. And he helps them rewrite stories that work. Minuchin has always been interested in literature and storytelling;

perhaps he likes the doctrine of constructivism simply because it legitimizes his storytelling. But, he cautions, when constructivism isn't grounded in structural understanding or when it neglects the emotional side of human beings, it can become arid intellectualism. Minuchin has moved toward eclecticism in technique, but not in theory. Although Minuchin the therapist has changed since 1974, his basic perspective on families, described in structural family theory, still stands, and continues to be the most widely used way of understanding what goes on in the nuclear family.

—Recommended Readings

Colapinto J. 1991. Structural family therapy. In *Handbook of family therapy*, Vol. II, A. S. Gurman and D. P. Kniskern, eds. New York: Brunner/Mazel.

Minuchin, S. 1974. *Families and family therapy.* Cambridge, MA: Harvard University Press.

Minuchin, S., and Fishman, H. C. 1981. *Family therapy techniques.* Cambridge, MA: Harvard University Press.

Minuchin, S., Lee, W-Y., and Simon, G. M. 1996. *Mastering family therapy: Journeys of growth and transformation.* New York: Wiley.

Minuchin, S., Montalvo, B., Guerney, B., Rosman, B., and Schumer, F. 1967. *Families of the slums.* New York: Basic Books.

Minuchin, S., and Nichols, M. P. 1993. *Family healing: Tales of hope and renewal from family therapy.* New York: Free Press.

Minuchin, S., Rosman, B. L., and Baker, L. 1978. *Psychosomatic families: Anorexia nervosa in context.* Cambridge, MA: Harvard University Press.

Nichols, M. P. 1999. *Inside family therapy.* Boston: Allyn & Bacon.

Nichols, M. P., and Minuchin, S. 1999. Short-term structural family therapy with couples. In *Short-term couple therapy*, J. M. Donovad, ed. New York: Guilford Press.

—References

Barkley, R., Guevremont, D., Anastopoulos, A., and Fletcher, K. 1992. A comparison of three family therapy programs for treating family conflicts in adolescents with attention-deficit hyperactivity disorder. *Journal of Consulting and Clinical Psychology. 60:*450–463.

Campbell, T., and Patterson, J. 1995. The effectiveness of family interventions in the treatment of physical illness. *Journal of Marital and Family Therapy. 21:*545–584.

Chamberlain, P., and Rosicky, J. 1995. The effectiveness of family therapy in the treatment of adolescents with conduct disorders and delinquency. *Journal of Marital and Family Therapy. 21:*441–459.

Colapinto, J. 1991. Structural family therapy. In *Handbook of family therapy*, Vol. II, A. S. Gurman and D. P. Kniskern, eds. New York: Brunner/Mazel.

Elizur, J., and Minuchin, S. 1989. *Institutionalizing madness: Families, therapy, and society.* New York: Basic Books.

Grief, G., and Dreschler, L. 1993. Common issues for parents in a methadone maintenance group. *Journal of Substance Abuse Treatment. 10:* 335–339.

Minuchin, S. 1974. *Families and family therapy.* Cambridge, MA: Harvard University Press.

Minuchin, S., Baker, L., Rosman, B., Liebman, R., Milman, L., and Todd, T. C. 1975. A conceptual model of psychosomatic illness in children. *Archives of General Psychiatry. 32:*1031–1038.

Minuchin, S., and Fishman, H. C. 1981. *Family therapy techniques.* Cambridge, MA: Harvard University Press.

Minuchin, S., Lee, W-Y., and Simon, G. M. 1996. *Mastering family therapy: Journeys of growth and transformation.* New York: Wiley.

Minuchin, S., Montalvo, B., Guerney, B., Rosman, B., and Schumer, F. 1967. *Families of the slums.* New York: Basic Books.

Minuchin, S., and Nichols, M. P. 1993. *Family healing: Tales of hope and renewal from family therapy.* New York: Free Press.

Minuchin, S., Rosman, B., and Baker, L. 1978. *Psychosomatic families: Anorexia nervosa in context.* Cambridge, MA: Harvard University Press.

Santisteban, D., Coatsworth, J., Perez-Vidal, A., Mitrani, V., Jean-Gilles, M., and Szapocznik, J. 1997. Brief structural/strategic family therapy with African American and Hispanic high-risk youth. *Journal of Community Psychology. 25:*453–471.

Simon, G. M. 1995. A revisionist rendering of structural family therapy. *Journal of Marital and Family Therapy. 21:*17–26.

Stanton, M. D., and Todd, T. C. 1979. Structural family therapy with drug addicts. In *The family therapy of drug and alcohol abuse,* E. Kaufman and P. Kaufmann, eds. New York: Gardner Press.

Szapocznik, J., Rio, A., Murray, E., Cohen, R., Scopetta, M., Rivas-Vazquez, A., Hervis, O., Posada, V., and Kurtines, W. 1989. Structural family versus psychodynamic child therapy for problematic Hispanic boys. *Journal of Consulting and Clinical Psychology. 57:*571–578.

8

Experiential Family Therapy

Family Therapy as an Emotional Encounter

An experiential branch of family ther-apy emerged from the humanistic wing of psychology that, like the ex-pressive therapies that inspired it, emphasized immediate, **here-and-now experience.** Ex-periential therapy was most popular when family therapy was young, when therapists talked about systems but borrowed their tech-niques from individual and group therapies. From Gestalt therapy and encounter groups came evocative techniques such as *role-playing* and *emotional confrontation,* while other ex-pressive methods such as *sculpting* and *family drawing* bore the influence of the arts and of psychodrama.

In focusing more on emotional experience than on the dynamics of interaction, experien-tial therapists seemed a little out of step with the rest of family therapy. Indeed, by emphasizing individuals and their feelings, experiential treat-ment may never have been as well suited to fam-ily therapy as were approaches that dealt with systems and action. With the passing of the in-spirational leaders of this tradition, Virginia Satir and Carl Whitaker, the methods they pop-ularized began to seem a little dated, more a product of the 1960s than of today's world.

Recently, however, experiential approaches have been enjoying a revival and, as we shall see, two of the newer models, Greenberg and Johnson's (1985) emotionally focused couples therapy and Schwartz's (1995) internal family systems model have combined the emotional impact of an experiential focus on the individ-ual with a more sophisticated understanding of family systems.

As the first great cathartic therapist, Sig-mund Freud, discovered, getting in touch with painful feelings is not, by itself, a sufficient model of psychotherapy. On the other hand, ig-noring or rationalizing unhappy emotions may cheat clients out of the opportunity to get to the heart of their problems. Thus the experiential emphasis on unblocking emotional expression continues to be a useful counterweight to the reductionistic emphasis on behavior and cog-nition common to today's problem-solving approaches.

Sketches of Leading Figures

Two giants stand out in the development of experiential family therapy: Carl Whitaker and Virginia Satir. Whitaker was the leading exponent of a freewheeling, intuitive approach aimed at puncturing pretense and liberating family members to be themselves. He was among the first to do psychotherapy with families and, although he was once considered something of a maverick, he eventually became one of the most admired therapists in the field. Iconoclastic, even outrageous at times, Whitaker nevertheless retained the respect of the family therapy establishment. He may have been their Puck, but he was one of them.

Whitaker grew up on a dairy farm in upstate New York. Rural isolation bred a certain shyness but also conditioned him to be less bound by social convention. After medical school and a residency in obstetrics and gynecology, Whitaker went into psychiatry, where he became fascinated by the psychotic mind. Unfortunately—or fortunately—back in the 1940s Whitaker couldn't rely on neuroleptic drugs to blunt the hallucinatory imaginings of his patients; instead he listened and learned to understand thoughts crazy but human, thoughts most of us usually keep buried.

After working at the University of Louisville College of Medicine and the Oakridge Hospital,

Carl Whitaker used a free-wheeling approach to wake family members up to their own inner longings.

Whitaker accepted the chair of Emory University's Department of Psychiatry, where he remained from 1946 to 1955, when, in the face of mounting pressure to make the department more psychoanalytic, Whitaker and his entire faculty, including Thomas Malone, John Warkentin, and Richard Felder, resigned to establish the Atlanta Psychiatric Clinic. Experiential psychotherapy was born of this union, and the group produced a number of provocative and challenging papers (Whitaker & Malone, 1953). In 1965 Whitaker moved to the University of Wisconsin Medical School. After his retirement in the late 1980s, he traveled widely to share his wisdom and experience at conventions and workshops. His death in 1995 was a great loss. Among Whitaker's best-known associates are August Napier, now in private practice in Atlanta, and David Keith, at the State University of New York in Syracuse.

The other towering figure among experiential family therapists was Virginia Satir. As an early member of the Mental Research Institute (MRI), Satir emphasized communication as well as emotional experiencing, and so her work must be considered in both the communications (see Chapters 3 and 6) and experiential traditions.

Satir began seeing families in private practice in Chicago in 1951. In 1955 she was invited to set up a training program for residents at the Illinois State Psychiatric Institute (where one of her students was Ivan Boszormenyi-Nagy). In 1959 Don Jackson invited her to join him at MRI, where Satir became the first director of training and remained until 1966, when she left to become the director of the Esalen Institute in Big Sur, California.

Satir was the archetypal nurturing therapist in a field enamored of abstract concepts and strategic maneuvers. Her warmth and genuineness gave her tremendous appeal as she traveled the country leading demonstrations and workshops. Her ability to move large audiences made her family therapy's most celebrated humanist. Satir died of pancreatic cancer in 1988.

Among the most recent experiential approaches is the emotionally focused couples therapy of Leslie Greenberg and Susan Johnson, which draws on Perls, Satir, and the MRI group (Greenberg & Johnson, 1985, 1986, 1988). Another specialized approach to the inner emotional life of families is Richard Schwartz's (1995) internal family systems therapy, in which clients' conflicting inner voices are personified as "parts" and then reintegrated using a variety of psychodramatic techniques. Schwartz lives in Chicago where he now has his own clinic and training program.

Theoretical Formulations

Experiential family therapy is founded on the premise that the cause and effect of family problems is emotional suppression. While children must learn that they can't always do whatever they feel like doing, many parents have an unfortunate tendency to confuse the *instrumental* and *expressive* functions of emotion. They try to regulate their children's actions by controlling their feelings. As a result, children learn to blunt their emotional experience to avoid making waves. Although this process is more or less universal, dysfunctional families tend to be less tolerant of the emotions that signal individuality than most. As a result, children in such families often grow up estranged from themselves and feeling only the residues of repressed affect: boredom, apathy, and anxiety.

While systemic therapists see the roots of symptomatic behavior in the dance of family interactions, experientialists view those interactions as the result of family members shadow dancing with the projections of each other's defenses. From this perspective, attempts to bring about positive change in families are more likely to be successful if family members first get in touch with their real feelings—their hopes and desires as well as fears and anxieties. Thus experiential family therapy works from the inside out—helping individuals uncover their honest emotions, and then forging more genuine family ties out of this enhanced authenticity.

●

Carl Whitaker summed up the experiential position on theory in a paper entitled, "The Hindrance of Theory in Clinical Work" (Whitaker, 1976a). Theory may be useful for beginners, Whitaker said, but his advice was to give up calculation as soon as possible in favor of just being yourself.

Being antitheoretical is, of course, itself a theoretical position. To say that therapy shouldn't be constrained by theories is to say that it should be creative and spontaneous. Despite Whitaker's disdain for theory, however, experiential family therapy is very much a product of the existential-humanistic tradition.

Much of the theorizing of existential psychologists (e.g., Binswanger, 1967; Boss, 1963) was in reaction to perceived shortcomings of psychoanalysis and behaviorism. In place of *determinism*, existentialists emphasized freedom and the immediacy of experience. Where psychoanalysts posited a structuralized model of the mind, existentialists treated persons as wholes, and offered a positive model of humanity in place of what they saw as a pessimistic psychoanalytic model. Instead of settling for resolution of their neuroses, existentialists believed that people should aim for fulfillment.

Despite their disinclination to theorize, there are certain basic premises that define the experiential position. Whitaker emphasized that self-fulfillment depends on family cohesiveness, and Satir stressed the importance of good communication among family members; but the basic commitment was to *individual self-expression*. While there was some talk about family systems (e.g., Satir, 1972), the experiential model of families was more like a democratic group than a structured organization. There is great emphasis on *flexibility* and *freedom* with respect to family roles and the distribution of power. Treatment is generally designed to help individual family members find fulfilling roles for themselves, with less concern for the family as a whole. This is not to say that the needs of the family are denigrated, but that they are thought to follow on the heels of individual enhancement.[1]

After reading the previous paragraph, David Keith (in a personal letter) helped put into perspective the experiential position on the claims of the individual versus the claims of the family:

> There is a dialectical tension between the individual and the family—between dependence and independence. To overemphasize either individuality or family connectedness is to distort the human condition.

Theories of families as systems are translated into techniques that promote communication and interaction. The emphasis on altering interactions implies an acceptance of whatever level of individual experience is already present. This is where experiential theory differs (as does psychoanalysis) from most systems approaches. Here the emphasis is on expanding experience. The assumption is that opening up individuals to their experience is a prerequisite to breaking new ground for the family group.

The underlying premise of experiential family therapy is that the way to promote individual growth and family cohesion is to liberate affects and impulses. Efforts to reduce defensiveness and unlock deeper levels of experiencing rest on an assumption of the basic goodness of human nature.

The exception to the experiential deemphasis on theory is Greenberg and Johnson's emotionally focused couples therapy, which draws on attachment theory (Bowlby, 1969). According to Greenberg and Johnson, emotion organizes attachment responses and serves a communicative function in relationships. When people express their vulnerability directly, for example, they're likely to elicit a compassionate response from their partners. But when an insecurely attached person fears vulnerability and shows anger instead, the response is more likely to be withdrawal. Thus the person most in need of attachment may, by being afraid to expose that need, push away the loved ones he or she longs to get close to. The antidote for this dilemma is what experiential therapy is all about: helping people relax defensive fears so that deeper and more genuine emotions can emerge.

The rediscovery of attachment theory is consistent with a larger effort to reclaim dependency as a natural human proclivity. In Bowlby's (1969) terms, attachment security provides a person with a safe haven and a secure base—the ability to regulate emotions, the positive expectations of others, and the confidence to explore the world, risk intimacy, and give of oneself to other people. When attachment security is threatened, the first response is likely to be anger and protest, followed by some form of clinging, which eventually gives way to despair. Finally, if attachment figures do not respond, detachment and separation will occur (Bowlby, 1969).

Although attachment security may be founded in the earliest years of childhood, Bowlby (1988) believed that every meaningful interaction with important others throughout life continues to mold beliefs about other people's availability and supportiveness. While attachment security may be fairly general, people also develop relationship-specific beliefs based

---

1. Though, at one time, the family was portrayed as the enemy of freedom and authenticity (Laing & Esterson, 1970).

on experiences with a particular partner (Collins & Read, 1994). The process is, of course, circular. The more secure and trusting a person, the more likely she is to be open to—and in—relationships; and, thus, the more likely she is to develop relationships that confirm her sense of worth in connection. The converse is, unfortunately, also true: Partners who are afraid to express their attachment needs may remain stuck in negative patterns that preclude the responsiveness necessary to build secure relationships.

Whether attachment patterns in childhood continue to play a critical role in close relationships in adulthood remains to be demonstrated (see Chapter 4). But, as with most clinical hypotheses, the value of attachment theory in the practice of therapy rests more with its usefulness than with its empirical proof.

Normal Family Development

Experiential therapists subscribe to the humanistic faith in the natural wisdom of honest emotion. Left alone, people tend to flourish, according to this point of view. Problems arise because this innate tendency toward *self-actualization* (Rogers, 1951) runs afoul of social pressures. Society enforces repression to tame people's instincts and make them fit for group living. Unhappily, self-control is achieved at the cost of "surplus repression" (Marcuse, 1955). Families add their own controls to achieve peace and quiet, perpetuating outmoded **family myths** (Gehrke & Kirschenbaum, 1967) and relying on **mystification** (Laing, 1967) to alienate children from their experience.

In the ideal situation, parental control isn't excessive, and children grow up in an atmosphere of support for their feelings and creative impulses. Parents listen to their children, accept their feelings, and validate their experience. Affect is valued and nurtured; children

are encouraged to experience life fully and to express the full range of human emotions.

Experiential therapists describe the family as a place of sharing experience (Satir, 1972). Functional families are secure enough to support and encourage a wide range of experiencing; dysfunctional families are frightened and bloodless. Neither problem-solving skills nor particular family structures are considered as important as expanding open, natural, and spontaneous experiencing. In short, the healthy family offers its members the freedom to be themselves.

Development of Behavior Disorders

From an experiential perspective, denial of impulses and suppression of feeling are the root of family problems. Dysfunctional families are locked into self-protection and avoidance (Kaplan & Kaplan, 1978). In Harry Stack Sullivan's (1953) terms, they seek *security*, not *satisfaction*. Their presenting complaints are many, but the basic problem is that they smother emotion and desire.

According to Whitaker (Whitaker & Keith, 1981), there's no such thing as a marriage—only two scapegoats sent out by their families to perpetuate themselves. Together they must work out the inherent conflict in this situation. Couples who remain together eventually reach some kind of accommodation. Whether based on compromise or resignation, reconciling themselves to each other lessens the previous friction. Dysfunctional families, terrified of conflict, adhere rigidly to the rituals that they work out together. Having experienced the anxiety of uncertainty, they now cling to their routines.

In her portrayal of troubled families, Satir (1972) emphasized the atmosphere of emotional deadness. Such families are cold; they seem to stay together out of habit or duty. The adults don't enjoy their children, and the children learn not to value themselves or care about their parents. In consequence of the lack of warmth in the family, these people avoid each other, and preoccupy themselves with work and other distractions.

It's important to notice that the "dysfunction" Satir described isn't the kind found in diagnostic manuals. Like others in the experiential camp, Satir was as concerned with "normal" people who lead lives of quiet desperation as with the officially recognized patients families usually focus on. As she (Satir, 1972) put it,

> It is a sad experience for me to be with these families. I see the hopelessness, the helplessness, the loneliness. I see the bravery of people trying to cover up—a bravery that can still bellow or nag or whine at each other. Others no longer care. These people go on year after year, enduring misery themselves or in their desperation, inflicting it on others. (p. 12)

Satir stressed the role of destructive communication in smothering feeling and said that there were four dishonest ways people communicate: *blaming, placating,* being *irrelevant,* and being *super reasonable.* What's behind these patterns of inauthentic communication? *Low self-esteem.* If people feel badly about themselves, it's hard to tell the truth about their feelings—and threatening to let others tell them honestly what they feel.

Goals of Therapy

Growth, not stability, is the goal of experiential family therapy. Symptom relief is secondary to increased personal integrity and expanded experiencing (Malone, Whitaker, Warkentin, & Felder, 1961). The problems families present with are regarded as tickets of admission (Whitaker & Keith, 1981); the real problem is emotional sterility.

Most experiential therapists focus on individuals and their experience more than on family organization. In Kempler's (1981) case the commitment to the individual is acknowledged: "I consider my primary responsibility to people—to each individual within the family—and only secondarily to the organization called family" (p. 27). This emphasis on the individual over the family is *not* true of the more systems-wise experiential family therapists, such as Carl Whitaker, David Keith, and Gus Napier.

In common with others in the existential-humanistic tradition, experiential therapists believe that the way to emotional health is to uncover deeper levels of experiencing. Virginia Satir (1972) stated it this way:

> We attempt to make three changes in the family system. First, each member of the family should be able to report congruently, completely, and honestly on what he sees and hears, feels and thinks, about himself and others, in the presence of others. Second, each person should be addressed and related to in terms of his uniqueness, so that decisions are made in terms of exploration and negotiation rather than in terms of power. Third, differentness must be openly acknowledged and used for growth. (p. 120)

When experiential methods are applied to treating family systems (rather than to individuals who happen to be assembled in family groups), the goal of individual growth is merged with the goal of achieving a strengthened family unit. Carl Whitaker's work nicely embodied this dual goal. According to him, personal growth requires family integration, and vice versa. Belongingness and individuation go hand in hand. In fact, it's often necessary to bring parents closer together to enable their children to leave home, since many children can't leave unless they sense that their parents can be happy without them.

Experientialists emphasize the feeling side of human nature: creativity, spontaneity, and the ability to play—and, in therapy, the value of experience for its own sake.

New experience for family members is thought to break down rigid expectancies and unblock awareness—all of which promotes individuation (Kaplan & Kaplan, 1978). Bunny and Fred Duhl (1981) speak of their goals as a heightened sense of competence, well-being, and self-esteem. In emphasizing self-esteem, the Duhls echo Virginia Satir (1964) who believed that low self-esteem, and the destructive communication responsible for it, were the main problems in unhappy families.

Most family therapists consider increased sensitivity and growth in individuals as serving the broad aim of enhanced family functioning. Some experiential family therapists keep the family-systems goal implicit and devote relatively few of their interventions to promote it; others see individual growth as linked to family growth, and so devote more of their attention to promoting family interactions. The Duhls (1981) espouse "new and renewed integration" within and between family members as mutually reinforcing goals of treatment. Whitaker (1976a) presumed that families come to treatment because they're unable to be close, and therefore unable to individuate. By helping family members recover their own potential for experiencing, he believed that he was also helping them recover their ability to care for one another.

Conditions for Behavior Change

Among the misconceptions of those new to family therapy is that families are fragile and therapists must be careful to avoid breaking them. A little experience teaches the opposite: Effective treatment requires powerful interventions—and for experiential family therapists that power comes from emotional experiencing.

Experiential clinicians use evocative techniques and the force of their own personalities to create therapeutic encounters. The vitality of the therapist as a person is one major force in therapy; the vitality of the *encounter* is an-

other. This powerfully personal experience is thought to help establish caring, person-to-person relationships among all family members. Gus Napier (Napier & Whitaker, 1978) wrote, in *The Family Crucible,* a nice description of what experiential therapists think causes change. Breakthroughs occur when family members risk being "more separate, divergent, even angrier" as well as "when they risk being closer and more intimate." To help clients dare to take those risks, experiential therapists are alternately provocative and warmly supportive. This permits family members to drop protective defenses and open up to each other.

Existential encounter is believed to be the essential force in the psychotherapeutic process (Kempler, 1973; Whitaker, 1976a). These encounters must be reciprocal; instead of hiding behind a professional role, the therapist must be a genuine person who catalyzes change using his or her personal impact on families. As Kempler (1968) said:

> In this approach the therapist becomes a family member during the interviews, participating as fully as he is able, hopefully available for appreciation and criticism as well as he is able to dispense it. He laughs, cries and rages. He feels and shares his embarrassments, confusions and helplessness. (p. 97)

For Satir, caring and acceptance were the keys to helping people open up to experience, and open up to each other:

> Some therapists think people come into therapy not wanting to be changed; I don't think that's true. They don't think they *can* change. Going into some new, unfamiliar place is a scary thing. When I first begin to work with someone, I am not interested in changing them. I am interested in finding their rhythms, being able to join with them, and helping them go inside to those scary places. Resistance is mainly the fear of going somewhere you have not been. (quoted in Simon, 1989, pp. 38–39)

Some experiential therapists pay more attention to resistance to feeling within family members than to resistance of family systems to change. Kempler's conception of interlocking family patterns is that they're easily resolved by pointing them out. "Often in families, merely calling attention to the pattern is sufficient for one or more members to stop their part in it, thereby eliminating the possibility of continuing that interlocking behavior" (Kempler, 1981, p. 113). Kempler believes the objective of experiential therapy is to complete interpersonal encounters. He tries to promote this objective by simply pushing family members through impasses. But, just as is true with encounter groups (Lieberman, Yalom, & Miles, 1973), these changes will probably not be sustained without repetition, working through, and some kind of cognitive insight.

Dysfunctional families have conservative (homeostatic) predilections; they opt for safety rather than satisfaction. Since passions are messy, unhappy families are content to submerge them; experiential therapists are not. Clinicians like Whitaker believe that it is important to be effective, not safe. Therefore he deliberately aimed to destabilize the families he worked with.

Just as stress opens up family dialogues and makes change possible, therapeutic regression enables family members to discover and reveal hidden aspects of themselves. Most approaches aim to help family members tell each other what's on their minds. But this means that they'll only share what they're conscious of feeling. They'll have fewer secrets from each other, but they'll continue to have secrets from themselves, in the form of unconscious needs and feelings. Experiential therapists, on the other hand, believe that increasing the experience levels of individual family members will lead to more honest and intimate family interactions. The following example demonstrates this "inside out" process of change.

—Case Study—

After an initial, information-gathering session, the L. family was discussing ten-year-old Tommy's misbehavior. For several minutes Mrs. L. and Tommy's younger sister took turns cataloging all the "terrible things" Tommy did around the house. As the discussion continued, the therapist noticed how uninvolved Mr. L. seemed to be. Although he dutifully nodded agreement to his wife's complaints, he seemed more depressed than concerned. When asked what was on his mind, he said very little, and the therapist got the impression that, in fact, very little *was* on his mind—at least consciously. The therapist didn't know the reason for his lack of involvement, but she did know that it annoyed her, and she decided to say so.

> *Therapist:* (To Mr. L.) Are you hearing this? What's going on with you?
>
> *Mr. L.:* What? (He was shocked; people he knew just didn't speak that way.)
>
> *Therapist:* I said, What's going on with you? Here your wife is concerned and upset about Tommy, and you just sit there like a bump on a log. You're about as much a part of this family as that lamp in the corner.
>
> *Mr. L.:* You have no right to talk to me that way (getting angrier by the minute). I work hard for this family. Who do you think puts bread on the table? I get up six days a week and drive a delivery truck all over town. All day long I have to listen to customers bitching about this and that. Then I come home and what do I get? More bitching. *"Tommy did this, Tommy did that."* I'm sick of it.
>
> *Therapist:* Say that again, louder.
>
> *Mr. L.:* I'm sick of it! I'm sick of it!!

This interchange dramatically transformed the atmosphere in the session. Suddenly, the reason for Mr. L.'s disinterest became clear. He was furious at his wife for constantly complaining about Tommy. She, in turn, was displacing much of her feeling for her husband onto Tommy, as a result of Mr. L.'s emotional unavailability. In subsequent sessions, as Mr. and Mrs. L. spent more time talking about their relationship, less and less was heard about Tommy's misbehavior.

Following her own emotional impulse, the therapist in this example increased the affective intensity in the session by confronting a member of the family. The anxiety generated as she did so was sufficient to expose a hidden problem. Once the problem was uncovered, it didn't take much cajoling to get the family members to fight it out.

Although the reader may be uncomfortable with the idea of a therapist so aggressively confronting a family member, it's not unusual in experiential therapy. What makes this move less risky than it may seem is the presence of other family members. When the whole family is there, it seems safer for therapists to be provocative than is true in individual treatment. And as Carl Whitaker (1975) pointed out, families will accept a great deal from a therapist, once they're convinced that he or she genuinely cares about them.

While experiential family therapists emphasize expanded experiencing for individuals as the vehicle for therapeutic change, they are now beginning to advocate inclusion of as many family members as possible in treatment. As experientialists, they believe in immediate personal experiencing; as family therapists, they believe in the interconnectedness of the family.

Carl Whitaker (1976b) liked a crowd in the room when he did therapy. He pushed for at least a couple of meetings with the larger family network, including parents, children, grandparents, and divorced spouses. Inviting these extended family members is an effective way to help them support treatment, instead of opposing or undermining it.

In order to overcome reluctance to attend, Whitaker invited extended family members as consultants, "to help the therapist," not as patients. In these interviews grandparents were asked for their help, for their perceptions of the family (past and present), and sometimes to talk about the problems in their own marriage (Napier & Whitaker, 1978). Parents may begin

to see that the grandparents are different from the images they introjected twenty years before. Grandparents, in turn, may begin to realize that their children are now adults.

Therapy

Experiential family therapists share the humanistic belief that people are naturally resourceful and if left to their own devices will be energetic, creative, loving, and productive (Rogers, 1951). The task of therapy is therefore seen as unblocking defenses and releasing people's innate vitality.

Assessment

Because experientialists are less interested in solving problems than in enhancing family functioning, they pay limited attention to the specifics of the presenting problem. Moreover, because they focus on individuals and their experience more than on family organization, they have little interest in assessing the structure of family dynamics.

The following quotation illustrates the experientialist disdain for evaluation. "Diagnoses are the tombstones of the therapist's frustration, and accusations such as defensive, resistant, and secondary gain, are the flowers placed on the grave of his buried dissatisfaction" (Kempler, 1973, p. 11). The point seems to be that the objective distance necessary for formal assessment fosters a judgmental attitude and isolates therapists from emotional contact with families.

For most experientialists, assessment takes place automatically as the therapist gets to know a family. In the process of developing a relationship, the therapist learns what kind of people he or she is dealing with. Whitaker began by asking each family member to describe the family and how it works. In this way, he got a composite picture of individual family members and their perceptions of the family group. But this kind of inquiry is about as formal as most experiential therapists get in sizing up families. The vast majority of what serves for assessment in this approach is an attempt to decode the defenses that emerge in the ongoing course of trying to help family members open up to each other.

Therapeutic Techniques

According to Walter Kempler (1968), in experiential therapy there are no techniques, only people. This epigram neatly summarizes the faith in the curative power of the therapist's personality. It isn't so much what therapists do that matters, but who they are.

To foster openness and authenticity in their patients, therapists must themselves be open and genuine. However, this point is at least partly rhetorical. Whoever they *are*, therapists must also *do* something. Even if what they do isn't carefully planned, it can nevertheless be described. Moreover, experiential therapists tend to do a lot; they're highly active and some (including Kempler) use quite a number of evocative techniques.

Some employ structured devices such as *family sculpting* and *choreography* to stimulate affective intensity in therapy; others such as Virginia Satir and Carl Whitaker rely on the spontaneity of just being themselves.

Virginia Satir had a remarkable ability to communicate. Like many great therapists, she was a dynamic personality who engaged clients energetically from the first encounter. But she didn't rely merely on personal warmth. Rather, she worked actively to clarify communication, turned people away from complaining toward finding solutions, supported the self-esteem of every member of the family, pointed out positive intentions (long before "positive connotation" became a strategic device), and showed by example the way for family members to be af-

fectionate (Satir & Baldwin, 1983). She was a loving but forceful healer.

One of Satir's hallmarks was the use of touch. Hers was the language of tenderness. She often began by making physical contact with children, as evidenced in her case "Of Rocks and Flowers." Bob, a recovering alcoholic, was the father of two boys, Aaron (four) and Robbie (two), whose mother had abused them repeatedly—pushing them down stairs, burning them with cigarettes, and tying them up under the sink. At the time of the interview, the mother was under psychiatric care and didn't see the children. Bob's new wife, Betty, had been abused by her previous husband, also an alcoholic. She was pregnant and afraid that the boys would abuse the baby. The boys had already been expressing the anger and violence they'd been exposed to—slapping and choking other children. Bob and Betty, acting out of frustration and fear, responded roughly to the boys, which only increased their violence.

Throughout the session, Satir showed the parents how to touch the children tenderly and how to hold them firmly when they wanted to stop them from misbehaving. When Bob started to tell Aaron something from a distance, Satir insisted on proximity and touch. She sat Aaron down directly in front of his father and asked Bob to take the little boy's hands and speak directly to him.

*V*irginia Satir focused more on helping family members connect than on the psychological and systemic forces that kept them apart.

The following fragments from the session are taken from Andreas (1991).

─Case Study─

Those little hands know a lot of things; they need to be reeducated. OK. Now, there is a lot of energy in both these youngsters, like there is in both of you. And I am going to talk to your therapist about making some room for you to have some respite (from the children). But use every opportunity you can to get this kind of physical contact. And what I would also recommend that you do is that the two of you are clear about what you expect.

And if you (Bob) could learn from Betty how to pay attention (to the kids) more quickly. I would like you to be able to get your message without a "don't" in it, without a "don't"—and that your strength of your arms when you pick them up—I don't know if I can illustrate it to you, but let me have your arm for a minute (reaching for Bob's forearm). Let me show you the difference. Pick up my arm like you were going to grab me. (Bob grabs her arm.) All right. Now when you do that, my muscles all start to tighten, and I want to hit back. (Bob nods.) Now pick up my arm like you wanted to protect me. (Bob holds her arm.) All right. I feel your strength now, but I don't feel like I want to pull back like this. (Bob says, "yeah.")

And what I'd like you to do is to do *lots* and lots of touching of both of these children. And when things start (to get out of hand), then you go over—don't say anything—go over to them and just take them (demonstrating the protective holding on both of Robbie's forearms) but you have to know in your inside that you're not pulling them (Aaron briefly puts his hands on top of Virginia's and Robbie's arms) like this (demonstrating), but you are taking them in a strong way (stroking Bob's arm with both hands), like you saw the difference. I'll demonstrate it to you (Bob), too. First of all I am going to grab you (demonstrating) like that. (Bob says, "yeah.") You see you want to pull back. All right. Now, at this time what I am going to do is give you some strength (demonstrating holding his arm with both hands. Robbie pats Virginia's hand). But I am not going to ask you to retaliate. Now this is the most important thing for you to start with.

(Virginia turns to Betty and offers her forearm.) OK. Now I'd like to do the same with you. So, take my arm really tight. . . . (Betty grabs Virginia's arm, and Aaron does, too.) Yeah, that's right, like you really wanted to give me "what for." OK. All right. Now give it to me like you want to give me support, but you also want to give me a boundary. (Aaron reaches toward Betty's hand and Virginia takes Aaron's free hand in her free hand.) It's a little bit tight, a little bit tight.

So the next time you see anything coming, what you do is you go and make that contact (Virginia demonstrates by holding Aaron's upper arm) and then let it go soft. (Virginia takes Aaron's hands and begins to draw him out of Betty's lap.) Now, Aaron, I'd like you to come up here so I could demonstrate something to your mother for a minute. (Aaron says, "OK.") Now, let's suppose some moment I'm not thinking and I take you like that (grabbing Betty's arms suddenly with both hands). You see what you want to do? (Betty nods.) All right. Now I am going to do it another way. I am giving you the same message (Virginia holds Betty's arm firmly with both hands, looking directly into her eyes, and starts to stand up), but I am doing it like this. And I am looking at you, and I'm giving you a straight message. OK. Now your body at that point is not going to respond negatively to me. It is going to feel stopped, but not negative. And then I will take you like this. (Virginia puts one arm around Betty's back and the other under her upper arm.) Just like this (Virginia puts both arms around Betty and draws her close) and now I will hold you. I will hold you like that for a little bit.

──────

Following this session, Satir commented on her technique:

There had been so many things happening, and the fear was so strong in relation to these children that if you thought of one image it was like they were monsters. So one of the things that I wanted to do was also to see that they had the capacity to respond with a touch, using myself in that regard by having them put their hands on my face—that was a kind of mirror for the family itself, the people in the family. And then allowing them, and encouraging them to do that with their own parents. See, touch, that comes out of the kind of ambience which was there at the time, says things no words can say.

To encourage empathy and bring family members closer together, Satir often used the following exercise (adapted from Satir & Baldwin, 1983):

1. Think of a difficult situation with your child. Perhaps your child has been doing something that you haven't known how to handle or that drives you up the wall.
2. Run your movie of this situation from your own point of view. Imagine you are going through this situation with your child again. Notice how you feel, what you see, what you hear.
3. Reexperience this situation, but this time as your child. Visualize the entire situation, slowly and in detail, as you would imagine seeing it through the eyes of your child. Let your self feel what your child must be feeling. Do you notice any feelings that you weren't aware your child might be having? Do you notice something that your child might need or want that you hadn't been aware of?
4. Reexperience the same situation, this time as an observer. Watch and listen to what's happening, and allow yourself to observe both your child and yourself. Do you notice anything about the way you and your child respond to each other? What do you see more clearly about yourself and your child?

Because he favored a personal encounter over a calculated approach, it's not surprising that Whitaker's style was the same with individuals, couples, or groups (Whitaker, 1958). He assiduously avoided directing real-life decisions, preferring instead to open family members up to their feelings and join them in sharing their uncertainty. This may sound trite, but it's an important point. As long as a therapist (or anyone else for that matter) is anxious to change people, it's hard, very hard, to help them feel understood—and even harder to really empathize with them.

A comparison between Whitaker's early (Whitaker, Warkentin, & Malone, 1959; Whitaker, 1967) and later work (Napier & Whitaker, 1978) shows how he changed over the years. He started out as deliberately outlandish. He might fall asleep in sessions and then report his dreams; he wrestled with patients; he talked about his own sexual fantasies. In later years he was less provocative. This seems to be what happens to therapists as they mature; they have less need to impose themselves and more willingness to listen.

Because Whitaker's treatment was so intense and personal, he believed it essential that two therapists work together. Having a cotherapist to share the burden keeps therapists from being absorbed in the emotional field of the family. All family therapy tends to activate therapists' own feelings toward certain types of family members. A detached, analytic stance minimizes such feelings; emotional involvement maximizes them.

The trouble with countertransference is that it tends to be unconscious. Therapists are more likely to become aware of such feelings after sessions are over. Easier still is to observe countertransference in others. Consider the example of Dr. Fox, a married man who specializes in individual therapy, but occasionally sees married couples in distress. In 75 percent of such cases, Dr. Fox encourages the couple to seek a divorce, and his patients follow his advice at a high rate. Perhaps if Dr. Fox were happier in his own marriage or had the courage to change it, he'd be less impelled to guide his patients where he fears to go.

To minimize countertransference, Whitaker recommended sharing feelings openly with a family. If feelings are openly expressed they're less likely to be acted out. At times, however, most therapists are unaware of their own feelings. This is where a cotherapist can be useful. Often a cotherapist can recognize, and counteract, reactive feelings in a colleague. A strong investment in the cotherapy relationship (or treatment team) keeps therapists from being *inducted* (drawn into families). Therapists who see families without a cotherapist may seek out supervision to help achieve the objectivity necessary to stay balanced.

Whitaker's first sessions (Napier & Whitaker, 1978) were fairly structured, and they included taking a family history. For him, the first contacts with families were opening salvos in "the battle for structure" (Whitaker & Keith, 1981). He made an effort to gain enough control to be able to exert maximum therapeutic leverage.[2] He wanted the family to know that the therapists were in charge. This began with the first telephone call. Whitaker (1976b) insisted that the largest possible number of family members attend; he believed that three generations were necessary to ensure that grandparents would support, not oppose, therapy, and that their presence would help correct distortions. If significant family members wouldn't attend, Whitaker generally refused to see the family. Why begin with the cards stacked against you?

Along with Virginia Satir, Whitaker was among the foremost exponents of the therapist's use of self as a catalyst for change. But whereas Satir offered a warm, supportive presence, Whitaker was at times blunt, even confrontational. Actually, the provocative interventions of someone like Whitaker (or Minuchin) only become acceptable to families after the therapist has proven to be an understanding and caring person. Before challenging people, it is first necessary to win their trust.

But whether they are provocative or supportive, experiential therapists are usually quite active. Instead of leaving them to work out their own issues with each other, family members are told, "Tell him (or her) what you feel!" or asked, "What are you feeling right now?" Just as the best way to get a school teacher's attention is to misbehave, the best way to get an experiential therapist's attention is to show signs of emotion without actually expressing it.

—Case Study——

Therapist: I see you looking over at Dad whenever you ask Mom a question, what's that about?

Kendra: Oh, nothing. . . .

Therapist: It must mean *something.* Come on, what were you feeling?

Kendra: Nothing!

Therapist: You must have been feeling something. What was it?

Kendra: Well, sometimes when Mom lets me do something, Dad gets mad. But instead of yelling at her, he yells at *me* (crying softly).

Therapist: Tell him.

Kendra: (Angrily, to the therapist) Leave me alone!

Therapist: No, it's important. Tell your Dad how you feel.

Kendra: (Sobbing hard) You're always picking on me! You never let me do anything!

Experiential therapists use a number of expressive techniques in their work, including family sculpture (Duhl, Kantor, & Duhl, 1973), family puppet interviews (Irwin & Malloy, 1975), family art therapy (Geddes & Medway, 1977), conjoint family drawings (Bing, 1970), and Gestalt therapy techniques (Kempler, 1973). Among the accoutrements of experiential therapists' offices are toys, dollhouses, clay, teddy bears, drawing pens and paper, and batacca bats.

In **family sculpture,** originated by David Kantor and Fred Duhl, the therapist asks one member of the family to arrange the others in

---

2. We might add that there is a big difference between trying to control the structure of sessions and trying to control people's lives.

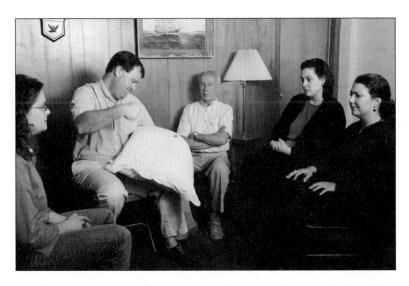

*E*xperiential therapists use expressive techniques to help families get at underlying feelings.

a tableau. This is a graphic means of portraying each person's perceptions of the family and his or her place in it. This was also a favorite device of Virginia Satir, who frequently used ropes and blindfolds to dramatize the constricting roles family members trap each other into (Satir & Baldwin, 1983).

The following example of sculpting occurred when a therapist asked Mr. N. to arrange the members of his family into a scene typical of the time when he comes home from work.

—Case Study——————

Mr. N.: When I come home from work, eh? Okay (to his wife) honey, you'd be by the stove, wouldn't you?
Therapist: No, don't talk. Just move people where you want them to be.
Mr. N.: Okay.

He guided his wife to stand at a spot where the kitchen stove might be, and placed his children on the kitchen floor, drawing and playing.

Therapist: Fine, now, still without any dialogue, put them into action.

Mr. N. then instructed his wife to pretend to cook, but to turn frequently to see what the kids were up to. He told the children to pretend to play for awhile, but then to start fighting and complaining to Mommy.

Therapist: And what happens, when you come home?
Mr. N.: Nothing. I try to talk to my wife, but the kids keep pestering her, and she gets mad and says to leave her alone.
Therapist: Okay, act it out.

Mrs. N. acted out trying to cook and referee the children's fights. The children, who thought this a great game, pretended to fight, and tried to outdo each other getting Mommy's attention. When Mr. N. "came home," he reached out for his wife, but the children came between them, until Mrs. N. finally pushed all of them away.

Afterwards, Mrs. N. said that she hadn't realized her husband felt ignored. She just thought of him as coming home, saying hello, and then withdrawing into the den with his newspaper and a bottle of beer.

Family sculpture is also used to illuminate scenes from the past. A typical instruction is, "Remember standing in front of your childhood home. Walk in and describe what typically happened." The idea is to make a tableau portraying one's perceptions of family life. It's a device to focus awareness and heighten sensitivity. Such dramatizations are probably most useful if they suggest changes, which can then be acted on.

Another expressive exercise is *family art therapy*. Kwiatkowska (1967) instructs families to produce a series of drawings, including a "joint family scribble," in which each person makes a quick scribble and then the whole family incorporates the scribble into a unified picture. Elizabeth Bing (1970) describes the **conjoint family drawing** as a means to warm families up and free them to express themselves. In this procedure families are told to "Draw a picture as you see yourselves as a family." The resulting portraits may disclose perceptions that haven't previously been discussed, or may stimulate the person drawing the picture to realize something that he or she had never thought of before.

—Case Study—

Afather drew a picture of the family that showed him off to one side, while his wife and children stood holding hands. Although he was portraying a fact well-known to his wife and himself, they hadn't spoken openly of it. Once he showed his drawing to the therapist, there was no avoiding discussion. In another case, when the therapist asked each of the family members to draw the family, the teenage daughter was uncertain what to do. She had never thought much about the family or her role in it. When she started to work, her drawing just seemed to emerge. She was surprised to discover that she'd drawn herself closer to her father and sisters than to her mother. This provoked a lively discussion between her and her mother about their relationship. Although the two of them spent time together, the daughter didn't feel close because she thought her mother treated her like a child, never talking about her own concerns, and showing only superficial interest in the daughter's life. For her part, the mother was surprised, and not at all displeased, that her daughter felt ready to establish a relationship on a more mutual, caring basis.

In *family puppet interviews*, Irwin and Malloy (1975) ask one of the family members to make up a story using puppets. This technique, originally used in play therapy with small children, is designed as a vehicle for highlighting conflicts and alliances. In fact, its usefulness is probably limited to working with children. Most adults resist expressing anything really personal through such a childlike medium. Even a reticent eight-year-old knows what's up when a therapist says, "Tell me a story."

Role-playing is another favorite device. Its use is based on the premise that experience, to be real, must be brought to life in the present. Recollection of past events and consideration of hoped-for or feared future events can be made more immediate by role-playing them in the immediacy of the session. Kempler (1968) encourages parents to fantasize and role-play scenes from childhood. A mother might be asked to role-play what it was like when she was a little girl, or a father might be asked to imagine himself as a boy caught in the same dilemma as his son.

When someone who isn't present is mentioned, therapists may introduce the Gestalt *empty chair technique* (Kempler, 1973). If a child talks about her grandfather, she might be asked to speak to a chair, which is supposed to personify grandfather. Whitaker (1975) used a similar role-playing technique, which he called "psychotherapy of the absurd." This consists of augmenting the unreasonable quality of a patient's response to the point of absurdity. It often amounts to calling a person's bluff, as the following example illustrates:

Patient: I can't stand my husband!

Therapist: Why don't you get rid of him, or take up a boyfriend?

At times this takes the form of sarcastic teasing, such as mock fussing in response to a fussy child. The hope is that patients will get objective distance by participating in the therapist's distancing; the danger is that patients will feel hurt at being made fun of.

These techniques have proved useful in individual therapy (Nichols & Zax, 1977) to intensify emotional experiencing by bringing memories into focus and acting out suppressed reactions. Whether such devices are necessary in family therapy is open to question. In individual treatment patients are isolated from the significant figures in their lives, and role-playing may be useful to approximate being with those people. But since family therapy is conducted with significant people present, it seems doubtful that role-playing or other means of fantasy are necessary. If emotional action is wanted, plenty is available simply by opening dialogue between family members.

●

Two recent emotive approaches to family therapy that represent a more sophisticated understanding of family dynamics are emotionally focused couples therapy and the internal family systems model.

Emotionally Focused Couples Therapy.
Emotionally focused couples therapy works on two levels in succession—uncovering the hurt and longing beneath defensive expressions of anger and withdrawal, and then helping couples understand how these feelings are played out in their relationship. To begin with the therapist acknowledges each client's immediate feelings—hurt and anger, say—to make them feel understood (Johnson, 1998).

—Case Study—

"You're getting angrier and angrier. It's upsetting for you to hear Will picture himself as innocent, isn't it?"

By interrupting a couple's quarrel and reflecting what each of them is feeling, the therapist defuses hostility and helps them focus on their experience, rather than on each other's crimes. Then, to explore the perceptions that un-

*S*usan Johnson's focus on emotional longings can be seen as an antidote to the field's current preoccupation with cognition.

derlie the partners' emotional responses to each other, the therapist asks for a description of what happens at home.

"Oh, so part of you believes him, but part of you is suspicious?"

"Part of you is watching and expecting that he'll hurt you?"

"Can you tell me about the part that believes he's being honest?"

Next the therapist points out how the couple's emotions are driving them into cycles of escalating polarization.

The cycle was formulated in terms of Will's protecting himself by staying distant and avoiding Nancy's anger, and Nancy's being vigilant and fighting to avoid being betrayed again. As she became more insecure and distrustful, Will then felt more helpless and distanced himself further. As he distanced, she felt betrayed and became more enraged. Both were framed as victims of the cycle, which I continually framed as a common problem that the partners need to help each other with. (Johnson, 1998, pp. 457–458)

The couple's growing awareness of how their emotional reactivity frustrates their longings sets the stage for uncovering and expressing the deep emotions that lie beneath their sparring. The resulting cathartic expression makes it possible for the couple to deepen their understanding of their destructive pattern with each other, and this circular process continues to be explored in the process of working through.

Attachment theory helps the emotionally focused couples therapist pinpoint the issues that get stirred up when couples talk about their hurts and longings.

"Maybe you feel like no one really loves you?"

"You feel helpless and alone, don't you?"

The impact of this emotional evocation is enhanced by the fact that the partner is present to be addressed in this new and more "feelingful" way.

"So, can you tell her that?"

The ultimate aim of this work is to enable the partners to risk being vulnerable with each other by acknowledging and expressing their attachment needs.

"Only you can face your fear and decide to risk depending on Will. He can't do it, can he? The only one who can drop your defenses and risk trusting him is you, isn't it?"
"What's the worst thing that could happen?"

Again, working together with the couple means that once the partners risk expressing their needs and fears, their mates can be encouraged to respond.

"What happens to you, Will, when you hear this?"

The response to this question will of course be very different once the partners let down their guard and begin to talk about what they're afraid of, and what they really want from each other.

The emotionally focused couples therapist frames family members' experiences in terms of deprivation, isolation, and loss of secure connectedness. This perspective, from attachment theory, helps family members focus on their longings rather than each other's faults and failings. The process of therapeutic intervention has been described in nine treatment steps (Johnson, Hunsley, Greenberg, & Schindler, 1999):

1. Assessment—creating an alliance and explicating the core issues in the couple's conflict using attachment theory
2. Identifying the problematic interaction cycle that maintains attachment insecurity and relationship distress
3. Uncovering the unacknowledged emotions underlying interactional positions

4. Reframing the problem in terms of a problematic cycle with underlying emotions and attachment needs
5. Encouraging acceptance and expression of disowned needs and aspects of the self
6. Encouraging acceptance of the partner's new openness
7. Encouraging the expression of specific needs and wants and creating an intimate, emotional engagement
8. Facilitating new solutions to unresolved relationship issues
9. Consolidating new positions and more honest expression of attachment needs

In all of these steps the therapist moves between helping partners uncover and express their emotional experience and helping them reorganize the pattern of their interactions. For example:

The therapist might, then, first help a withdrawn, guarded spouse formulate his sense of paralyzed helplessness that primes his withdrawal. The therapist will validate this sense of helplessness by placing it within the context of the destructive cycle that has taken over the relationship. The therapist will heighten this experience in the session and then help his partner to hear and accept it, even though it is very different from the way she usually experiences her spouse. Finally, the therapist moves to structuring an interaction around this helplessness, as in, "So can you turn to her and can you tell her, 'I feel so helpless and defeated. I just want to run away and hide.'" This kind of statement, in and of itself, represents a move away from passive withdrawal and is the beginning of active emotional engagement. (Johnson, Hunsley, Greenberg, & Schindler, 1999, p. 70)

Internal Family Systems Therapy. In the **internal family systems model** (Schwartz, 1995) conflicting inner voices are personified as subpersonalities or "parts." What makes this device powerful is that although client family members are often at odds with each other, their conflicts are frequently based on polarizations of only one aspect of what each of them feels. The truth is that people in conflict with each other are also often in conflict within themselves.

The adolescent's defiance and her parents' distrust are only one aspect of the complex feelings they have for each other. Or, to choose a different example, the couple caught in a pursuer–distancer pattern may be acting out only those parts of them that are terrified of abandonment and engulfment. By dramatizing the elements of their inner conflicts and ambivalence, internal family systems therapy helps family members sort out their feelings and reconnect with each other in less polarized ways.

To help clients' begin to distinguish among their conflicting inner voices Schwartz begins by introducing the language of parts.

—Case Study—

"So there's a part of you that gets upset and angry when your son gets down on himself. Do you think that if that part didn't get so stirred up, it would be easier for you to help him?"

"It sounds like part of you agrees with your husband about getting stricter with the kids, but there's another part that says he's being too harsh. What is that second part? What does it say to you? What is it afraid of?"

By listening carefully to what clients are feeling and then construing their reactions as coming from a part of them, the therapist initiates a shift in family polarizations. It's easier for people to acknowledge that "a part of them" feels—angry, helpless, or whatever—than that "they" (as in all of them) feel that way. A parent who has trouble admitting that he's angry at his son for not doing well in school may find it easier to acknowledge that a part of him gets angry at his son's failures—and, moreover, that the angry part gets in the way of his sympathetic part.

Once the idea is introduced that various parts of family members are reacting to each other, instead of seeing themselves intrinsically at odds, they can begin to see that parts of one are triggering parts of another. The obvious implication is that if their aggravating emotions are contained in only parts of them, they have other feelings and other possibilities for interaction.

Thus: "So that angry part of your father seems to trigger a sad and helpless part of you, is that right?"

And, since many such polarizations become triangles, it might be that the father's angry part also triggers a protective part in his wife.

"So when you see your husband's angry part responding to your son that triggers a protective part in you? A part of you feels that you need to fight your husband to protect your son?"

So instead of having a son who is a failure, a father who is unsympathetic, and parents who can't agree, the family discovers that each of them is having trouble with some of their parts. The father is transformed from a tyrant to a parent struggling with a frustrated and angry part of him. His wife ceases to be basically at odds with him and instead is seen as having a protective part that gets triggered by his angry part. And instead of being a failure, the son becomes a boy with a part of him that feels helpless in the face of his father's angry part and his parents' conflict.

Like all experiential models, internal family systems therapy is founded on the belief that underneath people's emotionally reactive parts lies a healthy self at the core of the personality. When the therapist notices various parts taking over, he or she asks the person first to visualize them, and then help them to calm down. If, for example, an angry part were seen as a snarling dog, that person might find that she could calm her anger by approaching the dog and petting it until it felt reassured and settled down. Or to use another example (cited by Schwartz, 1998), if a frightened part were imagined as a rag doll, the client might relax her fears by imagining holding and comforting that doll. Thus, by personifying people's polarizing emotional reactions as parts and then helping them to visualize and reassure these reactive parts, internal family systems therapy releases people from the domination of fear and anger, which in turn allows them to work together more ef-fectively to solve personal and family problems.

Evaluating Therapy Theory and Results

Experiential therapy helps family members get beneath the surface of their interactions to ex-plore the deeper feelings that drive them. At its best this approach helps people drop their de-fenses and come together with more immedi-acy and authenticity. Given family therapy's emphasis on behavior and cognition, the effort to help clients uncover the feeling side of their experience is surely a welcome addition.

Regardless of what approach to family ther-apy one takes, shifting to individuals and their experience is a powerful way to break through defensive squabbling. When family members argue, they usually lead with their defenses. Instead of saying, *"I'm hurt,"* they say, *"You make me mad"*; instead of admitting they're afraid, they criticize each other's behavior. An effective way to interrupt the unproductive es-calation of arguments is to explore the affect of the participants, one at a time. By talking to in-dividuals about what they're feeling—and the roots of such feelings—family members can be helped to get past the defensiveness that keeps them apart, and to reconnect at a more gen-uine level.

But just as approaches that focus entirely on families and their interactions leave something out, so too does an approach that concentrates too narrowly on individuals and their emotional experience. At the peak of their popularity, in the 1970s, experiential therapists approached family therapy as if it were an encounter group for relatives. They put great faith in the value of individual emotional experiencing and limited appreciation of the role family structure plays in regulating that experience. Not surprisingly, therefore, as family therapy focused more on or-ganization, interaction, and narrative in the

1980s and 1990s, the experiential model fell out of favor.

As we have already suggested, a therapy de-signed primarily to elicit feelings may be more suited to encounter groups than to family ther-apy. However, the prevailing behavioral and cognitive models of family therapy could do with a little more attention to people's feelings. If "more attention to people's feelings" sounds a little vague, allow us to make it more con-crete. Helping family members get in touch with their feelings accomplishes two things: It helps them as individuals to discover what they really think and feel—what they want and what they're afraid of—and it helps them as a family get beyond defensiveness and begin to relate to each other in a more honest and im-mediate way.

Two particularly creative approaches to helping individuals get in touch with their inner experience are emotionally focused couples therapy and internal family systems therapy. What sets Johnson and Greenberg's therapy apart is its sophisticated combination of emotional expressiveness and attention to the dynamic patterns of interaction between couples. Emotionally focused couples therapy begins, as any emotive approach must, by elic-iting and acknowledging the feelings clients come in with—even, or especially, if those feelings are defensive. You don't get beneath the surface of what people are feeling by ig-noring it.

The combination of uncovering deeper and more vulnerable emotions and teaching cou-ples about the reactive patterns their feelings drive them through creates a meaningful cog-nitive experience. As Lieberman, Yalom, and Miles (1973) demonstrated with encounter groups, an emotionally intense therapeutic ex-perience only brings lasting value when paired with an intellectual understanding of the sig-nificance of those emotions. The only caveat we might offer is that explanations are most useful when tailored to the specific experience of the clients, following an emotionally significant process of uncovering—which is what distinguishes psychotherapy from a conversation with your Aunt Harriet.

Like emotionally focused therapy, Schwartz's internal family systems approach helps family members come together with more understanding by helping individuals sort out their own conflicted experience. Personifying unruly emotions as "parts" is a powerful device for helping people achieve a clarifying distance from their conflicts. Unlike emotionally focused therapy, internal family systems therapy does not lean heavily on didactic explanations. In this approach emotional experiencing is clarified, but by learning to differentiate among one's own feelings rather than by explanations offered by the therapist.

In addition to anecdotal reports of successful outcomes (Napier & Whitaker, 1978; Duhl & Duhl, 1981) and descriptions of techniques that are effective in catalyzing emotional expression within sessions (Kempler, 1981), emotionally focused couples therapy has received a good deal of empirical support (e.g., Johnson & Greenberg, 1985, 1988; Johnson, Maddeaux, & Blouin, 1998; Johnson, Hunsley, Greenberg, & Schindler, 1999).

Recently, researchers seeking to study the effectiveness of experiential techniques have followed Mahrer's (1982) suggestion to focus on the process, rather than the outcome, of therapy. Because he believes that studies of outcome have little impact on practitioners (who already "know" that what they do works), Mahrer recommends studying "in-therapy outcomes"—that is, what kinds of interventions produce desired results (emotional expression, more open communication) within sessions. Following Mahrer (1982) and others (Pierce, Nichols, & DuBrin, 1983) who looked at such in-therapy outcomes in individual treatment, Leslie Greenberg and Susan Johnson have found that helping an angry and attacking partner to reveal his or her softer feelings characterizes the best session of successful cases (Johnson & Greenberg, 1988) and that intimate self-disclosure leads to deeper emotional experiencing and more productive sessions (Greenberg, Ford, Alden, & Johnson, 1993).

Once feeling and expression occupied center stage in psychological therapies; today that place is held by behavior and cognition. Psychotherapists have discovered that people think and act; but that doesn't mean we should ignore the immediate emotional experience that is the main concern of experiential family therapy.

—Summary—

Experiential therapy works from the inside out—strengthening families by encouraging individual self-expression, reversing the usual direction of effect in family therapy. Experiential family therapy is also distinguished by a commitment to emotional well-being as opposed to problem-solving. Personal integrity and self-fulfillment are seen as innate human capacities that will emerge spontaneously once defensiveness is overcome. To challenge the familiar and enhance experiencing, therapists use their own lively personalities as well as a host of expressive techniques.

Although the experiential model lost popularity in the 1980s, it is now enjoying something of a resurgence, especially in the innovative work of emotionally focused couples therapy and the internal family systems approach. Once, the idea that families were systems was both novel and controversial; today it is the new orthodoxy. Now that the pendulum has swung so far in the direction of systems thinking, individuals and their private joys and pains are rarely mentioned. Surely one of the major contributions of experiential family therapy is to remind us not to lose sight of the self in the system.

—Recommended Readings

Duhl, B. S., and Duhl, F. J. 1981. Integrative family therapy. In *Handbook of family therapy*, A. S. Gurman and D. P. Kniskern, eds. New York: Brunner/Mazel.

Duhl, F. J., Kantor, D., and Duhl, B. S. 1973. Learning, space and action in family therapy: A primer of sculpture. In *Techniques in family therapy*, D. A. Bloch, ed. New York: Grune & Stratton.

Greenberg, L. S., and Johnson, S. M. 1988. *Emotionally focused therapy for couples.* New York: Guilford Press.

Keith, D. V., and Whitaker, C. A. 1977. The divorce labyrinth. In *Family therapy: Full-length case studies*, P. Papp, ed. New York: Gardner Press.

Laing, R. D., and Esterson, A. 1970. *Sanity, madness and the family.* Baltimore: Penguin Books.

Napier, A. Y., and Whitaker, C. A. 1978. *The family crucible.* New York: Harper & Row.

Neill, J. R., and Kniskern, D. P., eds. 1982. *From psyche to system: The evolving therapy of Carl Whitaker.* New York: Guilford Press.

Satir, V. M. 1988. *The new peoplemaking.* Palo Alto, CA: Science and Behavior Books.

Satir, V. M., and Baldwin, M. 1983. *Satir step by step: A guide to creating change in families.* Palo Alto, CA: Science and Behavior Books.

Schwartz, R. C. 1995. *Internal family systems therapy*, New York: Guilford Press.

Schwartz, R. C. 1998. Internal family systems therapy. In *Case studies in couple and family therapy*, F. M. Dattilio ed. New York: Guilford Press.

Whitaker, C. A., and Bumberry, W. M. 1988. *Dancing with the family: A symbolic experiential approach.* New York: Brunner/Mazel.

Whitaker, C. A., and Keith, D. V. 1981. Symbolic-experiential family therapy. In *Handbook of family therapy*, A. S. Gurman and D. P. Kniskern, eds. New York: Brunner/Mazel.

—References

Andreas, S. 1991. *Virginia Satir: The patterns of her magic.* Palo Alto, CA: Science and Behavior Books.

Bing, E. 1970. The conjoint family drawing. *Family Process.* 9:173–194.

Binswanger, L. 1967. Being-in-the-world. In *Selected papers of Ludwig Binswanger*, J. Needleman, ed. New York: HarperTorchbooks.

Boss, M. 1963. *Psychoanalysis and daseinanalysts.* New York: Basic Books.

Bowlby, J. 1969. *Attachment and loss: Vol. 1. Attachment.* New York: Basic Books.

Bowlby, J. 1988. *A secure base.* New York: Basic Books.

Collins, N. L., and Read, S. J. 1994. Cognitive representations of attachment: The structure and function of working models. In *Attachment processes in adulthood*, K. Bartholomew and D. Perlman, eds. London: Jessica Kingsley.

Duhl, B. S., and Duhl, F. J. 1981. Integrative family therapy. In *Handbook of family therapy*, A. S. Gurman and D. P. Kniskern, eds. New York: Brunner/Mazel.

Duhl, F. J., Kantor D., and Duhl, B. S. 1973. Learning, space and action in family therapy: A primer of sculpture. In *Techniques of family psychotherapy*, D. A. Bloch, ed. New York: Grune & Stratton.

Geddes, M., and Medway, J. 1977. The symbolic drawing of family life space. *Family Process.* 16: 219–228.

Gehrke, S., and Kirschenbaum, M. 1967. Survival patterns in conjoint family therapy. *Family Process.* 6:67–80.

Greenberg, L. S., Ford, C. L., Alden, L., and Johnson, S. M. 1993. In-session change in emotionally focused therapy. *Journal of Consulting and Clinical Psychology.* 61: 78–84.

Greenberg, L. S., and Johnson, S. M. 1985. Emotionally focused couple therapy: An affective systemic approach. In *Handbook of family and marital therapy,* N. S. Jacobson and A. S. Gurman, eds. New York: Guilford Press.

Greenberg, L. S., and Johnson, S. M. 1986. Affect in marital therapy. *Journal of Marital and Family Therapy.* 12:1–10.

Greenberg, L. S., and Johnson, S. M. 1988. *Emotionally focused therapy for couples.* New York: Guilford Press.

Irwin, E., and Malloy, E. 1975. Family puppet interview. *Family Process.* 14:179–191.

Johnson, S. M. 1998. Emotionally focused couple therapy. In *Case studies in couple and family therapy,* F. M. Dattilio, ed. New York: Guilford Press.

Johnson, S. M., and Greenberg, L. S. 1985. Emotionally focused couples therapy: An outcome study. *Journal of Marital and Family Therapy.* 11:313–317.

Johnson, S. M., and Greenberg, L. S. 1988. Relating process to outcome in marital therapy. *Journal of Marital and Family Therapy.* 14:175–183.

Johnson, S. M., Hunsley, J., Greenberg, L., and Schindler, D. 1999. Emotionally focused couples therapy: Status and challenges. *Clinical Psychology: Science and Practice.* 6:67–79.

Johnson, S. M., Maddeaux, C., and Blouin, J. 1998. Emotionally focused therapy for bulimia: Changing attachment patterns. *Psychotherapy.* 35: 238–247.

Kaplan, M. L., and Kaplan, N. R. 1978. Individual and family growth: A Gestalt approach. *Family Process.* 17:195–205.

Kempler, W. 1968. Experiential psychotherapy with families. *Family Process.* 7:88–89.

Kempler, W. 1973. *Principles of Gestalt family therapy.* Oslo: Nordahls.

Kempler, W. 1981. *Experiential psychotherapy with families.* New York: Brunner/Mazel.

Kwiatkowska, H. Y. 1967. Family art therapy. *Family Process.* 6:37–55.

Laing, R. D. 1967. *The politics of experience.* New York: Ballantine.

Laing, R. D., and Esterson, A. 1970. *Sanity, madness and the family.* Baltimore, MD: Penguin Books.

Lieberman, M. A., Yalom, I. D., and Miles, M. B. 1973. *Encounter groups: First facts.* New York: Basic Books.

Mahrer, A. R. 1982. *Experiential psychotherapy: Basic practices.* New York: Brunner/Mazel.

Malone, T., Whitaker, C. A., Warkentin, J., and Felder, R. 1961. Rational and nonrational psychotherapy. *American Journal of Psychotherapy.* 15:21–220.

Marcuse, H. 1955. *Eros and civilization.* New York: Beacon Press.

Napier, A. Y. 1977. Follow-up to divorce labyrinth, In *Family therapy: Full-length case studies,* P. Papp, ed. New York: Gardner Press.

Napier, A. Y., and Whitaker, C. A. 1978. *The family crucible.* New York: Harper & Row.

Nichols, M. P., and Zax, M. 1977. *Catharsis in psychotherapy.* New York: Gardner Press.

Pierce, R., Nichols, M. P., and DuBrin, J. 1983. *Emotional expression in psychotherapy.* New York: Gardner Press.

Rogers, C. R. 1951. *Client-centered therapy.* Boston: Houghton Mifflin.

Satir, V. M. 1964. *Conjoint family therapy.* Palo Alto, CA: Science and Behavior Books.

Satir, V. M. 1972. *Peoplemaking.* Palo Alto, CA: Science and Behavior Books.

Satir, V. M., and Baldwin, M. 1983. *Satir step by step: A guide to creating change in families.* Palo Alto, CA: Science and Behavior Books.

Schwartz, R. C. 1995. *Internal family systems therapy.* New York: Guilford Press.

Schwartz, R. C. 1998. Internal family systems therapy. In *Case studies in couple and family therapy,* F. M. Dattilio, ed. New York: Guilford Press.

Simon, R. 1989. Reaching out to life: An interview with Virginia Satir. *The Family Therapy Networker.* 13(1):36–43.

Sullivan, H. S. 1953. *The interpersonal theory of psychiatry.* New York: Norton.

Whitaker, C. A. 1958. Psychotherapy with couples. *American Journal of Psychotherapy.* 12:18–23.

Whitaker, C. A. 1967. The growing edge. In *Techniques of family therapy,* J. Haley and L. Hoffman, eds. New York: Basic Books.

Whitaker, C. A. 1975. Psychotherapy of the absurd: With a special emphasis on the psychotherapy of aggression. *Family Process.* 14:1–16.

Whitaker, C. A. 1976a. The hindrance of theory in clinical work. In *Family therapy: Theory and practice,* P. J. Guerin, ed. New York: Gardner Press.

Whitaker, C. A. 1976b. A family is a four-dimensional relationship. In *Family therapy: Theory and practice,* P. J. Guerin, ed. New York: Gardner Press.

Whitaker, C. A., and Keith, D. V. 1981. Symbolic-experiential family therapy. In *Handbook of family therapy,* A. S. Gurman and D. P. Kniskern, eds. New York: Brunner/Mazel.

Whitaker, C. A., and Malone, T. P. 1953. *The roots of psychotherapy.* New York: Blakiston.

Whitaker, C. A., Warkentin, J., and Malone, T. P. 1959. The involvement of the professional therapist. In *Case studies in counseling and psychotherapy,* A. Burton, ed. Englewood Cliffs, NJ: Prentice Hall.

9

Psychoanalytic Family Therapy

Rediscovering Psychodynamics

Many of the pioneers of family therapy, including Nathan Ackerman, Murray Bowen, Ivan Boszormenyi-Nagy, Carl Whitaker, Don Jackson, and Salvador Minuchin, were psychoanalytically trained. But with the eager enthusiasm so essential to innovation they turned away from the old—psychodynamics—and toward the new—systems dynamics. Some, like Jackson and Minuchin, moved far indeed from their psychoanalytic roots. Others, like Bowen and Nagy, retained a distinctly analytic influence in their work.

In the 1960s and 1970s family therapy followed Jackson and Minuchin in not only ignoring psychoanalytic thinking but denigrating it. Jackson (1967) went so far as to declare the death of the individual, and Minuchin (1989) proclaimed that, "We understood that the decontexted individual was a mythical monster, an illusion created by psychodynamic blinders."

Then in the 1980s a surprising shift occurred: Family therapists took a renewed interest in the psychology of the individual. This revival of interest reflected changes in psychoanalysis—from the individualism of Freudian theory to the more relationship-oriented object relations theories and self psychology—as well as changes in family therapy itself, especially dissatisfaction with the mechanistic elements of the cybernetic model. Among the books calling for a rapprochement with psychoanalysis were: *Object Relations: A Dynamic Bridge between Individual and Family Treatment* (Slipp, 1984); *Object Relations Family Therapy* (Scharff & Scharff, 1987); and *The Self in the System* (Nichols, 1987).

The reason these psychodynamic voices found a receptive audience was that while family therapists discovered profound truths about systemic interactions, many believed they were wrong to turn their backs on depth psychology. Anyone who does not flee from self-awareness knows that the inner life is awash in conflict and confusion, most of it never expressed. While systems therapists focused on the outward expression of this inner life—family interaction and communication—psychoanalytic therapists probed beneath family dialogues to explore individual family members' private fears and longings.

Sketches of Leading Figures

Freud was interested in the family but saw it as old business—the place where people learned neurotic fears, rather than the contemporary context where such fears were maintained. Faced with a phobic Little Hans, Freud (1909) was more interested in analyzing the boy's Oedipus complex than in trying to understand what was going on in his family.

Major advances were achieved in the understanding of family dynamics by child psychiatrists who began to analyze mothers and children concurrently (Burlingham, 1951). One example of the fruits of these studies was Adelaide Johnson's (Johnson & Szurek, 1952) explanation of *superego lacunae,* gaps in personal morality passed on by parents who do things such as telling their children to lie about how old they are to save a couple of bucks at the movies.

Subsequently, the concurrent analysis of married couples revealed the family as a group of interlocking, intrapsychic systems (Oberndorf, 1938; Mittlemann, 1948). This notion of interlinked psyches remains an important feature of the psychoanalytic view of families (Sander, 1989). Most family therapists view the family as a unit, but psychoanalytic therapists are less concerned with the workings of the whole than with the inner worlds of family members and the pasts that shaped them as individuals.

From the 1930s to the 1950s psychoanalytic researchers became more interested in the contemporary family. Erik Erikson explored the sociological dimensions of ego psychology. Erich Fromm's observations about the struggle for individuality foreshadowed Bowen's work on differentiation of the self. Harry Stack Sullivan's interpersonal theory emphasized the mother's role in transmitting anxiety to her children.

In the 1950s American psychoanalysis was dominated by ego psychology (which focuses on intrapsychic structures), while object relations theory (which lends itself to interpersonal analysis) flourished an ocean away in Britain. In the 1940s Henry Dicks (1963) established the Family Psychiatric Unit at the Tavistock Clinic in England, where teams of social workers attempted to reconcile couples referred by the divorce courts. By the 1960s Dicks (1967) was applying object relations theory to the understanding and treatment of marital conflict. His classic text, *Marital Tensions* (Dicks, 1967), is still one of the most profound and useful books ever written about the inner life of couples.

Meanwhile, the psychoanalysts who helped create family therapy were moving away from psychodynamics, and the analytic influence in their work was deliberately muted. The exception was Nathan Ackerman, who of all the pioneers retained the strongest allegiance to psychoanalysis. Students, among them Salvador Minuchin, flocked to New York to observe this master therapist at work.

Edith Jacobson (1954) and Harry Stack Sullivan (1953) helped bring American psychiatry to an interpersonal point of view. Less well-known, but more important to the development of family therapy, was the work carried out at the National Institute of Mental Health (NIMH). When NIMH opened in 1953, Irving Ryckoff moved from Chestnut Lodge, where he'd been working with schizophrenics, to develop a research project on families of schizophrenics under the leadership of Robert Cohen. This group introduced such concepts as *pseudomutuality* (Wynne, Ryckoff, Day, & Hirsch, 1958), *trading of dissociations* (Wynne, 1965), and *delineations* (Shapiro, 1968). But perhaps their most important contribution was the application of *projective identification* (from Melanie Klein) to family relationships.

In the 1960s Ryckoff and Wynne inaugurated a course in family dynamics at the Washington School of Psychiatry, which led to a family therapy training program. They were joined by Shapiro and Zinner and Robert Winer. In 1975 they recruited Jill Savege (now Scharff) and David Scharff. By the mid-1980s the Washington School of Psychiatry, under the directorship of David Scharff, had become a leading center of psychoanalytic family therapy. The Scharffs left in 1994 to form their own institute.

Among others who have incorporated psychoanalytic theory into family therapy are Helm Stierlin (1977), Robin Skynner (1976), William Meissner (1978), Arnon Bentovim and Warren Kinston (1991), Fred Sander (1979, 1989), Samuel Slipp (1984, 1988), Michael Nichols (1987), Nathan Epstein, Henry Grunebaum, and Clifford Sager.

Theoretical Formulations

The essence of psychoanalytic treatment is uncovering and interpreting unconscious impulses and defenses against them. It isn't a question of analyzing individuals instead of family interactions: It's knowing where to look to discover some of the basic wants and fears that keep those individuals from interacting in a mature way. Consider the case of Carl and Peggy.[1]

—Case Study—

Whenever Peggy talked to Carl about their relationship, she got upset and started criticizing. Carl, feeling attacked, was cowed into submission. The more Peggy complained, the quieter Carl became. Only after enduring her tirades for several minutes did Carl get mad

---
1. This case is taken from *The Self in the System* (Nichols, 1987).

and start to shout back at her. As a result, Peggy got the opposite of what she was looking for. Instead of understanding her concerns, Carl felt threatened and withdrew. When that didn't work, he lost his temper. At home, he sometimes slapped her.

The therapist concentrated on interrupting this cycle and then helping the two of them see the pattern so that they could prevent its recurrence. Unfortunately, while Carl and Peggy learned to relate more effectively in the therapist's office, at home they forgot. Week after week it was the same story. They'd manage to listen to each other in their sessions, but at least once a month they'd lose it at home. Eventually, when they got discouraged enough to stop coming, the therapist decided that they just weren't motivated enough to make the necessary changes.

As actors, perhaps we take ourselves too seriously; as observers, we take other selves not seriously enough. As family therapists we see the actions of our clients as a product of their interactions. Yes, people are connected, but that connectedness should not obscure the fact that the nature of their interactions is partly dictated by psychic organization of unsuspected depth and complexity.

—Case Study—

Why couldn't (wouldn't) Carl stop hitting his wife? The fact that she provoked him doesn't really explain anything. Not every husband who is provoked hits his wife. Looking back, the therapist remembered how Carl used to say with exaggerated concern, "I *must* control my temper!" She also remembered how dramatically he described his intimidating outbursts and his wife's cowering. And she remembered that when Peggy talked about Carl's brutality a smile played around the corner of his mouth. These hints of a willful, motivated quality to Carl's abuse could be described in the jargon of psychodynamics, which, because it is alien, might lead some people to dismiss it as a relic of outmoded thinking. Psychodynamic language might imply that Carl's unconscious was responsible for his abusing his wife; he was helpless in the face of his inner conflicts.

Psychodynamic theory may be useful to understand the self in the system, but it isn't necessary to be highly technical. If we were to write a dramatic narrative about Carl, we could say that he was misrepresenting, even to himself, his feelings and intentions. He fooled his wife, he fooled himself, and he fooled his therapist. Carl, who thinks himself concerned about his "temper" (his version of nonhuman agency), is actually pleased with his power to intimidate his wife, and the "manliness" it implies. This explanation does not replace the interactional one, only complicates it. Carl's attacks were triggered by their interactions, but they were propelled by his own unrecognized insecurities. Knowing the motives behind his behavior enables us to help Carl understand that he hits his wife to make up for feeling weak, and to help him find some other way to feel more powerful. As long as therapists stay at the simple behavioral level of interaction, with a certain number of their cases, they will make little headway.

Recognizing that people are more complicated than billiard balls means that we sometimes have to delve deeper into their experience. Psychoanalytic theory gets so complex when you get into the specifics that it's easy to get lost. Here are the basics.

Freudian Drive Psychology

At the heart of human nature, according to Freud, are the drives—sexual and aggressive. Mental conflict arises when children learn, and mislearn, that acting on these impulses may lead to punishment. The resulting conflict is signaled by unpleasant affect: Anxiety is unpleasure associated with the idea (often unconscious) that one will be punished for acting on a particular impulse—for example, the anger you're tempted to express might make your partner stop loving you. Depression is unpleasure plus the idea (often unconscious) that the feared calamity *has already happened*—for ex-

ample, your anger at your mother long ago made her stop loving you; in fact, nobody loves you.

The balance of conflict can be shifted in one of two ways: by strengthening the defenses against one's impulses or by relaxing defenses to permit a healthy modicum of gratification.

Self Psychology

The essence of **self psychology** (Kohut, 1971, 1977) is that every human being longs to be appreciated. If, when we're young, our parents demonstrate their appreciation, we internalize this acceptance in the form of strong, self-confident personalities. But to the extent that our parents insufficiently demonstrate admiring acceptance, then our craving for it is retained in an archaic manner. As adults we alternately suppress the desire for attention and then allow it to break through whenever we're in the presence of a receptive audience.

The child lucky enough to grow up with appreciative parents will be secure, able to stand alone as a center of initiative, and able to love. The unhappy child, cheated out of loving affirmation, will move through life forever craving the attention he or she was denied.

Object Relations Theory

Psychoanalysis is the study of individuals and their deepest motives (drives and the need for attachment); family therapy is the study of social relationships. The bridge between them is **object relations theory.** While the details of object relations theory can be complicated, its essence is simple: We relate to others on the basis of expectations formed by early experience. The residue of these early relationships leaves **internal objects**—mental images of self and other built up from experience and expectation.

Freud's original focus was on bodily appetites, particularly sex. While these appetites may involve other people, they are primarily biological; relationships are secondary. Sex can't be divorced from object relations, but sexual relations can be more physical than personal. This is less true of aggression (to which Freud turned his interest in later years), because aggression isn't an organic appetite. As Guntrip (1971) put it, aggression is a personal reaction to "bad" object relations. Therefore as Freud's interest shifted from sex to aggression, the interpersonal side of his thinking came to the fore.

Melanie Klein combined Freud's psychobiological concepts with her own brilliant insights into the mental life of children to develop object-relational thinking. Klein's theory (Segal, 1964) stemmed from her observations of the infant's developing relationship with the first significant object, namely, the mother. According to Klein, an infant doesn't form impressions of mother based solely on real experience, but instead sifts experience through a rich fantasy life.

Klein has been criticized for failing to follow her own observations to their logical conclusion—namely, that object relations are more relevant than instincts to personality development. Ronald Fairbairn went further in the direction of object relations and away from drive psychology. His radical version of object relations theory redefined the ego as object-seeking and downplayed the role of instincts—making love more important than sex.

Because internal object relations are developed from the earliest and most primitive forms of interpersonal interaction, it's not surprising that the major advances in this field were made by people like Klein and Fairbairn who treated young children and disturbed adults. In the late 1930s and 1940s, based on his work with schizoid patients, Fairbairn (1952) elaborated the concept of *splitting.* Freud originally described splitting as a defense mechanism of the ego; he defined it as a lifelong coexistence of two contradictory positions that do not influence each other.

Fairbairn's view of splitting is that the ego is divided into structures that contain (a) part of the ego; (b) part of the object; and (c) the affect associated with the relationship. The external object is experienced in one of three ways: (1) an ideal object, which leads to satisfaction; (2) a rejecting object, which leads to anger; or (3) an exciting object, which leads to longing. As a result of internalizing split objects, the resulting structure of the ego is: (1) a *central ego,* conscious, adaptable, satisfied with its ideal object; (2) a *rejecting ego,* unconscious, inflexible, frustrated by its rejecting object; or (3) an *exciting ego,* unconscious, inflexible, forever longing for a tempting but unsatisfying object. To the degree that splitting isn't resolved, object relations retain a kind of "all good" or "all bad" quality.

In their observations of infants and young children, Rene Spitz and John Bowlby emphasized the child's profound need for **attachment** to a single and constant object. If the child's need for attachment is denied, the result is *anaclitic depression* (Spitz & Wolf, 1946), a turning away from the world and withdrawal into apathy. According to Bowlby (1969), attachment isn't simply a secondary phenomenon, resulting from being fed, but a basic need in all creatures. Those who don't have this experience are vulnerable to even the slightest lack of support, and may become chronically dependent or isolated. This, in psychoanalytic terms, explains the genesis of *enmeshed* and *disengaged* relationships.

Margaret Mahler observed young children and described a process of **separation-individuation.** After an initial period of total merger, the child begins a gradual process of separation from the mother, progressively renouncing symbiotic fusion with her. The result of successful separation and individuation is a well-differentiated self (Mahler, Pine, & Bergman, 1975). Failure to achieve individuation undermines the development of a differentiated identity, resulting in overly intense emotional attachments. Depending on the severity of the failure to separate, crises are liable to develop when a child reaches school age, enters adolescence, or prepares to leave home as an adult.

The shift from drives to object relations can also be seen in the interpersonal psychiatry of Harry Stack Sullivan (1953) who emphasized the crucial importance of early mother–child interactions. When mother is warm and nurturing, the child feels good; when mother rebuffs or frustrates the child's need for tenderness, the child feels bad; and when the child is exposed to extreme pain or frustration, he dissociates to escape anxiety that would otherwise be intolerable. These experiences create the self-dynamisms: *good me, bad me,* and *not me,* which then become part of the person's response to future interpersonal situations.

The internal world of object relations never corresponds exactly to the actual world of real people. It's an approximation, strongly influenced by the earliest object images, introjections, and identifications. This inner world gradually matures and develops, becoming progressively synthesized and closer to reality. The individual's internal capacity for dealing with conflict and failure is related to the depth and maturity of the internal world of object relations. Trust in one's self and in the goodness of others is based on the confirmation of love from internalized good objects.

Normal Family Development

A child doesn't mature in sublime indifference to the interpersonal world. From the start, we need a facilitating environment in order to thrive. This environment doesn't have to be ideal; an *average expectable environment* featuring *good-enough mothering* (Winnicott, 1965a) is sufficient. The parents' capacity to provide security for the baby's developing ego depends on whether they themselves feel secure. To begin with, the mother must be secure enough to channel her energy into caring for her infant. She withdraws interest from herself and her marriage and focuses it on the baby.

The early attachment between mother and child has been shown to be a critical aspect of healthy development (Bowlby, 1969). Close physical proximity and attachment to a single maternal object are necessary preconditions for

Psychoanalysts see early childhood experience as the key to later problems in relationships.

healthy object relations in childhood and adulthood. The infant needs a state of total merging and **identification** with the mother as a foundation for future growth of a strongly formed personal self.

As the baby comes to need less, the mother gradually recovers her self-interest, which allows her to permit the child to become independent (Winnicott, 1965b). If the early relationship with mother is secure and loving, the infant will gradually be able to give her up, while retaining her loving support in the form of a good internal object. In the process, most little children adopt a *transitional object* (Winnicott, 1965b) to ease the loss—a soft toy or blanket that the child clings to when she starts to realize that mother is a separate object and can go away. The toy that Mommy gives reassures her anxious baby; it's a reminder that stands for her and keeps alive the mental image of her until she returns. When Mommy says, "Goodnight," the child hugs the teddy bear until morning when Mommy reappears.

After passing through the normal autistic and symbiotic phases, the child enters a long *separation–individuation period* at approximately six months (Mahler, Pine, & Bergman, 1975). First efforts at separation are tentative and brief, as symbolized playfully in the game of peekaboo. Soon the child begins to creep and then crawl, first away from and then back to mother. What enables the child to practice separating is the awareness that mother is constantly there for assurance, like a safe harbor.

Recently, Otto Kernberg and Heinz Kohut have brought theories of the self to center stage in psychoanalytic circles. According to Kernberg (1966), the earliest **introjections** occur in the process of separating from mother. If separation is successful and securely negotiated, the child establishes himself or herself as an independent being. A mother must have the capacity to tolerate separation in order to accept her child's growing independence. If the child is excessively dependent and clings in fear of separation, or if the mother is made anxious by the loss of the symbiotic relationship, or is excessively rejecting, the process is subverted. The child with a backlog of good object relations matures with the ability to tolerate closeness as well as separateness.

To the very young child, parents are not quite separate individuals; they are, in Kohut's (1971, 1977) term, **selfobjects,** experienced as part of the self. As a selfobject, the mother transmits her love by touch, tone of voice, and gentle words, as though they were the child's own feelings. When she whispers, "Mommy loves you," the baby learns that he or she is (1) a person and (2) lovable.

In self psychology, two qualities of parenting are thought to be essential for the development of a secure and cohesive self. The first is **mirroring**—understanding plus acceptance. Attentive parents convey a deep appreciation of how their children feel. Their implicit "I see how you feel" validates the child's inner experience. Parents also offer models for **idealization.** The little child who can believe "My mother (or father) is terrific, and I am part of her (or him)" has a firm base of self-esteem. In the best of circumstances, the child, already basically secure in his or her self, draws additional strength from identifying with the power and strength of the parents.

According to Kohut, children begin life with fantasies of a grandiose self and ideal parents. As the child develops, these illusions are tamed and integrated into a mature personality. Grandiosity gives way to self-esteem; idealization of our parents becomes the basis for our strongest values. But if trauma occurs, the most primitive version of the self persists. The grandiose self is not subdued, and the result is what Kohut termed narcissistic personality disorder.

The narcissistic personality—which Christopher Lasch (1979) once described as characteristic of our age—is lonely, craves attention, and is easily angered. The narcissistic person longs to be a hero. Yet it's hard to live up to such grandiose aspirations. The result, frequently, is rage, turned against the self and sometimes the outside world. Freud took this to be a biologically based eruption of self-preserving instinct. Kohut viewed rage as the response to a narcissistic wound, a blow to the idealized sense of who and what we are. By analyzing rage—what kinds of slights result in blowups—Kohut believed that we might come to see where our narcissistic illusions lie, and perhaps even do something about them.

The most significant recent contribution to the psychoanalytic study of normal family development is the work of Daniel Stern (1985). Stern has painstakingly traced the development of the self through detailed observations of infants and small children. The most revolutionary of Stern's findings is that child development is *not* a gradual process of separation and individuation. Rather, infants differentiate themselves almost from birth, and then progress through increasingly complex modes of relatedness. From *attunement* (reading and sharing the child's affective state) to *empathy*, attachment and dependency are needs throughout life.

From a psychoanalytic perspective the fate of the family is largely determined by the early development of individual personalities that make up the family. If the parents are mature and healthy adults, the family will be happy and harmonious.

Some of the most interesting and productive psychoanalytic ideas are contained in descriptions of the psychodynamics of marriage. In the 1950s the marital bond was described as a result of unconscious fantasy (Stein, 1956). We marry a blurry blend of real and hoped-for mates. But more recently, and more interestingly, psychoanalysts have described the overlapping and interlocking of fantasies and projections (Blum, 1987; Sander, 1989). Some authors have described this as "mutual projective identification" (Zinner, 1976; Dicks, 1967), others as "neurotic complementarity" (Ackerman, 1966), "marital collusion" (Dicks, 1967), "mutual adaptation" (Giovacchini, 1958), and "conscious and unconscious contracts" (Sager, 1981).

Among psychodynamic family therapists, few have made more important contributions than Ivan Boszormenyi-Nagy's **contextual therapy,** which emphasizes the ethical dimension of family development. Boszormenyi-Nagy considers relational ethics to be a fundamental dynamic force holding families and communities together. In a field that often seeks refuge in the illusion of clinical neutrality, Nagy reminds us of the importance of decency and fairness.

For marital partners, Boszormenyi-Nagy's criterion of health is a balance between rights and responsibilities. Depending on their integrity and the complementarity of their needs, partners can develop a trustworthy give-and-take (Boszormenyi-Nagy, Grunebaum, & Ulrich, 1991). When needs clash, negotiation and compromise are necessary.

Development of Behavior Disorders

According to classical psychoanalytic theory, symptoms are attempts to cope with unconscious conflicts over sex and aggression. As psychoanalytic thinkers shifted emphasis from instincts to object relations, infantile dependence and incomplete ego development replaced the oedipal complex and repressed instincts as the core problems in development. Fear-dictated flight from object relations, which begins in early childhood, is now considered the deepest root of psychological problems.

One important reason for relationship problems is that children distort their perceptions by attributing the qualities of one person to someone else. Freud (1905) discovered this phenomenon and called it **transference** when his patient Dora displaced feelings for her father onto him and terminated treatment abruptly just as it was on the threshold of success. Others have observed similar phenomena and called it "scapegoating" (Vogel & Bell, 1960); "trading of dissociations" (Wynne, 1965); "merging" (Boszormenyi-Nagy, 1967); "irrational role assignments" (Framo, 1970); "delineations" (Shapiro, 1968); "symbiosis" (Mahler, 1952); and "family projection process" (Bowen, 1965). Regardless of the name, all are variants of Melanie Klein's (1946) concept, *projective identification.*

Projective identification is a process whereby the subject perceives an object as if it contained unwelcome elements of the subject's personality *and* evokes responses from the object that conform to those perceptions. Unlike projection, projective identification is a truly interactional process. Not only do parents project anxiety-arousing aspects of themselves onto their children, the children collude by behaving in a way that confirms their parents' fears. By doing so, they may be stigmatized or scapegoated, but they also gratify aggressive impulses, as, for instance, in delinquent behavior (Jacobson, 1954); realize their own omnipotent fantasies; receive subtle reinforcement from their families; and avoid the terrible fear of rejection for not conforming (Zinner & Shapiro, 1976). Meanwhile the parents are able to avoid the anxiety associated with unhousebroken impulses, experience vicarious gratification, and still punish their children for expressing these impulses. In this way, intrapsychic conflict becomes externalized, with the parent acting as a superego, punishing the child for acting on the dictates of the parental id. That's one reason parents overreact: They're afraid of their own impulses.

—Case Study———————

The J. family sought help controlling fifteen-year-old Paul's delinquent behavior. Arrested several times for vandalism, Paul seemed neither ashamed of nor able to understand his compulsion to strike out against authority. As therapy progressed, it became clear that Paul's father harbored a deep but unexpressed resentment of the social conditions that made him work long hours for low wages in a factory, while the "fat cats didn't do shit, but still drove around in Cadillacs." Once the therapist became aware of Mr. J.'s strong but suppressed hatred of authority, she also began to notice that he smiled slightly whenever Mrs. J. described Paul's latest exploits.

———————————————————

Parents' failure to accept that their children are separate beings can take extreme forms, leading to the most severe psychopathology. Lidz (Lidz, Cornelison, & Fleck, 1965) described a mother of identical twins who, when she was constipated, would give her two sons an enema.

Poorly differentiated children face a crisis in adolescence, when developmental pressures for independence conflict with infantile attachments. The outcome may be a retreat to dependence or an attack of violent rebellion. But the teenager who rebels as a reaction to unresolved dependency needs is ill-equipped for mature relationships. Behind their facade of proud self-reliance, such individuals harbor deep longings for dependence. When they marry, they may seek constant approval, automatically reject any influence, or both.

—Case Study———————

Mr. and Mrs. B.'s complaints were mirror images. He claimed she was "bossy and demanding"; she said that he "had to have everything his own way." Mr. B. was the youngest in a close-knit family of five. He described his mother as warm and loving, but said she tried to smother him, and that she discouraged all his efforts to be independent. Subjected to these same pressures, his two older sisters knuckled under and still remain unmarried, living with their parents. Mr. B., however, rebelled against his mother's domination and left home to join the Marines at seventeen. As he related his experience in the Marine

Corps and successful business ventures, it was clear that he was fiercely proud of his independence.

Once the story of Mr. B.'s success in breaking away from his domineering mother was brought into the open, both Mr. and Mrs. B. had a clearer understanding of his tendency to overreact to anything he perceived as controlling. Deeper analysis revealed that while Mr. B. staunchly rejected what he called "bossiness," he nevertheless craved approval. He had learned to fear his deep-seated dependency needs and protect himself with a facade of "not needing anything from anybody"; nevertheless, the needs were still there, and had in fact been a powerful determinant of his choice of wife.

When it comes to marital choice, psychoanalysts assure us, love is blind. Freud (1921) wrote that the overvaluation of the loved object when we fall in love leads us to make poor judgments based on *idealization*. The "fall" of falling in love reflects an overflow of narcissistic libido, so that the object of our love is elevated as a substitute for our own unattained ideals. Naturally, our own identity glows in the reflected radiance of an idealized companion.

Further complicating marital choice is the fact that we learn to hide some of our own needs and feelings in order to win approval. Children tend to suppress feelings they fear may lead to rejection. Winnicott (1965a) dubbed this phenomenon the *false self*—children behave as if they were perfect angels, pretending to be what they are not. In its most extreme form, a false self leads to schizoid behavior (Guntrip, 1969); even in less severe manifestations it affects the choice of a mate. During courtship most people present themselves in the best possible light. Powerful dependency needs, **narcissism,** and unruly impulses may be submerged before marriage; but once married, spouses relax into themselves, warts and all.

Marriage, on the surface, appears to be a contract between two responsible people; at a deeper level, however, marriage is a transaction between hidden internalized objects. Contracts in marital relations are usually described using the terms of behavioral or communications theories; but Sager's (1981) treatment of marital contracts also considers unconscious factors: Each contract has three levels of awareness:

1. Verbalized, though not always heard
2. Conscious but not verbalized, usually because of fear of anger or disapproval
3. Unconscious

Each partner acts as though the other ought to be aware of the terms of the contract, and is hurt and angry if the spouse doesn't live up to these terms. Every one of us wants our mates to conform to an internalized model, and we are anything but understanding when these unrealistic expectations are disappointed (Dicks, 1963).

It's useful to emphasize individual rights and responsibilities in relationships (Boszormenyi-Nagy, 1972), but it's also true that at an unconscious level a marital pair may represent a single personality, with each spouse playing the role of half self and half the other's projective identifications. This is why people tend to marry those with needs complementary to their own (Meissner, 1978).

A similar dynamic operates between parents and children. Even before they're born, children exist as part of their parents' fantasies (Scharff & Scharff, 1987). The anticipated child may represent, among other things, a more devoted love object than the spouse, someone to succeed where the parent has failed, or a peace offering to reestablish loving relations with grandparents. Zinner and Shapiro (1976) coined the term *delineations* for parental actions that communicate parental fantasies to their children. Pathogenic delineations are based more on parents' defensive needs than on realistic perceptions of the children; moreover, parents are strongly motivated to maintain defensive delineations despite anything the children actually do. Thus it's not uncommon to see parents who insist on seeing their children as bad, helpless, and sick—or brilliant, normal, and fearless—regardless of the truth.

Any and all of the children in a family may suffer from such distortions, but usually only one is identified as "the patient" or the "sick one." He or she is chosen because of some trait that makes him or her a suitable target for the parents' projected emotions. These children shouldn't, however, be thought of as helpless victims. In fact, they collude in the projected identification in order to cement attachments, assuage unconscious guilt, or preserve their parents' shaky marriages. Often the presenting symptom is symbolic of the denied parental emotion. A misbehaving child may be acting out her father's repressed anger at his wife; a dependent child may be expressing his mother's fear of leading her own independent life; and a bully may be counterphobically compensating for his father's projected insecurity.

Intrapsychic personality dynamics are obscured by psychological defenses, which mask the true nature of an individual's feelings, both from himself and from others. **Family myths** (Ferreira, 1963) serve the same function in families, simplifying and distorting reality. Stierlin (1977) elaborated on Ferreira's view of family myths and developed the implications for family assessment and therapy. Myths protect family members from facing certain painful truths, and also serve to keep outsiders from learning embarrassing facts. A typical myth is that of family harmony, familiar to family therapists, especially those who have worked with conflict-avoiding families. In the extreme, this myth takes the form of the "pseudomutuality" (Wynne, Ryckoff, Day, & Hirsch, 1958) found in schizophrenic families. Often the myth of family harmony is maintained by the use of projective identification; one family member is delegated to be the bad one, and all the others insist that they are well-adjusted. This bad seed

may be the identified patient or even a deceased relative.

Families as well as individuals experience **fixation** and **regression.** Most families function adequately until they're overtaxed, at which time they become stuck in dysfunctional patterns (Barnhill & Longo, 1978). When faced with too much stress, families tend to decompensate to earlier levels of development. The amount of stress a family can tolerate depends on its level of development and the type of fixations its members have.

●

Ivan Boszormenyi-Nagy believes that family members owe one another *loyalty,* and that they acquire *merit* by supporting each other. To the degree that parents are fair and responsible, they engender loyalty in their children; however, parents create loyalty conflicts when they ask their children to be loyal to one parent at the expense of the other (Boszormenyi-Nagy & Ulrich, 1981).

Pathological reactions may develop from **invisible loyalties**—unconscious commitments children take on to help their families to the detriment of their own well-being. For example, a child may get sick to unite parents in concern. Invisible loyalties are problematic because they're not subject to rational awareness and scrutiny.

Goals of Therapy

The goal of psychoanalytic family therapy is to free family members of **unconscious** constraints so that they'll be able to interact with one another as healthy individuals. Plainly this is an ambitious task. Couples in crisis are treated with understanding and support to help them through their immediate difficulty. Once the crisis is resolved, the psychoanalytic family therapist hopes to engage the couple in long-term therapy. Some couples accept, but many do not.

When a family is motivated only for symptom relief, the therapist should support their decision to terminate.

When psychoanalytic family therapists opt for crisis resolution with symptom reduction as the only goal (e.g., Umana, Gross, & McConville, 1980), they function much like other family therapists. They focus more on supporting defenses and clarifying communication than on analyzing defenses and uncovering repressed impulses. In general, however, behavioral changes that in other therapy models would be seen as the goal of treatment (e.g., getting a school-phobic child to attend class) are seen by psychodynamic family therapists as by-products of the resolution of underlying conflicts.

It's easy to say that the goal of psychoanalytic therapy is personality change, rather more difficult to specify precisely what's meant by that. The most common objective is described as *separation-individuation* (Katz, 1981) or *differentiation* (Skynner, 1981); both terms emphasize independence from families, and thus reflect the prominent influence of object relations theory. (Perhaps an additional reason for emphasizing separation-individuation is that enmeshed families are more likely to seek treatment than are isolated or disengaged families.) Individual therapists often think of individuation in terms of physical separation. Thus adolescents and young adults may be treated in isolation from their families in order to help them become more independent. Family therapists, on the other hand, believe that emotional growth and autonomy are best achieved by working through the emotional bonds within the family. Rather than remove individuals from their families, psychoanalytic family therapists convene families to help them learn how to let go of one another in a way that allows individuals to be independent as well as related. The following example illustrates how the goals of psychoanalytic family therapy were implemented with a particular family.

—Case Study—

Three months after he went away to college, Barry J. had his first psychotic break. A brief hospital stay made it clear that Barry was unable to withstand separation from his family without decompensating; therefore, the hospital staff recommended that he should live apart from his parents in order to help him become more independent. Accordingly, he was discharged to a supportive group home for young adults and seen twice weekly in individual psychotherapy. Unfortunately, he suffered a second breakdown and was rehospitalized.

As the time for discharge from this second hospitalization approached, the ward psychiatrist decided to convene the family in order to discuss plans for Barry's posthospital adjustment. During this meeting it became painfully obvious that powerful forces within the family were impeding any chance for genuine separation. Barry's parents were pleasant and effective people who separately were most engaging and helpful. Toward each other, however, they displayed an icy disdain. During the few moments in the interview when they spoke to each other, rather than to Barry, their hostility was palpable. Only their concern for Barry prevented their relationship from becoming a battleground—a battleground on which Barry feared one or both of them might be destroyed.

At the staff conference following this interview, two plans for disposition were advanced. One group recommended that Barry be removed as far as possible from his parents and treated in individual therapy. Others on the staff disagreed, arguing that only by treating them conjointly could the collusive bond between Barry and his parents be resolved. After lengthy discussion the group reached a consensus to try the latter approach.

Most of the early family meetings were dominated by the parents' anxious concern about Barry: about the apartment complex where he lived, his job, his friends, how he was spending his leisure time, his clothes, his grooming—in short, about every detail of his life. Gradually, with the therapist's support, Barry was able to limit how much of his life was open to his parents' scrutiny. As he did so, and as they were less able to preoccupy themselves with him, they began to focus on their own relationship. As Barry became more successful at handling his own affairs, his parents became openly combative with each other.

Following a session during which the parents' relationship was the primary focus, the therapist recommended that the couple come for a few separate sessions. Unable to divert their attention to Barry, the J.s fought viciously, leaving no doubt that theirs was a seriously destructive relationship. Rather than getting better in treatment, their relationship got worse.

After two months of internecine warfare—during which time Barry continued to improve—Mr. and Mrs. J. sought a legal separation. Once they were separated, both parents seemed to become happier, more involved with their friends and careers, and less worried about Barry. As they released their stranglehold on their son, both parents began to develop a warmer and more genuine relationship with him. Even after the parents divorced they continued to attend family sessions with Barry.

In Boszormenyi-Nagy's contextual therapy the goal is a balance of fairness in the burdens and benefits of adult life. The well-being of the individual is seen to include giving as well as taking. Family members are helped to overcome irrational, unproductive guilt and to claim their own **entitlements.** However, facing realistic guilt—based on actual harm done to others, even inadvertently—is seen as essential to expanding accountability within families. Thus, each person works toward self-fulfillment by asserting his or her rights and by living up to his or her obligations.

Conditions for Behavior Change

As any student knows, psychoanalytic therapy works through insight; but the idea that insight cures is a myth. Insight may be necessary, but it is not sufficient for successful analytic treatment. In psychoanalytic family therapy, family members expand their insight by learning that their psychological lives are larger than their conscious experience, and by coming to accept repressed parts of their personalities. Just as in individual therapy, to be effective, interpretations should be limited to preconscious material—that which the patient is almost aware of. (Interpretations of unconscious material arouse anxiety, which means they will be rejected.) Whatever insights are achieved, however, must be *worked through* (Greenson, 1967)— that is, translated into new and more productive ways of interacting.

Some (Kohut, 1977) have even suggested that psychoanalytic treatment works not as much by insight as by reducing defenses so that patients can become more truly themselves. From this point of view, it may be more important for family members to stop fighting their unconscious needs than to analyze them. Most therapists work to do both—that is, foster insight and encourage people to accept who they are (Ackerman, 1958).

Analytic therapists foster insight by looking beyond behavior to the hidden motives below. Naturally, families defend against baring their innermost feelings. After all, it's a great deal to ask of anyone to expose old wounds and deep longings. Psychoanalysts deal with this problem by creating a climate of trust and proceeding slowly. Once an atmosphere of security is established, the analytic therapist can begin to identify projective mechanisms and bring them back into the marital relationship. Once they no longer need to rely on projective identification, partners can acknowledge and accept previously split-off parts of their own egos.

Projective identification can seem like one of those mystical processes that make some people reject psychoanalysis as just so much mumbo jumbo. But it isn't necessary to think of projective identification as some mysterious force by which one person's experience is passed to another completely outside both parties' awareness. Rather, feelings are communicated and provoked by subtle but recognizable signals.

Just as it is possible to drive down a crowded highway while concentrating on a conversation or listening to a book on tape, so it is possible to pick up cues from a partner without thinking about them.

Intervening in a sequence of projective identification involves first interrupting the couple's quarrel in order to help one or both partners think about what they are feeling, and avoiding. To intervene effectively the therapist should have a basic grasp of each partner's core conflicts. What are they struggling with? What are they likely to disavow? Otherwise the therapist's interventions are only shots in the dark.

The therapist helps couples begin to recognize how their present difficulties emerged from unconscious perpetuation of conflicts from their own families. This work is painful and cannot proceed without the security offered by a supportive therapist. Nichols (1987) emphasizes the need for *empathy* to create a "holding environment" for the whole family.

Therapy

Assessment

Analysts don't postpone treatment until they've made an exhaustive study of their cases; on the contrary, they may not even arrive at a final formulation until the latter stages of treatment. However, although analytic clinicians may continue to refine their understanding over the course of treatment, effective therapy cannot proceed without some dynamic formulation. Beginning therapists—who lack theory as well as experience—sometimes proceed on the assumption that if they merely sit back and listen, understanding will emerge. This is rarely true in individual therapy and almost never true in family therapy. The following is an abbreviated sketch of an initial psychoanalytic evaluation of a family.

—Case Study—

A fter two sessions with the family of Sally G., who was suffering from school phobia, the therapist made a preliminary formulation of the family's dynamics. In addition to the usual descriptions of the family members, the presenting problem, and the family history, the formulation included assessments of the parents' object relations and the collusive, unconscious interaction of their marital relationship.

Mr. G. had been initially attracted to his wife as a libidinal object who would fulfill his sexual fantasies, including his voyeuristic propensities. Counterbalancing this was a tendency to idealize his wife. Thus he was deeply conflicted and intensely ambivalent in sexual relations with her.

At another level, Mr. G. had unconscious expectations that his wife would be the same long-suffering, self-sacrificing kind of person that his mother was. Thus he longed for motherly consolation. However, these dependent longings were threatening to his sense of masculinity, so he behaved outwardly as though he were self-sufficient and needed no one. That he had a dependent inner object inside himself was shown by his tender solicitude toward his wife and children when they were ill. But they had to be in a position of weakness and vulnerability to enable him to overcome his defenses enough for him to gratify his own infantile dependency needs vicariously.

Mrs. G. expected marriage to provide her with an ideal father. Given this unconscious expectation, the very sexuality that attracted men to her was a threat to her wish to be treated like a little girl. Like her husband, she was highly conflicted about sexual relations. Raised as an only child, she expected to come first. She was even jealous of her husband's warmth toward Sally and attempted to maintain distance between father and daughter by her own intense attachment to Sally.

At the level of her early selfobject images, she was a greedy, demanding little girl. Her introjection of her mother provided her with a model of how to treat a father figure. Unfortunately, what worked for her mother didn't work for her.

Thus, at an object-relations level, both spouses felt themselves to be deprived children, each wanting to be taken care of without having to ask. When these magical wishes weren't granted, both seethed with resentment. Eventually they reacted to trivial provocations with the underlying rage, and horrible quarrels erupted.

When Sally witnessed her parents' violent altercations, she became terrified that her own murderous fantasies might come true. Although her parents hated their own internalized bad-parent figures, they seemed to act them out with each other. Further enmeshing Sally in their conflict was the fact that the ego boundaries between herself and her mother were blurred–almost as though mother and daughter shared one joint personality.

Dynamically, Sally's staying home from school could be seen as a desperate attempt to protect her mother-herself from her father's attacks, and to defend both parents against her own, projected, murderous fantasies.

An excellent model for developing a psychodynamic focus is the work of Arnon Bentovim and Warren Kinston in Great Britain (Bentovim & Kinston, 1991), who offer a five-step strategy for formulating a focal hypothesis:

1. How does the family interact around the symptom, and how does the family interaction affect the symptom?
2. What is the function of the current symptom?
3. What disaster is feared in the family that keeps them from facing their conflicts more squarely?
4. How is the current situation linked to past trauma?
5. How would the therapist summarize the focal conflict in a short, memorable statement?

Among the metaphors used to describe psychoanalytic treatment, "depth" and "uncovering" feature prominently. All therapies aim to uncover something. Even behaviorists make inquiries to uncover unnoticed contingencies of reinforcement before switching to a directive stance. What sets analytic therapy apart is that the process of discovery is protracted and directed not only at conscious thoughts and feelings, but also at fantasies and dreams.

David Scharff (1992) related the following example of the use of dreams in couples treatment.

—Case Study—

L ila and Clive played the all-too-familiar complementary roles whereby the more she sought closeness, the more he retreated. Unlike a systemic therapist, however, Scharff was interested not merely in the synchronicity of their behavior but in the inner experience underlying it. Because Clive had little awareness of his internal life and few memories of his early years, the therapist was frustrated in his attempts to understand what pushed Clive into retreat. The following dream proved instructive.

Clive dreamed about a baby with a wound on its buttocks. A woman, he thought to be the sister, was supposed to take care of the baby, but because she wasn't doing much, Clive stepped in and took the baby from her. When asked for his thoughts–"Does anything come to mind in connection with the dream?"–Clive's association was to the prospect of having children and his concern that he might have to take all the responsibility. After acknowledging this worry, Dr. Scharff pointed out that the dream also suggested a fear of something being terribly wrong, so bad that Clive wouldn't be able to fix it. This triggered a memory of a time when Lila was upset and crying. Clive held her and tried to comfort her, but when her crying didn't subside, he got upset and went into the other room. Thus the dream could also symbolize Clive's fear of taking care of his wife. When she's upset, he may overestimate the depth of her hurt and, since he feels he's the only one who can take care of her, the responsibility feels overwhelming.

Now Lila spoke up, saying that when she gets upset and Clive tries to comfort her, she ends up having to reassure him that she's okay, that what he's doing *is* enough. Thus, even when she's in need of comfort, she has to take care of him. (As Lila's response demonstrates, dreams in couples therapy not only suggest how the dreamer experiences self and object, but also the way dreams are told

*Jill and David Scharff
are leading exponents
of object-relations
family therapy.*

and related to in the session provides additional information about the partners' dynamics.)

When asked if she had any other thoughts about Clive's dream, Lila hesitated, then said she wondered if Clive thinks of her as the baby. This led to the interpretation that in addition to Clive's thinking of Lila in some ways as a baby, he also thought of himself as a baby, deeply wounded by childhood hurts. This insight—that Clive's lifelong fear of female engulfment was superimposed on his own sense of infantile neediness and childhood losses—turned out to be pivotal. Lila began to see Clive's withdrawing less as a rejection of her than as a sign of his own vulnerability. She therefore felt less threatened by abandonment, which she now saw more as her own deep worry than any real possibility. Clive, meanwhile, began to understand his anxiety in the face of his wife's emotional needs not so much as her doing, but as something in him, his own vulnerability. As a result of this understanding he felt less urgency to withdraw from moments of intimacy and emotion.

Therapeutic Techniques

For all the complexity of psychoanalytic theory, psychoanalytic therapy is relatively simple—

not easy, but simple. There are four basic techniques: listening, empathy, interpretations, and analytic neutrality. Two of these—listening and analytic neutrality—may not sound terribly different from what other family therapists do, but they are.

Listening is a strenuous but silent activity, rare in our culture. Most of the time we're too busy waiting to get a word in edgewise to listen more than perfunctorily. This is especially true in family therapy where therapists feel a tremendous pressure to do something to help the troubled and troubling families they treat. And this is where the importance of *analytic neutrality* comes in. To establish an analytic atmosphere, it's essential to concentrate on understanding without worrying about making changes or solving problems. Change may come about as a by-product of understanding, but the analytic therapist suspends anxious involvement with outcomes. It's impossible to overestimate the importance of this frame of mind in establishing a climate of analytic exploration.

The analytic therapist resists the temptation to be drawn in to reassure, advise, or confront families in favor of a sustained, but silent, immersion in their experience. When analytic therapists do intervene, they express *empathy* in order to help family members open up, and they make *interpretations* to clarify hidden aspects of experience.

Most psychoanalytic family therapy is done with couples, where conflict between partners is taken as the starting point for exploring interpersonal psychodynamics. Take, for example, a couple who reported having an argument over the breakfast table. A systemic therapist might ask them to talk with each other about what happened, hoping to observe in their interaction what they were doing to keep the argument from getting settled. The focus would be on communication and interaction. A psychoanalytic therapist would be more interested in helping the partners understand their emotional reactions. Why did they get so angry? What do they want from each other? What did they expect? Where did these feelings come from? Rather than trying to resolve the argument, the analytic therapist would explore the fears and longings that lay underneath it.

The signal of intrapsychic conflict is affect. Instead of focusing on who did what to whom, analytic therapists key in on strong feeling and use it as a starting point for detailed inquiry into its origins. What were you feeling? When have you felt that way before? And before that? What do you remember? Rather than stay on the horizontal plane of the couple's current behavior, the therapist looks for openings into the vertical dimension of their internal experience.

To summarize, psychoanalytic couples therapists organize their explorations along four channels: (1) internal experience, (2) the history of that experience, (3) how the partner triggers that experience, and, finally, (4) how the context of the session and therapist's input might contribute to what's going on between the partners. Here's a brief example:

—Case Study—

Having made great strides in understanding over the course of their first few couples sessions, Andrew and Gwen were all the more upset by their inability to discuss, much less settle, an angry disagreement about buying a new car. It wasn't the car but how to pay for it that set them so infuriatingly at odds. Andrew wanted to take money out of savings for the down payment, to keep the monthly payments low. This made Gwen furious. How could he even consider cutting into their savings! Didn't he understand that their mutual fund paid twice as much interest as they'd have to pay on a car loan?

Unfortunately, they were both too bent on changing the other's mind to make any real effort to understand what was going on inside it. The therapist interrupted their arguing to ask each of them what they were feeling and what they were worried about. He wasn't primarily interested in settling the disagreement—although asking about the feelings underlying an altercation is often an effective opening to understanding and compromise; rather, he felt that the intensity of their reactions indicated that this issue touched key concerns.

Inquiry into the partners' inner experience revealed that Andrew was worried about the burden of monthly expenses. "Don't you see," he implored, "if we don't take out enough to make a substantial downpayment, we'll have to worry every month about making the payments?" Gwen was ready to dispute this, but the therapist cut her off. He was more interested in the roots of Andrew's worry than in the couple's trying to convince each other of anything.

It turned out that Andrew had a lifelong fear of not having enough money. Having enough money turned out to mean, not a big house or a fancy car, but enough to spend on things that might be considered indulgent—nice clothes, going out to dinner, flowers, presents. Andrew connected his urge to reward himself with modest material luxuries to memories of growing up in a spartan household. His parents were children of the Depression who thought that things like going out to dinner and buying clothes except when absolutely necessary were frivolous and wasteful. At a deeper level, Andrew's memories of austerity were a screen for his never having gotten the attention and affection he craved from his rather reserved mother.[2] And so he'd learned to soothe himself with a new shirt or fancy dinner at times when he was feeling low. One of Gwen's chief attractions was her giving and expressive nature. She was openly affectionate and almost always happy to indulge Andrew's wish to buy something for himself.

Gwen connected her anxiety about having a cushion against the unexpected to memories of her father as an unreliable breadwinner. Unlike Andrew's parents, hers spent freely. They went out to dinner three or four times a week, took expensive vacations, and everyone in the family wore nice clothes. But, although he was a free spender, Gwen remembered her father as lacking the discipline and foresight to invest wisely or to expand his business beyond its modest success. Although it had never been part of her conscious memories, it seemed that although her father lavished attention and affection on her, he never really took her seriously as a person. He treated her, in the familiar phrase, like "Daddy's little girl," as adorable—and insubstantial—as a kitten. That's why she was so attracted to what she saw as Andrew's serious and self-disciplined nature—and his high regard for her.

How did these two trigger such virulent reactions in each other? Not only did Gwen's anxious need to have money in the bank conflict with Andrew's need to have money to spend, but they each felt betrayed by the other. Part of Gwen's unconscious bargain with Andrew was that she could count on him to be a secure, steady pillar, and to build for the future. Part of his unconscious expectations of her were that she would indulge him. No wonder they were so reactive to each other on this issue.

And the therapist's role in all this? On reflection he realized that he'd been a little too anxious to smooth things over with this couple. Out of his own desire to see marital happiness he'd controlled the level of conflict in the sessions, intervening actively as a peacemaker. As a result, the couple's progress had come at a price. Deep longings and resentments had been pushed aside rather than explored and resolved. Perhaps, the therapist thought, he'd picked up the couple's fears of facing their own anger.

What use should a therapist make of such countertransferential reactions? Should he disclose his feelings? To say that **countertransference** may contain useful information isn't to say that it's oracular. Perhaps the most useful thing to do is look to countertransference for hypotheses that need confirming evidence from the patients' side of the experience. In this case the therapist acknowledged his sense that he'd been trying too hard to smooth things over, and he asked Gwen and Andrew whether they, too, were a little afraid to open up their anger.

Like many descriptions of clinical work, this one may seem a little pat. How did we get from arguing about buying a car to a hunger for a mirroring selfobject on Andrew's part and someone to idealize on Gwen's? Part of the explanation lies in the inevitably condensed account. But it's also important to recognize that one of the things that enables psychoanalysts to see beneath the surface of things is knowing where to look.

Sessions begin with the therapist inviting family members to discuss current concerns, thoughts, and feelings. In subsequent meetings, the therapist might begin either by saying nothing or perhaps, "Where would you like to begin today?" The therapist then leans back and lets the family talk. Questions are limited to requests for amplification and clarification. "Could you tell me more about that?" "Have the two of you discussed how you feel about this?"

When initial associations and spontaneous interactions dry up, the therapist probes gently, eliciting history, people's thoughts and feelings, and their ideas about family members' perspectives. "What does your father think about your problems? How would he explain them?" This technique underscores the analytic therapist's interest in assumptions and projections. Particular interest is paid to childhood memories and associations to parents. The following vignette shows how transitions are made from the present to the past.

---

2.   In Kohut's terms, Andrew's mother provided an inadequate *mirroring* selfobject function.

—Case Study—————

Among their major disappointments in each other, Mr. and Mrs. S. both complained that the other one "doesn't take care of me when I'm sick, or listen to my complaints at the end of the day." Not only did they share the perception of the other's lack of "mothering," they both steadfastly maintained that *they* were supportive and understanding. Mrs. S.'s complaint was typical: "Yesterday was an absolute nightmare. The baby was sick and fussy, and I had a miserable cold. Everything was twice as hard and I had twice as much to do. All day long I was looking forward to John's coming home. But when he finally did, he didn't seem to care about how I felt. He only listened to me for a minute before starting to tell me some dumb story about his office." Mr. S. responded by telling a similar account, but with the roles reversed.

At this point the therapist intervened to ask both spouses to describe their relationships with their mothers. What emerged were two very different but revealing histories.

Mr. S.'s mother was a taciturn woman, for whom self-reliance, personal sacrifice, and unremitting struggle were paramount virtues. Though she loved her children, she withheld indulgence and affection, lest they become "spoiled." Nevertheless, Mr. S. craved his mother's attention and constantly sought it. Naturally, he was often rebuffed. A particularly painful memory was of a time he came home in tears after getting beaten up by a bully in the schoolyard. Instead of the consoling he hoped for, his mother scolded him for "acting like a baby." Over the years he learned to protect himself from these rebuffs by developing a facade of independence and strength.

With the second significant woman in his life, his wife, Mr. S. maintained his rigid defensiveness. He never talked about his problems, but since he continued to yearn for compassionate understanding, he resented his wife for not drawing him out. His own failure to risk rejection by asking for support served as a self-fulfilling prophecy, confirming his expectation, "She doesn't care about me."

Mrs. S.'s background was quite different from her husband's. Her parents were indulgent and demonstrative. They doted on their only child, communicating their love by expressing constant, anxious concern for her well-

being. When she was a little girl, the slightest bump or bruise was an occasion for lavish expressions of concern. She came to marriage used to talking about herself and her problems. At first Mr. S. was enchanted. "Here is someone who really cares about feelings," he thought. But when he discovered that she didn't ask him to talk about his own concerns, he became resentful and progressively less sympathetic. This convinced her, "He doesn't care about me."

After the roots of current family conflicts have been uncovered, interpretations are made about how family members continue to reenact past, and often distorted, images from childhood. The data for such interpretations come from transference reactions to the therapist or to other family members, as well as from actual childhood memories. Psychoanalytic therapists deal less with recollections of the past than with reenactments of its influence in the present.

Psychoanalytic family therapists are aware that their influence isn't confined to rational analysis, but also includes a kind of reparenting. Thus therapists may act in a more controlling or permissive fashion depending on their assessment of the particular needs of a family. One therapist who was acutely aware of his personal influence on families was Nathan Ackerman. His interventions (Ackerman, 1966) were designed to penetrate family defenses in order to surface hidden conflicts over sex and aggression. Unlike the traditionally reserved analyst, Ackerman related to families in a very personal manner. In this regard he wrote:

> It is very important at the outset to establish a meaningful emotional contact with all members of the family, to create a climate in which one really touches them and they feel they touch back. (1961, p. 242)

Ackerman encouraged honest expression of feeling by being honest himself. His spontaneous disclosure of his own thoughts and feelings made it hard for family members to resist doing likewise. Ackerman made full use of his charisma, but he did more than simply "be himself." He made deliberate use of confrontive techniques to bring out family conflicts from behind defensive facades. His memorable phrase to describe this was "tickling the defenses."

Psychoanalytic family therapists emphasize that much of what is hidden in family dialogues is not consciously withheld, but rather repressed into unconsciousness. The approach to this material is guarded by resistance often manifest in the form of transference. The following vignette illustrates the interpretation of resistance.

—Case Study—————

Mr. and Mrs. Z. had endured ten years of a loveless relationship in order to preserve the fragile security that being married offered them. Mrs. Z.'s totally unexpected and uncharacteristic affair forced the couple to acknowledge the problems in their relationship, and so they consulted a family therapist.

Although they could no longer deny the existence of conflict, both spouses exhibited major resistance to confronting their problems openly. Their resistance represented a reluctance to acknowledge certain of their feelings, and collusion to avoid frank discussions of their relational problems.

In the first session, both partners said that married life had been "more or less okay"; that Mrs. Z. had some kind of "midlife crisis"; and that it was she who needed therapy. This request for individual therapy was seen as a resistance to avoid the painful examination of the marriage, and the therapist said so. "It seems, Mr. Z., that you'd rather blame your wife than consider how the two of you might both be contributing to your difficulties. And you, Mrs. Z., seem to prefer accepting all the guilt in order to avoid confronting your husband with your dissatisfaction and anger."

Accepting the therapist's interpretation and agreeing to examine their relationship deprived the couple of one form of resistance, as though an escape hatch had been closed to two reluctant combatants. In the next few ses-

sions both partners attacked each other vituperatively, but they talked only about her affair and his reactions rather than about problems in the relationship. These arguments weren't productive because whenever Mr. Z. felt anxious he attacked his wife, and whenever she felt angry she became guilty and depressed.

Sensing that their fighting was unproductive, the therapist said, "It's clear that you've put each other through a lot of unhappiness and you're both quite bitter. But unless you get down to talking about specific problems in your marriage, there's little chance that you'll get anywhere."

Thus focused, Mrs. Z. timidly ventured that she'd never enjoyed sex with her husband and wished that he would take more time with foreplay. He snapped back, "Okay, so sex wasn't so great, is that any reason to throw away ten years of marriage and start whoring around!" At this, Mrs. Z. buried her face in her hands and sobbed uncontrollably. After she regained her composure, the therapist intervened, again confronting the couple with their resistance: "It seems, Mr. Z., that when you get upset, you attack. What makes you so anxious about discussing sex?" Following this the couple was able to talk about their feelings about sex in their marriage until near the end of the session. At this point, Mr. Z. again lashed out at his wife calling her a whore and a bitch.

Mrs. Z. began the following session by saying that she'd been depressed and upset, crying off and on all week. "I feel so guilty," she sobbed. "You *should* feel guilty!" retorted her husband. Once again, the therapist intervened. "You use your wife's affair as a club. Are you still afraid to discuss problems in your marriage? And you, Mrs. Z., cover your anger with depression. What is it that you're angry about? What was missing in the marriage? What did you want?"

This pattern continued for several more sessions. The spouses who had avoided discussing or even thinking about their problems for ten years used a variety of resistances to veer away from them in therapy. The therapist persisted in pointing out their resistance and urging them to talk about specific complaints.

Psychoanalytic family therapists endeavor to foster insight and understanding; they also urge families to consider what they're going to do about the problems they discuss. This effort—part of the process of working through—is more prominent in family therapy than in individual therapy. Boszormenyi-Nagy, for example, considers that family members must not only be made aware of their motivations, but also held accountable for their behavior. In contextual therapy, Boszormenyi-Nagy (1987) points out that the therapist must help people face the stifling expectations involved in invisible loyalties, and then help them find more positive ways of making loyalty payments in the family ledger. What this boils down to is developing a balance of fairness.

Ackerman too stressed an active working through of insights by encouraging families to constructively express the aggressive and libidinal impulses uncovered in therapy. In order to alleviate symptoms, impulses must become conscious; but an emotional experience must be associated with increased self-awareness in order for lives to change. To modify thinking and feeling is the essential task of psychoanalytic therapy, but family therapists are also concerned with supervising and analyzing changes in behavior.

Evaluating Therapy Theory and Results

Too many family therapists neglect psychology in general and psychoanalytic theory in specific. Regardless of what other approaches a therapist uses, the writings of psychoanalytically informed clinicians are a rich resource.

Having said this, we also wish to make a cautionary point. Doctrinaire psychoanalytic family therapies are powerful in the hands of trained psychoanalysts. However, many therapists who get discouraged with the usual contentious family dialogues, gravitate to psychoanalytic methods as a way to break through the defensive wrangling. Interrupting a family's arguments to explore the individuals' feelings is an excellent way to avoid arguments. But if therapists make themselves overly central (by directing all conversation through themselves), or if they overemphasize individuals and neglect family interactions, then the power of family therapy—addressing relationship problems directly—may be lost. Interrupting defensive sparring to get to the hopes and fears that lie beneath is all to the good. But unless these interrogatories are followed by extensive and free-flowing interchanges among family members themselves, these explorations may only produce the illusion of change as long as the therapist is present to act as detective and referee.

Psychoanalytic therapists have generally been opposed to attempts to evaluate their work using empirical standards. Because symptom reduction isn't the goal, it can't serve as the measure of success. And since the presence or absence of unconscious conflict isn't apparent to outside observers, whether an analysis is successful depends on subjective judgment. Psychoanalytic clinicians consider the therapist's observations as a valid means of evaluating theory and treatment. The following quotation from the Blancks (1972) illustrates this point. Speaking of Margaret Mahler's ideas, they wrote:

> Clinicians who employ her theories technically question neither the methodology nor the findings, for they can confirm them clinically, a form of validation that meets as closely as possible the experimentalist's insistence upon replication as criterion of the scientific method. (p. 675)

Another example of this point of view can be found in the writing of Robert Langs. "The ultimate test of a therapist's formulation," says Langs (1982), "lies in the use of the therapist's impressions as a basis for intervention" (p 186). What then determines the validity and effectiveness of these interventions? Langs doesn't hesitate; the patient's reactions, conscious and unconscious, constitute the ultimate litmus test. "True validation involves responses from the patient in both the cognitive and interpersonal spheres."

Is the ultimate test of therapy then the patient's reactions? Yes and no. First, patients' reactions are open to various interpretations—especially since validation is sought not only in manifest responses but also in unconsciously encoded derivatives. Moreover, this point of view doesn't take into account the changes in patients' lives that occur outside the consulting room. Occasionally therapists report on the outcome of psychoanalytic family therapy, but mostly in uncontrolled case studies. One such report is Dicks's (1967) survey of the outcome of psychoanalytic couples therapy at the Tavistock Clinic, in which he rated as having been successfully treated 72.8 percent of a random sample of cases.

—Summary

Psychoanalytically trained clinicians were among the first to practice family therapy, but when they began treating families most of them traded in their ideas about depth psychology for systems theory. Since the mid-1980s there's been a resurgence of interest in psychodynamics among family therapists, an interest dominated by object relations theory and self psychology. In this chapter we've sketched the main points of these theories and shown how they're relevant to a psychoanalytic family therapy, integrating depth psychology and systems theory. A few practitioners (e.g., Kirschner & Kirschner, 1986; Nichols, 1987; Slipp, 1984) have combined elements of both; some have developed more frankly psychoanalytic approaches (notably Scharff & Scharff, 1987; Sander, 1989); none has achieved a true synthesis.

—Recommended Readings

Ackerman, N. W. 1966. *Treating the troubled family.* New York: Basic Books.

Boszormenyi-Nagy, I. 1972. Loyalty implications of the transference model in psychotherapy. *Archives of General Psychiatry. 27:* 374–380.

Boszormenyi-Nagy, I. 1987. *Foundations of contextual therapy.* New York: Brunner/Mazel.

Dicks, H. V. 1967. *Marital tensions.* New York: Basic Books.

Meissner, W. W. 1978. The conceptualization of marriage and family dynamics from a psychoanalytic perspective. In *Marriage and marital therapy,* T. J. Paolino and B. S. McCrady, eds. New York: Brunner/Mazel.

Nadelson, C. C. 1978. Marital therapy from a psychoanalytic perspective. In *Marriage and marital therapy,* T. J. Paolino and B. S. McCrady, eds. New York: Brunner/Mazel.

Nichols, M. P. 1987. *The self in the system.* New York: Brunner/Mazel.

Sander, F. M. 1989. Marital conflict and psychoanalytic theory in the middle years. In *The middle years: New psychoanalytic perspectives,* J. Oldham and R. Liebert, eds. New Haven: Yale University Press.

Scharff, D., and Scharff, J. S. 1987. *Object relations family therapy.* New York: Jason Aronson.

Stern, M. 1985. *The interpersonal world of the infant.* New York: Basic Books.

Zinner, J., and Shapiro, R. 1976. Projective identification as a mode of perception of behavior in families of adolescents. *International Journal of Psychoanalysts. 53:*523–530.

References

Ackerman, N. W. 1958. *The psychodynamics of family life.* New York: Basic Books.

Ackerman, N. W. 1961. The emergence of family psychotherapy on the present scene. In *Contemporary psychotherapies,* M. I. Stein, ed. Glencoe, IL: Free Press.

Ackerman, N. W. 1966. *Treating the troubled family.* New York: Basic Books.

Barnhill, L. R., and Longo, D. 1978. Fixation and regression in the family life cycle. *Family Process.* 17:469–478.

Bentovim, A., and Kinston, W. 1991. Focal family therapy. In *Handbook of family therapy,* Vol. II, A. S. Gurman and D. P. Kniskern, eds. New York: Brunner/Mazel.

Blanck, G., and Blanck, R. 1972. Toward a psychoanalytic developmental psychology. *Journal of the American Psychoanalytic Association.* 20:668–710.

Blum, H. P. 1987. Shared fantasy and reciprocal identification: General considerations and gender disorder. In *Unconscious fantasy: Myth and reality,* H. P. Blum et al., eds. New York: International Universities Press.

Boszormenyi-Nagy, I. 1967. Relational modes and meaning. In *Family therapy and disturbed families,* G. H. Zuk and I. Boszormenyi-Nagy, eds. Palo Alto, CA: Science and Behavior Books.

Boszormenyi-Nagy, I. 1972. Loyalty implications of the transference model in psychotherapy. *Archives of General Psychiatry.* 27: 374–380.

Boszormenyi-Nagy, I. 1987. *Foundations of contextual therapy.* New York: Brunner/Mazel.

Boszormenyi-Nagy, I. Grunebaum, J., and Ulrich, D. 1991. Contextual therapy. In *Handbook of family therapy,* Vol. II, A. S. Gurman and D. P. Kniskern, eds. New York: Brunner/Mazel.

Boszormenyi-Nagy, I., and Ulrich, D. N. 1981. Contextual family therapy. In *Handbook of family therapy,* A. S. Gurman and D. P. Kniskern, eds. New York: Brunner/Mazel.

Bowen, M. 1965. Family psychotherapy with schizophrenia in the hospital and in private practice. In *Intensive family therapy,* I. Boszormenyi-Nagy and J. L. Framo, eds. New York: Harper & Row.

Bowlby, J. 1969. *Attachment and loss.* Vol. 1: *Attachment.* New York: Basic Books.

Burlingham, D. T. 1951. Present trends in handling the mother–child relationship during the therapeutic process. *Psychoanalytic study of the child.* New York: International Universities Press.

Dare, C. 1979. Psychoanalysis and systems in family therapy. *Journal of Family Therapy.* 1:137–151.

Dicks, H. V. 1963. Object relations theory and marital studies. *British Journal of Medical Psychology.* 36:125–129.

Dicks, H. V. 1967. *Marital tensions.* New York: Basic Books.

Fairbairn, W. D. 1952. *An object-relations theory of the personality.* New York: Basic Books.

Ferreira, A. 1963. Family myths and homeostasis. *Archives of General Psychiatry.* 9:457–463.

Framo, J. L. 1970. Symptoms from a family transactional viewpoint. In *Family therapy in transition,* N. W. Ackerman, ed. Boston: Little, Brown & Co.

Freud, S. 1905. Fragment of an analysis of a case of hysteria. *Collected papers.* New York: Basic Books, 1959.

Freud, S. 1909. Analysis of a phobia in a five-year-old boy. *Collected papers, Vol. III.* New York: Basic Books, 1959.

Freud, S. 1921. Group psychology and the analysis of the ego. *Standard edition.* 17:1–22. London: Hogarth Press, 1955.

Giovacchini, P. 1958. Mutual adaptation in various object relations. *International Journal of Psychoanalysis.* 39:547–554.

Greenson, R. R. 1967. *The theory and technique of psychoanalysis.* New York: International Universities Press.

Guntrip, H. 1969. *Schizoid phenomena, object relations theory and the self.* New York: International Universities Press.

Jackson, D. D. 1967. The individual and the larger context. *Family Process.* 6:139–147.

Jacobson, E. 1954. *The self and the object world.* New York: International Universities Press.

Johnson, A., and Szurek, S. 1952. The genesis of antisocial acting out in children and adults. *Psychoanalytic Quarterly.* 21:323–343.

Katz, B. 1981. Separation–individuation and marital therapy. *Psychotherapy: Theory, Research and Practice.* 18: 195–203.

Kernberg, O. F. 1966. Structural derivatives of object relationships. *International Journal of Psychoanalysis. 47:* 236–253.

Kirschner, D., and Kirschner, S. 1986. *Comprehensive family therapy: An integration of systemic and psychodynamic treatment models.* New York: Brunner/Mazel.

Klein, M. 1946. Notes on some schizoid mechanisms. *International Journal of Psycho-Analysis. 27:*99–110.

Kohut, H. 1971. *The analysis of the self.* New York: International Universities Press.

Kohut, H. 1977. *The restoration of the self.* New York: International Universities Press.

Langs, R. 1982. *Psychotherapy: A basic text.* New York: Jason Aronson.

Lasch, C. 1979. *The culture of narcissism: American life in an age of diminishing expectations.* New York: Basic Books.

Lidz, T., Cornelison, A., Fleck, S. 1965. *Schizophrenia and the family.* New York: International Universities Press.

Mahler, M. S. 1952. On child psychosis and schizophrenia: Autistic and symbiotic infantile psychoses. *Psychoanalytic Study of the Child,* vol. 7.

Mahler, M., Pine, F., and Bergman, A. 1975. *The psychological birth of the human infant.* New York: Basic Books.

Meissner, W. W. 1978. The conceptualization of marriage and family dynamics from a psychoanalytic perspective. In *Marriage and marital therapy,* T. J. Paolino and B. S. McCrady, eds. New York: Brunner/Mazel.

Minuchin, S. 1989. Personal communication. Quoted from *Institutionalizing madness,* J. Elizur and S. Minuchin, eds. New York: Basic Books.

Mittlemann, B. 1948. The concurrent analysis of married couples. *Psychoanalytic Quarterly. 17:* 182–197.

Nichols, M. P. 1987. *The self in the system.* New York: Brunner/Mazel.

Oberndorf, C. P. 1938. Psychoanalysis of married couples. *Psychoanalytic Review. 25:*453–475.

Sager, C. J. 1981. Couples therapy and marriage contracts. In *Handbook of family therapy,* A. S. Gurman and D. P. Kniskern, eds. New York: Brunner/Mazel.

Sander, F. M. 1979. *Individual and family therapy: Toward an integration.* New York: Jason Aronson.

Sander, F. M. 1989. Marital conflict and psychoanalytic therapy in the middle years. In *The middle years: New psychoanalytic perspectives,* J. Oldham and R. Liebert, eds. New Haven, CT: Yale University Press.

Scharff, D. 1992. *Refining the object and reclaiming the self.* New York: Jason Aronson.

Scharff, D., and Scharff, J. 1987. *Object relations family therapy.* New York: Jason Aronson.

Segal, H. 1964. *Introduction to the work of Melanie Klein.* New York: Basic Books

Shapiro, R. L. 1968. Action and family interaction in adolescence. In *Modern psychoanalysis,* J. Marmor, ed. New York: Basic Books.

Shapiro, R. L. 1979. Family dynamics and object relations theory. In *Adolescent psychiatry,* S. C. Feinstein and P. L. Giovacchini, eds. Chicago: University of Chicago Press.

Skynner, A. C. R. 1976. *Systems of family and marital psychotherapy.* New York: Brunner/Mazel.

Skynner, A. C. R. 1981. An open-systems, group analytic approach to family therapy. In *Handbook of family therapy,* A. S. Gurman and D. P. Kniskern, eds. New York: Brunner/Mazel.

Slipp, S. 1984. *Object relations: A dynamic bridge between individual and family treatment.* New York: Jason Aronson.

Slipp, S. 1988. *Technique and practice of object relations family therapy.* New York: Jason Aronson.

Spitz, R., and Wolf, K. 1946. Anaclitic depression: An inquiry into the genesis of psychiatric conditions early in childhood. *Psychoanalytic Study of the Child. 2:*313–342.

Stein, M. 1956. The marriage bond. *Psychoanalytic Quarterly. 25:*238–259.

Stern, M. 1985. *The interpersonal world of the infant.* New York: Basic Books.

Stierlin, H. 1977. *Psychoanalysis and family therapy.* New York: Jason Aronson.

Sullivan, H. S. 1953. *The interpersonal theory of psychiatry.* New York: Norton.

Szasz, T. S. 1961. *The myth of mental illness.* New York: Hoeber-Harper.

Umana, R. F., Gross, S. J., and McConville, M. T. 1980. *Crisis in the family: Three approaches.* New York: Gardner Press.

Vogel, E. F., and Bell, N. W. 1960. The emotionally disturbed as the family scapegoat. In *The family,* N. W. Bell and E. F. Vogel, eds. Glencoe, IL: Free Press.

Winnicott, D. W. 1965a. *The maturational process and the facilitating environment.* New York: International Universities Press.

Winnicott, D. W. 1965b. *The maturational process and the facilitating environment: Studies in the theory of emotional development.* New York: International Universities Press.

Wynne, L. C. 1965. Some indications and contradictions for exploratory family therapy. In *Intensive family therapy,* I. Boszormenyi-Nagy and J. L. Framo, eds. New York: Harper & Row.

Wynne, L., Ryckoff, I., Day, J., and Hirsch, S. 1958. Pseudomutuality in the family relations of schizophrenics. *Psychiatry. 21:205–220.*

Zinner, J. 1976. The implications of projective identification for marital interaction. In *Contemporary marriage: Structure, dynamics, and therapy,* H. Grunebaum and J. Christ, eds. Boston: Little, Brown.

Zinner, J., and Shapiro, R. 1976. Projective identification as a mode of perception and behavior in families of adolescents. *International Journal of Psychoanalysis. 53:523–530.*

Cognitive-Behavioral Family Therapy

Beyond Stimulus and Response

When they first began working with families in the 1970s behavior therapists applied learning theory to train parents in behavior modification and teach couples communication skills. These approaches proved effective with discrete, behavioral problems and well-motivated individuals. However, anchored as they were in individual psychology, behavior therapists had little appreciation of the ways in which misbehavior and poor communication were embedded in relationship problems.

In addition to their unfamiliarity with systems dynamics, behavior therapists generally worked in academic settings and, despite developing a whole armamentarium of useful techniques, remained relatively isolated from mainstream family therapy. The past ten years, however, have seen sweeping changes in behavioral family therapy, with increasing sophistication about family dynamics and the incorporation of cognitive principles. Unfortu-

nately, advances in cognitive-behavior therapy have continued to have limited impact on the field of family therapy, a situation that should change with the current emphasis on cross-fertilization among various models.

Sketches of Leading Figures

Behavior therapy is a direct descendent of the investigations of Ivan Pavlov, the Russian physiologist whose work on conditioned reflexes led to the development of **classical conditioning.** In classical conditioning, an *unconditioned stimulus* (UCS), such as food, which leads to a reflex *unconditioned response* (UCR), like salivation, is paired with a *conditioned stimulus* (CS), such as a bell. The result is that the conditioned stimulus begins to evoke the same response (Pavlov, 1932, 1934). Subsequently John B. Watson used classical conditioning to experimentally induce a phobia in "Little Albert"

(Watson & Raynor, 1920), while Mary Cover Jones successfully resolved a similar phobia in the case of "Peter" (Jones, 1924).

In 1948 Joseph Wolpe introduced *systematic desensitization,* with which he achieved great success in the treatment of phobias and generated enormous interest in behavioral methods. According to Wolpe (1948) anxiety is a persistent response of the autonomic nervous system acquired through classical conditioning. Systematic desensitization deconditions the anxiety through *reciprocal inhibition,* by pairing responses incompatible with anxiety to the previously anxiety-arousing stimuli. For example, if Indiana Jones were frightened of snakes, Wolpe would teach Dr. Jones deep muscle relaxation and then have him imagine approaching a snake in a graded hierarchy of stages. Each time Indy became anxious, he would be told to relax. In this way the anxiety evoked by imagining snakes would be systematically extinguished.

Systematic desensitization proved to be a powerful technique for reducing anxiety, and even more effective when it included actual practice in approaching the feared object or situation (*in vivo desensitization*).

The application of classical conditioning theory to family problems was primarily in the treatment of anxiety-based disorders, including agoraphobia and sexual dysfunction, pioneered by Wolpe (1958) and later elaborated by Masters and Johnson (1970). Effective behavioral treatments for enuresis were also developed using classical conditioning (Lovibond, 1963).

By far the greatest influence on behavioral family therapy came from B. F. Skinner's **operant conditioning.** The term *operant* refers to voluntary responses, as opposed to involuntary reflexes. The frequency of operant responses is determined by their consequences. Responses that are *positively reinforced* will be repeated more frequently; those that are *punished* or ignored will be *extinguished.*

The operant conditioner carefully observes target behavior and then quantifies its frequency and rate. Then, to complete a **functional analysis of the behavior,** the consequences of the behavior are noted to determine the *contingencies of reinforcement.* For example, someone interested in a child's temper tantrums would begin by observing when they occurred and what the consequences were. A typical finding might be that the child threw a tantrum whenever his parents denied his requests, and that the parents frequently gave in if the tantrums were prolonged. Thus the parents would be reinforcing the very behavior they least wanted. To eliminate the tantrums, they would be taught to ignore them. Moreover they would be told that giving in, even occasionally, would maintain the tantrums, because behavior that is partially or *intermittently reinforced* is the most difficult to extinguish. If the child were aware of the contingencies, he might think, "They're not giving in now, but if I keep fussing they eventually will; if not this time, then the next."

Operant conditioning is particularly effective with children because parents have considerable control over reinforcers and punishments. Boardman (1962) trained parents in effective use of punishment to deal with the aggressive antisocial behavior of their five-year-old. Wolpe (1958) described how to employ parents as cotherapists in anxiety management. Risley and Wolf (1967) trained parents in the operant reinforcement of speech in their autistic children. In technical terms, these parents were trained to eliminate the contingencies that maintained the deviant behavior and to reinforce behavior patterns that were incompatible with the deviant behavior (Falloon, 1991). In plain English, they were taught to ignore inappropriate and to reward appropriate behavior.

Although no single figure was responsible for the development of behavioral family therapy, three leaders played a dominant role: a psychologist, Gerald Patterson, a psychiatrist, Robert Liberman, and a social worker, Richard Stuart.

Gerald Patterson, at the University of Oregon, was the most influential figure in developing behavioral parent training. Patterson and his colleagues developed methods for sampling periods of family interaction in the home, trained parents in the principles of **social learning theory,** developed programmed workbooks (e.g., Patterson, 1971b), and worked out careful strategies for eliminating undesirable behavior and substituting desirable behavior. Among others prominent in this field are Anthony Graziano, Rex Forehand, Daniel and Susan O'Leary, and Roger McAuley.

The second major figure in the development of behavioral family therapy was Robert Liberman. In his 1970 paper, "Behavioral Approaches to Family and Couple Therapy," he outlined the application of an operant learning framework to the family problems of four adult patients with depression, intractable headaches, social inadequacy, and marital discord. In addition to employing contingency management of mutual reinforcers, Liberman introduced the use of *role rehearsal* and **modeling** (Bandura & Walters, 1963) to family therapy.

The third major influence on behavioral family therapy was the **contingency contracting** approach of Richard Stuart (1969). Rather than focus on how the undesired behavior of one family member could be modified, Stuart focused on how the exchange of positive behavior could be maximized using the principle of **reinforcement reciprocity.**

During the 1970s behavioral family therapy evolved into three major packages: parent training, behavioral couples therapy, and sexual therapy. At present the leading figures in behavioral couples therapy include Robert Weiss, Richard Stuart, Michael Crowe, Ian Falloon, Norman Epstein, and Gayola Margolin.

Recently there has been a rapprochement between stimulus-response conditioning models and cognitive theories (e.g., Epstein, Schlesinger, & Dryden, 1988; Dattilio, 1998). **Cognitive-behavior therapy** refers to those approaches inspired by the work of Albert Ellis (1962) and Aaron Beck (1976) that emphasize the need for attitude change to promote and maintain behavioral modification. Among the leaders in cognitive-behavioral family therapy are Donald Baucom at the University of North Carolina, Norman Epstein at the University of Maryland, and Frank Dattilio in private practice in Pennsylvania.

Theoretical Formulations

The basic premise of behavior therapy is that behavior is maintained by its consequences. Consequences that accelerate behavior are called *reinforcers,* while those that decelerate behavior are known as *punishers.*

Some responses may not be recognized as operants—something done to get something— just because people aren't aware of the reinforcing payoffs. For example, whining is usually reinforced by attention, although the people supplying the reinforcement may not realize it. In fact, a variety of undesired behaviors, including nagging and temper tantrums, are often reinforced by attention. Thus, family problems are often maintained under conditions that are counterintuitive.

Extinction occurs when no reinforcement follows a response. Ignoring it is, of course, often the best response to behavior you don't like. The reason some people fail to credit this is because withholding response rarely leads to *immediate* cessation of unwanted behavior. This is because most behavior problems have been partially or intermittently reinforced, and therefore take time to extinguish.

Despite the mechanistic sound of "schedules of reinforcement" and "controlling behavior," behavior therapists have increasingly become aware that people not only act but also think and feel. This recognition has taken the form of efforts to integrate pure stimulus-response behaviorism (Skinner, 1953) with cognitive theories (Mahoney, 1977). The central tenet of the cognitive approach is that our interpretation of other people's behavior affects the way we respond to them. Among the most troublesome of *automatic thoughts* are those based on "arbitrary inference," distorted conclusions, shaped by a person's **schemas,** core beliefs about the world and how it functions. What makes these underlying beliefs problematic is that although they are generally not conscious, they bias how we approach and respond to one another.

As behavior therapists shifted their attention from individuals in isolation to family relationships, they came to rely on Thibaut and Kelley's (1959) **theory of social exchange,** according to which people strive to maximize "rewards" and minimize "costs" in relationships. In a successful relationship both partners work to maximize mutual rewards, while minimizing costs. By contrast, in unsuccessful relationships the partners are too busy trying to protect themselves from getting hurt to consider ways to make each other happy. According to Thibaut and Kelley, behavior exchanges follow a norm of reciprocity over time, so that aversive or positive stimulation from one person tends to produce reciprocal behavior from the other. Kindness begets kindness; nastiness begets nastiness.

Normal Family Development

According to the behavior exchange model (Thibaut & Kelley, 1959), a good relationship is one in which giving and getting are balanced— or, in the model's terms, there is a high ratio of benefits to costs. Put as generally as this, little is added to commonsense notions of family satisfaction. But behaviorists have begun to spell out, in empirical studies, some of the details of what makes for relationship satisfaction. For example, Weiss and Isaac (1978) found that affection,

communication, and child care are the most important elements in marital satisfaction. Earlier, Wills, Weiss, and Patterson (1974) found that unpleasant behavior reduced marital satisfaction significantly more than pleasant behavior increased it. A good relationship, then, is one in which there is an exchange of pleasant responses and, even more important, minimal unpleasantness. Another way of putting this is that good relationships are under *positive reinforcing control.*

Communication skills—the ability to talk, especially about problems—is considered by behaviorists to be the most important feature of good relationships (Gottman, Markman, & Notarius, 1977; Jacobson, Waldron, & Moore, 1980). (It's also the most easily observed feature of relationships.) Good communication increases the rewards of relating by leading to effective stimulus control over behavior.

In time all couples run into conflict and, therefore, a critical skill in maintaining family harmony is skill in conflict resolution (Gottman & Krokoff, 1989). Unfortunately, problems are part of life. Healthy families aren't problem free but have the ability to cope with problems when they do arise. Recognizing this, behavior therapists stress the need for *problem-solving skills* and the ability to resolve conflicts as criteria for successful marriages (Jacobson & Margolin, 1979).

In a good relationship partners are able to speak openly about conflicts. They focus on issues and keep them in perspective, and they discuss specific behavior that is of concern to them. They describe their own feelings and request changes in the behavior of others, as opposed to just criticizing and complaining. "I've been kind of lonely and I wish you and I could go out and do things more often" is more likely to get a positive response than, "You never care what I want! All you care about is yourself!"

Some people assume that good relationships will evolve naturally if people are well matched and if they love each other. Behaviorists, on the other hand, emphasize the need to develop relationship skills. Good marriages, they believe, aren't made in heaven, but are a product of learning effective coping behavior. The late Neil Jacobson (1981) described a good relationship as one in which the partners maintain a high rate of rewards.

> Successful couples . . . expand their reinforcement power by frequently acquiring new domains for positive exchange. Spouses who depend on a limited quantity and variety of reinforcers are bound to suffer the ill effects of satiation. As a result, over time their interaction becomes depleted of its prior reinforcement value. Successful couples cope with this inevitable reinforcement erosion by varying their shared activities, developing new common interests, expanding their sexual repertoires, and developing their communication to the point where they continue to interest one another. (p. 561)

Development of Behavior Disorders

Behaviorists view symptoms as learned responses. They don't look for underlying motives, nor do they posit marital conflict as leading to children's problems. Instead they concentrate on the symptoms themselves and look for responses that reinforce problem behavior.

At first glance it would seem puzzling that family members reinforce undesirable behavior. Why would parents reward temper tantrums? Why would a wife reinforce her husband's withdrawal, when it appears to cause her so much pain? The answer lies not in some kind of convoluted motive for suffering but in the simple fact that people often inadvertently reinforce precisely those responses that cause them the most distress.

Parents often inadvertently reinforce temper tantrums by giving in or merely by giving the tantruming child extra attention.

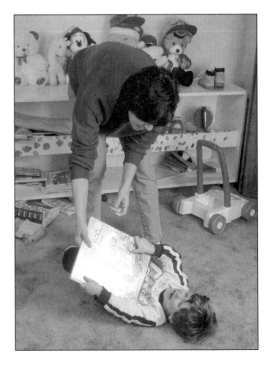

Parents usually respond to problem behavior in their children by scolding and lecturing. These reactions may seem like punishment, but they may in fact be reinforcing, because attention—even from a critical parent—is a powerful *social reinforcer* (Skinner, 1953). The truth of this is reflected in the sound advice to "Ignore it, and it will go away." The problem is, most parents have trouble ignoring bad behavior. Notice, for example, how quickly children learn that certain words get a big reaction. Moreover, even when parents do resolve to ignore misbehavior, they usually don't do so consistently. This can make things even worse, because *intermittent reinforcement* is the most resistant to extinction (Ferster, 1963).

In addition to behavior problems unwittingly maintained by parental attention, other problems persist because parents are unaware of how to make effective use of punishment. They make threats they don't follow through on; they punish too long after the fact; they use punishments so mild as to have no effect; or they use punishments so severe as to generate more anxiety than discriminative learning.

Learning, moreover, is not just a one-way street. Consider the behavior of a mother and daughter in the supermarket.

—Case Study———————

The little girl asks her mother for a candy bar. The mother says, "No." The child begins crying and complaining. The mother says, "If you think I'm going to buy you candy when you make such a fuss, you have another think coming, young lady!" But the child escalates her tantrum, getting louder and louder. Finally, exasperated and embarrassed, the mother gives in: "All right, if you'll quiet down, I'll buy you some cookies."

Obviously, the child has been reinforced for throwing a temper tantrum. Not so obviously,

but also true, the mother has been reinforced for giving in—by the child's calming down after being promised cookies. Thus a spiral of undesirable behavior is maintained by *reciprocal reinforcement.*

The use of **aversive control**—nagging, crying, withdrawing—is often cited as a major determinant of marital unhappiness (Stuart, 1975). Spouses typically reciprocate their partners' use of aversive behavior, and a vicious circle develops (Patterson & Reid, 1970). People in distressed relationships also show poor problem-solving skills (Vincent, Weiss, & Birchler, 1975; Weiss, Hops, & Patterson, 1973). When discussing a problem, they frequently change the subject; they phrase wishes and complaints in vague and critical ways; and they respond to complaints with countercomplaints. The following exchange demonstrates sidetracking, cross-complaining, and name-calling, all typical of distressed marriages.

—Case Study———————

"I'd like to talk about all the sweets you've been giving the kids lately." "What sweets! Talk about *me,* you're always stuffing your face. And what do you ever do for the kids? You just come home and complain. Why don't you just stay at the office! The kids and I get along better without you."

Most behavioral analyses point to a lack of reinforcement for adaptive strivings in distressed families. The old adage, "The squeaky wheel gets the grease," seems to apply. Depressions, headaches, and temper tantrums tend to elicit concern and therefore more attention than pleasant behavior. Because this process is unwitting, family members are often mystified about their role in reinforcing annoying behavior.

According to cognitive-behaviorists, the schemas that plague relationships are learned in the process of growing up. Some of these dysfunctional beliefs are assumptions about specific family roles while others are about family life in general. These schemas are the underlying basis of the "shoulds," self-fulfilling prophesies, mind reading, jealousy, and bad faith that poison relationships by distorting family members' responses to each other's actual behavior.

The following eight types of cognitive distortion are taken from Datillio (1998):

1. *Arbitrary inference:* Conclusions are drawn from events in the absence of supporting evidence; for example, a man whose wife is consistently late concludes that she doesn't care about his feelings.
2. *Selective abstraction:* Certain details are highlighted while other important information is ignored; for example, parents of a teenager remember the times she defies them, but not the times she goes out of her way to please them.
3. *Overgeneralization:* Isolated incidents are taken as general patterns; for example, a wife rejects her husband's advances twice in a month and he decides that she isn't interested in sex.
4. *Exaggeration and minimization:* The significance of events is unrealistically magnified or diminished; for example, a husband considers the two times in one month he shops for groceries as fulfilling his share of the household duties, while his wife thinks that he "never does anything."
5. *Personalization:* Events are arbitrarily interpreted in reference to oneself; for example, a teenager wants to spend more time with his friends, so his father assumes that his son doesn't enjoy his company.
6. *Dichotomous thinking:* Experiences are interpreted as all good or all bad; for example, Jack and Diane have some good times

and some bad times, but he remembers only the good times, while she remembers only the bad times.
7. *Labeling:* Behavior is attributed to undesirable personality traits; for example, a woman who avoids talking with her mother about her career because her mother always criticizes is considered "withholding."
8. *Mind reading:* People don't communicate because they assume that they know what others are thinking; for example, a man doesn't ask an attractive classmate out on a date because he assumes that she wouldn't be interested.

Goals of Therapy

The goal of behavior therapy is to modify specific patterns of behavior to alleviate the presenting symptom. This focus on behavior, rather than on the organization of the family or the health of its relationships, gives cognitive-behavior therapy a more technical flavor than most systemic family therapies.

The behavior therapist tailors treatment to fit the case, but the general intent is to extinguish undesired behavior and reinforce positive alternatives as defined by the family (Azrin, Naster, & Jones, 1973). Thus, for example, parents of a child with temper tantrums might be taught to ignore the tantrums and reward the child for putting his feelings into words.

Sometimes it may be necessary to redefine a family's goal of decreasing negative behavior in terms of increasing incompatible, positive responses (Umana, Gross, & McConville, 1980). Couples, for example, often state goals of reducing aversive behavior (Weiss, 1978), but the behavioral therapist will also establish a goal of helping them increase satisfaction by accelerating positive behavior.

Behavior therapy also has an educational agenda. In addition to applying learning theory principles to alleviate specific behavioral problems, behavior therapists also teach communication, problem-solving, and negotiation skills. Similarly, cognitive-behavioral therapists not only use their technology of helping clients reexamine distorted beliefs to solve specific complaints, but also make an effort to teach families how to use cognitive strategies to prevent or resolve problems in the future.

Conditions for Behavior Change

The basic premise of behavior therapy is that behavior will change when the contingencies of reinforcement are altered. Behavioral family therapy aims to resolve specific targeted family problems through identification of behavioral goals, learning theory techniques for achieving these goals, and use of social reinforcers to facilitate this process. Significant others are trained to use contingency management techniques to influence family members and to provide appropriate consequences for desired behavior.

The hallmarks of behavioral family therapy are: (1) careful and detailed assessment to determine the baseline frequency of problem behavior, to guide therapy, and to provide accurate feedback about the success of treatment; and (2) strategies designed to modify the contingencies of reinforcement in each unique client family.

The first task of the therapist is to observe and record the frequency and duration of problem behavior, as well as the stimulus conditions that precede it and the reinforcement that follows it. This enables the therapist to design an individually tailored treatment program.

Moving out of the playroom and the office into the natural world of the home and classroom enabled behavior therapists to discover that some of their previous notions about child aggression were fundamentally erroneous.

Contrary to Skinner's assumptions, for example, punishment *does* have long-term effects. The data show that reinforcement of positive behavior, such as cooperation and compliance, doesn't lead to reductions in antisocial behavior. Introducing punishment (time out, point loss) produces long-term reductions in antisocial behavior (Patterson, 1988).

Furthermore, behavioral family therapists now realize that the manner in which problems are reinforced in families is often complex (Falloon, 1991). In addition to the reinforcing responses that immediately follow a specific problem behavior, more remote reinforcers may also play a part. These may include tacit approval of aggressive behavior, particularly by men in the family, often accompanied by modeling of this behavior. Spanking children for fighting demonstrates by example the violence that a parent may wish to discourage. In addition, behavior that is approved by peers or others outside the family may be extremely difficult to modify at home—especially if the therapist fails to take this wider context into account.

Most behavioral family therapy uses operant rather than classical conditioning (with the exception of treating sexual dysfunctions), and the focus is on changing dyadic interactions (parent–child or spouse–spouse). This dyadic focus differs from the triadic approach of systems-oriented family therapists. Although behavioral family therapists (Liberman, 1970; Falloon & Lillie, 1988) have disputed this distinction, we believe this is a major difference between behavioral and nonbehavioral family therapists.

Although behavior change remains the primary focus, more and more behavioral family therapists are recognizing the role of cognitive factors in resolving relationship problems. In a classic study, Margolin and Weiss (1978) first demonstrated the effectiveness of a cognitive component to behavioral marital therapy by comparing couples treatment using a strictly behavioral approach with a group that also received a cognitive component. The treatment that included cognitive restructuring proved significantly more effective than behavioral marital therapy alone.

The cognitive approach first gained attention as a supplement to behavioral-oriented couples and family therapy (Margolin, Christensen, & Weiss, 1975). In addition to the work of Ellis (1977), the Margolin and Weiss study (1978) sparked intense interest in cognitive techniques with dysfunctional couples (Baucom & Epstein, 1990; Baucom & Lester, 1986; Beck, 1988; Dattilio, 1990; Dattilio & Padesky, 1990; Doherty, 1981; Ellis et al., 1989; Epstein, 1992; Finchman, Bradbury, & Beach, 1990; Schindler & Vollmer, 1984; Weiss, 1984). This interest in cognitive-behavioral approaches to couples therapy eventually led to the recognition by behavioral family therapists that cognition plays a significant role in the events that mediate family interactions (Alexander & Parsons, 1982). The important role of cognitive factors, not only in determining relationship distress but also in mediating behavioral change, has become a topic of increasing interest (Epstein, Schlesinger, & Dryden, 1988; Alexander, 1988; Dattilio, 1993).

Although marital and family therapists began to realize decades ago that cognitive factors were important in the alleviation of relationship dysfunction (Dicks, 1953), it took some time before cognition was formally included as a primary component of treatment (Munson, 1993).

Barton and Alexander, who call their approach *functional family therapy* (Barton & Alexander, 1981; Morris, Alexander, & Waldron, 1988), point out that members of unhappy families tend to attribute their problems to negative traits (laziness, irresponsibility, poor impulse control) in other members. Such views block therapeutic change by projecting blame in a way that makes it impossible for anyone to change. Such negative and incomplete views leave family members with a limited sense of

control over their lives. After all, what can one person do to change another person's "laziness," "irresponsibility," or "poor impulse control"? Cognitive behavior therapists believe that attributional shifts are necessary to make behavior change possible, but that, in turn, behavior change is necessary to reinforce new and more productive attributions.

In general, behaviorists deemphasize the "art" of therapy, treating it instead as a technical procedure dependent largely on the application of learning theory. Some behavioral writers have argued that change will occur if current behavioral principles are applied regardless of the individual personality or style of the therapist (Stuart, 1969; Hawkins, Peterson, Schweid, & Bijou, 1966). But contemporary behavior therapists now realize that successful treatment requires complex skills and great tact. According to Ian Falloon (1991), the supportive therapeutic alliance essential for effective treatment is maintained by displaying respect for the family, reliably adhering to the agreed-on time and place and focus of therapy (this means not shifting from parenting to marital problems without the explicit agreement of the couple), and appreciating that family members are doing the best they can. "The role of the therapist is not to confront the inadequacies of these best efforts, but to facilitate efforts to overcome manifest deficits and to improve the efficiency of the family members' responses" (Falloon, 1991, p. 85). Falloon advises that confrontation, coercion, and criticism be minimized and that therapists concentrate instead on validating the efforts family members are making.

Traditionally, behaviorists have been little concerned with resistance, despite the fact that systems theorists have established that any ongoing social system resists change, either from within or without. Although behavior therapists have lately recognized the importance of resistance (Birchler, 1988), most have tended to assume that people seeking psychotherapy are capable of rational, collaborative effort to change. As Spinks and Birchler (1982) put it:

> Most behaviorists view so-called resistance phenomena as the results of ineffective case management. That is, resistance is a sign that the treatment model or the therapist have been unsuccessful, not that the clients inherently resist change, or will not change. (p. 172)

Cognitive-behavioral therapists have become more concerned with resistance (Birchler, 1988), but their view of it differs from systemic family therapists in two ways. First, they see resistance as primarily a property of individuals, rather than a homeostatic tendency in systems. Second, they assume that although family members may have beliefs or expectancies that interfere with change, these beliefs are relatively easily reexamined and reevaluated. Once an individual's concerns are addressed, therapy can continue. While this happy optimism seems preferable to those systemic therapists who assume family members are blindly driven by mechanical forces they're powerless to resist, it also seems a little naive.

As their experience with families increased in the 1970s and 1980s, behavioral therapists began to incorporate more principles and techniques from systems theory into their work. Gerald Patterson, for example, studied Minuchin's structural family therapy, and Gary Birchler integrated systems theory and behavioral marital therapy (Birchler & Spinks, 1980; Spinks & Birchler, 1982). According to Birchler, straight behavioral family therapy is overly structured and fails to deal with underlying relationship dynamics.

A major tenet of behavioral family treatment is that behavior change is better achieved by accelerating positive behavior than by decelerating negative behavior. Although, as we've seen, there may be a need to introduce punishment to eliminate antisocial behavior in aggressive children, behavior therapists generally try to minimize coercion by aversive control or extinction. It's believed that most distressed families already use these approaches to excess. Therefore only positive reinforcement is consistently and widely used in behavioral family therapy.

Behavioral therapists directly manipulate contingencies of reinforcement in the families they treat, and may provide reinforcement themselves when family members comply with

*B*ehavior therapists teach parents to use positive reinforcement rather than aversive control.

their instructions. Once new behaviors are established, therapists counsel family members to use intermittent positive reinforcement and then to fade out material reinforcements in favor of social ones. Following this direct control, therapists teach family members how to observe and modify their own contingencies of reinforcement to maintain their initial gains using self-control procedures.

Learning theory may have been developed by observing white rats in laboratory mazes, but applying learning theory to families is a different matter. In behavioral family therapy it's important not to make simplistic assumptions about what may be rewarding and what may be punishing. Instead, it's critical to examine the interpersonal consequences of behavior. The therapist must find out what is reinforcing for each person and each family, rather than assume that certain things are universally rewarding. Moreover, a variety of different behaviors may be aimed at the same payoff. For example, a child might throw tantrums, whine, or drop things at various times, but all of these may be reinforced by parental attention. Therefore, in order to understand how to help families change, the therapist must shift attention from the behavior (R) to the consequences (KC).

Therapy

Behavioral Parent Training

Most family therapists begin with the assumption that the family, not the individual, is the problem, so that the whole family should be convened to solve the problem. Behavior therapists, on the other hand, accept the parents' view that the child is the problem and generally meet with only one parent (guess which one) and the child, although some behaviorists (Gordon & Davidson, 1981) recommend that both parents and even older siblings be included.

Perhaps it's more accurate to say that behavioral parent training therapy accepts that the child *has* the problem rather than *is* the problem. The assumption is that the root of children's problems lies in providing inconsistent or inappropriate consequences for problem behavior (Patterson & Brodsky, 1966) as well as failing to support positive behavior (Patterson & Forgatch, 1995).

> Parents of antisocial children ignore prosocial behavior and tend to be ineffective in their use of punishment. Periodically, they explode and physically assault their children. In nonproblem families, prosocial behaviors are reinforced frequently, and parents consistently set limits on deviant behavior. As children enter school, the family training is supplemented with rich schedules of both positive and negative reinforcement provided by peers and teachers. (Forgatch & Patterson, 1998, p. 86)

The most commonly used intervention is operant conditioning, where the reinforcers employed may be tangible or social. In fact, smiling, praise, and attention have been found to be as effective as money or candy (Bandura, 1969). Operant techniques may be further divided into shaping, token economies, contingency contracting, contingency management, and time-out.

Shaping (Schwitzgebel & Kolb, 1964) consists of reinforcing change in small steps that gradually approximate the desired goals. **Token economies** (Baer & Sherman, 1969) use a system of points or stars to reward children for successful behavior. *Contingency contracting* (Stuart, 1971) involves agreements by parents to make certain changes following changes made by their children. *Contingency management* (Schwitzgebel, 1967) consists of giving and taking away rewards and punishments based on the children's behavior. *Time-out* (Rimm & Masters, 1974) is a punishment where children are made to sit in the corner or sent to their rooms.

Assessment. In common with other forms of behavior therapy, parent training begins with a thorough assessment. While the exact procedure varies from clinic to clinic, most assessments are based on Kanfer and Phillips's (1970) SORKC model of behavior: *S* for stimulus, *O* for the state of the organism, *R* for the target response, and *KC* for the nature and contingency of consequences. The following example illustrates how this assessment model is applied.

—Case Study—

In the case of parents who complain that their son pesters them for cookies between meals and throws tantrums if they don't give him any, the tantrums would be considered the target behavior, *R. O,* the state of the organism, might turn out to be mild hunger or, more likely, boredom. The stimulus, *S,* might be the sight of cookies in the cookie jar; and the contingency of consequences, *KC,* might be that the parents give in by feeding the boy cookies occasionally, especially if he makes enough of a fuss.

In simple cases, such as the one above, applying the SORKC model is straightforward, but it quickly becomes more complex with families, in which there are long chains of interrelated behavior. Consider the following.

—Case Study—

Mr. and Mrs. J. complain that their two small children whine and fuss at the dinner table. A home observation reveals that when Mr. J. yells at the children for misbehaving they start to whine and stand by their mother's chair.

Given this sequence it's not difficult to apply the SORKC model. Imagine, however, that the above sequence is only part of a more complex picture.

In the morning, Mr. J. makes a sexual overture to his wife, but she, tired from taking care of the children, rolls over and goes back to sleep. Mr. J. is hurt and leaves for work after making some unkind remarks to his wife. She, feeling rejected by her husband, spends the entire day playing with the children for solace. By the time she has to cook dinner, Mrs. J. is exhausted and exasperated with the children. Mr. J. comes home after a hard day at the office and tries to make up with his wife by hugging her. She responds but only perfunctorily because she's busy trying to cook. While she's at the stove, the children and Mr. J. vie for her attention, each one wanting to tell her something. Finally, she blows up at her husband: "Can't you see I'm busy!" He goes into the den and sulks until dinner is ready. Just as his wife finds it difficult to express her anger at the children and takes it out on him, Mr. J. has trouble directing anger at his wife and so tends to divert it toward the children. At the dinner table he yells at them for the slightest infraction, at which point they whine and turn to their mother. She lets one sit on her lap while she strokes the other's hair.

In this longer, but not atypical sequence, what is stimulus and what is response? Obviously these definitions become circular, and their application depends on the perspective of the observer.

Assessment in behavioral parent training entails defining, observing, and recording the frequency of the behavior to be changed, as well as the events that precede it and those that follow. Interviews, usually with the mother, are designed to provide a definition of the problem and a list of potential reinforcers. Observations may be conducted behind a one-way mirror or during a home visit. Baseline data, collected prior to the initiation of therapy, may be recorded by therapists or family members. Typically, parents are trained to pinpoint problem behavior, to observe and record its occurrence, and to note the occurrence and frequency of various events that might serve as stimuli and reinforcers. Checklists and questionnaires provide information that may have been omitted or overlooked in interviews. The final product of this stage of the assessment is the selection of target behaviors for modification.

The measurement and functional analysis stage consists of actually observing and recording the target behavior, as well as its antecedents and consequences. This may be done by the parents at home or by therapists in the clinic—and now, more and more, by therapists in the natural setting (Arrington, Sullaway, & Christensen, 1988).

Therapeutic Techniques.   Once the assessment is complete, the therapist decides which behaviors should be increased and which decreased. To accelerate behavior, the **Premack principle** (Premack, 1965) is applied; that is, high probability behavior (particularly pleasant activities) is chosen to reinforce behavior with a low probability of occurrence. Where once it was thought that reinforcers must satisfy some basic drive, such as hunger or thirst, it's now known that any behaviors chosen more frequently (given a wide variety of choices) can serve as reinforcers for those chosen less frequently.

—Case Study—

Mrs. G. stated that she couldn't get her five-year-old son Adam to clean up his room in the morning. She went on to say that she tried rewarding him with candy, money, and toys, but "Nothing works!" A functional analysis of Adam's behavior revealed that, given his choice of things to do, the most probable behaviors were watching television, riding his bicycle, and playing in the mud behind his house. Once these activities were made contingent on tidying his room, he quickly learned to do so.

A variety of material and social reinforcers have been employed to accelerate desired behaviors, but as the Premack principle demonstrates, to be effective, reinforcers must be popular with the child in question. While money and candy seem like powerful rewards, they may not be as effective for some children as a chance to play in the mud.

Once effective rewards are chosen, parents are taught to **shape** the desired behavior by reinforcing successive approximation to the final goal. They are also taught to raise the criteria for reinforcement gradually, and to present reinforcement immediately contingent on the desired behavior.[1] Once the child is regularly performing the desired response, reinforcement becomes intermittent in order to increase the durability of the new behavior.

The most common technique for decelerating behavior is **time-out.** This means ignoring or isolating the child after he or she misbehaves. Studies have shown that a duration of about five minutes is most effective (Pendergrass, 1971). Children are first warned, to give them a chance to control their own behavior, before they are put into time-out. Other techniques used to decelerate behavior include verbal reprimand, ignoring, and isolation. Simply repeating commands to children has been shown to be the most ineffective way to change their behavior (Forehand et al., 1976).

Because of the inconvenience of reinforcing behavior immediately after it occurs, token systems have been very popular with parent trainers. Points are earned for desirable behavior and lost for undesirable behavior (Christophersen, Arnold, Hill, & Quilitch, 1972). The principles of behavioral parent training described above are exemplified and more clearly delineated in the following case study.

—Case Study—

Mrs. F. is a mother of two small children who came to the clinic complaining of headaches and crying spells. The intake interviewer found her to be

---

1.   The importance of immediate proximity is what makes time-out such an effective punishment and grounding second only to lecturing as an ineffective one.

Time-outs are a highly effective form of punishment for young children.

mildly depressed and concluded that the depression was primarily a reaction to difficulty coping with the children. Suzie, age five, was a shy child who rarely played with other children and had frequent temper tantrums. Robert, who was eight, was more outgoing and sociable but did poorly in school. The children were a handful, and Mrs. F. felt helpless and resentful in her dealings with them.

A functional analysis of behavior revealed that Suzie's shyness resulted in her getting extra attention from her anxious mother. Whenever Suzie declined an invitation to play with other children, her mother spent a great deal of time doing things to make her feel better. The therapist selected social behavior (not shyness) as the first target response, and instructed Mrs. F. to reinforce all efforts at socializing and to ignore Suzie when she avoided social contact. Thereafter, whenever Suzie made any attempt to socialize with other children, Mrs. F. would immediately reinforce her with attention and praise. When Suzie chose to stay home rather than play with other children, her mother ignored her, instead busying herself with her own activities. In three weeks, Mrs. F. reported that Suzie "seemed to have gotten over her shyness."

Following this initial success the therapist felt it was time to help Mrs. F. tackle the more difficult problem of Suzie's tantrums. Since the tantrums were unlikely to occur while the family was at the clinic or during home visits, the therapist instructed Mrs. F. to make observational notes for

a week. These notes revealed that Suzie generally had her tantrums when her parents denied her requests for a treat or some special indulgence, such as staying up to watch television. Moreover, tantrums were especially likely to occur at the end of the day when Suzie (and her parents) were tired. As for how the parents responded to these maddening outbursts, Mrs. F. reported that "We've tried everything. Sometimes we try to ignore her, but that's impossible; she just screams and shrieks until we can't stand it anymore. Then sometimes we spank her—or give her what she wants, just to shut her up. Sometimes after we spank her she cries so much that we let her watch television until she calms down. That usually works."

After listening to this description, the therapist explained how Mr. and Mrs. F. had inadvertently been reinforcing the tantrums, and told them what they would have to do to stop them. For the next week, the F.'s were instructed to ignore fits of temper whenever they occurred. If they occurred at bedtime, Suzie was to be put in her bed; if she continued to cry and fuss, she was to be left alone until she stopped. Only when she stopped were her parents to talk with her about what was on her mind. The following week Mrs. F. reported that the tantrums had indeed decreased, except for one night when they took on a new and more troubling form. When Suzie was told that she wouldn't be able to stay up late to watch television she began to yell and cry as usual. Instead of relenting, Mrs. F. put Suzie in her room and told her to get ready for bed. However, realizing that her parents were going to ignore her, as they had earlier in the week, Suzie began to scream and smash things in her room. "It was awful, she was completely out of control. She even smashed the little dog-shaped lamp I bought her. We didn't know what to do, so just that once we let her stay up." Again the therapist described the consequences of such behavior, and explained to Mrs. F. how, should Suzie again become destructive, both parents should hold her until the tantrum subsided.

At the next session, Mrs. F. described how Suzie did "get out of control again." This time, however, instead of giving in, the parents held her as they had been told. Mrs. F. was amazed at the fury and duration of the resulting tantrum. "But we remembered what you said—there was no way we were going to give in!" It took twenty minutes, but Suzie finally calmed down. This, it turned out, was the last time Suzie ever became so violent during a temper tantrum. Nevertheless she did continue to have an occasional flare-up during the next few weeks. According to Mrs. F., the few tantrums that did occur seemed to take place in different settings or under different conditions than the usual episodes at home (which Suzie had now learned would not be reinforced). For example, one episode took place in the supermarket, when Suzie was told she couldn't have a candy bar. By this time, however, Mrs. F. was thoroughly convinced of the necessity of not reinforcing the tantrums, and so she didn't. Because she was embarrassed at all the noise her daughter was making in public, she did find it necessary to take her out of the store. But she made Suzie sit in the car and took pains not to let it be a pleasant experience. Very few tantrums followed this one.

Next the therapist turned her attention to Robert's poor school performance. A careful assessment revealed that Robert rarely brought assignments home and when asked usually denied that he had any homework. After checking with Robert's teacher the therapist discovered that the children generally did have homework, and that they were expected to work between thirty minutes and an hour a night. Mrs. F. selected a high-probability behavior, watching television, and made it contingent on Robert's having first completed his homework. For the first two weeks of this regimen, Mrs. F. found it necessary to call the teacher every night to verify the assignments. But soon this was no longer necessary. Doing homework fairly quickly

became a habit for Robert, and his grades increased from Ds and Cs to Bs and As by the end of the school year. At this point, everyone was happier, and Mrs. F. felt the family no longer needed help.

A follow-up session in the fall found things continuing to go well. Suzie was now much more sociable and hadn't had any temper tantrums in months. Robert was doing well in school, although he had begun to neglect some of his more difficult assignments. To address this, the therapist explained to Mrs. F. how to institute a token system, and she was able to use it with excellent results in a short amount of time.

The preceding example illustrates a form of behavioral parent training in which the therapist meets with the mother and instructs her in the use of operant conditioning principles. Another format is to observe parent and child interacting behind a one-way mirror in the clinic. In this way, the therapist can get a firsthand look at what actually transpires. With this approach, parents can be taught how to play with their children, as well as how to discipline them, and how to negotiate with them. Sometimes the observing therapist may communicate to the parents through a remote microphone, called a "bug in the ear."

Currently, the most widely used approach to behavioral parent training involves teaching prosocial behavior through contingent encouragement with incentive charts. Chores are broken down into clearly defined steps, with points given for each step. The number of points can reflect the difficulty of the behavior or the value the parents place on it.

Common rewards include food treats, special time with a parent, household resources (e.g., computer or TV time), privileges, and things that cost money. Items used as rewards are changed regularly to keep things interesting. When a child learns a given task or responsibility, the chart is altered to include something new.

Disciplinary techniques are usually introduced after progress has been made in reinforcing positive behavior. For preadolescent children, the most widely used disciplinary technique is *time-out.* Time-out usually begins with removal to a boring place for 5 minutes. (Older children are sent to college and required to take large lecture classes.) When a child refuses to go to time-out, the parent is taught to add time minute by minute, up to a 10-minute maximum. If the child continues to refuse, a privilege is removed. When parents are consistent, children soon learn to go to time-out rather than lose the opportunity to watch TV or use the computer for up to an hour.

Families are encouraged to meet weekly to discuss important issues, such as changes in the family rules, negotiation of rights and responsibilities, and planning special events (Forgatch & Patterson, 1998). Parents of problem children are also taught to monitor their children when they are at school or elsewhere by networking with parents of their children's friends and keeping in touch with teachers as well as leaders of extracurricular activities. Therapists may call parents during the week to check on their progress and encourage their efforts.

As part of the educational component of parent training, parents are taught to make requests in a way that increases the likelihood of compliance. Effective requests are short and sweet; are made in the physical proximity of the child; are phrased as statements, not questions; and ask for only one thing at a time. "Please put your dish in the sink," not "What is your dish doing on the living room rug!"

The techniques that have been described are particularly effective with young children. With teenagers the use of *contingency contracting* (Alexander & Parsons, 1973; Rinn, 1978) is more widely used. Contracting is introduced as a way for everybody in the family to get something by compromising. Parents and teenagers are asked to specify what behavior they'd like each other to change. These requests form the nucleus of the initial contract. In order to help family members arrive at contracts, the therapist models, prompts, and reinforces (a) clear communication of content and feelings and (b) clear presentation of demands, leading to (c) negotiation, with each person receiving something in exchange for some concession.

Alexander and Parsons (1973) recommend starting with easy issues while the family is learning the principles of contingency contracting. Success in dealing with minor issues will increase the family's willingness to deal with more difficult problems. Some parents are reluctant to negotiate with their children to do things "that they *should do anyway,* without being bribed." In fact, these parents have a legitimate point, and they should be helped to understand the difference between rules (which are nonnegotiable) and privileges (which can be negotiated).

Behavioral parent training is also conducted in packaged training programs, designed for preventive education. The content of these programs varies from general principles of operant behavior to specific techniques for dealing with specific problems. Many of these programs include instruction in charting, or graphing, the target behavior. Parents are also taught how to state and enforce rules, and the necessity for being consistent. Training in the use of positive reinforcement includes helping parents increase the frequency and range of reinforcers that they apply. In addition to increasing behavior that their children are already engaging in, parents are taught to develop new behaviors through shaping, modeling, instruction, and prompting.

Behavioral Couples Therapy

Assessment. As with parent training, behavioral couples therapy begins with an elaborate, structured assessment. This process usually includes clinical interviews, ratings of specific target behaviors, and marital assessment questionnaires. The most widely used of the latter is the Locke-Wallace Marital Adjustment Scale (Locke & Wallace, 1959), a twenty-three-item questionnaire covering various aspects of marital satisfaction, including communication, sex, affection, social activities, and values. Other widely used self-report measures include the Marital Satisfaction Inventory (Snyder, 1979), a sort of MMPI for couples, which produces ratings of marital functioning on a variety of dimensions, and the Areas-of-Changes Questionnaire (Weiss, Hops, & Patterson, 1973), which asks couples to indicate partner behaviors they would like to see changed.

Weiss and Patterson developed an instrument to aid couples in collecting observational data at home. The Spouse Observation Checklist (Weiss, Hops, & Patterson, 1973) consists of about 400 spouse behaviors grouped into twelve categories: companionship, affection, consideration, communication, sex, coupling, child care, household maintenance, financial management, work (school) activities, personal habits, and self- and spouse-independence. Partners are to check each behavior that occurs in a given twenty-four-hour period and to rate their daily satisfaction with the relationship on a nine-point scale.

Assessments are designed to reveal strengths and weaknesses of the couple's relationship and the manner in which rewards and punishments are exchanged. Interviews are used to specify and elaborate target behaviors first revealed on the structured assessment devices. Some attempt is also made during interviews to understand the etiology of the problems couples describe as well as to observe problems other than those noted by the spouses themselves. In general, however, behavior therapists deemphasize interviews (Jacobson & Margolin, 1979) in favor of written questionnaires and direct observation of couples' interactions. Jacobson (1981) offers an outline for pretreatment assessment (see Table 10.1).

Unlike with most nonbehavioral approaches, a behavioral assessment (1) is concerned with identifying specific behavioral excesses and deficits that produced the current dissatisfaction and the variables responsible for their occurrence; (2) relies on direct measurement of behavior rather than accepting vague descriptions or focusing on personality traits; (3) has a treatment plan that is directly related to the results of the assessment; and (4) is continuous, taking place throughout treatment to provide therapist and clients with feedback on progress and to detect and modify ineffective treatment strategies.

Therapeutic Techniques. After completing an assessment, the behavioral clinician presents the couple with an analysis of their relationship in social learning terms. In doing so, therapists take pains to accentuate the positive, striving to maintain positive expectancies and a collaborative set (Jacobson, 1981).

One of the things that makes couples therapy difficult is that partners in distressed relationships often see themselves as victims of the other's withholding or demandingness. By presenting an analysis of the relationship in learning terms, the therapist introduces a focus that implies mutual responsibility for problems—and mutual possibility of change. Although both partners may have an investment in viewing themselves as innocent, which is unlikely to yield to preaching about shared responsibility, the broader perspective provided by a behavioral analysis makes it clear that each one has some control over the contingencies that govern the relationship.

Married partners often state their goals negatively: "I wish he wouldn't always argue with me"; or "She nags too much." Most have difficulty describing behavior that they want their

TABLE 10.1 Jacobson's Pretreatment Assessment for Marital Therapy

A. Strengths and skills of the relationship

What are the major strengths of this relationship?

Specifically, what resources do these spouses have to explain their current level of commitment to the relationship?

What is each spouse's current capacity to reinforce the other?

What behaviors on the part of each spouse are highly valued by the other?

What shared activities does the couple currently engage in?

What common interests do they share?

What are the couple's competencies and skills in meeting the essential tasks of a relationship: problem-solving, provision of support and understanding, ability to provide social reinforcement effectively, sexual capabilities, childrearing and parenting skills, ability to manage finances, household responsibilities, interpersonal skills regarding interaction with people outside the relationship?

B. Presenting problems

What are the major complaints, and how do these complaints translate into explicit behavioral terms?

What behaviors occur too frequently or at inappropriate times from the standpoint of each spouse?

Under what conditions do these behaviors occur?

What are the reinforcers that are maintaining these behaviors?

What behaviors occur at less than the desired frequency or fail to occur at appropriate times from the standpoint of each spouse?

Under what conditions would each spouse like to see these behaviors occur?

What are the consequences of these behaviors currently, when they occur?

How did the current problems develop over time?

How are current lines of decision-making authority drawn?

Is there a consensus on who makes important decisions in regard to various areas of the relationship?

What kinds of decisions are made collectively as opposed to unilaterally?

C. Sex and affection

Are the spouses physically attracted to one another?

Is either currently dissatisfied with rate, quality, or diversity of sex life together?

If sex is currently a problem, was there a time when it was mutually satisfying?

What are the sexual behaviors that seem to be associated with current dissatisfaction?

Are either or both partners dissatisfied with the amount or quality of nonsexual physical affection?

Are either or both partners currently engaged in an extramarital sexual relationship?

If so, is the uninvolved partner aware of the affair?

What is the couple's history regarding extramarital affairs?

(continued)

TABLE 10.1   Continued

D. Future prospects

Are the partners seeking therapy to improve their relationship, to separate, or to decide whether
  the relationship is worth working on?
What are each spouse's reasons for continuing the relationship despite current problems?
What steps has each spouse taken in the direction of divorce?

E. Assessment of social environment

What are each person's alternatives to the present relationship?
How attractive are these alternatives to each person?
Is the environment (parents, relatives, friends, work associates, children) supportive of either
  continuance or dissolution of present relationship?
Are any of the children suffering from psychological problems of their own?
What would the probable consequences of relationship dissolution be for the children?

F. Individual functioning of each spouse

Does either spouse exhibit any severe emotional or behavioral problems?
Does either spouse represent a psychiatric history of his/her own? Specify.
Have they been in therapy before, either alone or together? What kind of therapy? Outcome?
What is each spouse's past experience with intimate relationships?
How is the present relationship different?

Adapted from: Jacobson, N. S. 1981. Behavioral marital therapy. In *Handbook of Family Therapy*, A. S. Gurman and D. P. Kniskern, eds.
(pp. 565–566) New York: Brunner/Mazel.

mates to accelerate. To help them do so, some therapists (Azrin, Naster, & Jones, 1973) ask couples to make a list of pleasing things their partners do during the week. Reviewing these lists in the following session provides the opportunity to emphasize the importance of positive feedback.

Stuart (1975) lists five strategies that summarize the behavioral approach to troubled marriages. First, couples are taught to express themselves in clear, behavioral descriptions, rather than in vague, critical complaints. Second, couples are taught new behavior exchange procedures, emphasizing positive control in place of aversive control. Third, couples are helped to improve their communication. Fourth, couples are encouraged to establish clear and effective means of sharing power and making decisions. Fifth, couples are taught strategies for solving future problems, as a means to maintain and extend gains initiated in therapy.

Behavior exchange procedures are taught to help couples increase the frequency of desired behavior. Couples are advised to express their wishes specifically and behaviorally. Thus, "You should be more aware of my needs" might translate into "I want you ask me what's wrong when you see that I'm upset." A typical device is to ask each partner to list three things he or she would like the other to do more often. While explicitly exchanging "strokes" in this way, couples are implicitly learning ways of influencing each other through positive reinforcement. An alternative tactic is to ask each partner to think of things the other might want, do them, and see what happens. Weiss and his associates direct couples to have "love days," where one partner doubles his or her pleasing behavior toward the other (Weiss & Birchler, 1978). Stuart (1976) has couples alternate "caring days," where one partner demonstrates caring in as many ways as possible.

In a carefully designed longitudinal study Gottman and Krokoff (1989) found that disagreement and angry exchanges, which have often been considered destructive to relationships, may not be harmful in the long run. These patterns were correlated with immediate dissatisfaction but were predictive of improved satisfaction after three years. Defensiveness, stubbornness, and withdrawal from conflict, on the other hand, *did* lead to long-term deterioration in marriages. Passive compliance may create a facade of harmony, but it doesn't work in the long run—as many dominating partners with compliant mates discover when their partners, who "used to be so agreeable," suddenly become "so critical."

Conflict engagement may make couples uneasy, but it may be an essential prelude to facing and solving problems. The anger that accompanies direct expression of dissatisfaction may be painful, but it may also be healthy. Gottman and Krokoff conclude (1989): "If the wife must introduce and elaborate disagreements in marriages, our data suggest that, for the sake of long-term improvement in marital satisfaction, she may need to do this by getting her husband to confront areas of disagreement and to openly vent disagreement and anger" (p. 51). In other words, confrontation is effective only if it doesn't make the partner defensive. It isn't just honesty that counts, but honesty expressed in a way the partner can tolerate.

Training in communications skills may be done in a group format (Ely, Guerney, & Stover, 1973; Hickman & Baldwin, 1971; Pierce, 1973) or with individual couples. The training includes instruction, modeling, role-playing, structured exercises, behavior rehearsal, and feedback (Jacobson, 1977; Patterson, Hops, & Weiss, 1973; Stuart, 1976). Couples are taught to be specific, phrase requests in positive terms, respond directly to criticism instead of cross-complaining, talk about the present and future rather than the past, listen without interruption, minimize punitive statements, and eliminate questions that sound like declarations (O'Leary & Turkewitz, 1978).

Once a couple has been taught to communicate in ways that are conducive to problem solving, they are introduced to the principles of *contingency contracting*—agreeing to make changes contingent on the partner making changes. In **quid pro quo** contracts (Knox, 1971; Lederer & Jackson, 1968), one partner agrees to make a change after a prior change by the other. Each partner specifies desired behavior changes, and with the therapist's help they negotiate agreements. At the end of the session a written list is made and both partners sign it. Such a contract might take the following form:

Date _____

This week I agree to:
(1) Come home from work by 6:00 P.M.
(2) Play with the children for half an hour after supper.

_____

Husband's signature

Contingent on the above changes, I agree to:
(1) Go bowling once a week with my husband.
(2) Not serve leftovers for supper on weeknights.

_____

Wife's signature

An alternative form of contracting is the *good faith contract*, in which both partners agree to make changes that aren't contingent on what the other does (Weiss, Hops, & Patterson, 1973). Each partner's independent changes are independently reinforced. In the example above, the husband who comes home each night by 6:00 P.M. and plays with the children after supper might reward himself by buying a new shirt at the end of the week, or be rewarded by his wife with a back rub.

Problem-solving training is used to deal with problems that are too conflictual or complicated for simple exchange agreements. The key to successful problem solving is developing a collaborative set. Negotiations are preceded by a careful and specific definition of problems. Only when partners agree on the definition of a problem can they effectively begin to discuss a solution. Discussions are limited to one problem at a time. Each begins by paraphrasing what the other has said, and they are taught to avoid inferences about motivation—especially inferences of malevolent intent. They're also encouraged to avoid aversive responses. When defining a problem it's most effective to begin with a positive statement; instead of saying, "You never . . . ," partners are taught to say, "I appreciate the way you . . . and, in addition I wish. . . ."

As we move into the twenty-first century the most significant advance in behavioral treatment is the increasing use and sophistication of cognitive-behavioral methods (Epstein, Schlesinger, & Dryden, 1988; Dattilio, 1998). The cognitive mediation model (Beck, 1976) posits that emotions and actions are mediated by specific cognitions. Understanding these cognitions (*beliefs, attributions,* and *expectancies*) makes it possible to identify factors that trigger and maintain the dysfunctional emotional and behavioral patterns that families bring to treatment. In practice this boils down to ferreting out and confronting negative assumptions that keep people stuck.

The Cognitive-Behavioral Approach to Family Therapy

Cognitive family therapy followed the same progression as cognitive couples therapy—first as a supplemental component to the behavioral approach and then as a more comprehensive system of intervention. Munson (1993) noted at least eighteen different types of cognitive therapy used by various practitioners, but the focus of this discussion will be limited to those approaches proposed by the rational-emotive (Ellis, 1978, 1982; DiGiuseppe & Zeeve, 1985) and cognitive-behavioral theories (Beck, 1988; Dattilio, 1993, 1994; Teichman, 1984, 1992).

The rational-emotive approach, as proposed by Albert Ellis (1978), concentrates on individual interpretations of events that occur in the family. The rational-emotive therapist helps family members see how illogical beliefs serve as the foundation for their emotional distress. The use of the "*A-B-C* theory" is introduced, according to which family members blame their problems on certain activating events in the family (*A*) and are taught to look for irrational beliefs (*B*), which are then challenged (*C*). The goal is to modify beliefs and expectations by putting them on a more rational basis (Ellis, 1978). The therapist's role is to teach the family that emotional problems are caused by unrealistic beliefs and that by revising these self-defeating ideas, they may improve the overall quality of family life.

With rational-emotive therapy it's a little hard to separate the approach from its creator. Ellis didn't merely challenge people's assumptions, he punctured them with fierce and gleeful sarcasm. It isn't necessary to imitate Ellis's acerbic style to take advantage of his insights. It seems fair to say, however, that rational-emotive therapists generally content themselves with lecturing people about generic assumptions rather than probing for more personal and closely held beliefs.

The cognitive-behavioral approach, which balances the emphasis on cognition and behavior, takes a more expansive and inclusive approach by focusing in greater depth on patterns of family interaction (Epstein, Schlesinger, & Dryden, 1988; Leslie, 1988). Family relationships, cognitions, emotions, and behavior are viewed as exerting mutual influence on one another, so that a cognitive inference can evoke emotion and behavior, and emotion and behavior can influence cognition.

The cognitive-behavioral approach to families is also compatible with systems theory and includes the premise that members of a family simultaneously influence and are influenced by each other. Consequently, the behavior of one family member triggers behavior, cognitions, and emotions in other members, which, in turn, elicit reactive cognitions, behavior, and emotions in the original member. As this process plays out, the volatility of family dynamics escalates, rendering the family vulnerable to negative spirals of conflict. Epstein and Schlesinger (1991, 1996) cite four means by which family members' cognitions, behavior, and emotions may interact and build to a volatile climax:

1. The individual's own cognitions, behaviors, and emotions regarding family interaction (e.g., the person who notices himself or herself withdrawing from the rest of the family)
2. The actions of individual family members toward him or her
3. The combined (and not always consistent) reactions several family members have toward him or her
4. The characteristics of the relationships among other family members (e.g., noticing that two other family members usually are supportive of each other's opinions)

As the number of family members involved increases, so does the complexity of the dynamics, adding momentum to the escalation process.

Cognitive therapy, as set forth by Aaron Beck (1976), places a heavy emphasis on *schemas* or "core beliefs" about the world and how it functions (Beck, Rush, Shaw, & Emery, 1979;

DeRubeis & Beck, 1988). Therapeutic intervention is aimed at distorted assumptions whereby family members interpret and evaluate one another unrealistically.

Just as individuals maintain core beliefs about themselves, their world, and their future, they also maintain beliefs about their families. Frank Dattilio (1993) suggests that individuals maintain two separate sets of schemata about families: schemata related to the parents' family of origin and schemata related to families in general. Both types of schemata have a major impact on how individuals think, feel, and behave within the family setting. Schwebel and Fine (1992) elaborated on the concept of *family schemata* by describing it as follows:

All of the cognitions that individuals hold about their own family life and about family life in general. Included in this set of cognitions are an individual's schema about family life, attributions about why events occur in the family, and beliefs about why events occur in the family, and beliefs about what should exist within the family unit (Baucom & Epstein, 1990). The family schema also contains ideas about how spousal relationships should work, what different types of problems should be expected in marriage and how they should be handled, what is involved in building and maintaining a healthy family, what responsibilities each family member should have, what consequences should be associated with failure to meet responsibilities or to fulfill roles, and what costs and benefits each individual should expect to have as a consequence of being in a marriage. (p. 50)

Beliefs, conscious and unconscious, passed down from the family of origin contribute to jointly held beliefs that lead to the development of the current family schema. This set of beliefs is conveyed and applied in the rearing of children and, when mixed with their own individual thoughts and perceptions of their environment and life experiences, contributes to the further development of the family schema.

In some sessions, a cognitive-behavioral therapist will focus primarily on cognitions, while in other sessions the focus will shift to behavior, including all the usual elements in behavior therapy: training in reinforcement reciprocity, communication training, problem-solving training, behavior change agreements, and training in parenting skills. Cognitive interventions are designed to increase family members' skills at monitoring and testing the validity and appropriateness of their own cognitions. This is an important point: Cognitive therapy should not be reduced to generic interpretations ("It's a mistake to be dependent on others," "Who says it's disastrous when things go wrong?"), nor should the therapist do all the work. Rather, for cognitive intervention to be effective, specific cognitive distortions must be uncovered and clients must learn to test their own assumptions.

An early goal of the cognitive approach is to help family members develop skills in identifying automatic thoughts that flash through their minds. The importance of identifying such automatic thoughts ("She's crying—she's must be mad at me") is that they often reflect underlying schemas ("Women always hold men responsible for their unhappiness") that may be distorted and counterproductive.

To improve their skill in identifying automatic thoughts, clients are encouraged to keep a diary and jot down situations that provoke automatic thoughts and the resulting emotional responses. The therapist's role then is to ask a series of questions about these assumptions, rather than to challenge them directly. Here's an example:

—Case Study——

When thirteen-year-old Frankie's parents caught her walking home from school with a boy she was forbidden to see, they responded by saying "We just can't

trust you!" and grounded her for a week. Frankie's automatic thought was "They'll never trust me again," which made her feel, by turns, worried and then angry. This conclusion was followed by the thought, "Now I'll never have any freedom."

After helping Frankie identify these thoughts, the therapist asked her to test these assumptions and then to consider alternative explanations. "What evidence exists to substantiate this thought?" "Might there be alternative explanations?" "How would you test these assumptions?"

Frankie decided that it was too soon to be sure how her parents would treat her in the future, and she decided to test the proposition that if she stopped lying to them they would eventually start to trust her again and that, in this way, she could slowly win back her freedom.

The late 1980s and early 1990s saw the cognitive-behavioral approach applied more widely in family therapy. Edited books by Epstein, Schlessinger, and Dryden (1988) and a short text produced by Huber and Baruth (1989) were among the first works to address the cognitive approach to family therapy. This was elaborated in subsequent articles by Schwebel and Fine (1992), Dattilio (1993, 1994, 1997), and Teichman (1992). Most recently, Dattilio (1998) has produced a major casebook that discusses the integration of cognitive-behavioral strategies with various modalities of couples and family therapy. This important work discusses the compatibility of cognitive-behavior therapy with a wide array of modalities.

Treatment of Sexual Dysfunction

Wolpe's (1958) introduction of *systematic desensitization* led to major advances in the treatment of sexual dysfunction. According to Wolpe most sexual problems are the result of conditioned anxiety. His therapy consists of instructing couples to engage in a series of progressively intimate encounters, while avoiding thoughts about erection or orgasm. Another approach that frequently proved effective was *assertiveness training* (Lazarus, 1965; Wolpe, 1958). In assertive training, socially and sexually inhibited persons are encouraged to accept and express their needs and feelings.

While these behavioral remedies were often helpful, the real breakthrough came with the publication of Masters and Johnson's (1970) approach. This was followed by others who applied and extended Masters and Johnson's basic procedure (Lobitz & LoPiccolo, 1972; Kaplan, 1974, 1979).

Although the details vary, there is a general approach followed by most sex therapists. As with other behavioral methods, the first step is a thorough assessment, including a complete medical examination and extensive interviews to determine the nature of the dysfunction and establish goals for treatment. In the absence of organic problems, cases involving lack of information, poor technique, and poor communication are most amenable to sexual therapy.

Therapists following Masters and Johnson tended to lump sexual problems into one category—anxiety that interferes with couples' ability to relax into arousal and orgasm. Helen Singer Kaplan (1979) pointed out that there are three stages of the sexual response and, hence, three types of problems: disorders of desire, arousal disorders, and orgasm disorders. *Disorders of desire* range from "low sex drive" to sexual aversion. Treatment focuses on (a) deconditioning anxiety, and (b) helping clients resist negative thoughts. *Arousal disorders* include decreased emotional arousal and difficulty achieving and maintaining an erection or dilating and lubricating. These problems are often helped with a combination of relaxation and teaching couples to focus on the physical sensations of touching and caressing, rather than worrying about what comes next. *Orgasm disorders* include the timing of orgasm (e.g., premature or delayed), the quality of the orgasm, or the requirements for orgasm (e.g.,

some people only have orgasm during masturbation). Premature ejaculation usually responds well to sex therapy; lack of orgasm in women may respond to sex therapy, usually involving teaching the woman to practice on her own and learning to fantasize.

Following the assessment, clients are presented with an explanation of the role of conditioned anxiety in problems with sex, and they are told how anxiety developed and is being maintained in their sexual relationship. Insight and attitude change are thus a fundamental part of this "behavioral" therapy.

Although sex therapy must be tailored to specific problems, most treatments are initiated with *sensate focus*, in which couples are taught how to relax and enjoy touching and being touched. They're told to go home and find a time when they're both reasonably relaxed and free from distraction, and then get in bed together naked. Then they take turns gently caressing each other. The person being touched is told to simply relax and concentrate on the feeling of being touched. Later the one being touched will let the partner know which touch is most pleasing and which is less so. At first couples are told not to touch each other in the sensitive breast or genital areas, in order to avoid undue anxiety.

After they learn to relax and exchange gentle, pleasant caressing, couples are encouraged to gradually become more intimate—but to slow down if either should feel anxious. Thus sensate focus is a form of *in vivo desensitization.* Couples who are highly anxious and fearful of "having sex" (which some people reduce to a hectic few minutes of poking and panting) learn to overcome their fears through a gradual and progressively intimate experience of mutual caressing. As anxiety decreases and desire mounts, they're encouraged to engage in progressively more intimate exchanges. In the process, couples are also taught to communicate what they like and don't like. So, for example, instead of enduring something unpleasant until she finally gets so upset that she snaps at her partner or avoids sex altogether, a woman might be taught how to gently show him, "No, not like that, like this."

Once sensate focus exercises have gone smoothly, the therapist introduces techniques to deal with specific problems. Among women the most common sexual dysfunctions are difficulties with orgasm (Kaplan, 1979). Frequently these problems are rooted in lack of information. The woman and her partner may be expecting her to have orgasms reliably during intercourse without additional clitoral stimulation. In men, the most common problem is premature ejaculation, for which part of the treatment is the *squeeze technique* (Semans, 1956), in which the woman stimulates the man's penis until he feels the urge to ejaculate. At that point, she squeezes the frenulum (at the base of the head) firmly between her thumb and first two fingers until the urge to ejaculate subsides. Stimulation begins again until another squeeze is necessary.

Techniques to deal with erectile failure are designed to reduce performance anxiety and increase sexual arousal. These include desensitization of the man's anxiety; discussions in which the partners describe their expectations; increasing the variety and duration of foreplay; the *teasing technique* (Masters & Johnson, 1970), in which the woman alternately starts and stops stimulating the man; and beginning intercourse with the woman guiding the man's flaccid penis into her vagina.

Successful sex therapy usually ends with the couple's sex life much improved, but not as fantastic as frustrated expectations had led them to imagine—expectations that were part of the problem in the first place. As in any form of directive therapy, it's important for sex therapists to gradually fade out their involvement and control. Therapeutic gains are consolidated and extended by reviewing the changes that have occurred; by anticipating future trouble spots; and by planning in advance to deal with problems according to principles learned in treatment.

Evaluating Therapy Theory and Results

Behavioral family therapists started by applying learning theory techniques devised for treating individuals; but in the thirty years since its inception, the technology of behavioral family therapy has become increasingly sophisticated and its practitioners increasingly aware that family life is more complicated than the sum of observable behavior in its individual members. Behavior therapists have developed a host of experimentally tested techniques that they administer to a variety of family problems, but most of the emphasis remains on parent training, behavioral couples therapy, and treatment of sexual dysfunctions.

The distinctive methods of behavioral family therapy are derived from classical and operant conditioning and, increasingly, cognitive theory. Target behavior is precisely specified in operational terms; operant conditioning, classical conditioning, social learning theory, and cognitive strategies are then used to produce change. As behavior therapists have gained experience with family problems, they have begun to address such traditionally nonbehavioral concerns as the therapeutic alliance, the need for empathy, the problem of resistance, communication, and problem-solving skills. However, even when dealing with such mainstream issues, behaviorists are distinguished by their methodical approach. More than by any technique, behavioral therapy is characterized by careful assessment and evaluation. Analysis of behavioral sequences prior to treatment, assessment of therapy in progress, and evaluation of final results are the hallmarks of behavioral therapy.

Behavior therapy was born and bred in a tradition of research, and so it's not surprising that behavioral family therapy is the most carefully studied form of family treatment. Two trends emerge from this substantial body of evidence. The first is that both behavioral parent training and behavioral couples therapy have repeatedly been demonstrated to be effective interventions. Among the most well-supported versions of these approaches are Gerald Patterson's parent training therapy (e.g., Patterson, Dishion, & Chamberlain, 1993; Patterson & Forgatch, 1995) and Neil Jacobson's behavioral couples therapy (e.g., Crits-Christoph, Frank, Chambless, Brody, & Karp, 1995).

The second trend in research on behavioral family therapy is that the leading exponents of these approaches have begun to see the need to extend their approaches beyond the basic contingency contracting and operant learning procedures of traditional behavior therapy. As already noted, one form this has taken has been the incorporation of cognitive theories and techniques into more traditional stimulus-response behaviorism (e.g., Baucom & Epstein, 1990; Dattilio & Padesky, 1990).

Another new direction being undertaken by practitioners of behavioral family therapy is the incorporation of principles from more systemically oriented family therapies. Gerald Patterson, for example, has begun to use elements of strategic family therapy in his approach to parent training (Forgatch & Patterson, 1998). When parents appear to be unsuccessful using time-outs and the withholding of privileges, Patterson and his colleagues introduce such strategic devices as paradoxical assignments and pretend techniques to overcome parental resistance to what they still consider the core of their approach—changing the contingencies of reinforcement for children's behavior.

The late Neil Jacobson in partnership with Andrew Christensen has gone even further in modifying traditional behavioral couples therapy along the lines of more traditional family therapy approaches. They retained the behavioral change techniques but added novel strategies to bring about increased emotional acceptance in clients. In other words, before they start working with couples to produce changes in the partners' behavior, they endeavor to help them learn to be more accepting of each other. So different, in fact, is the resulting approach that we will consider it more extensively in our chapter on integrative approaches (Chapter 14).

Gordon and Davidson (1981) summarized studies of behavioral parent training and found that the majority of measures yielded positive results in the majority of cases. They reported hundreds of documented successes with a wide variety of problem children. Outcome criteria are usually based on parents' and observers' frequency counts of prosocial and deviant behavior. Researchers have found that more advantaged families show distinctly better results from behavior parent training (O'Dell, 1974). This isn't surprising considering the heavy emphasis on education in this approach.

A typical finding is that targeted behavior improves; only marginal changes, however, can be seen for nontargeted problem behavior. Apparently the specific focus on presenting problems lends leverage to resolving focal complaints, but only minimally generalizes to overall family functioning. Moreover, improvements don't generalize from home to other settings, such as school (Gurman & Kniskern, 1978). Finally, therapeutic gains tend to decrease sharply between termination and follow-up.

The behavioral literature also contains a large number of empirical studies of couples therapy. These studies are usually done on brief treatment (approximately nine sessions) and the most common criteria of success are observers' ratings and couples' self-reports. Gurman and Kniskern (1978) found that six of seven naturalistic comparative studies favored behavioral couples therapy. These findings support the efficacy of this approach; however, as the authors noted, behavioral therapy is still relatively untested on couples with severe marital problems. When they updated their survey, Gurman and Kniskern (1981) found similar results and concluded that behavioral marriage therapy appears to be about as effective for mild to moderate marital problems as are nonbehavioral approaches.

Several studies have shown that the most effective ingredient in any form of couples therapy is increasing communication skills (Jacobson, 1978; Jacobson & Margolin, 1979). Jacobson's studies strongly support his approach, based on observational measures of communication and self-reported marital satisfaction. Liberman and his colleagues (1976) found that on objective measures of marital communication, behavioral couples therapy in a group setting was more effective than insight-oriented couples groups. However, the two approaches didn't differ in effecting increased marital satisfaction. O'Leary and Turkewitz (1978) have shown that behavior exchange procedures are effective, especially with young couples; older couples tend to respond more favorably to communications training.

Despite the growth of public and professional interest in sex therapy, there are few well-controlled studies of its effectiveness. In a careful review, Hogan (1978) found that most of the literature consists of clinical case studies. These reports are little more than box scores of successes and failures. Absent are pre- and post-measures, specification of techniques, points of reference other than the therapists, and follow-up data. Moreover, since most of these reports come from the same handful of therapists, it's impossible to discern what's being evaluated—the techniques of sex therapy or the skill of these particular therapists. This state of the research hadn't changed much by 1990, according to later summary reports (Crowe, 1988; Falloon & Lillie, 1988).

The greatest success rates with sexual therapy have been found in treating vaginismus, orgasmic dysfunction, and premature ejaculation. Vaginismus, the spastic contraction of vagina muscles, has been successfully treated in 90 to 95 percent of cases (Fuchs et al., 1973). Eighty-five to 95 percent of the women who had never previously achieved orgasm did so after treatment. Success rates are lower, 30 to 50 percent, when limited to those who had previously reached orgasm during coitus (Heiman, LoPiccolo, & LoPiccolo, 1981). The reported success rates for treatment of premature ejaculation using the squeeze technique (Masters & Johnson, 1970) are uniformly high, 90 to 95 percent.

For men who had never had erectile functioning, the success rates are between 40 and 60 percent—though, as Michael Crowe (1988) has noted, this problem turns out to be medically related more often than we used to think. For those who once had adequate erectile functioning and then developed difficulty, success rates average 60 to 80 percent (Heiman, LoPiccolo, & LoPiccolo, 1981). Retarded ejaculation or failure to ejaculate is relatively uncommon; consequently there are fewer reported treatment cases. Among this small sample, reported success rates range from 50 to 82 percent (Heiman, LoPiccolo, & LoPiccolo, 1981). Treatment of individuals with very low levels of interest in sex is relatively new (Kaplan, 1979), but apparently such cases respond well to treatment (LoPiccolo & LoPiccolo, 1978).

Sex therapy appears to be an effective approach to some very vexing problems. Most observers (Gurman & Kniskern, 1981) agree that it should be considered the treatment of choice when there is an explicit complaint about a couple's sex life.

Three areas of research in family intervention seem ready to move to a more advanced stage of development. These areas are conduct disorders in children (Patterson, 1986; Morris, Alexander, & Waldron, 1988), marital conflict (Follette & Jacobson, 1988), and schizophrenic adults (Falloon, 1985).

—Summary—

Although behavior therapists have been applying their techniques to family problems for over twenty years, they have done so for the most part within a linear frame of reference. Family symptoms are treated as learned responses, involuntarily acquired and reinforced. Treatment is generally time-limited and symptom-focused. The behavioral approach to families is based on social learning theory, according to which behavior is learned and maintained by its consequences, and can be modified by altering those consequences. An essential adjunct to social learning theory is Thibaut and Kelley's theory of social exchange, according to which people strive to maximize interpersonal "rewards" while minimizing "costs."

The general goals of behavioral family therapy are to increase the rate of rewarding exchanges, decrease aversive exchanges, and teach communication and problem-solving skills. Specific techniques are applied to target behaviors; in the process, families are also taught general principles of behavior management.

The behaviorists' focus on modifying the consequences of problem behavior accounts for the strengths and weaknesses of this approach. By concentrating on presenting problems, behaviorists have been able to develop an impressive array of effective techniques. Even such relatively intractable problems as delinquent behavior in children and severe sexual dysfunctions have yielded to behavioral technology. On the other hand, behavior is only part of the person, and the problem person is only part of the family. You can't simply teach people to change if unresolved conflict is keeping them stuck.

Unhappiness may center around a behavioral complaint, but resolution of the behavior may not resolve the unhappiness. Treatment may succeed with the symptom but fail the family. Attitudes and feelings may change along with changes in behavior, but not necessarily. And teaching communication skills may not be sufficient to resolve real conflict. Mere behavior change may not be enough for family members whose ultimate goal is to feel better. "Yes, he's doing his chores now," a parent may agree. "But I don't think he *feels* like helping out. He still isn't really part of our family." Behavior isn't all that family members in distress are concerned about, and to be responsive to all their needs therapists need to deal with cognitive and affective issues as well.

Behaviorists rarely treat whole families. Instead they see only those subsystems they consider central to the targeted behavior. Unfortunately, failure to include—or even consider—the entire family in treatment may be disastrous. A therapeutic program to reduce a son's aggressiveness toward his mother can hardly succeed if the father wants an aggressive son, or if the father's anger toward his wife isn't addressed. Moreover, if the whole family isn't involved in change, new behavior may not be reinforced and maintained.

Despite these shortcomings, behavioral family therapy offers impressive techniques for treating the problems of children and within troubled marriages. Furthermore, its weaknesses can be corrected by broadening the focus of conceptualization and the scope of treatment to include families as systems. Perhaps the greatest strength of behavior therapy is its insistence on observing what happens and then measuring change. Behaviorists have developed a wealth of reliable assessment methods and applied them to evaluation, treatment planning, and monitoring progress and outcome. A second important advance has been the gradual movement from eliminating or reinforcing discrete "marker" behaviors to the teaching of general problem-solving, cognitive, and communicational skills. A third major advance in current behavioral family therapy is modular treatment interventions organized to meet the specific and changing needs of the individual and the family. Finally, the shift to address distorted cognitions that may underlie problematic family interactions has added a powerful new dimension to the behavioral approach.

—Recommended Readings

Barton, C., and Alexander, J. F. 1981. Functional family therapy. In *Handbook of family therapy,* A. S. Gurman and D. P. Kniskern, eds. New York: Brunner/Mazel.

Bornstein, P., and Bornstein, M. 1986. *Marital therapy: A behavioral-communications approach.* New York: Pergamon.

Dattilio, F. M. 1998. *Case studies in couple and family therapy: Systemic and cognitive perspectives.* New York: Guilford Press.

Dattilio, F. M., and Reinecke, M. 1996. *Casebook of cognitive-behavior therapy with children and adolescents.* New York: Guilford Press.

Epstein, N., Schlesinger, S. E., and Dryden, W. 1988. *Cognitive-behavioral therapy with families.* New York: Brunner/Mazel.

Falloon, I. R. H. 1988. *Handbook of behavioral family therapy.* New York: Guilford Press.

Falloon, I. R. H. 1991. Behavioral family therapy. In *Handbook of family therapy,* Vol. II, A. S. Gurman and D. P. Kniskern, eds. New York: Brunner/Mazel.

Gordon, S. B., and Davidson, N. 1981. Behavioral parent training. In *Handbook of family therapy,*

A. S. Gurman and D. P. Kniskern, eds. New York: Brunner/Mazel.

Jacobson, N. S., and Margolin, G. 1979. *Marital therapy: Strategies based on social learning and behavior exchange principles.* New York: Brunner/Mazel.

Kaplan, H. S. 1979. *The new sex therapy: Active treatment of sexual dysfunctions.* New York: Brunner/Mazel.

Masters, W. H., and Johnson, V. E. 1970. *Human sexual inadequacy.* Boston: Little, Brown.

Patterson, G. R. 1971. *Families: Application of social learning theory to family life.* Champaign, IL: Research Press.

Sanders, M. R., and Dadds, M. R. 1993. *Behavioral family intervention.* Needham Heights, MA: Allyn & Bacon.

Stuart, R. B. 1980. *Helping couples change: A social learning approach to marital therapy.* New York: Guilford Press.

Weiss, R. L. 1978. The conceptualization of marriage from a behavioral perspective. In *Marriage and marital therapy,* T. J. Paolino and B. S. McCrady, eds. New York: Brunner/Mazel.

—References

Ables, B. S., and Brandsma, S. J. 1977. *Therapy for couples.* San Francisco: Jossey-Bass.

Alexander, J. F., and Barton, C. 1976. Behavioral systems therapy with families. In *Treating relationships,* D. H. Olson, ed. Lake Mills, IA: Graphic Publishing.

Alexander, J. F., and Parsons, B. V. 1973. Short-term behavioral intervention with delinquent families: Impact on family process and recidivism. *Journal of Abnormal Psychology.* 51:219–225.

Alexander, J., and Parsons, B. V. 1982. *Functional family therapy.* Pacific Grove, CA: Brooks/Cole.

Alexander, P. 1988. The therapeutic implications of family cognitions and constructs. *Journal of Cognitive Psychotherapy.* 2:219–236.

Anderson, C. M., and Stewart, S. 1983. *Mastering resistance.* New York: Guilford Press.

Arrington, A., Sullaway, M., and Christensen, A. 1988. Behavioral family assessment. In *Handbook of behavioral family therapy,* I. R. H. Falloon, ed. New York: Guilford Press.

Azrin, N. H., Naster, J. B., and Jones, R. 1973. Reciprocity counseling: A rapid learning-based procedure for marital counseling. *Behavior Research and Therapy.* 11:365–383.

Baer, D. M., and Sherman, J. A. 1969. Reinforcement control of generalized imitation in young children. *Journal of Experimental Child Psychology.* 1:37–49.

Bancroft, J. 1975. The behavioral approach to marital problems. *British Journal of Medical Psychology.* 48:147–152.

Bandura, A. 1969. *Principles of behavior modification.* New York: Holt, Rinehart & Winston.

Bandura, A., and Walters, R. 1963. *Social learning and personality development.* New York: Holt, Rinehart & Winston.

Barton, C., and Alexander, J. F. 1975. Therapist skills in systems-behavioral family intervention: How the hell do you get them to do it? Paper presented at the annual meeting of the Orthopsychiatric Association, Atlanta, Georgia.

Barton, C., and Alexander, J. F. 1981. Functional family therapy. In *Handbook of family therapy,* A. S. Gurman and D. P. Kniskern, eds. New York: Brunner/Mazel.

Baucom, D. H. 1981. Cognitive-behavioral strategies in the treatment of marital discord. Paper presented at the annual meeting of the Association of the Advancement of Behavior Therapy, Toronto, Canada.

Baucom, D. H., and Epstein, N. 1990. *Cognitive-behavioral marital therapy.* New York: Brunner/Mazel.

Baucom, D. H., and Lester, G. W. 1986. The usefulness of cognitive restructuring as an adjunct to behavioral marital therapy. *Behavior Therapy.* 17:385–403.

Beck, A. T. 1976. *Cognitive therapy and the emotional disorders.* New York: International Universities Press.

Beck, A. T. 1988. *Love is never enough.* New York: Harper & Row.

Beck, A. T., Rush, J. A., Shaw, B. F., and Emery, G. 1979. *Cognitive therapy of depression.* New York: Guilford Press.

Birchler, G. R. 1988. Handling resistance to change. In *Handbook of behavioral family therapy,* I. R. H. Falloon, ed. New York: Guilford Press.

Birchler, G. R., and Spinks, S. H. 1980. Behavioral-systems marital therapy: Integration and clinical application. *American Journal of Family Therapy.* 8:6–29.

Boardman, W. K. 1962. Rusty: A brief behavior disorder. *Journal of Consulting Psychology.* 26:293–297.

Christophersen, E. R., Arnold, C. M., Hill, D. W., and Quilitch, H. R. 1972. The home point system: Token reinforcement procedures for application by parents of children with behavioral problems. *Journal of Applied Behavioral Analysis.* 5:485–497.

Crits-Christoph, P., Frank, E., Chambless, D. L., Brody, F., and Karp, J. F. 1995. Training in empirically validated treatments: What are clinical psychology students learning? *Professional Psychology: Research and Practice.* 26:514–522.

Crowe, M. 1988. Indications for family, marital, and sexual therapy. In *Handbook of behavioral family therapy,* I. R. H. Falloon, ed. New York: Guilford Press.

Dattilio, F. M. 1989. A guide to cognitive marital therapy. In *Innovations in clinical practice: A source book,* Vol. 8, P. A. Keller and S. R. Heyman, eds. Sarasota, FL: Professional Resource Exchange.

Dattilio, F. M. 1990. Cognitive marital therapy: A case study. *Journal of Family Psychotherapy.* 1:15–31.

Dattilio, F. M. 1993. Cognitive techniques with couples and families. *The Family Journal.* 1:51–65.

Dattilio, F. M. 1994. Families in crisis. In *Cognitive-behavioral strategies in crisis interventions,* F. M. Dattilio and A. Freeman, eds. New York: Guilford Press.

Dattilio, F. M. 1997. Family therapy. In *Casebook of cognitive therapy,* R. Leahy, ed. Northvale, NJ: Jason Aronson.

Dattilio, F. M. 1998. *Case studies in couple and family therapy: systemic and cognitive perspectives.* New York: Guilford Press.

Dattilio, F. M., and Padesky, C. A. 1990. *Cognitive therapy with couples.* Sarasota, FL: Professional Resource Exchange.

DeRubeis, R. J., and Beck, A. T. 1988. Cognitive therapy. In *Handbook of cognitive-behavioral therapies,* K. S. Dobson, ed. New York: Guilford Press.

Dicks, H. 1953. Experiences with marital tensions seen in the psychological clinic. In Clinical Studies in Marriage and the Family: A symposium on methods. *British Journal of Medical Psychology.* 26:181–196.

DiGiuseppe, R. 1988. A cognitive-behavioral approach to the treatment of conduct disorder in children and adolescents. In *Cognitive-behavioral therapy with families*, N. Epstein, S. E. Schlesinger, and W. Dryden, eds. New York: Brunner/Mazel.

DiGiuseppe, R., and Zeeve, C. 1985. Marriage: Rational-emotive couples counseling. In *Clinical applications of rational-emotive therapy*, A. Ellis and M. Bernard, eds. New York: Springer.

Doherty, W. J. 1981. Cognitive processes in intimate conflict: 1. Extending attribution theory. *American Journal of Family Therapy*. 9:5–13.

Ellis, A. 1962. *Reason and emotion in psychotherapy*. New York: Lyle Stuart.

Ellis, A. 1977. The nature of disturbed marital interactions. In *Handbook of rational-emotive therapy*, A. Ellis and R. Greiger, eds. New York: Springer.

Ellis, A. 1978. Family therapy: A phenomenological and active-directive approach. *Journal of Marriage and Family Counseling*. 4:43–50.

Ellis, A. 1982. Rational-emotive family therapy. In *Family counseling and therapy*, A. M. Horne and M. M. Ohlsen, eds. Itasca, IL: Peacock.

Ellis, A., Sichel, J. L., Yeager, R. J., DiMattia, D. J., and DiGiuseppe, R. 1989. *Rational emotive couples therapy*. Needham Heights, MA: Allyn & Bacon.

Ely, A. L., Guerney, B. G., and Stover, L. 1973. Efficacy of the training phase of conjugal therapy. *Psychotherapy: Theory, Research and Practice*. 10:201–207.

Epstein, N. 1982. Cognitive therapy with couples. *American Journal of Family Therapy*. 10:5–16.

Epstein, N. 1992. Marital Therapy. In *Comprehensive casebook of cognitive therapy*, A. Freeman and F. M. Dattilio, eds. New York: Plenum.

Epstein, N., and Schlesinger, S. E. 1991. Marital and family problems. In *Adult clinical problems: A cognitive-behavioral approach*, W. Dryden and R. Rentoul, eds. London: Routledge.

Epstein, N., and Schlesinger, S. E. 1996. Cognitive-behavioral treatment of family problems. In *Casebook of cognitive-behavior therapy with children and adolescents*, M. Reinecke, F. M. Dattilio, and A. Freeman, eds. New York: Guilford Press.

Epstein, N., Schlesinger, S. E., and Dryden, W., eds. 1988. *Cognitive-behavioral therapy with families*. New York: Brunner/Mazel.

Falloon, I. R. H. 1985. *Family management of schizophrenia: A study of the clinical, social, family and economic benefits*. Baltimore: Johns Hopkins University Press.

Falloon, I. R. H., ed. 1988. *Handbook of behavioral family therapy*. New York: Guilford Press.

Falloon, I. R. H. 1991. Behavioral family therapy. In *Handbook of family therapy*, Vol. II, A. S. Gurman and D. P. Kniskern, eds. New York: Brunner/Mazel.

Falloon, I. R. H., and Liberman, R. P. 1983. Behavioral therapy for families with child management problems. In *Helping families with special problems*, M. R. Textor, ed. New York: Jason Aronson.

Falloon, I. R. H., and Lillie, F. J. 1988. Behavioral family therapy: An overview. In *Handbook of behavioral family therapy*, I. R. H. Falloon, ed. New York: Guilford Press.

Ferster, C. B. 1963. Essentials of a science of behavior. In *An introduction to the science of human behavior*, J. I. Nurnberger, C. B. Ferster, and J. P. Brady, eds. New York: Appleton-Century-Crofts.

Fincham, F. D., Bradbury, T. N., and Beach, S. R. H. 1990. To arrive where we began: A reappraisal of cognition in marriage and in marital therapy. *Journal of Family Psychology*. 4:167–184.

Follette, W. C., and Jacobson, N. S. 1988. Behavioral marital therapy in the treatment of depressive disorders. In *Handbook of behavioral family therapy*, I. R. H. Falloon, ed. New York: Guilford Press.

Forehand, R., and McDonough, T. S. 1975. Response-contingent time out: An examination of outcome data. *European Journal of Behavioral Analysis and Modification*. 1:109–115.

Forehand, R., Roberts, M. W., Doleys, D. M., Hobbs, S. A., and Resnick, P. A. 1976. An examination of disciplinary procedures with children. *Journal of Experimental Child Psychology*. 21:109–120.

Forgatch, M. S., and Patterson, G. R. 1998. Behavioral family therapy. In *Case studies in couple and family therapy*, F. M. Datillio, ed. New York: Guilford Press.

Friedman, P. H. 1972. Personalistic family and marital therapy. In *Clinical behavior therapy*, A. A. Lazarus, ed. New York: Brunner/Mazel.

Fuchs, K., Hoch, Z., Paldi, E., Abramovici, H., Brandes, J. M., Timor-Tritsch, I., and Kleinhaus, M. 1973. Hypnodesensitization therapy of vaginismus: Part 1. "In vitro" method. Part 11. "In vivo" method. *International Journal of Clinical and Experimental Hypnosis*. 21:144–156.

Goldenberg, I., and Goldenberg, H. 1991. *Family therapy: An overview*. Pacific Grove, CA: Brooks/Cole.

Goldiamond, I. 1965. Self-control procedures in personal behavior problems. *Psychological Reports.* 17:851–868.

Goldstein, M. K. 1971. Behavior rate change in marriages: Training wives to modify husbands' behavior. *Dissertation Abstracts International.* 32 (18):559.

Goldstein, M. K., and Francis, B. 1969. Behavior modification of husbands by wives. Paper presented at the National Council on Family Relations, Washington, DC.

Gordon, S. B., and Davidson, N. 1981. Behavioral parent training. In *Handbook of family therapy,* A. S. Gurman and D. P. Kniskern, eds. New York: Brunner/Mazel.

Gottman, J., and Krokoff, L. 1989. Marital interaction and satisfaction: A longitudinal view. *Journal of Consulting and Clinical Psychology.* 57:47–52.

Gottman, J., Markman, H., and Notarius, C. 1977. The topography of marital conflict: A sequential analysis of verbal and nonverbal behavior. *Journal of Marriage and the Family.* 39:461–477.

Graziano, A. M. 1977. Parents as behavior therapists. In *Progress in behavior modification,* M. Hersen, R. M. Eisler, and P. M. Miller, eds. New York: Academic Press.

Guerin, P. J., Fay, L., Burden, S. L., and Kautto, J. B. 1987. *The evaluation and treatment of marital conflict: A four-stage approach.* New York: Basic Books.

Gurman, A. S., and Kniskern, D. P. 1978. Research on marital and family therapy: Progress, perspective and prospect. In *Handbook of psychotherapy and behavior change: An empirical analysis,* S. L. Garfield and A. E. Bergin, eds. New York: Wiley.

Gurman, A. S., and Kniskern, D. P. 1981. Family therapy outcome research: Knowns and unknowns. In *Handbook of family therapy,* A. S. Gurman and D. P. Kniskern, eds. New York: Brunner/Mazel.

Gurman, A. S., and Knudson, R. M. 1978. Behavioral marriage therapy: A psychodynamic-systems analysis and critique. *Family Process.* 17:121–138.

Hawkins, R. P., Peterson, R. F., Schweid, E., and Bijou, S. W. 1966. Behavior therapy in the home: Amelioration of problem parent-child relations with a parent in the therapeutic role. *Journal of Experimental Child Psychology.* 4:99–107.

Heiman, J. R., LoPiccolo, L., and LoPiccolo, J. 1981. The treatment of sexual dysfunction. In *Handbook of family therapy,* A. S. Gurman and D. P. Kniskern, eds. New York: Brunner/Mazel.

Hickman, M. E., and Baldwin, B. A. 1971. Use of programmed instruction to improve communication in marriage. *The Family Coordinator.* 20:121–125.

Hogan, D. R. 1978. The effectiveness of sex therapy: A review of the literature. In *Handbook of sex therapy,* J. LoPiccolo and L. LoPiccolo, eds. New York: Plenum Press.

Huber, C. H., and Baruth, L. G. 1989. *Rational-emotive family therapy: A systems perspective.* New York: Springer.

Jacobson, N. S. 1977. Problem solving and contingency contracting in the treatment of marital discord. *Journal of Consulting and Clinical Psychology.* 45:92–100.

Jacobson, N. S. 1978. Specific and nonspecific factors in the effectiveness of a behavioral approach to the treatment of marital discord. *Journal of Consulting and Clinical Psychology.* 46:442–452.

Jacobson, N. S. 1981. Behavioral marital therapy. In *Handbook of family therapy,* A. S. Gurman and D. P. Kniskern, eds. New York: Brunner/Mazel.

Jacobson, N. S., and Margolin, G. 1979. *Marital therapy: Strategies based on social learning and behavior exchange principles.* New York: Brunner/Mazel.

Jacobson, N. S., and Martin, B. 1976. Behavioral marriage therapy: Current status. *Psychological Bulletin.* 83:540–556.

Jacobson, N. S., Waldron, H., and Moore, D. 1980. Toward a behavioral profile of marital distress. *Journal of Consulting and Clinical Psychology.* 48:696–703.

Jones, M. C. 1924. A laboratory study of fear: The case of Peter. *Journal of Geriatric Psychology.* 31:308–315.

Kanfer, F. H., and Phillips, J. S. 1970. *Learning foundations of behavior therapy.* New York: Wiley.

Kaplan, H. S. 1974. *The new sex therapy: Active treatment of sexual dysfunctions.* New York: Brunner/Mazel.

Kaplan, H. S. 1979. *Disorders of sexual desire and other new concepts and techniques in sex therapy.* New York: Brunner/Mazel.

Katkin, E. S. 1978. Charting as a multipurpose treatment intervention in family therapy. *Family Process.* 17:465–468.

Keefe, F. J., Kopel, S. A., and Gordon, S. B. 1978. *A practical guide to behavior assessment.* New York: Springer.

Kimmel, C., and Van der Veen, F. 1974. Factors of marital adjustment in Locke's Marital Adjustment Test. *Journal of Marriage and the Family.* 36:57–63.

Knox, D. 1971. *Marriage happiness: A behavioral approach to counseling.* Champaign, IL: Research Press.

Lazarus, A. A. 1965. The treatment of a sexually inadequate male. In *Case studies in behavior modification,* L. P. Ullmann and L. Krasner, eds. New York: Holt, Rinehart & Winston.

Lazarus, A. A. 1968. Behavior therapy and group marriage counseling. *Journal of the American Society of Medicine and Dentistry.* 15:49–56.

Lazarus, A. A. 1971. *Behavior therapy and beyond.* New York: McGraw-Hill.

LeBow, M. D. 1972. Behavior modification for the family. In *Family therapy: An introduction to theory and technique,* G. D. Erickson and T. P. Hogan, eds. Monterey, CA: Brooks/Cole.

Lederer, W. J., and Jackson, D. D. 1968. *The mirages of marriage.* New York: Norton.

Leslie, L. A. 1988. Cognitive-behavioral and systems models of family therapy: How compatible are they? In *Cognitive-behavioral therapy with families,* N. Epstein, S. E. Schlesinger, and W. Dryden, eds. New York: Brunner/Mazel.

Liberman, R. P. 1970. Behavioral approaches to family and couple therapy. *American Journal of Orthopsychiatry.* 40:106–118.

Liberman, R. P. 1972. Behavioral approaches to family and couple therapy. In *Progress in group and family therapy,* C. J. Sager and H. S. Kaplan, eds. New York: Brunner/Mazel.

Liberman, R. P., Levine, J., Wheeler, E., Sanders, N., and Wallace, C. 1976. Experimental evaluation of marital group therapy: Behavioral vs. interaction-insight formats. *Acta Psychiatrica Scandinavia* Supplement.

Lobitz, N. C., and LoPiccolo, J. 1972. New methods in the behavioral treatment of sexual dysfunction. *Journal of Behavior Therapy and Experimental Psychiatry.* 3:265–271.

Locke, H. J., and Wallace, K. M. 1959. Short-term marital adjustment and prediction tests: Their reliability and validity. *Journal of Marriage and Family Living.* 21:251–255.

LoPiccolo, J., and LoPiccolo, L. 1978. *Handbook of sex therapy.* New York: Plenum.

Lovibond, S. H. 1963. The mechanism of conditioning treatment of enuresis. *Behavior Research and Therapy.* 1:17–21.

Madanes, C. 1981. *Strategic family therapy.* San Francisco: Jossey-Bass.

Mahoney, M. J. 1977. Reflections on the cognitive learning trend in psychotherapy. *American Psychologist.* 32:5–13.

Margolin, G., Christensen, A., and Weiss, R. L. 1975. Contracts, cognition and change: A behavioral approach to marriage therapy. *Counseling Psychologist.* 5:15–25.

Margolin, G., and Weiss, R. L. 1978. Comparative evaluation of therapeutic components associated with behavioral marital treatments. *Journal of Consulting and Clinical Psychology.* 46:1476–1486.

Markman, H. J. 1981. Prediction of marital distress: A 5-year follow up. *Journal of Consulting and Clinical Psychology.* 49:760–762.

Masters, W. H., and Johnson, V. E. 1970. *Human sexual inadequacy.* Boston: Little, Brown.

McCauley, R. 1988. Parent training: Clinical application. In *Handbook of behavioral family therapy,* I. R. H. Falloon, ed. New York: Guilford Press.

McGuire, R. J., and Vallance, M. 1964. Aversion therapy by electric shock: A simple technique. *British Medical Journal.* 1:151–153.

Meichenbaum, D. 1977. *Cognitive behavior modification.* New York: Plenum.

Minuchin, S. 1974. *Families and family therapy.* Cambridge, MA: Harvard University Press.

Minuchin, S., Rosman, B. L., and Baker, L. 1978. *Psychosomatic families.* Cambridge, MA: Harvard University Press.

Mischel, W. 1973. On the empirical dilemmas of psychodynamic approaches: Issues and alternatives. *Journal of Abnormal Psychology.* 82:335.

Morris, S. B., Alexander, J. F., and Waldron, H. 1988. Functional family therapy. In *Handbook of behavioral family therapy,* I. R. H. Falloon, ed. New York: Guilford Press.

Morton, T. L., Twentyman, C. T., and Azar, S. T. 1988. Cognitive-behavioral assessment and treatment of child abuse. In *Cognitive-behavioral therapy with families,* N. Epstein, S. E. Schlesinger, and W. Dryden, eds. New York: Brunner/Mazel.

Munson, C. E. 1993. Cognitive family therapy. In *Cognitive and behavioral treatment: Methods and applications*, D. K. Granvold, ed. Pacific Grove, CA: Brooks/Cole.

O'Dell, S. 1974. Training parents in behavior modification: A review. *Psychological Bulletin. 81:*418–433.

O'Leary, K. D., O'Leary, S., and Becher, W. C. 1967. Modification of a deviant sibling interaction pattern in the home. *Behavior Research and Therapy. 5:*113–120.

O'Leary, K. D., and Turkewitz, H. 1978. Marital therapy from a behavioral perspective. In *Marriage and marital therapy*, T. J. Paolino and B. S. McCrady, eds. New York: Brunner/Mazel.

O'Leary, K. D., and Wilson, G. T. 1975. *Behavior therapy: Application and outcome.* Englewood Cliffs, NJ: Prentice-Hall.

Patterson, G. R. 1971a. Behavioral intervention procedures in the classroom and in the home. In *Handbook of psychotherapy and behavior change: An empirical analysis*, A. E. Bergin and S. L. Garfield, eds. New York: Wiley.

Patterson, G. R. 1971b. *Families: Application of social learning theory to family life.* Champaign, IL: Research Press.

Patterson, G. R. 1986. The contribution of siblings to training for fighting; A microsocial analysis. In *Development of antisocial and prosocial behavior: Research, theories, and issues*, D. Olweus, J. Block, and M. Radke-Yarrow, eds. Orlando, FL: Academic Press.

Patterson, G. R. 1988. Foreword. In *Handbook of behavioral family therapy*, I. R. H. Falloon, ed. New York: Guilford Press.

Patterson, G. R., Dishion, T. J., and Chamberlain, P. 1993. Outcomes and methodological issues relating to treatment of anti-social children. In *Effective psychotherapy: A handbook of comparative research*, T. R. Giles, ed. New York: Plenum Press.

Patterson, G. R., and Forgatch, M. S. 1995. Predicting future clinical adjustment from treatment outcomes and process variables. *Psychological Assessment. 7:*275–285.

Patterson, G. R., and Hops, H. 1972. Coercion, a game for two. In *The experimental analysis of social behavior*, R. E. Ulrich and P. Mountjoy, eds. New York: Appleton-Century-Crofts.

Patterson, G. R., Hops, H., and Weiss, R. L. 1973. A social learning approach to reducing rates of marital conflict. In *Advances in behavior therapy*, R. Stuart, R. Liberman, and S. Wilder, eds. New York: Academic Press.

Patterson, G. R., and Reid, J. 1970. Reciprocity and coercion; two facets of social systems. In *Behavior modification in clinical psychology*, C. Neuringer and J. Michael, eds. New York: Appleton-Century-Crofts.

Patterson, G. R., Weiss, R. L., and Hops, H. 1976. Training in marital skills: Some problems and concepts. In *Handbook of behavior modification and behavior therapy*, H. Leitenberg, ed. Englewood Cliffs, NJ: Prentice-Hall.

Pavlov, I. P. 1932. Neuroses in man and animals. *Journal of the American Medical Association. 99:*1012–1013.

Pavlov, I. P. 1934. An attempt at a physiological interpretation of obsessional neurosis and paranoia. *Journal of Mental Science. 80:*187–197.

Pendergrass, V. E. 1971. Effects of length of timeout from positive reinforcement and schedule of application in suppression of aggressive behavior. *Psychological Record. 21:*75–80.

Pierce, R. M. 1973. Training in interpersonal communication skills with the partners of deteriorated marriages. *The Family Coordinator. 22:*223–227.

Premack, D. 1965. Reinforcement theory. In *Nebraska symposium on motivation*, D. Levine, ed. Lincoln, NB: University of Nebraska Press.

Rappaport, A. F., and Harrell, J. A. 1972. A behavior-exchange model for marital counseling. *Family Coordinator. 21:*203–213.

Rimm, D. C., and Masters, J. C. 1974. *Behavior therapy: Techniques and empirical findings.* New York: Wiley.

Rinn, R. C. 1978. Children with behavior disorders. In *Behavior therapy in the psychiatric setting*, M. Hersen and A. S. Bellack, eds. Baltimore: Williams & Wilkins.

Risley, T. R. 1968. The effects and side effects of punishing the autistic behaviors of a deviant child. *Journal of Applied Behavior Analysis. 1:*21–34.

Risley, T. R., and Wolf, M. M. 1967. Experimental manipulation of autistic behaviors and generalization into the home. In *Child development: Readings in experimental analysis*, S. W. Bijou and D. M. Baer, eds. New York: Appleton.

Romanczyk, R. G., and Kistner, J. J. 1977. The current state of the art in behavior modification. *The Psychotherapy Bulletin. 11*:16–30.

Sanders, M. R., and Dadds, M. R. 1993. *Behavioral family intervention.* Boston, MA: Allyn & Bacon.

Satir, V. 1967. *Conjoint family therapy.* Palo Alto, CA: Science and Behavioral Books.

Schindler, L., and Vollmer, M. 1984. Cognitive perspectives in behavioral marital therapy: Some proposals for bridging theory, research and practice. In *Marital interaction: Analysis and modification,* K. Hahlwag and N. S. Jacobson, eds. New York: Guilford Press.

Schwebel, A. I., and Fine, M. A. 1992. Cognitive-behavioral family therapy. *Journal of Family Psychotherapy. 3*:73–91.

Schwitzgebel, R. 1967. Short-term operant conditioning of adolescent offenders on socially relevant variables. *Journal of Abnormal Psychology. 72*:134–142.

Schwitzgebel, R., and Kolb, D. A. 1964. Inducing behavior change in adolescent delinquents. *Behaviour Research and Therapy. 9*:233–238.

Semans, J. H. 1956. Premature ejaculation: A new approach. *Southern Medical Journal. 49*:353–357.

Skinner, B. F. 1953. *Science and human behavior.* New York: Macmillan.

Snyder, D. K. 1979. Multidimensional assessment of marital satisfaction. *Journal of Marriage and the Family. 41*:813–823.

Spinks, S. H., and Birchler, G. R. 1982. Behavior systems marital therapy: Dealing with resistance. *Family Process. 21*:169–186.

Stuart, R. B. 1969. An operant-interpersonal treatment for marital discord. *Journal of Consulting and Clinical Psychology. 33*:675–682.

Stuart, R. B. 1971. Behavioral contracting within the families of delinquents. *Journal of Behavior Therapy and Experimental Psychiatry. 2*:1–11.

Stuart, R. B. 1975. Behavioral remedies for marital ills: A guide to the use of operant-interpersonal techniques. In *International symposium on behavior modification,* T. Thompson and W. Docken, eds. New York: Appleton.

Stuart, R. B. 1976. An operant interpersonal program for couples. In *Treating relationships,* D. H. Olson, ed. Lake Mills, IA: Graphic Publishing.

Teichman, Y. 1984. Cognitive family therapy. *British Journal of Cognitive Psychotherapy. 2*:1–10.

Teichman, Y. 1992. Family treatment with an acting-out adolescent. In *Comprehensive casebook of cognitive therapy,* A. Freeman and F. M. Dattilio, eds. New York: Plenum.

Thibaut, J., and Kelley, H. H. 1959. *The social psychology of groups.* New York: Wiley.

Umana, R. F., Gross, S. J., and McConville, M. T. 1980. *Crisis in the family: Three approaches.* New York: Gardner Press.

Vincent, J. P., Weiss, R. L., and Birchler, G. R. 1975. A behavioral analysis of problem solving in distressed and nondistressed married and stranger dyads. *Behavior Therapy. 6*:475–487.

Watson, J. B., and Raynor, R. 1920. Conditioned emotional reactions. *Journal of Experimental Psychology. 3*:1–14.

Weiss, R. L. 1978. The conceptualization of marriage from a behavioral perspective. In *Marriage and marital therapy,* T. J. Paolino and B. S. McCrady, eds. New York: Brunner/Mazel.

Weiss, R. L. 1984. Cognitive and strategic interventions in behavioral marital therapy. In *Marital interaction: Analysis and modification,* K. Hahlwag and N. S. Jacobson, eds. New York: Guilford Press.

Weiss, R. L., and Birchler, G. R. 1978. Adults with marital dysfunction. In *Behavior therapy in the psychiatric setting,* M. Hersen and A. S. Bellack, eds. Baltimore: Williams & Wilkins.

Weiss, R. L., Hops, H., and Patterson, G. R. 1973. A framework for conceptualizing marital conflict, a technology for altering it, some data for evaluating it. In *Behavior change: Methodology, concepts and practice,* L. A. Hamerlynch, L. C. Handy, and E. J. Marsh, eds. Champaign, IL: Research Press.

Weiss, R. L., and Isaac, J. 1978. Behavior vs. cognitive measures as predictors of marital satisfaction. Paper presented at the Western Psychological Association meeting, Los Angeles.

Williams, C. D. 1959. The elimination of tantrum behavior by extinction procedures. *Journal of Abnormal and Social Psychology. 59*:269.

Wills, T. A., Weiss, R. L., and Patterson, G. R. 1974. A behavioral analysis of the determinants of marital satisfaction. *Journal of Consulting and Clinical Psychology. 42*:802–811.

Wodarski, J., and Thyer, B. 1989. Behavioral perspectives on the family: An overview. In *Behavioral family therapy,* B. Thyer, ed. Springfield, IL: Charles C. Thomas.

Wolpe, J. 1948. An approach to the problem of neurosis based on the conditioned response. Unpublished M.D. thesis. University of Witwatersrand, Johannesberg, South Africa.

Wolpe, J. 1958. *Psychotherapy by reciprocal inhibition.* Stanford, CA: Stanford University Press.

Wolpe, J. 1969. *The practice of behavior therapy.* New York: Pergamon Press.

Wright, J. H., and Beck, A. T. 1993. Family cognitive therapy with inpatients: Part II. In *Cognitive therapy with inpatients: Developing a cognitive milieu,* J. H. Wright, M. E. Thase, A. T. Beck, and J. W. Ludgate, eds. New York: Guilford Press.

Family Therapy in the Twenty-First Century

The Shape of Family Therapy Today

From a radical new experiment in the 1960s, family therapy grew into an established force, complete with its own literature, organizations, and legions of practitioners. Unlike other fields organized around a single conceptual model (psychoanalysis, behavior therapy), family therapy was always a diverse enterprise, with competing schools and a multitude of theories. What they shared was a belief that problems run in families. Beyond that, however, each school was a well-defined and distinct enterprise, with its own leaders, texts, and ways of doing therapy.

Today, all of that has changed. The field is no longer neatly divided into separate schools, and its practitioners no longer share a universal adherence to systems theory. As family therapists have always been fond of metaphors, we might say that the field has grown up. No longer cliquish or cocksure, the family therapy movement has been shaken and transformed by a series of challenges—to the idea that any one approach has all the answers, about the nature

of men and women, about the American family—indeed, about the possibility of knowing anything with certainty. In this chapter, we'll examine those challenges and see what family therapy looks like in the twenty-first century.

Erosion of Boundaries

The boundaries between schools of family therapy gradually eroded in the 1990s to the point where now fewer and fewer therapists would characterize themselves as purely Bowenian or structural, or what have you. One reason for this decline in sectarianism was that, as they gained experience, practitioners found no reason not to borrow from each other's arsenal of techniques. Suppose, for example, that a card-carrying structural therapist were to read White and Epston's little gem of a book, *Narrative Means to Therapeutic Ends,* and start spending more and more time exploring the stories clients tell about their lives. Would this therapist still be a structuralist? A narrative therapist? Or perhaps a little of both?

Suppose that our hypothetical therapist were to hear Jim Keim at a conference describing his strategic approach to families with oppositional children and started using it in her own practice. What would we call this therapist now? Structural-narrative-strategic? Eclectic? Or simply "a family therapist"?

Another reason for the erosion of orthodoxy was the growing recognition of the need for individualized techniques to deal with specific problems and populations. Once family therapists cherished their models. If a particular family didn't quite fit the paradigm, maybe they just weren't "an appropriate treatment case." Today, one-size-fits-all therapies are no longer seen as viable. Now therapists approach families less as experts confident of fixing them than as partners hoping to shore up their resources. These resources are constrained not only by a family's structure but also by political and economic forces beyond their control. Some of the change in status of the classic schools was due to the death or retirement of the pioneers and the absence of dominating figures to replace them. Our current era of questioning and uncertainty is also related to a growing recognition that doctrinaire models aren't always relevant to the specific needs of clients. Family therapy is one of many social sciences that has been turned upside down by the postmodern revolution.

Postmodernism

Advances in science at the beginning of the twentieth century gave us a sense that the truth of things could be uncovered through objective observation and measurement. The universe was a mechanism whose laws of operation awaited discovery. Once these universal laws were known, we could control our environment. This modernist perspective influenced the way family therapy's pioneers approached their clients—as cybernetic systems to be decoded and reprogrammed. The therapist was the expert. Structural and strategic blueprints were used to search out flaws that needed repair, regardless of whether families saw things that way themselves.

Postmodernism was a reaction to this kind of hubris. Not only are we losing faith in the validity of scientific, political, and religious truths, we're also coming to doubt whether absolute truth can ever be known. As Walter Truett Anderson (1990) writes in *Reality Isn't What It Used To Be*, "Most of the conflicts that tore the now-ending modern era were between different belief systems, each of which professed to have the truth: this faith against that one, capitalism against communism, science against religion. On all sides the assumption was that somebody possessed the real item, a truth fixed and beyond mere human conjecture" (p. 2). In family therapy it was structural truth versus psychodynamics; Bowen versus Satir.

Einstein's relativity undermined our faith in certainties. Marx challenged the right of one class to dominate another. In the 1960s we lost trust in the establishment and gained a sense that there were other realities besides those of ordinary consciousness. The feminist movement challenged patriarchal assumptions about gender that had been considered laws of nature. As the world shrank and we were increasingly exposed to people of different cultures, we had to reexamine our assumptions about their "primitive" beliefs.

This mounting skepticism became a major force in the 1980s and shook the pillars of every human endeavor. In literature, education, religion, political science, and psychology, accepted practices were **deconstructed**—that is, shown to be social conventions developed by people with their own agendas. French philosopher Michel Foucault interpreted the accepted principles in many fields as stories perpetuated to protect power structures and silence alternative voices. The first and perhaps most influential of those voices to be raised in family therapy was the feminist critique.

The Feminist Critique

Feminism prompted family therapy's rudest awakening. In an eye-opening critique heralded by an article of Rachel Hare-Mustin's in 1978, feminist family therapists not only exposed the gender bias inherent in existing models, they also advocated a style of therapy that called into question systems theory itself.

It became painfully clear that cybernetics and functionalism had blinded us to the endemic cultural inequality of women. Cybernetics encouraged us to view a family system as a flawed machine. Judith Myers Avis (1988) described this family machine as one that

> . . . functions according to special systemic rules and is divorced from its historical, social, economic, and political contexts. By viewing the family out of context, family therapists locate family dysfunction entirely within interpersonal relationships in the family, ignore broader patterns of dysfunction occurring across families, and fail to notice the relationship between social context and family dysfunction. (p. 17)

The Batesonian version of cybernetics had claimed that personal control in systems was impossible because all elements are continually influencing one another in repetitious feedback loops. If all parts of a system are equally involved in its problems, no one is to blame. This idea appealed to family therapists because family members often enter therapy pointing fingers at each other and failing to see their role in the problems that plague them.

To feminists, however, the notion of equal responsibility for problems looked suspiciously like a sophisticated "version of blaming the victim and rationalizing the status quo" (Goldner, 1985, p. 33). This criticism was particularly germane in crimes against women, such as battering, incest, and rape, for which psychological theories have long been used to imply that women either provoked or consented to their own abuse (James & MacKinnon, 1990).

The family constellation most commonly cited as contributing to problems was the peripheral father, the overinvolved mother, and the symptomatic child caught up in their relationship. For years, psychoanalysts had blamed mothers for their children's symptoms. Family therapy's contribution was to show how the father's lack of involvement contributed to the mother's overinvolvement, and so therapists tried to pry the mother loose by inserting the father in her place. This wasn't the boon for women that it might have seemed because, in too many cases, mothers were viewed no less negatively. Mothers were still enmeshed and incompetent, but now a new solution appeared—bringing in good old dad to the rescue.

What feminists contended that therapists failed to see, and to help their clients see, was that "the archetypal 'family case' of the overinvolved mother and peripheral father is best understood not as a clinical problem, but as the product of an historical process two hundred years in the making" (Goldner, 1985, p. 31). Mothers were overinvolved and insecure not because of some personal flaw but because they were in emotionally isolated, economically dependent, overresponsible positions in families, positions that were crazy-making.

Gender-sensitive therapists sought to help families reorganize so that no one, male or female, remained stuck in such positions. Thus, instead of further diminishing a mother's self-esteem by replacing her with a peripheral father (who was likely to have been critical of her parenting all along), a feminist family therapist might help the family reexamine the roles that kept mothers down and fathers out. Fathers might be encouraged to become more involved with parenting—not because mothers are in-

*P*eggy Papp, Olga Silverstein, Marianne Walters, and Betty Carter, founding members of the Women's Project in Family Therapy.

competent, but because it's a father's responsibility (Goodrich, Rampage, Ellman, & Halstead, 1988; Walters, Carter, Papp, & Silverstein, 1988).

Feminists weren't simply asking therapists to be more sensitive to gender issues in working with families. Rather, they asserted that issues of gender or, more specifically, patriarchy, permeated therapists' work, even though they had been conditioned not to notice them. They therefore believed that gender inequality should be a primary concern for family therapists (Goldner, 1988; Luepnitz, 1988).

Only when therapists become more gender sensitive will they stop blaming mothers and looking to them to do all of the changing. Only then will they be able to fully counter the unconscious bias toward seeing women as ultimately responsible for childrearing and housekeeping; as needing to support their husbands' careers by neglecting their own; as needing to be married or at least to have a man in their lives (Anderson, 1995). Only then can they stop relying on traditional male traits, such as rationality, independence, and competitiveness, as their standards of health and stop denigrating or ignoring traits traditionally encouraged

in women, like emotionality, nurturance, and relationship focus.

As one might anticipate, the feminist critique wasn't initially welcomed by the family therapy establishment. The early to mid-1980s was a period of polarization between male and female therapists, as feminists tried to exceed the establishment's "threshold of deafness." By the 1990s that threshold had been exceeded. The major feminist points are no longer debated and the field is evolving toward a more collaborative and socially enlightened form of therapy.

Lest we get too complacent about family therapy's acceptance of feminism, it's important to remember that women still face political, economic, and social problems on a daily basis. Women still earn less than men for their labor. Women are still assigned most domestic work. Women are still often blamed for family problems. Men's violence against women is still tolerated by many families, peers, and cultural forces. Moreover, although some men resist, the masculine ideal still influences most men, who strive to be "manly" and reject less macho men as geeks, wimps, or wusses. Although many men do not experience themselves as powerful within their own families, men still benefit from arrangements that give them power in society. As Rachel Hare-Mustin says, "Although it is true that men can cry now, too, they still have less to cry about."[1]

Social Constructionism and the Narrative Revolution

Constructivism was the crowbar that pried family therapy away from its belief in objectivity—the assumption that what one sees in families is what *is* in families. Understanding behavior is never simply a process of seeing it, grasping it, or decoding it. Human experience is fundamentally ambiguous. Fragments of experience are understood only through a process that organizes it, selects what's salient, and assigns meaning and significance.

Instead of focusing on patterns of family interaction, constructivism shifted the emphasis to exploring and reevaluating the perspectives that people with a problem have about it. Meaning itself became the primary target.

In the 1980s and 1990s Harlene Anderson and Harry Goolishian translated constructivism into an approach that democratized the therapist–client relationship. Along with Lynn Hoffman and others, these *collaborative therapists* were united in their opposition to the cybernetic model and its mechanistic implications. Their version of postmodernism focused more on caring than curing, and they sought to move the therapist out of the position of expert into a more egalitarian partnership with clients.

Perhaps the most striking example of this democratization of therapy was introduced by the Norwegian psychiatrist Tom Andersen, who leveled the playing field by hiding nothing

from his clients. He and his team openly discuss their reactions to what a family says. This **reflecting team** (Andersen, 1991) has become a widely used aspect of the collaborative model's therapy by consensus. Observers come out from behind the one-way mirror to discuss their impressions with the therapist and family. This process creates an open environment in which the family feels part of a larger team and the team feels more empathy for the family.

What these collaborative therapists shared was the conviction that too often clients aren't heard because therapists are doing therapy *to* them rather than *with* them. To redress this authoritarian attitude, Harlene Anderson (1993) recommended that therapists adopt a position of "not knowing," which leads to genuine conversations with clients in which "both the therapist's and the client's expertise are engaged to dissolve the problem" (p. 325).[2]

This new perspective was in the tradition of an approach to knowledge that emerged from biblical studies called **hermeneutics,** a term derived from the Greek word for interpretation. Before it surfaced in family therapy, hermeneutics had already shaken up psychoanalysis. In the 1980s Donald Spence, Roy Schafer, and Paul Ricoeur were challenging the Freudian notion that there was one correct and comprehensive interpretation of a patient's symptoms, dreams, and fantasies. The analytic method isn't, they argued, archaeological or reconstructive; it's constructive and synthetic, organizing whatever is there into patterns it imposes (Mitchell, 1993).

From a hermeneutic perspective, what a therapist knows is not simply discovered or revealed through a process of free association and analysis—or enactment and circular questioning—it's organized, constructed, and

---

1. Rachel Hare-Mustin (2001). "Family therapy and the future—2001." Plenary Address, American Family Therapy Academy Conference of the Americas, Miami, FL, June 27.

2. Collaborative therapists distinguish these conversations from the nondirective, empathic Rogerian style because they don't just reflect but also offer ideas and opinions, though always tentatively.

fitted together by the therapist alone, or collaboratively with the patient or family. Although there's nothing inherently democratic about hermeneutic exegesis, its challenge to essentialism went hand in hand with the challenge to authoritarianism. In family therapy, the hermeneutic tradition seemed a perfect partner to efforts to make treatment more collaborative.

It's hard to give up certainty. A lot is asked of a listener who, in order to be genuinely open to the speaker's story, must put aside his or her own beliefs and, at least temporarily, enter the other's world. In so doing, the listener may find those beliefs challenged and changed. This is more than some therapists are willing to risk.

Constructivism focused on how individuals create their own realities, but family therapy has always emphasized the power of interaction. As a result, another postmodern psychology called **social constructionism** now influences many family therapists. Social psychologist Kenneth Gergen (1985), its main proponent, emphasized the power of social interaction in generating meaning for people.

Gergen challenged the notion that we are autonomous individuals holding independent beliefs and argued instead that our beliefs are fluid and fluctuate with changes in our social context. Gergen (1991b) asks, "Are not all the fragments of identity the residues of relationships, and aren't we undergoing continuous transformation as we move from one relationship to another?" (p. 28).

This view has several implications. The first is that no one has a corner on the truth; all truths are social constructions. This idea invites therapists to help clients understand the origins of their beliefs, even those they had assumed were laws of nature. The second implication is that therapy is a linguistic exercise; if therapists can lead clients to new constructions about their problems, the problems may open up. Third, therapy should be collaborative. Since neither therapist nor client brings truth to the table, new realities emerge through conversa-

tions in which both sides share opinions and respect each other's perspective.

Social constructionism was welcomed with open arms by those who were trying to shift the focus of therapy from action to cognition, and it became the basis for an approach that took family therapy by storm in the 1990s, **narrative therapy** (Chapter 13). The narrative metaphor focuses on how experience generates expectations, and how expectations shape experience through the creation of organizing stories. Narrative therapists follow Gergen in considering the "self" a socially constructed phenomenon.

The question for the narrative therapist isn't one of truth but of which points of view are useful and lead to preferred outcomes. Problems aren't in persons (as psychoanalysis had it) or in relationships (as systems theory had it); rather, problems are embedded in points of view about individuals and their situations. Narrative therapy helps people reexamine these points of view.

Family Therapy's Answer to Managed Care: Solution-Focused Therapy

Solution-focused therapy was the other new model to rise to prominence in the 1990s. Steve de Shazer and his colleagues (Chapter 12) took the ideas of constructivism in a different, more pragmatic, direction. The goal of this approach is to get clients to shift from "problem talk"—trying to understand their problems—to "solution talk"—focusing on what's working—as quickly as possible. The idea is that focusing on solutions, in and of itself, often eliminates problems.

The popularity of solution-focused model exploded during a period in which agency budgets were slashed and managed care began to dictate the number of sessions for which practitioners could be reimbursed. This produced a tremendous demand for a brief, easy-to-apply approach, to which solution-focused seemed the perfect answer.

Family Violence

In the early 1990s family therapy took a hard look at the dark side of family life. For the first time, books and articles on wife battering and sexual abuse began appearing in the mainstream family therapy literature (e.g., Trepper & Barrett, 1989; Goldner, Penn, Sheinberg, & Walker, 1990; Sheinberg, 1992). The field was shaken out of its collective denial regarding the extent of male-to-female abuse in families.

Judith Myers Avis (1992) delivered a barrage of shocking statistics regarding the number of women who have experienced sexual abuse before the age of eighteen (37 percent), the percent of abusers who are male (95 percent), the number of women abused each year by the men with whom they live (one in six), the percent of male college students who had coerced sex from an unwilling partner (25 percent), and those who said they would commit rape if guaranteed immunity from punishment (20 percent). After reiterating the indictment of theories that call for therapist neutrality and that treat the abused as partially responsible for their abuse, she concluded that:

> As long as we train therapists in systemic theories without balancing that training with an understanding of the non-neutrality of power dynamics, we will continue producing family therapists who collude in the maintenance of male power and are dangerous to the women and children with whom they work. (p. 231)

Michele Bograd (1992) summarized one of the central predicaments for family therapy in this decade.

> In working with family violence, how do we balance a relativistic world view with values about

human safety and the rights of men and women to self-determination and protection? When is the clinical utility of neutrality limited or counterproductive? When is conviction essential to the change process? How do we confront the batterer about the destructive nature of his behavior without condemning him? How strongly and passionately do we employ our values to therapeutic advantage while maintaining a caring and respectful connection with family members struggling with the trauma of violence? (pp. 248, 249)

The systemic view, now under attack, was that family violence was the outcome of cycles of mutual provocation, an escalation, albeit unacceptable, of the emotionally destructive behavior that characterizes many marriages. Advocates for women rejected this point of view. From their perspective, violent men don't lose control, they *take* control—and will stop only when they are held accountable.

While the claim made by some women's advocates that couples therapy has no place in the treatment of violent marriages was controversial, their warnings provided a wake-up call. Domestic violence—let's call it what it is, wife battering and child beating—is a major public health problem, right up there with alcoholism and depression.

Multiculturalism

Family therapy has always billed itself as a treatment of people in context. In the postwar America of family therapy's birth, this principle was translated into a pragmatic look at the influence of a family's relationships on its members. Now as we've become once again a more diverse country enriched by a flow of immigrants from Asia, Central and South America, Africa, and Eastern Europe, family therapy as a profession has shown its willingness to embrace this influx of diversity. Not only are we learning to respect that families from other cul-

*N*ancy Boyd-Franklin's Black Families in Therapy *was one of the first— and best—books on treating ethnic minority families.*

tures have their own valid ways of doing things but our journals and professional organizations are making an effort to become more diverse and inclusive.

Monica McGoldrick and her colleagues (McGoldrick, Pearce, & Giordano, 1982) dealt the first blow to our ethnocentricity with a book describing the characteristic values and structure of a host of different ethnic groups. Following this and a spate of related works (e.g., Falicov, 1983, 1998; Boyd-Franklin, 1989; Saba, Karrer, & Hardy, 1989; Mirkin, 1990; Ingoldsby & Smith, 1995; Okun, 1996; McGoldrick, 1998), we are now more sensitive to the need to know something about the ethnic background of our client families, so we don't assume they're sick just because they're different. As Monica McGoldrick (1993) writes,

> Ethnicity patterns our thinking, feeling, and behavior in both obvious and subtle ways, although generally operating outside our awareness. It plays a major role in determining what we eat, how we work, how we relate, how we celebrate holidays and rituals, and how we feel about life, death, and illness. (p. 335)

Multiculturalism has become a prevailing theme in family therapy, as reflected in conference agendas, journal articles, and graduate school curriculums. The attention to these issues represents a welcome sensitizing to the influence of ethnicity.

Multiculturalism is certainly an advance over ethnocentrism. Yet in highlighting differences, there is a danger of overemphasizing identity politics. Segregation, even in the name of ethnic pride, isolates people and fosters prejudice. Perhaps *pluralism* is a better term than *multiculturalism* because it implies more balance between ethnic identity and connection to the larger group.

As we suggested in Chapter 4, ethnic sensitivity does not require becoming an expert—or thinking you're an expert—on every culture you might conceivably work with. If you don't know how a rural Mexican family feels about their children leaving home or what Korean parents think about their teenage daughter dating American boys, you can always ask. Curiosity and respect for other people's ways of doing things is probably a more useful aspiration than encyclopedic knowledge.

Race

In the early days of family therapy, African American families received some attention (e.g., Minuchin et al., 1967), but for many years it seemed that the field, like the rest of the country, tried to ignore people of color and the racism they live with every day. Finally, however, African American family therapists such as Nancy Boyd-Franklin (1993) and Ken Hardy

*K*en Hardy advises *therapists not to overlook the impact of racism on their clients—or in the therapeutic relationship.*

(1993) brought these issues out of the shadows and forced them into the field's consciousness.

White therapists still, of course, have the option to walk away from these issues. Nonwhite therapists and clients don't have that luxury (Hardy, 1993):

> To avoid being seen by whites as troublemakers, we suppress the part of ourselves that feels hurt and outraged by the racism around us, instead developing an "institutional self"—an accommodating facade of calm professionalism calculated to be nonthreatening to whites. . . . Familiar only with our institutional selves, white people don't appreciate the sense of immediate connection and unspoken loyalty that binds black people together. . . . We are united by being raised with the same messages most black families pass on to their children: "You were born into one of the most despised groups in the world. You can't trust white people. You are somebody. Be proud, and never for one minute think that white people are better than you." (pp. 52–53)

Laura Markowitz (1993) quotes a black woman's therapy experience:

> I remember being in therapy years ago with a nice white woman who kept focusing me on why I was such an angry person and on my parents as inadequate individuals. . . . We never looked at my father as a poor black man, my mother as a poor black woman and the context in which they survived and raised us. . . . Years later, I saw a therapist of color and the first thing out of her mouth was, "Let's look at what was going on for your parents." It was a joyous moment to be able to see my dad not as a terrible person who hated us but as a survivor living under amazingly difficult conditions. I could embrace him, and I could understand my anger instead of blaming myself for feeling that way. (p. 29)

It's hard for whites to realize how many doors were open to them based on their skin color, and to understand how burdened by racism nonwhites are. African American families not only have to overcome barriers to opportunity and achievement but also the anxiety, frustration, and despair that such obstacles create.

The task of therapists working with nonwhite families is to understand their reluctance to engage in treatment (particularly if the therapist is white) in the context of their environment and their history of negative interaction with white people, including many of

Nonwhite clients may feel that white therapists can't fully understand their experiences.

the social service agents they encounter. In addition, the therapist must recognize the family's strengths and draw from their networks, or help them create networks of support if the family is isolated.

Finally, therapists must look inside and face their own attitudes about race, class, and poverty. Toward this end, several authors recommend curricula that go beyond lectures to personal encounters—that is, confronting our own demons of racism (Pinderhughes, 1989; Boyd-Franklin, 1989; Green, 1998).

Poverty and Social Class

Money and social class are not subjects that most helping professionals like to discuss. The shame of economic disadvantage is related to the pervasive individualist ethic that people are responsible for their own success or lack of it. If you're poor, it must be your own fault.

Despite decreasing fees due to managed care, most therapists are able to maintain a reasonably comfortable lifestyle. They often have little appreciation of the obstacles their poor clients face and the psychological impact of those conditions. When poor clients don't show up for appointments or don't comply with directives, some therapists are quick to see them as apathetic or irresponsible. In many cases, this is also the way poor people come to see themselves—and that negative self-image can become the biggest obstacle of all.

How can we counter this tendency to think that poor people just can't cut it? First, therapists need to educate themselves to the social and political realities of being poor in the U.S.A. Recently, investigative journalist Barbara Ehrenreich (1999) spent a year trying to live like a former welfare recipient coming into the workforce. Living in a trailer park and working as a waitress left her with virtually nothing after expenses.

How former welfare recipients and single mothers will (and do) survive in the low-wage workforce, I cannot imagine. Maybe they will figure out how to condense their lives—including child-raising, laundry, romance and meals—into the couple of hours between full-time jobs. Maybe they will take up residence in their vehicles [as she found several fellow workers had done], if they have one. All I know is that I couldn't hold two jobs and I couldn't make enough money to live on with one. And I had advantages unthinkable to many of the long-term poor—health, stamina, a working car, and no children to care for or support. . . . The thinking behind welfare reform was that even the humblest jobs are morally uplifting and psychologically buoying. In reality these are likely to be fraught with insult and stress. (p. 52)

The fact is, this isn't the land of equal opportunity. The economy has built-in disparities that make it extremely difficult for anyone to climb out of poverty and that keep nearly one in four children living in privation (Walsh, 1998).

These days, it isn't just families of poverty who live with financial insecurity. As mortgages, car payments, and college tuitions mount up, and corporations frequently lay off employees suddenly and ruthlessly, family life at all but the wealthiest levels is increasingly dominated by economic anxiety. Median family income has declined in the past two decades to the point where young families can't hope to do as well as their parents, even with the two incomes needed to support a very modest standard of living (Rubin, 1994).

Therapists can't help their clients pay the rent, but they can help them appreciate that the burdens they live with are not all of their own making. Even when they don't bring it up, a sensitive therapist should be aware of the role financial pressures play in the lives of their client families. Asking about how they manage to get by not only puts this issue on the table, it can also lead to a greater appreciation of the effort and ingenuity that it takes to make ends meet these days.

Gay and Lesbian Rights

Family therapy's consciousness was raised about gay and lesbian rights in the same way it was for race. After a long period of neglect and denial, family therapy in the late 1980s began to face the discrimination that a sizable percentage of the population lives with (Krestan, 1988; Roth & Murphy, 1986; Carl, 1990; Laird, 1993; Sanders, 1993). The release in 1996 of a major clinical handbook (Laird & Green, 1996) and the magazine *In the Family* (edited by Laura Markowitz) indicate that gay and lesbian issues are finally out of family therapy's closet.

Despite gains in tolerance in some segments of our society, however, gays and lesbians continue to face humiliation, discrimination, and even violence because of their sexuality. After a childhood of confusion, shame, and fear of discovery, many gays and lesbians are rejected by their families once they come out. Due to the lack of social support, the bonds in gay and lesbian relationships can be strained by the pressures of isolation, generating stress and jealousy.

Parents often feel guilty, in part because early psychoanalytic studies blamed them for their children's sexual orientation. Parental reactions range from denial, self-blame, and fear for their child's future, to hostility, violence, and disowning (LaSala, 1997). Therapists should remember that, while gay or lesbian children may have struggled for years to come to grips with their identity, their parents may need some time to catch up after the initial shock.

When working with gay, lesbian, bisexual, or transgendered clients, we recommend that therapists get as much information as they can about the unique identify formation and relationship issues that these groups face. Therapists who aren't well informed about gay and lesbian experience should seek supervision from someone who is, or refer these clients to a clinician with more experience. It simply isn't true that individuals and families, regardless of their cultural context, all struggle with the same issues.

We hope the day will arrive soon when gay and lesbian families, bisexual and transgendered persons, African Americans, and other marginalized groups are studied by family therapists to learn not only about the problems they face but also about how they survive and thrive against such great odds. For example, gays and lesbians often create "families of choice" out of their friendship networks (Johnson & Keren, 1998). As Joan Laird (1993) suggested, these families have much to teach us "about gender relationships, about parenting, about adaptation to tensions in this society, and especially about strength and resilience" (p. 284). The question is whether we are ready to learn.

Spirituality

Throughout the twentieth century psychotherapists, wanting to avoid any association with what science considers irrational, have avoided bringing religion into the consulting room. We've also tried to stay out of the moralizing business, striving to remain neutral so that clients could make up their own minds about their lives.

At the turn of the twenty-first century, however, as increasing numbers of people found modern life isolating and empty, spirituality and religion emerged as antidotes to a widespread feeling of alienation—both in the popular press (making covers of both *Time* and *Newsweek*) and in the family therapy literature (Brothers, 1992; Burton, 1992; Prest & Keller, 1993; Doherty, 1996; Walsh, 1999).

Some of a family's most powerful organizing beliefs have to do with how they find meaning in their lives and their ideas about a higher power. Yet most therapists never ask about such matters. Is it possible to explore a family's spiritual beliefs without proselytizing or scoffing? More and more therapists believe that it's not only possible, it's crucial. They believe that people's answers to those larger questions are intimately related to their emotional and physical health.

Tailoring Treatment to Populations and Problems

In recent years, family therapists have come down from the ivory towers of their training institutes to grapple with the messy problems of the real world. They find it increasingly necessary to fit their approaches to the needs of their clients, rather than the other way around. The maturing of family therapy is reflected in its literature. Once most of the writing was about the classic models and how they applied to families in general (e.g., Haley, 1976; Minuchin & Fishman, 1981). Beginning in the 1980s, books no longer tied to any one school began to focus on how to do family therapy with a host of specific types of problems and family constellations.

Books are now available on working with families of people who abuse drugs (Stanton, Todd, & Associates, 1982; Barth, Pietrzak, & Ramier, 1993), alcohol (Steinglass, Bennett, Wolin, & Reiss, 1987; Treadway, 1989; Elkin, 1990), food (Root, Fallon, & Friedrich, 1986; Schwartz, 1995), and each other (Trepper & Barrett, 1989; Friedrich, 1990; Madanes, 1990). There are books about treating single-parent families (Morawetz & Walker, 1984), stepparent families (Visher & Visher, 1979, 1988), divorcing families (Sprenkle, 1985; Wallerstein & Kelley, 1980; Ahrons & Rogers, 1989; Emery, 1994), blended families (Hansen, 1982; Sager et al., 1983), and families in transition among these states (Pittman, 1987; Falicov, 1988).

There are also books on treating families with young children (Combrinck-Graham,

1989; Wachtel, 1994; Gil, 1994; Freeman, Epston, & Lobovits, 1997; Selekman, 1997; Smith & Nylund, 1997; Bailey, 1999), with troubled adolescents (Price, 1996; Micucci, 1998; Sells, 1998) and young adults (Haley, 1980); and with problems among siblings (Kahn & Lewis, 1988). There are even books on normal families (Walsh, 1982, 1993) and "successful families" (Beavers & Hampson, 1990).

There are books for working with schizophrenic families (Anderson, Reiss, & Hogarty, 1986), families with bipolar disorder (Miklowitz & Goldstein, 1997), and families with AIDS (Walker, 1991; Boyd-Franklin, Steiner, & Boland, 1995); families who have suffered trauma (Figley, 1985), chronic illness or disability (Rolland, 1994; McDaniel, Hepworth, & Doherty, 1992); families who are grieving a death (Walsh & McGoldrick, 1991), have a child with a disability (Seligman & Darling, 1996), or have an adopted child (Reitz & Watson, 1992); poor families (Minuchin, Colapinto, & Minuchin, 1998); and families of different ethnicities (Boyd-Franklin, 1989; Okun, 1996; McGoldrick, Giordano, & Pearce, 1996; Lee, 1997; Falicov, 1998). There are also several books in the works about treating gay and lesbian families (e.g., Laird & Green, 1996; Greenan & Tunnell, 2003).

In addition to these specialized books, the field has broadened its scope and extended systems thinking beyond the family to include the impact of larger systems like other helping agents or social agencies and schools (Schwartzman, 1985; Imber-Black, 1988; Elizur & Minuchin, 1989), the importance of family rituals and their use in therapy (Imber-Black, Roberts, & Whiting, 1988), and the sociopolitical context in which families exist (Mirkin, 1990; McGoldrick, 1998).

There are practical guides to family therapy not connected to any one school (Taibbi, 1996; Patterson, Williams, Graul-Grounds, & Chamow, 1998), and edited books that include contributions from all of the schools but that are focused on specific problems or cases (Dattilio, 1998;

Donovan, 1999). Thus, as opposed to the earlier days of family therapy when followers of a particular model read little outside of what came from that school, the trend toward specialization by content rather than by model has made the field more pluralistic in this postmodern age.

Home-Based Services

Like traditional versions of family therapy, home-based services target the family as the primary recipient of mental health care (Friesen & Koroloff, 1990). Unlike conventional models, however, the home-based approach focuses more on expanding the network of a family's resources than on repairing family dysfunction (Henggeler & Borduin, 1990). While home-based services recognize and address problems in the family system, the primary emphasis is on building relationships between the family and various community resources.

Home-based services are a descendent of the "friendly visitor movement," in which social workers, inspired by Mary Richmond, called on families in their own homes. In the past social workers, more often than not, found themselves removing vulnerable children from harm's way. Unfortunately, this misguided altruism often undermined the family unit. Beginning in the 1970s, and influenced by the principles of deinstitutionalization and community care, there has been more of an effort to keep fragile families together and to prevent placement of children (McGowen & Meezan, 1983).

Family-focused outreach services entail more than just visiting families in their homes. Instead of precipitously removing troubled children from the home, in-home therapists use family crises to promote change within the family. In addition, rather than responding to every expressed problem with a referral to external services, home-based services are designed to work with the family's own internal resources.

Home-based therapists approach families with a collaborative mind-set and positive expectations. This "strength-based" approach, which assumes that families contain the resources to deal with their own problems, can also be applied to the expectation that competence is inherent in other agencies as well, such as other organizations involved with the family. Consequently, agencies and other influences are viewed not as adversaries but as potential partners in the treatment process.

Home-based services generally include four elements: family support services, therapeutic intervention, case management, and crisis intervention (Lindblad-Goldberg, Dore, & Stern, 1998). *Family support services* include respite care as well as concrete assistance with food, clothing, and shelter. *Therapeutic intervention* may include individual, family, or couples treatment. The overriding therapeutic goal is strengthening and stabilizing the family unit. Families are empowered by helping them utilize their own strengths and resources for solving problems rather that relying on out-of-home placement of the children. *Case management* involves developing links to community resources, including such things as medical care, welfare, education, job training, and legal services. *Crisis intervention* means making available twenty-four-hour emergency services, either with the home-based agency staff or by contracting with an outside mental health emergency service.

Marion Lindblad-Goldberg, one of the most articulate voices in the home-based movement, recommends introducing the concept of home-based services to the family in a session that includes as many members of the helping team as possible. From the start, it is important that parents be treated with respect and encouraged to form a collaborative partnership with the professional staff. Goals should be negotiated between the family and workers, and the structure of services being offered should be made as clear as possible.

When meeting a family in their home, it's a good idea to invite them to help create a task-oriented atmosphere so that home visits don't became either an annoyance or just a social occasion. Family members, for example, may be able to make suggestions about how best to reduce distractions.

Visiting a family at home gives a therapist the opportunity to show interest in the things family members may be proud of or that define their identity—such as children, pets, religious artifacts, mementos, awards, and so on. Looking through photo albums can be a valuable method in joining with a family and learning about their history and their hopes and dreams. Once a positive relationship has been established—but not before—the therapist can ask the family directly to reduce such distractions as heavy smoking, loud television playing, or barking dogs. (Barking cats are less likely to be a problem.)

Roles, rules, and boundaries that are implicit in an office setting may need to be spelled out in home-based work. Clarifying roles while in the home begins with defining what the process of treatment entails, the ground rules for sessions, and what the therapist's and family members' roles will be. The following comments illustrate the process of clarifying roles.

—Case Study—

"**B**efore we start, I want to say that I have no intention of coming here and telling you how to run your lives. I don't have any power to take your kids away or to make you do anything. My job is to help you figure out how you want to deal with your children. I can't solve your problems. Only you can do that.

"In our meetings, it's important for you to say whatever you think and feel. We need to be honest. If you're not honest with each other—and with me—therapy won't work. Tell me what you expect of me, and I'll tell you what I expect of you. I won't act like I have all the answers, because I don't.

"Will Grandmother be coming tonight? If not, that's okay, but I would like her to attend future sessions, because I'm sure she has valuable ideas to contribute.

"Tonight, I'd like to get to know each of you a little bit. After that, I'd like to hear what concerns each of you have about your family life and what you'd like to change."[3]

While many family therapists speak glibly about their "eco-systemic" orientation, home-based workers really must coordinate their efforts with a variety of other service systems. To do so, it is imperative to understand the concerns of other agencies involved with the family and to develop collaborative relationships with them. Rather than being critical of school personnel or juvenile justice workers who don't seem to support both the family and the child, home-based workers must learn to appreciate that these other agencies are equally concerned about the needs of their clients, even though their approaches may differ. A family served by multiple agencies that don't see eye to eye is no different from a child caught in a triangle between parents who can't function together as a team in the best interests of their child.

Operating with a systemic perspective begins with working collaboratively with other agencies. It also means keeping the entire family constellation in mind even when meeting with subsystems. Thus, for example, a therapist who meets individually with a disgruntled adolescent should remember that there are two sides to every story and that often the best way to support children is to support their parents' constructive efforts rather than to side uncritically with the children.

While in-home therapy offers a unique opportunity to influence families directly in their natural environment, seeing people in their living rooms also increases the pressures of *induction* into a family's problematic patterns. Working with a cotherapist may help minimize the tendency to be drawn unwittingly into the family's unproductive way of seeing things.

---

3. Adapted from Lindblad-Goldberg, Dore, & Stern, 1998.

Home-based therapists who don't work with cotherapists must make special efforts to maintain professional boundaries and to avoid being inducted into playing missing roles in the family. For example, if a child needs comforting, it is far better to support the parents in providing it than it is to take over that function.

The first priority in home-based work should be to demonstrate that the therapist is consistent and genuine. Having a connection with someone who can be counted on may be more important to families with a history of unmet dependency needs than having a worker who is powerful, smart, or controlling.

One of the most important things that happens in any form of psychotherapy is that client(s) create with their therapists the same but unsatisfying kind of relationship they have with most people. Perhaps the most important thing a therapist can do is to avoid being drawn into the usual pattern. The most dangerous pattern for home-based workers to repeat is moving in too close and then pushing clients to go where they are afraid or don't want to go. Rather than start pushing for change right away, it's often more effective to begin by recognizing the obstacles to change.

Beleaguered families fear abandonment; insecure therapists fear not being helpful. The worker who feels a pull to do everything for a client may subsequently feel overwhelmed by the family's needs and back away by setting rigid limits and withholding support. The "rescuer" then becomes another "abuser." This process reactivates the clients' anxiety and inevitably pushes them away. The lessons for the family are clear: Nothing will ever change—and don't trust anyone.

Medical Family Therapy and Psychoeducation

Over the past fifteen years a new conception of family therapy has emerged. Rather than solving problems, the goal of this approach is to help families cope with disabilities. This represents a shift from the idea that families cause problems to the idea that problems, like natural disasters, sometimes befall families. **Psychoeducational family therapy** emerged from working with schizophrenic patients and their families, whereas *medical family therapy* developed from helping families struggle with chronic illnesses such as cancer, diabetes, and heart disease.

Psychoeducation and Schizophrenia

The search for a cure for schizophrenia launched the field of family therapy in the 1950s. Ironically, five decades later, when we now know that schizophrenia involves a biological vulnerability of unknown origin, family therapy, or at least the psychoeducational model, is once again considered part of the most effective treatment for this baffling disorder.

The psychoeducational model was born of dissatisfaction with both traditional family therapy and psychiatric approaches to schizophrenia. As Carol Anderson, Douglas Reiss, and Gerald Hogarty (1986) lamented,

> We have blamed each other, the patients themselves, their parents and grandparents, public authorities, and society for the cause and for the too often terrible course of these disorders. When hope and money become exhausted, we frequently tear schizophrenic patients from their families, consigning them to the existential terror of human warehouses, single room occupancy hotels, and more recently to the streets and alleys of American cities. (p. vii)

In their attempts to get at the function of the schizophrenic's symptoms, family therapists urged family members to express bottled-up feelings and thus created sessions of highly charged emotion, which often did little more than stir up tension. After noticing the frequent decline in functioning of patients and increased anxiety in their families after such sessions, Anderson and her colleagues (1986) "began to wonder if most 'real' family therapy was in fact antitherapeutic" (p. 2).

Meanwhile, studies began to show that the patients who fared best after hospitalization were those who returned to the least stressful households. A British group, including George Brown, John Wing, Julian Leff, and Christine Vaughn, focused on what they called "expressed emotion" (EE) in the families of schizophrenics—particularly criticism, hostility, and emotional overinvolvement—and found that patients returning to high EE households had higher rates of relapse (Brown, Birley, & Wing, 1972; Vaughn & Leff, 1976; Vaughn et al., 1984).

With this in mind, three different groups in the late 1970s and early 1980s began experimenting with ways to reduce stress in the most common environments for schizophrenic patients—their parents' homes. Michael Goldstein led a group at UCLA (Goldstein et al., 1978) who designed a brief, structured model focused on anticipating the stresses a family was likely to face and reducing conflict around the patient. Following the Goldstein study, groups headed by Ian Falloon at the University of Southern California (whose model is primarily behavioral) and Carol Anderson at the Western Psychiatric Institute in Pittsburgh experimented with psychoeducational models.

Psychoeducators try not only to help families change their ideas about and interactions with patients but also to reverse the damage done by insensitive professionals. Instead of providing the information, support, and sense of control that these families need when in crisis, many mental health professionals ignore family members except to gather information—information about what went wrong. The implications of this line of questioning add to the guilt and shame family members already feel. No wonder many families either give up or get into antagonistic battles with these authoritarian professionals.

Psychoeducators seek to establish a collaborative partnership in which family members feel supported and empowered to deal with the patient. To achieve this kind of partnership, Anderson and her colleagues (1986) find that they must reeducate professionals to give up ideas that the family is somehow responsible for schizophrenia, reinforce family strengths, and share information with the family about schizophrenia. It is this information-sharing that constitutes the educational element of *psychoeducation*. Information about the nature and course of schizophrenia helps family members develop a sense of mastery—a way to understand and anticipate the often chaotic and apparently uncontrollable process.

One of psychoeducation's key interventions is to lower expectations, to reduce pressure on the patient to perform normally. For example, the goals for the first year following an acute episode are primarily the avoidance of a relapse and the gradual taking on of some responsibilities in the home. Family members are to view the patient as someone who's had a serious illness and needs to recuperate. Patients may need a great deal of sleep, solitude, and limited activity for some time following an episode; they may also seem restless and have trouble concentrating. By predicting these developments, psychoeducators try to prevent conflict between the patient and the family.

Anderson's psychoeducational approach looks very much like structural family therapy, except that the family's structural flaws are construed as the *result* of rather than *cause* of the presenting problem. Much of the therapy follows familiar themes: reinforcing generational boundaries, opening up the family to the outside world and developing support networks, urging parents to reinvest in their marriage, and getting family members to not speak or do for the patient.

Is the psychoeducational model effective? Yes. For example, in the study by Anderson and colleagues (1986),

Among treatment takers (n=90), 19% of those receiving family therapy alone experienced a psychotic relapse in the year following hospital discharge. Of those receiving the individual behavioral therapy, 20% relapsed, but *no* patient in the treatment cell that received both family therapy and social skills training experienced a relapse. These relapse rates constitute significant effects for both treatments when contrasted to a 41% relapse rate for those receiving only chemotherapy and support. (p. 24)

Other studies have shown equally impressive results (Falloon et al., 1982; Leff et al., 1982). There seems to be little question that psychoeducation can delay relapse and readmission to a hospital better than other approaches to schizophrenia.

Medical Family Therapy

If one considers schizophrenia a chronic disease, then psychoeducational family therapy can be seen as a specialized form of medical family therapy. Medical family therapists work with families struggling with illness or disability in much the same way as just described for families of schizophrenics.

Chronic illness often has a devastating impact. It can take over a family's life, ravaging health, hope, and peace of mind. As Peter Steinglass says, "it can be like a terrorist, who has appeared on the doorstep, barged inside the home and demanded everything the family has" (quoted in McDaniel et al., 1992, p. 21).

The demands of the illness interact with the qualities of the family, such as the family's life-cycle stage and the role the stricken family member plays; the family's leadership resources and degree of isolation; and their beliefs about illness and who should help, derived from their ethnicity and history with illness. With an awareness of these factors, therapists can help families prepare to deal with an illness or, if the

illness has been with them for years, gain perspective on their resulting polarizations and enmeshments.

Medical family therapists work in collaboration with pediatricians, family practitioners, rehabilitation specialists, and nurses. They advocate that near the time of diagnosis, families should receive a routine consultation to explore their resources relative to the demands of the illness or disability. They cite the growing body of research suggesting a strong relationship between family dynamics and the clinical course of medical conditions (Campbell, 1986) and more recent research showing that family therapy has a positive effect on physical health and health care usage (Law & Crane, 2000).

In the early 1990s the field came of age, with three books setting the pace (McDaniel et al., 1992; Ramsey, 1989; Rolland, 1994). It has now mushroomed into a whole new paradigm called *collaborative family health care,* with a large annual conference that began in 1996 and now offers fourteen plenaries and more than fifty workshops. There, well-known medical family therapists, such as John Rolland, Bill Doherty, Lorraine Wright, Susan McDaniel, and Thomas Campbell, present their work alongside experts in medicine, nursing, social work, and hospital administration. The hope and promise of this movement are to provide new careers for family therapists but also to become a new model for cost-effective and humane health care nationally.

In conclusion, psychoeducational and medical family therapy share many elements with the other models in this chapter which together represent a significant trend: a move away from an antagonistic relationship with families, toward a collaborative partnership. Therapists are now encouraged to look for a family's strengths rather than deficits and find ways to lift families out of the guilt and blame that often accompany their problems.

Managed Care

It seems ironic that with all the exciting developments in family therapy, the most powerful influence on the field today has nothing to do with clinical theory. **Managed care** companies increasingly control not only access to clients but also what kinds of therapy they receive, how long they can be treated, and how much therapists are paid.

In the first wave of managed care, therapists applied to be on panels to receive referrals. Once they received a referral, they had to ask permission from a case manager for more sessions and had to justify their treatment plans. Increasingly, managed care companies are finding this micromanagement too expensive, so the second wave involves incentives for therapists themselves to reduce costs. In this second wave therapists agree to "capitated" contracts under which they provide mental health services for a specific group at a preset annual fee. While the capitated system may discourage therapists from offering some services, at least therapists will be wrestling with their own consciences rather than with faceless strangers.

Therapists have reacted in a variety of ways. Some see managed care as a positive, or at least inevitable, correction to a situation that was out of control. They suggest that before managed care, psychotherapy was unaccountable and exploitative, with no incentive to contain runaway costs. These therapists learn how to please managed care companies and have plenty of business, even though they make less per hour. Others are trying to survive by increasing their marketing to clients who can pay out-of-pocket and by finding other ways to use their skills, such as divorce mediation; consulting to businesses, schools, and courts; teaching and leading workshops; and working in human resource departments. Still others are actively fighting the managed care tidal wave by organizing in groups that offer alternatives to managed care, by feeding the media a constant stream of managed care horror stories, and by pursuing antitrust suits.[4]

The final verdict on managed care isn't in yet. While there are huge profits to be made by those who want to restrict services, there is growing dissatisfaction with those restrictions. It's unlikely that we will return to the unrestricted days that some long for, and perhaps that's as it should be. It is likely, however, that as consumers realize they aren't getting the help they need, new alternatives will emerge to fill the demand, and these new alternatives will be more palatable to clients and therapists alike.

---

4.   One such group is the National Coalition of Mental Health Professionals and Consumers (telephone: 516-424-5232).

—Summary

During the past two decades, the family therapy movement ran into a series of hard-hitting critiques—from feminists, postmodernists, social constructionists, multiculturalists, and those who work with the abused, gays and lesbians, the poor, and the chronically ill. Therapists were challenged to become more collaborative; sensitive to differences in ethnicity, race, class, gender, and sexual orientation; and interested in beliefs and values rather than just actions and interactions. The family therapy expert was dethroned by the compassionate conversationalist.

This new interest in collaboration is no accident—it reflects a maturing of the field. The pioneers first encountered the family as a powerful adversary—"homeostatic," "resistant"— in part because they approached it with a built-in prejudice. Bent on rescuing "family scapegoats," they saw mothers as enemies to be overcome and fathers as peripheral figures to be ignored. Systems do resist change; but one reason family therapists encountered so much resistance was that they were too eager to change people, and too slow to understand them.

Family therapists taught us to see past individual personalities to the patterns that make them a family—an organization of interconnected lives governed by strict but unspoken rules. But in the process they created a mechanistic entity—the family system—and then set about doing battle with it. Most of the challenges that have rocked and reshaped family therapy have been in reaction to this mechanism. But if the systemic revolution went too far in one direction, the same may be true of some of its critics.

The feminist critique was the first and perhaps most influential of the challenges to family therapy's traditions. In taking a stand against mother bashing, feminists challenged the essence of systems thinking by pointing out that concepts like complementarity and circular causality can imply that subjugated women were as much to blame as their oppressors.

Family therapy's bridge to the twenty-first century was social constructionism. Much as was the case when the pioneers shifted their focus from individuals to families, this recent shift from behavior to cognition, and from challenging to collaborating, is opening up a new world of possibilities. We'll see just how exciting some of those possibilities are in the next few chapters.

Since Paul Watzlawick first brought out the constructivist implications of the MRI model in *The Invented Reality* (1984), family therapists have become increasingly aware of the power of the stories people tell themselves to shape their actions. As we shall see in Chapter 13, Michael White and his colleagues in the narrative movement have translated this insight into a powerful new approach to treatment. Helping clients construct new and more useful stories of their experience is surely an advance on the manipulative attempts to control and outwit them. But to the extent that narrative therapists merely substitute cognition for action and interaction, they risk ignoring all that we've learned about how family dynamics shape the lives of family members—regardless of what stories they tell themselves.

The two great values of postmodern skepticism are diversity and democracy. Surely, respecting multiple perspectives is a good thing. Two very positive expressions of this value are the rise of integrative models and a renewed respect for diverse forms of family organization. But it's not so good if we reject all norms and treat every individual as absolutely unique. This means we have no need for knowledge and no room for guidelines. Family therapists have embraced democracy by advocating nonhierarchical approaches and opposing the imposition of influence. But, as Bateson pointed out, hierarchy is inherent in nature; certainly families in treatment, like other social systems, need some kind of executive decision-making team.

The headline story of family therapy's evolution from first- to second-order cybernetics, from MRI to solution-focused therapy, from Milan systemic to Hoffman and Goolishian, and from constructivism to social constructionism and now narrative, is what's been in the forefront of intellectual discussion. All the while these front-page developments were taking place, family therapists practicing less trendy approaches (behavioral, psychoanalytic, structural, Bowenian, and experiential) have continued their work. So it can be a mistake to think that what's new and gets attention is the only or even major thing going on in the field.

The collaborative movement has raised new questions about the therapist's style of leadership. When Harlene Anderson and Harry Goolishian advocated a "collaborative approach," what was being rejected was the medical model—an authoritarian role model in which the clinician plays the expert, to whom the patient looks for answers. But being an expert doesn't mean being an ogre. Here the advance is challenging the medical model that, ironically, was perpetuated in such avant garde models of family therapy as the strategic and Milan systemic approaches. No longer do

we see the therapist as a technocrat of change. But that doesn't mean therapists shouldn't be experts—leaders in the process of change.

Finally, it should be said that, just as family therapy hasn't stood still in recent years, neither has the family. Today's family is evolving and stressed. We've gone from the complementary model of the family in the 1950s to a symmetrical version—though we haven't come to terms with the new model yet. Perhaps it's time to ask the question: As the American family struggles through this stressful time of transition, what concepts does family therapy offer to help us understand and deal with the protean family forms of the twenty-first century?

—Recommended Readings

Andersen, T. 1991. *The reflecting team.* New York: Norton.

Anderson, C. M., Reiss, D., and Hogarty, B. 1986. *Schizophrenia and the family: A practitioner's guide to psychoeducation and management.* New York: Guilford Press.

Avis, J. M. 1992. Where are all the family therapists? Abuse and violence within families and family therapy's response. *Journal of Marital and Family Therapy.* 18:225–232.

Fowers, B., and Richardson, F. 1996. Why is multiculturalism good? *American Psychologist.* 51:609–621.

Gergen, K. 1985. The social constructionist movement in modern psychology. *American Psychologist.* 40:266–275.

Goldner, V. 1985. Feminism and family therapy. *Family Process.* 24:31–47.

Goodrich, T. J., ed. 1991. *Women and power: Perspectives for family therapy.* New York: Norton.

Greenan, D. E., and Tunnell, G. 2002. *Couples therapy with gay men: A family systems model for healing relationships.* New York: Guilford Press.

Hare-Mustin, R. T., and Marecek, J. 1988. The meaning of difference: Gender theory, postmodernism

and psychology. *American Psychologist.* 43:455–464.

Held, B. S. 1995. *Back to reality: A critique of postmodern theory in psychotherapy.* New York: Norton.

Kellner, D. 1991. *Postmodern theory.* New York: Guilford Press.

Krestan, J., and Bepko, C. 1980. The problem of fusion in the lesbian relationship. *Family Process.* 19:277–289.

Laird, J., and Green, R. J. 1996. *Lesbians and gays in couples and families: A handbook for therapists.* San Francisco: Jossey-Bass.

Luepnitz, D. 1988. *The family interpreted: Feminist theory in clinical practice.* New York: Basic Books.

McDaniel, S., Hepworth, J., and Doherty, W. 1992. *Medical family therapy.* New York: Basic Books.

McGoldrick, M., Giordano, J., and Pearce, J. 1996. *Ethnicity and family therapy,* 2nd ed. New York: Guilford Press.

Rolland, J. 1994. *Helping families with chronic and life-threatening disorders.* New York: Basic Books.

Walsh, F., ed. 1993. *Normal family processes,* 2nd ed. New York: Guilford Press.

—References—

Ahrons, C., and Rogers, R. 1989. *Divorced families: Meeting the challenges of divorce and remarriage.* New York: Norton.

Andersen, T. 1991. *The reflecting team.* New York: Norton.

Anderson, C. M. 1995. *Flying solo.* New York: Norton.

Anderson, C. M., Reiss, D., and Hogarty, G. E. 1986. *Schizophrenia and the family: A practitioner's guide to psychoeducation and management.* New York: Guilford Press.

Anderson, H. 1993. On a roller coaster: A collaborative language systems approach to therapy. In *The new language of change,* S. Friedman, ed. New York: Guilford Press.

Anderson, H. 1997. *Conversation, language, and possibilities.* New York: Basic Books.

Anderson, H., and Goolishian, H. 1988. Human systems as linguistic systems: Preliminary and evolving ideas about the implications for clinical theory. *Family Process. 27:*371–394.

Anderson, W. T. 1990. *Reality isn't what it used to be.* San Francisco: Harper & Row.

Avis, J. M. 1988. Deepening awareness: A private study guide to feminism and family therapy. In *Women, feminism, and family therapy,* L. Braverman, ed. New York: Haworth Press.

Avis, J. M. 1992. Where are all the family therapists? Abuse and violence within families and family therapy's response. *Journal of Marital and Family Therapy. 18:*223–230.

Bailey, E. 1999. *Children in therapy: Using the family as a resource.* New York: Norton.

Barth, R., Pietrzak, J., and Ramier, M. 1993. *Families living with drugs and HIV.* New York: Guilford Press.

Beavers, W., and Hampson, R. 1990. *Successful families: Assessment and intervention.* New York: Norton.

Bograd, M. 1992. Values in conflict: Challenges to family therapists' thinking. *Journal of Marital and Family Therapy. 18:*243–253.

Boyd-Franklin, N. 1989. *Black families in therapy: A multisystems approach.* New York: Guilford Press.

Boyd-Franklin, N. 1993. Race, class, and poverty. In *Normal family processes,* F. Walsh, ed. New York: Guilford Press.

Boyd-Franklin, N., Steiner, G., and Boland, M. 1995. *Children, families, and HIV/AIDS.* New York: Guilford Press.

Brothers, B. J., ed. 1992. *Spirituality and couples: Heart and soul in the therapy process.* New York: Haworth Press.

Brown, G. W., Birley, J. L. T., and Wing, J. K. 1972. The influence of family life on the course of schizophrenic disorders: A replication. *British Journal of Psychology. 121:*241–258.

Burton, L. A., ed. 1992. *Religion and the family.* New York: Haworth Press.

Campbell, T. 1986. Family's impact on health: A critical review and annotated bibliography. *Family Systems Medicine. 4:*135–148.

Carl, D. 1990. *Counseling same-sex couples.* New York: Norton.

Combrinck-Graham, L. 1989. *Children in family contexts.* New York: Guilford Press.

Dattilio, F., ed. 1998. *Case studies in couple and family therapy.* New York: Guilford Press.

Doherty, W. 1991. Family therapy goes postmodern. *Family Therapy Networker. 15:*36–42.

Doherty, W. 1996. *The intentional family.* Reading, MA: Addison-Wesley.

Donovan, J. M., ed. 1999. *Short-term couple therapy.* New York: Guilford Press.

Ehrenreich, B. 1999. Nickel-and-dimed: On (not) getting by in America. *Harpers.* Jan. 37–52.

Elizur, J., and Minuchin, S. 1989. *Institutionalizing madness: Families, therapy and society.* New York: Basic Books.

Elkin, M. 1990. *Families under the influence.* New York: Norton.

Emery, R. 1994. *Renegotiating family relationships: Divorce, child custody, and mediation.* New York: Guilford Press.

Falicov, C. 1983. *Cultural perspectives in family therapy.* Rockville, MD: Aspen Systems.

Falicov, C. 1988. *Family transitions: Continuity and change over the life cycle.* New York: Guilford Press.

Falicov, C. 1995. Training to think culturally: A multidimensional comparative framework. *Family Process. 34:*373–388.

Falicov, C. 1998. *Latino families in therapy.* New York: Guilford Press.

Falloon, I. J. R., Boyd, J. L., McGill, C. W., Razani, J., Moss, H. B., and Gilderman, A. M. 1982. Family management in the prevention of exacerbations of schizophrenia. *New England Journal of Medicine. 306:*1437–1440.

Figley, C. 1985. *Trauma and its wake: The study and treatment of post-traumatic stress disorder.* New York: Brunner/Mazel.

Freeman, J., Epston, D., and Lobovits, D. 1997. *Playful approaches to serious problems.* New York: Norton.

Friedrich, W. 1990. *Psychotherapy of sexually abused children and their families.* New York: Norton.

Friesen, B. J., and Koroloff, N. M. 1990. Family-centered services: Implications for mental health administration and research. *Journal of Mental Health Administration. 17* (1):13–25.

Gergen, K. 1985. The social constructionist movement in modern psychology. *American Psychologist. 40:*266–275.

Gergen, K. 1991a. *The saturated self.* New York: Basic Books.

Gergen, K. 1991b. The saturated family. *Family Therapy Networker. 15:*26–35.

Gil, E. 1994. *Play in family therapy.* New York, Guilford Press.

Goldner, V. 1985. Feminism and family therapy. *Family Process. 24:*31–47.

Goldner, V. 1988. Generation and gender: Normative and covert hierarchies. *Family Process. 27:*17–33.

Goldner, V., Penn, P., Sheinberg, M., and Walker, G. 1990. Love and violence: Gender paradoxes in volatile attachments. *Family Process. 29:*343–364.

Goldstein, M. J., Rodnick, E. H., Evans, J. R., May, P. R., and Steinberg, M. 1978. Drug and family therapy in the aftercare treatment of acute schizophrenia. *Archives of General Psychiatry. 35:*1169–1177.

Goodrich, T. J., Rampage, C., Ellman B., and Halstead K., 1988. *Feminist family therapy: A casebook.* New York: Norton.

Green, R. J. 1998. Training programs: Guidelines for multicultural transformations. In *Re-visioning family therapy,* M. McGoldrick, ed. New York: Guilford Press.

Greenan, D. E., and Tunnell, G. 2003. *Couple therapy with gay men.* New York: Guilford Press.

Haley, J. 1976. *Problem-Solving therapy,* San Francisco: Jossey-Bass.

Haley, J. 1980. *Leaving home.* New York: McGraw-Hill.

Hansen, J. C. 1982. *Therapy with remarried families.* Rockville, MD: Aspen Systems.

Hardy, K. 1993. War of the worlds. *Family Therapy Networker. 17:*50–57.

Henggeler, S. W., and Borduin, C. M., eds. 1990. *Family therapy and beyond: A multisystemic approach to treating the behavior problems of children and adolescents.* Pacific Grove, CA: Brooks/Cole.

Imber-Black, E. 1988. *Families and larger systems: A family therapist's guide through the labyrinth.* New York: Guilford Press.

Imber-Black, E., Roberts, J., and Whiting, R. 1988. *Rituals in families and family therapy.* New York: Norton.

Ingoldsby, B., and Smith, S. 1995. *Families in multicultural perspective.* New York: Guilford Press.

James, K., and MacKinnon, L. 1990. The "incestuous family" revisited: A critical analysis of family therapy myths. *Journal of Marital and Family Therapy. 16:*71–88.

Johnson, T., and Keren, M. 1998. The families of lesbian women and gay men. In *Re-visioning family therapy,* M. McGoldrick, ed. New York: Guilford Press.

Kahn, M., and Lewis, K. G. 1988. *Siblings in therapy.* New York: Norton.

Krestan, J. 1988. Lesbian daughters and lesbian mothers: The crisis of disclosure from a family systems perspective. *Journal of Psychotherapy and the Family. 3:*113–130.

Laird, J. 1993. Lesbian and gay families. In *Normal family processes,* 2nd ed. F. Walsh, ed. New York: Guilford Press.

Laird, J., and Green, R. J. 1996. *Lesbians and gays in couples and families: A handbook for therapists.* San Francisco: Jossey-Bass.

LaSala, M. 1997. The need for thick skin: Coupled gay men and their relationships with their parents and in-laws. *Dissertation Abstracts International. 58:*4444-A.

Law, D., Crane, D., and Russell, D. 2000. The influence of marital and family therapy on health care utilization in a health-maintenance organization. *Journal of Marital and Family Therapy. 26:*281–291.

Lee, E. 1997. *Working with Asian Americans.* New York: Guilford Press.

Leff, J., Kuipers, L., Berkowitz, R., Eberlein-Vries, R., and Sturgeon, D. 1982. A controlled trial of social intervention in the families of schizophrenic patients. *British Journal of Psychiatry. 141*:121–134.

Lindblad-Goldberg, M., Dore, M. M., and Stern, L. 1998. *Creating competence from chaos.* New York: Norton.

Luepnitz, D. 1988. *The family interpreted: Feminist theory in clinical practice.* New York: Basic Books.

Madanes, C. 1990. *Sex, love and violence.* New York: Norton.

Markowitz, L. 1993. Walking the walk. *Family Therapy Networker. 17*:18–24, 27–31.

McDaniel, S., Hepworth, J., and Doherty, W. 1992. *Medical family therapy.* New York: Basic Books.

McGoldrick, M. 1993. Ethnicity, cultural diversity, and normality. In *Normal family processes,* F. Walsh, ed. New York: Guilford Press.

McGoldrick, M., ed. 1998. *Re-visioning family therapy.* New York: Guilford Press.

McGoldrick, M., Anderson, C., and Walsh, F., eds. 1989. *Women in families: A framework for family therapy.* New York: Norton.

McGoldrick, M., Giordano, J., and Pearce, J. 1996. *Ethnicity and family therapy,* 2nd ed. New York: Guilford Press.

McGoldrick, M., Pearce, J., and Giordano, J. 1982. *Ethnicity and family therapy.* New York: Guilford Press.

McGowen, B. G., and Meezan, W. 1983. *Child welfare: Current dilemmas, future directions.* Itasca, IL: Peacock.

Micucci, J. 1998. *The adolescent in family therapy.* New York: Guilford Press.

Miklowitz, D., and Goldstein, M. 1997. *Bipolar disorder: A family-focused treatment approach.* New York: Guilford Press.

Minuchin, P., Colapinto, J., and Minuchin, S. 1998. *Working with families of the poor.* New York: Guilford Press.

Minuchin, S. 1984. *Family kaleidoscope.* Cambridge, MA: Harvard University Press.

Minuchin, S., and Fishman, H. C. 1981. *Techniques of family therapy.* Cambridge, MA: Harvard University Press.

Minuchin, S., Montalvo, B., Guerney, B., Rosman, B., and Schumer, F. 1967. *Families of the slums.* New York: Basic Books.

Mirkin, M. P. 1990. *The social and political contexts of family therapy.* Boston: Allyn & Bacon.

Mirkin, M. P., and Koman, S. L., eds. 1985. *Handbook of adolescents and family therapy.* New York: Gardner Press.

Mitchell, S. 1993. *Hope and dread in psychoanalysis.* New York: Basic Books.

Morawetz, A., and Walker, G. 1984. *Brief therapy with single-parent families.* New York: Bruner/Mazel.

Ogbu, J. 1989. Cultural models and educational strategies of non-dominant people. 1989 Catherine Molony Memorial Lecture. New York: City College Workshop Center.

Okun, B. 1996. *Understanding diverse families.* New York: Guilford Press.

Patterson, J., Williams, L., Graul-Grounds, C., and Chamow, L. 1998. *Essential skills in family therapy.* New York: Guilford Press.

Pinderhughes, E. 1989. *Understanding race, ethnicity and power: The key to efficacy in clinical practice.* New York: Free Press.

Pittman, F. 1987. *Turning points: Treating families in transition and crisis.* New York: Norton.

Prest, L., and Keller, J. 1993. Spirituality in family therapy. *Journal of Marital and Family Therapy. 19*:137–148.

Price, J. 1996. *Power and compassion: Working with difficult adolescents and abused parents.* New York: Guilford Press.

Ramsey, R. N. ed. 1989. *Family systems in medicine.* New York: Guilford Press.

Reitz, M., and Watson, K. 1992. *Adoption and the family system.* New York: Guilford Press.

Rolland, J. 1994. *Helping families with chronic and life-threatening disorders.* New York: Basic Books.

Root, M., Fallon, P., and Friedrich, W. 1986. *Bulimia: A systems approach to treatment.* New York: Norton.

Roth, S., and Murphy, B. 1986. Therapeutic work with lesbian clients: A systemic therapy view. In *Women and family therapy,* M. Ault-Riche and J. Hansen, eds. Rockville, MD: Aspen Systems.

Rubin, L. 1994. *Families on the faultline.* New York: HarperCollins.

Saba, G., Karrer, B., and Hardy, K. 1989. *Minorities and family therapy.* New York: Haworth Press.

Sager, C., Brown, H. S., Crohn, H., Engel, T., Rodstein, E., and Walker, L. 1983. *Treating the remarried family.* New York: Brunner/Mazel.

Sanders, G. 1993. The love that dares not speak its name: From secrecy to openness in gay and lesbian affiliations. In *Secrets in families and family therapy,* E. Imber-Black, ed. New York: Norton.

Schwartz, R. C. 1995. *Internal family systems therapy.* New York: Guilford Press.

Schwartzman, J. 1985. *Families and other systems: The macrosystemic context of family therapy.* New York: Guilford Press.

Selekman, M. 1997. *Solution-focused therapy with children.* New York: Guilford Press.

Seligman, M., and Darling, R. B. 1996. *Ordinary families, special children: A systems approach to childhood disability,* 2nd ed. New York: Guilford Press.

Sells, S. 1998. *Treating the tough adolescent.* New York: Guilford Press.

Sheinberg, M. 1992. Navigating treatment impasses at the disclosure of incest: Combining ideas from feminism and social constructionism. *Family Process.* 31:201–216.

Smith, C., and Nylund, D. 1997. *Narrative therapies with children and adolescents.* New York: Guilford Press.

Sprenkle, D. 1985. *Divorce therapy.* New York: Haworth Press.

Stanton, M. D., Todd, T., and Associates. 1982. *The family therapy of drug abuse and addiction.* New York: Guilford Press.

Steinglass, P., Bennett, L., Wolin, S. J., and Reiss, D. 1987. *The alcoholic family.* New York: Basic Books.

Taibbi, R. 1996. *Doing family therapy.* New York: Guilford Press.

Treadway, D. 1989. *Before it's too late: Working with substance abuse in the family.* New York: Norton.

Trepper, T. S., and Barrett, M. J. 1989. *Systemic treatment of incest: A therapeutic handbook.* New York: Brunner/Mazel.

Vaughn, C., and Leff, J. 1976. The measurement of expressed emotion in the families of psychiatric patients. *British Journal of Psychology.* 15:157–165.

Vaughn, C. E., Snyder, K. S., Jones, S., Freeman, W. B., and Falloon, I. R. H. 1984. Family factors in schizophrenic relapse: Replication in California of British research on expressed emotion. *Archives of General Psychiatry.* 41:1169–1177.

Visher, E., and Visher, J. 1979. *Stepfamilies: A guide to working with stepparents and stepchildren.* New York: Brunner/Mazel.

Visher, E., and Visher, J. 1988. *Old loyalties, new ties: Therapeutic strategies with stepfamilies.* New York: Brunner/Mazel.

Wachtel, E. 1994. *Treating troubled children and their families.* New York: Guilford Press.

Walker, G. 1991. *In the midst of winter: Systemic therapy with families, couples, and individuals with AIDS infection.* New York: Norton.

Wallerstein, J., and Kelly J. 1980. *Surviving the breakup: How children and parents cope with divorce.* New York: Basic Books.

Walsh, F. 1982. *Normal family processes.* New York: Guilford Press.

Walsh, F. 1993. *Normal family processes,* 2nd ed. New York: Guilford Press.

Walsh, F. 1998. *Strengthening family resistance.* New York: Guilford Press.

Walsh, F., ed. 1999. *Spirituality in families and family therapy.* New York: Guilford Press.

Walsh, F., and McGoldrick, M., eds. 1991. *Living beyond loss: Death in the family.* New York: Norton.

Walters, M., Carter, B., Papp, P., and Silverstein, O. 1988. *The invisible web: Gender patterns in family relationships.* New York: Guilford Press.

Watzlawick, P., ed. 1984. *The invented reality.* New York: Norton.

Solution-Focused Therapy

Building on Past Successes

Judging by its popularity, solution-focused therapy may be the treatment for our times. Its pragmatic minimalism, cognitive emphasis, and easily teachable techniques have combined to make it the hottest thing on the workshop circuit—and its promise of quick solutions has endeared it to the managed care industry. Indeed, when asked to indicate their therapeutic orientation, many applicants for provider status call themselves "solution-focused" regardless of whether they have any training in this approach. The spate of books on the model is further evidence of its popularity (de Shazer, 1988, 1991b, 1994; O'Hanlon & Weiner-Davis, 1989; Walter & Peller, 1992; Furman & Ahola, 1992; Cade & O'Hanlon, 1993; O'Hanlon & Martin, 1992; Miller, Hubble, & Duncan, 1996; Berg & Dolan, 2001; Lipchik, 2002), as well as to the model's application to couples (Weiner-Davis, 1992; Hudson & O'Hanlon, 1992) and to alcoholism (Berg & Miller, 1992).

What is it—besides its remarkably appealing name—that has made the solution-focused approach so popular? Solution-focused therapy takes the elegance of the MRI model and turns it on its head. While the one aims to help clients do less of what doesn't work, the other promotes more of what does. Both of these deliberately pragmatic approaches focus on the presenting complaint and aim to resolve it as parsimoniously as possible. The MRI model does so by looking for failed attempts to solve the presenting problem, while the solution-focused approach focuses on **exceptions**—times when the problem wasn't a problem.

The real difference between these two approaches, however, isn't merely a matter of where they punctuate problem sequences but that, while the MRI model focuses on behavior, the solution-focused model emphasizes cognition. It's assumed that people who come to therapy are already capable of behaving effectively but that their effectiveness has been blocked by a negative mind-set. Drawing their attention to times when they were doing well helps clients to see things differently:

Problems are seen to maintain themselves simply because they maintain themselves and because clients depict the problem as *always happening.* Therefore, times when the complaint is absent are dismissed as trivial by the client or even remain completely unseen, hidden from the client's view. Nothing is actually hidden, but although these exceptions are open to view, they are not seen by the clients as differences that make a difference. For the client, the problem is seen as primary (and the exceptions, if seen at all, are seen as secondary), while for the therapists the exceptions are seen as primary; interventions are meant to help clients make a similar inversion, which will lead to the development of a solution. (de Shazer, 1991b, p. 58)

The art of solution-focused therapy then becomes a matter of helping clients not only see that their problems have exceptions, but also to realize that these exceptions are solutions that they still have in their repertoires. To get past the idea that exceptions just happen, the solution-focused therapist asks questions like, "How did you do that?"

Sketches of Leading Figures

Solution-focused therapy grew from the work of Steve de Shazer, Insoo Berg, and their colleagues at the Brief Family Therapy Center (BFTC) in Milwaukee, Wisconsin. This private training institute was started in 1979 when some of the staff at a Milwaukee community agency who were drawn to the MRI model became dissatisfied with the agency's constraints and broke off to form the BFTC. The initial group included married partners Steve de Shazer and Insoo Berg, Jim Derks, Elaine Nunnally, Marilyn La Court, and Eve Lipchik. Their students included John Walter, Jane Peller, and Michele Weiner-Davis. De Shazer is considered the primary developer of solution-focused theory, though he no longer does much clinical work, preferring to devote his time to research and writing. De Shazer had worked earlier in Palo Alto, and was strongly influenced by the MRI approach.

*S*teve de Shazer, *founder of solution-focused therapy.*

Insoo Kim Berg is known primarily as a clinician but has also contributed substantially to theory. She has trained therapists all over the world and has applied the model to alcoholism (Berg & Miller, 1992), marital therapy (Berg, 1994a), and family-based services to the poor (Berg, 1994b).

Other notable figures include Eve Lipchik, who worked at the BFTC for eight years until she left in 1988 to found ICF Consultants with Marilyn Bojean. Lipchik pioneered the application of the solution-focused model to wife battering (Lipchik & Kubicki, 1996), and recently published one of the most useful books about how to do solution-focused therapy (Lipchik, 2002).

After training with de Shazer, Michele Weiner-Davis converted an agency program in Woodstock, Illinois, to the solution-focused

*I*nsoo Kim Berg, a *leading practitioner of the solution-focused model.*

model. Weiner-Davis (1992) applied the model to marital problems in her popular book *Divorce-Busting.* Scott Miller, now based in Chicago, was with the BFTC for three years, directing the alcohol and drug treatment services, and has written widely about the model.

John Walter and Jane Peller are in private practice together in Chicago. They trained at the BFTC and, after writing a book laying out the steps of the approach (Walter & Peller, 1992), have become popular presenters on the workshop circuit.

Bill O'Hanlon, who has recently moved his practice from Omaha, Nebraska, to Santa Fe, New Mexico, was never formally associated with the BFTC but, having been trained by Milton Erickson and as a prominent translator of Erickson's ideas, the step toward the solution-focused approach was an easy one. He and Weiner-Davis (O'Hanlon & Weiner-Davis, 1989) have collaborated to expand on the groundwork laid by de Shazer.

Yvonne Dolan lives in Hammond, Indiana, and teaches workshops in solution-focused therapy and Ericksonian hypnosis. Along with Insoo Berg, she recently published *Tales of Solutions,* a collection of case studies illustrating various solution-focused techniques (Berg & Dolan, 2001).

Theoretical Formulations

The assumptions that form the basis of solution-focused therapy are straightforward and uncomplicated. As Insoo Berg said, "We are very proud of our simplicity. It took a great deal of discipline to become so simple" (Wylie, 1990, p. 27).

One of the defining characteristics of family therapy has always been its focus on the present, where problems are maintained, not on the past that "caused" them. Solution-focused therapists prefer to focus on the future, where problems can be solved. They contend that

therapists don't need to know a great deal about the nature of the problems that bring people to therapy. Indeed, a problem's solution may be totally unrelated to how it developed.

Like the MRI model, solution-focused therapists believe that people are constrained by narrow, pessimistic views of their problems into perpetuating rigid patterns of false solutions. As O'Hanlon and Weiner-Davis (1989) put it:

> So, the meanings people attribute to behavior limit the range of alternatives they will use to deal with a situation. If the methods used do not produce a satisfactory outcome, the original assumption about the meaning of the behavior is generally not questioned. If it were, new meanings might be considered, which in turn might prompt a different, perhaps more effective, approach. Instead, people often redouble their efforts to solve the problem in an ineffective way, thinking that by doing it more, harder or better (e.g., more punishments, more heart-to-heart talks, and so on) they will finally solve it. (p. 48)

Solution-oriented therapists reject the notion that problems serve ulterior motives or that people are ambivalent about their problems. They assume that clients *really do* want to change. De Shazer (1984), in fact, declared the death of resistance as a concept, suggesting that when clients don't follow directives, it's their way of "cooperating" by teaching the therapist the best way to help them.

The MRI model was strongly influenced by Milton Erickson's view of people as containing untapped, unconscious resources. According to this view, people may only need slight shifts of perspective to release their potential. Early solution-focused theory showed more evidence of this Ericksonian view of people as resourceful. Since the postmodern revolution, the theorizing has moved increasingly from releasing resources to changing the way people talk about their problems.

Constructivists believe that language shapes reality. Through the influence of the analytic philosopher Ludwig Wittgenstein (1958), de Shazer has gradually moved toward a more radical position—namely, that language *creates* reality. "Language constitutes 'the human world and the human world constitutes the whole world' " (de Shazer & Berg, 1993, p. 73). Nothing exists outside of language. Thus, de Shazer (1993) asserts that "There are no wet beds, no voices without people, no depressions. There is only *talk* about wet beds, *talk* about voices without people, *talk* about depression" (p. 89). If one accepts that language is reality, therapy becomes a relatively simple procedure. All that's needed is to change the way people talk. From this idea flows the solution-focused goal to steer clients from "problem-talk" to "solution-talk."

Recently a number of authors have shifted their attention from the idea that the "words are magic" (to paraphrase the title of de Shazer's last book [1994]) to look at the power of the therapist–client relationship (Tuyn, 1992; Metcalf, Thomas, Duncan, Miller, & Hubble, 1996; Butler & Powers, 1996; Simon, 1996; Lipchik, 1997). As William Butler and Keith Powers (1996) assert, "[Solution-focused therapy] works . . . but it is not the model or the techniques that really matter. It is the attitude of the therapist and the interchange between the client and the therapist that is the real key" (p. 245). Eve Lipchik (1997) echoes this sentiment, saying that "solution-focused therapy is a philosophy, not a collection of techniques."

Dvorah Simon (1996) suggests that the ability of the therapist to bring clients a sense of hope "seems to me to be at the spiritual heart of this work—placing longing, desire, and the belief that a better life is not only possible but available in a central position around which everything else can flow" (p. 46). Others suggest that solution-focused therapy works by making clients feel good about themselves, by highlighting their strengths and successes—the cheerleader effect (Metcalf, et al., 1996).

Normal Family Development

Solution-focused therapists borrow from constructivism the idea that there are no absolutes; therefore therapists shouldn't impose their views of normality. The search for structural flaws that characterizes most other forms of psychotherapy is rejected. As de Shazer (1991b) writes, "Structuralist thought points to the idea that symptoms are the result of some underlying problem, a psychic or structural problem such as incongruent hierarchies, covert parental conflicts, low self-esteem, deviant communication, repressed feelings, 'dirty games,' etc." The solution-focused therapist dispenses with such speculations and instead is interested only in language—the way people describe themselves and their problems.

Therapy, then, is highly relativistic. The therapist should be concerned only with the complaints that families present and shouldn't impose values by suggesting that clients address other, unpresented, problems (O'Hanlon & Weiner-Davis, 1989).

> Solution-oriented therapists don't believe that there is any single "correct" or "valid" way to live one's life. We have come to understand that what is unacceptable behavior in one family or for one person is desirable behavior in another. Therefore, clients, not therapists, identify the goals to be accomplished in treatment. (p. 44)

Development of Behavior Disorders

In the solution-focused world, this subject is closed. Just as they steer clients away from speculating about problem formation, solution-focused therapists also dissuade therapists from such conjecture. Their conviction is that solutions to problems are often unrelated to the way the problems developed, and that tracking etiological factors is engaging in "problem talk"—exactly what they seek to avoid.

Problem talk and the related preoccupation with the problem is the furthest solution-focused therapists go in identifying etiological factors. They believe that problem-focused thinking keeps people from recognizing the effective solutions they've already used or could come up with in the future.

Goals of Therapy

As with the MRI model, the goal of solution-focused therapy is to resolve presenting complaints by helping clients do or think something different so as to become more satisfied with their lives. More than MRI therapists, however, solution-focused therapists trust clients to reach their own goals. They believe that people already have the skills to solve their problems but have lost sight of these abilities because their problems loom so large to them that their strengths are crowded out of the picture. Sometimes a simple shift in focus from what's not going well to what they're already doing that works can remind clients of, and expand their use of, these resources. At other times, people may have to search for abilities that they aren't currently using and bring those dormant skills to bear on their problems.

At another level, the goal is simply to help clients begin to shift their language from talking about problems to talking about solutions. Once people begin speaking about what they can do effectively, what resources they have, what they've done in the past that worked, solution-focused therapists have achieved their primary aim. From that point on the work is to build on solutions that emerge from those more optimistic conversations.

Because solution-focused therapists aren't out to reorganize personalities or family structures, they're willing to settle for modest goals. A homeless woman may simply need to find a place to live, a single man may want the courage to ask someone for a date. If a client's goal is vague—"I'd like to feel happier"—or utopian—"I never want to be sad again"—they ask questions designed to translate the goal into something clear and specific. Helping clients set clear and achievable goals is a major intervention in itself, and the process of thinking about the future and what one wants to be different is a large part of what solution-focused therapists do (Walter & Peller, 1996).

Conditions for Behavior Change

The task of solution-focused therapy is to help clients amplify *exceptions* to their problems—effective solutions of which they are already in possession. The therapist strives to work from the client's understanding of the problem and seeks behavioral change. But, although the model is consistent with the brevity and pragmatism of strategic approaches, solution-focused therapists emphasize the collaborative construction of solution-oriented narratives.

From Berg and de Shazer's (1993) point of view, what's needed for change is that therapist and client engage in a discussion that shifts the way the problem is "languaged."

> Rather than looking behind and beneath the language that clients and therapists use, we think that the language they use is all that we have to go on. . . . What we talk about and how we talk about it makes a difference, and it is these differences that can be used to make a difference (to the client) . . . we have come to see that the meanings arrived at in a therapeutic conversation are developed through a process more like negotiation than the development of understanding or an uncovering of what it is that is "really" going on. (p. 7)

Thus, changing the way people talk about their problems is all one needs to accomplish because "as the client and therapist talk more and more about the solution they want to construct together, they come to believe in the truth or reality of what they are talking about. This is the way language works, naturally" (Berg & de Shazer, 1993, p. 9). This is why solution-focused therapy can be so brief—it's a lot easier to get clients to talk differently about their problems than it is to produce significant changes in behavior patterns or intrapsychic structure. The assumption is, of course, that getting people to talk positively will help them think positively—and, ultimately, to act positively to solve their own problems.

From the Ericksonian perspective that informed de Shazer's early thinking, the therapist is to create an atmosphere in therapy in which people's strengths can move out of the shadows and into the foreground. De Shazer (1985, 1986) found these strengths lurking in the spaces between problems—in the "behaviors, perceptions, thoughts, feelings, and expectations that are outside the complaint's constraints. These exceptions . . . can be used as building blocks in the construction of a solution . . . solutions involve determining what 'works' so that the client can do more of it" (de Shazer, 1986, p. 48).

To illustrate this process, de Shazer (1986) used the metaphor of a man whose problem is that he wants to leave Chicago. To solve this problem much of the following information has little relevance: how the man got to Chicago; how long he's been there; what's kept him from leaving earlier; or the nature of Chicago. Instead, the traveler need only focus on where he wants to go, and on the resources at his disposal for getting there.

It may be, however, that in discussing his wishes, he remembers some good days in Chicago, and that while these exceptions had seemed insignificant, in thinking about what made them exceptional, he realizes that those were days when he was having fun with other people. He decides that he doesn't really have to

leave Chicago after all, and instead directs his energy toward spending more time with people he enjoys. It's this focus on goals, resources, and exceptions to the problem that characterizes the solution-focused model. With that focus people will either find a solution to their original problem (leaving Chicago) or decide that their problem is something else (not enough time with friends) and find a solution for that.

Therapy

Assessment

Therapists using the solution-focused model studiously avoid any assessment of how problems develop. Nor are they interested in evaluating patterns of behavior that might be perpetuating those problems. What they are concerned with identifying are those patterns of behavior that existed when the problem wasn't operative.

Instead of dwelling on past problems, solution-focused therapists concentrate on assessing future goals. Clarifying goals is a proactive process that begins in the first session and continues throughout therapy, and that might take the form of some of the following questions (adapted from Lipchik, 2002):

1. What do you think the problem is now?
2. How will you know when the problem is solved?
3. How will you know you don't have to come here anymore? What will the signs be?
4. What will have to be different for that to happen in terms of your behavior, thoughts, and feelings?
5. What will you notice that is different about others involved in the situation?
6. What is your wildest fantasy about what you want to have happen?

Because they aren't interested in assessing family dynamics, solution-focused therapists don't feel the need to convene any particular grouping of people, like whole families. Instead, they say that anyone who's concerned about the problem should attend sessions. They also need very little intake information because they want to hear clients' constructions of their problems firsthand and without preconceptions.

Following de Shazer (1988), practitioners of this approach distinguish between relationships with clients of varying levels of motivation. Some clients have complaints but seem unwilling to work on them, while others seem ready and eager to make changes. The point de Shazer makes is that these distinctions aren't qualities of character but qualities of the therapeutic relationship, and are therefore fluid. With an apparently unmotivated complainer the therapist's job is to engage in a solution-focused conversation, compliment the client, and possibly give an assignment to observe exceptions to the problem. By not pushing for change but shifting attention away from problems and toward solutions, the relationship may evolve into one in which the client becomes a customer for change. Once a client becomes a customer for change, the therapist can take a more active role in helping the client look for exceptions.

Therapeutic Techniques

Interventions are delivered in a three-step process: The therapist (1) actively reframes the problem in a more positive, functional light and compliments clients on their perseverance and resourcefulness; (2) clarifies the logical bind clients have created for themselves; and (3) links a hypnotic-like directive to an inevitable sign of progress.

For example, parents of a misbehaving child might be complimented on their persistent concern and the child's equally persistent way of getting their attention. The therapist might further say, "You continue to be concerned, yet none of your punishments is working." And, fi-

nally, "I don't know what you'll be doing differently the next time your child acts out."

In the early 1980s, de Shazer's team began experimenting with this orientation toward solutions by giving all clients the same assignments, which they called "formula tasks." Some of these assignments seemed to be universally effective regardless of the problem. One of these tasks, given in the first session, was to ask clients to observe what happens in their life or relationships that they want to continue (de Shazer, 1985). This assignment helped reorient people from focusing on the bad things in their lives to thinking about and expecting the good. These therapists also found that this shift in perspective seemed to build on itself—to create a more positive outlook that led to better interactions, which in turn reinforced and expanded that positive outlook.

This has become known as the **formula first-session task** and is the standard assignment given at the end of the first session. "Between now and the next time we meet, I would like you to observe, so you can describe to me next time, what happens in your (family, life, marriage, relationship) that you want to continue to have happen" (de Shazer, 1985, p. 137).

With the success of these formula tasks, it began to dawn on the team that the process of change could be initiated without much knowledge of the problem or the personalities of those suffering from it. They began to focus on ways to foster and amplify this problem-solving faculty in people, which they believed was inhibited by a focus on problems and deficits. This thinking led to the development of the "exception question" and the "miracle question," two mainstays of the solution-focused approach (de Shazer, 1985, 1988).

The *exception question* ignores the picture of the problems clients hold up and, instead, directs their attention to the negative of that image—to times when they didn't have the problems. By exploring these times and what was different about them, clients find clues to what they can do to expand those *exceptions*. In addition, clients may find that in light of the fact that they were able to change or eliminate the problem, their outlook toward it may change. It seems less insurmountable.

—Case Study—

Mary, who suffers from bulimia, may remember several times the previous week when she had the urge to binge and purge but didn't. She discovers that at those times she was away from her parents and didn't feel like she was disappointing them. She decides that it's time to become more independent.

"Thus, a solution is a joint product of therapist and client talking together about whatever it is that the problem/complaint is not" (Berg & de Shazer, 1993, p. 21).

Eve Lipchik (2002) recommends asking for exceptions using some of the following questions: "Are there times when you don't have this problem?" "What is different at those times?" "How does that make a difference to you?" "For others?" "What will make it possible for more of that to happen?" "What small changes will you notice?" "What will others notice about you?"

Asking for exceptions allows the therapist and client to build on past successes. Failing that, the therapist can ask why things aren't worse—"How did you manage that?"—and then build on that accomplishment. "Coping questions" can help clients realize that they are more resourceful, simply for enduring, than they realize. "What keeps you going under such difficult circumstances?" "How come things aren't worse?" "What have you done to keep them from getting worse?" If the client provides an answer, the therapist can build on it with questions about how that endurance can be maintained, and how more of that effort can be brought to bear. If the client offers no evidence of having done anything to keep matters from getting worse, the therapist can ask, "Do you think things can get worse?" "What will that be like for you?" "For others?" "What is the smallest thing you can imagine doing that could make a difference?"

When finding and building on exceptions is effective, there may be little need for further intervention. But in cases where it is difficult for clients to come up with past success, it may be useful to ask them to imagine future success, using the miracle question.

The **miracle question** is: "Suppose one night, while you were asleep, there was a miracle and this problem was solved. How would you know? What would be different?" This question activates a problem-solving mind-set by giving people a vision of their goal, perhaps in the same way that visualization of the perfect serve helps a tennis player. It also helps clients look beyond the problem to see that what they really want may not be the elimination of the problem per se, but instead to be able to do the things that the problem has been obstructing. If the therapist can encourage them to begin doing those things despite the problem, suddenly the problem may not loom as large.

—Case Study—

Mary, who suffers from bulimia, says that if not for her symptoms she'd get closer to people and have more fun. If, with her therapist's encouragement, Mary begins to take interpersonal risks and has more fun, then her bulimia may become less of a problem, less of an obstacle in her life, which might also increase her ability to control it.

The miracle question is most effectively introduced when clients complain in vague terms.

—Case Study——————

A therapist working with a distressed couple tried to shift them away from complaining and toward solutions by asking a series of constructive questions, such as: "How do you usually solve problems like this?" "When you're feeling more appreciated by your partner, what is he doing differently?" Although the couple had plenty of complaints about each other, the husband was able to respond positively to the therapist's question, "So you both agree, the other feels as bad as you do; any ideas what the solution might be?"

> *Husband:* "Yeah, the solution would be more acceptance."
>
> *Therapist:* "On her part? On your part?"
>
> *Husband:* "Well, for both of us."
>
> *Wife:* "Well, the only solution I see is similar, but I've lost trust in him."

When the therapist asked her to elaborate on what a solution might look like, the wife kept coming back to her complaints. And so the therapist asked a modified form of the miracle question in hopes of shifting her toward a more specific vision of a direction for positive change. "And if by some miracle that trust would be there tomorrow, how would you know? What would the signs be?"[1]

———

More recently, **scaling questions** have become an important ingredient in solution-focused therapy. Scaling questions were first introduced to help therapists and clients talk about vague topics such as depression and communication, where it's difficult to identify concrete behavioral changes and goals (Berg & de Shazer, 1993).

The therapist asks the depressed client, for example, "On a scale of one to ten, with one being how depressed you felt when you called me and

———

1. This vignette is paraphrased from Friedman and Lipchik (1999).

ten being how you feel the day after the miracle, how do you feel right now?"

The client might say two and the therapist might say, "So you feel a little better than when you called. How did you achieve this improvement?" Or the therapist might ask, "What do you think you need to do to achieve a three?" In this way, the therapist and client can recognize and nurture small changes toward the goal rather than being stuck in the "I'm either depressed or I'm not" kind of thinking that typifies such problems.

Scaling questions are often used to ask clients to quantify their confidence that they can maintain their resolve. "On a scale of 1 to 10, how confident are you that you will be able to avoid losing your temper this week?" In practice this device has a kind of "prove it" implication. The response is followed up by asking clients what they might do to increase the odds of success. "What do you have to do to stick to your guns this time?" Scaling questions are a clever way of anticipating and disarming resistance and backsliding, and of encouraging commitment to change.

Scaling questions can also be used to reduce goals that might seem dauntingly far off to more manageable small steps. "On a scale of 1 to a 100, with 1 being never and 100 being always, what percentage of the time would you say you are experiencing the problem?" Then, in response to the answer, "How many points would it have to go down for you to feel slightly better?" "What would a step from 75 to 70 look like?" "What would you be doing differently?" "What would others be doing differently?"

A Woman Who Was Stronger Than She Thought. To illustrate the process of solution-focused therapy we will summarize a session reported by Insoo Berg and Peter De Jong (1996). The client, Lucinda, is a nineteen-year-old African American mother of two children, ages three and four, who had been removed from Lucinda and placed with foster parents eighteen months earlier. Lucinda had been physically abused by a former partner. This is all the information the therapist chose to know before seeing Lucinda.

—Case Study—

Rather than asking about what her problems are, the therapist begins the session by asking "What can I do that would be helpful to you?" Lucinda says that she is depressed and stressed out and wants someone to talk to because her kids aren't with her. She also alludes to the abusive relationship with a man she no longer sees.

Without any further discussion of Lucinda's feelings or predicament, the therapist asks a series of questions about how Lucinda was able to break off from the abusive relationship. Lucinda says it was hard because the man, Marvin, didn't want to leave and was threatening to kill her and that he beat her when he saw her. The therapist said, "So that's when most women sort of become weak and they take him back. How come you didn't?" Lucinda replied, "A couple of times I did because I was scared. And the more I kept getting back with him, it got worse and worse. And then he ended up hurting my son." She goes on to describe how Marvin broke the child's leg, which is why she lost custody of her children, and that's when she drew the line and wouldn't take him back. The therapist punctuates her story with comments highlighting Lucinda's competence in protecting her kids like, "But some women . . . would either get scared of him or, you know, somehow think that he's gonna change and take him back," and "Wow, I'm amazed by this. How did you do this?"

After letting Lucinda know she's impressed with her competence, the therapist turns to goal-setting questions. Lucinda says she wants her kids back and doesn't want to be afraid of Marvin anymore. She wants advice on how to be strong with Marvin. The therapist says, "Sounds like you already are, though."

To clarify Lucinda's goal, the therapist asks her the miracle question. She asks Lucinda to imagine that after she goes to bed that night a miracle will happen and her problems–that she wants her kids back and wants to be stronger–will be solved. How would Lucinda be able to tell

that the miracle has happened? Lucinda responds that her kids would be home and she would be very excited. The therapist asks her to elaborate on that miracle picture and Lucinda spends much of the session happily describing what she'd do with her children and how she and they would feel, with the therapist interjecting questions like, "Where did you learn to be such a good, loving mother?"

The therapist asks a scaling question, "On a scale of 1 to 10, 10 stands for how you will be when you finally get your kids back and 1 is what you were like when your children were taken away from you, where would you say things are today?" Lucinda says between 8 and 9. The therapist asks how she was able to climb that high. Lucinda says it's because she's sure her kids are coming back soon.

After giving more compliments, the therapist takes a break and returns to summarize her feedback. She says that it makes sense that Lucinda would be depressed given what she's lost and what she's experienced in her life, but the therapist is amazed at how Lucinda's used what she's learned. "And that's really absolutely amazing to me. For someone as young as you are . . . you are very wise already." The therapist also compliments her again on breaking up with Marvin. Lucinda agrees with all this, so the therapist says, "At this point I'm not sure if we even need to get together again. What do you think?" Lucinda agrees that she doesn't need any more help and they end the session. She never called for another appointment and her children were returned to her.

Berg and De Jong (1996) believe that during the solution-focused conversation Lucinda's perceptions of herself as depressed and her passive demeanor shifted. They think she left with a clearer sense of what she wanted and how to make it happen.

Solution-focused therapists hold that if both client and therapist can reorient themselves in the direction of strengths—exceptions to the problem, clarified goals, and strategies to achieve them—then therapy can be quite brief. Two assumptions justify this belief. The first draws again from constructivism and the power of suggestion. As O'Hanlon and Weiner-Davis (1989) explain,

> Since what you expect influences what you get, solution-oriented therapists maintain those presuppositions that enhance client-therapist cooperation, empower clients, and make our work more effective and enjoyable. We hold assumptions which focus on strengths and possibilities; fortunately, these assumptions also help create self-fulfilling prophecies. (p. 34)

If one perspective is as valid as the next, why not assume that solutions can be found easily and quickly?

The second assumption is borrowed from the MRI model—that a small change is usually all that's needed because it can snowball into bigger changes. As O'Hanlon and Weiner-Davis (1989) put it, "Once a small positive change is made, people feel optimistic and a bit more confident about tackling further changes" (p. 42).

With these two assumptions about change, the solution-focused theorists have fashioned a set of pivotal questions and tasks designed to create an optimistic perspective and start the snowball rolling. In Lucinda's case, the therapist used the miracle question, exception questions, coping questions ("How did you do that?"), in-session compliments, and end-of-session feedback that emphasized and summarized her competencies. Lucinda left with the sense that the therapist thought she could achieve her goals.

Compliments, which are an important part of solution-focused therapy, are conveyed with questions that take the general form of "How did you do that?"—or, to be more accurate, "Wow! How did you do that?" Notice that this phrasing calls attention to the fact that the person has already done something. Rather than asking questions like "Have you ever had a job before," asking "What kinds of jobs have you had before" invites clients to describe their successes and thus helps foster more self-confidence (Berg & Dolan, 2001).

To be effective, compliments should point toward what to do more, not what to eliminate. Most clients know what's wrong but have run out of ideas about what to do to avoid repeating the same old ineffective solutions. Compliments, both direct and indirect, can be used to highlight successful strategies and keep clients focused on those that work (Berg & Dolan, 2001).

Solution-focused therapy is often practiced using a team approach, with one therapist in the session and one or more colleagues observing behind a one-way mirror. Whether working with a team or alone, the interviewing therapist usually takes a five- or ten-minute break near the end of the session. During this time the therapist (with the team or alone) composes a summary message to the clients. The summary message consists of four elements (Lipchik, 2002):

1. Feedback on what the therapist has heard during the session
2. Compliments on positive steps already taken
3. A framework within which to place the client's predicament, usually emphasizing the normality of the situation
4. A suggested task to be carried out between sessions

The overall goal of the summary message is to provide a new and more hopeful perspective on the problem and to engender hope and positive expectations.

> So, for example, the therapist might begin by saying, "What I heard you say today is. . . ." This statement includes what the therapist heard the clients say (using the clients' language as much as possible), their goals, progress, and comments about their feelings or emotions. Next, the therapist offers compliments, reinforces positive changes, normalizes, reframes, or presents information from a developmental perspective. Finally, a suggestion is made. This can be as simple as "Continue doing what you're already doing" or one more specifically designed to

guide the clients toward doing something different. (Friedman & Lipchik, 1999, p. 332)

The summary message begins with a summation of what the therapist heard the clients say during the interview, including the problem, its background, the clients' goals, and pre-session progress and strengths. "What I heard you tell me today, Mr. and Mrs. X, is that. . . ." "Did I hear all of you correctly?" "Is there anything of importance that I omitted or that you want to add?"

This summary is followed by a statement reflecting the therapist's reaction, including an expression of empathy ("I'm not surprised you're so depressed!"), a reflection of the emotional impact on the client ("My sense is that you must really be hurting a lot"), compliments on presession changes or strengths ("I was impressed by how many things you've tried to make things better"), and some comment on the clients' shared goals.

The therapist then makes a suggestion about noticing or building on positives. "I would suggest that you notice what Patrick is doing at school that you want him to continue doing." "Patrick, I would suggest that you try to notice what you like about what's happening at school with the kids and your teacher and what you want to continue to have happen."

Among the suggestions used commonly in solution-focused therapy are the following:

1. Assign the formula first session task (de Shazer, 1985). "Between now and next time we meet, I would like you to observe what happens in your family that you want to continue to have happen."

2. Do more of what works. "Since you said that you usually can talk together when you go for a walk, maybe you should try that once or twice and see what happens."

3. Do something different. "You mentioned that when you rely on Janine to be responsible for her own homework, she often fails to do it.

Maybe you should try something different?" If a client says, "I've said the same thing over and over again until I'm blue in the face," the suggestion to try something different invites the client to discover his or her own solution.

The suggestion to do something different can be given as an experiment, as illustrated by Insoo Berg's example of parents, exasperated by their son's encopresis, who when given the suggestion to try something different, started filling the boy's potty seat with water and a toy boat, telling him that his job was to sink the boat (Berg & Dolan, 2001). It worked!

4. Go slowly. This suggestion, taken from the MRI model, is designed to help clients overcome fear and resistance to change by asking about possible negative consequences of changing and warning against trying to change too rapidly. "I have what may seem like a strange question: Could there possibly be any advantages to things staying the way they are?"

5. Do the opposite. This suggestion, also taken from the MRI model, is based on the notion that many problems are maintained by the attempted solution. Suggesting that client(s) try the opposite of what they have been doing is especially useful for problems that exist between just two people (one member of a couple, or one parent who's having trouble with a child).

If scolding a child for being bad isn't working, parents can be encouraged to start praising her for being good. If a husband's attempts to avoid conversations with his wife about their relationship aren't working, he could try initiating them when he's in the mood.

6. Assign the "prediction task" (de Shazer, 1988). "Before you go to bed tonight predict whether the problem will be better or the same tomorrow. Tomorrow night rate the day and compare it with your prediction. Think about what may have accounted for the right or wrong prediction. Repeat this every night until we meet again."

As you can see, the compliments and suggestions of the summary message continue the basic thrust of the solution-focused approach, drawing attention to the family's resources and encouraging them to capitalize on their strengths in order to focus on solutions rather than problems.

Evaluating Therapy Theory and Results

Although some have criticized solution-focused therapy as being simplistic, there are useful ingredients in the approach that can help clients step out of their pessimism and move toward constructive action. Like any model in the early stages of evolution, it has been presented at times in a cookbook style that has led therapists with limited experience to use it as a set of formulaic techniques. More recently, some solution-focused therapists have recognized this problem and have stressed the importance of the overall philosophy and the relationship with clients.

Eve Lipchik, for example, points out that the "speed and success of solution construction depend on the therapist's ability to stay connected with the clients' reality throughout the course of therapy. This is the underpinning for the whole collaborative process, the grease that keeps the axles turning" (Lipchik, 1999, p. 329). Like any other therapy, the solution-focused approach isn't likely to be very effective if therapists, in a rush to get to their own agenda, fail to listen to clients and make them feel understood.

To their credit, solution-focused therapists have done research and reported results that weren't necessarily what they expected. One study of the process of solution-focused therapy stirred things up a bit. Linda Metcalf (1993; Metcalf et al., 1996) interviewed six couples who were considered to have achieved good outcome at the BFTC. She also interviewed their therapists. She found that in several ways what the therapists said happened (and what solution-focused theory says should happen) didn't match the clients' experiences.

For example, in discussing what was helpful, therapists focused primarily on the techniques they used, whereas clients were far more likely to point to qualities of their relationship with the therapist. In addition, while all the therapists believed that the decision to terminate therapy had been reached collaboratively, four of the six couples thought that their therapist had made the decision unilaterally, and some of them felt pushed out prematurely. The study also found that the therapists generally took a more directive role than is suggested by the solution-focused literature.

In reviewing Lucinda's experience, described earlier, a case could be made that the therapist steered the interview in a certain upbeat direction and that the decision to stop after one session was less than mutual. After the therapist said, "At this point I'm not sure if we even need to get together again. What do you think?" It would have taken a very assertive client to say "No, I need more sessions."

The issue of whether solution-focused therapy is genuinely collaborative or directive has been raised frequently (Wylie, 1990; Storm, 1991; Lipchik, 1992, 1993, 1996; Efron & Veendendaal, 1993; Efran & Schenker, 1993; Miller, 1994; Nylund & Corsiglia, 1994; O'Hanlon, 1996). It has even been called "solution-forced" therapy by some people because of the perceived tendency for therapists to pressure clients into discussing only the positive and aggressively disregarding anything negative. As Efran and Schenker (1993) ask, "what assurance is there that clients of solution-focused therapists haven't simply learned to keep their complaints to themselves in the presence of the therapist?" Acknowledging this concern, Eve Lipchik (1997) writes that "I have occasionally worked with clients who describe their experience with their past solution-focused professional as he or she having been too positive and not providing opportunity for talking about things that really bothered them" (p. 167).

Solution-focused therapists themselves have expressed reservations about the model's injunction to remain constantly upbeat (Storm, 1991; Lipchik, 1992, 1993; Efron & Veenendaal, 1993). As Cheryl Storm (1991) reported, "I have found that being relentlessly solution-focused is a mismatch for some clients. These individuals insist on talking about the problem in detail and, if ignored, fire the therapist. I thought I was misapplying the approach but now believe . . . I overemphasized change." Others echo these sentiments: "When we attempt to use these models and stances exclusively, we build up a sense of wrongness and futility, as if we were somehow pulling the wool over the eyes of clients and ourselves" (Efron & Veenendaal, 1993, p. 17).

Like Lipchik, some solution-focused therapists are reading the feedback. According to Bill O'Hanlon (1996) "Carl Rogers taught us years ago that listening respectfully to clients and letting them know we can hear their perceptions and feelings and that we accept them as they currently are is a prerequisite for most people to cooperate in the change process" (p. 85).

Similarly, William Butler and Keith Powers (1996) stress the importance of validating the client's experience of the problem, and note the absence of such validation in the solution-focused literature.

> During the first interview the client complained about feeling increasingly depressed due to recent losses. . . . The therapist listened intently, reflected her feelings, and made many empathic comments. The most important thing the therapist did, however, was to *not ask* a series of future-oriented questions. . . . In the second interview, one week later, the client again told details of her long history of depression and loss. The therapist picked up on the theme of multiple losses and the many years of struggle. (p. 230)

It was only after going over in detail and empathizing with the large number of losses over the past ten years that the therapist introduced a solution-focused question: "But when I look over this long list [of losses] and consider what you've been through, I can't help but wonder— how do you keep it from getting worse?" (p. 230). The authors conclude that it was crucial to allow the client to fully express her struggles and have her experience validated before shifting the conversation to her strengths.

The problem some solution-focused therapists may have with this line of thinking is that the model could lose its claim to being distinctively brief. It may take several sessions before some clients feel fully understood and acknowledged. If they added an acknowledgement stage to the current model, wouldn't solution-focused therapy begin to resemble the usual supportive therapy, both in duration and in practice?

In other words, the refusal to talk about problems, which is what makes solution-focused therapy unique, turns out to be problematic. Reassuring someone who's worried that there's nothing to worry about isn't very reassuring. It can make you believe that your feelings aren't valid, because you wouldn't have them if you would only look at the bright side of things. Most people aren't very eager to be changed by someone they feel doesn't understand them.

We hope that this debate helps solution-focused therapists continue to move away from the formulaic way the model was originally packaged. Many of the techniques are no doubt valuable to clients if properly timed and flexibly applied. But techniques can obscure therapists' intuitive humanity. We hope students will remember Michele Weiner-Davis's (1993) candid confession that she doesn't always practice what she preaches: " . . . my clients cry and express pain, anger, disappointment and fears just as they might in any other therapist's office. And I respond with compassion . . . my therapy story [what she presents in workshops] is not the total picture of how I do therapy" (p. 157).

—Summary———————————————

Solution-focused therapy is a direct descendant of the MRI approach, though it reverses the emphasis from what doesn't work to what does. Where the MRI approach is totally focused on problems, solution-focused therapy is totally focused on solutions. The idea is that people often get stuck in their problems because by trying to get to the bottom of them they overlook solutions that are sometimes right under their noses.

This notion has led to the development of a set of techniques for changing "problem talk" into "solution talk." These techniques include: exception questions (e.g., "Can you think of a time when you didn't have the problem? What were you doing then?"); the miracle question (e.g., "Suppose you went to sleep and a miracle happened such that when you awoke, your problem was solved. What would be different?"); scaling questions (e.g., "On a scale from 1 to 10, how do you feel now compared to when you called?"); coping questions (e.g., "Given how bad that was, how were you able to cope?"); the formula first-session task ("After you leave today, observe what happens that you want to continue during the next week."); and giving compliments ("Wow, you must be very smart to have thought of that!"). These techniques are put into practice as soon as possible to keep the work brief and to discourage clients from dwelling on the negative side of their experience.

More recently, therapists have questioned the model's emphasis on technique and speculated that qualities of the therapist–client relationship may be at the heart of the model's effectiveness. This has led to a call for greater collaboration with clients such that their feelings are acknowledged and validated before introducing solution-focused techniques.

Solution-focused therapy continues to have enormous appeal in the world of psychotherapy. Some of its popularity relates to the number of therapists who are struggling to find ways to feel effective while living with managed care's limited number of sessions. Because of its reputation for brevity, solution-focused treatment is favored by managed care companies, so therapists can get approval to use it. In addition, its formula version is relatively easy to learn—the basics can be picked up in a few workshops—and its upbeat nature makes it more enjoyable for many therapists. Yet its easy-to-learn formula leads some therapists to dismiss it as superficial once they get stuck. They don't understand that the techniques only work within the context of the solution-oriented philosophy, which takes time to assimilate.

Critics question if the therapist is really having a respectful conversation with a client when the therapist only praises, searches for exceptions, and coaxes optimism. Do such insistently upbeat dialogues have the effect of silencing people's doubts and their pain? Can the solution-focused therapist find a way to honor client perceptions that don't fit into the formula? Can clients trust the feedback of someone who constantly strives to find things to praise and never challenges or questions them? Can clients be honest regarding the outcome of their therapy with someone who seems to want so much for them to feel better about things?

Other questions highlight the model's strengths; for example, isn't it important for therapists to have clear, concrete guidelines so therapy doesn't become vague and directionless? Isn't it more empowering to help people envision their future goals and focus on their strengths than on their problems and deficits? If people's experience of pain is tied to the way they think or talk about it, then isn't it better to use language to lead people out of pain than to dwell on it?

Solution-focused therapy is struggling to answer all these questions and thereby find a coherent identity for the twenty-first century. We hope that this evolution won't be dictated entirely by the constraints of managed care or dogmatic adherence to doctrine. Instead, we imagine that the maturing of solution-focused therapy will reflect a growing appreciation that while a focus on solutions can be helpful, people need acknowledgement for their lived experience, which isn't always upbeat.

—Recommended Readings

de Shazer, S. 1988. *Clues: Investigating solutions in brief therapy.* New York: Norton.

de Shazer, S. 1991. *Putting difference to work.* New York: Norton.

Lipchik, E. 2002. *Beyond technique in solution-focused therapy.* New York: Guilford Press.

Miller, S., Hubble, M., and Duncan, B. 1996. *Handbook of solution-focused brief therapy.* San Francisco: Jossey-Bass.

Walter, J., and Peller, J. 1992. *Becoming solution-focused in brief therapy.* New York: Brunner/Mazel.

—References

Berg, I. K. 1994a. A wolf in disguise is not a grandmother. *Journal of Systemic Therapies. 13:* 13–14.

Berg, I. K. 1994b. *Family-based services: A solution-focused approach.* New York: Norton.

Berg, I. K., and De Jong, P. 1996. Solution-building conversations: Co-constructing a sense of competence with clients. *Families in Society: The Journal of Contemporary Human Services.* June, 376–391.

Berg, I. K., and de Shazer, S. 1993. Making numbers talk: Language in therapy. In *The new language of change,* S. Friedman, ed. New York: Guilford Press.

Berg, I. K., and Dolan, Y. 2001. *Tales of solutions: A collection of hope-inspiring stories.* New York: Norton.

Berg, I., and Miller, S. 1992. *Working with the problem drinker: A solution-focused approach.* New York: Norton.

Butler, W., and Powers, K. 1996. Solution-focused grief therapy. In *Handbook of solution-focused brief therapy,* S. Miller, M. Hubble, and B. Duncan, eds. San Francisco: Jossey-Bass.

Cade, B., and O'Hanlon, W. 1993. *A brief guide to brief therapy.* New York: Norton.

de Shazer, S. 1984. The death of resistance. *Family Process. 23:* 11–21.

de Shazer, S. 1985. *Keys to solutions in brief therapy.* New York: Norton.

de Shazer, S. 1986. An indirect approach to brief therapy. In *Indirect approaches in therapy,* S. de Shazer and R. Kral, eds. Rockville, MD: Aspen Systems.

de Shazer, S. 1987. Minimal elegance. *Family Therapy Networker.* September/October, 59.

de Shazer, S. 1988. *Clues: Investigating solutions in brief therapy.* New York: Norton.

de Shazer, S. 1991a. Muddles, bewilderment, and practice theory. *Family Process. 30:* 453–458.

de Shazer, S. 1991b. *Putting difference to work.* New York: Norton.

de Shazer, S. 1993. Creative misunderstanding: There is no escape from language. In *Therapeutic conversations,* S. Gilligan and R. Price, eds. New York: Norton.

de Shazer, S. 1994. *Words were originally magic.* New York: Norton.

de Shazer, S., and Berg, I. K. 1993. Constructing solutions. *Family Therapy Networker. 12:* 42–43.

Efran, J., and Schenker, M. 1993. A potpourri of solutions: How new and different is solution-focused therapy? *Family Therapy Networker. 17* (3): 71–74.

Efron, D., and Veenendaal, K. 1993. Suppose a miracle doesn't happen: The non-miracle option. *Journal of Systemic Therapies. 12:* 11–18.

Friedman, S., and Lipchik, E. 1999. A time-effective, solution-focused approach to couple therapy. In *short-term couple therapy,* J. M. Donovan, ed. New York: Guilford Press.

Furman, B., and Ahola, T. 1992. *Solution talk: Hosting therapeutic conversations.* New York: Norton.

Hudson, P., and O'Hanlon, W. H. 1992. *Rewriting love stories: Brief marital therapy.* New York: Norton.

Lipchik, E. 1986. Purposeful interview. *Journal of Strategic and Systemic Therapies. 5:* 88–99.

Lipchik, E. 1992. Interview. *Journal of Strategic and Systemic Therapies. 11* (4): 22–26.

Lipchik, E. 1993. "Both/and" solutions. In *The new language of change,* S. Friedman, ed. New York: Guilford Press.

Lipchik, E. 1996. Mr. Spock goes to therapy. *Family Therapy Networker.* Jan/Feb, 79–84.

Lipchik, E. 1997. My story about solution-focused brief therapist/client relationships. *Journal of Systemic Therapies.* 16:159–172.

Lipchik, E. 2002. *Beyond technique in solution-focused therapy.* New York: Guilford Press.

Lipchik, E., and Kubicki, A. 1996. Solution-focused domestic violence views: Bridges toward a new reality in couples therapy. In *Handbook of solution-focused brief therapy,* S. Miller, M. Hubble, and B. Duncan, eds. San Francisco: Jossey Bass.

Metcalf, L. 1993. The pragmatics of change in solution-focused brief therapy. Unpublished doctoral dissertation. Texas Women's University, Denton.

Metcalf, L., Thomas, F., Duncan, B., Miller, S., and Hubble, M. 1996. What works in solution-focused brief therapy: A qualitative analysis of client and therapist's perceptions. In *Handbook of solution-focused brief therapy,* S. Miller, M. Hubble, and B. Duncan, eds. San Francisco: Jossey-Bass.

Miller, S. 1994. The solution-conspiracy: A mystery in three installments. *Journal of Systemic Therapies. 13:* 18–37.

Miller, S., Hubble, M., and Duncan, B. 1996. *Handbook of solution-focused brief therapy.* San Francisco: Jossey-Bass.

Nylund, D., and Corsiglia, V. 1994. Becoming solution-focused in brief therapy: Remembering something important we already knew. *Journal of Systemic Therapies. 13:* 5–12.

O'Hanlon, W. 1996. Case commentary. *Family Therapy Networker.* Jan/Feb: 84–85.

O'Hanlon, W., and Martin, M. 1992. *Solution oriented hypnosis: An Ericksonian approach.* New York: Norton.

O'Hanlon, W. H., and Weiner-Davis, M. 1989. *In search of solutions: A new direction in psychotherapy.* New York: Norton.

Satir, V. 1964. *Conjoint family therapy.* Palo Alto, CA: Science and Behavior Books.

Simon, D. 1996. Crafting consciousness through form: Solution-focused therapy as a spiritual path. In *Handbook of solution-focused brief therapy,* S. Miller, M. Hubble, and B. Duncan, eds. San Francisco: Jossey-Bass.

Storm, C. 1991. The remaining thread: Matching change and stability signals. *Journal of Strategic and Systemic Therapies.* 10:114–117.

Tuyn, L. K. 1992. Solution-focused therapy and Rogerian nursing science: An integrated approach. *Archives of Psychiatric Nursing.* 6:83–89.

Walter, J., and Peller, J. 1992. *Becoming solution-focused in brief therapy.* New York: Brunner/Mazel.

Walter, J., and Peller, J. 1996. Rethinking our assumptions: Assuming anew in a postmodern world. In *Handbook of solution-focused brief therapy,* S. Miller, M. Hubble, and B. Duncan, eds. San Francisco: Jossey-Bass.

Weiner-Davis, M. 1992. *Divorce-busting.* New York: Summit Books.

Weiner-Davis, M. 1993. Pro-constructed realities. In *Therapeutic conversations,* S. Gilligan and R. Price, eds. New York: Norton.

Wittgenstein, L. 1958. *The blue and brown books.* New York: Harper & Row.

Wylie, M. S. 1990. Brief therapy on the couch. *Family Therapy Networker. 14:* 26–34, 66.

Narrative Therapy

Restoring Lives

The narrative approach that now dominates family therapy is a perfect expression of the postmodern revolution. When all knowledge is regarded as constructed rather than discovered, it's fitting that the leading approach to family therapy is concerned with the ways people construct meanings rather than the ways they behave.

The central assumption is that personal experience is fundamentally ambiguous. This doesn't mean that experience isn't real or that it's necessarily mysterious or opaque, but that understanding human experience, including one's own, is never simply a process of seeing it or analyzing it. The elements of human experience are understood only through a process that organizes those elements, puts them together, assigns meaning, and prioritizes them. To say that experience is fundamentally ambiguous is to say that its meaning isn't inherent or apparent, but that it lends itself to multiple interpretations.

To illustrate how experience is shaped by the language we use to describe it, consider the difference between calling the heart-racing tension most people feel before speaking in public "stage fright" or "excitement." The first description makes this familiar agitation a problem, something to overcome. The second suggests that it's a natural, almost inevitable, response to standing up in front of people whose approval you hope to win.

Whether people experience stage fright or excitement depends on how they interpret their arousal. Strategic therapists gave clients reframes—new interpretations—for their experience: "The next time you're speaking, just think of yourself as excited rather than frightened." Narrative therapists recognize that such interpretations don't take unless they fit the stories people construct about themselves. A man whose life story is that he's boring will have trouble seeing his trembling hands as due to excitement, no matter how hard someone tries to sell that frame. If the same man were helped to construct a new, more positive, story about himself, the reframe becomes unnecessary. He will automatically begin to interpret his reactions as excitement because, if he thinks he's interesting, he will expect people to enjoy what he has to say.

Life is complicated, so we find ways to explain it. These explanations, the stories we tell ourselves, organize our experience and shape our behavior. Unfortunately, the stories most clients bring to treatment are discouraging. They selectively highlight past events that confirm negativism and minimize contradictory events.

The stories we tell ourselves are powerful because they determine what we notice and remember, and therefore, how we face the future. Imagine, for example, what things a woman who thought of herself as "reasonably successful" would remember from high school and how this version of events would affect her approach to college. Then picture what the same past and future would look like if that woman thought of herself as "never quite good enough."

Unlike the cybernetic metaphor, which focused the field on self-defeating patterns of *behavior*, the narrative metaphor focuses on self-defeating *cognitions*—the stories people tell themselves about their problems. With the cybernetic metaphor, therapy meant blocking maladaptive patterns of interaction—with or without the clients' understanding of the process. The narrative metaphor, on the other hand, focuses on clients' understanding and experience, expanding their attention to allow them to consider alternative ways of looking at themselves and their problems.

Systems thinking was once the inspiration for the field, but narrative therapists criticize systems thinking and replace it with the narrative metaphor. Family therapists used to work mainly with whole families and rarely addressed the issues of individuals; narrative therapists spend more time helping individuals reexamine themselves than discussing family conflicts. Family therapists were interested in the family's impact on the problem; narrative therapists are interested in the problem's impact on the family.

Stories don't mirror life, they shape it. That's why people have the interesting habit of becoming the stories they tell about their experience. It's also why therapists in too much of a hurry to impose their own perspectives on clients often fail—and why, by delving deeply into people's stories, narrative therapists are able to understand and influence what makes them act as they do.

Sketches of Leading Figures

Michael White, avatar of the narrative movement, lives in Adelaide, South Australia. He and his wife, Cheryl White, are based at the Dulwich Centre in Adelaide, out of which comes training, clinical work, and publications related to White's approach. The *Dulwich Centre Newsletter,* a quarterly journal, is the major vehicle through which White's ideas are disseminated. In addition, the Dulwich Centre has published several collections of his writings and interviews (available by writing to Dulwich Centre Publications, Hutt Street, P.O. Box 7192, Adelaide, South Australia 5000).

Now in his fifties, White initially worked as an electrical and mechanical draftsman before realizing that he preferred working with people to working with machines. Not surprisingly, he became staunchly antimechanistic and rejects systems thinking and cybernetics because of their mechanical qualities. In 1967 he trained to be a social worker and has been struggling

*M*ichael White, founder of the narrative approach to family therapy.

for over thirty years to find ways to help people. Some of his early experiences on inpatient units soured him on traditional approaches to therapy and piqued his interest in the writings of Michel Foucault and Erving Goffman, who criticized the dehumanizing processes of institutions and expert discourses.

In the late 1970s White became interested in the work of Gregory Bateson but found himself more interested in what Bateson said about how people construe the world than in the behavioral patterns of systems-based models. Under the influence of Bateson and Foucault, White crystallized his original ideas about "externalizing" problems (regarding them as something operating on persons, rather than as something they're doing).

David Epston, a family therapist from Auckland, New Zealand, is the second most influential shaper of the narrative movement. Through his interest in anthropology, Epston encountered the narrative metaphor and convinced White that it was more useful for clients than cybernetics. He'd always had an interest in literature and for years was known as a storyteller, writing the "Story Corner" for the *Australian and New Zealand Journal of Family Therapy*.

Epston has contributed to most aspects of narrative theory and practice, but in particular has emphasized that to maintain their new narratives, clients need supportive communities. He fostered the development of "leagues"—groups of clients battling the same problem, such as the Anti-Anorexia/Anti-Bulimia League of New Zealand. He serves as archivist for a number of such leagues, collecting tapes and letters that provide ideas to others about the resourceful ways that people have escaped from their problems.

He also pioneered the use of letter writing to clients, pointing out that long after the influence of the therapist's presence has faded, clients can read letters that bolster their new stories and resolve. Epston coauthored with White two collections of writings that have served as bibles for the narrative model (White & Epston, 1990; Epston & White, 1992), and has more recently coauthored a book of creative narrative techniques for working with children and their families (Freeman, Epston, & Lobovits, 1997).

Jill Freedman and Gene Combs direct a small training center in Evanston, Illinois. Before joining the narrative camp, they were strategic therapists and political activists, drawn to White's approach in large part by its emphasis on issues of social justice. This combination of former strategic therapist and political activist characterizes the backgrounds of many prominent narrative therapists. Their book, *Narrative Therapy* (Freedman & Combs, 1996) is an excellent, practical guide to doing narrative therapy.

Jeffrey Zimmerman and Vicki Dickerson are codirectors of the Bay Area Family Therapy Training Associates and together with John Neal conduct training in narrative therapy for the Mental Research Institute (MRI) in Palo Alto. These two creative therapists pioneered the use of narrative therapy with difficult adolescents and with couples (Dickerson & Zimmerman, 1992; Zimmerman & Dickerson, 1993). Their most recent book, *If Problems Talked: Adventures in Narrative Therapy* (Zimmerman & Dickerson, 1996), is a useful explication of narrative practice, animated by the novel device of personifying problems and having them speak about how "they" conspire to take over peoples' lives.

Stephan Madigan (1994; Madigan & Epston, 1995) is a therapist in Vancouver, British Columbia, who has contributed to narrative theory and founded the Vancouver Anti-Anorexia/Anti-Bulimia League, a grassroots organization that provides support for members and has become politically active, educating public and professional groups and protesting images in the media that promote "body-guilt." This group represents a logical extension of the narrative movement's therapy of liberation, helping people organize not only to create a supportive subculture but also to take an active role in trying to humanize the dominant culture.

Other prominent narrative therapists include Kathe Weingarten and Sallyann Roth at the Family Institute of Cambridge, and Janet Adams-Wescott in Tulsa, Oklahoma.

Harlene Anderson and the late Harry Goolishian, who developed a collaborative, conversational approach to family therapy (described in Chapter 10), can be seen as forerunners of the narrative model. Their work was based on the premise that problems are maintained in language and are subsequently dissolved through conversation. By adopting a "not-knowing" stance, Goolishian and Anderson subsumed their expertise to allow clients to become the experts on their own lives. The link between this work and the narrative school was the belief that conversation generates meaning, and that therapy should be a collaborative enterprise.

Theoretical Formulations

The narrative approach first found its way into psychotherapy in the hermeneutic tradition in psychoanalysis. Following Freud, classical analysts believed that there was one correct way to interpret experience. Patients might not understand their dreams or symptoms, because their motives were unconscious, but an analyst possessed of the truth of psychoanalytic theory could discover unconscious meaning much like an archeologist uncovers the buried remains of the past. Then in the 1980s, revisionists such as Donald Spence, Roy Schafer, and Paul Ricoeur began to argue against this positivistic conception of psychoanalytic reality.

The truth of experience, they said, isn't discovered, it's created. The goal of therapy shifted from historical truth to narrative intelligibility. The challenge was to construct truths in the service of self-coherence—not a true picture of the past. The therapist became more of a poet or novelist than an archeologist.

Family therapists found this narrative metaphor extremely useful. As they began to ask clients about their stories, therapists came to recognize how much narrative accounts affected clients' perceptions and interpretations of those perceptions. Life stories function as filters that screen out experiences that don't fit the plot line or, if they can't be screened out, distort events until they somehow fit. Consider the following example:

─Case Study─────────

According to Tim, Kayla was never satisfied. All she did was complain. Their apartment, the furniture, her wardrobe—nothing was ever good enough. No matter what they had, she wanted more.

Kayla had no idea what Tim was talking about. She was, in fact, perfectly content. Well, except maybe for one thing. Every time she'd see a picture in a magazine of a beautiful sofa or a pretty dress, she'd point it out to Tim. "Wow, look at that," she'd say, "maybe we should get one of those." She was just dreaming out loud. But to Tim, who was brought up never to ask for anything, Kayla's fantasies felt like complaints. Notice, however, that it wasn't so much what Kayla said that hurt Tim, but how he interpreted it.

Looking deeper, it turned out that Tim was never satisfied with his own accomplishments. Growing up with a mother who wasn't given much to praise, Tim dreamt of someday doing great things. Unfortunately, his own very real achievements never lived up to his fantasies. Sure, other people praised him, but he still secretly dreamed the grand and glorious dreams of childhood.

Until he could begin to accept himself, it was hard for Tim to believe that anyone else could truly appreciate him. Trying to get such a man to change his behavior without addressing his controlling life story is futile, because no matter how many successes he has, he'll still find ways to dismiss them and continue to dwell on his failures—and his partner's (presumed) dissatisfaction.

Narrative therapists believe that systems thinking encourages therapists to view families from the position of objective, outside observers as one might study a broken machine, without reference to its history, point of view, or environment. In contrast, narrative theory is viewed as encouraging therapists to (1) take a collaborative, empathic position with strong interest in the client's story; (2) search for times in a client's history when he or she was strong or resourceful; (3) use questions to take a nonimposing, respectful approach to any new story put forth; (4) never label people but instead treat them as human beings with unique personal histories; and (5) help people separate from the dominant cultural narratives they have internalized so as to open space for alternative life stories (White, 1995; Freedman & Combs, 1996).

Narrative therapists also oppose the functionalist elements in family systems and psychoanalytic models that led therapists to believe that problems are inherent in individuals (as psychoanalysis would have it) or families (as family systems would have it). Instead, they believe that problems arise because people are indoctrinated into narrow and self-defeating views of themselves and the world.

To counter the way society convinces people that they are their problems, narrative therapists **externalize** problems. Instead of *having* a problem or *being* a problem, they encourage clients to think of themselves as struggling against their problems. Neither the patient nor the family is the problem; the problem is the problem. Accordingly, narrative therapists aren't interested in problem-maintaining interactions or structural flaws. They aren't interested in the family's impact on the problem but rather in the problem's impact on the family.

As narrative therapists shifted their attention from families as the source of problems to cultural beliefs and practices, they turned to the writings of Michel Foucault (1965, 1980), the French social philosopher, who devoted his life to exposing how various social discourses objectified and dehumanized various marginalized groups. Foucault not only believed that those constructing the dominant narratives in a society (those deemed to have expert knowledge in various fields) had the power to subjugate, but that the narratives themselves become internalized truths within all citizens of the society, such that people come to judge their bodies, achievements, and personalities on the basis of standards set by society's judges (doctors, educators, clergy, psychotherapists, politicians, celebrities). Thus Foucault influenced White to take the social constructionist axiom that there are no absolute truths in the world in a political direction, toward deconstructing (reexamining) the established truths that oppress peoples lives.

Narrative therapists applied Foucault's political analysis to understand how individuals and families are dominated by oppressive narratives from which they need liberation. They drew from the work of Jerome Bruner (1986, 1991) to understand how personal narratives are constructed and can be deconstructed.[1]

Normal Family Development

Narrative therapists not only avoid judgments about what is normal, they reject the very idea of categorizing people. Recall how Foucault criticized the way theories of normality have been used to perpetuate patterns of privilege and oppression. Too often in human history the

---

1. The term *deconstructionism* is most closely associated with Jacques Derrida (1992), who analyzed literary texts to show that they had no one true meaning. Narrative therapists use the term in a political way, as subverting dominant discourses, whereas Derrida's intent was more relativistic.

judgments made by people in power regarding normality and abnormality have been imposed in ways that subjugated those with no voice in the matter.

While it's easy to see the dangers of reducing people to DSM-IV diagnoses, family therapists may have trouble seeing their favorite concepts, such as rigid boundaries, cross-generational coalitions, or differentiation of self, as dehumanizing. But becoming a postmodern narrative therapist means giving up all such categories. Not only do they avoid pigeonholing people by diagnosis or normality and abnormality, they also avoid the idea of general principles of what causes problems or what resolves them. They try not to stand over people in judgment—in any way—but instead strive to help them make sense of their own experience.

In the spirit of collaboration, narrative therapists endeavor to "situate" themselves with clients—that is, disclose the beliefs that inform their therapy so that clients can know what they're getting into. Clients are also encouraged to educate therapists regarding their cultural predicaments and to correct therapists when they make assumptions that don't fit their experience (Freedman & Combs, 1996).

Although narrative therapists try not to make judgments, it may be impossible not to have some assumptions about people and how they change. From the ideas described in the previous section we can distill the basic assumptions narrative therapists make about normal families. People (1) have good intentions—they don't need or want problems; (2) are profoundly influenced by the discourses around them; (3) are not their problems; and (4) can develop alternative, empowering stories once separated from their problems and from the common wisdom they have internalized.

Development of Behavior Disorders

When the stories people tell themselves lead them to construe their experience in unhelpful ways, they tend to get bogged down with problems. Such problems are likely to persist as long as these unhelpful stories remain fixed, obscuring more optimistic versions of events.

Thus, for example, a single mother whose life narrative is that she can't trust that anyone loves her reacts furiously whenever her daughter breaks curfew. This narrative makes the mother notice all the times her daughter stays

*F*amily arguments are often fueled by negative story lines about other family members.

out late or leaves cigarette butts on the porch and not notice the times when she gets her homework done or volunteers to wash the dishes. Each of the daughter's transgressions confirms the mother's story line that, like all the other people in her life, her daughter doesn't really love her. The daughter, in turn, is keenly aware of how often her mother criticizes her friends or explodes over small mistakes, but doesn't remember the times her mother showed respect for her opinion or praised her achievements. The daughter gradually develops a narrative around never being able to satisfy people and becomes increasingly controlled by "rebelliousness," which makes her not care what her mother thinks, and instead indulges in whatever makes her feel better, like partying late into the night. In short, both sides remain stuck not simply in a pattern of control and rebellion but, more specifically, of noticing only incidents of control or rebellion.

This analysis might not sound all that different from one which other schools of family therapy might make for an escalating cycle of antagonism between a mother and a daughter. The difference is that the narrative approach doesn't focus on their behavior. They reject the cybernetic notion that the mother and daughter are stuck in a dysfunctional feedback loop—acting and reacting to each other in unhelpful ways. Instead, they concentrate on the way mother and daughter narrate their exchange. It's their stories (being unloved, being picked on) that affect not only what they notice (lateness, scolding) but also how they interpret it.

Narrative therapists refer to these patterns of tunnel vision as **problem-saturated stories,** which, once they take hold, encourage people to respond to each other in ways that perpetuate the problem story. As long as they focus on their children's misbehavior, parents will concentrate on criticizing and controlling them. As long as they think of their parents primarily as hassling them, youngsters are likely to remain reactive and rebellious. Their responses to each other be-

come invitations to more of the same and support further hardening of problem stories.

Such closed and rigid narratives make people vulnerable to being overtaken by destructive emotional states that narrative therapists like to portray as external invaders. Narrative therapists don't really see problematic feelings or beliefs as alien entities, but they do believe that such emotional responses *are* external in the sense that they are socially constructed. Externalizing problems cuts down on guilt and blame. The daughter isn't the problem, "rebelliousness" is. Mother isn't the problem, "oversensitivity" is. Mother and daughter can unite to combat rebelliousness and oversensitivity rather than each other.

Instead of looking inside families for the source of their problems, narrative therapists look outside to the toxic effects of cultural narratives that govern our lives. In Michael White's (1995) words:

> The discourses of pathology make it possible for us to ignore the extent to which the problems for which people seek therapy are the outcome of certain practices of relationship and practices of the self, many of which are actually informed by modern notions of "individualism" . . . [and] are so often mired in the structures of inequality of our culture, including those pertaining to gender, race, ethnicity, class, economics, age, and so on. (p. 115)

Anorexia nervosa, for example, can be viewed as an internalization of our obsession with thinness and beauty, and the worship of self-discipline and competitiveness. By seeing women who starve themselves as having a disease or a dysfunctional family, we not only ignore the bigger picture but also avoid having to confront our own participation in these cultural stereotypes.

Goals of Therapy

Narrative therapists aren't problem-solvers. Instead, they help people separate themselves from problem-saturated stories (and destructive cultural assumptions) in order to open space for new and more constructive views of themselves. Narrative therapy transforms identities from flawed to heroic, not by getting family members to confront their conflicts, but rather by separating persons from problems and then uniting the family to fight a common enemy. It's also done by combing the family's history for **unique outcomes** or "sparkling events"—times when they resisted the problem or behaved in ways that contradicted the problem story.

If Alice sees herself as "codependent" because of the way she relates to men, a narrative therapist wouldn't explore the reasons for this condition, nor would she give Alice suggestions for altering this pattern. Instead, she would ask questions about the effect of *Self-blame* on her life, ask family members to help her defeat *Self-blame*, and highlight times in her life when she related to men in ways she prefers. She might also invite Alice to explore how our society's view of women contributed to *Self-blame*'s grip on her life.

Thus, narrative therapists see their work as a political enterprise—freeing people from oppressive cultural assumptions and empowering them to become active agents in charge of their own lives. Once liberated from problem-saturated stories, family members can unite with one another and with communities of support to deal with their problems with more agency, optimism, and persistence.

Conditions for Behavior Change

Narrative therapy works by helping clients **deconstruct** unproductive stories in order to *reconstruct* new and more productive ones. Deconstruction, a term borrowed from literary criticism, means questioning assumptions. Narrative therapists *externalize* problems from persons as one way to deconstruct the disempowering assumptions that often surround problems. Rather than talk of "Sally's laziness," for example, they'll inquire about times when "*Procrastination* takes hold of her." Once the problem is externalized and redefined in more experience-near terms, the person can begin to resist it. By viewing the problem as an external entity, narrative therapists free families to challenge its influence on their lives.

After externalizing the problem, narrative therapists ask about unique outcomes—times when clients resisted the problem's influence. Unique outcomes open room for counterplots, new and more empowering ways of constructing events. A man who identifies himself as depressed sees his life through a glass darkly. Depression becomes a career, a life-style. But if the man begins to think of, say, "*Self-doubt* getting the best of him," then he may be able to remember times when he didn't let *Self-doubt* get him down. These newly attended to times of effectiveness provide openings around which to weave a new and more optimistic story.

Just as externalization is used to shift clients' perceptions of themselves, narrative therapists also endeavor to shift family members' perceptions of each other from "totalizing views" (reducing them to one set of frustrating responses) that lead to antagonism and polarization. Thus parents who see their teenagers as "irresponsible"—as though that were the sum total of their being—are likely to be seen in return as "not really caring." Likewise, parents who totalize their children as "lazy" may be seen as "pushy" or "demanding." As long as both sides remain fixed in such polarized perspectives, they may be too busy to think about their own preferences. In unhappy families, people may be so busy *not* being what others expect, that they have no time to figure out how they themselves want to be.

Michael White sets an inspiring example of seeing the best in people even when they've lost faith in themselves. He's famous for his persistence in questioning negative stories. He just won't allow people to slip away into their misery. You can tell that he is absolutely convinced that people are not their problems. His voice, his posture, his whole being radiates possibility and hope.

The tenacious confidence in people that narrative therapists convey with genuine respect and caring is contagious. As clients come to trust their therapist, they can borrow that confidence and use it in dealing with their problems.

Therapy

Assessment

A narrative assessment means getting the family's story—including not only their experience with their problems but also their presuppositions about those problems. "Getting the family's story" is not just information gathering. It is a reconstructive inquiry, designed to move clients from passivity and defeatism toward a sense that they already have at least some power over the problems that plague them.

The narrative therapist approaches assessment as both an anthropologist and a hypnotist. As an anthropologist, the therapist asks, as it were, "Tell me this story—let us see what we can make of it together." Always, the therapist conveys respect: "What would you prefer to happen?" "What are you hoping to accomplish here?" "Is this what you intend for your future?"

This anthropological investigation slides so imperceptibly into the hypnotic process of asking questions to empower clients that assessment can be differentiated from intervention in narrative therapy only in an abstract way. Although we will describe certain elements of narrative inquiry as belonging to the assessment phase, we will revisit these same elements in the following section on therapeutic intervention.

Once problems are personified as alien entities, the narrative therapist first maps the influence of the problem on the family and then maps the influence of the family over the problem. In *mapping the influence of the problem on the family*, the therapist explores the distressing impact of the problem on their lives. Clients' responses to this line of inquiry usually highlight their own sense of incompetence and despair.

—Case Study—

Alesha Jackson, a single mother of four with a live-in boyfriend, sought therapy because Jermaine, her four-year-old, was getting into trouble at preschool. Two or three times a week Jermaine got into arguments that resulted in his hitting and biting other children. Jermaine "was also a problem" at home. Although he got along reasonably well with his brothers and sisters, he frequently threw tantrums when his mother tried to make him do something. Alesha sheepishly admitted that she was probably too easy on Jermaine, but she had gotten to the point where she felt helpless.

"I don't know what to do," she said. "I've tried everything. Nothing I do makes any difference. Luke, that's my boyfriend, he can make Jermaine behave, but he can get mean about it. He thinks I spoil Jermaine. Lately, Luke's been getting mad and going out after supper by himself. Which leaves me all alone with the kids."

The therapist listens not just to get Alesha's story of the problem (what Jerome Bruner [1991] called "the landscape of action") but also to explore the conclusions ("the landscape of consciousness") that she has drawn from her experience.

"What conclusions about yourself as a mother have you drawn because of your problems with Jermaine?"

"What conclusions have you drawn about your relationship with Luke because of this problem?" Note that it is the problem affecting the relationship, rather than the relationship causing the problem.

This line of questioning not only allows Jermaine's mother to tell her unhappy story but also tries to make her aware that the problem is burdening her and begins to suggest that rather than she and her family being somehow dysfunctional—that they're struggling against an enemy.

In *mapping the family members' influence in the life of the problem,* the therapist explores to what extent they have been able to stand up to the problem's oppression of them. To supply this information, family members are encouraged to recognize their own competence and sufficiency. Questions of the following form are useful:

- How is it that you've been able to avoid making mistakes that most people with similar problems usually make?
- Were there times in the recent past when this problem may have tried to get the better of you, and you didn't let it?
- How did you do that?

The therapist can then express surprise that things are not a lot worse.

—Case Study——

Although Jermaine's mother continued to disparage her abilities as a mother, she was able to describe a few times when she had been firm with Jermaine and insisted that he do what he was told—"even though that boy pitched one heck of a fit!"

In this phase of the assessment, the therapist did not try to coax Alesha to be more optimistic. Rather she confined herself to helping her client remember incidents of effectiveness that didn't fit her idea of herself as being at her problems' mercy.

We tend to think of memory as a recorder or a camera, where the past is filed and can be called up at will. But memory is none of these things. Memory is a storyteller. It creates shape

and meaning by emphasizing some things and leaving other things out. The narrative therapist's assessment explores two sides of the clients' memory—beginning with the problem narrative, a story of affliction (not pathology). These problem stories are understood not as personal failings but as stories of domination, alienation, and frustration. From here the therapist helps clients search their memories for the other side of the story—the side that honors their courage and persistance, the side that opens the way to hope.

Therapeutic Techniques

Almost all narrative interventions are delivered in the form of questions. They almost never assert anything or make interpretations. They just ask question after question, often repeating back the answers and writing them down.

In the first session, narrative therapists begin by finding out how people spend their time. This gives the therapist a chance to appreciate how clients see themselves, without getting into a lengthy history, and the attributions of blame so frequently a part of such histories. They pay special attention to people's talents and competencies. As a further means of establishing a collaborative atmosphere, Zimmerman and Dickerson (1996) encourage clients to ask any questions they might have about the therapists. They also invite clients to read their notes if they wish. And they often take notes as each person talks, which not only helps them retain important points, but also gives clients a sense that their point of view is respected.

Externalizing: The Person Is Not the Problem. Narrative therapists begin by asking clients to tell their problem-saturated story, and they listen long enough to convey their appreciation for what the family has been going through. After a sense of trust has been established, the therapist begins asking questions that externalize the problem and make its destructive effects apparent.

From the outset, the problem is seen as separate from people and as influencing them—"*It* brought them there"—and each person is asked for his or her own perspective on *It*. Externalizing language is used from the beginning. One major way of doing this is to ask about the problem's effects rather than its causes (causative questions usually lead to attributions of blame), or mapping the influence of the problem. "How does *Guilt* affect you?" "What other effects does it have?" "What does *Guilt* 'tell' you?"

The therapist's questions about the identified problem immediately imply that it isn't possessed by anyone, but instead is trying to possess them. For example, in a case where parents describe the problem as a lack of trust in their daughter because of her sneakiness, the therapist doesn't reflect back, "So your daughter's sneakiness bothers you." Instead the therapist might say, "So *Sneakiness* made your daughter act in ways that caused a rift between you, is that right?"

Sometimes whole patterns of interaction are externalized. For example, in the case in which a teenager's parents were responding to her sneakiness with increasing control, Vicki Dickerson chose to highlight the rift that was encouraging this pattern—because one thing they could all agree on was that they didn't like the breach that was splitting them apart. Thus instead of identifying the daughter's sneakiness or the parent's distrust as the problem, the *Rift* became the enemy that encouraged sneakiness and control. The *Rift* told the parents that their daughter couldn't be trusted; the *Rift* made the daughter more secretive and told her to pull away from her parents. The *Rift* was something they could join forces against (Zimmerman & Dickerson, 1996).

Problems are always personified—portrayed as unwelcome invaders that try to dominate people's lives. For example, while discussing her eating problems, a woman is asked how *Anorexia* convinces her to starve herself. A phobic child is asked how often *Fear* is able to make him do what it wants and how often he is able to stand up to it. A guilt-ridden mother is asked how *Self-hate* is making her feel bad about her parenting.

This line of questioning is often disconcerting for families, unaccustomed as they are to talking about imaginary entities living in their households. Consequently, therapists who treat externalization merely as a gimmick may lack the conviction necessary to overcome the initial awkwardness of talking this way. On the other hand, therapists will find that externalizing questions flow freely if they actually learn to think of problems as enemies that feed on polarizations and misunderstandings. White suggests that problems are dependent on their effects for their survival, so by standing up to a problem and not allowing it to affect them, clients cut off the problem's "life-support system."

Sallyann Roth and David Epston (1996) developed an exercise to help therapists grasp what it's like to think of problems as external. They have a group of trainees take turns being a problem—such as *Self-hatred*—while others interview them. The interviewers might ask the person playing *Self-hatred* such questions as: "Under what circumstances do you manage to get into X's world?" "How are you intervening in the lives of X's family and friends?"

Externalizing, by itself, can have a powerful impact. Over time, people become identified with their problems. They believe that the problem's existence is proof of their flawed character. This way of thinking poisons confidence. When the problem is externalized, it's as if the person can peek out from behind it; and family members can see that there is a healthier person that the problem has been hiding from them.

Bill no longer *is* a depressed person, instead he is overcome at times by *Depression*, an antagonist he dislikes as much as his family does. As the therapist queries him about *Depression's* tactics and effects, Bill becomes motivated to fight back.

Who's in Charge, the Person or the Problem? Over many sessions therapists ask a multitude of questions that explore how the problem has managed to disrupt or dominate the family, versus how much they have been able to control it. These are called **relative influence questions.** By including all family members in the discussion it usually becomes clear that the problem has succeeded in disturbing their relationships with each other—dividing and conquering them.

"How much has the *Bulimia* that's taken over Jenny kept you from being the way you want to be with her?" "When *Depression* gets the better of Dad, how does that affect family life?" "When *Tantrums* convince Joey to yell and scream, do you think your response gives *Tantrums* more or less fuel?"

Reading between the Lines of the Problem Story. While asking relative influence questions, the therapist listens for sparkling events or unique outcomes when clients were able to avoid the problem's effects, and then asks for elaboration on how that was done.

"Can you remember a time when *Anger* tried to take you over, but you didn't let it? How did you do that?" "Have there been times when your daughter didn't believe the lies that *Anorexia* tells her about her body?" "When Jenny has withstood the tremendous pressure she feels from *Alcoholism,* have you appreciated the magnitude of that accomplishment?" These unique outcomes become the building blocks of new, more heroic stories.

Reauthoring the Whole Story. Evidence of competence relative to the problem, gathered from sifting through the clients' history, can serve as the start of new narratives regarding what kind of people they are. To make this connection, the therapist begins by asking about what the series of past and present victories over the problem say about the client. For example: "What does it say about you as a person that you were able to defeat *Depression* on those occasions?" "What qualities of character must your son possess to be able to do that?" The therapist can also expand the historical purview beyond episodes relating to the problem to find more evidence to bolster the new self-narrative. "What else can you tell me about your past that helps me understand how you were able to handle *Anger* so well?" "Who knew you as a child who wouldn't be surprised that you have been able to stand up to *Fear* on these occasions?"

As the new self-narrative begins to take shape, the therapist can shift the focus to the future, inviting the client or family to envision the upcoming changes that will fit the new story. "Now that you've discovered these things about yourself, how do you think these discoveries will affect your relationship with *Self-hate.*" The self-story now has a past, present, and future—it's a complete narrative.

Reinforcing the New Story. Because they believe that the self is constituted in social interaction and, therefore, that people are susceptible to having their new stories undermined by the same contexts that bred the old ones, narrative therapists make a point of helping clients find an audience to support their progress in constructing new stories for themselves.

Clients might be asked to contact people from their past who can authenticate their new story—who can confirm and add to examples of the person's acting capably. Clients are also encouraged to recruit people in their lives who can serve as a supportive witnesses to their new story. Sometimes "leagues" are formed, ongoing groups of people with similar problems to support one another's efforts to resist the problem. For example, the Vancouver Anti-Anorexia/Anti-Bulimia League (Madigan, 1994) has a newsletter and monitors the media, writing letters to company presidents, newspapers, and magazines that portray an emaciated ideal for women and encourage them to diet.

David Epston has pioneered the use of letter writing to extend the therapeutic conversation beyond the session. These letters often convey a deep appreciation of what the client endured, the outline of a new story, and the therapist's confidence in the client's ability to continue to progress. The advantage of this technique is that the words in a letter don't vanish the way words do after a conversation. Clients have reported to Epston that they regularly reread letters he sent them years earlier to remind themselves what they went through and how far they have come (Epston, 1994).

All of these efforts—recruiting authenticators and audiences, forming teams and leagues, writing letters and making certificates—are in keeping with the social constructionist emphasis on interaction in creating and maintaining change. For people to solidify new identities, they need communities that confirm and reinforce re-visioned narratives and that counter cultural and familial messages to the contrary. What happens in a session is just a beginning, because the goal isn't just to solve a problem; it's to change a whole way of thinking and living.

At the end of each session, narrative therapists often summarize what happened, being sure to use externalizing language and emphasizing any unique outcomes that were mentioned. These summaries are what Epston often puts into his letters to clients. The effect of these summaries is to convey to clients that the therapist is with them and celebrates their blossoming new identity. This sense of being cheered on by the therapist can be extremely encouraging.

Deconstructing Destructive Cultural Assumptions. There are times when narrative therapists will make the connection to cultural narratives more explicit. For example, an anorexic woman might be asked how she was recruited into the belief that her worth depended on her appearance. This would lead to other questions regarding the position of women in our society. Similarly, a violent man might be asked how he came to believe that men should never be weak or tender, and a deconstructing of the messages men receive would ensue.

To clarify what this deconstructing of cultural attitudes might look like, we will present one of White's cases as described by Mary Sikes Wylie (1994):

> John . . . came to see White because, says White, "he was a man who never cried"—he had never been able to express his emotions—and he felt isolated and cut off from his own family. As a child, John had been taught, both at home and at his Australian grammar school, that any show of gentleness or "softness" was unmanly and would be met with harsh punishment and brutal public humiliation. White asks John a series of questions that are at once political and personal, eliciting information about the man's "private" psychological suffering and linking it to the "public" cultural practices, rigidly sexist and aggressively macho, that dominated his youth. "How were you recruited into these thoughts and habits [of feeling inadequate, not sufficiently masculine, etc.]? What was the training ground for these feelings? Do you think the rituals of humiliation [public caning by school authorities, ridicule by teachers and students for not being good at sports or sufficiently hard and tough] alienated you from your own life? Were they disqualifications of you? Did these practices help or hinder you in recognizing a different way of being a male?" (p. 43)

After deconstructing the masculine image in this way, White helped John remember times when he resisted it and to recognize the nobility of his efforts to remain gentle and loving in spite of his socialization.

A Case of Sneaky Poo. White's therapy comes to life in his case descriptions, as in the following excerpt from his (1989) description of a family with an encopretic child:

> When mapping the influence of family members in the life of what we came to call "Sneaky Poo," we discovered that:
>
> 1. Although Sneaky Poo always tried to trick Nick into being his playmate, Nick could recall a number of occasions during which he had not allowed Sneaky Poo to "outsmart" him. These were occasions during which Nick could have co-operated by "smearing," "streaking" or "plastering," but he declined to do so. He had not allowed himself to be tricked into this.
> 2. There was a recent occasion during which Sneaky Poo could have driven Sue into a heightened sense of misery, but she resisted and turned on the stereo instead. Also, on this occasion, she refused to question her competence as a parent and as a person.
> 3. Ron could not recall an occasion during which he had not allowed the embarrassment caused by Sneaky Poo to isolate him from others. However, after Sneaky Poo's requirements of him were identified, he did seem interested in the idea of defying these requirements. . . .
> 4. . . . It was established that there was an aspect to Sue's relationship with Nick that she thought she could still enjoy, that Ron was still making some attempts to persevere in his relationship with Nick, and that Nick had an idea that Sneaky Poo had not destroyed all of the love in his relationship with his parents.

After identifying Nick's, Sue's, and Ron's influence in the life of Sneaky Poo, I introduced questions that encouraged them to perform meaning in relation to these examples, so that they might "re-author" their lives and relationships.

> How had they managed to be effective against the problem in this way? How did this reflect on them as people and on their relationships? . . . Did this success give them any ideas about further steps that they might take to reclaim their lives from the problem? . . . In response to these questions, Nick thought that he was ready to stop Sneaky Poo from outsmarting him so much, and decided that he would not be tricked into being its playmate anymore. (pp. 10–11)

Two weeks later White found that Nick had fought Sneaky Poo valiantly, having only one minor episode, and he seemed happier and stronger. Sue and Ron had also done their parts in the battle. In her effort to not cooperate with Sneaky Poo's requirements for her to feel guilty, Sue had begun to "treat herself" when Sneaky Poo was getting her down, and Ron had fought Sneaky Poo's attempts to keep him isolated by talking to friends about the problem.

> I encouraged the family to reflect on and to speculate about what this success said about the qualities that they possessed as people and about the attributes of their relationships. I also encouraged them to review what these facts suggested about their current relationship with Sneaky Poo. In this discussion, family members identified further measures that they could take to decline Sneaky Poo's invitations to them to support it. (p. 11)

White reports that the family expanded these efforts in the interim, and by the third session they felt confident that Sneaky Poo had been defeated. At a six-month follow-up they were still doing well.

Evaluating Therapy Theory and Results

By externalizing problems, deconstructing pessimistic life stories, and conveying unswerving confidence in their clients, narrative therapists have constructed a powerful recipe for change. Packaging their input in the form of questions makes their input less like advice to be resisted and fosters a sense of partnership with clients.

The two most powerful ingredients in narrative therapy are the narrative metaphor itself and the technique of externalizing problems. The strength and weakness of the narrative approach is its cognitive focus. In rejecting the cybernetic model—families stuck in dysfunctional feedback loops—narrative therapists repudiated the idea that families with problems have something wrong with them. Unfortunately, they also turned their backs on the three defining characteristics of family therapy: (1) recognizing that psychological symptoms are often related to family conflict; (2) thinking about human problems as interactional, which means thinking in terms of twos (complementarity, reciprocity) and threes (triangles); and (3) treating the family as a unit.

Treating problems as stories to be deconstructed overlooks the fact that some families have real conflicts that don't disappear because they join together temporarily to fight an externalized problem. For example, parents whose lives are empty may have trouble letting their children grow up. Does that emptiness evaporate while they help their children battle *Rebelliousness?*

In the process of helping people restory their experience, narrative therapists often subscribe to a view of unhappy emotions— anger, fear, anxiety, depression—much like that of cognitive-behaviorists: as annoyances to avoid rather than explore. They ask how anger or fear "defeats" clients, but rarely why clients are angry or what they are afraid of?

Early versions of family therapy *did* cast families in a bad light and blamed them for maintaining problems. The narrative movement has helped shift the field toward more respect and collaboration with families. In the process of rejecting the patronizing consciousness of that earlier age, however, narrative therapists have rejected systems thinking, emphasizing its mechanistic elements while ignoring more humanistic versions (derived from theorists like von Bertalanffy). One of family therapy's greatest contributions was to bring a contextual understanding of people and their problems to psychotherapy. Nonsystemic therapists, influenced by the disease model, had encouraged people to fight problems (with medication, support groups, education) rather than explore the network of relationships in which their problems were embedded. While opposed to the disease model, narrative therapists advocate returning to a similarly acontextual view of problems as things to be fought, and eschew efforts to understand their ecological contexts.

In looking beyond families to the cultural assumptions in which they're embedded, narrative therapists have given a distinctly political cast to their work. Most narrative therapists would agree with Vicki Dickerson's statement that narrative therapy is "primarily about situating problems in their cultural context" (Freedman, 1996). That is, it's about helping clients identify and challenge the ubiquitous, but commonly unexamined, prescriptions that permeate society and make self-worth and harmonious relating difficult at best. But how does one do that without imposing one's own political biases?

Although some therapists still make a case for strict therapeutic neutrality, many now agree that it is sometimes necessary to question invidious cultural assumptions. It's true that popular culture promotes many unhelpful values. The question is, what is the best way to help people free themselves from those influences without imposing one's own values? This is a complex question, and narrative therapy answers it one way. We hope that example inspires all family therapists to grapple with this question.

—Summary—

The narrative approach is built around two organizing metaphors: personal narrative and social construction. When memory speaks it tells a "narrative truth," which comes to have more influence than "historical truth." The "facts" presented to a therapist are partly historical truth and partly constructions. The constructions that make up the shared reality of a family represent mutual understandings and shared prejudices, some of which are useful, some of which are not.

Narrative therapists break the grip of unhelpful stories by externalizing problems. By challenging pessimistic versions of events, therapists make room for flexibility and hope. Uncovering unique outcomes provides an opening through which new and more optimistic stories can be envisioned. Finally, clients are encouraged to create audiences of support to witness and promote their progress in restorying their lives along preferred lines.

The strategies of narrative therapy fall into three stages: (1) the problem narrative stage: recasting the problem as an affliction (externalizing) by focusing on its effects, rather than its causes; (2) finding exceptions: partial triumphs over the problem and instances of effective action; and (3) the recruitment of support. Encouraging some kind of public ritual to reinforce new and preferred interpretations moves cognitive constructions past private insight into not just action but socially supported action.

The tactics by which these strategies are put into practice involve an elaborate series of questions:

- *Deconstruction questions:* Externalizing the problem. "What does *Depression* whisper in your ear?" "What conclusions about your relationship have you drawn because of this problem?"
- *Opening space questions:* Uncovering unique outcomes. "Has there ever been a time when *Arguing* could have taken control of your relationship but didn't?"
- *Preference questions:* Making sure unique outcomes represent preferred experiences. "Was this way of handling things better or worse?" "Was that a positive or negative development?"
- *Story development questions:* Developing a new story from the seeds of (preferred) unique outcomes. "How is this different from what you would have done before?" "Who played a part in this way of doing things?" "Who will be the first to notice these positive changes in you?"
- *Meaning questions:* Challenging negative images of self and emphasizing positive agency. "What does it say about you that you were able to do that?"
- *Questions to extend the story into the future:* Supporting changes and reinforcing positive developments. "What do you predict for the coming year?"

The social constructionist foundation of narrative therapy gives the approach its political cast and deemphasizes family dynamics and conflict. Instead of looking within families for dysfunctional interactions, narrative therapists look outside for destructive influences of certain cultural values and institutions. They invite family members to pull together to oppose these values and practices. Instead of neutrality, they offer advocacy.

—Recommended Readings

Bruner, J. S. 1986. *Actual minds, possible worlds.* Cambridge, MA: Harvard University Press.

Diamond, J. 2000. *Narrative means to sober ends: Treating addiction and its aftermath.* New York: Guilford Press.

Dickerson, V. C., and Zimmerman, J. 1992. Families with adolescents: Escaping problem lifestyles. *Family Process.* 31:341–353.

Eron, J., and Lund, T. 1996. *Narrative solutions in brief therapy.* New York: Guilford Press.

Freedman, J., and Combs, G. 1996. *Narrative therapy: The social construction of preferred realities.* New York: Norton.

Gilligan, S., and Price, R. 1993. *Therapeutic conversations.* New York: Norton.

Minuchin, S. 1998. Where is the family in narrative family therapy? *Journal of Marital and Family Therapy.* 24:397–403.

White, M. 1989. *Selected papers.* Adelaide, Australia: Dulwich Centre Publications.

White, M. 1995. *Re-authoring lives: Interviews and essays.* Adelaide, Australia: Dulwich Centre Publications.

White, M., and Epston, D. 1990. *Narrative means to therapeutic ends.* New York: Norton.

Zimmerman, J., and Dickerson, V. 1996. *If problems talked: Adventures in narrative therapy.* New York: Guilford Press.

—References

Anderson, C. M., Reiss, D., and Hogarty, B. 1986. *Schizophrenia and the family.* New York: Guilford Press.

Bruner, J. S. 1986. *Actual minds, possible worlds.* Cambridge, MA: Harvard University Press.

Bruner, J. S. 1991. The narrative construction of reality. *Critical Inquiry.* 18:1–21.

Derrida, J. 1992. *Derrida: A critical reader.* D. Wood, ed. Oxford: Blackwell.

Dickerson, V., and Zimmerman, J. 1992. Families with adolescents: Escaping problem lifestyles. *Family Process.* 31:341–353.

Epston, D. 1994. Extending the conversation. *Family Therapy Networker.* 18:30–37, 62.

Epston, D., and White, M. 1992. *Experience, contradiction, narrative, and imagination: Selected papers of David Epston and Michael White, 1989–1991.* Adelaide, Australia: Dulwich Centre Publications.

Foucault, M. 1965. *Madness and civilization: A history of insanity in the age of reason.* New York: Random House.

Foucault, M. 1975. *The birth of the clinic: An archeology of medical perception.* London: Tavistock.

Foucault, M. 1980. *Power/knowledge: Selected interviews and other writings.* New York: Pantheon.

Foucault, M. 1984. *The history of sexuality.* Great Britain: Peregrine Books.

Freedman, J. 1996. AFTA voices on the annual meeting. *American Family Therapy Academy Newsletter.* Fall, 30–32.

Freedman, J., and Combs, G. 1996. *Narrative therapy: The social construction of preferred realities.* New York: Norton.

Freeman, J., Epston, D., and Lobovits, D. 1997. *Playful approaches to serious problems.* New York: Norton.

Gergen, K. 1991. *The saturated self.* New York: Basic Books.

Held, B. 1995. *Back to reality: A critique of postmodern theory in psychotherapy.* New York: Norton.

Madigan, S. 1994. Body politics. *Family Therapy Networker.* 18:27.

Madigan, S., and Epston, D. 1995. From "spy-chiatric gaze" to communities of concern: From professional monologue to dialogue. In *The reflecting team in action,* S. Friedman, ed. New York: Guilford Press.

Minuchin, S. 1998. Where is the family in narrative family therapy? *Journal of Marital and Family Therapy.* 24:397–403.

Nichols, M. 1995. *The lost art of listening.* New York: Guilford Press.

O'Hanlon, W. 1994. The third wave. *Family Therapy Networker. 18:*18–26, 28–29.

Roth, S. A., and Epston, D. 1996. Developing externalizing conversations: An introductory exercise. *Journal of Systemic Therapies. 15:*5–12.

Tamasese, K., and Waldegrave, C. 1993. Cultural and gender accountability in the "Just therapy" approach. *Journal of Feminist Family Therapy. 5:* 29–45.

Tomm, K. 1993. The courage to protest: A commentary on Michael White's work. In *Therapeutic conversations,* S. Gilligan and R. Price, eds. New York: Norton.

Waldegrave, C. T. 1990. Just therapy. *Dulwich Centre Newsletter. 1:*5–46.

Weingarten, K. 1991. The discourses of intimacy: Adding a social constructionist and feminist view. *Family Process. 30:*285–305.

Waters, D. 1994. Prisoners of our metaphors. *Family Therapy Networker. 18:*73–75.

White, M. 1989. *Selected papers.* Adelaide, Australia: Dulwich Centre Publications.

White, M. 1991. Deconstruction and family therapy. *Dulwich Centre Newsletter. 3:*21–40.

White, M. 1993. Deconstruction and therapy. In *Therapeutic conversations,* S. Gilligan and R. Price, eds. New York: Norton.

White, M. 1995. *Re-authoring lives: Interviews and essays.* Adelaide, South Australia: Dulwich Centre Publications.

White, M. 1997. *Narratives of therapists' lives.* Adelaide, South Australia: Dulwich Centre Publications.

White, M. 1998. Liberating conversations: New dimensions in narrative therapy. Workshop at the Family Therapy Network's Annual Symposium, Washington, DC.

White, M., and Epston, D. 1990. *Narrative means to therapeutic ends.* New York: Norton.

Wylie, M. S. 1994. Panning for gold. *Family Therapy Networker. 18:*40–48.

Zimmerman, J., and Dickerson, V. 1993. Bringing forth the restraining influence of pattern in couples therapy. In *Therapeutic conversations,* S. Gilligan and R. Price, eds. New York: Norton.

Zimmerman, J., and Dickerson, V. 1996. *If problems talked: Adventures in narrative therapy.* New York: Guilford Press.

Integrative Models

A More Flexible Approach to Treatment

In breaking with the dominant paradigm of the time, family therapists defined themselves in opposition to all things psychoanalytic. Did psychoanalysis maintain that behavior was an artifact of unconscious forces, that family relationships were a function of individual psychodynamics, and that only insight brought about lasting change? Then family therapists would insist that an individual's behavior was dictated by the structure of the family and that "insight" was completely unnecessary to problem solving.

Similarly, as they worked out the implications of their own insights, the various schools of family therapy emphasized not only their own strengths but also their differences. Bowen sought to reason with family members by talking to them one at a time; Minuchin insisted that the way to really get at relationships was to have people to talk directly to each other. Nor are the new schools immune from this us-against-them mentality; both solution-focused and narrative therapists have made a point of rejecting some of the defining features of the traditional schools. They are antimechanistic,

decidedly not behavioral, and they pretty much ignore conflict as a source of family problems.

For this very reason, radical revisionists often remain trapped within old categories. They represent an antithesis, not a new synthesis; and they are condemned to the dispensibility of all merely partial and polemical views. Just as it took systems therapists years to get beyond their denigration of psychodynamics, it will probably take time for these postmodernists to bring back what we've learned about family dynamics into their work.

In any field of endeavor, it seems that integration is only possible after a period of differentiation. It's no surprise, then, that in the early years of family therapy the idea of *integration* had a negative connotation. At a time when the energies of the emerging schools were devoted to differentiating, integration was seen as a watering down, rather than an enrichment, of the classic models.

During the past decade, however, there has been a growing awareness that no single approach has a monopoly on clinical effectiveness. The time of distinct and competitive schools of family therapy has passed. As family therapy enters its fifth decade, the dominant trend is integration.

When it's described as respect for the multiplicity of truth, integration seems like an unquestionably good idea. The obvious argument in favor of incorporating elements from different approaches is that human beings are complicated—thinking, feeling, and acting creatures who exist in a complex system of biological, psychological, and social influences. No therapy can succeed without having an impact on all of these dimensions. There is also, however, a valid argument that eclecticism robs therapy of the intensity made possible by focusing on certain elements of experience. There may be many ways to skin a cat, but it might not be advisable to try all of them at once.

As we will see in this chapter "integration" refers to three very different kinds of approaches. First there is *eclecticism*, which draws from a variety of models and methods. Second is *selective borrowing*, in which even relative purists will occasionally use techniques from other approaches. Third are the *specially designed integrative models*. Of these there are theoretical models that draw on several influences, including the integrative approaches of William Nichols (1996) and Bill Pinsof (1995); pragmatic models that combine elements of two complementary approaches, such as Eron and Lund's (1996) narrative solutions therapy and Jacobson and Christensen's (1996) integrative couples therapy; and integrative models developed for specific clinical problems, such as Virginia Goldner and Gillian Walker's couples therapy for marital violence (Goldner, 1998).

Eclecticism

One of the advantages of graduate training is that students are exposed to a variety of approaches and taught to think critically about them. Unfortunately, graduate schools sometimes produce better critics than clinicians. In the long run, a certain amount of professional agnosticism is probably a good thing; in the short run it can be confusing.

What do you do in the first session? Well, try to make sure that everyone shows up, greet each of them, and try to make them comfortable. Ask about the presenting problem, of course. But then what? Suppose a mother says that her fourteen-year-old has become rude and disrespectful. Do you focus on her feelings? Ask what her husband thinks? Set up an enactment in which she talks to her teenager? Inquire about exceptions? Any one of these options might be useful. But trying to do all of them may lead to a lack of focus.

Effective integration involves more than taking a little of this and a little of that from various models. In creating a workable integration, there are two things to avoid. The first is sampling techniques from diverse approaches without conceptual focus. The problem here isn't so much theoretical inelegance as clinical inconsistency.

—Case Study——————

A student who was being supervised in a psychodynamic approach asked to present at a case conference when, after some good initial progress, the therapy bogged down. Most of the people at the case conference weren't familiar with the psychodynamic model, and they were interested and impressed by what the student had thus far accomplished. But when it came time for discussion, several of those present suggested that the way to get the case moving again might be to try a different approach—cognitive-behavioral, structural, narrative, or what have you, depending on who was doing the suggesting.

The second thing to avoid is switching horses in midstream. Almost every treatment runs into difficulty at some point. When this happens, beginners may be tempted to shift to an entirely different model. If a structural approach isn't working, maybe a narrative one will. The problem here is that almost any strategy will work for a while—and then stall. Getting stuck isn't necessarily a reason to change models; rather it should be a signal that you and your clients are getting to what may be the heart of their problems. This is the time to sharpen your tools, not discard them.

Postgraduate training programs once provided an antidote to unfocused eclecticism through intensive instruction in one consistent approach. Unfortunately, fewer and fewer therapists these days take the time and expense to seek out advanced training. Many recent graduates would like to get more training, but they have loans to pay off, they want to settle down, or they feel they already know enough to get started. Those who do make the sacrifice to get postdoctoral training are likely to consider it the best professional decision they ever made.

Selective Borrowing

While postmodernism has made the field more inclusive, the same thing tends to happen to experienced practitioners. When family therapy's elders were asked to discuss their careers in an issue of the *American Family Therapy Academy Newsletter* (Winter, 1999), many said that over the years they'd become less doctrinaire and had adopted ideas from other models—but they had held on to the core of their original theory as a base. For example, feminist family therapist Betty Carter was trained in Bowen's model and believed it to be substantial enough to evolve with her. "I never felt I had to trash the whole theory and start over again. Though, of course, Bowen theory had the same blind spot that all the early theories had about power, so that all had to be added" (Mac Kune-Karrer, 1999, p. 24). Today there are few purists among seasoned therapists. Most, like Carter, become selective borrowers.

To borrow selectively, you need a solid foundation in one paradigm. Which one you choose will depend in part on what is available in your training program. It's a good idea to take advantage of what's offered by learning as much as you can from whomever you happen to be supervised by. However, the approach you eventually specialize in should also make sense to you. At some point you will be free to seek out training and supervision, and the approach you choose should be consistent with how you think about people and how you like to interact with them. If narrative therapy inspires you, seek out training in this approach. In graduate school you may not have a lot of choice about what your instructors offer. But after that it can be a mistake to settle for a particular kind of training merely because it's convenient.

Therapists who do eventually manage to combine approaches, or successfully master more than one, usually don't try to learn them all at once. Using techniques from here and there without conceptual focus produces a muddled form of eclecticism in which therapists shift back and forth without consistency or conviction. Effective borrowing doesn't mean a hodgepodge of techniques, and it doesn't mean switching from one approach to another whenever therapy reaches a temporary impasse. Borrowing techniques from other approaches is more likely to be effective if you do so in a way that fits into the basic paradigm within which you are operating.

—Case Study—

Consider, for example, a structural therapist treating a mother and daughter who are locked in a battle in which the mother constantly criticizes the daughter for being irresponsible, and the daughter constantly acts irresponsibly. If the mother would back off and stop criticizing, the girl might feel less browbeaten and begin to take more responsibility for herself—or if the daughter would start to take more responsibility, maybe the mother would back off. But as long as each of them remains preoccupied with the other one, and the awful things she's doing, neither is likely to break this cycle.

Suppose the therapist were to try the narrative technique of externalizing the problem. Instead of "nagging" and "irresponsibility" polarizing the mother and daughter, perhaps they could be convinced to start thinking in terms of a "breach" that's come between them. This shift in thinking might open space for them to recapture a more cooperative way of relating together. But if the mother and daughter's quarrelling was a product of enmeshment, attempting to bring them together in a more harmonious way might not solve the problem.

In fact, the case we've just described isn't hypothetical. Here's how the therapist actually did introduce the technique of externalizing in this situation.

—Case Study————————

Because he saw the mother and daughter's quarrelling as a result of their enmeshment, the therapist concentrated first on helping the mother address with her husband some of the conflicts that were keeping them distant. As they started to get closer, the mother began to spend less time worrying about what her daughter was or wasn't doing.

Then in separate sessions with the daughter, the therapist found a useful way to introduce the externalizing technique. As a result of her mother's nagging, the daughter had gotten into the habit of actively shirking responsibility, and as a result her school performance had plummeted. It was as though when she had a homework assignment, she felt the same kind of oppression she felt from her mother's nagging.

The therapist pointed this out, but found that the girl had begun to internalize her mother's harsh characterizations. "I guess I'm just lazy," she'd say, in what was becoming a self-fulfilling prophesy. The therapist responded by

asking her about times when "Procrastination" got the better of her, and times when "It" didn't. This device proved effective in helping the girl separate herself from the negative introject she'd adopted and, thus energized, she was able to start getting back on track with her school work.

Specially Designed Integrative Models

While most practitioners eventually become selective borrowers, grafting ideas and practices onto their basic model, some therapists create a new synthesis out of complementary aspects of existing models. Some of these integrative efforts are comprehensive systems that include a whole range of approaches under one umbrella, while others simply combine elements of one approach with another, forming a hybrid model.

Comprehensive, Theoretically Inclusive Models

In order to deal with the complexity of family life, the founders of family therapy developed specific models, each of which concentrated on certain aspects of human experience. Although this selectivity enabled the various schools to consolidate their approaches, it eventually created a competitive environment, which emphasized differences and discouraged therapists from taking advantage of insights from other models. The maturing of the field has seen an erosion of sectarianism and a more pragmatic approach to practice. For some this has meant not limiting one's practice to any one model but drawing on a variety of existing approaches.

The advantage of these comprehensive approaches is that they bring a wider range of human experience into focus. They also offer more options for intervention. For example, rather than simply trying to pry apart an enmeshed mother and child, a therapist whose purview includes cultural issues might help the mother to reexamine the assumptions keeping her from getting more satisfaction out of her own life.

The disadvantage of comprehensive approaches is that they require a great deal of therapists. First, therapists can't just specialize in, say, untangling family triangles; they have to consider a variety of other issues—intrapsychic, transgenerational, even political—and a greater range of interventions. In addition, therapists who adopt a more comprehensive framework must guard against the tendency mentioned previously to give up too quickly and switch haphazardly from one strategy to another.

Here we will present two examples of models designed to increase comprehensiveness. The first, *metaframeworks*, selects key ideas that run through the different schools of family therapy and connects them with superordinate principles. The second, *integrative problem-centered therapy*, links several different approaches in sequence and provides a decision tree for shifting from one to another when therapists get stuck.

The Metaframeworks Model. Metaframeworks grew out of the collaboration among three family therapy teachers who worked at the Institute for Juvenile Research in Chicago: Douglas Breunlin, Richard Schwartz, and Betty Mac Kune-Karrer. This approach offers a unifying theoretical framework operationalized with six core domains of human functioning, or metaframeworks: intrapsychic process, family organization, sequences of family interaction, development, culture, and gender (Breunlin, Schwartz, & Mac Kune-Karrer, 1992).

The application of metaframeworks is conceived in terms of releasing the constraints, at whatever level, keeping a family from solving its problems.

—Case Study—

For example, a depressed woman may be constrained on many fronts simultaneously. At the level of internal process, she may be burdened by guilt over wanting a little time for herself or because her children complain that they have no friends. (If children are unhappy, it must be their mother's fault, right?) At the level of family organization, she may be stuck in a stale second marriage to a man obsessed with his career while she's left to run the house and raise the kids. In addition, she may be preoccupied with her hyperactive son and polarized with her own mother over how to deal with him. This pattern may be part of a sequence in which her son's behavior gets worse after monthly visits with her ex-husband. Finally, the woman's situation may be part of a transgenerational pattern maintained by the family and cultural belief that women should be devoted to their families and never be "selfish."

As the therapist considers the network of constraints impeding this woman and her family, one framework often emerges as a point of departure, but the therapist is always aware of the others and can shift when necessary. Thus therapy may start in the gender metaframework by reexamining the woman's beliefs about selfishness and her husband's unbalanced expectations about the proper roles of men and women. At some point the focus might shift to the internal framework when the therapist asks about the parts of each partner that hold these beliefs, and what they are related to from their pasts. This exploration might make the woman want to reorganize the family responsibilities and the shift is to the organizational metaframework. At another point the couple might discuss their son's oscillating between acting younger and older than his age, and they're in the developmental framework, and so on.

The metaframeworks model isn't simple. In an age when therapists often seek to fall back on formulaic techniques, it challenges clinicians to consider a wide range of possibilities. Yet, for many therapists who've felt boxed in by the narrow scope of sectarian models, the metaframeworks approach offers a more comprehensive view and a broader range of options.

Integrative Problem-Centered Therapy.
Whereas metaframeworks distills key elements
from different theories into a new synthesis, integrative problem-centered therapy incorporates
a variety of family and individual approaches in
sequence, without trying to combine them. Integrative problem-centered therapy has been developed over the past twenty years by William
Pinsof (1995, 1999) and his colleagues at the
Family Institute at Northwestern University.

Like many therapists, Pinsof began his career convinced that the model he was trained in
(strategic family therapy) could be effective
with any and every sort of problem. Unlike selective borrowers, however, when he ran up
against his theory's limitations, he didn't just
add new techniques, he added whole new approaches. For example, if his strategic model
didn't seem to be working, he might help family
members explore and express their emotions
à la Virginia Satir or Susan Johnson. In other
cases, if problems persisted, he might recommend a psychopharmacological assessment.
With continued failure he might bring in
grandparents or even offer individual therapy
to some family members.

This sequencing made sense to Pinsof
(1999) partly because it reflected his own personal development. But it also makes sense
that some problems are deep-seated while others are not. Some families will respond to behavioral or structural interventions while
others may need more of an in-depth focus.
Why not consider the whole spectrum of psychotherapies if necessary rather than assume
that all troubles should be treated with just one
approach?

—Case Study————

To illustrate Pinsof's approach, consider a couple in
their sixties who have been caught up in picky but intense fights for the past year. They relate the fighting to the
husband's increasing impotence. In exploring the meaning
each attaches to these events, the therapist finds that the
wife sees her husband's lack of sexual response as a reflection of her diminished attractiveness, while he considers it
a sign of waning virility. These conclusions are painful to
each of them, and so they avoid discussing, much less
having, sex.

The therapist forms an alliance with each of them so
they feel safe enough to disclose their private pain and
clear up their misconceptions about the other's feelings. If
at that point they respond well—fewer fights and more satisfactory sex—therapy can stop. If not, the therapist would
explore possible physiological causes of the impotence—
fatigue, depression, incipient diabetes. If improvements
don't follow the exploration at that level, the therapist
might discuss with each partner the unexamined assumptions that they have about the aging process. If the problem still remains unsolved, the focus would shift to
intrapsychic blocks, and either or both of them might be
engaged in individual therapy.

By now the reader may be daunted at the
prospect of having to master so many different
therapeutic models. But Pinsof doesn't expect
therapists to be competent in all these approaches. Integrative therapy often involves
teamwork among a number of therapists, particularly when key family members are vulnerable and need their own therapists. While
separate therapists with differing orientations
can be a nightmare, the integrative framework
provides common ground for collaboration.

The metaframeworks and integrative approaches represent two possible reactions to the
realization many family therapists have that the
models they'd adopted as cure-alls all have their
limitations. One solution (metaframeworks) is
almost alchemical—taking pieces from here
and there to forge a new synthesis. The other
(integrative) is additive—linking whole models
together without trying to revise them or connect them theoretically.

Models That Combine Two Distinct Approaches

Some theorists who found one approach too limiting were satisfied to improve their model by combining it with just one other, believing that two heads were better than one—and probably also better than five or six. The advantage is that one can expand one's horizons without losing the focus that comes with having a fairly steady compass.

The Narrative Solutions Approach. One of the things that troubles some seasoned practitioners is the tendency for solution-focused and narrative therapists to turn their backs on valuable elements of the older models. That's why Eron and Lund's narrative solutions model (Eron & Lund, 1993, 1996), which combines the MRI model with narrative techniques, is a welcome addition.

Among the reasons strategic therapy fell into disfavor were its mechanistic assumptions and manipulative techniques. The way some strategists applied the cybernetic model, families were seen as stubborn and not to be reasoned with. You don't talk sense to a machine.

Family histories were dismissed as irrelevant. Therapy was ideological and therefore to a certain extent impersonal. The meretriciousness of this kind of thinking, however, wasn't essential to the insight that families often get stuck applying more-of-the-same solutions that don't work. Eron and Lund resuscitated that insight and incorporated it into a blend of strategic and narrative therapy.

Joseph Eron and Thomas Lund of the Catskill Family Institute in New York began collaborating in the early 1980s as brief strategic therapists. Although they were attracted to the narrative movement, there were aspects of the strategic approach they didn't want to give up. So they combined the two. The resulting narrative solutions approach revolves around the concept of the **preferred view:**

- Preferred views include the qualities people would like to possess and have noticed by others; for example, "determined," "caring," "responsible."
- Preferred views shape the *attributions* one makes about behavior. "I did that (got into that fight) because I am cool, independent, able to manage my own affairs."

Eron and Lund's narrative solutions therapy combines narrative techniques with the MRI insight that people often perpetuate their problems with misguided attempted solutions.

- Preferred views also include people's hopes, dreams, and intentions for living their lives. "I want to be different from my mother who was selfish and critical."
- Preferred views may or may not have anything to do with one's actual behavior. "I may not have done well in school, but I like to think of myself as a hard-working and self-disciplined person. I expect to go to a good graduate school, even though, given my grades, it isn't likely."

People are at their best when they act in line with their preferred views. On the other hand, people experience frustration and anger when they aren't acting in line with their preferred view, or when they imagine that they are seen by others in ways that contradict their preferred view.

Eron and Lund (1996) assume that people have strong preferences for how they like to see themselves and to be seen by others. Problems arise when people aren't living according to their preferred views. To address this discrepancy, Eron and Lund use a combination of reframing from the MRI model and restorying from the narrative approach.

Eron and Lund subscribe to the basic premise of the MRI model that problems develop from the mishandling of life transitions. However, Eron and Lund are more specific. They propose that people begin to think and act in problematic ways when they experience a discrepancy between their preferred view of themselves and their perception of their actions or their impression of how others regard them.

Note that while Eron and Lund follow the MRI model in looking for more-of-the-same cycles, they differ in focusing not just on behavior, but also on what people think about their problems. Conflict, according to this model, is driven by disjunctions between individuals' preferred views of themselves and how they perceive others as responding to them.

Eron and Lund (1996) offer the following guidelines to therapists for managing helpful conversations.

Maintain an Interest in Clients' Preferences and Hopes. The therapist must pay attention to stories that reflect how clients prefer to see themselves, and how they want to be seen by significant others. The following questions may be asked to help clients get in touch with their preferred views:

- When are you at your best—at home, work, school, with friends?
- Who notices—family, colleagues, teachers, friends?
- What do they notice about you at these times?
- Who are your favorite relatives, friends, teachers, other adults?
- What do they like about you?
- What do they see in you?
- When you think back on your life, are there other times when you felt at your best?
- When you look to the future and you are the person you would like to be, what do you envision?

—Case Study—

In *Narrative Solutions in Brief Therapy,* Eron and Lund (1996) offer the example of Al, who became depressed in the wake of retirement and the onset of emphysema. Al preferred to think of himself as productive and useful. Yet he worried that he might not be able to remain as active as in the past and that his family would no longer view him as someone to rely on. The disjunction between Al's preferences and his perceptions led to his feeling sad and listless. The more depressed Al seemed, the more family members began to do for him, finishing projects he started and trying to cheer him up, which only deepened his despondency. The negative *frame* through which Al viewed his current circumstances affected the *stories* he recalled from the past. He pictured himself following in the footsteps of his own father, who had deteriorated rapidly after retiring. According to Eron and Lund, negative frames of the present shape the stories people recall from the past, which in turn influence their perspectives on the future.

When Al was asked when he had felt he was the person he wanted to be, he recalled several stories. These stories revealed a man who felt close to this family and liked being helpful. Al also recalled times when he had taken control of his life under challenging circumstances. For example, he decided to stop drinking because it was having a bad effect on his family relationships. When Al recounted these occasions in which he had acted in line with his preferred attributes, (e.g., being helpful, caring, in control, connected with family members), he became more hopeful. He also noticed the gap between the person he wanted to be and how he was currently acting.

In describing their approach to working with couples, Eron and Lund (1998) offer the following example.

—Case Study—

Jim came to counseling after his wife consulted an attorney about a separation. Rita told Jim that she had hoped that their relationship would improve after he got sober, but his violent outbursts continued. When the therapist asked Jim when he felt at his best, he said it was when he made the decision to seek sobriety. He felt he was finally taking control of his life, and taking a stand to separate himself from his brothers and father who remained raging alcoholics. When asked how this action fit with his wife's account of his temper, her fear, and her decision to seek a separation, Jim became thoughtful and began talking of his experience growing up in an alcoholic household. The therapist's questions reoriented Jim to the person he wanted to be, creating a motivational spark rather than defensiveness and resistance.

Explore the Effects of Behavior. The therapist helps clients examine the effects of their behavior on themselves and others. The following are typical questions.

- What happened when you did *X* or didn't do *Y?*
- How was that for you? A good thing? A bad thing?
- How do others (parents, teachers, friends, relatives) react? What do they think? What do they say?
- How is that for you? Does anything feel good about it? Bad about it? What do you do?
- Has *X* happened in the past?
- How was that for you?

—Case Study—

With Jim, the violent husband, the therapist asked, "How is it for you when your temper gets the best of you?"

Jim, looking perplexed, responded, "What do you mean?"

The therapist elaborated, "How do you feel about yourself when you wind up banging the door down, getting in your wife's face and threatening to hurt her?"

"Not very good," Jim said.

The therapist then asked, "What effect does this have on Rita?"

Jim hesitated. "She gets scared. She doesn't want to talk with me."

"How is that for you?"

"I hate it when Rita doesn't talk to me."

The therapist asked about the effects of Jim's rage on his children. Jim looked down and said that his kids feared and avoided him.

The therapist then highlighted Jim's preferences: "You'd like to be in control, and you said you felt best about yourself when you made the decision to get sober—and you stuck to it." He reminded Jim of how Rita regarded him when he took control of his drinking. "Rita said that she was proud of you for taking charge of your life." The therapist also highlighted the effects of Jim's current behavior. "You don't like it when Rita pulls away from you. You said that you'd like to talk with her and understand her."

—**Case Study**—————————

When Al was asked about the effects of his current behavior on his family, he said that they were avoiding him. He also told a story about a recent incident in which he tried shoveling off the snow in his driveway. He went at it full tilt, as usual. But five minutes into the task, he started having trouble breathing. In disgust, he threw down the shovel and retreated to the house, where he collapsed on the couch for the rest of the afternoon. When asked what happened to the driveway, a pained look came over Al's face. "My son had to finish it."

Effects questions "externalize" problems; they separate the person from the problem. This allows clients to talk about problematic behavior without feeling ashamed or judged.

Effects questions also hold people accountable for the discrepancy between who they would like to be and the impact of their actions on themselves and others. When therapists simply challenge and confront negative behavior without taking into account this discrepancy, clients are apt to become resistant, to deny and minimize their responsibility. However, when therapists help clients to confront the gap in the context of noticing their preferred selves, clients are more likely to think of creative ways to bridge the gap. They come up with solutions.

Use Past and Present Stories. The therapist helps clients find past and present stories that are line

with their preferences and that contradict problem-maintaining behavior.

—**Case Study**—————————

When the therapist asked Jim about what motivated his decision to get sober, Jim told a story about riding in a car with his brothers who were drinking. Jim was in the passenger seat and his younger brother was driving recklessly while his older brothers were fighting in the back seat. Jim managed to quiet his brothers, convince them to stop the car, and turn over the driving to him. After this incident, Jim vowed to get sober. While telling this story, Jim appeared calm and in control, a contrast to his current aggressive behavior at home. As therapy progressed, the therapist often reminded Jim of this story, and of his capacity to be in control.

Discuss the Future. The therapist asks clients to imagine what the future will look like when the problem is resolved.

—**Case Study**—————————

When the therapist asked Al to envision a future without his problems, he pictured being less depressed and more involved with his family. He imagined himself coping with the emphysema while remaining useful to others; not following in the footsteps of his father who deteriorated with retirement and illness.

—**Case Study**—————————

Jim imagined a future in which he was more in control of his temper, in which he counted to ten and didn't explode. He also pictured himself having more positive conversations with Rita, in which he didn't criticize her or get angry, and in which she didn't run away from him.

Pose Mystery Questions. The therapist asks clients **mystery questions**—for example, how did a person with *X* preferred attributes (hard-working, productive) wind up in *Y* situation (acting listless, feeling depressed) and being seen by people in *Z* ways (uncaring, lazy)?

Mystery questions invite clients to reconcile the discrepancy between who it is they would like to be and the hard facts of their problematic behavior. Mystery questions inspire reflection in a nonthreatening way. People often begin to rethink their predicaments, how it is they came to act out of line with their preferred views, and what they can do about it. Eron and Lund recommend asking these questions in a puzzled rather than confrontive way.

—**Case Study**—————————

A I was asked how it was that someone who had always been there for his family would find himself so withdrawn. How could someone who had faced previous challenges by taking control and setting realistic limits (as with quitting drinking) wind up acting out of character in the wake of emphysema? Al seemed curious to find an explanation, and he asked the therapist to meet with his family to explore how his behavior had affected them. He reflected on his father's deterioration, and on how he was following in his footsteps, even though he didn't want to. Al realized that his family was foundering and needed his guidance about how to be helpful. He began to rethink his approach to emphysema and to his family.

—————————————————

Coauthor Alternative Explanations. The therapist works with clients to develop new explanations for the evolution of the problem that fits with how they prefer to be seen, and inspires new actions.

—**Case Study**—————————

J im was asked how it was that a man who had taken a stand against violence and taken control of his drinking would wind up losing control of his temper and being seen by his wife as untrustworthy. Jim grew thoughtful. He talked about growing up in an alcoholic family, where violence and loss of control was the norm. Jim hated it when his mother and father fought. He felt protective of his mother and brothers, but he was afraid. Remembering these scenes from his past helped Jim see the effect of his temper on Rita's withdrawal. Perhaps she was doing what he had done as a boy. Perhaps his own aggressive behavior was the reason for her withholding love and affection, not his unlovablity. Armed with this alternative explanation, Jim became more motivated to alter his approach to Rita.

—————————————————

Encourage Discussion. The therapist prompts clients to talk to significant others about their preferences, hopes, and intentions.

—**Case Study**—————————

A I felt empowered to talk to his doctor about his illness after he was able to recall preferred experiences indicating that he was a take-charge kind of guy. He also began reframing the motives of family members away from the belief that they saw him as useless to viewing them as bewildered, not knowing how to help him. Al's depression lifted after he met with his family and told them what was and wasn't helpful.

—————————————————

—**Case Study**—————————

J im sat down and talked with Rita about what he'd like in their relationship. He said that he missed their closeness and wanted to be able to talk with her without becoming angry. Rita said she admired Jim for staying sober, but no longer wanted rage or violence in her marriage. What she wanted was understanding and support. This preference-focused, nonblaming conversation between Rita and Jim set the stage for other helpful conversations in which Jim demonstrated control of his temper and a willingness to support Rita in her dreams and aspirations. Rita chose to stay with Jim, and their relationship improved.

Integrative Couples Therapy. Neil Jacobson of the University of Washington, one of the preeminent behavioral family therapists, teamed with Andrew Christensen of UCLA to figure out how to improve the limited success rates they were finding with traditional behavioral couples therapy. They discovered that their results improved when they added a humanistic element to the standard behavioral mix of communication training, conflict resolution, and problem solving. The approach they developed is described in *Integrative Couple Therapy* (Jacobson & Christensen, 1996).

Traditional behavioral couples therapy is based on the behavior exchange model. After a "functional analysis" showing how partners in a relationship influence one another, they're taught to reinforce changes they wish to bring about in each other. Anyone who's been married for a long time can tell you what's missing from this approach. Therapy may be about change, but a successful relationship also involves a certain amount of acceptance of differences and disappointments. Some things in an unhappy marriage may need to change for the relationship to improve; but some things about our partners are part of the package, and couples who survive the break-in period learn to accept these things. It's this element, *acceptance*, that Jacobson and Christensen have added in their new approach to couples therapy.

In contrast to the teaching and preaching characteristic of traditional behavioral therapy, integrative couples therapy emphasizes support and empathy, the same qualities that therapists want couples to learn to show each other. To create a conducive atmosphere, this approach begins with a phase called the *formulation*, which is aimed at helping couples let go of

blaming and open themselves to acceptance and personal change. The formulation consists of three components: a *theme* that defines the primary conflict; a *polarization process* that describes their destructive pattern of interaction; and the *mutual trap*, which is the impasse that prevents the couple from breaking the polarization cycle once it's triggered.

Common themes in couples' problems include conflicts around closeness and distance, a desire for control but unwillingness to take responsibility, and disagreements about sex. Whereas partners view these differences as indicating deficiencies in the other person and as problems to be solved, Jacobson and Christensen encourage couples to see that some differences are inevitable. This kind of acceptance can break the cycles that build up when each is constantly trying to change the other. Also, as the formulation phase continues, the partners begin to see that they aren't victims of each other, but of the *pattern* in which they've both been trapped. As with Michael White's externalizing, the couple can unite to fight a mutual enemy, the pattern. For example, when Jacobson asked a couple to describe their pattern,

> The husband replied, "We fight over whether or not to be close. When she is not as close to me as she wants to be, she pressures me into being close, and I withdraw, which leads to more pressure. Of course, sometimes I withdraw before she has a chance to pressure me. In fact, that's how it usually starts." (Jacobson & Christensen, 1996, p. 100)

Notice how the formulation process helps this couple describe their fight as a pattern to which they both contribute, rather than in the accusatory language more typical of distressed couples.

To further foster acceptance, Jacobson and Christensen encourage partners to talk about their own experience rather than attack their mates. Shifting from statements like, "She never shows me any affection!" to disclosure of vulnerability—"I'm not always sure she cares about me"—is more likely to promote understanding. The listening partner is encouraged to convey empathy for such disclosures.

Strategies to produce change include the two basic ingredients of behavioral couples therapy: behavior exchange and communication skills training. Behavior exchange interventions (described more fully in Chapter 10) involve quid pro quo and good faith contracts by which couples learn to exchange favors or to initiate pleasing behavior in the hope of getting the same in return. For example, each partner might be asked to generate a list of things they could do that would lead to greater satisfaction for the other. (Ask not what your partner can do for you; ask what you can do for your partner.) After each compiles a list, they're instructed to start doing some of the things they think will please their partners— and to observe the effect of this benevolence on the relationship.

The second ingredient—communication training—involves teaching couples to listen and to express themselves in direct but non-blaming ways. Learning to use active listening and to make I-statements is taught by assigned reading, instruction, and practice. As they learn to communicate less defensively, couples not only are better able to resolve conflicts, but they also become more accepting of each other.

It's too soon to evaluate the effectiveness of integrative couples therapy, but it seems to be an improvement over traditional behavioral therapy. Its significance isn't only in improving a model, but in the shift it represents toward the humanizing of behavioral technology. In emphasizing acceptance and compassion, integrative couples therapy joins other family therapies of the twenty-first century—from solution-focused to strategic to narrative—in recognizing the importance of nurturing relationships. Carl Rogers would be proud.

The narrative solutions model illustrates a principle that every good matchmaker knows: make sure the partners aren't incompatible before pushing them together. Because MRI techniques are similar to narrative ones, and because both traditions emphasize changing cognitions rather than emotions and downplay psychic conflict and developmental history, they're fairly compatible. Had they tried to combine either with, say, psychoanalytic therapy, it might be like trying to mix oil and water.

Jacobson and Christensen's amalgamation also involved compatible marriage candidates— behavioral and experiential. Both models are concerned with the communication that takes place between couples. They just have different emphases. Behaviorists focus on contracts and reinforcement while experientialists are interested in emotions and empathy. Blending some of the latter into the former is not a huge stretch. Encouraging partners to show each other more compassion doesn't necessarily interfere with helping them learn to be better problem solvers.

Other Integrative Models. Although we've singled out some of what we consider the most innovative examples, there are in fact so many integrative approaches to family therapy that it's impossible to list them all. While many of the models described as integrative are new, some of them have been around so long they don't always get the attention they deserve. To cite just one example, Carol Anderson and Susan Stewart wrote one of the most useful integrative guides to family therapy back in 1983. Two other integrative approaches that have been around for a while are those designed by Larry Feldman (1990) and William Nichols (1995). The tradition of offering practical advice that transcends schools of family therapy is upheld in a splendid book by Robert Taibbi (1996) called *Doing Family Therapy.* Others have attempted to integrate structural and strategic therapies (Stanton, 1981; Liddle,

1984), strategic and behavioral (Alexander & Parsons, 1982), psychodynamic and systems theory (Sander, 1979; Kirschner & Kirschner, 1986; Nichols, 1987; Scharff, 1989; Slipp, 1988), and experiential and systems theory (Duhl & Duhl, 1981; Greenberg & Johnson, 1988).

One particularly elegant model that's been around for a while (first described in 1981) is Alan Gurman's *brief integrative marital therapy,* which combines social learning theory and psychodynamics. As in behavior therapy, marital problems are seen as due to poor communication and problem solving, but, as in object relations theory, these deficits are understood as having roots in the unconscious conflicts of the partners. What might seem like simply a deficit—poor relationships skills—may turn out to serve a protective function of limiting intimacy to a level that a couple can tolerate without undue anxiety and conflict.

Gurman's assessment begins with looking for problematic themes in a couple's relationship. In a recent chapter on brief integrative marital therapy, Gurman (2002) describes a case in which Sue is angry and critical of her husband Karl's emotional unavailability. This familiar demand-and-withdraw pattern is assumed to reflect not only the couple's interaction but also the intrapsychic conflicts that motivate this interaction.

Like an analyst, Gurman sees Sue's attacking as serving the defensive function of avoiding dealing with her own fears of abandonment. Meanwhile Karl's distance helps him avoid his own conflicts about intimacy. The partners' complaints about each other ("nagging," "withdrawing") allow them to maintain a consistent and tolerable sense of themselves, even if it limits the satisfaction they share in their relationship.

Like a behaviorist, Gurman also looks at the *consequences* of the couple's problematic interaction, noting what positive and negative reinforcements or punishments may be main-

taining these patterns. Karl negatively reinforced Sue's criticism by apologizing and coming closer to her after her complaints reached the shouting and crying stage. Sue inadvertently punished Karl's closeness by venting her pent up anger and frustration whenever the couple did spend time together—thus violating the first law of social learning theory.[1]

In order to explore the impact of one or both partners' personal conflicts on the couple's relationship, Gurman may talk at some length to each partner individually while the other just listens. Talking separately to the partners, rather than having them talk to each other (à la Murray Bowen), helps minimize anxiety and thus makes therapy a safer "holding environment."

Gurman's blocking of Sue's criticism allowed Karl to explore how he felt about trying to balance his commitments to career and family. As Karl opened up about his fears of failure, Sue softened enough to empathize with his struggles—and to share her own fears of being alone and of not being able to manage.

In addition to addressing couples' problematic interactions and the conflicts underlying them, Gurman's brief integrative marital therapy also includes practical problem-solving discussions, advice, teaching of self-control techniques, exploration of the past, modeling, coaching, bibliotherapy—in short, the wide and flexible variety of interventions that characterize the best kinds of integration.

Other integrative approaches haven't received as much attention in mainstream family therapy as they have by federal funding agencies. These include Scott Henggeler's multisystemic model (Henggeler & Borduin, 1990) and Howard Liddle's multidimensional family therapy (Liddle, Dakoff, & Diamond, 1991). These approaches both evolved out of research pro-

---

1.   You catch more flies with honey.

jects with difficult adolescents, a population that challenges theorists to expand their views beyond the limits of one school of therapy or one level of system.

Liddle developed his integrative approach while working with drug-abusing, inner-city adolescents in a federally funded project. His multidimensional family therapy brings together the risk factor models of drug and problem behavior, developmental psychopathology, family systems theory, social support theory, peer cluster theory, and social learning theory. In practice, the model applies a combination of structural family therapy, parent training, skills training for adolescents, and cognitive-behavioral techniques.

One of the most useful aspects of Liddle's approach is the way he integrates individual and systems interventions. While he makes liberal use of the structural technique of enactment, he frequently meets with individual family members to coach and prepare them to participate more effectively in these family dialogues. Liddle also uses these individual sessions to focus on teenagers' experiences outside the home. Here, sensitive subjects like drug use and sexual behavior can be explored more safely than when the whole family is present. The need to meet with teenagers to focus on their lives outside the family reflects a growing recognition of the limited influence families have in comparison to peers and culture.

Scott Henggeler of the University of South Carolina and a number of research-oriented colleagues who work with "difficult-to-treat" children tried to improve on their systems-oriented family therapy by (1) more actively considering and intervening into the extrafamilial systems in which families are embedded, in particular their school and peer contexts; (2) including individual developmental issues in assessments; and (3) incorporating cognitive-behavioral interventions (Henggeler & Borduin, 1990). This multisystemic model has shown promising results in several well-

designed outcome studies of juvenile offenders and families referred for abuse or neglect. For that reason, it is highly regarded among governmental funding agencies, and Henggeler has received a number of large grants.

Models Designed for Specific Clinical Problems

One sign that family therapy was maturing was when therapists began focusing on specific clinical problems rather than generic "families." Some groups applied their preexisting models to the problems they were wrestling with; for example, structural family therapy was used with anorexia nervosa and brittle diabetes (Minuchin, Rosman, & Baker, 1978). Other groups had to be more creative because they decided to tackle problems that weren't typically seen in the practice of family therapy. Such problems often require more than any single approach offers.

Working with Violent Families. One of the most impressive integrative efforts is the approach to treating spousal abuse developed by Virginia Goldner and Gillian Walker at the Ackerman Institute in New York (Goldner, Penn, Sheinberg, & Walker, 1990; Walker & Goldner, 1995; Goldner, 1998). When Goldner and Walker began studying violence in couples, the standard approach involved separating the partners and treating the man in a group with other offenders and the abused woman in a support group. This treatment was informed by the feminist critique of systems-based therapies that implied that both partners were responsible for the violence and, consequently, could be treated together like any other couple.

Goldner and Walker share the feminist conviction that regardless of the woman's role, the man is responsible for his violent behavior, no matter what provocation he might feel. But they also believe that there is value to treating the couple together and to attending to the

*V*irginia Goldner's work with violent couples combines a highly sophisticated clinical approach with a passionate feminist sensitivity.

woman's part in these couples' dangerous dramas. Instead of taking sides in the systems theory versus feminism battles, they bridged the polarized thinking that pervaded the field of family violence. Could it be possible to take both positions simultaneously? Yes, the man is responsible for controlling his violence; but both partners participate in a process of interaction that must change. As Goldner says, "A battered woman is not equally responsible for

her broken nose, even if she acknowledges having been angry or 'provocative'; just as the victim of sexual abuse is not equally responsible for what happened in the middle of the night, even if she felt aroused" (Goldner, 1988, p. 266). With this more nuanced position, it became possible to examine both partners' roles in their escalations of conflict without blaming the victim.

Rather than seeing each partner individually and insisting that they separate, Goldner and Walker work with the couple together, but insist that the violence must cease immediately and the man must take responsibility for making that happen. Here they combine the feminist emphasis on safety and responsibility with a systemic interest in the way the couple interacts. Goldner points out that separating violent couples rarely promotes safety because they are often so symbiotically attached that they quickly reunite, and those women who do manage to leave are the most likely to be attacked. On the other hand, if they are together

*L*earning to control patterns of escalating emotion is one of the keys to working with violent couples.

in treatment, the victim can explain to the abuser how damaging his aggression is in the presence of the therapist who can emphasize the moral imperative to stop.

Goldner and Walker use the language of "parts" to help the partners detach from global labels like abuser and victim and to bring intrapsychic insights into the conversation. That is, he can talk about the angry part of himself and she the part that needs to protect him rather than look after herself. As they inquire into the origin of these parts, Goldner and Walker find themselves listening to painful stories from each partner's past. "Here we typically find ourselves back in a time when the man was a boy, subject to sadistic acts of violence, power and control" (Goldner, 1998, p. 275). This compassionate witnessing helps reduce the partners' sense of antagonism toward each other.

Goldner and Walker also incorporate a kind of active listening format so that not only are past traumas witnessed but also the man listens to the woman describe the pain and terror she suffered from his attacks. Here again there's a both/and message to the man: Yes, you suffered as a boy and that's related to your violent behavior, but you are still choosing to be violent, and that's unacceptable. Similarly, regardless of how passive the woman has been in the past, she can choose to protect herself without feeling guilty or disloyal. This nondichotomous position is an advance over the either/or positions of both the feminist and psychoanalytic models. That is, feminist therapists believe that to explore a man's troubled childhood would imply excusing his violence, while psychoanalysts too often see violence as a symptom of underlying pathology for which they don't hold anyone accountable. Goldner (1998) writes that "From a both/and perspective, violence is best conceptualized as simultaneously willful and impulse-ridden, as both instrumental and dissociative" (p. 279).

While Goldner and Walker's approach was designed for violent couples, it offers important lessons for the integration of therapy models in general. It illustrates the value of stepping out of the dichotomies that dominate clinical work (especially around volatile issues like domestic violence) to see that more than one perspective has validity and can coexist with others. Too often, "Ideas that could mutually enrich one another have instead been set up as oppositional positions, creating a polarizing context of forced choices between adequate alternatives" (Goldner, 1998, p. 264). The depolarizing effect is a major virtue of integration.

Community Family Therapy

Many family therapists start out working in agencies with poor families, but as they realize how powerless family therapy alone is to deal with many of the problems impoverished families face, they get discouraged and opt for private practice with middle-class families. This recognition of family therapy's limits had the opposite effect on Ramon Rojano.

According to Rojano, the greatest obstacle poor people face is the sense of powerlessness that comes with being controlled by a multitude of dehumanizing bureaucracies and the futility of having no hope of achieving the American dream of a decent job and a comfortable home. Rojano uses his knowledge of and personal connections with the helping systems to make clients feel reconnected to their communities and empowered to advocate for what they need. Not only does he help families find the resources to survive—child care, jobs, food stamps, housing—which is the essence of traditional casework, but he also begins encouraging aspirations beyond mere survival.

Laura Markowitz (1997) describes Rojano's work this way.

> Ramon Rojano is a professional nudge. Let's say you're a single mother on welfare who goes to him because your teenage son is skipping school and on the verge of being expelled. Leaning forward in his chair, the

stocky, energetic Rojano will start prodding and poking with this questions in his Spanish accent, zeroing in on your son like he's herding a stray lamb back into the fold. After some minutes of this interrogation, you actually hear your boy admit what's going on with him and promise in a small, sincere voice you haven't heard come out of him in a long time, that he will go to school regularly if he can graduate. As your mouth opens in surprise, Rojano won't even pause. Now he'll urge the 15-year-old boy to apply for an after-school job he just heard about from someone who runs a program . . . Rojano will write the phone number down and put it directly into the boy's hand, look him in the eye and use his name a few times to make sure he knows Rojano actually cares whether or not this kid ends up on the streets or in a gang . . . You think the session is over, right? Not quite. He has plans for you too. Be prepared—he might ask you something outrageous, like whether you've thought about owning your own house. You may be a single mother barely getting by, but as he leans toward you it's like the force of his confidence in you pulls you in, and now he's pressing a piece of paper into your hand with the number of a woman he knows who runs a program that helps people with no money buy a home of their own. (pp. 25–26)

He'll ask clients about things that they, in their state of hopelessness and disconnection, never considered—running for the school board, going to college, starting a business or an advocacy program—in such a way that these things seem possible. This is partly because Rojano can see strengths that disheartened clients have forgotten and partly

because he has the connections to get the ball rolling.

Rojano also recognizes that community empowerment by itself is not enough. Without ongoing family therapy, it wouldn't be long before the single parent in the previous scenario might start being late for work because of renewed conflicts with her son, and that dream of a house would evaporate.

So this is the integration: family therapy with community psychology and social work. Rojano has taken a version of structural family therapy and bolstered it with hands-on advocacy. Structural family therapy was developed in the Wiltwyck agency in Harlem in the late 1950s. Retrospectively, Braulio Montalvo, one of its developers, said, "We couldn't get the resources around the family to uphold the changes they were able to make in family therapy" (quoted in Markowitz, 1997, p. 28). Forty years later, someone has taken the next step by incorporating those resources. Whereas narrative therapy coauthors with clients a new story about their past in the hope of inspiring a sense of agency, Rojano goes one better by not only encouraging a new attitude, but also leading clients along the path toward their dreams.

Once again we see that integration requires a new way of thinking. Rojano had to step out of the mind-set that said therapy takes place in an office, even though clients are often constrained by forces untouched in the office. Why not take it to the street so the whole system is addressed? It seems like an obvious question—but maybe not so obvious when you're trapped in your circumstances.

—Summary

In the founding decades of family therapy, a number of clearly articulated models were developed, and most family therapists became

disciples of one of these approaches. Each of the major schools concentrated on a particular aspect of family life. Experientialists opened people up to feeling, behaviorists helped them reinforce more functional behavior, and Bowenians taught them to think for themselves. By concentrating their attention this way, practitioners of the classic models focused their power for change. If in the process they got a little parochial and competitive, what was the harm?

The harm was that by ignoring valuable insights of other approaches, orthodox disciples of the various schools may have limited their impact and applicability. But maybe this parochialism is better understood from a developmental perspective—as a necessary stage in the consolidation of the original insights of the founding models. Perhaps it was useful for the schools to pursue the truth as they knew it in order to mine the full potential of their essential ideas. If so, that time has passed.

Most of the schools of family therapy have been around long enough to have solidified their approach and proven their worth. That's why the time is ripe for integration.

Valuable as integrative efforts are, however, there remains a serious pitfall in mixing ingredients from different approaches. You don't want to end up with what happens when you blend three or more colors from a set of poster paints. The trick is to find unifying conceptual threads that can tie together disparate ideas, and to add techniques from various models without subtracting the power that focusing offers. A successful integrative approach draws on existing therapies in such a way that they can be practiced coherently within one consistent theoretical framework. Adding techniques willy-nilly from here and there just doesn't work.

To succeed, a synthesizing effort must strike a balance between breadth and focus. Breadth may be particularly important when it comes to conceptualization. Contemporary family therapists are wisely adopting a broad, bio-psychosocial perspective in which biological, psychological, relational, community, and even societal processes are viewed as relevant to understanding people's problems. When it comes to techniques, on the other hand, the most effective approaches don't overload therapists with scores of interventions.

Finally, an effective integration must have clear direction. The trouble with being too flexible is that families have strong and subtle ways of inducting therapists into their habits of avoidance. Good family therapy creates an environment where conversations that should happen at home, but don't, can take place. These dialogues won't happen, however, if therapists abruptly shift from one type of intervention to another in the face of resistance.

Family therapy is ultimately a clinical enterprise, its worth measured in results. The real reason to combine elements from various approaches is to maximize their usefulness, not merely their theoretical inclusiveness. To contradict Billy Crystal, it's better to be effective than to look marvelous.

—Recommended Readings

Anderson, C., and Stewart, S. 1983. *Mastering resistance: A practical guide to family therapy.* New York: Guilford Press.

Breunlin, D. C., Schwartz, R. C., and Mac Kune-Karrer, B. 1992. *Metaframeworks: Transcending the models of family therapy.* San Francisco: Jossey-Bass.

Eron, J., and Lund, T. 1996. *Narrative solutions in brief therapy.* New York: Guilford Press.

Goldner, V. 1998. The treatment of violence and victimization in intimate relationships. *Family Process.* 37:263–286.

Jacobson, N. S., and Christensen, A. 1996. *Integrative couple therapy.* New York: Norton.

Pinsof, W. M. 1995. *Integrative problem-centered therapy.* New York: Basic Books.

Taibbi, R. 1996. *Doing family therapy.* New York: Guilford Press.

—References

Alexander, J., and Parsons, B. 1982. *Functional family therapy.* Pacific Grove, CA: Brooks/Cole.

American Family Therapy Academy Newsletter, Winter 1999, Washington, DC.

Anderson, C., and Stewart, S. 1983. *Mastering resistance: A practical guide to family therapy.* New York: Guilford Press.

Breunlin, D., Schwartz, R., and Mac Kune-Karrer, B. 1992. *Metaframeworks: Transcending the models of family therapy.* San Francisco: Jossey-Bass.

Duhl, B., and Duhl, F. 1981. Integrative family therapy. In *Handbook of family therapy,* A. Gurman and D. Kniskern, eds. New York: Brunner/Mazel.

Eron, J., and Lund, T. 1993. An approach to how problems evolve and dissolve: Integrating narrative and strategic concepts. *Family Process.* 32:291–309.

Eron, J., and Lund, T. 1996. *Narrative solutions in brief therapy.* New York: Guilford Press.

Feldman, L. 1990. *Multi-dimensional family therapy.* New York: Guilford Press.

Goldner, V. 1998. The treatment of violence and victimization in intimate relationships. *Family Process.* 37:263–286.

Goldner, V., Penn, P., Sheinberg, M., and Walker, G. 1990. Love and violence: Gender paradoxes in volatile attachments. *Family Process.* 29:343–364.

Greenberg, L. S., and Johnson, S. M. 1988. *Emotionally focused therapy for couples.* New York: Guilford Press.

Gurman, A. S. 1981. Integrative marital therapy: Toward the development of an interpersonal approach. In *Forms of brief therapy,* S. H. Budman, ed. New York: Guilford Press.

Gurman, A. S. 2002. Brief integrative marital therapy: A depth-behavioral approach. In *Clinical handbook of couple therapy,* 3rd ed., A. S. Gurman and N. S. Jacobson, eds. New York: Guilford Press.

Henggeler, S., and Borduin, C. 1990. *Family therapy and beyond: A multisystemic approach to treating the behavior problems of children and adolescents.* Pacific Grove, CA: Brooks/Cole.

Jacobson, N., and Christensen, A. 1996. *Integrative couple therapy.* New York: Norton.

Kirschner, D., and Kirschner, S. 1986. *Comprehensive family therapy.* New York: Brunner/Mazel.

Liddle, H. A. 1984. Toward a dialectical-contextual-coevolutionary translation of structural-strategic family therapy. *Journal of Strategic and Systemic Family Therapies.* 3:66–79.

Mac Kune-Karrer, B. 1999. A conversation with Betty Carter. *American Family Therapy Academy Newsletter,* Winter, Washington, DC.

Markowitz, L. 1997. Ramon Rojano won't take no for an answer. *Family Therapy Networker.* 21:24–35.

Minuchin, S., Rosman, B., and Baker, L. 1978. *Psychosomatic families: Anorexia in context.* Cambridge, MA: Harvard University Press.

Nichols, M. P. 1987. *The self in the system.* New York: Brunner/Mazel.

Nichols, W. C. 1995. *Treating people in families: An integrative framework.* New York: Guilford Press.

Pinsof, W. 1995. *Integrative problem-centered therapy.* New York: Basic Books.

Pinsof, W. 1999. Choosing the right door. *Family Therapy Networker.* 23:48–55.

Sander, F. M. 1979. *Individual and family therapy: Toward an integration.* New York: Jason Aronson.

Scharff, J., ed. 1989. *The foundations of object relations family therapy.* New York: Jason Aronson.

Slipp, S. 1988. *Technique and practice of object relations family therapy.* New York: Jason Aronson.

Stanton, M. D. 1981. An integrated structural/strategic approach to family and marital therapy. *Journal of Marital and Family Therapy.* 7:427–440.

Taibbi, R. 1996. *Doing family therapy.* New York: Guilford Press.

Walker, G., and Goldner, V. 1995. The wounded prince and the women who love him. In *Gender and power in relationships,* C. Burcke, and B. Speed, eds. London: Routledge, Chapman and Hall.

Comparative Analysis

The Essential Differences among Models

The exponential growth of family therapy crowded the field with competing models, each of which made important contributions. This diversification produced a rich and varied literature, bearing witness to the vitality of the profession, while at the same time creating a confusing array of concepts and techniques. See Table 15.1 for a summary of these models.

In this chapter we offer a comparative analysis of the various models. Each school proclaims a set of truths, yet despite some overlap there are notable conflicts among these truths.

Theoretical Formulations

Theories can bias observation, but they also bring order out of chaos. They organize our awareness and help us make sense of what families are doing. Instead of seeing a "blooming, buzzing confusion," we begin to see patterns of pursuit and distance, enmeshment and disengagement, and problem-saturated stories. The minute you begin to see ineffectual attempts to settle arguments between children as enmeshment, your goal shifts from intervening more effectively to backing off and letting the children settle their own disputes. Here we evaluate theories in terms of their pragmatic function: understanding families in order to better help them.

Families as Systems

Communications therapists introduced the idea that families are systems. More than the sum of their parts, **systems** are the parts *plus* the way they function together. Once, not accepting systems theory was like not believing in apple pie and motherhood. Now the postmodern movement has challenged systems thinking as just another modernist framework, a metaphor taken too literally, and has shifted emphasis from action to meaning and from the organization of the family to the thinking of its members. It's easy to say that a good therapist takes into account both the self *and* the system. In practice, however, deciding when to delve into individual experience or

TABLE 15.1 Schools

	Bowenian	Strategic	Structural
Founder(s)	Murray Bowen	Don Jackson Jay Haley	Salvador Minuchin
Key Theoretical Constructs	Differentiation of self	Homeostasis Feedback loops	Subsystems Boundaries
Core Problem Dynamic	Triangles Emotional reactivity	More-of-the-same solutions	Enmeshment/ disengagement
Key Techniques	Genogram Process questions	Reframing Directives	Enactments Boundary making

	Experiential	Psychodynamic	Cognitive-Behavioral
Founder(s)	Virginia Satir Carl Whitaker	Nathan Ackerman Henry Dicks Ivan Boszormenyi- Nagy	Gerald Patterson Robert Liberman Richard Stuart
Key Theoretical Constructs	Authenticity Self-actualization	Drives Selfobjects Internal objects	Reinforcement Extinction Schemas
Core Problem Dynamic	Emotional suppression Mystification	Conflict Projective identification Fixation and regression	Inadvertent reinforcement Aversive control
Key Techniques	Confrontation Structured exercises	Silence Interpretation	Functional analysis Teaching positive control

	Solution-Focused	Narrative
Founder(s)	Steve de Shazer Insoo Kim Berg	Michael White David Epston
Key Theoretical Contructs	Language creates reality	Narrative theory Social constructionism
Core Problem Dynamic	Problem talk	Problem-saturated stories
Key Techniques	Focusing on solutions Identifying exceptions	Externalization Identifying unique outcomes Creating audiences of support

focus on interactional patterns presents a host of hard choices.

Stability and Change

Communications theorists described families as rule-governed systems with a tendency toward stability or homeostasis (Jackson, 1965). But in order to adjust to changing circumstances, families must also be capable of revising their rules and modifying their structure.

The dual nature of families—*homeostatic* and *changing*—is best appreciated by the communications, structural, and strategic schools. They don't presume that symptomatic families are inherently dysfunctional but merely that they have failed to adapt to changing circumstances.

Anyone who ignores this developmental principle runs the risk of placing undue emphasis on pathology. A therapist who sees a family having trouble, but fails to consider that they may be stuck at a transitional impasse, is apt to think they need an overhaul, when a tune-up might do. Therapies that emphasize long-range goals are all susceptible to this therapeutic overkill. Psychoanalytic, experiential, and extended family practitioners are inclined to assume that families need fundamental reorganization. Because they have the equipment for major surgery—long-term therapy—they tend to see their clients as needing it.

The pioneers of family therapy (with the notable exception of Virginia Satir) tended to overestimate homeostatic forces in families and underestimate their flexibility and resourcefulness. This viewpoint encouraged therapists to act as provokers, controllers, and strategizers. The corollary of the family trapped by systemic forces they can't understand was the clever therapist who would do the understanding for them. Many of the newer approaches are designed to elicit families' resources rather than battle with their re-

sistance. These models encourage therapists to collaborate with families to work out solutions rather than assume that they won't change unless provoked. But when some of these "collaborative" approaches—like solution-focused therapy, for example—presume that change is easy, that seems as much naive as optimistic.

Process/Content

Most schools of family therapy emphasize the **process** of family interaction. Psychoanalysts and experientialists try to reduce defensiveness and foster open expression of thoughts and feelings; communications therapists increase the flow of interactions and help family members reduce the incongruence between levels of communication; Bowenians block triangulation and encourage "I-position" stances; strategic therapists counter problem-maintaining interactions; behaviorists teach parents to use positive control and couples to eliminate coercive communication; structural therapists realign boundaries and strengthen hierarchical organization.

Despite their commitment to process, however, therapists often get distracted by content issues. Psychoanalysts lose sight of process when they concentrate on individual family members and their memories of the past. Experientialists are prone to become overly central while working with individual family members to help them overcome emotional defensiveness. The danger is that by so doing the therapist will neglect interactional processes that affect individual expression.

Behavior therapists neglect process in favor of content when they isolate behavior from its context and ignore the interactional patterns surrounding it. They often interfere with the process of family interaction by assuming a directive, teaching role. (As long as a teacher stands in front of the class lecturing, there's little opportunity to find out what the students can do on their own.)

Process concepts are so central to Bowen systems therapy that there's little danger of forgetting them. Only naive misunderstanding of Bowen's theory would lead someone to think merely of reestablishing family ties, without also being aware of processes of triangulation, fusion, and differentiation. The same is true of structural family therapy and communications therapy; process issues are always at center stage.

The newer models, with their deemphasis on systems thinking, have moved away from process. Narrative constructivists are less interested in interactional patterns than in the ways family members understand their problems. They're less interested in changing behavior than in expanding stories. Similarly, because solution-focused therapists have no interest in how problems got started, they too ignore the family processes that surround problems. The only processes they do attend to are interactions that constitute "exceptions"—times when the problem wasn't a problem.

Monadic, Dyadic, or Triadic Model

Some therapists (e.g., psychoeducational) continue to think of individuals as the patient and include the rest of the family as an adjunct to that person's treatment. Keep in mind that psychoeducational therapists work primarily with serious mental illness (schizophrenia, bipolar disorder), where the family's influence is almost certainly less than in the majority of cases treated by family therapists.

The same cannot, however, be said for narrative therapists, whose focus on cognition leads them to concentrate on individuals and largely ignore the three defining characteristics of family therapy: (1) recognizing that psychological symptoms are often the result of family conflict; (2) thinking about human problems as interactional, which means thinking in twos and threes (complementarity, triangles); and (3) treating the family as a unit. Although narrative thera-

pists disregard family conflict in their formulations, their efforts to redefine problems as alien invaders have the effect of uniting families to overcome the problem's influence. It would be interesting to speculate on whether ignoring family conflict but rallying family members to unite in concern would be more effective in cases like anorexia, where problems take on a life of their own, than in others, like school refusal or misbehavior, where the problem is more likely to be a result of family conflicts.

Psychoanalysts tend to think about personality dynamics, whether they meet with individuals or with families. They see family life as a product of internalized relationships from the past, and they're often more concerned with these mental ghosts than with the flesh-and-blood families of the present. Behavior therapists use a **monadic model** when they accept a family's definition of a symptomatic child as the problem and set about teaching parents to modify the child's behavior. Experiential therapists focus on individuals to help them uncover and express their feelings.

Actually, no living thing can adequately be understood in terms of the monadic model. A bird's egg may be the closest thing in nature to a self-contained unit. The fetus is locked away inside its shell with all the nutrients it needs to survive. Even this view is incomplete, however, for there is an exchange of heat between the egg and the surrounding environment. Without its mother's warmth, the baby bird will die.

Dyadic concepts are necessary to explain the fact that people act in relation to one another. Even the psychoanalytic patient, free-associating on the couch, filters memories and dreams through reactions to the analyst. Most of the time family therapists operate with dyadic concepts. Even with a large family in treatment, the focus is usually on various pairs or units of the family.

Helping two people learn to relate better doesn't always mean that the therapist thinks in dyadic terms. Behavior therapists work with couples but treat them as individuals, each deficient in the art of communicating. A true **dyadic model** is based on the recognition that two people in a relationship aren't independent entities interacting with each other; they each define the other. Using this model, a wife's agoraphobia would be understood as a reaction to her husband and as a means of influencing him. Likewise, his decision to send her for behavior modification reflects his reluctance to accept his role in her life.

Family therapists of all schools use some dyadic concepts: unconscious need complementarity, expressive/instrumental, projective identification, symbiosis, intimacy, quid pro quo, double bind, symmetrical/complementary, pursuer/distancer, and behavioral contract. Some terms are based on dyadic thinking even though they may involve more than two people: compliant (referring to a family's relationship to a therapist) or defiant. Some seem to involve only one: countertransference, dominant, and supercompetent. Still other concepts are capable of encompassing units of three or more but are often used to refer to units of two: boundary, coalition, fusion, and disengagement.

Too often family therapists neglect triadic complications. Murray Bowen, who introduced the concept of emotional triangles, did more than anyone to point out that human behavior is always a function of triangles. Structural therapists have consistently emphasized that enmeshment or disengagement between two people is a function of reciprocal relationships with third parties. Communications therapists wrote about triadic relationships but tended to think in units of two. The same is true of most strategic therapists, although Haley, Selvini Palazzoli, and Lynn Hoffman are consistently aware of triangles.

The advantage of the **triadic model** is that it permits a more complete understanding of behavior in context. If a child misbehaves when his mother doesn't use firm discipline, teaching her to be stricter won't work if her behavior is a function of her relationship with her husband. Perhaps she allows her child to misbehave as a way of undermining her husband's authority, or she and her husband may have worked out a relationship where her ineffectiveness reassures him that he's the strong one.

The fact that triadic thinking permits a more complete understanding doesn't mean that family therapists must always include all parties in treatment. The issue isn't how many people are in the consulting room, but whether the therapist considers problems in their full context.

The Nuclear Family in Context

Just as most family therapists endorse the ideas of systems theory, most also describe families as **open systems.** The family is open in that its members interact not only with each other but also with extrafamilial systems. Indeed, a major emphasis in contemporary family therapy has been to expand the focus of attention to include how families are affected by race, gender, ethnicity, class, and sexual orientation. For today's therapist, talking about the social context of families is no longer an idle abstraction.

Members of the Palo Alto group introduced the concept of open systems but actually treated families as self-contained units. They paid little attention to stressors outside the family and rarely considered the impact of the community or extended family. The first to take the extrafamilial into account were Murray Bowen and Ross Speck. Bowen stressed the critical role of extended family relationships, and Speck mobilized networks of friends and neighbors to aid in treatment.

Bowen systems therapists and network therapists virtually always include people outside the nuclear family in treatment; psychoanalytic, solution-focused, behavioral, and narrative therapists rarely do. Among experientialists, Whitaker routinely included members of the extended family for one or two sessions. Including extended family members or friends in treatment is often useful, sometimes essential. It is not, however, the same thing as thinking of the family as an open system. An open system isn't a larger system; it's a system that interacts with its environment.

Nowhere is the idea of families as open systems better articulated than in Minuchin's (1974) *Families and Family Therapy*. Writing about "Man in His Context," Minuchin contrasts family therapy with psychodynamic theory. The latter, he says, draws on the concept of man as a hero, remaining himself despite the circumstances.[1] On the other hand, "The theory of family therapy is predicated on the fact that man is not an isolate. He is an acting and reacting member of social groups" (p. 2). Minuchin credits Gregory Bateson with erasing the boundary between inner and outer space and goes on to say that, just as the boundary separating the individual from the family is artificial, so too is the boundary separating the family from the social environment.

One of the things that anyone who works with agency families quickly learns is that attempts to help them often get caught in a sticky web of competing influences from courts, probation departments, child protective agencies, family services, housing programs, group homes, domestic violence agencies, and so on. If middle-class families can be treated as organizationally closed units, with poor families that's impossible. Poor families live in homes without walls.

As services proliferate, fiefdoms multiply. The most obvious problem is lack of coordination. Take, for example, a recent case involving a fifteen-year-old boy who had sexually abused his two adolescent sisters and younger brother. There were agencies working with the female victims, one with the older girl, and another with the younger one. One agency worked with the younger boy, one worked with the perpetrator, and one worked with the mother of the victims. There was an art therapist in the public school working with the sexually abused children, and the fifteen-year-old was in a residential school where he had individual and group therapy. Is it any wonder that these helpers were pulling in different directions? A second, more invidious, problem is that most agencies are mandated to serve individuals—victims or victimizers, adults or children. By addressing themselves to the rights of persons in need of protection or correction, these agencies support individuals, not the family unit.

The usual reaction of therapists who run into these networks of unorganized altruism is first to make an effort to coordinate the various inputs, and then, when they discover their lack of leverage with all these agencies and helpers, to give up and do the best they can with the family in the office. Among those who aren't willing to give up, Evan Imber-Black (1988) and Richard Kagan and Shirley Schlosberg (1989) have written practical books about working with families in "perpetual crisis." Patricia Minuchin, Jorge Colapinto, and Salvador Minuchin (1998) published an inspiring account of their efforts to bring coordination and a family focus to agency social work with families of the poor.

Under the influence of social constructionism, the newer models of family therapy have become acutely aware of the social context of the families they treat. This awareness is, however, less likely to take the form of including people outside the family in treatment than

---

1.   Although we recognize that it was until recently the rule, use of the masculine pronoun here may be particularly apt. The model of the hero is of a man who keeps his moral integrity hard and intact. He is an isolate, stoic and enduring, cut off from family, community, and faith—that is, the trivial, suffocating world of women.

*I*t's impossible to understand relationships without taking into account the social and cultural forces impinging on the partners.

being sensitive to social and political influences on the modern family.

The Personal as Political

At one time it was axiomatic that therapists should maintain therapeutic neutrality: They shouldn't make judgments, take sides, or tell people what to do. They should remain steadfastly objective, encouraging communication or making interpretations, but refrain from imposing their personal opinions and values. Today, however, many practitioners believe that therapists should stand for some things and against others.

Since feminist family therapists first challenged us to face up to gender inequality (e.g., Hare-Mustin, 1978; Goldner, 1985), a growing number of practitioners in the narrative tradition have begun to help family members iden-

tify the harmful influence of certain cultural values and practices on their lives and relationships (e.g., White & Epston, 1990; Freedman & Combs, 1996). Indeed, one of the most powerful ways they motivate people to become more active in their own destinies is to help them think of themselves as not flawed but oppressed. Once they start to make progress, the narrative therapist seeks to recruit other people as witnesses and a cheering squad to support the client's new and more positive sense of self.

There is certainly a case to be made for helping people question values that may be contributing to their problems. Who says women should be as thin as runway models? That adolescence must be a time of turmoil? That a man's first obligation is to his career? Moreover, by defining certain destructive assumptions as culturally imposed, narrative therapists invite family members to pull together in opposing those values. Questions can be raised, however, about how this political awareness is put into practice.

Sometimes a readiness to identify oppressive cultural attitudes can lead to ignoring a client's role in his or her own problems in favor of projecting blame outward. Take, for example, the case of a woman who starts to wonder if something about what she's doing might be responsible for her lack of success with men. What happens if the therapist redefines the woman's problem as "The Voice of Insecurity" and urges her to consider this doubt as part of a cultural pattern whereby women learn to conform to the expectations of men? It may be true that women do more accommodating than men, but what about *this* woman? If her consideration of how she might be contributing to the pattern of unsuccessful relationships in her life is blamed on society, does this empower her?

It's fine to be sympathetic, even to be the client's champion, but when therapists start assuming that their patients are victims of patriarchy, men, racism, or heterosexism, they may fall into the kind of linear, blaming mentality that family therapy was designed to combat in the first place.

At times the readiness to identify cultural influences as villains in the lives of clients seems like posturing, with the therapist as a knight in shining armor against the forces of oppression. On the other hand, ignoring racism, sexism, ethnocentrism, poverty, crime, and alienation— thinking of families as though they were living on a desert island—makes about as much sense as hiding your head in the sand. What is the proper role of a family therapist with respect to larger issues of social injustice?

Given the impact of social conditions on families, do family therapists have a unique role to play in politics and society, or are they, at least in their professional capacity, primarily clinicians, trained to treat psychological problems but having no special authority or exper-

tise to right social wrongs? These are important questions without easy answers.

Boundaries

The most useful concepts of interpersonal boundaries are found in the works of Murray Bowen and Salvador Minuchin. Bowen is best at describing the boundary between the self and the family; Minuchin is best at identifying boundaries among various subsystems of the family. In Bowen's terms, individuals vary on a continuum from fusion to differentiation, while Minuchin describes boundaries as ranging from diffuse to rigid, with resultant **enmeshment** or **disengagement.**

Bowen's thinking reflects the psychoanalytic emphasis on *separation* and *individuation* (Mahler, Pine, & Bergman, 1975), with special attention to the resolution of oedipal attachments and leaving home. In this model, we become ourselves by learning to stand alone. Bowen paid less attention to the emotional isolation stemming from too rigid boundaries, treating this as an artifact—a defense against—a lack of psychological separateness. Bowen used a variety of terms—*togetherness, fusion, undifferentiation, emotional reactivity*—all referring to the danger that people will lose themselves in relationships.

Minuchin offers a more balanced view, describing the problems that result when **boundaries** are either too weak *or* too strong. *Diffuse boundaries* allow too much interference into the functioning of a subsystem; *rigid boundaries* allow too little support between members of the family. Bowen described only one boundary problem—fusion—and only one goal— differentiation. Fusion is like a disease—you can have a bad case or a mild one. Minuchin speaks of two possibilities—enmeshment or disengagement—and his therapy is designed to fit the specific case.

Bowen's "fusion" and Minuchin's "enmeshment" both deal with blurred boundaries, but they aren't synonymous. **Fusion** is a psychological quality of individuals, the opposite of individuation. The dynamics of fusion have an impact on relationships (especially in the form of reactivity and triangulation), but fusion is *within* the person. Enmeshment is *between* people.

These conceptual differences also lead to differences in treatment. Bowenian therapists encourage relationships but emphasize autonomy. Success is measured by **differentiation** of self. Structuralists encourage authenticity but strive to restructure family relationships either by strengthening *or* weakening boundaries. Success is measured by the harmonious functioning of the whole family.

Normal Family Development

As a rule family therapists have had little to say about developmental issues.[2] One of the distinguishing characteristics of family therapy is its focus on here-and-now interactions. Normal family development, which involves the past and what's healthy, has therefore been underemphasized.

Most therapists have assumptions about what's normal, and these ideas influence their work. The problem is that these implicit models are based largely on personal experience; as long as they remain unarticulated they may reflect personal bias as much as anything else. When it comes to setting goals for family treatment, the choice isn't between having or not having a model of what's healthy, but between using a model that's been spelled out and examined or operating on the basis of ill-defined, personal standards.

---

2. This is true despite the current popularity of disavowing impositional models of normality. It's one thing to challenge universals in favor of the particular, but accusing traditional family therapists of operating with fixed views of normality is a straw man argument.

Family therapists concerned with the past, especially members of Bowenian and psychoanalytic schools, have had the most to say about normal development. Although most schools of family therapy aren't concerned with how families get started, Bowenians and psychoanalysts have a great deal to say about marital choice. Bowen talked about *differentiation, fusion,* and *triangles,* while psychoanalytic writers speak of *unconscious need complementarity, projective identification,* and *idealization;* however, they seem to be using different terms to describe similar phenomena. Psychoanalysts speak of marital choice as an object of *transference* from the family of origin and of people choosing partners to match their own level of maturity; Bowen said that people pick partners who replicate familiar patterns of family interaction and select mates at the same level of differentiation.

These are descriptions of ways in which people marry their own alter egos. Both schools also discuss how people choose mates who appear to be different, at least on the surface, in ways that are exciting and seem to make up for deficiencies in the self. Obsessive individuals tend to marry hysterical individuals and, according to Bowen, togetherness-oriented people often marry distancers. This brings up another way in which the Bowenian and psychodynamic schools are similar to each other and different from others. Both recognize that personalities have layers. Both think that the success of a relationship depends not only on the partners' shared interests and values but also on the nature of their internal, introjected object images.

Even if they don't emphasize the past, most of the other schools of family therapy have concepts for describing processes of normal family development. For example, communications therapists speak of the *quid pro quos* (Jackson, 1965) exchanged in normal marriages, while behaviorists describe the same phenomenon in terms of *social exchange theory* (Thibaut & Kelley, 1959).

Virginia Satir described normal families as those in which communication is direct and honest, where differences are faced rather than hidden, and where emotions are openly expressed. Under these conditions, she believed, people develop healthy *self-esteem*, which enables them to take the risks necessary for authentic relationships.

According to Minuchin (1974), clinicians should have some appreciation of the facts of ordinary family life to become effective therapists. Clinicians need to distinguish functional from dysfunctional structures, as well as pathological structures from structures that are simply transitional.

Because structural therapy begins by assessing the adequacy of a family's structure, it sometimes appears to impose a standard. In fact, however, normality is defined in terms of functionality, and structural therapists recognize that diverse patterns may be equally functional. The clarity of subsystem boundaries is more important than the composition of the subsystem. For example, a parental subsystem made up of a single parent and oldest child can function effectively if the lines of authority are clearly drawn. Patterns of enmeshment and disengagement are viewed as preferred styles, not necessarily as indications of abnormality.

Most therapists don't think in terms of remaking families and therefore believe they have little need for models of what a family should be like. Instead, they intervene around specific problems—problem-maintaining interactions, problem-saturated stories, forgotten solutions—conceptualized in terms of function, not structure. The patterns they observe are dysfunctional; therefore, by implication, what's functional must be just the opposite.

Although it may not be necessary to have a way of understanding a family's past in order to help them, it is useful to have a way of understanding the family's organization of the present, using a model of normal behavior to set goals for treatment. Such a model should include a design for the present and for change over time. Among the ideas presented in this book, the most useful for a basic model of normal family functioning include *structural hierarchy, effective communication,* and *family life cycle development.*

Development of Behavior Disorders

In the early days of family therapy, patients were seen as innocents—**scapegoats**—whose deviance maintained family stability. Much of the literature was about dysfunctional ways of keeping the peace: scapegoating, pseudomutuality, family projection process, double bind, mystification, and so on. These malignant mechanisms may have driven young people crazy but they helped keep families together. It was a simple and satisfying tale of malevolence. No one exactly blamed the parents—their coercions weren't really deliberate—but these explanations did rest on parental faults and failings, and as such had mythic force. The idea that schizophrenia was a sacrifice children made for their families was absolutely riveting—and absolutely untrue.

Today, family therapists think less about what causes problems than how families unwittingly perpetuate them.

Inflexible Systems

Early observers of schizophrenic families emphasized their inflexibility. Wynne coined the term **rubber fence** to dramatize how psychotic families resist outside influence and **pseudomutuality** to describe their rigid facade of harmony. R. D. Laing showed how parents, unable to tolerate their children's individuality, used **mystification** to deny their experience. Communication theorists thought that the most striking disturbance in schizophrenic families was that they lacked mechanisms for changing their rules. They were programmed for negative feedback, treating novelty and change as deviations to be resisted.

This tradition of viewing families of mentally ill patients as rigidly homeostatic was taken into the 1980s by Selvini Palazzoli in the form of her concept of "dirty games." Carol Anderson and Michael White countered this negative perspective by suggesting that rigidity might be the result of living with serious problems and of being blamed for them by mental health professionals.

Explaining family problems in terms of homeostatic inflexibility became one of the cornerstones of the strategic school. Dysfunctional families respond to problems with a limited range of solutions. Even when the solutions don't work, these families stubbornly keep trying. Behaviorists use a similar idea when they explain symptoms as resulting from faulty efforts to control behavior. Often when parents think they're punishing misbehavior, they're actually reinforcing it with attention.

According to psychoanalytic and experiential theories, intrapsychic rigidities, in the forms of *conflict, developmental arrest,* and *emotional suppression,* are the individual's contribution to family inflexibility. Psychoanalysts consider unhealthy families as closed systems that resist change. When stressed, inflexible families regress to earlier levels of development, where unresolved conflicts left them fixated.

Experientialists describe dysfunctional families as emotionally stagnant. If it's true that you sometimes have to try something different just to know you're alive, families afraid of rocking the boat become timid and lifeless. The symptom-bearer is a victim of the family's opposition to the life force.

Structural therapists locate the inflexibility of families in the boundaries between subsystems. But structural problems are not necessarily the result of some flaw in the family. Otherwise normal families may develop problems if they are unable to modify a previously functional structure to cope with an environmental or developmental crisis. Family therapists should be extremely clear on this point: Symptomatic families are often basically sound; they may simply need help adjusting to a change in circumstances.

Solution-focused and narrative therapists avoid notions that implicate family members in the development of their problems. Both camps prefer to focus on the strengths of individuals in the family and on times when they used their resources to triumph over their troubles. What these models do identify as problematic are rigid habits of thought that lead people to consider themselves defeated. Solution-focused therapists leave it at that; they don't speculate about the origins of defeatist thinking. Narrative therapists point to what they consider toxic systems of belief in the culture that are internalized by family members. It's society, not the family, that's inflexible.

The Function of Symptoms

The first family therapists described the identified patient as serving a function in disturbed families by detouring conflict and thus stabilizing the family. Vogel and Bell (1960) described emotionally disturbed children as "family scapegoats," singled out as objects of parental projection on the basis of traits that set them apart. Thereafter, the patient's deviance promotes cohesion in the family by uniting the parents in concern.

Today, many family therapists deny that symptoms have either meaning or function. Indeed, narrative, solution-focused, and psychoeducational therapists are so diametrically opposed to the idea that symptoms serve a purpose that these approaches can be seen as inspired to counter that idea. Narrative therapy is built around the metaphor of symptoms as alien entities, and the psychoeducation approach is devoted to exonerating families from responsibility for mental illness.

Behaviorists have always argued against the idea that symptoms are a sign of underlying pathology. Behavioral family therapists treat problems as skill deficits or as the uncomplicated result of faulty efforts to change behavior. Restricting their focus to symptoms is one reason they're successful in discovering the contingencies that reinforce them; it's also one reason why they aren't very successful with cases where a child's behavior problems function to stabilize a conflicted marriage or where a couple's arguments protect them from dealing with deeper conflicts.

Some schools of family therapy continue to believe that symptoms signal deeper problems and may serve to maintain family stability. In families that can't tolerate open conflict, a symptomatic member may act as a smokescreen and a diversion. In psychoanalytic, Bowenian, and structural formulations, a couple's inability to form an intimate bond may be ascribed to the fact that one or both of them are still embroiled in the relationship between their parents. In this way symptomatic behavior is transmitted across generations and serves to stabilize the multigenerational family system.

Sometimes it's possible to see how a symptomatic child motivates a depressed or disengaged parent to become more involved in the family. According to Jay Haley, a child's misbehavior is often part of a repetitive cycle that keeps the parents energized. In a typical sequence, father becomes unhappy and withdraws; the child misbehaves; mother fails to discipline the child; father steps in, reinvolving himself with the mother through the child.

The following example of how "dysfunctional" behavior may have its uses is from an interview conducted by Harry Aponte (a noted structural family therapist), quoted in Hoffman (1981).

> The interview is with a poor black family that fully answers to the description "multiproblem." Everybody—the mother, six grown or nearly grown children, and two grandchildren—is at risk, from breakdown, illness, nerves, violence, accident, or a combination of all these factors. In addition, the family members are noisy, disruptive, and hard to control.
>
> At a certain point Aponte asks the mother, "How do you handle all this?" The mother, who has been apathetic and seemingly unconcerned as the therapist tries to talk with the children, says, "I put on my gorilla suit." The children laugh as they describe just how terrible their mother is when she puts on her gorilla suit.
>
> An incident occurs shortly after this conversation which suggests that a circular causal sequence is at work, one of those redundancies that may have to do with family balance. Mother is still apathetic and looks tired, and the therapist begins to ask about her nerves. At first the children are somewhat quiet, listening. As she begins to admit that she has had bad nerves and that she is taking pills, they begin to act up. One boy pokes the baby; another boy tries to restrain the baby from kicking back; the baby starts to yell. The therapist asks the twenty-year-old daughter (the baby's mother) if she can control him; she says no. At this point the mother gets up and smacks her daughter's baby with a rolled-up newspaper, rising out of her lethargy like some sleeping giant bothered by a gnat. She sits the baby down with a bump, and he makes no further trouble. During this sequence the rest of the children jump and shriek with joy, causing their mother to reprimand them, after which they calm down and the mother sits back, more watchful now and definitely in control. (p. 83)

Here a mother overwhelmed by stress becomes depressed; as she talks about her depression the children become anxious and misbehave; the misbehavior triggers a reaction in the mother, rousing her from withdrawal to control the chaos. The children's symptomatic misbehavior functions as cause and cure of the mother's depression, in a recurring cycle.

Underlying Dynamics

In the 1950s family therapists challenged the psychoanalytic notion that symptoms were only surface phenomena and that the real problems were internal. Instead, they showed how focusing on behavioral interactions was sufficient to treat most problems.

Today many family therapists still deny that it's necessary to consider underlying dynamics in order to explain or treat symptomatic behavior. These clinicians believe that it's sufficient to observe patterns of interaction in the family. Some strategic therapists, like the MRI group, focus on interactions around symptomatic behavior; others, like the Milan group, take a broader view of the whole family. Behaviorists maintain that to account for unwanted behavior it's necessary only to observe its reinforcing consequences.

Despite the tradition of explaining problem behavior without bringing in underlying dynamics, many therapists believe that neither the presenting symptoms nor the surrounding interactions are the real problem; the real problem is an underlying family dysfunction. These therapists look beneath—or beyond—behavioral sequences for some flaw in the family. Minuchin's notion of family structure is the leading example of such a concept. Structural therapists pay attention to the complaints families bring in, but their real focus is on underlying structural problems.

Family structure is now one of the central concepts in family therapy, and the field can be divided into those who do or don't include structure in their analyses. Haley (1980) does, and for this reason many people consider him a structuralist as much as a strategist. John Weakland of the MRI group emphatically denied the need to include structural concepts in family assessment, and he considered doing so a

return to discredited psychodynamic theorizing. Others, whose focus is more on here-and-now interactions, including behaviorists (Patterson) and some experientialists (Whitaker), eventually came to accept the usefulness of structural concepts.[3] Their doing so was one of the early signs of a growing convergence among competing systems.

The postmodern revolution is also poststructural in the sense that conceptions of an underlying structure are viewed as modernist (falsely absolutist) and therefore problematic. Postmodernists like Michael White, Steve de Shazer, and Harlene Anderson all avoid structural speculations.

Psychoanalytic and Bowenian therapists have their own concepts of underlying dynamics. Psychoanalysts originated the idea of underlying dynamics; present-day psychoanalytic family therapy practitioners use this idea in concepts of intrapsychic structural conflict (id, ego, superego); developmental arrest; internal object relations; and interlocking pathological structures among family members. According to the psychoanalytic model, difficulties may develop in interaction, but it's the interacting individuals who have the real problems.

In Bowen's theory the major concepts describing family dynamics are fusion, family projection process, and interlocking triangles. So much are these underlying issues emphasized that Bowenians probably spend less time than anyone else dealing directly with presenting symptoms.

Bowenian theory uses a *diathesis–stress* model of psychological problems. This is a model from genetic research, in which a person develops a disorder when a genetic flaw is triggered by stress in the environment. In Bowenian theory,

---

3.   Not incidentally, both Patterson and Whitaker visited the Philadelphia Child Guidance Clinic to study with Minuchin at a point in their careers when they felt the need for a more systemic understanding of the families they worked with.

people who develop symptoms in the face of anxiety-arousing stress have low levels of differentiation and are emotionally cut off from support systems, especially in the extended family. The diathesis may not be genetic, but it is passed from one generation to the next.

Pathological Triangles

Pathological triangles lie at the heart of several family therapy explanations of behavior disorder. Among these, Bowen's theory is the most elegant. Bowen explained how, when two people are in conflict, the one who experiences the most anxiety will "triangle in" a third person. This model not only provides an explanation of systems pathology but also serves as a warning: As long as a therapist remains tied to one party in an emotional conflict, he or she is part of the problem, not part of the solution.

In psychoanalytic theory, oedipal conflicts are considered the root of neurosis. Here the triangle is triggered by family interactions but lodged in the individual psyche. Mother's tenderness may be seductive and father's jealousy threatening, but the wish to do away with the father and possess the mother is a figment of fantasy. Pathological fixation of this conflict may be caused by developments in the outer space of the family, but the conflict is harbored in the inner space of the child's mind.

Structural family theory is based on triangular configurations where a dysfunctional boundary between two subsystems is the reciprocal of a boundary with a third. Father and son's enmeshment reflects father and mother's disengagement; a single mother's disengagement from her children is the counterpart of her overinvolvement outside the family. Structural theory also uses the concept of pathological triangles to explain *conflict-detouring triads,* whereby parents divert their conflict onto their child. Minuchin, Rosman, and Baker (1978) have even demonstrated that physiological

changes occur when parents in conflict transmit their stress to a psychosomatic child.

Strategic therapists typically work with a dyadic model, in which one person's symptoms are maintained by others' efforts to resolve them. Haley and Selvini Palazzoli, however, used a triangular model in the form of **cross-generational coalitions.** These "perverse triangles," as Haley (1977) calls them, occur when a parent and child, or a grandparent and child, collude to form a bastion of covert opposition to the other parent.

Triangular functioning is less central to the newer models because they're not concerned with *how* families develop problems. It might even be argued that ignoring family dynamics is one of the strengths of narrative and solution-focused approaches, if doing so helps these therapists zero in on the constricting habits of thought they're interested in. It might also be said, however, that ignoring family dynamics is one of the weaknesses of these approaches, especially in cases in which conflict in the family isn't just going to go away because family members work together to solve a common problem.

●

When things go wrong it's tempting to look for someone to blame. Your partner never talks about his feelings? He must be from Mars. Families drop out after the first couple of sessions? They must be resistant. Before we get too judgmental, let's recognize that it's perfectly natural to attribute our problems to other people's influence. Because we look out at life from inside our own skins, we're most aware of other people's contributions to our mutual problems. But therapists, we'd hope, aren't handicapped by this egocentric bias. No, they're handicapped by another bias.

Whenever we hear one side of an unhappy story, it's only natural to sympathize with the person doing the telling. If a friend tells you her boss is a jerk, your sympathy puts you automatically on her side. Experience suggests that most stories have two sides. But when your impulse is to show solidarity with someone who's telling you his or her troubles, the temptation is to look abroad for villains. Among professional helpers, this temptation is too often not resisted.

One reason for blaming family problems on easily vilified influences—men, racism, mothers—is that it's hard to see past individual personalities to the patterns of interaction that make them a family, unless you see the whole group and see them in action. That's why family therapy was invented in the first place.

Goals of Therapy

The goal of all psychotherapy is to help people change in order to relieve their distress. This is true of individual therapy, group therapy, and family therapy. Why then is so much written about the goals of various schools of therapy? Some of it has to do with differing ideas about how people change, some of it merely with alternate vocabularies for describing that change. When Bowenians speak of "differentiation of self" and psychoanalysts speak of "increased ego strength," they mean pretty much the same thing.

If we strip away the semantic differences, models of family therapy vary on two major dimensions of goals. First, schools differ with respect to their intermediate goals; they seek change through different aspects of personal and family functioning. Second, schools differ in terms of how much change they seek. Some are content with symptom resolution, others aspire to transform the whole family system.

All therapists are interested in resolving problems, but they vary from concentrating exclusively on symptom resolution to being concerned with the health of the entire family system. Strategic, solution-focused, and behavioral therapists are least concerned with changing the whole system; psychoanalytic and Bowenian therapists are most concerned with systems change.

The goal of structural family therapy is both symptom resolution and structural change. But the structural change sought has the modest aim of reorganizing that part of the family that's failed to adjust to meet changing circumstances. Narrative, communications, and experiential therapists also aim midway between symptomatic improvement and systematic family reorganization. Practitioners from these schools focus neither on presenting complaints nor on the overall family system. Instead they pay special attention to processes that they believe underlie symptoms: cognitive constructions, patterns of communication, and emotional expressivity. Improvements in these processes are thought to resolve symptoms and promote growth.

The focus of strategic therapy and its solution-focused offshoot is on problem solving. The goal is simply to resolve whatever complaints clients present. Narrative therapists, many of whom rebelled against the mechanistic aspects of their own strategic background (cf. Freedman & Combs, 1996), aim to help clients solve the problems they come in with, but also to leave with an enhanced sense of personal agency.

In our view, the primary goal of family therapy must be to resolve the presenting complaint. If a family asks for help with a specific problem and the therapist helps them express their feelings but doesn't solve the problem, then he or she has failed them in an important way. One of the virtues of behavioral and strategic therapists is that they don't fool themselves (or their clients) about whether these problems get solved. Some of the approaches with larger aspirations run the risk of losing sight of this first responsibility of a professional helper. If success is defined as accepting the therapist's point of view and working toward his or her conceptual goal, then therapy becomes a power struggle or an indoctrination. To some extent this happens in all therapies, but it's justified only when achieving the therapist's goals also meets the family's goals.

The advantage of working toward symptom change is that it eliminates obfuscation about whether or not therapy is successful. The disadvantage of working *only* at the level of symptom-maintaining behavior is that it may produce change that doesn't last.

A final note on goals. Resolving problems has been family therapy's trademark, emblematic of the optimism of its practitioners. Now, however, by embracing the disease model (Yes, Virginia, there is such a thing as schizophrenia), some family therapists, notably those who practice psychoeducation, advocate coping with, rather than curing, serious psychopathology as a worthy goal. This modest but realistic goal has been hard for some family therapists to accept. What's at stake is a question of which is more powerful, family therapy or certain entrenched conditions—psychopathology, arrested psychodynamics, poverty and despair, or even failures of nerve that make it hard for some people to risk change.

Conditions for Behavior Change

To establish family treatment as a distinct and innovative approach, family therapists began by emphasizing their differences with individual therapy. Later they emphasized differences among themselves. Today there is much cross-fertilization among the schools, but although most schools share a broad consensus about principles of change, they still differ on many specific issues.

Action or Insight?

One of the first distinctions between family therapy and individual therapy had to do with insight. Individual therapists stressed intellec-

tual and emotional insight; family therapists stressed action. However, although they emphasized action in their writing, most of the techniques of early family therapists were designed to affect action through understanding. Actually, since people think, feel, and act, no form of therapy can succeed without influencing all three aspects of the human personality.

Action and insight are the primary vehicles of change in family therapy. Most therapists use both mechanisms, but some schools emphasize either action (strategic, behavioral) or insight (psychoanalytic, narrative).

The case for action is based on the observation that people often don't change even though they understand why they should. The truth of this is familiar to anyone who's ever tried to lose weight, stop smoking, or spend more time with the kids. Behaviorists make the case for action by pointing out that behavior is often reinforced unwittingly; explanations, they say, don't change behavior, reinforcement does.

Like behaviorists, strategic therapists focus on behavior and aren't concerned with insight. They don't believe in fostering understanding and they don't believe in teaching; instead they believe that the way to change behavior is through manipulation. They box stuck families into a corner from which the only way out is to become unstuck.

The case for insight is based on the belief that if people understand themselves better they'll be free to act in their own best interests. Psychoanalysts believe that people are blind to their real motives. Without insight into hidden conflicts, action can be self-defeating, even dangerous. Unexamined action can be self-defeating because symptomatic relief without insight fosters denial and repression; it can be dangerous if repressed impulses are acted on precipitously.

What some people consider action may be regarded by psychoanalysts as acting-out—diversions to mask the anxiety that signals underlying conflicts. Only by understanding their impulses and the dangers involved in expressing them can people achieve lasting change. Moreover, since the important conflicts are unconscious, only methodical interpretation of the hidden springs of behavior brings about lasting change. In psychoanalytic therapy, unanalyzed action initiated by families is called acting out; unanalyzed action initiated by therapists is considered manipulation. Insight can only be achieved if families verbalize their thoughts and feelings rather than act on them, and therapists interpret unconscious meaning rather than suggest or manipulate action.

Discussions of insight are often divisive, because insight is a buzzword; proponents extol it, opponents ridicule it. Advocates of insight endow it with pseudomedical properties: Insight, like medicine, cures. Actually, insight doesn't cure anything; it's something through which cure occurs. To say that a family acquires insight means that family members learn what they intend by their actions and what they want from each other; how they act on such insights is up to them.

In contrast to the polar positions taken by some schools, others work with action *and* insight. In structural family therapy, change is initiated in action and then supported by understanding. According to Minuchin (Minuchin & Nichols, 1993), family structure and family beliefs support and reinforce each other; the only way to achieve lasting change is to challenge both. Action comes first because it leads to new experiences that make insight possible.

In Bowen systems theory, interventions also affect both levels—action and understanding; but the order of effect is reversed. Bowenians begin by calming people down, so that they'll stop blaming each other and start reflecting on the relationship processes they're caught up in. Once they begin to see their role in triangles and polarizations like the pursuer/distancer dy-

namic, family members are encouraged to carry out relationship experiments in which they alter their participation in these patterns.

The Milan model and the later work of Cecchin, Boscolo, and Hoffman elevated the importance of working with systems of meaning. Thus systems-oriented family therapists became less tied to behavioral analyses and action-oriented interventions. Taking into account the "externalizing" technique of Michael White and David Epston, the therapy as conversation model of the late Harry Goolishian and Harlene Anderson, the popularity of social constructionism, and the reemergence of psychodynamic influence, the trend in the field is definitely away from action and toward, if not insight, at least cognition.[4]

A growing number of family therapists would reject the notion of insight as tied to outmoded beliefs in objective truth. Being good postmodernists, they prefer the idea of "narrative reconstruction" to "insight," and see the therapist as helping clients construct new and more hopeful stories rather than excavating some buried truth. However, regardless of whether we speak in declassé terms of insight or in more contemporary terms of coconstructing reality, the fact is that the contemporary interest in narrative and the popularity of reflecting teams are symptoms of family therapy's drift from action to cognition (or meaning, if you prefer).

This emphasis on meaning is especially attractive to therapists who favor a collaborative approach, but while the individuals who make up families are certainly feeling, thinking, and acting beings, we wonder if what ties them

---

4. The difference is that insight refers to an understanding of the true nature of things; in the context of psychotherapy this means the underlying motivations behind one's thoughts and behavior. Cognition, on the other hand, refers more narrowly to one's point of view. In the context of therapy, cognitive change involves a shift to a more productive point of view—not necessarily one that is more "true," only more useful.

most strongly together in creating and maintaining problems isn't that their actions are coordinated and interlocking. Helping people reconsider the way they perceive their dilemmas may help them discover new ways to address them. But all too often seeing what we need to do somehow doesn't quite get us to do it. Perhaps working with meaning *as well as* action would be a better idea for family therapists than trading one for the other.

Resistance

Families are notoriously **resistant** to change. In addition to the recalcitrance of individual family members, the system itself resists change—or, to bring this abstraction down to earth, the structure that holds a family together is supported by the habits of every one of its members.

The same device that gives family therapy its greatest leverage—bringing all the players together—also carries with it the seeds of resistance. With all parties to a problem present, it's hard to resist the temptation to blame someone else—or at least to wait for that person to change first. Even when a therapist conscientiously points out each person's contribution, it's only human for people to hear what they already believe: "It isn't me; it's them."

It's popular these days to speak of "the death of resistance," and many of the newer schools claim that resistance isn't a problem in their "nonhierarchical" approaches. This is partly true, partly posturing. While it is true that resistance is more to be expected to the highly visible confrontations of a Minuchin or a Whitaker, resistance, or reluctance to change, is still an issue even for today's persuasive, cognitive approaches. Narrative therapists neither argue with clients nor confront them about their contribution to family conflicts; but what they describe as "externalizing" and "deconstructive conversations" are part of an effort to impose their own narrative shape on clients' stories. Resistance may not be overt, but people do not as readily give up their "problem-saturated stories" as you might think.[5]

Behavior therapists ignore resistance and succeed only when their clients are willing to follow instructions. Other schools of family therapy consider resistance a major obstacle and have devised various ways to overcome it.

Psychoanalytic practitioners believe that resistance is motivated by unconscious defenses, which first must be made manifest and then resolved through interpretation. This is an intrapsychic model, but it doesn't ignore conscious and interactional resistances. Instead, psychoanalytic therapists believe that interactional conflict—among family members or between the family and therapist—have their roots in unconscious resistance to basic drives. Experiential therapists have a similar model; they see resistance to emotional expression, and they blast away at it using confrontations and emotive exercises. Experientialists believe that breaching defenses automatically releases healthy strivings; change occurs from the inside out.

People do avoid knowing painful things about themselves, but even more strenuously do they conceal painful truths from other members of their family. It's one thing to tell a therapist that you're angry at your partner; it's another thing to tell your partner.

Minuchin's solution to the problem of resistance is straightforward: He wins families over by joining and accommodating to them. This gives him the leverage to utilize powerful confrontations designed to restructure family interactions. Resistance is seen as a product of the interaction between therapist and family; change is accomplished by alternately challenging the family and then rejoining them to repair breaches in the therapeutic relationship.

---

5.   People come to therapy not just to solve problems but also to complain. They want to talk about their troubles, and, because they aren't at home, they expect someone to listen.

Strategic therapists avoid power struggles by going with resistance rather than challenging it head on. They assume that families don't understand their own behavior and will oppose attempts to change it. In response, some strategic practitioners try to gain control by deliberately provoking families to resist. Once the family begins to react against therapeutic directives, the therapist can manipulate them to change in the desired direction. In practice, this can result in doggedly pursuing reverse psychology or in creative forms of therapeutic jujitsu.

Steve de Shazer denies the existence of resistance, saying that it's the family's way of cooperating. It's up to the therapist to learn to use it. Richard Schwartz sees resistance as a proper reaction of protective parts of family members whose job it is to not allow anyone into the family until it's clear that person won't harm or humiliate them. Schwartz goes to great lengths to respect and reassure those protective parts.

Finally, under the heading of resistance, we should consider the phenomenon of *induction.* Induction is what happens when a therapist is drawn into the family system and abides by its rules. When this happens the therapist becomes just another member of the family; this may stabilize the system, but it undermines therapeutic leverage. A therapist is inducted when he or she is drawn in to fulfill a missing family function, such as disciplining children or sympathizing with a husband whose wife doesn't, or when the therapist does what everybody else does, such as avoid challenging the patriarch or minimize a drinking problem.

Induction is so subtle that it's hard to see, so seductive that it's hard to resist. As helpers and healers, therapists are prone to take over for people, doing for them what they don't do for themselves. But taking over—being inducted— precludes real change. As long as families have someone to do for them, they don't have to learn to do for themselves.

One reason early family therapists encountered so much resistance was that they were eager to change people, and slow to understand them. It turns out that families, like you and me, resist efforts to change them by people they feel don't understand and accept them. Family therapists learned to see nagging and withdrawal as circular, but they were slow to see them as human. Only later did therapists come to see through the nagging to the pain behind it, and to understand the anxiety that motivates withdrawal.

Rigidly stuck families are run by their fears, and therapists, eager to be liked, are vulnerable to those fears. Families quickly teach therapists what's threatening: "Don't ask *him* about *that.*" The art of therapy is understanding and sympathizing with those fears, but avoiding induction enough to be able to challenge them. As in so many things, progress sometimes means doing what you're afraid to do.

Family–Therapist Relationship

While individual therapists have long believed that the fundamental pillar of treatment was the bond between patient and therapist, early family therapists minimized the importance of the therapeutic relationship. When the dominant metaphor was the cybernetic machine, therapists were seen as technocrats of change. In recent years the wind has shifted 180 degrees, and the prevailing view of the therapist is anything but technological.

The first shift occurred in the 1980s, when the cybernetic model was rejected because it placed the therapist outside and above the family. *Second-order cybernetics* was the term used to emphasize that the therapist was part of the system in treatment and therefore incapable of detached objectivity. An even more fundamental shift occurred in the 1990s when family therapists began to reject the role of expert in favor of a more collaborative model.

Unlike the distinction between **first-** and **second-order cybernetics,** which was largely academic, the **collaborative model** was a turning point in how family therapy is practiced. What was rejected was the medical model, an authoritarian role model, with the clinician as the expert-in-charge to whom the patient turned for answers. Early practices were seen as ranging from benign paternalism to a dogmatic emphasis on power and control. Harlene Anderson and Harry Goolishian called their alternative a "collaborative language-systems approach." This shift from a directive, hierarchical position to a collaborative one was consistent with Maturana and Varela's (1980) idea that systems are self-creating and cannot be manipulated like machines. The ultimate expression of this attempt to demystify therapy was Tom Andersen's reflecting team, in which the clinical team came out from behind the mirror to join the family in equal and open dialogue.

The advocates of a collaborative model have provoked a backlash from those who say that it's fine to renounce authoritarianism, but not so fine if this means abdicating leadership (e.g., Nichols, 1993). But while the idea of therapy as collaboration has become almost a cliché, what may matter more than whether therapists describe themselves as experts or "coparticipants" is whether they act to manipulate or empower people.

In thinking about the stance a therapist takes in treatment, it's important to realize that what the therapist does reflects not only what he or she believes, but also who he or she is. No matter what model a therapist subscribes to, personal style will have a large impact on his or her posture with families. John Weakland's "one-down" stance was as consistent with his own shy and unassuming character as Betty Carter's bluntness was with her outspoken nature.

The variations of patient–therapist relationship are a function of individual practitioners, but they also tend to characterize different schools of treatment. The hallmark of the *subject–object* paradigm is objective observation. In this model the therapist is a natural scientist. Personal and emotional reactions are regarded as intrusions. Therapist and family are separate entities. This isn't a popular conception, and few family therapists would describe themselves in these terms; nevertheless, aspects of behavioral, psychoanalytic, Bowenian, strategic, solution-focused, and structural therapy fit this model.

Behavior therapists think of themselves as objective observers and rational scientists. Psychoanalysts operate within this model when they think of themselves as blank screens on whom patients project distorted perceptions and fantasies. Although some clinicians still maintain this assumption, it's not consistent with current psychoanalytic thinking. The blank screen is a metaphor and a myth. Therapists reveal themselves in a thousand ways, and patients' reactions are always influenced by the therapist's behavior as well as by personal distortions. Bowenians think of themselves as objective observers who act as teachers or coaches to help clients overcome their emotionality. The strategic school has produced some of the most sophisticated concepts of the intricate relationship between therapists and families (Hoffman, 1981). The subject–object paradigm isn't a feature of this school, but it creeps in when therapists think of themselves as outsiders, locked in contest with families. Solution-focused therapists talk about being collaborative but come across like sales agents, aggressively promoting visions of a bright future.

The *interpersonal* paradigm treats therapy as a two-way interaction. This model acknowledges that therapists and families constantly influence each other. Psychoanalysts employ this idea in their concepts of transference/countertransference, projective identification, and introjection. The model of influence is transversal. In fact, this paradigm describes most family therapists most of the time. However, the constructivist movement in the 1980s represents an even more explicit attempt to include the effects of the therapist's presuppositions and behavior on the families they treat. Most of the newer therapies adopt this language—they favor "generative conversations"—though whether individual practitioners remain open may be more a matter of personal sensitivity than professional identity.

The *phenomenological* paradigm is one in which the therapist tries to adopt the patient's frame of reference. It's what happens when psychoanalytic practitioners identify with their patients, when structuralists join families, when narrative therapists empathize with clients' stories, and when therapists of any persuasion try to understand that families are doing the best they can. Stanton and Todd (1981) used this concept in their technique of "ascribing noble intention" to families. This tactic fits the phenomenological model when it's done sincerely but not when it's used as a strategic ploy—for example, in most reframing. Selvini Palazzoli's positive connotation is far more effective when done with sincerity. (Although the idea of positive connotation seems supportive, it was often experienced as patronizing, especially when delivered by the same therapists who held secret discussions behind a one-way mirror.) Boszormenyi-Nagy's recognition that symptomatic behavior is an act of unconscious loyalty to the family definitely represents a sincere position. Experientialists speak of accepting the patient's frame of reference but often follow an encounter paradigm, in which they loudly proclaim their own feelings and challenge families to do the same.

The *encounter* paradigm calls attention to the direct engagement between the therapist's personality and that of the client. It involves mutuality, honesty, openness, and self-disclosure, and its use in family therapy is primarily restricted to experientialists. During an encounter the therapist becomes a full participant, something most therapists don't really let happen. However, it's possible to let yourself go and confront a family if you do so with clear therapeutic indications and not simply because you feel like it. Minuchin engages in genuine encounters from time to time, but he appears to do so without sacrificing his objectivity.

Ultimately, the relationship you form with clients will depend on your view of human nature. If you believe that people have problems because they lack something, whether that something is information, good-enough parenting, ego strength, serotonin, or self-reflective awareness, you may feel obliged to take a hierarchical, expert position. To really collaborate with clients, you must trust that family members already have the capacity to handle their problems themselves but that for some reason that capacity is blocked. With this view, therapists will work with clients to help them release whatever is constraining their abilities rather than trying to give them something they lack. It's this faith in the human capacity for self-healing that characterizes the best therapists, whether from old schools or new.

Therapy

Comparing techniques by reading about them is difficult because clinicians often describe their interventions in abstract terms. When techniques are described in theoretical jargon—restructuring, unbalancing, externalizing, differentiating—it's not always clear precisely what's meant. In this section, we treat issues of technique as a series of practical questions about how to conduct therapy.

Assessment

Each school of family therapy has a theory about families that determines where they look for problems and what they see. Some consider the whole family (Milan, structural, Bowenian); some concentrate on individuals (psychoanalytic, experiential); some focus narrowly on sequences that maintain symptoms (strategic, behavioral); and some pay very little attention to what causes problems, preferring instead to mobilize people to work against them (solution-focused, narrative).

Behaviorists place the greatest value on assessment and use the most formal procedures. Assessment is the first order of business. The advantage of the behavioral emphasis on assessment is that it provides clear baseline data, definite goals, and a reliable way to determine whether therapy succeeds. The disadvantage is that, by using standardized interviews and questionnaires, you don't see families in natural interaction. By looking only at part of the family (mother and child, or marital couple), you miss the total context; by relying on questionnaires, you learn only what the family reports.

Structural therapists also emphasize assessment, but their evaluations are based on observation. Enactments give the therapist a chance to observe patterns of enmeshment and disengagement. The positive aspects of this school's assessment procedure are that it uses the family's patterns of interaction among themselves, it includes the entire family, and it's organized in simple terms that point directly to desired changes.

A potential disadvantage to structural assessment is that it may lose sight of individuals while focusing on their roles in the family. This doesn't necessarily happen, but it's an error often made by beginners.

The Bowenian school also does an excellent job of considering the whole family in its assessment. Unlike structuralists, however, Bowenians rely on what they're told, and they're interested in the past as well as the present.

The breadth of psychoanalytic theory enables practitioners to speculate well ahead of their data; a little information suggests a great deal. The advantage is that the theory organizes the data and provides valuable leads to uncovering hidden meanings. The danger is

that the theory may distort the data, leading clinicians to see only what they expect to see. Experientialists have neither these advantages nor disadvantages. Their evaluations are guided by a simple theory about feelings and how they are suppressed; they tend not to uncover much that's hidden, but they also tend not to see things that aren't there.

Two of the newer schools, narrative and solution-focused, eschew any form of assessment. Solution-focused therapists believe that dwelling on problems and their causes undermines the positive thinking they hope to generate. They also believe that solutions aren't necessarily related to the ways problems come about. Narrative therapists believe that looking within families for problems perpetuates the therapist-as-expert stance they want to get away from. By personifying problems and talking about their effects rather than their causes, they circumvent the finger pointing that often accompanies family discussions of how problems got started. The danger is that by disregarding how problems arise they may overlook real conflicts. And conflict, as you may have noticed, doesn't necessarily go away simply because you ignore it.

Decisive Interventions

Family therapists use a wide variety of techniques, some dictated by their model, others by the therapist's personality and experience. Even if we limited our attention to the techniques specific to each of the schools, the list would be long and confusing. Some techniques are used by virtually everyone who practices family therapy—asking questions, reflecting feelings, clarifying communication—and this list has been growing as the field has become more integrated. Each school, however, relies on one or two techniques that are unique and decisive.

In psychoanalytic therapy there are two definitive techniques. The first of these, *interpretation*, is well known but not well understood.

Properly used, interpretation refers to elucidating unconscious meaning. It does not mean statements of opinion—"You need to express your feelings before you can really be close"; advice—"As long as you continue writing to him, the affair isn't over"; theory—"Some of the reasons you were attracted to him were based on unconscious needs"; or confrontations—"You said you didn't care, but you were really angry." Interpretations are statements about unconscious meaning. "You've been complaining about your son's arguing with you all the time. Based on what you've said previously, I think that some of your anger is deflected from your husband. He does the same thing, but you're afraid to tell him so, and that's why you get so mad at your son."

By refraining from asking questions or giving advice, the psychoanalytic practitioner maintains a stance of listening and fostering understanding. By limiting interventions to interpretations, the therapist makes it clear that treatment is designed for learning; whether families take advantage of this atmosphere and change their behavior as a result of what they learn is up to them.

The second decisive technique in analytic treatment is *silence*. The therapist's silence permits him or her to discover what's on a patient's mind and to test the family's resources; it also lends force to the eventual interpretations. When a therapist is silent, family members talk, following their own thoughts rather than responding to the therapist's. When they learn that the therapist won't interrupt, they react and respond to each other. This produces a wealth of information that might not otherwise emerge. If a father begins by saying, "The problem is my depression," and the therapist immediately asks, "How long have you been depressed?" he or she may not discover what thoughts are associated in the man's mind with his depression or how the man's wife responds to his complaint.

The decisive technique in experiential therapy is *confrontation*. Confrontations are de-

signed to provoke emotional reactions and are often aggressively blunt. It isn't unusual for experiential therapists to tell clients to shut up or to mock them for being insincere. Confrontations are often combined with *personal disclosure*, the second primary technique of this school. Experientialists use themselves as emotionally expressive models. Finally, most experiential therapists also use *structured exercises.* These include role playing, psychodrama, sculpting, and family drawings. The rationale for these techniques is that they stimulate emotional experiencing in the session; their drawback is that, because they're artificial, the reactions they provoke may be divorced from ordinary experience. Family members may get something off their chests in a structured exercise but may not transfer this to their interactions at home.

Most people associate reinforcement with behavior therapy, but reinforcement isn't a technique used in behavioral family therapy; *observation* and *teaching* are the vehicles of this approach. Behavioralists begin by observing the contingencies of reinforcement in the families they work with. Their aim is to discover the antecedents and consequences of problem behavior. Once they've completed a *functional analysis of behavior,* they become instructors, teaching families how they inadvertently reinforce undesirable behavior. As teachers, their most useful lesson is the use of positive control. They teach parents that it's more effective to reward good behavior than to punish bad behavior; they teach married couples to substitute being nice to each other for their usual bickering.

Positive control—rewarding desirable behavior—is one of the most useful principles in family therapy. It's a valuable lesson for families, and for therapists. Therapists, like parents, tend to chide their charges for mistakes; unfortunately, if you're told that you're suppressing your feelings, spoiling your children, or using coercive control, you're apt to feel picked on and put down. Although it may be necessary to point out people's mistakes, it's more effective to concentrate on praising the positive aspects of their behavior. Among practicing family therapists this point seems best understood by structuralists, who speak of working with the family's strengths; by strategists and Milan therapists, who use reframing and positive connotation to support efforts to do the right thing; and of course by solution-focused and narrative therapists, who have raised the power of positive thinking to an art form.

Bowen systems therapists are also teachers, but they follow a different curriculum. They *teach people to be responsible for themselves* and how by doing so they can transform their entire families. Being responsible for yourself means getting clear about what you think and feel—not what your mother says or what you read in the *New York Times* but what you really believe—and then being true to your beliefs in dealings with other people. You don't take responsibility by changing others or wishing they were different; you do so by speaking for yourself and maintaining your own values. The power of this position is tremendous. If a client can accept who he or she is and that other people are different from themselves, then he or she no longer has to approach relationships with the idea that someone has to change. This enables the client to be in contact with people without becoming unduly upset or emotionally reactive.

In addition to teaching differentiation, Bowenian therapists promote two corollary lessons: *avoiding triangulation* and *reopening cut-off family relationships.* Taken together these three lessons enable one person to transform the whole network of his or her family system. Even if her spouse nags, if his children are disobedient, if her mother never comes to visit, the *client* can create a change. Other schools of therapy gain leverage by including the entire family in treatment; Bowenians teach individuals to be themselves, to make

contact with others, and to deal directly with the people they have conflicts with. This gives a person a tool for change that's portable and lasting.

Communications family clinicians contributed so much to the theoretical base of family therapy that it's difficult to single out their interventions. Perhaps their greatest achievement was pointing out that communication is multilayered and that often the most important things being said are said covertly. Therapy was designed to make the covert overt. Initially this was done by *clarifying communication* and pointing out hidden messages. When this direct approach met with resistance, therapists began using directives to make the rules of family functioning explicit and to provoke changes in the rules.

Strategic therapy is an offshoot of communications theory, and the techniques used by strategists are refinements of those used by communicationists. Principal among these are *reframing, directives,* and *positive connotation.* Strategic practitioners begin by getting concrete descriptions of problems and attempts to solve them. In the process, they pay particular attention to the family's language and expectations. They try to grasp the family's point of view and acknowledge it—in a positive connotation; then they use reframing to shift the family's point of view and directives to interrupt problem-maintaining behavior.

Directives are designed to interrupt homeostatic patterns, they are assigned to be carried out when the family is at home, and they are often paradoxical. Although strategic therapists emphasize fitting the treatment to the patient, they often assumed that indirect interventions are necessary to outwit resistance. This is sometimes but not always true. It's not so much that some families are resistant and others aren't, but that resistance isn't a property *in* families; it's a quality of interaction *between* therapist and family. A therapist who proceeds on the assumption that families are unable and unwilling to follow advice is likely to encounter the expected resistance.

Structural family therapy is also a therapy of action, but in this approach the action occurs in the session. The decisive techniques are *enactments* and *boundary making.* Rigid boundaries are softened when the therapist gets people to talk with each other and blocks attempts to interrupt them. Diffuse boundaries are strengthened when the therapist works to support autonomy of individuals and subsystems.

Several promising techniques emerged in the 1980s around which whole models of therapy were built. Steve de Shazer and his colleagues expanded the technique of *focussing on successful solutions* that family members had already tried but abandoned. The result was solution-focused therapy. Michael White did the same with the technique of *externalization*—personifying problems and attributing oppressive intentions to them, which is a powerful device for getting family members to unite against a common enemy.

Actually, externalization is a concept, not a technique. The decisive technique of narrative

therapy is a persistent and forceful series of *questions*—whereby the therapist begins by trying to understand the client's experiences of suffering but then switches from understanding to prodding the clients to think about their problems as malevolent agents. Narrative therapists also use a relentless series of questions to challenge negative images and convince clients that they have reason to be proud of themselves and that their fates are in their own hands.

In reaction to the sectarian techniquism that reached a peak in the early 1980s, family therapists today borrow freely from other approaches and deemphasize technique in favor of a less hierarchical and more respectful quality of therapist–family relationship. Both trends are healthy, but we would like to end this section with two questions. When is cross-fertilization enriching, and when does eclecticism rob separate approaches of their muscle by watering down their distinctive elements? How best can family therapists get away from a formulaic emphasis on technique without losing leverage altogether by practicing a more congenial but less effective form of treatment?

Summary

The theme of the early years in the development of family therapy was the proliferation of competing schools, each advertised as unique and uniquely effective. Now, as family therapy moves into the twenty-first century, the theme is integration. So many talented therapists have been working for so long that the field has accumulated a number of useful ways of looking at and treating families. In what follows, we offer some very subjective comments about a few of the concepts and methods that have proven themselves classics of family therapy.

Theories of family functioning have both a scientific and a practical purpose. The most

useful theories treat families as systems; have concepts to describe forces of stability and change; notice the process underlying the content of family discussions; recognize the triadic nature of human relationships; remember to consider the context of the nuclear family rather than viewing it as a closed system; and appreciate the function of boundaries in protecting the cohesiveness of individuals, subgroups, and families.

Clinicians are more concerned with pathology and change than with normality, but it's useful to have some ideas about normal family functioning, both to mold treatment goals and to distinguish what's problematic and needs changing, from what is normal and doesn't. Some of the most useful concepts of normal family functioning include the structural model of families as open systems in transformation; the communications model of direct, specific, and honest communication in a family, with rules clear enough to ensure stability and flexible enough to allow change; the behavioral model of equitable exchange of interpersonal costs and benefits, the use of positive control instead of coercion, and mutual reinforcement between partners; the strategic model of systemic flexibility, which allows adjustment to changing circumstances and the ability to find new solutions when old ones don't work; and the Bowenian model, which explains how differentiation of self enables people to be independent at times, intimate at others.

Most family therapy concepts of behavior disorder focus on systems and interactions, but the psychoanalytic, Bowenian, narrative, and experiential models add psychological depth to the interactional view, bridging the gap between inner experience and outward behavior. The fact that many divorced people repeat the mistakes of their first marriages supports the idea that some of what goes on in families is a product of individual character. Some of the most valuable concepts of personal dysfunction in families are Bowen's concept of fusion; the experiential concepts of repressed affect and fear of taking risks; and the psychoanalytic concepts of developmental arrest, internal object relations, instinctual conflict, and hunger for appreciation.

These concepts of individual dynamics are useful adjuncts, but the major ideas in the field explain behavior disorder in terms of systems theory. The most influential of these are about inflexible systems, too rigid to accommodate individual strivings or adjust to changing circumstances; symptomatic family members promoting cohesion by stabilizing the nuclear and extended families; inadequate hierarchical structure; families too tightly or too loosely structured; and pathological triangles.

Some of the goals of family therapy are practically universal—clarifying communication, solving problems, promoting individual autonomy—and some are unique. Some of the schools take presenting problems at face value, whereas others treat them as metaphors and signs. In either case, goals shouldn't be so broad as to neglect symptom resolution, or too narrow to ensure the stability of symptom resolution. Incidentally, values are seldom discussed in the family therapy literature, the notable exception being Boszormenyi-Nagy. Too little consideration has been given to practicing therapists' ethical responsibilities, including the possibility of conflicting responsibilities to individuals, families, and the larger community.

If narrative therapists have tended to ignore family dynamics in order to emphasize the ills of the culture, perhaps this will turn out to be one of those swings of the pendulum that inevitably corrects itself. There's surely no need to neglect systems theory to introduce an ethical dimension to working with people in context.

Some of the major differences among family therapists about how behavior is changed are focused on the following issues: action or insight; change in the session or change at home; duration of treatment; resistance; family–therapist relationship; paradox; and the extent to which it's important to work with the whole family system, part of it, or just motivated individuals. Even though general consensus exists about some issues—for example, once most family therapists believed that action was primary and insight was secondary—there have always been divergent opinions on every one of these points. Strategic therapists, for example, flatly denied that insight is useful.

We've looked at some of the major methodological issues and tried to separate out the decisive techniques of the different systems. As is always the case when a number of variables are involved in a final result, it's not easy to know how much each variable contributes to that result or how important each one is. Furthermore, the more we talk about techniques, the greater the danger of seeing family therapy as a purely technological enterprise. Studying families is like solving a riddle; the art of treating them is to relieve suffering and

anguish. The job of the theoretician is to decode or decipher, which requires theory and ingenuity. The job of the therapist is healing, which requires theory but also conviction, perseverance, and caring. Treating families isn't only a matter of theory and technique; it's also an act of love.

—Recommended Readings

Dattilio, F. M. 1998. *Case studies in couple and family therapy: Systemic and cognitive perspectives.* New York: Guilford Press.

Gurman, A. S. 1978. Contemporary marital therapies: A critique and comparative analysis of psychoanalytic, behavioral and systems theory approaches. In *Marriage and marital therapy,* T. J. Paolino and B. S. McCrady, eds. New York: Brunner/Mazel.

Madanes, C., and Haley, J. 1977. Dimensions of family therapy. *Journal of Nervous and Mental Diseases.* 165:88–98.

Piercy, F. P., Sprenkle, D. H., and Wetchler, J. L. 1996. *Family therapy sourcebook,* 2nd ed. New York: Guilford Press.

Sluzki, C. E. 1983. Process, structure and world views: Toward an integrated view of systemic models in family therapy. *Family Process.* 22:469–476.

Sluzki, C. E. 1987. Family process: Mapping the journey over 25 years. *Family Process.* 26:149–153.

—References

Bowen, M. 1966. The use of family theory in clinical practice. *Comprehensive Psychiatry.* 7:345–374.

Freedman, J., and Combs, G. 1996. *Narrative therapy: The social construction of preferred realities.* New York: Norton.

Goldner, V. 1985. Feminism and family therapy. *Family Process.* 24:31–47.

Gordon, S. B., and Davidson, N. 1981. Behavioral parent training. In *Handbook of family therapy,* A. S. Gurman and D. P. Kniskern, eds. New York: Brunner/Mazel.

Haley, J. 1963. *Strategies of psychotherapy.* New York: Grune & Stratton.

Haley, J. 1976. *Problem-solving therapy.* San Francisco: Jossey-Bass.

Haley, J. 1977. Toward a theory of pathological systems. In *The interactional view,* P. Watzlawick and J. Weakland, eds. New York: Norton.

Haley, J. 1980. *Leaving home: The therapy of disturbed young people.* New York: McGraw-Hill.

Hare-Mustin, R. T. 1978. A feminist approach to family therapy. *Family Process.* 17:181–194.

Hoffman, L. 1981. *The foundations of family therapy.* New York: Basic Books.

Imber-Black, E. 1988. *Families and larger systems: A family therapist's guide through the labyrinth.* New York: Guilford Press.

Jackson, D. D. 1965. Family rules: The marital quid pro quo. *Archives of General Psychiatry.* 12:589–594.

Jasnow, A. 1978. The psychotherapist—artist and/or scientist? *Psychotherapy: Theory, Research and Practice.* 15:318–322.

Kagan, R., and Schlosberg, S. 1989. *Families in perpetual chaos.* New York: Norton.

Madanes, C. 1980. Protection, paradox and pretending. *Family Process.* 19:73–85.

Madigan, S., and Epston, D. 1995. From "spy-chiatric gaze" to communities of concern: From professional monologue to dialogue. In *The reflecting team in action,* S. Friedman, ed. New York: Guilford Press.

Mahler, M. S., Pine, F., and Bergman, A. 1975. *The psychological birth of the human infant.* New York: Basic Books.

Maturana, H., and Varela, F. 1980. *Autopoesis and cognition: The realization of living.* Boston: D. Reidel.

Minuchin, P., Colapinto, J., and Minuchin, S. 1998. *Working with families of the poor.* New York: Guilford Press.

Minuchin, S. 1974. *Families and family therapy.* Cambridge, MA: Harvard University Press.

Minuchin, S., and Fishman, H. C. 1981. *Family therapy techniques.* Cambridge, MA: Harvard University Press.

Minuchin, S., and Nichols, M. P. 1993. *Family healing: Tales of hope and renewal from family therapy.* New York: Free Press.

Minuchin, S., Rosman, B., and Baker, L. 1978. *Psychosomatic families: Anorexia nervosa in context.* Cambridge, MA: Harvard University Press.

Nadelson, C. C. 1978. Marital therapy from a psychoanalytic perspective. In *Marriage and marital therapy,* T. J. Paolino and B. S. McCrady, eds. New York: Brunner/Mazel.

Nichols, M. P. 1987. *The self in the system.* New York: Brunner/Mazel.

Nichols, M. P. 1993. The therapist as authority figure. *Family Process. 32:*163–165.

Paul, W. L. 1967. The use of empathy in the resolution of grief. *Perspectives in Biology Medicine. 11:*153–169.

Pierce, R., Nichols, M. P., and DuBrin, J. 1983. *Emotional expression in psychotherapy.* New York: Gardner Press.

Rabkin, R. 1977. *Strategic psychotherapy.* New York: Basic Books.

Schwartz, R. 1995. *Internal family systems therapy.* New York: Guilford Press.

Selvini Palazzoli, M., Boscolo, L., Cecchin, G., and Prata, G. 1978. *Paradox and counterparadox.* New York: Jason Aronson.

Stanton, M. D., Todd, T. C., and Associates. 1981. *The family therapy of drug addiction.* New York: Guilford Press.

Thibaut, J. W., and Kelley, H. H. 1959. *The social psychology of groups.* New York: Wiley.

Vogel, E. F., and Bell, N. W. 1960. The emotionally disturbed child as the family scapegoat. In *The family,* N. W. Bell and E. F. Vogel, eds. Glencoe, IL: Free Press.

Whitaker, C. A., and Keith, D. V. 1981. Symbolic-experiential family therapy. In *Handbook of family therapy,* A. S. Gurman and D. P. Kniskern, eds. New York: Brunner/Mazel.

White, M. 1995. *Re-authoring lives: Interviews and essays.* Adelaide, Western Australia: Dulwich Centre Publications.

White, M., and Epston, D. 1990. *Narrative means to therapeutic ends.* New York: Norton.

(16)

Advances in Family Therapy Research

Howard A. Liddle and Cindy L. Rowe
Center for Treatment Research on Adolescent Drug Abuse
University of Miami School of Medicine

Bridging Gaps and Expanding Frontiers

In the past two decades, family therapy research has come of age (Baucom, Shoham, Mueser, Daiuto, & Stickle, 1998; Diamond & Siqueland, 2001; Lebow & Gurman, 1995; Liddle, Bray, Levant, & Santisteban, 2001; Pinsof & Wynne, 1995). Family therapy has been applied to virtually every type of disorder among children, adolescents, and adults, and has demonstrated efficacy with each population studied (Pinsof & Wynne, 2000). Family-based interventions enhance engagement of clients and their family members (e.g., Prinz & Miller, 1994; Sisson & Azrin, 1986) and demonstrate impressive retention rates with the most difficult clients (e.g., Henggeler, Pickrel, Brondino, & Crouch, 1996), as well as reducing symptoms and facilitating prosocial development in a number of domains (Lebow & Gurman, 1995). Meta-

analyses, which examine the magnitude of therapy's effects across many studies, reveal that family therapy generally demonstrates superior effects in comparison to no-treatment controls or alternative treatments (Hazelrigg, Cooper, & Borduin, 1987; Shadish et al., 1993; Shadish, Ragsdale, Glaser, & Montgomery, 1995). Family therapy appears to be particularly effective in the treatment of substance use disorders, child behavior problems, marital/relationship distress, and as one element of multicomponent interventions for schizophrenia.

Still, significant challenges lie ahead in the science of family intervention. We have little empirical basis to judge the superiority of one type of family intervention over any other (Jacobson & Addis, 1993; Pinsof & Wynne, 1995; Shadish et al., 1993; Smith, Sayger, & Szykula,

395

1999). Accurate measurement of family patterns remains challenging, and assessment of family change over time in treatment is even more complex (Snyder, Cozzi, & Mangrum, 2001). Although well-specified theories of change guide family interventions, we don't know if the domains targeted, such as improvements in parenting, affect regulation, and family communication and organization, are related to outcomes. Yet identification of the ways in which families change in therapy and the therapists' contributions to these important shifts may be the key to bridging the gap now separating family therapy research from clinical practice (Pinsof & Wynne, 2000). Clearly, the significant strides made in family therapy research have yet to make a major impact on the practice of front-line clinicians (Fals-Stewart & Birchler, 2001). This unfortunate circumstance is exacerbated by the fact that very few studies of family therapy examine cost questions that affect the funding of empirically supported interventions at the policy level (Coffey, Olson, & Sessions, 2001; Hawley, Bailey, & Pennick, 2000).

Nowhere is the frequently cited and bemoaned "research-practice gap" more evident than in family therapy (Liddle, 1991). Family therapy research remains largely divorced from the realities of front-line practice, as interventions with substantial empirical support have yet to be adopted and practiced by clinicians in the community. Responsibility for this circumstance lies not only in the constraints and realities of daily practice and gaps in marriage and family therapy training programs, but also in the complexities of the models developed in state-of-the-art clinical trials (NIDA, 2002). Many practicing therapists feel that research-based therapies are biased toward the interests of academics (e.g., heavy emphasis on behavioral techniques) and that this research tends to be removed from the realities facing therapists in practice settings (Hawley et al., 2000). Thus family therapists may have

a sense that empirical research fails to address realistic issues or practically outline the steps to implementing interventions into practice (Pinsof & Wynne, 2000). While certainly not all family therapy research is directly relevant to the practicing clinician, some aspects of research are applicable and potentially useful to family therapists. For instance, effects of specific models of family therapy for particular disorders should be important, because they give therapists a gauge of what might be possible with a given client. Process studies are particularly relevant because they explore what goes on within sessions to make therapy effective, which is, of course, of primary concern to supervisors and therapists alike.

Potential avenues for reconciling the research–practice disconnect have been identified in recent reviews. These reviews highlight a new era of family therapy research in which investigations relevant to practitioners, such as process studies, are being undertaken (Diamond & Diamond, 2001; Pinsof & Hambright, 2001). The new generation of empirically supported family therapy models are more systems oriented and integrative (Kaslow & Lebow, 2002), incorporating components from traditions as diverse as individual psychotherapy (Josephson & Serrano, 2001), child and adolescent psychiatry (Malone, 2001), in-home therapy (Rowe, Liddle, McClintic, & Quille, 2002), and case management (Fishman, Andes, & Knowlton, 2001). McCrady and Epstein (1996, p. 117) declare that "the mental health field has made the second half of the twentieth century the era of the family," with new funding initiatives and training programs developing. Funding opportunities from federal agencies have supported family-based intervention research (e.g., CSAP/OJJDP's Strengthening Families Initiative) and a sprinkling of research training programs focused specifically on training family intervention scientists (e.g., NIDA's Center for Treatment Research on Adolescent Drug Abuse; NIMH's Family Research Consortium). Professional practice guidelines for many disorders, such as ADHD, conduct disorder, and substance abuse, now prescribe family interventions as essential aspects of treatment (Bukstein et al., 1997; Dulcan et al., 1997; McCrady & Ziedonis, 2001; Steiner et al., 1997). Further, family therapy research has become increasingly clinically relevant (e.g., Liddle, et al., 2002; Rotunda & O'Farrell, 1997). In fact, clinical research has already influenced practice in some areas (Alexander, Sexton, & Robbins, 2001; Henggeler, Schoenwald, & Pickrel, 1995; Liddle, 2002a), even though its potential for widespread influence remains unfulfilled. Clinicians in all settings and using all types of psychotherapy are facing new demands for accountability and outcomes (Law & Crane, 2000). Yet the process of how research outcomes (e.g., the effects of certain kinds of treatments for particular disorders) can shape practice remains uncertain (Newman & Tejeda, 1996). At the same time, we are clear that new economic, training, and research conditions converge to make empirical findings increasingly important for therapists to consider and incorporate into practice (Liddle, Bray, et al., 2001).

This chapter explores the major empirical findings in clinically important practice areas, including developmental psychopathology, prevention, and treatment of major diagnostic categories. We include only the highest quality scientific findings, and those that have the most clinical significance. Research means many different things, and it comes in many different forms. Treatment outcome findings are but one class of research that can inform practice. Process studies have begun to illuminate the workings of therapy and shed light on important family therapy change mechanisms (e.g., Nichols & Fellenberg, 2000). Thus, clinically relevant conclusions about process research and studies of change mechanisms in family therapy are provided. Finally, we conclude with suggestions for increasing the interface between family therapy research and practice.

Family Therapy Outcome

Childhood and Adolescent Behavior Disorders

Family Risk and Protective Factors for Behavior Problems. Childhood and adolescent behavior problems, including oppositional defiant disorder (ODD), attention-deficit hyperactivity disorder (ADHD), and conduct disorder (CD), have been strongly and consistently linked to a number of family factors such as conflict and aggression (Dadds, Sanders, Morrison, & Rebgetz, 1992; Lindahl, 1998). In fact, evidence strongly suggests that antisocial behavior is learned at an early age in the home through negative reinforcement of coercive patterns (e.g., a child's aggressive behavior reinforced by the cessation of his parents' arguments), and then generalizes to the school and peer group environments (Patterson, 1995; Snyder & Patterson, 1995). For instance, coercive parenting and poor parental monitoring at age four and a half each predict conduct problems among socioeconomically disadvantaged minority children as early as age six (Kilgore, Snyder, & Lentz, 2000). Further, longitudinal studies show that ineffective parenting practices in childhood maintain antisocial behavior into adolescence (Vuchinich, Bank, & Patterson, 1992) and young adulthood (Klein, Forehand, Armistead, & Long, 1997). Parental substance abuse and antisocial personality disorder, as well as conflict between parents, are also risk factors for oppositional defiant disorder and conduct disorder (Frick et al., 1992; Marcus, Lindahl, & Malik, 2001). Positive family factors, including parental responsiveness, acceptance, and strong connections among parents and children serve as protective factors against ADHD, ODD, and CD (Lindahl, 1998).

Family-Based Interventions for Child Behavior Problems. Because of the role of coercive family patterns in initiating and exacerbating disruptive behavior problems, a number of family-based interventions have been designed to prevent conduct problems among high-risk children and reduce antisocial behavior among children and adolescents with behavioral disorders. Family interaction is accessible, as family therapists well know (Minuchin, 1974). This is fortunate since some contributors to dysfunction, such as deviant peer influence, are less available to therapeutic observation and intervention (Liddle, in press). These family therapy approaches specifically target the coercive family patterns maintaining the behavior problems while at the same time bolstering protective factors in the family and other systems impacting the child (Blechman & Vryan, 2000; Liddle, 1996; Rutter, 1999). In several reviews of treatments for child and adolescent behavior problems, family-based treatments have been highlighted as among the most promising interventions (Carr, 2000; Estrada & Pinsof, 1995; Kazdin, 1987, 1991).

Engagement and Retention in Therapy. Family-based approaches have the advantage of addressing many of the very barriers, such as parental resistance to change (Stoolmiller, Duncan, Bank, & Patterson, 1993), family adversity (Prinz & Miller, 1994), perceived challenges of therapy itself, and a disconnected relationship with the therapist (Kazdin, Holland, & Crowley, 1997), that keep troubled children from getting the help they need (Coatsworth, Santisteban, McBride, & Szapocznik, 2001; Fishman et al., 2001; Miller & Prinz, 1990; Spoth & Redmond, 1995). In fact, one of family therapy's major contributions is an increased focus on strategies for engaging difficult youth and their families in treatment (e.g., Donohue et al., 1998; Henggeler et al., 1996). For instance, in early studies using specialized

engagement strategies within a structural family therapy model for Hispanic boys with behavior problems, Jose Szapocznik and colleagues demonstrated that their intervention was more successful than alternative treatments in retaining families (Szapocznik et al., 1988, 1989). They went on to refine these engagement techniques, successfully retaining families and reducing behavioral problems among more severe cases, and identifying cultural factors that influence engagement (Coatsworth et al., 2001; Santisteban et al., 1996). Miller and Prinz (1990) suggest that these types of multisystemic, broad-based engagement-focused enhancements to existing family-based interventions are promising and warrant further investigation. Indeed, the lack of systematic incorporation of these successful engagement strategies into training and regular therapy sessions remains puzzling.

Parent Management Training (PMT). Of the family-based interventions for child and adolescent behavior problems, parent management training has received the most empirical attention and support (Kazdin, 1987; Mabe, Turner, & Josephson, 2001). The basic approach, aimed at developing parents' skills and correcting parenting behaviors that contribute to negative coercive cycles (Wierson & Forehand, 1994), is characterized by:

1. Focusing on the parent in treatment
2. Helping parents to identify, observe, and react to the child's problem behavior in new ways
3. Applying social learning principles to increase positive parenting skills (e.g., praise for prosocial behaviors, appropriate and effective use of mild punishment such as time-out) to shape the child's behavior
4. Providing opportunities to practice new parenting skills and apply them in the home (Kazdin, 1991)

Gerald Patterson and his colleagues at the Oregon Social Learning Center have produced significant support for the effects of PMT with a range of ages and samples, demonstrating impressive changes in children's and adolescent's behavior in comparison to standard family therapy, attention-placebo, peer group intervention, services as usual in the community, and no treatment (Bank, Marlowe, Reid, & Patterson, 1991; Dishion & Andrews, 1995; Patterson, 1986). These investigators developed a prototype for the application of basic scientific findings about family functioning into an elegant and effective clinical model. Their groundbreaking research program has paved the way for major advances in this important area.

Other researchers have explored PMT techniques with different disorders and populations. For instance, Barkley, Guevremont, Anastopoulos, and Fletcher (1992) reported preliminary evidence supporting the use of PMT with adolescents suffering from ADHD, although the effects were not significantly greater than structural family therapy or a family problem-solving approach, nor did many adolescents in any of the treatments show clinically significant change. A recent study by the same group with ADHD adolescents similarly showed few differences in either a combination PMT (first stage of therapy) plus family problem solving (second stage of therapy) versus family problem solving alone, although PMT techniques appear to be important in the first stage of treatment to reduce drop out from family therapy (Barkley et al., 2001). PMT is also promising as a preventive approach with young children identified as at risk for conduct problems (Nye, Zucker, & Fitzgerald, 1995; Sanders, Markie-Dadds, Tully, & Bor, 2000). Other groups have shown that a combination of parent and child management training appears to be superior to either approach alone in reducing child aggression and promoting positive functioning among both parents and children up to one year posttreat-

ment (Kazdin, Siegel, & Bass, 1992; Webster-Stratton & Hammond, 1997). Carolyn Webster-Stratton has also developed and tested an innovative, promising version of PMT using videotape review to provide feedback and training to parents (Webster-Stratton, 1994). Positive long-term effects of PMT have consistently been demonstrated from one year (Dishion & Andrews, 1995; Webster-Stratton & Hammond, 1997; Webster-Stratton, Hollinsworth, & Kolpacoff, 1989) up to fourteen years following treatment (Long, Forehand, Wierson, & Morgan, 1994).

Functional Family Therapy. Functional family therapy (FFT; Alexander & Parsons, 1982) is another promising family-based approach for the prevention and treatment of childhood and adolescent conduct problems. This model is based on the assumption that children's behavior problems serve a function within the family system and are initiated and maintained by maladaptive interpersonal processes. Treatment therefore targets change in these destructive interactional patterns and uses behavioral interventions to reinforce positive ways of responding and to establish more effective problem-solving approaches within the family. Early research, among the first well-controlled trials of family therapy for adolescent behavior problems (Alexander & Parsons, 1973; Barton et al., 1985), established that functional family therapy improved family functioning and reduced recidivism among delinquent teens to a greater extent than juvenile court–mandated group therapy, group home therapy, psychodynamic therapy, or no treatment. The preventive promise of this model was revealed with younger siblings of the adolescents treated in the original trial, who were assessed two and a half years later and found to have significantly lower rates of juvenile justice involvement than younger siblings of teens in the alternative treatments (Klein, Alexander, & Parsons, 1977). FFT has also fared well in replication studies (e.g., Gordon, Graves, & Arbuthnot, 1995) and, as will be discussed later, investigators have conducted a series of process studies designed to outline the specific therapeutic steps necessary to bring about client change (e.g., Robbins, Alexander, & Turner, 2000).

Multisystemic Therapy (MST). Among the new generation of multisystems family-based interventions is perhaps the most promising therapeutic approach for the treatment of juvenile delinquency, multisystemic therapy (MST; Henggeler et al., 1991, 1993, 1996). In a series of rigorously controlled trials implemented with serious juvenile offenders, Scott Henggeler and his colleagues have demonstrated impressive results of the model's ability to engage youth and families into treatment (Henggeler et al., 1996) and to reduce recidivism up to four years posttreatment (Borduin et al., 1995). In comparison to juvenile court services as usual and individual therapy, MST has not only shown significantly lower recidivism rates and reduced time incarcerated, but has also demonstrated greater positive effects on family functioning and aggression with peers (Henggeler, Melton, & Smith, 1992). Further, MST has shown positive effects when implemented by community practitioners in mental health clinics, although therapeutic impact varied depending on the therapists' adherence to the MST model (Henggeler et al., 1997). Finally, these investigators conducted one of the only cost-effectiveness studies of family-based interventions. In comparison to outpatient treatment, MST significantly reduced the youth's involvement with the legal system within six months after treatment, and this decrease was not offset by an increase in out-of-home placements (Schoenwald et al., 1996). However, because the comparison treatments in each of these studies involved standard treatment in the community, the relative impact of MST in comparison to other state-of-the-art treatment

models is not known. In sum, the MST research program has accumulated significant support for the model's effectiveness in reducing juvenile delinquency and in altering maladaptive family patterns known to maintain antisocial behavior, and recent investigations have begun to outline process–outcome links.

To summarize, the evidence supporting family-based interventions for child and adolescent behavior problems is quite strong. Several different models have demonstrated efficacy and are generating effectiveness evidence in community-based replication studies. State-of-the-art, family-based interventions for child and adolescent behavioral disorders are increasingly focused on issues of ecological validity and devising strategies for intervening in the many systems that influence these youth and their families (Blechman & Vryan, 2000; Fishman et al., 2001). These therapies promote positive outcomes such as more prosocial peer relationships and family functioning, as well as reducing conduct problems. Yet progress in this area can be further advanced with increased attention to methodological issues such as more careful specification of the clinical problems of children treated in these studies, measurement of treatment integrity, and assessment of intervention effects at longer follow-up points (Kazdin, 1991). More attention to the clinical significance of symptom reduction—the extent to which these interventions make practical differences in the lives of children and families—is needed (Kazdin, 1999). Next steps necessary to advance this research specialty, some of which are currently underway, include the further investigation of the effectiveness of these models as applied in real-world clinic settings and their cost-effectiveness in comparison to standard community care (e.g., Henggeler, Schoenwald, & Pickrel, 1995). Given the accumulation of research support for these models, training in these approaches should be incorporated as standard components of marital and family therapy training programs.

Family Therapy for Depression and Anxiety

Family Risk and Protective Factors for Depression and Anxiety. There is evidence for particular family processes in the development and maintenance of anxiety and depression among children, adolescents, and adults. For instance, insecure and difficult attachment relationships (Sexson, Glanville, & Kaslow, 2001), dysfunctional, incongruent communication patterns (Slesnick & Waldron, 1997), generally negative messages communicated by parents (Stark et al., 1993), and other family factors increase risk for child and adolescent depression (Kaslow & Racusin, 1994). Parent–adolescent conflict (Cole & McPherson, 1993; Forehand et al., 1988), parental rejection (Whitbeck et al., 1992), and parental depression (Downey & Coyne, 1990; Fendrich, Warner, & Weissman, 1990) have also been linked to depression in childhood and adolescence. Conversely, adolescents' perceptions of family cohesion, support, and adaptability serve as protective factors against depression (Cumsille & Epstein, 1994). Among adults, investigators have outlined characteristics of marital interactions that are linked to depressive symptoms, such as marital infidelity and separation (Cano & O'Leary, 2000), marital dissatisfaction and lack of intimacy (Basco et al., 1992), and negative/poor communication and problem-solving skills (Basco et al., 1992; Goldman Sher & Baucom, 1993). Further, family dysfunction predicts poor prognosis and relapse of depressive illness (Miller et al., 1992; Moos, Cronkite, & Moos, 1998a), particularly perceived criticism from one's spouse (Hooley & Teasdale, 1989) and high expressed emotion among family members (Hinrichsen & Pollack, 1997).

Although less research has focused on the role of the family in the development of anxiety disorders, there is evidence that maternal characteristics such as low warmth, negativity, catastrophizing, and low autonomy granting, as well as psychopathology (Fristad & Clayton, 1991) and alcoholism (Chassin, Pitts, DeLucia, & Todd, 1999) may leave children vulnerable to anxiety (Whaley, Pinto, & Sigman, 1999). Anxious children's tendencies to interpret information as threatening and to develop avoidant responses have been shown to increase during problem-solving family interactions (Barrett, Rapee, Dadds, & Ryan, 1996). Anxiety has also been linked to marital negativity and dissatisfaction (Caughlin, Huston, & Houts, 2000). Thus a constellation of family factors have been linked to depression and anxiety across the lifespan, and potentially leave patients at risk for relapse if not adequately addressed in therapy.

Family-Based Treatment for Child and Adolescent Emotional Problems. Despite the strong evidence for family influence on child and adolescent depression and anxiety, very few family-based treatments for these disorders have been developed or tested (Diamond & Siqueland, 2001). Brent et al. (1997) tested systemic behavior family therapy (SBFT, which utilizes functional family therapy, communication, and problem-solving techniques) in a randomized controlled trial for depressed adolescents in comparison to individual cognitive behavior therapy and individual nondirective supportive therapy. Results favored individual CBT over the other interventions in the rate of recovery of both interviewer-rated and self-reported depressive symptoms, although all three treatments were associated with similar reductions in suicidality and functional impairment from intake to posttreatment. In one- and two-year follow-up analyses, however, all three treatments were equally effective in helping adolescents achieve recovery from symptoms and remission from a diagnosable depressive disorder (Birmaher et al., 2000). Further analyses revealed that SBFT was more effective in addressing parent–adolescent conflict than either of the other treatments (Kolko et al., 2000). Results of studies testing combination treatments for depression with parent components have been mixed. Lewinsohn, Clarke, Hops, and Andrews (1990) demonstrated no additional benefit from adding a parent psycho-educational and skills training module to a CBT group intervention for adolescent depression, yet Stark (1990) reported significantly greater reduction in children's depressive symptoms using a combination school-based CBT approach with family therapy sessions in comparison to traditional supportive counseling. Thus, the few studies that have been conducted on family-based interventions provides limited support for its efficacy with depressed children and adolescents.

Family-based interventions for child anxiety disorders have only slightly more support. Dadds and colleagues have conducted several studies testing combination CBT and family-based interventions with anxious children and their parents. For instance, Dadds et al. (1997) tested a ten-week school-based cognitive-behavioral and family-based group early intervention for children screened for anxiety problems in comparison to a monitoring condition. Both treatments reduced anxiety symptoms from pre- to posttest, yet only the CBT family-based intervention maintained treatment gains at six months and up to two years following the intervention (Dadds et al., 1999). Another investigation of this approach tested CBT-group, CBT-group plus family management (problem solving and skills training and support for parents in helping manage their child's anxiety), and a wait-list control group for children with anxiety disorders (Barrett, 1998; Barrett, Dadds, & Rapee, 1996). Both interventions were superior to the wait-list control in terms of the percentage of youth no longer meeting diagnosis at posttreatment and twelve-month follow-up. Further, the addition of the family management component demonstrated slightly better effects in children's internalizing and externalizing symptoms than CBT-group alone, with younger children and fe-males responding particularly well to the CBT-group plus family management intervention (Barrett et al., 1996). These results suggest that parent involvement in the treatment of child and adolescent anxiety disorders can have important benefits over CBT alone.

Family-Based Treatment for Adult Depression and Anxiety. Family-based interventions for adult depression have focused almost entirely on the application of behavioral couples therapy, due to the strong link between depression and marital problems, the evidence that marital distress commonly precedes depressive episodes, and the finding that continued marital problems are associated with relapse following acute episodes (Jacobson, Holtzworth-Munroe, & Schmaling, 1989). Behavioral or social learning based marital therapies for depression focus on teaching couples to communicate and problem solve more effectively, while increasing positive, pleasing interactions and reducing negative interchanges. Generally, these marital interventions have been shown to be as effective as state-of-the-art alternative treatments (e.g., interpersonal psychotherapy and cognitive therapy) and wait-list controls in reducing depressive symptoms and are more effective than these other treatments in improving the quality of the marital relationship (Jacobson et al., 1989; O'Leary & Beach, 1990). Behavioral couples therapy appears to work equally well in decreasing marital dissatisfaction, eliminating negative communication, and improving psychological functioning for distressed couples and couples with a depressed partner (Goldman Sher, Baucom, & Larus, 1990). However, Jacobson et al. (1991) reported that BMT was less effective than cognitive therapy in reducing depressive symptoms among women who were not maritally distressed at intake. Further, there is no evidence to suggest that marital and couples therapy is superior to cognitive therapy in reducing relapse rates in the year following treatment (Jacobson et al., 1993), contrary to expectations from research documenting the important role of family and marital problems in the chronicity of depression (Moos, Cronkite, & Moos, 1998b). Generally, couples therapy has generated convincing empirical support in the treatment of depression, particularly among women whose depressive symptoms are related to marital distress.

One noteworthy study of family-based psychoeducational treatment for bipolar disorder was conducted by Simoneau et al. (1999). Family-focused psychoeducational therapy (FFT; Miklowitz & Goldstein, 1997) is similar in structure to behavioral family therapy, incorporating didactic information sessions about the disorder, communication-enhancement training, and problem-solving skills training, as well as behavioral techniques designed to provide opportunities to practice and refine new skills. Patients were randomly assigned to either nine months of FFT or crisis management with follow-up (both conditions involving medication management). Results demonstrated the superiority of FFT in increasing positive nonverbal family exchanges and reducing patients' symptoms in the year following treatment entry, although verbal interactions and negative nonverbal interactions did not improve significantly. These results suggest that psychoeducational family interventions need further investigation, but offer promise in the treatment of bipolar patients.

Family-based interventions for adult anxiety disorders have been infrequently tested and have not demonstrated great success. For instance, behavioral family therapy as applied to PTSD symptoms among combat veterans had no additional impact when delivered in combination with exposure therapy (Glynn et al., 1999). Involvement of the spouse in therapy for agoraphobia and OCD appears to have some beneficial effects, although the mechanisms by which partner-assisted therapy achieves outcomes is not well understood and the evidence for these interventions is inconsistent (Baucom et al., 1998; Jacobson et al., 1989).

●

In sum, family-based interventions for child and adolescent emotional disorders have lagged behind the progress seen in the application of family approaches for behavioral disorders. There is slightly more evidence for the effectiveness of family interventions for child anxiety than depression, although these studies need replication. Guy Diamond and his colleagues are in the process of studying a structural-strategic approach to the treatment of childhood depression, which appears to hold promise given its focus on the reparation of parent–adolescent attachment relationships (Diamond & Siqueland, 2001). A pilot study of this model with a small sample of depressed adolescents indicates that it is more effective than a wait-list control in reducing depressive and anxiety symptoms as well as family conflict (Diamond et al., in press). Nadine Kaslow and her colleagues have developed and piloted an interpersonal family therapy approach with encouraging initial results; it blends family systems theory, cognitive-behavioral psychology, object relations theory, and basic knowledge of developmental psychopathology in treating depressed youngsters (Schwartz, Kaslow, Racusin, & Carton, 1998). Certainly family-based interventions for both childhood depression and anxiety have promise, yet further study of these approaches is necessary.

In the treatment of adult emotional disturbances, significant support exists for the use of behavioral couples therapy with depressed patients and their partners, yet little evidence supports the use of family-based interventions for adults with anxiety disorders. Couples therapy may be a useful adjunct to exposure therapy for adult anxiety disorders, although further study of this approach is needed. The knowledge base of family interventions for depression and anxiety is limited, although several lines of research show encouraging results.

Family Therapy for Substance Use Disorders

Family Risk and Protective Factors for Substance Abuse.
Family factors have been strongly and consistently linked to substance abuse problems. Further, substance abuse wreaks havoc on the cohesion of the family as a unit and the functioning of its members (Rotunda, Scherer, & Imm, 1995). Relationship factors such as parent–adolescent attachment consistently predict adolescent drug use across cultures (Brook et al., 2001). Parenting practices such as low monitoring, ineffective discipline, and poor communication are also implicated in substance abuse problems among youth (Liddle, Rowe, Dakof, & Lyke, 1998; McGillicuddy, Rychtarik, Duquette, & Morsheimer, 2001), although parenting clearly interacts with a host of other factors in predicting the onset of drug abuse and related problems (Dishion & Kavanagh, 2000). Other family factors have been shown to exert a strong protective influence against drug problems (Morojele & Brook, 2001). For instance, youth whose parents strongly disapprove of drug use were significantly less likely to report current use of an illicit drug (SAMHSA, 2001). Studies with adults show that couple and marital factors, such as the partners' poor coping strategies for dealing with the substance abuse (Barber, 1995) and generally negative communication patterns within the marriage (Fals-Stewart & Birchler, 1998) are associated with the substance abuser's more frequent use. Further, research shows that maintaining close relationships within healthy families of origin may buffer adult substance abusers from relapse (Lavee & Altus, 2001).

Family-Based Interventions for Adolescent Substance Abuse.
Family-based treatments have been heralded in a number of recent reviews as among the most promising approaches for the treatment of adolescent drug problems (Stanton & Shadish, 1997; Williams & Chang, 2000; Winters, Latimer, & Stinchfield, 1999). The first wave of randomized controlled trials of family-based interventions for adolescent drug abuse (Joanning, Quinn, Thomas, & Mullen, 1992; Lewis, Piercy, Sprenkle, & Trepper, 1990; Szapocznik et al., 1988) utilized state-of-the-art methods available at that time. These studies established the significant promise of family-based treatments in reducing adolescent drug abuse and related problems (Liddle & Dakof, 1995).

A second wave of family-based intervention studies has been conducted since this first generation of trials, building on the foundations set by these early studies and adhering to more rigorous standards of clinical research now held in the fields of psychotherapy and drug abuse treatment research. Several of these studies have tested multisystems, integrative family-based models designed to alter the life ecology of the drug abusing teen as well as changing maladaptive family patterns, such as home-based sessions, case management, and extrafamilial work in the domains of school, work, and legal involvement (Henggeler et al., 1991; Rowe et al., 2002; Szapocznik & Williams,

Jose Szapocznik's studies demonstrate that making family treatment responsive to cultural context greatly increases its effectiveness with high-risk individuals and families.

2000). The use of therapy manuals has facilitated the dissemination and replication of family-based therapies in various adolescent treatment and research settings (Liddle et al., 2002). Greater attention to methodological challenges such as accurate assessment of family processes (Liddle & Rowe, 1998), evaluation of therapist adherence to treatment protocols (Henggeler et al., 1997; Hogue et al., 1998), and investigation of the links between therapeutic process and outcome (Diamond & Diamond, 2001) are evident. While significant challenges remain, the past decade has seen major advances from different research programs investigating family-based treatments for adolescent drug abuse (Liddle, in press).

Strong and consistent empirical support exists for the comparative efficacy of family-based therapy in reducing levels of adolescent drug use and increasing adaptive functioning in a number of well-controlled clinical trials (Liddle & Dakof, 1995; Stanton & Shadish, 1997; Waldron, 1997). Family-based interventions have been found to have superior pre- to posttreatment effects on levels of adolescent drug use compared to individual therapy (Azrin et al., 1994; Henggeler et al., 1991; Liddle, 2002a; Waldron et al., 2001), adolescent group therapy (Joanning et al., 1992; Liddle, Dakof, et al., 2001), and family psychoeducational drug counseling (Joanning et al., 1992; Lewis et al., 1990; Liddle, Dakof, et al., 2001). These reductions in drug use seen in family-oriented treatments have demonstrated long-term effects up to twelve months after termination. Further, family-based treatments exert positive effects on family functioning (Joanning et al., 1992; Liddle, Dakof, et al., 2001), school performance (Azrin et al., 2001; Brown et al., 1999; Liddle, Dakof, et al., 2001), comorbid symptomatology (Azrin et al., 1994, 2001; Liddle, Dakof, et al., 2001; Liddle, 2002a), and delinquency (Henggeler, Pickrel, & Brondino, 1999). Finally, family-based prevention approaches that help parents institute effective practices against

drug use are being implemented and tested in school (Dishion & Kavanagh, 2000) and community settings (Hogue, Liddle, Becker, & Johnson-Leckrone, 2002).

The multidimensional family therapy (MDFT) approach (Liddle, 2002b) has been the focus of consistent empirical development and refinement since 1985 and continues to be tested in important federal research initiatives. MDFT has been recognized as one of the most promising interventions in a new generation of comprehensive, multicomponent, theoretically derived and empirically supported adolescent drug abuse treatments (CSAT, 1999; Drug Strategies, 2002; Lebow & Gurman, 1995; NIDA, 1999; Nichols & Schwartz, 1998). MDFT has demonstrated efficacy in comparison to alternative treatments in four controlled trials, including a prevention study, with mainly juvenile justice involved and comorbid drug-abusing youth (Dennis et al., in press; Hogue et al., 2002; Liddle, Dakof, et al., 2001; Liddle, 2002a). The clinical outcomes achieved in these randomized studies indicate that MDFT is effective in comparison to state-of-the-art treatments (individual cognitive-behavioral treatment, peer group treatment, and family education models) in significantly reducing substance use and related problems up to one year following treatment completion. MDFT demonstrates superior therapeutic benefits in relation to the costs of delivering the approach in comparison to standard community drug treatment and other state-of-the-art models (French et al., in press). In an ongoing transporting study, investigators have demonstrated that the treatment can be adapted, refined, and successfully integrated into a day treatment drug abuse program by community therapists (Liddle et al., 2002). MDFT investigators have also outlined important change mechanisms in a series of therapy process studies reviewed below. Thus, the empirical support for the efficacy and effectiveness of specific multisystems family-based interventions for adolescent substance abuse such as MDFT continues to grow.

Family-Based Interventions for Adult Substance Abuse. The subspecialty of family-based interventions for adult substance abusers has also made major strides in the past two decades, particularly in the area of alcoholism (Edwards & Steinglass, 1995; Heath & Stanton, 1998; Rotunda & O'Farrell, 1997). Empirical support for both behavioral family therapy and family systems approaches in treating adult substance abusers has accumulated, although like alcoholism treatments generally, neither model has established superiority. More recently, research has focused on developing and testing engagement strategies designed to mobilize natural supports and utilize leverage within the family to motivate substance abusers into treatment (e.g., Miller, Meyers, & Tonigan, 1999). In the drug abuse area, progress has been slower. Stanton and Shadish (1997) concluded from their meta-analysis of family therapy for drug abuse that family interventions work equally well for adults and adolescents, and that family therapy studies with adults and adolescents tend to be of good design quality, show better results than nonfamily approaches, and, with adult narcotic addicts, is a cost-effective component of methadone maintenance. Yet reviewers agree that the subspecialty of family-based treatment for adult drug problems has lagged behind the field of family-based adult alcoholism treatment (McCrady & Epstein, 1996; O'Farrell & Fals-Stewart, 1999). Several authors have suggested that the application of effective family-based models for alcoholics hold promise for the treatment of adult drug abusers (Epstein & McCrady, 1998; Liddle & Dakof, 1995), and in recent years there have been increased efforts in this direction.

Family-Based Interventions with Adult Alcoholics. Given the importance of couples' interactional patterns in the substance abusers' level of use and relapse after treatment (e.g., Fals-Stewart & Birchler, 1998), much of the family-based treatment for adult alcoholics has centered on behavioral couples therapy (BCT). The approach generally involves an initial agreement for the alcoholic to commit to sobriety and the partner to reinforce this commitment daily, as well as strategies to help the alcoholic cope with cravings and for the couple to deal with crises concerning relapse, communicate more effectively, and increase enjoyable activities that don't involve substance use. BCT delivered in group and individual formats has been instrumental in helping alcoholics reduce their drinking as well as incidents of domestic violence, improve marital functioning, and shows significant cost savings in reduced hospitalizations and jail costs up to two years post-treatment (Epstein & McCrady, 1998; Jacobson et al., 1989; O'Farrell & Fals-Stewart, 1999). The use of BCT with alcoholics has ignited significant interest due to its efficacy evidence and applicability to practice settings (Baucom et al., 1998; Rotunda & O'Farrell, 1997).

Behavioral family therapy techniques have also been adapted by family intervention researchers in designing interventions aimed at increasing engagement of substance abusers into treatment by mobilizing family supports. Azrin's (1976) broad-based Community Reinforcement Approach serves as the foundation for much of this work. This model is based on behavioral principles and targets specific interventions with the substance abuser and family members to provide reinforcement for abstinence and removing reinforcement for drinking. Early studies revealed that community reinforcement techniques demonstrated greater efficacy than treatment as usual in engaging alcoholics into treatment (e.g., Sisson & Azrin, 1986). The Community Reinforcement and Family Training (CRAFT) program (Meyers & Smith, 1995), which incorporates skills training strategies aimed at reducing significant others' distress, has shown promise in engaging substance abusers into treatment (Meyers, Miller, & Smith, 2001). For instance, in a rigorously controlled study comparing CRAFT with two commonly practiced interventions (Al-Anon facilitation therapy and Johnson Institute confrontation intervention), Miller, Meyers, and Tonigan (1999) found that CRAFT was more effective in engaging unmotivated alcoholic patients into treatment, although the functioning of significant others was comparable across conditions up to twelve months follow-up. Thus the community reinforcement approach offers promise in the area of treatment engagement for alcoholic patients, and further investigation of interventions using these strategies and principles throughout treatment (not only in the initial stage of therapy) is warranted.

Family-Based Interventions with Adult Drug Abusers. Early studies by Duncan Stanton and his colleagues were among the first controlled trials of family-based interventions for substance-abusing adults. Stanton and Todd (1982) reported that an innovative and integrative structural-strategic family therapy model reduced drug use more effectively than a family movie condition or standard drug counseling. In a subsequent study, this research group showed that a home detoxification program was more effective than standard detoxification for substance abusers (Stanton, 1985). While this encouraging line of research has unfortunately not been pursued further, other family-based interventions for drug-abusing adults have been recently developed based largely on the work in the alcoholism treatment field. Two areas in particular have benefited from this type of empirical attention: (1) the application of behavioral couples therapy, previously demonstrating efficacy with alcoholic populations, to drug abusers and their partners; and (2) the adaptation of community reinforcement techniques and other engagement strategies that work with significant family members to facilitate engage-

ment of the drug abuser into treatment (e.g., Landau et al., 2000).

Epstein and McCrady (1998) suggest that the application of behavioral couples therapy to treating drug abusers offers one of the most promising areas of family-based treatment research with substance abusers. In fact, recent studies by William Fals-Stewart and his colleagues suggest that behavioral couples therapy (BCT) may in fact have considerable promise in the treatment of drug abusers as well as alcoholic patients. Fals-Stewart, Birchler, and O'Farrell (1996) demonstrated the efficacy of BCT in a randomized trial comparing BCT and individual-based therapy for male drug abusers. BCT couples had better relationship outcomes and husbands had fewer days of drug use, longer periods of abstinence, and fewer drug-related arrests and hospitalizations up to one year follow-up than those in individual therapy. An extension of this study found that a larger proportion of drug abusers in BCT significantly reduced their drug use and improved their relational functioning than did those in individual behavior therapy (Fals-Stewart et al., 2000). Winters et al. (2002) replicated these results with seventy-five female drug abusers, showing longer periods of continuous abstinence and lower levels of drug, alcohol, and family problems up to one year follow-up among female drug abusers in BCT than those in individual behavior therapy only. Finally, Kelley and Fals-Stewart (2002) demonstrated that children's behavioral functioning improved more dramatically from intake to twelve months follow-up when their drug-abusing fathers participated in BCT than when they received individual behavioral therapy or a psychoeducational control treatment. Fathers' drug use and couples' relationship quality also improved most significantly in BCT from intake to twelve months in this study. Taken together, these encouraging results suggest that BCT benefits both male and female drug abusers, as well as their relationships with their partners and overall family functioning, and their children's adjustment more significantly than alternative treatments.

Family-based engagement interventions for adult drug abusers are also gaining empirical support. For instance, Gayle Dakof and her colleagues developed and tested the efficacy of a manualized, in-home drug abuse treatment that intervenes at the level of the individual and family. The Engaging Moms program has roots in the relational model of women's development (Dakof, 2000), family systems models of drug abuse treatment (Liddle, Dakof, & Diamond, 1991), and family preservation models of service delivery (Wells, 1995). Results demonstrated that significantly more women assigned to the Engaging Moms program enrolled in drug abuse treatment than did women assigned to the community engagement as usual (control) condition. Eighty-eight percent of women in the Engaging Moms program entered a drug treatment program compared to 46 percent of the women who received community services as usual, and 67 percent of the women assigned to the experimental condition remained in treatment for at least four weeks compared to 38.5 percent of controls (Dakof et al., in press). Kirby et al. (1999) randomized thirty-two family members and significant others of drug abusers to either a Community Reinforcement Training (CRT) intervention, adapted from Sisson and Azrin's (1986) approach with alcoholics and their wives, or a Twelve-step self-help group. Follow-up assessments conducted ten weeks later revealed significantly greater retention of significant others in treatment as well as higher rates of treatment engagement among drug abusers whose significant others were assigned to CRT. Thus preliminary evidence for the success of engagement interventions with family members and significant others suggests that these interventions hold promise for enlisting these natural supports to motivate drug abusers into treatment. Longer follow-up of these interven-

tions will increase enthusiasm for their efficacy with drug abusing populations.

To summarize, family-based approaches for both adolescent and adult substance abusers hold significant promise (Stanton & Shadish, 1997). Several reviews, including those by Ozechowski and Liddle (2000), Waldron (1997), and Winters, Latimer, and Stinchfield (1999), outline a number of suggestions for improving empirical efforts in the adolescent substance abuse treatment area, including greater attention to family measurement issues, standardized operationalization and measurement of core constructs such as drug use and behavior problems, investigation of therapist variables that impact outcome, assessment of longer-term outcomes, and further study of process and mechanisms of change.

Family-based interventions for adult substance abusers might be advanced with the investigation of nonbehaviorally based models, the integration of behavioral models with other approaches, and interventions beyond the initial stage of therapy, as well as the study of mechanisms of change and treatment matching studies (Epstein & McCrady, 1998; O'Farrell & Fals-Stewart, 1999). With both adolescent and adult substance abusers, the interventions used most commonly in community practice have yet to be adequately tested, and the models described here with accumulating empirical support have not made their way into the very settings in which substance abusers need them most (Fals-Stewart & Birchler, 2001; Liddle, Rowe, et al., 2002; Rotunda & O'Farrell, 1997). New directions in family-based intervention research with substance abusers are focused on addressing this critical research–practice gap.

Family Therapy for Schizophrenia

Family Risk and Protective Factors for Schizophrenia. Family researchers have been intrigued by the family dynamics of schiz-ophrenic patients since the 1960s and 1970s, when relational patterns known as "communi-cation deviance" (Singer & Wynne, 1965) and "expressed emotion" (Vaughn & Leff, 1976) were posited as having unique explanatory power in the web of factors influencing the de-velopment of psychotic disorders. Subsequent research strongly supports the role of disturbed family dynamics as a contributing factor, per-haps secondary to biological processes, but contributing nonetheless, in the onset and chronicity of schizophrenia. For instance, a number of studies have linked family "commu-nication deviance," a general label for unclear, distorted, discontinuous, and vague interac-tions, to schizophrenia (Doane et al., 1989; Goldstein, 1987; Miklowitz et al., 1991). These studies have associated communication de-viance with schizophrenia over time and across cultures.

Other studies have focused on the link be-tween "expressed emotion" (EE), a pattern of emotional over involvement and criticism, to schizophrenia. Relatives of schizophrenic pa-tients have been shown to make more nega-tive, intrusive statements than relatives of bipolar patients (Miklowitz, Goldstein, & Nuechterlein, 1995). Further, relatives of schizophrenics characterized as high-EE tend to make causal attributions about the patient's illness to factors that are internal to and con-trollable by the patient (Brewin, MacCarthy, Duda, & Vaughn, 1991), and families' attribu-tions and criticism of the patient are important in determining the course of illness (Lopez, Nelson, Snyder, & Mintz, 1999). However, EE in families of schizophrenics has been shown to be bidirectional in nature (Rosenfarb, Gold-stein, Mintz, & Nuechterlein, 1995) and its im-pact on the patient and on family exchanges is likely mediated by the patient's level of symp-toms and social skills (Mueser et al., 1993). High EE in the family has been consistently linked to greater risk for relapse after treat-

ment (Parker & Hadzi-Pavlovic, 1990), thus interventions are increasingly devoted to as-sisting families cope with the stress of taking care of their loved ones and modifying their at-titudes and interactions to support the pa-tients' recovery (Backer & Richardson, 1989; Marsh & Johnson, 1997).

Family-Based Interventions for Schizo-phrenia. The advent of psychoactive medi-cation in the 1960s, which revolutionized institutional treatment for mentally ill patients, also left communities and families with much of the burden of caring for schizophrenic patients. Family interventions were subsequently devel-oped based on the accumulating evidence of family risk factors noted above in schizophrenia onset and relapse and the significant stress of caring for mentally ill family members. These family-based treatments have been designed to augment pharmacological interventions, with the aim of improving the family environment (including reducing criticism and hostility and increasing stability and structure) and assisting families with the management of the illness (Hahlweg & Wiedemann, 1999). The interven-tions generally consist of engagement strategies, psychoeducation, coping and problem-solving skills training to lower family stress, and crisis in-tervention. Considerable support now exists for the use of these family-based interventions within a multimodal treatment regimen for schizophrenic patients (Goldstein & Miklowitz, 1995).

Several family-based interventions have documented success in reducing symptoms from pre- to posttreatment and in decreasing risk for relapse following treatment (Baucom et al., 1998). For instance, in an early study of combination medication management and family therapy, Michael Goldstein and his team (1978) reported relapse rates at six months as low as 0 percent among patients receiving fam-ily therapy and moderate medication dose, in comparison to almost 50 percent relapse rates with low medication dose alone. Research supports the positive effects of behavioral family management (incorporating psychoeducation with communication and problem-solving skills) in increasing the schizophrenic's social skills, decreasing the family's stress, and improving family communication, as well as significantly reducing relapse rates in comparison to standard psychiatric care up to two years following treatment (Falloon, Boyd, & McGill, 1984).

Tarrier et al. (1989) also demonstrated impressive results with two versions of family therapy against a brief family education condition and treatment as usual. Both family therapy approaches demonstrated significantly lower relapse rates than the comparison conditions up to two years after treatment. A recent investigation by this same group tested an integrated multi-component model consisting of motivational interviewing, CBT, and family therapy for schizophrenics with comorbid substance use disorders. The integrated approach was superior to standard care in terms of reductions in patients' positive symptoms as well as substance use from intake to twelve months (Barrowclough et al., 2001). Mueser et al. (2001) compared supportive family management (consisting of two years of monthly support groups) and applied family management (involving one year of behavioral family therapy, with support groups continuing for a second year), with all patients receiving medication management. Their results showed slight advantages of adding behavioral family therapy in terms of less rejection of the patient and reduced friction among family members, yet the interventions did not differ in relation to patients' social functioning or family burden at the two-year follow-up point. There was no evidence to support the hypothesis that more intensive family intervention would enable patients to be maintained on lower medication doses. Finally, William McFarlane and his colleagues (1995) developed a multiple-family supportive intervention with emphasis on improving family members' social support. The model demonstrated lower relapse rates than individual family therapy approaches up to four years posttreatment.

Thus there is clear evidence to support the use of family interventions as one component of multimodal strategies for the treatment of schizophrenics. Certain family patterns, most notably high criticism and rejection, complicate the recovery process for schizophrenics returning to their families after treatment. Further, the stress of managing a family member's illness necessitates social support and skill development for all involved family members. Therefore the line of evidence supporting these interventions is encouraging. Further research designed to specify the mechanisms of change and essential ingredients of these complex interventions will facilitate treatment development in this area. As advocacy for the families of chronically mentally ill patients increases, the utilization of these empirically supported family-based models into the community will become more common in standard practice (Backer & Richardson, 1989; Baucom et al., 1998).

Family Therapy for Eating Disorders

Family Risk and Protective Factors for Disordered Eating. Salvador Minuchin's classic work with eating disordered girls and their families (Minuchin, Rosman, & Baker, 1978) was inspired largely by the clinical observation that the families of these patients were deficient in providing nurturance and support to developing adolescents and young adults. In fact, research supports these clinical observations. Parents of eating disordered individuals have been characterized in empirical studies as overprotective (Wade, Treloar, & Martin, 2001), enmeshed and overly critical (Polivy & Herman, 2002), and as having diffuse boundaries with their adolescents (Rowa, Kerig, & Geller, 2001). Interactional patterns in families of eating disordered patients tend to constrain autonomy and the expression of intimacy (Maharaj et al., 2001), disrupt attachment relations (Ratti, Humphrey, & Lyons, 1996), and are characterized by destructive communication (Lattimer, Wagner, & Gowers, 2000). Parental substance abuse may also increase vulnerability for eating disorders (Lyon et al., 1997). However, some evidence suggests that the influence of family dysfunction on the development of eating disorders is indirect; high conflict, low cohesion, and childhood abuse may impact disordered eating through depressive symptoms (Mazzeo & Espelage, 2002). Yet there is little doubt that family problems not only affect the development of eating disorders, but that family factors such as high criticism also predict poorer treatment prognosis among both bulimics and anorexics (Reiss & Johnson-Sabine, 1995; van Furth et al., 1996).

Family-Based Interventions for Eating Disorders. Since Minuchin's groundbreaking application of structural family therapy to the treatment of anorexia (Minuchin et al., 1978), several controlled trials lend support to family-based interventions for both bulimic and anorexic patients (Lemmon & Josephson, 2001). A series of studies from investigators at the Maudsley Hospital in London have tested a multimodal family-based treatment that emphasizes collaboration with the family as a valuable resource in the patient's recovery and avoids blaming the parents. The model borrows heavily from Minuchin's original structural family therapy techniques using a family meal in the first stage of therapy and reorganizing parental coalitions in later therapeutic work, as well as aspects of the Milan approach in examining and addressing the intergenerational context of the patient's problems. The model has demonstrated impressive results in weight gain and maintenance up to five years post-treatment in comparison to individual supportive therapy particularly for adolescents with more recent onset of problems (Russell, Dare, Eisler, & LeGrange, 1994; Russell, Szmukler, Dare, & Eisler, 1987).

Behavioral family systems therapy, which emphasizes parental control over eating and incorporates cognitive restructuring and problem-solving training, has also been tested in comparison to individual therapy for anorexic patients. The model was more effective than an individual approach focused on building ego strength and facilitating autonomy in terms of increasing body weight from pre- to posttreatment (approximately sixteen months of therapy), although the treatments were equally effective in most of the outcomes measured, including eating attitudes, body shape dissatisfaction, and depressive symptoms (Robin et al., 1994). Further, a comparison of a structural family therapy approach and a family psychoeducation group approach revealed no statistically significant differences in the use of the two approaches for anorexic patients (Geist et al., 2000). Finally, multiple family therapy approaches have recently been developed and pilot tested with encouraging results (Asen, 2002; Colahan & Robinson, 2002). This type of model treats families together in hospital settings using a multidisciplinary approach and actively involves family members in the treatment of the eating disordered patient in intensive family work (Scholz & Asen, 2001). Further investigation of these approaches is certainly warranted given their promising preliminary efficacy findings. Taken together, the support for family-based interventions with eating disordered patients is growing, although questions remain about the most effective dosage of family work within the generally multimodal programs necessary to treat these patients.

Efficacy of Marital and Couples Therapy

As discussed earlier, marital and couples therapy has demonstrated efficacy in the treatment of several disorders, including alcoholism, drug abuse, and depression (Baucom et al., 1998). A range of approaches, including behavioral, cognitive-behavioral, insight-oriented, systemic, and psychoeducational models, have generated positive findings in the main outcome of improving couples' relationships (e.g., Goldman & Greenberg, 1992; Kaiser, Hahlweg, Fehm-Wolfsdorf, & Groth, 1998; Snyder, Wills, & Grady-Fletcher, 1991). Next we present clinically relevant findings in the research on marital and couple interventions for relationship problems more generally and discuss new directions in this specialty.

Behavioral couples therapy (BCT) has been the most extensively studied of all couples therapy approaches (Jacobson et al., 2000). As previously noted, the approach is based on social learning principles and involves behaviorally oriented interventions designed to reinforce effective communication, problem solving, and positive interactions, and to decrease negative exchanges between couples. Behavioral techniques include contracting for follow-through of specific tasks or activities and homework assignments to generalize skills outside of therapy. Consensus has been reached that BCT effectively improves marital adjustment and satisfaction in comparison to waiting list controls (Dunn & Schwebel, 1995; Jacobson & Addis, 1993; Lebow & Gurman, 1995; Shadish et al., 1993) and results in clinically significant change for the majority of participants (Baucom et al., 1998). Follow-up results are somewhat disappointing, with treatment gains maintained in most studies up to one year (Hahlweg & Markman, 1988), although a significant percentage (38 percent) of couples divorce within four years of receiving BCT (Snyder et al., 1991).

BCT interventions have expanded with shifting foci in recent years (Baucom & Epstein, 1991). For instance, a new approach, integrative behavioral couples therapy (Jacobson et al., 2000; see Chapter 14), addresses some of the limitations of BCT, including its reduced impact over time (Hahlweg & Markman, 1988). The integrative approach emphasizes acceptance of partners' characteristics that are most difficult to change and uses these obstacles as platforms for establishing greater intimacy. The integrative approach has demonstrated preliminary comparative efficacy in comparison to traditional BCT using effect sizes and clinical significance ratings to measure marital satisfaction, and has also been adapted successfully into a group format (Jacobson et al., 2000). In addition, an enhanced version of BCT with cognitive restructuring and affect exploration techniques was also tested in comparison to standard BCT but found to be equally effective as the more traditional behavioral approach in decreasing negative communications and cognitions in session and at home (Halford, Sanders, & Behrens, 1993). In sum, Jacobson and Addis (1993) assert that BCT is the most well established and validated of any couples approach.

Cognitive behavioral marital therapy (CBMT) builds on the strong foundation of BCT but also seeks to change the unrealistic expectations and beliefs that interfere with adaptive relationships and intimacy. In Dunn and Schwebel's (1995) meta-analysis of fifteen methodologically sound randomized trials of marital therapy, CBMT was superior to both BCT and insight-oriented marital therapy in changing spouses' relationship-related cognitions from pre- to posttreatment. However, studies in which cognitive techniques were tested against standard BCT or used to augment standard behavioral marital therapy failed to provide any evidence that cognitive interventions are more effective than BCT or increase BCT's efficacy (Fincham, Bradbury, & Beach, 1990). Baucom et al. (1998) describe CBMT as "possibly efficacious," given small sample sizes in the studies reviewed and the lack of evidence suggesting added benefits of cognitive techniques over traditional BCT.

Insight-oriented approaches, including insight-oriented couples therapy and emotionally focused couples therapy, have also been subjected to clinical trial investigations and found to be superior to no treatment (Jacobson & Addis, 1993), with some evidence for their superiority in comparison to other established approaches (Baucom et al., 1998). The insight-oriented marital therapy approach (IOMT; Snyder & Wills, 1989) has increased in popularity and focus in empirical investigations. IOMT blends Gestalt and systemic techniques to increase couples' insight into their own intrapersonal and the relationships' dynamics, with focus on the affective nature of interactions and facilitation of partners' responses to the emotional needs expressed by their spouse. Dunn and Schwebel's (1995) meta-analysis revealed that IOMT is more successful than BCT or CBMT in improving spouses' perceptions of general relationship quality. Snyder, Wills, and Grady-Fletcher (1991) discovered few differences between IOMT and BCT in marital outcomes from pre- to posttest or at six month follow-up, but a four-year follow-up study indicated that a significantly greater percentage of couples in BCT had subsequently divorced than those in IOMT (38 percent versus 3 percent). Clearly, IOMT is a promising approach in the treatment of marital distress and dissatisfaction.

Emotionally focused couples therapy (Greenberg & Johnson, 1988; see Chapter 8) maintains that relationship difficulties generally stem from the disowning of feelings and attachment needs, creating negative interactional cycles and ineffective communication patterns. The model identifies these issues and negative cycles; helps clients to acknowledge the emotions underlying these cycles; assists in the acceptance of partners' positions; and encourages partners to communicate needs and emotions more effectively in the spirit of generating solutions and solidifying new relationship positions to increase intimacy. Emotionally focused couples therapy has shown greater efficacy than no-treatment wait list controls (Goldman & Greenberg, 1992; Jacobson & Addis, 1993) and demonstrated superior efficacy to BCT in improving marital adjustment from pre- to posttest in one study with moderately distressed couples (Johnson & Greenberg, 1985). One study with parents of chronically ill children showed that emotionally focused marital therapy more effectively reduced marital distress at posttreatment and five-month follow-up than a wait list control condition (Walker, Johnson, Manion, & Cloutier, 1996). Given its replication across research programs and its comparative efficacy against the well-established BCT model, emotionally focused therapy has significant potential in the treatment of relationship distress (Baucom et al., 1998).

Finally, evidence for the use of strategic therapy techniques in the context of couples therapy is provided by Goldman and Greenberg (1992) and Davidson and Horvath (1997). Goldman and Greenberg (1992) found that an integrated systemic therapy model was equally effective as emotionally focused couple therapy and more effective than a wait-list control in alleviating relationship distress and improving target complaints and conflict resolution. Further, couples in integrated treatment showed greater maintenance of treatment gains at the four-month follow-up than couples in emotionally focused couple therapy. Davidson and Horvath (1997) developed and tested a brief (three-session) couple therapy approach based on the MRI brief therapy model incorporating refraining and restraining interventions as well as homework assignments. The brief strategic couples therapy model was more effective in improving relationship adjustment, conflict resolution, and target complaints than a wait-list control condition from intake to six-week follow-up. These initial results in support of strategic techniques with couples suggest that further investigation of such approaches has potential to broaden the scope of marital and couples intervention research.

New Directions in Couples Therapy Research. Snyder et al.'s (1991) findings suggesting the superior long-term effects of IOMT over BCT sparked a series of comments and recommendations from leading researchers on the state-of-the-art in couples therapy research and the necessary next steps of this specialty. Neil Jacobson (1991), who initiated the debate with his criticisms of the Snyder et al. (1991) study, suggested that the future of couples therapy research lies in greater attention to measuring and controlling for therapeutic competence across conditions and operationalization of specific interventions in treatment manuals. He advocated less focus on "horse-race" studies comparing different models, and more attention to within-model studies of change mechanisms to identify the essential ingredients of successful treatment, as well as matching studies to identify the clients who respond best to various treatments. While there is certainly agreement that the investigation of within-model change processes is critical, researchers suggest that it may be premature for couples therapy to abandon comparative studies of different models, given the limited existing knowledge of the efficacy of specific approaches (Gurman, 1991; Johnson & Greenberg, 1991).

Howard Markman (1991) recommends broader conceptualization and measurement of relationship functioning and other important outcomes in couples therapy research, including increased reliance on observational data and longer follow-up periods in controlled trials. More recent recommendations for couples therapy research include the use of more sophisticated statistical and conceptual models, such as structural equation modeling, that account for the interdependence of intervention and interpersonal processes which occur over treatment (Cook, 1998). In sum, couples therapy researchers have produced solid empirical support for the use of several approaches to intervene with distressed couples, and these innovative treatment developers are exploring new areas of investigation.

Contributions of Family Therapy Process Research

Identifying Mechanisms of Therapeutic Change in Family Therapy. Although the findings reviewed above are valuable in establishing what types of family interventions have potential for alleviating psychological and interpersonal problems, they offer only limited information about the essential ingredients of family therapy. Questions about *why* certain therapies are effective, *how* families change, *what* specific techniques of treatment are most important, and *which* client and therapist variables impact change directly and indirectly cannot be addressed in comparative outcome studies. These questions can only be answered by looking inside the therapies discussed and using different types of methodologies and strategies (e.g., task analysis; Heatherington & Friedlander, 1990a) and analytic tools (e.g., growth modeling; Willett, Ayoub, & Robinson, 1991) to link specific therapeutic factors to the "mini-outcomes" throughout treatment and the ultimate outcomes at the end of treatment and at follow-up periods months later (Pinsof, 1989). Process research has the potential to lead to the development of more effective treatments and to bridge the gap between science and practice by increasing the relevance of empirical findings to practitioners (Diamond & Diamond, 2001; Pinsof & Wynne, 2000). This section discusses some of the most important family therapy process research findings to date, although a complete presentation of this area would require at least an entire chapter. We suggest further reading in this area for a more comprehensive exploration of family therapy process research (e.g., Alexander, Holtzworth-Munroe, & Jameson, 1994; Diamond & Diamond, 2001; Friedlander, Wildman, Heatherington, & Skowron, 1994; Pinsof, 1989).

Process of Therapeutic Alliance Formation in Family Therapy. The process of building and negotiating multiple therapeutic alliances is more complex in couples and family therapy than in individual therapy (Rait, 2000). Some family therapy models have emphasized the formation of multiple therapeutic alliances rather than a conceptualization of a single therapeutic alliance (Liddle, 2002b). Several family therapy process researchers have focused on the investigation of how therapists establish and maintain the important therapeutic alliance with different family members. For instance, Heatherington and Friedlander (1990b) explored relational control communication patterns and their impact on the development of the therapeutic alliance in systemic family therapy. They found that therapists and family members tended to interact in complementary ways, rather than having symmetrical, or competitive exchanges. However, neither pattern was related to family members' perceptions of the quality of the therapeutic relationship.

In family therapy with adolescent substance abusers, investigators examined the impact of adolescent engagement interventions on improving initially poor therapist–adolescent alliances over the first three sessions of multidimensional family therapy (MDFT; Diamond, Liddle, Hogue, & Dakof, 1999). Significant gains in working alliance were evident when therapists emphasized the following alliance-building interventions: attending to the adolescent's experience, formulating personally meaningful goals, and presenting one's self as the adolescent's ally. Lack of improvement or deterioration in alliance was associated with

the therapist spending too much time explaining the nature of therapy, thus waiting too long to discuss how the therapy could be personally meaningful for the teenager. A second examination of the alliance-building process in MDFT attended to the role of culturally important theme development. Jackson-Gilfort, Liddle, Dakof and Tejeda (2001) investigated whether therapeutic discussion of culturally specific themes enhanced treatment engagement of African American male substance-abusing youths. Exploration of particular themes—anger and rage, alienation, and the journey from boyhood to manhood (i.e., what it means to become an African American man)—were associated with both increased participation and decreased negativity by adolescents in the very next treatment session. These and other studies of the alliance in family therapy have yielded clinically important findings; however, future research needs to examine the links between the therapeutic relationship and outcomes in family therapy.

Critical Change Events in Family Therapy. Process research also focuses on the nature and sequences that determine important change events in family therapy, or those interventions that lead to resolution of problems or relational shifts within the family. For example, Friedlander, Heatherington, Johnson, and Skowron (1994) studied the dynamics of structural family therapy cases in which families were able to successfully move from disengagement to engagement. Using a modified analytic induction method, successful sustaining engagement events were identified and examined, and found to involve both interpersonal and personal learning experiences by each family member. Although no consistent pattern characterized the resolution of each family's impasse, sustained engagement generally involved active solicitation by the therapist of each family member's thoughts and feelings about the impasse and the benefits of reengagement, and helping other family members to hear each other's point of view. Similarly, in process studies of emotionally focused couple therapy, Greenberg, Ford, Alden, and Johnson (1993) found that peak session events were more frequently associated with affiliative, self-focused positive (e.g., self-disclosing, expressing) statements and accepting, friendly statements by partners than poor session events. Further, partners were significantly more likely to respond with an affiliative statement after therapists facilitated self-disclosure from the other partner.

Michael Nichols and his colleagues recently validated a rating scale to facilitate the examination of the complex process of successful enactments in family therapy (Allen-Eckert et al., 2001). Their research with highly trained and experienced family therapists suggests that breaking through family conflict and helping families shift their relational stance is a complex process that requires active, directive facilitation by the therapist (Nichols & Fellenberg, 2000). Essential ingredients of successful enactments include preenactment preparation with family members, specification of an agenda and explanation of the need for dialogue, direction about how the discussion should go, avoiding interrupting unless absolutely necessary, keeping the action going by pushing family members to work harder in the process of communicating, and closing by providing clients with clear direction in how to communicate with each other. The development of this scale will undoubtedly advance this area of process research.

Diamond and Liddle (1996) used task analysis to identify the combination of clinical interventions and family interactions necessary to resolve in-session impasses in MDFT (clinical situations characterized by negative exchanges, emotional disengagement, and poor problem-solving between parents and adolescents). Therapist behaviors that contributed to defusing

these negative interactions included: (a) actively blocking or addressing and working through negative affect; (b) evoking and amplifying thoughts and feelings that promote constructive dialogue; and (c) creating emotional treaties among family members by alternately working in session with parents alone and adolescents alone—a kind of shuttle diplomacy. In cases with successful resolution of the impasse, the therapist transformed the nature and tone of the conversation in the session, shifting the parent's blaming to a focus on their feelings of regret and loss, and eliciting the adolescent's thoughts and feelings about relationship roadblocks with parents and others. The most conflicted families were least likely to move to a new conversational level. The study broke down in behavioral terms the components of the impasse, defining sequential contributions of both parents and adolescents, and specifying the relation of different therapist actions to the impasse.

In sum, process studies examining successful change events have illuminated some of the essential ingredients of effective family therapy. Taken together, the results of these investigations suggest that change events are facilitated in a range of family interventions by the therapist moving family members to a more vulnerable, self-disclosing, affective level, and helping other family members to listen and subsequently respond.

Gender in the Process of Family Therapy. Investigations of the role of gender in family therapy have also yielded important findings relevant to clinical practice. Newberry, Alexander, and Turner (1991) examined microsequences of therapist–client exchanges in the first stage of functional family therapy to examine the effects of therapist and client sex roles on the behaviors of each in therapy. They found that base rates of supportive and structuring interventions did not differ between male and female therapists in training, nor did they differ in the frequency of utilization with male and female clients; however, the sequences of behaviors between therapists and clients were determined in part by gender. Fathers responded more positively to structuring interventions than did mothers, and female therapists were more likely than male therapists to receive supportive responses from both male and female clients following their use of supportive interventions. Interestingly, female therapists subsequently responded with more structuring responses than males following client supportive responses. In an investigation of gender in the first interview using a structural/strategic family therapy approach, Shields and McDaniel (1992) similarly uncovered no differences in the frequency of supportive statements by male and female therapists, but they did find differences in the ways that family members respond to therapists depending on the therapists' gender. For instance, family members made more conflictual statements to each other in the presence of female therapists, and made more structuring comments to therapists who were male than female. Finally, Werner-Wilson, Price, Zimmerman, and Murphy (1997) analyzed videotapes of family therapy sessions to explore the role of gender in conversational control and found that family therapists in training interrupt women three times more than male clients. Given these initial findings, the investigation of gender as a variable in the process of family therapy is clearly a fruitful avenue for further investigation.

Process Investigations in Family Therapy with Child and Adolescent Behavior Problems. Process studies specific to family interventions with behavior problem children and adolescents have examined the links between parent and child/adolescent change in therapy and other important questions about working

effectively with difficult families. For instance, Patterson and Chamberlain's (1992) groundbreaking process study identified ways in which therapists contribute to parental resistance in therapy, and thus paved the way for treatment development advances in family interventions with problem children and adolescents. Schmidt, Liddle, and Dakof (1996) investigated the nature and extent of change in parenting behaviors in MDFT, as well as the link between parental subsystem change and reduction in adolescent drug abuse and other symptomatology. Parents showed significant decreases in negative parenting behavior (e.g., negative affect, verbal aggression) and increases in positive parenting (e.g., monitoring and limit-setting, positive affect, and commitment) over the course of therapy. Moreover, these changes in parenting behavior were associated with reductions in adolescent drug use and problem behavior. These results support a basic tenet of family-based treatments: Change in a fundamental aspect of the family system (parenting practices) is related to change at the critical level of interest—reduction of adolescent symptoms. Furthermore, these data suggest that parenting risk and protective factors for drug use are accessible to intervention within a therapeutic environment.

Mann, Borduin, Henggeler, and Blaske (1990) found that families with delinquent adolescents had more cross-generational coalitions and marital conflict at intake than healthy control families. Further, over the course of multisystemic therapy, decreases in adolescents' and fathers' symptoms were linked to improvements in the marital relationship. Although the results did not support the link between reductions in adolescents' symptoms and improved parent–adolescent relationships, these findings did show the negative impact of unhealthy, unbalanced coalitions in family therapy. However, a subsequent investigation revealed a clear association between improved family functioning (increased parental monitoring and cohesion) and reduced delinquency among adolescents, mediated by decreased affiliation with delinquent peers (Huey, Henggeler, Brondino, & Pickrel, 2000). This study was unique in that it investigated the extent to which therapeutic "dosage," or the extent of fidelity to the prescribed model, impacted the improvements of family functioning and adolescent symptoms. In fact, therapists' adherence to their model determined the extent of family change, which was associated with reduced affiliation with negative peers, and subsequently with decreased delinquency.

Finally, functional family therapy researchers have investigated the sequences of therapist and family behavior that lead to positive behavior from delinquent adolescents and their parents in session. Robbins, Alexander, Newell, and Turner (1996) found that therapist reframes were the only interventions that were met with positive responses from delinquent adolescents in first sessions of functional family therapy, suggesting that the reframe may have a particularly important role in engaging resistant adolescents during the early stage of therapy. Robbins, Alexander, and Turner (2000) subsequently studied the processes by which therapists were able to disrupt defensive interactions among delinquent adolescents and their parents in session. Similar to the first study, therapist reframes were the only interventions that effectively reduced family members' defensive statements. These studies have been instrumental in outlining specific in-session therapist behaviors that lead to changes in family members' behavior needed to shape longer-term positive outcomes.

This is only a sample of process research conducted by family intervention scientists. Without doubt, the field is moving toward greater specification of the interventions necessary to produce immediate and more durable changes among client and family members. For instance, an adherence evalua-

tion of the extent to which therapists delivered MDFT and CBT in a clinical trial with teenage drug abusers not only established that therapists achieved fidelity to their respective models, but also that the implementation of very specific interventions could be differentiated using a therapy rating instrument (Hogue et al., 1998). These and other coding systems are advancing the investigation of the sequencing and successful implementation of specific therapeutic interventions (Hogue, Liddle, & Rowe, 1996; Allen-Eckert et al., 2001). Yet while these process investigations have answered important questions about critical within-therapy patterns of change, the family therapy field has very limited knowledge about the ways in which interventions and therapy change processes are linked to short or long-term outcomes (Friedlander, 2001). Myrna Friedlander and her colleagues (1994) suggest that family therapy process research can also be advanced by studying the experiences and perspectives of family members in therapy and afterward, as well as examining in greater detail how interventions affect change among family members in different ways. Process research clearly offers important opportunities to advance the field of family therapy and continue to lessen the research and practice divide.

Conclusions and Future Directions

Any discussion of family therapy research would be remiss if it failed to address family therapy's record of neglect and at times even adversarial relationship with research. Despite early indications that empirical support for family therapy's efficacy would be integrated into family therapy's culture (Framo, 1976), there were sharp turns away from research over the years. The professional organizations most associated with family therapy, AFTA and AAMFT, were mixed or confused about the role that research should play in mainstream family therapy, including its role at conferences, in training programs and advocacy efforts, continuing professional education, and even in bread and butter, guild-oriented licensing and certification efforts. Thus, the leadership that could have been exercised by these professional groups relative to the integration of research sensibilities and content into the practice of family therapy never materialized. Absent too was leadership and successful execution of system change (i.e., relative to the research–practice connection) from the field. While some articles were written bemoaning the research–practice disconnect, change relative to these recommendations took a long time to materialize. Part of the difficulty in making progress with the research–practice gap had to do with the complexity of the issue, the nature of the research that had been done up to that time, and the culture of clinical work, including those aspects of the practice culture supported and taught in graduate training programs.

Today, however, there are signs of change. For instance, the AAMFT dedicated one of its recent annual conferences to addressing the theme of empirically supported therapies. This is a far cry from a research panel here or there at a meeting of this visibility and scope. Additionally, AFTA now regularly has research poster sessions, as does AAMFT, and a dedicated plenary to research topics. Whether these developments are merely attempts to alter the field's image or signs of genuine change remains to be seen. Additionally, even if these research-oriented events continue, the attempted influence process is more complex than researchers or practitioners have anticipated (Brown, 2000; IOM, 1998). Furthermore, researchers are more aware than ever before of the cost of producing work (e.g., clinical models, findings) that is insufficiently relevant to clinicians. Perhaps we now understand that the diatribes (i.e., "what's wrong with family therapy") of the past, ineffective as they were in promoting any change on the fundamental issues pertaining to the research–practice relationship, were a prelude to change or perhaps a stage of change.

Although the field has emphasized the need to make research relevant for clinicians, perhaps the problem in the research-practice gap has to do with the framing of the issue. For instance, should all research be directly relevant to the practice of therapy? Doubtful. Research and practice are two contexts of remarkable diversity, so the general admonitions about the importance of research and practice to each other may be insufficiently precise or misguided. Outcome studies are relevant for therapists in some ways, yet in other ways they are not. Generally speaking, it may be interesting and perhaps useful for clinicians to know about the extent of decrease in serious problems such as drug use or conduct disorder that have been obtained with a manual-guided treatment. But generally, this information is reported in terms of groups of individuals, whereas therapists work in terms of individual cases that may or may not be similar to those included in outcome studies.

Increasingly, studies also measure and report changes in protective factors such as family organizational change, parenting practices, and increased success at school as a result of family therapy. These findings are important for therapists to understand because they highlight the fact that it isn't sufficient to simply reduce symptoms, but that it is also important to increase positive adjustment in specific areas of family functioning—areas that are known to be instrumental to achieving good developmental outcomes and adjustment. Knowledge about what can change in effective therapy, what is important to change, and how the sequences of change might unfold makes an enormous contribution to clinical practice.

While this research-based knowledge may confirm what clinicians already "know," it is research's contribution of an additional way of "knowing," a classic family therapy dual description, that is interesting and important, and it is yet another way to understand the contribution of contemporary family therapy research.

Perhaps it is in the process study arena where it is the easiest to make a case for how contemporary research is useful for day-to-day practice (Pinsof & Wynne, 2000). Process research attempts to illuminate the inner workings of therapy and the therapeutic relationship. Knowing about therapeutic impasses and their successful resolution, the connection of therapeutic alliance to clinical outcomes, difficulties of and steps to effective engagement, the process of changing important behavior such as parenting practices in symptomatic families—all areas of current process research—are illustrations of therapy enhancing knowledge. In some ways, perhaps research has taken (or has been ascribed) too much responsibility for not changing practice, when there are other contextual and implementation issues, having to do with training and professional development issues and lack of opportunities to institute effective models in clinical settings that deserve some of the responsibility for research's limited influence on the practice of family therapy. This is where professional associations of all sorts, family therapy–oriented and not, and professional licensing and certification groups, come into play.

These professional organizations can do a great deal to support the inclusion of science-based therapies in everyday practice. State administrations of mental health, substance abuse, and juvenile justice now routinely link funds for services to the capacity of service providers to implement treatments with proven efficacy. Combined with the uniformly positive reception of family therapy research in federal funding circles, as well as in private foundation funding and policy-making groups, these developments suggest that family therapy research has made more of an impact outside of family therapy proper than within it. Not until family therapy research becomes one with the training programs in which the clinical methods are taught will the culture of family therapy relative to its research values and beliefs change once and for all.

There is cause for excitement in the family therapy research field, signs of progress in recent years, and positive changes on the horizon. Family therapy models offer a conceptual framework that organizes complex, multilevel information about the etiology and maintenance of problems, linking basic science knowledge about developmental psychopathology to specific interventions. Thus family therapy has in place a conceptual scaffolding within which clinically relevant research can be organized and treatments further developed, refined, and empirically evaluated. The popularity of family-based therapies has soared over the last decade or so, as therapists and researchers have confirmed that including parents and other family members in treatment is critical to successful engagement of clients and to overall effectiveness. Certain manual-guided family-based therapies are experienced by therapists not as constraining, but as providing sufficient flexibility (Godley et al., 2001). Numerous practice guidelines and reports of influential private foundations and policy-making groups have endorsed the importance of working with the parents and families of clients, representing a major shift from a decade ago. Research can, as we have seen in recent years, influence policy- and practice-level changes that support increased resources and opportunities for the dissemination of empirically supported family-based treatments into practice.

─Recommended Readings ─

Alexander, J. F., Holtzworth-Munroe, A., & Jameson, P. B. (1994). Research on the process and outcome of marriage and family therapy. In A. E. Bergin & S. L. Garfield (Eds.), *Handbook of Psychotherapy and Behavior Change,* 4th ed. New York: Wiley.

Baucom, D. H., Shoham, V., Mueser, K. T., Daiuto, A. D., & Stickle, T. R. (1998). Empirically supported couple and family interventions for marital distress and adult mental health problems. *Journal of Consulting and Clinical Psychology. 66*(1): 53–88.

Cook, W. L. (1998). Integrating models of interdependence with treatment evaluations in marital therapy research. *Journal of Family Psychology. 12*(4): 529–542.

Estrada, A. U., & Pinsof, W. M. (1995). The effectiveness of family therapies for selected behavioral disorders of childhood. *Journal of Marital and Family Therapy. 21:* 403–440.

Friedlander, M. L., Wildman, J., Heatherington, L., & Skowron, E. A. (1994). What we do and don't know about the process of family therapy. *Journal of Family Psychology. 8*(4): 390–416.

Goldstein, M. J., & Miklowitz, D. J. (1995). The effectiveness of psychoeducational family therapy in the treatment of schizophrenic disorders. *Journal of Marital and Family Therapy. 21:* 361–376.

Gottman, J. M., Ryan, K. D., Carrere, S., & Erley, A. M. (2001). Toward a scientifically based marital therapy. In *Family psychology: Science-based interventions* (pp. 147–174), H. A. Liddle, D. A. Santisteban, R. F. Levant, & J. H. Bray, eds. Washington, DC: American Psychological Association.

Jacobson, N. S., & Addis, M. E. (1993). Research on couples and couple therapy: What do we know? Where are we going? *Journal of Consulting and Clinical Psychology. 61*(1): 85–93.

Kazdin, A. E., Siegel, T. C., & Bass, D. (1992). Cognitive problem-solving skills training and parent management training in the treatment of antisocial behavior in children. *Journal of Consulting and Clinical Psychology. 60*(5): 733–747.

Lebow, J. L., & Gurman, A. S. (1995). Research assessing couple and family therapy. *Annual Review of Psychology. 46:* 27–57.

Liddle, H. A., Bray, J. H., Levant, R. F., & Santisteban, D. A. (2001). Family psychology intervention science: An emerging area of science and practice. In *Family psychology: Science-based interventions* (pp. 3–15), H. A. Liddle, D. A. Santisteban, R. F. Levant, & J. H. Bray, eds. Washington, DC: American Psychological Association.

Liddle, H. A., Rowe, C. L., Quille, T., Dakof, G., Sakran, E., & Biaggi, H. (2002). Transporting a research-developed adolescent drug abuse treatment into practice. *Journal of Substance Abuse Treatment,* Special Edition on Transferring Research to Practice (D. Simpson, Ed.).

Miller, G. E., & Prinz, R. J. (1990). Enhancement of social learning family interventions for childhood conduct disorder. *Psychological Bulletin. 108*(2): 291–307.

O'Farrell, T. J., & Fals-Stewart, W. (1999). Treatment models and methods: Family models. In *Addictions: A comprehensive guidebook* (pp. 287–305), B. S. McCrady & E. E. Epstein, eds. New York: Oxford University Press.

Patterson, G. R., & Chamberlain, P. (1992). A functional analysis of resistance (A neobehavioral perspective). In *Why don't people change? New perspectives on resistance and noncompliance,* H. Arkowitz, ed. New York: Guilford Press.

Pinsof, W. M., & Wynne, L. C. (1995). The efficacy of marital and family therapy: An empirical overview, conclusions and recommendations. *Journal of Marital and Family Therapy. 21:* 585–614.

Pinsof, W. M., & Wynne, L. C. (2000). Toward progress research: Closing the gap between family therapy practice and research. *Journal of Marital and Family Therapy. 26*(1): 1–8.

Rutter, M. (1999). Resilience concepts and findings: Implications for family therapy. *Journal of Family Therapy. 21:* 119–144.

Shadish, W. R., Ragsdale, K., Glaser, R. R., & Montgomery, L. M. (1995). The efficacy and effectiveness of marital and family therapy: A perspective from meta-analysis. *Journal of Marital and Family Therapy. 21:* 345–360.

Snyder, D. K., Cozzi, J. J., & Mangrum, L. F. (2001). Conceptual issues in assessing couples and families. In *Family psychology: Science-based interventions* (pp. 69–87), H. A. Liddle, D. A. Santisteban, R. F. Levant, & J. H. Bray, eds. Washington, DC: American Psychological Association.

References

Alexander, J. F., Holtzworth-Munroe, A., & Jameson, P. B. (1994). Research on the process and outcome of marriage and family therapy. In *Handbook of Psychotherapy and Behavior Change*, 4th ed. A. E. Bergin & S. L. Garfield, eds. New York: Wiley.

Alexander, J. F., & Parsons, B. V. (1973). Short-term behavioral intervention with delinquent families: Impact on family process and recidivism. *Journal of Abnormal Psychology. 81:* 219–225.

Alexander, J. F., & Parsons, B. V. (1982). *Functional family therapy.* Monterey, CA: Brooks/Cole.

Alexander, J. F., Sexton, T. L., & Robbins, M. S. (2001). The developmental status of family therapy in family psychology intervention science. In *Family psychology: Science-based interventions* (pp. 17–40), H. A. Liddle, D. A. Santisteban, R. F. Levant, & J. H. Bray, eds. Washington, DC: American Psychological Association.

Allen-Eckert, H., Fong, E., Nichols, M. P., Watson, N., & Liddle, H. A. (2001). Development of the Family Therapy Enactment Rating Scale. *Family Process. 40*(4): 469–478.

Asen, E. (2002). Multiple family therapy: An overview. *Journal of Family Therapy. 24*(1): 3–16.

Azrin, N. H. (1976). Improvements in the community-reinforcement approach to alcoholism. *Behavioral Research and Therapy. 14:* 339–348.

Azrin, N. H., Donohue, B., Teichner, G. A., Crum, T., Howell, J., & DeCato, L. A. (2001). A controlled evaluation and description of individual-cognitive problem solving and family-behavior therapies in dually-diagnosed conduct-disordered and substance-dependent youth. *Journal of Child and Adolescent Substance Abuse. 11*(1): 1–43.

Azrin, N. H., McMahon, P. T., Donohue, B., Besalel, V. A., Lapinski, K. J., Kogan, E. S., Acierno, R. E., & Galloway, E. (1994). Behavioral therapy for drug abuse: controlled treatment outcome study. *Behaviour Research and Therapy. 33:* 858–866.

Backer, T. E., & Richardson, D. (1989). Building bridges: Psychologists and families of the mentally ill. *American Psychologist. 44*(3): 546–550.

Bank, L., Marlowe, J. H., Reid, J. B., & Patterson, G. R. (1991). A comparative evaluation of parent-training interventions for families of chronic delinquents. *Journal of Abnormal Child Psychology. 19*(1): 15–33.

Barber, J. G. (1995). Working with resistant drug abusers. *Social Work. 40*(1): 17–23.

Barkley, R. A., Edwards, G., Laneri, M., Fletcher, K., & Metevia, L. (2001). The efficacy of problem-solving communication training alone, behavior management training alone, and their combination for parent-adolescent conflict in teenagers with ADHD and ODD. *Journal of Consulting and Clinical Psychology. 69*(6): 926–941.

Barkley, R. A., Guevremont, D. C., Anastopoulos, A. D., & Fletcher, K. E. (1992). A comparison of three family therapy programs for treating family conflicts in adolescents with Attention-Deficit Hyperactivity Disorder. *Journal of Consulting and Clinical Psychology. 60*(3): 450–462.

Barrett, P. M. (1998). Evaluation of cognitive-behavioral group treatments for childhood anxiety disorders. *Journal of Clinical Child Psychology. 27*(4): 459–468.

Barrett, P. M., Dadds, M. M., & Rapee, R. M. (1996). Family treatment of childhood anxiety: A controlled trial. *Journal of Consulting and Clinical Psychology. 64*(2): 333–342.

Barrett, P. M., Rapee, R. M., Dadds, M. M., & Ryan, S. M. (1996). Family enhancement of cognitive style in anxious and aggressive children. *Journal of Abnormal Child Psychology. 24*(2): 187–203.

Barrowclough, C., Haddock, G., Tarrier, N., Lewis, S. W., Moring, J., O'Brien, R., Schonfield, N., & McGovern, J. (2001). Randomized controlled trial of motivational interviewing, cognitive behavior therapy, and family intervention for patients with comorbid schizophrenia and substance use disorders. *American Journal of Psychiatry. 158:* 1706–1713.

Barton, C., Alexander, J. F., Waldron, H., Turner, C. W., & Warburton, J. (1985). Generalizing treatment effects of functional family therapy: Three replications. *American Journal of Family Therapy. 13:* 16–26.

Basco, M. R., Prager, K. J., Pita, J. M., Tamir, L. M., & Stephens, J. J. (1992). Communication and intimacy in the marriages of depressed patients. *Journal of Family Psychology. 6*(2): 184–194.

Baucom, D. H., & Epstein, N. (1991). Will the real cognitive-behavioral marital therapy please stand up? *Journal of Family Psychology. 4*(4): 394–401.

Baucom, D. H., Shoham, V., Mueser, K. T., Daiuto, A. D., & Stickle, T. R. (1998). Empirically supported couple and family interventions for marital distress and adult mental health problems. *Journal of Consulting and Clinical Psychology. 66*(1): 53–88.

Birmaher, B., Brent, D. A., Kolko, D. J., Baugher, M., Bridge, J., Iyengar, S., & Ulloa, R. E. (2000). Clinical outcome after short-term psychotherapy for adolescents with major depressive disorder. *Archives of General Psychiatry. 57:* 29–36.

Blechman, E. A., & Vryan, K. D. (2000). Prosocial family therapy: A manualized preventive intervention for juvenile offenders. *Aggression and Violent Behavior. 5*(4): 343–378.

Borduin, C. M., Mann, B. J., Cone, L. T., Henggeler, S. W., Fucci, B. R., Blaske, D. M., & Williams, R. A. (1995). Multisystemic treatment of serious juvenile offenders: Long-term prevention of criminality and violence. *Journal of Consulting and Clinical Psychology. 63*(4): 569–578.

Brent, D. A., Holder, D., Kolko, D., Birmaher, B., Baugher, M., Roth, C., Iyengar, S., & Johnson, B. A. (1997). A clinical psychotherapy trial for adolescent depression comparing cognitive, family, and supportive therapy. *Archives of General Psychiatry. 54:* 877–885.

Brewin, C. R., MacCarthy, B., Duda, K., & Vaughn, C. E. (1991). Attribution and expressed emotion in the relatives of patients with schizophrenia. *Journal of Abnormal Psychology. 100*(4): 546–554.

Brook, J. S., Brook, D. W., Arencibia-Mireles, O., Richter, L., & Whiteman, M. (2001). Risk factors for adolescent marijuana use across cultures and time. *Journal of Genetic Psychology. 162*(3): 357–374.

Brown, B. S. (2000). From research to practice: The bridge is out and the water's rising. *Advances in Medical Sociology. 7:* 345–365.

Brown, T. L., Henggeler, S. W., Schoenwald, S. K., Brondino, M. J., & Pickrel, S. G. (1999). Multisystemic treatment of substance abusing and dependent juvenile offenders: Effects on school attendance at posttreatment and 6-month follow-up. *Children's Services: Social Policy, Research, and Practice. 2:* 81–93.

Bukstein, O. G., & the Work Group on Quality Issues (1997). Practice parameters for the assessment and treatment of children and adolescents with substance use disorders. *Journal of the American Academy of Child and Adolescent Psychiatry. 36* (Suppl. 10): 140S–156S.

Cano, A., & O'Leary, K. D. (2000). Infidelity and separations precipitate major depressive episodes and symptoms of nonspecific depression and anxiety. *Journal of Consulting and Clinical Psychology. 68*(5): 774–781.

Carr, A. (2000). Evidence-based practice in family therapy and systemic consultation 1. Child-focused problems. *Journal of Family Therapy. 22:* 29–60.

Caughlin, J. P., Huston, T. L., & Houts, R. M. (2000). How does personality matter in marriage? An examination of trait anxiety, interpersonal negativity, and marital satisfaction. *Journal of Personality and Social Psychology. 78*(2): 326–336.

Center for Substance Abuse Treatment (CSAT). (1999). *Treatment of adolescents with substance use disorders. Treatment improvement protocol (TIP) Series, Number 32.* DHHS Publication No. (SMA) 01-3494. Washington, DC: U.S. Government Printing Office.

Chassin, L., Pitts, S. C., DeLucia, C., & Todd, M. (1999). A longitudinal study of children of alcoholics: Predicting young adult substance use disorders, anxiety, and depression. *Journal of Abnormal Psychology. 108*(1): 106–119.

Coatsworth, J. D., Santisteban, D. A., McBride, C. K., & Szapocznik, J. (2001). Brief strategic family therapy versus community control: Engagement, retention, and an exploration of the moderating role of adolescent symptom severity. *Family Process. 40*(3): 313–332.

Coffey, E. P., Olson, M. E., & Sessions, P. (2001). The heart of the matter: An essay about the effects of managed care on family therapy with children. *Family Process. 40*(4): 385–399.

Colahan, M., & Robinson, P. H. (2002). Multi-family groups in the treatment of young adults with eating disorders. *Journal of Family Therapy. 24*(1): 17–30.

Cole, D. A., & McPherson, A. E. (1993). Relation of family subsystems to adolescent depression: Implementing a new family assessment strategy. *Journal of Family Psychology. 77*(1): 119–133.

Cook, W. L. (1998). Integrating models of interdependence with treatment evaluations in marital therapy research. *Journal of Family Psychology.* 12(4): 529–542.

Cumsille, P. E., & Epstein, N. (1994). Family cohesion, family adaptability, social support, and adolescent depressive symptoms in outpatient clinic families. *Journal of Family Psychology.* 8(2): 202–214.

Dadds, M. R., Holland, D. E., Laurens, K. R., Mullins, M., Barrett, P. M., & Spence, S. H. (1999). Early intervention and prevention of anxiety disorders in children: Results at 2-year follow-up. *Journal of Consulting and Clinical Psychology.* 67(1): 145–150.

Dadds, M. R., Sanders, M. R., Morrison, M., & Rebgetz, M. (1992). Childhood depression and conduct disorder II. An analysis of family interaction patterns in the home. *Journal of Abnormal Psychology.* 101(3): 505–513.

Dadds, M. R., Spence, S. H., Holland, D. E., Barrett, P. M., & Laurens, K. R. (1997). Prevention and early intervention for anxiety disorders: A controlled trial. *Journal of Consulting and Clinical Psychology.* 65(4): 627–635.

Dakof, G. A. (2000). Understanding gender differences in adolescent drug abuse: Issues of comorbidity and family functioning. *Journal of Psychoactive Drugs.* 35: 25–32.

Dakof, G. A., Quille, T. J., Tejeda, M. J., Alberga, L. R., Bandstra, E., & Szapocznik, J. (in press). Enrolling and retaining cocaine abusing mothers into drug abuse treatment. *Journal of Consulting and Clinical Psychology.*

Davidson, G. N. S., & Horvath, A. O. (1997). Three sessions of brief couples therapy: A clinical trial. *Journal of Family Psychology.* 11(4): 422–435.

Dennis, M. L., Titus, J. C., Diamond, G., Babor, T., Donaldson, J., Godley, S. H., Tims, F., Webb, C., Liddle, H. A., & Scott, C. (in press). The cannabis youth treatment (CYT) experiment: A multi-site study of five approaches to outpatient treatment for adolescents. *Addiction.*

Diamond, G. M., Liddle, H. A., Hogue, A., & Dakof, G. A. (1999). Alliance-building interventions with adolescents in family therapy: A process study. *Psychotherapy.* 36: 355–368.

Diamond, G. S., & Diamond, G. M. (2001). Studying a matrix of change mechanisms: An agenda for family-based process research. In *Family psychology: Science-based interventions* (pp. 41–66), H. A. Liddle, D. A. Santisteban, R. F. Levant, & J. H. Bray, eds. Washington, DC: American Psychological Association.

Diamond, G. S., & Liddle, H. A. (1996). Resolving a therapeutic impasse between parents and adolescents in multidimensional family therapy. *Journal of Consulting and Clinical Psychology.* 64: 481–488.

Diamond, G. S., Reis, B. F., Diamond, G. M., Siqueland, L., & Isaacs, L. (in press). Attachment based family therapy for depressive adolescents: A treatment development study. *Journal of the American Academy of Child and Adolescent Psychiatry.*

Diamond, G. S., & Siqueland, L. (2001). Current status of family intervention science. *Child and Adolescent Psychiatric Clinics of North America.* 10(3): 641–661.

Dishion, T. J., & Andrews, D. W. (1995). Preventing escalation of problem behaviors with high-risk young adolescents: Immediate and 1-year outcomes. *Journal of Consulting and Clinical Psychology.* 63(4): 538–548.

Dishion, T. J., & Kavanagh, K. (2000). A multilevel approach to family-centered prevention in schools: Process and outcome. *Addictive Behaviors.* 25(6): 899–911.

Doane, J. A., Miklowitz, D. J., Oranchak, E., Flores de Apodaca, R., Karno, M., Strachan, A. M., & Jenkins, J. H. (1989). Parental communication deviance and schizophrenia: A cross-cultural comparison of Mexican- and Anglo-Americans. *Journal of Abnormal Psychology.* 98(4): 487–490.

Donohue, B., Azrin, N., Lawson, H., Friedlander, J., Teicher, G., & Rindsberg, J. (1998). Improving initial session attendance of substance abusing and conduct disordered adolescents: A controlled study. *Journal of Child and Adolescent Substance Abuse.* 8(1): 1–13.

Downey, G., & Coyne, J. C. (1990). Children of depressed parents: An integrative review. *Psychological Bulletin.* 108(1): 50–76.

Drug Strategies. (2002). *Treating teens: A guide to adolescent drug programs.* Washington, DC: American Psychological Association.

Dulcan, M. K., Benson, S., & the Work Group on Quality Issues. (1997). Summary of the practice parameters for the assessment and treatment of children, adolescents, and adults with ADHD.

Journal of the American Academy of Child and Adolescent Psychiatry. 36(9): 1311–1317.

Dunn, R. L., & Schwebel, A. 1. (1995). Meta-analytic review of marital therapy outcome research. *Journal of Family Psychology. 9*(1): 58–68.

Edwards, M. E., & Steinglass, P. (1995). Family therapy treatment outcomes for alcoholism. *Journal of Marital and Family Therapy. 21*(4): 475–509.

Epstein, E. E., & McCrady, B. S. (1998). Behavioral couples treatment of alcohol and drug use disorders: Current status and innovations. *Clinical Psychology Review. 18*(6): 689–711.

Estrada, A. U., & Pinsof, W. M. (1995). The effectiveness of family therapies for selected behavioral disorders of childhood. *Journal of Marital and Family Therapy. 21*: 403–440.

Falloon, l. R. H., Boyd, J. L., & McGill, C. W. (1984). *Family care of schizophrenia.* New York: Guilford Press.

Fals-Stewart, W., & Birchler, G. R. (1998). Marital interactions of drug-abusing patients and their partners: Comparisons with distressed couples and relationship to drug-using behavior. *Psychology of Addictive Behaviors. 12*(1): 28–38.

Fals-Stewart, W., & Birchler, G. R. (2001). A national survey of the use of couples therapy in substance abuse treatment. *Journal of Substance Abuse Treatment. 20*: 277–283.

Fals-Stewart, W., Birchler, G. R., & O'Farrell, T. J. (1996). Behavioral couples therapy for male substance-abusing patients: Effects on relationship adjustment and drug-using behavior. *Journal of Consulting and Clinical Psychology. 64*(5): 959–972.

Fals-Stewart, W., O'Farrell, T. J., Feehan, M., Birchler, G. R., Tiller, S., & McFarlin, S. K. (2000). Behavioral couples therapy versus individual-based treatment for male substance-abusing patients: An evaluation of significant individual change and comparison of improvement rates. *Journal of Substance Abuse Treatment. 18*: 249–254.

Fendrich, M., Warner, V., & Weissman, M. M. (1990). Family risk factors, parental depression, and psychopathology in offspring. *Developmental Psychology. 26*(1): 40–50.

Fincham, F. D., Bradbury, T. N., & Beach, S. R. H. (1990). To arrive where we began: A reappraisal of cognition in marriage and in marital therapy. *Journal of Family Psychology. 4*(2): 167–184.

Fishman, H. C., Andes, F., & Knowlton, R. (2001). Enhancing family therapy: The addition of a community resource specialist. *Journal of Marital and Family Therapy. 27*(1): 111–116.

Forehand, R., Brody, G., Slotkin, J., Fauber, R., McCombs, A., & Long, N. (1988). Young adolescent and maternal depression: Assessment, interrelations, and family predictors. *Journal of Consulting and Clinical Psychology. 56*(3): 422–426.

Framo, J. I. (1976). Chronicle of a struggle to establish a family unit within a community mental health center. In *Family therapy: Theory and practice,* P. Guerin, ed. New York: Gardner Press.

French, M. T., Roebuck, M. C., Dennis, M. L., Babor, T., Diamond, G., Godley, S., Tims, F., Liddle, H. A., & Herrell, J. (in press). The economic cost of outpatient marijuana treatment for adolescents: Findings from a multisite field experiment. *Journal of Substance Abuse Treatment.*

Frick, P. J., Lahey, B. B., Loeber, R., Stouthamer-Loeber, M., Christ, M. G., & Hanson, K. (1992). Familial risk factors to oppositional defiant disorder and conduct disorder: Parental psychopathology and maternal parenting. *Journal of Consulting and Clinical Psychology. 60*(1): 49–55.

Friedlander, M. L. (2001). Family therapy research: Science into practice, practice into science. In *Family therapy: Concepts and methods* (pp. 485–521), M. Nichols & R. Schwartz, eds. Boston: Allyn & Bacon.

Friedlander, M. L., Heatherington, L., Johnson, B., & Skowron, E. A. (1994). Sustaining engagement: A change event in family therapy. *Journal of Counseling Psychology. 41*(4): 438–448.

Friedlander, M. L., Wildman, J., Heatherington, L., & Skowron, E. A. (1994). What we do and don't know about the process of family therapy. *Journal of Family Psychology. 8*(4): 390–416.

Fristad, M. A., & Clayton, T. L. (1991). Family dysfunction and family psychopathology in child psychiatry outpatients. *Journal of Family Psychology. 5*(1): 46–59.

Geist, R., Heinmaa, M., Stephens, D., Davis, R., & Katzman, D. K. (2000). Comparison of family therapy and family group psychoeducation in adolescents with anorexia nervosa. *Canadian Journal of Psychiatry. 45*: 173–178.

Glynn, S. M., Eth, S., Randolph, E. T., Foy, D. W., Urbaitis, M., Boxer, L., Paz, G. G., Leong, G. B., Firman, G., Salk, J. D., Katzman, J. W., & Crothers, J.

(1999). A test of behavioral family therapy to augment exposure for combat-related posttraumatic stress disorder. *Journal of Consulting and Clinical Psychology.* 67(2): 243–251.

Godley, S. H., White, W. L., Diamond, G. S., Passetti, L., & Titus, J. C. (2001). Therapist reactions to manual-guided therapies for the treatment of adolescent marijuana users. *Clinical Psychology: Science and Practice.* 8(4): 405–417.

Goldman, A., & Greenberg, L. (1992). Comparison of integrated systemic and emotionally focused approaches to couples therapy. *Journal of Consulting and Clinical Psychology.* 60(6): 962–969.

Goldman Sher, T., & Baucom, D. H. (1993). Marital communication: Differences among martially distressed, depressed, and nondistressed-nondepressed couples. *Journal of Family Psychology.* 7(1): 148–153.

Goldman Sher, T., Baucom, D. H., & Larus, J. M. (1990). Communication patterns and response to treatment among depressed and nondepressed maritally distressed couples. *Journal of Family Psychology.* 4(1): 63–79.

Goldstein, M. J. (1987). Family interaction patterns that antedate the onset of schizophrenia and related disorders: A further analysis of data from a longitudinal prospective study. In *Understanding major mental disorder: the contribution of family interaction research* (pp. 11–32), K. Hahlweg & M. J. Goldstein, eds. New York: Family Process Press.

Goldstein, M. J., & Miklowitz, D. J. (1995). The effectiveness of psychoeducational family therapy in the treatment of schizophrenic disorders. *Journal of Marital and Family Therapy.* 21: 361–376.

Goldstein, M. J., Rodnick, E., Evans, J., May, P., & Steinberg, M. (1978). Drug and family therapy in the aftercare of acute schizophrenics. *Archives of General Psychiatry.* 35: 1169–1177.

Gordon, D. A., Graves, K., & Arbuthnot, J. (1995). The effect of functional family therapy for delinquents on adult criminal behavior. *Criminal Justice and Behavior.* 22: 60–73.

Greenberg, L. S., Ford, C. L., Alden, L. S., & Johnson, S. M. (1993). In-session change in emotionally focused therapy. *Journal of Consulting and Clinical Psychology.* 61(1): 78–84.

Greenberg, L. S., & Johnson, S. M. (1988). *Emotionally focused therapy for couples.* New York: Guilford Press.

Gurman, A. S. (1991). Back to the future, ahead to the past: Is marital therapy going in circles? *Journal of Family Psychology.* 4(4): 402–406.

Hahlweg, K., & Markman, H. J. (1988). Effectiveness of behavioral marital therapy: Empirical status of behavioral techniques in preventing and alleviating marital distress. *Journal of Consulting and Clinical Psychology.* 56: 440–447.

Hahlweg, K., & Wiedemann, G. (1999). Principles and results of family therapy in schizophrenia. *European Archives of Psychiatry and Clinical Neuroscience.* 249 (Supp. 4): 108–115.

Halford, W. K., Sanders, M. R., & Behrens, B. C. (1993). A comparison of the generalization of behavioral marital therapy and enhanced behavioral marital therapy. *Journal of Consulting and Clinical Psychology.* 61(1): 51–60.

Hawley, D. R., Bailey, C. E., & Pennick, K. A. (2000). A content analysis of research in family therapy journals. *Journal of Marital and Family Therapy.* 26(1): 9–16.

Hazelrigg, M. D., Cooper, H. M., & Borduin, C. M. (1987). Evaluating the effectiveness of family therapies: An integrative review and analysis. *Psychological Bulletin.* 101(3): 428–442.

Heath, A. W., & Stanton, M. D. (1998). Family-based treatment: Stages and outcomes. In *Clinical textbook of addictive disorders* (2nd ed., pp. 496–520), R. J. Frances & S. I. Miller, eds. New York: Guilford Press.

Heatherington, L., & Friedlander, M. L. (1990a). Applying task analysis to structural family therapy. *Journal of Family Psychology.* 4(1): 36–48.

Heatherington, L., & Friedlander, M. L. (1990b). Complementarity and symmetry in family therapy communication. *Journal of Counseling Psychology.* 37(3): 261–268.

Henggeler, S. W., Borduin, C. M., Melton, G. B., Mann, B. J., Smith, L. A., Hall, J. A., Cone, L., & Fucci, B. R. (1991). Effects of Multisystemic therapy on drug use and abuse in serious juvenile offenders: A progress report from two outcome studies. *Family Dynamics of Addiction Quarterly.* 1: 40–51.

Henggeler, S. W., Melton, G. B., Brondino, M. J., Scherer, D. G., & Hanley, J. H. (1997). Multisystemic Therapy with violent and chronic juvenile offenders and their families: The role of treatment fidelity in successful dissemination. *Journal of Consulting and Clinical Psychology.* 65(5): 821–833.

Henggeler, S. W., Melton, G. B., & Smith, L. A. (1992). Family preservation using Multisystemic Therapy: An effective alternative to incarcerating serious juvenile offenders. *Journal of Consulting and Clinical Psychology. 60*(6): 953–961.

Henggeler, S. W., Melton, G. B., Smith, L. A., Schoenwald, S. K., & Hanley, J. H. (1993). Family preservation using multisystemic treatment: Long-term follow-up to a clinical trial with serious juvenile offenders. *Journal of Child and Family Studies. 2:* 283–293.

Henggeler, S. W., Pickrel, S. G., & Brondino, M. J. (1999). Multisystemic treatment of substance abusing and dependent delinquents: Outcomes, treatment fidelity, and transportability. *Mental Health Services Research. 1:* 171–184.

Henggeler, S. W., Pickrel, S. G., Brondino, M. J., & Crouch, J. L. (1996). Eliminating (almost) treatment dropout of substance abusing or dependent delinquents through home-based multisystemic therapy. *American Journal of Psychiatry. 153:* 427–428.

Henggeler, S. W., Rodick, J. D., Borduin, C. M., Hanson, C. L., Watson, S. M., & Urey, J. R. (1996). Multisystemic treatment of juvenile offenders: Effects on adolescent behavior and family interaction. *Developmental Psychology. 22:* 132–141.

Henggeler, S. W., Schoenwald, S. K., & Pickrel, S. G. (1995). Multisystemic therapy: Bridging the gap between university- and community-based treatment. *Journal of Consulting and Clinical Psychology. 63*(5): 709–717.

Hinrichsen, G. A., & Pollack, S. (1997). Expressed emotion and the course of late-life depression. *Journal of Abnormal Psychology. 106*(2): 336–340.

Hogue, A., Liddle, H. A., Becker, D., & Johnson-Leckrone, J. (2002). Family-based prevention counseling for high-risk young adolescents: Immediate outcomes. *Journal of Community Psychology. 330:* 1–22.

Hogue, A., Liddle, H. A., & Rowe, C. (1996). Treatment adherence process research in family therapy: A rationale and some practical guidelines. *Psychotherapy: Theory, Research, Practice, & Training. 33:* 332–345.

Hogue, A., Liddle, H. A., Rowe, C., Turner, R. M., Dakof, G., & LaPann, K. (1998). Treatment adherence and differentiation in individual versus family therapy for adolescent substance abuse. *Journal of Consulting and Clinical Psychology. 45:* 104–114.

Hooley, J. M., & Teasdale, J. D. (1989). Predictors of relapse in unipolar depressives: Expressed emotion, marital distress, and perceived criticism. *Journal of Abnormal Psychology. 98*(3): 229–235.

Huey, S. J., Henggeler, S. W., Brondino, M. J., & Pickrel, S. G. (2000). Mechanisms of change in multisystemic therapy: Reducing delinquent behavior through therapist adherence and improved family and peer functioning. *Journal of Consulting and Clinical Psychology. 68*(3): 451–467.

Institute of Medicine [IOM]. (1998). *Bridging the gap between practice and research: Forging partnerships with community-based drug and alcohol treatment.* Washington, DC: National Academy Press.

Jackson-Gilfort, A., Liddle, H. A., Tejeda, M., & Dakof, G. (2001). Facilitating engagement of African American male adolescents in family therapy: A cultural theme process study. *Journal of Black Psychology. 27:* 321–340.

Jacobson, N. S. (1991). Toward enhancing the efficacy of marital therapy and marital therapy research. *Journal of Family Psychology. 4*(4): 373–393.

Jacobson, N. S., & Addis, M. E. (1993). Research on couples and couple therapy: What do we know? Where are we going? *Journal of Consulting and Clinical Psychology. 61*(1): 85–93.

Jacobson, N. S., Christensen, A., Prince, S. E., Cordova, J., & Eldridge, K. (2000). Integrative behavioral couple therapy: An acceptance-based, promising new treatment for couple discord. *Journal of Consulting and Clinical Psychology. 68*(2): 351–355.

Jacobson, N. S., Dobson, K., Fruzzetti, A. E., Schmaling, D. B., & Salusky, S. (1991). Marital therapy as a treatment for depression. *Journal of Consulting and Clinical Psychology. 59:* 547–557.

Jacobson, N. S., Fruzzetti, A. E., Dobson, K., Whisman, M., & Hops, H. (1993). Couple therapy as a treatment for depression II. The effects of relationship quality and therapy on depressive relapse. *Journal of Consulting and Clinical Psychology. 61*(3): 516–519.

Jacobson, N. S., Holtzworth-Munroe, A., & Schmaling, K. B. (1989). Marital therapy and spouse involvement in the treatment of depression, agoraphobia, and alcoholism. *Journal of Consulting and Clinical Psychology. 57*(1): 5–10.

Joanning, H., Quinn, Q., Thomas, F., & Mullen, R. (1992). Treating adolescent drug abuse: A comparison of family systems therapy, group therapy, and family drug education. *Journal of Marital and Family Therapy. 18:* 345–356.

Johnson, S. M., & Greenberg, L. S. (1985). Emotionally focused couples therapy: An outcome study. *Journal of Marital and Family Therapy. 11:* 313–317.

Johnson, S. M., & Greenberg, L. S. (1991). There are more things in heaven and earth than are dreamed of in BMT: A response to Jacobson. *Journal of Family Psychology. 4*(4): 407–415.

Josephson, A. M., & Serrano, A. (2001). The integration of individual therapy and family therapy in the treatment of child and adolescent psychiatric disorders. *Child and Adolescent Psychiatric Clinics of North America. 10*(3): 431–450.

Kaiser, A., Hahlweg, K., Fehm-Wolfsdorf, G., & Groth, T. (1998). The efficacy of a compact psychoeducational group training program for married couples. *Journal of Consulting and Clinical Psychology. 66*(5): 753–760.

Kaslow, F. W., & Lebow, J. (2002). *Comprehensive handbook of psychotherapy: Vol. 4. Integrative/eclectic.* New York: Wiley.

Kazdin, A. E. (1987). Treatment of antisocial behavior in children: Current status and future directions. *Psychological Bulletin. 102:* 187–203.

Kazdin, A. E. (1991). Effectiveness of psychotherapy with children and adolescents. *Journal of Consulting and Clinical Psychology. 59*(6): 785–798.

Kazdin, A. E. (1999). The meanings and measurement of clinical significance. *Journal of Consulting and Clinical Psychology. 67*(3): 332–339.

Kazdin, A. E., Holland, L., & Crowley, M. (1997). Family experience of barriers to treatment and premature termination from child therapy. *Journal of Consulting and Clinical Psychology. 65*(3): 453–463.

Kazdin, A. E., Siegel, T. C., & Bass, D. (1992). Cognitive problem-solving skills training and parent management training in the treatment of antisocial behavior in children. *Journal of Consulting and Clinical Psychology. 60*(5): 733–747.

Kelley, M. L., & Fals-Stewart, W. (2002). Couples- versus individual-based therapy for alcohol and drug abuse: Effects on children's psychosocial functioning. *Journal of Consulting and Clinical Psychology. 70*(2): 417–427.

Kilgore, K., Snyder, J., & Lentz, C. (2000). The contribution of parental discipline, parental monitoring, and school risk to early-onset conduct problems in African American boys and girls. *Developmental Psychology. 36*(6): 835–845.

Kirby, K. C., Marlowe, D. B., Festinger, D. S., Garvey, K. A., & LaMonaca, V. (1999). Community reinforcement training for family and significant others of drug abusers: A unilateral intervention to increase treatment entry of drug users. *Drug and Alcohol Dependence. 56:* 85–96.

Klein, K., Forehand, R., Armistead, L., & Long, P. (1997). Delinquency during the transition into early adulthood: Family and parenting predictors from early adolescence. *Adolescence. 32*(125): 61–80.

Klein, N. C., Alexander, J. F., & Parsons, B. V. (1977). Impact of family systems intervention on recidivism and sibling delinquency: A model of primary prevention and program evaluation. *Journal of Consulting and Clinical Psychology. 45:* 469–474.

Kolko, D. J., Brent, D. A., Baugher, M., Bridge, J., & Birmaher, B. (2000). Cognitive and family therapies for adolescent depression: Treatment specificity, mediation, and moderation. *Journal of Consulting and Clinical Psychology. 68*(4): 603–614.

Landau, J., Garrett, J., Shea, R. R., Stanton, M. D., Brinkman-Sull, D., & Baciewicz, G. (2000). Strength in numbers: The ARISE method for mobilizing family and network to engage substance abusers in treatment. *American Journal of Drug and Alcohol Abuse. 26*(3): 379–398.

Lattimer, P. J., Wagner, H. L., & Gowers, S. (2000). Conflict avoidance in anorexia nervosa: An observational study of mothers and daughters. *European Eating Disorders Review. 8*(5): 355–368.

Lavee, Y., & Altus, D. (2001). Family relationships as a predictor of post-treatment drug abuse relapse: A follow-up study of drug addicts and their spouses. *Contemporary Family Therapy: An International Journal. 23*(4): 513–530.

Law, D. D., & Crane, D. R. (2000). The influence of marital and family therapy on health care utilization in a health-maintenance organization. *Jour-*

nal of Marital and Family Therapy. 26(3): 281–291.

Lebow, J. L., & Gurman, A. S. (1995). Research assessing couple and family therapy. *Annual Review of Psychology. 46:* 27–57.

Lemmon, C. R., & Josephson, A. M. (2001). Family therapy for eating disorders. *Child and Adolescent Psychiatric Clinics of North America. 10*(3): 519–542.

Lewinsohn, P. M., Clarke, G. N., Hops, H., & Andrews, J. (1990). Cognitive-behavioral treatment for depressed adolescents. *Behavior Therapy. 21:* 385–401.

Lewis, R. A., Piercy, F. P., Sprenkle, D. H., & Trepper, T. S. (1990). Family-based interventions for helping drug-abusing adolescents. *Journal of Adolescent Research. 5:* 82–95.

Liddle, H. A. (1991). Empirical values and the culture of family therapy. *Journal of Marital and Family Therapy. 17*(4): 327–348.

Liddle, H. A. (1996). Family-based treatment for adolescent problem behaviors: Overview of contemporary developments. *Journal of Family Psychology. 10*(1): 3–11.

Liddle, H. A. (2002a). Advances in family-based therapy for adolescent substance abuse: Findings from the multidimensional family therapy research program. In *Problems of Drug Dependence 2001: Proceedings of the 63rd Annual Scientific Meeting* (pp. 113–115), L. S. Harris, ed. NIDA Research Monograph No. 182, NIH Publication 02-5097. Bethesda, MD: National Institute on Drug Abuse.

Liddle, H. A. (2002b). *Multidimensional family therapy for adolescent cannabis users, Cannabis youth treatment (CYT) series, Vol. 5.* Rockville, MD: Center for Substance Abuse Treatment (CSAT).

Liddle, H. A. (in press). Family-based treatments for adolescent substance abuse: Research contributions, advances and directions. *Addiction.*

Liddle, H. A., Bray, J. H., Levant, R. F., & Santisteban, D. A. (2001). Family psychology intervention science: An emerging area of science and practice. In *Family psychology: Science-based interventions* (pp. 3–15), H. A. Liddle, D. A. Santisteban, R. F. Levant, & J. H. Bray, eds. Washington, DC: American Psychological Association.

Liddle, H. A., & Dakof, G. A. (1995). Efficacy of family therapy for drug abuse: Promising but not definitive. *Journal of Marital and Family Therapy. 21:* 511–544.

Liddle, H. A., Dakof, G., & Diamond, G. (1991). Adolescent substance abuse: Multidimensional family therapy in action. In *Family therapy approaches with drug and alcohol problems* (2nd ed., pp. 120–171), E. Kaufman & P. Kaufmann, eds. Boston: Allyn & Bacon.

Liddle, H. A., Dakof, G. A., Parker, K., Diamond, G. S., Barrett, K., & Tejeda, M. (2001). Multidimensional family therapy for adolescent substance abuse: Results of a randomized clinical trial. *American Journal of Drug and Alcohol Abuse. 27*(4): 651–687.

Liddle, H. A., & Rowe, C. L. (1998). Family measures in drug abuse prevention research. In *Drug abuse prevention through family interventions* (pp. 324–372). R. Ashery, E. Robertson, & K. Kumpfer, eds. NIDA Monograph No. 177. Rockville, MD: National Institute on Drug Abuse.

Liddle, H. A., Rowe, C. L., Dakof, G. D., & Lyke, J. (1998). Translating parenting research into clinical interventions for families with adolescents. *Clinical Child Psychology and Psychiatry. 3*(3): 419–443.

Liddle, H. A., Rowe, C. L., Quille, T., Dakof, G., Sakran, E., & Biaggi, H. (2002). Transporting a research-developed adolescent drug abuse treatment into practice. *Journal of Substance Abuse Treatment* (Special Edition on Transferring Research to Practice. *22:* 231–243.

Lindahl, K. M. (1998). Family process variables and children's disruptive behavior problems. *Journal of Family Psychology. 12*(3): 420–436.

Long, P., Forehand, R., Wierson, M., & Morgan, A. (1994). Does parent training with young noncompliant children have long-term effects? *Behavior Research and Therapy. 32*(1): 101–107.

Lopez, S. R., Nelson, K. A., Snyder, K. S., & Mintz, J. (1999). Attributions and affective reactions of family members and course of schizophrenia. *Journal of Abnormal Psychology. 108*(2): 307–314.

Lyon, M., Chatoor, I., Atkins, D., Silber, T., Mosimann, J., & Gray, J. (1997). Testing the hypothesis of the multidimensional model of anorexia nervosa in adolescents. *Adolescence. 32*(125): 101–111.

Mabe, P. A., Turner, K., & Josephson, A. M. (2001). Parent management training. *Child and Adolescent*

Psychiatric Clinics of North America. 10(3): 451–474.

Maharaj, S., Rodin, G., Connolly, J., Olmsted, M., & Daneman, D. (2001). Eating problems and the observed quality of mother-daughter interactions among girls with type I diabetes. *Journal of Consulting and Clinical Psychology. 69*(6): 950–958.

Malone, C. A. (2001). Child and adolescent psychiatry and family therapy. *Child and Adolescent Psychiatric Clinics of North America. 10*(3): 395–413.

Mann, B. J., Borduin, C. M., Henggeler, S. W., & Blaske, D. M. (1990). An investigation of systemic conceptualizations of parent-child coalitions and symptom change. *Journal of Consulting and Clinical Psychology. 58*(3): 336–344.

Marcus, N. E., Lindahl, K. M., & Malik, N. M. (2001). Interparental conflict, children's social cognitions, and child aggression: A test of a mediational model. *Journal of Family Psychology. 15*(2): 315–333.

Markman, H. J. (1991). Backwards into the future of couples therapy and couples therapy research: A comment on Jacobson. *Journal of Family Psychology. 4*(4): 416–425.

Marsh, D. T., & Johnson, D. L. (1997). The family experience of mental illness: Implications for intervention. *Professional Psychology: Research and Practice. 28*(3): 229–237.

Mazzeo, S. E., & Espelage, D. L. (2002). Association between childhood physical and emotional abuse and disordered eating behaviors in female undergraduates: An investigation of the mediating role of alexithymia and depression. *Journal of Counseling Psychology. 49*(1): 86–100.

McCrady, B. S., & Epstein, E. E. (1996). Theoretical bases of family approaches to substance abuse treatment. In F. Rotgers & D. S. Keller (Eds.), *Treating substance abuse: Theory and technique. The Guilford substance abuse series* (pp. 117–142). New York: Guilford Press.

McCrady, B. S., & Ziedonis, D. (2001). American Psychiatric Association practice guidelines for substance use disorders. *Behavior Therapy. 32:* 309–336.

McFarlane, W. R., Link, B., Dushay, R., Marchal, J., & Crilly, J. (1995). Psychoeducational multiple family groups: Four-year relapse outcome in schizophrenia. *Family Process. 34:* 127–144.

McGillicuddy, N. B., Rychtarik, R. G., Duquette, J. A., & Morsheimer, E. T. (2001). Development of a skill training program for parents of substance-abusing adolescents. *Journal of Substance Abuse Treatment. 20:* 59–68.

Meyers, R. J., Miller, W., & Smith, J. E. (2001). Community reinforcement and family training (CRAFT). In *A community reinforcement approach to addiction treatment. International research monographs in the addictions* (pp. 147–160), R. J. Meyers & W. R. Miller, eds. New York: Cambridge University Press.

Meyers, R. J., & Smith, J. E. (1995). *Clinical guide to alcohol treatment: The community reinforcement approach.* New York: Guilford Press.

Miklowitz, D. J., & Goldstein, M. J. (1997). *Bipolar disorder: A family-focused treatment approach.* New York: Guilford Press.

Miklowitz, D. J., Goldstein, M. J., & Nuechterlein, K. H. (1995). Verbal interactions in the families of schizophrenic and bipolar affective patients. *Journal of Abnormal Psychology. 104*(2): 268–276.

Miklowitz, D. J., Velligan, D. I., Goldstein, M. J., Nuechterlein, K. H., Gitlin, M. J., Ranlett, G., & Doane, J. A. (1991). Communication deviance in families of schizophrenic and manic patients. *Journal of Abnormal Psychology. 100*(2): 163–173.

Miller, G. E., & Prinz, R. J. (1990). Enhancement of social learning family interventions for childhood conduct disorder. *Psychological Bulletin. 108*(2): 291–307.

Miller, I. W., Keitner, G. I., Whisman, M. A., Ryan, C. E., Epstein, N. B., & Bishop, D. S. (1992). Depressed patients with dysfunctional families: Description and course of illness. *Journal of Abnormal Psychology. 101*(4): 637–646.

Miller, W. R., Meyers, R. J., & Tonigan, J. S. (1999). Engaging the unmotivated in treatment for alcohol problems: A comparison of three strategies for intervention through family members. *Journal of Consulting and Clinical Psychology. 67*(5): 688–697.

Minuchin, S. (1974). *Families and family therapy.* Cambridge, MA: Harvard University Press.

Minuchin, S., Rosman, B. L., & Baker, L. (1978). *Psychosomatic families: Anorexia nervosa in context.* Cambridge, MA: Harvard University Press.

Moos, R. H., Cronkite, R. C., & Moos, B. S. (1998a). The long-term interplay between family and extrafamily resources and depression. *Journal of Family Psychology. 12*(3): 326–343.

Moos, R. H., Cronkite, R. C., & Moos, B. S. (1998b). Family and extrafamily resources and the 10-year course of treated depression. *Journal of Abnormal Psychology. 107*(3): 450–460.

Morojele, N. K., & Brook, J. S. (2001). Adolescent precursors of intensity of marijuana and other illicit drug use among adult initiators. *Journal of Genetic Psychology. 162*(4): 430–450.

Mueser, K. T., Bellack, A. S., Wade, J. H., Sayers, S. L., Tierney, A., & Haas, G. (1993). Expressed emotion, social skill, and response to negative affect in schizophrenia. *Journal of Abnormal Psychology. 102*(3): 339–351.

Mueser, K. T., Sengupta, A., Schooler, N. R., Bellack, A. S., Xie, H., Glick, I. D., & Keith, S. J. (2001). Family treatment and medication dosage reduction in schizophrenia: Effects on patient social functioning, family attitudes, and burden. *Journal of Consulting and Clinical Psychology. 69*(1): 3–12.

National Institute On Drug Abuse [NIDA]. (2002). *Modifying and testing efficacious behavioral therapies to make them more community friendly.* RFA-DA-02-006. National Institute on Drug Abuse (http://www.nida.nih.gov).

Newberry, A. M., Alexander, J. F., & Turner, C. W. (1991). Gender as a process variable in family therapy. *Journal of Family Psychology. 5*(2): 158–175.

Newman, F. L., & Tejeda, M. J. (1996). The need for research designed to support decisions in the delivery of mental health services. *American Psychologist. 51:* 1040–1049.

Nichols, M. P., & Fellenberg, S. (2000). The effective use of enactments in family therapy: A discovery-oriented process study. *Journal of Marital and Family Therapy. 26*(2): 143–152.

Nichols, M. P., & Schwartz, R. C. (1998). *Family therapy: Concepts and methods* (4th ed.). Needham Heights, MA: Allyn & Bacon.

Nye, C. L., Zucker, R. A., & Fitzgerald, H. E. (1995). Early intervention in the path to alcohol problems through conduct problems: Treatment involvement and child behavior change. *Journal of Consulting and Clinical Psychology. 63*(5): 831–840.

O'Farrell, T. J., & Fals-Stewart, W. (1999). Treatment models and methods: Family models. In *Addictions: A comprehensive guidebook* (pp. 287–305), B. S. McCrady & E. E. Epstein, eds. New York: Oxford University Press.

O'Leary, K. D., & Beach, S. R. H. (1990). Marital therapy: A viable treatment for depression and marital discord. *American Journal of Psychiatry. 147:* 183–186.

Ozechowski, T., & Liddle, H. A. (2000). Family-based therapy for adolescent drug abuse: Knowns and unknowns. *Clinical Child and Family Psychology Review. 3*(4): 269–298.

Parker, G., & Hadzi-Pavlovic, D. (1990). Expressed emotion as a predictor of schizophrenic relapse: An analysis of aggregated data. *Psychological Medicine. 20*(4): 961–965.

Patterson, G. R. (1986). Performance models for antisocial boys. *American Psychologist. 41:* 432–444.

Patterson, G. R. (1995). Coercion as a basis for early age of onset for arrest. In *Coercion and punishment in long-term perspectives* (pp. 81–105), J. McCord, ed. New York: Cambridge University Press.

Patterson, G. R., & Chamberlain, P. (1992). A functional analysis of resistance (A neobehavioral perspective). In *Why don't people change? New perspectives on resistance and noncompliance,* H. Arkowitz, ed. New York: Guilford Press.

Pinsof, W. M. (1989). A conceptual framework and methodological criteria for family therapy process research. *Journal of Consulting and Clinical Psychology. 57*(1): 53–59.

Pinsof, W. M., & Hambright, A. B. (2001). Toward preventive and clinical relevance: A preventive intervention model for family therapy research and practice. In *Family Psychology: Science-based interventions* (pp. 177–195), H. A. Liddle, D. A. Santisteban, R. F. Levant, & J. H. Bray, eds. Washington, DC: American Psychological Association.

Pinsof, W. M., & Wynne, L. C. (1995). The efficacy of marital and family therapy: An empirical overview, conclusions and recommendations. *Journal of Marital and Family Therapy. 21:* 585–614.

Pinsof, W. M., & Wynne, L. C. (2000). Toward progress research: Closing the gap between family therapy practice and research. *Journal of Marital and Family Therapy. 26*(1): 1–8.

Polivy, J., & Herman, P. C. (2002). Causes of eating disorders. *Annual Review of Psychology.* 53(1): 187–213.

Prinz, R. J., & Miller, G. E. (1994). Family-based treatment for childhood antisocial behavior: Experimental influences on dropout and engagement. *Journal of Consulting and Clinical Psychology.* 62(3): 645–650.

Rait, D. S. (2000). The therapeutic alliance in couples and family therapy. *JCLP/In Session: Psychotherapy in Practice.* 56(2): 211–224.

Ratti, L. A., Humphrey, L. L., & Lyons, J. S. (1996). Structural analysis of families with a polydrug-dependent, bulimic, or normal adolescent daughter. *Journal of Consulting and Clinical Psychology.* 64(6): 1255–1262.

Reiss, D., & Johnson-Sabine, E. (1995). Bulimia nervosa: Five-year social outcome and relationship to eating pathology. *International Journal of Eating Disorders.* 18(2): 127–133.

Robbins, M. S., Alexander, J. F., Newell, R. M., & Turner, C. W. (1996). The immediate effect of refraining on client attitude in family therapy. *Journal of Family Psychology.* 10(1): 28–34.

Robbins, M. S., Alexander, J. F., & Turner, C. W. (2000). Disrupting defensive family interactions in family therapy with delinquent adolescents. *Journal of Family Psychology.* 14(4): 688–701.

Robin, A. L., Siegel, P. T., Koepke, T., Moye, A. W., & Tice, S. (1994). Family therapy versus individual therapy for adolescent females with anorexia nervosa. *Developmental and Behavioral Pediatrics.* 15(2): 111–116.

Rosenfarb, I. S., Goldstein, M. J., Mintz, J., & Nuechterlein, K. H. (1995). Expressed emotion and subclinical psychopathology observable within the transactions between schizophrenic patients and their family members. *Journal of Abnormal Psychology.* 104(2): 259–267.

Rotunda, R. J., & O'Farrell, T. J. (1997). Marital and family therapy of alcohol use disorders: Bridging the gap between research and practice. *Professional Psychology: Research and Practice.* 28(3): 246–252.

Rotunda, R. J., Scherer, D. G., & Imm, P. S. (1995). Family systems and alcohol misuse: Research on the effects of alcoholism on family functioning and effective family interventions. *Professional Psychology: Research and Practice.* 26(1): 95–104.

Rowa, K., Kerig, P. K., & Geller, J. (2001). The family and anorexia nervosa: Examining parent-child boundary problems. *European Eating Disorders Review.* 9(2): 97–114.

Rowe, C. L., Liddle, H. A., McClintic, K., & Quille, T. (2002). Integrative treatment development: Multidimensional family therapy for adolescent substance abuse. In *Comprehensive handbook of psychotherapy, (Volume 4: Integrative/Eclectic therapies* (pp. 133–161), F. Kaslow & J. Lebow, eds. New York: Wiley.

Russell, G. F. M., Dare, C., Eisler, I., & LeGrange, P. D. F. (1994). Controlled trials of family treatments in anorexia nervosa. In *Psychobiology and the treatment of anorexia nervosa and bulimia nervosa* (pp. 237–262), K. A. Halmi, ed. Washington, DC: American Psychiatric Press.

Russell, G. F. M., Szmukler, G. I., Dare, C., & Eisler, I. (1987). An evaluation of family therapy in anorexia nervosa and bulimia nervosa. *Archives of General Psychiatry.* 44: 1047–1056.

Rutter, M. (1999). Resilience concepts and findings: Implications for family therapy. *Journal of Family Therapy.* 21: 119–144.

Sanders, M. R., Markie-Dadds, C., Tully, L. A., & Bor, W. (2000). The Triple P-Positive Parenting Program: A comparison of enhanced, standard, and self-directed behavioral family intervention for parents of children with early onset conduct problems. *Journal of Consulting and Clinical Psychology.* 68(4): 624–640.

Santisteban, D. A., Szapocznik, J., Perez-Vidal, A., Kurtines, W. M., Murray, E., & LaPerriere, A. (1996). Efficacy of intervention for engaging youth and families into treatment and some variables that may contribute to differential effectiveness. *Journal of Family Psychology.* 10(1): 35–44.

Schmidt, S. E., Liddle, H. A., & Dakof, G. A. (1996). Changes in parenting practices and adolescent drug abuse during multidimensional family therapy. *Journal of Family Psychology.* 10: 12–27.

Schoenwald, S. K., Ward, D. M., Henggeler, S. W., Pickrel, S. G., & Patel, H. (1996). MST treatment of substance abusing or dependent adolescent offenders: Costs of reducing incarceration, inpatient, and residential placement. *Journal of Child and Family Studies.* 5: 431–444.

Scholz, M., & Asen, E. (2001). Multiple family therapy with eating disordered adolescents: Concepts and preliminary results. *European Eating Disorders Review. 9:* 33–42.

Schwartz, J. A., Kaslow, N. J., Racusin, G. R., Carton, E. R. (1998). Interpersonal family therapy for childhood depression. In *Handbook of psychological treatment protocols for children and adolescents* (pp. 109–151), V. B. Van Hasselt & M. Hersen, eds. New York: Erlbaum.

Sexson, S. B., Glanville, D. N., & Kaslow, N. J. (2001). Attachment and depression: Implications for family therapy. *Child and Adolescent Psychiatric Clinics of North America. 10*(3): 465–486.

Shadish, W. R., Montgomery, L. M., Wilson, P., Wilson, M. R., Bright, I., & Okwumabua, T. (1993). Effects of family and marital psychotherapies: A meta-analysis. *Journal of Consulting and Clinical Psychology. 61*(6): 992–1002.

Shadish, W. R., Ragsdale, K., Glaser, R. R., & Montgomery, L. M. (1995). The efficacy and effectiveness of marital and family therapy: A perspective from meta-analysis. *Journal of Marital and Family Therapy. 21:* 345–360.

Shields, C. G., & McDaniel, S. H. (1992). Process differences between male and female therapists in a first family interview. *Journal of Family Psychology. 18:* 143–151.

Simoneau, T. L., Miklowitz, D. J., Richards, J. A., Saleem, R., & George, E. L. (1999). Bipolar disorder and family communication: Effects of a psychoeducational treatment program. *Journal of Abnormal Psychology. 108*(4): 588–597.

Singer, M., & Wynne, L. (1965). Thought disorder and family relations of schizophrenics: IV. Results and implications. *Archives of General Psychiatry. 12:* 201–212.

Sisson, R. W., & Azrin, N. H. (1986). Family-member involvement to initiate and promote treatment of problem drinkers. *Behavior Therapy and Experimental Psychiatry. 17:* 15–21.

Slesnick, N., & Waldron, H. B. (1997). Interpersonal problem-solving interactions of depressed adolescents and their parents. *Journal of Family Psychology. 11*(2): 234–245.

Smith, W. J., Sayger, T. V., & Szykula, S. A. (1999). Child-focused family therapy: Behavioural family therapy versus brief family therapy. *Australian and New Zealand Journal of Family Therapy. 20*(2): 83–87.

Snyder, D. K., Cozzi, J. J., & Mangrum, L. F. (2001). Conceptual issues in assessing couples and families. In *Family psychology: Science-based interventions* (pp. 69–87), H. A. Liddle, D. A. Santisteban, R. F. Levant, & J. H. Bray, eds. Washington, DC: American Psychological Association.

Snyder, D. K., & Wills, R. M. (1989). Behavioral versus insight-oriented marital therapy: Effects on individual and interspousal functioning. *Journal of Consulting and Clinical Psychology. 57:* 39–46.

Snyder, D. K., Wills, R. M., & Grady-Fletcher, A. (1991). Long-term effectiveness of behavioral versus insight-oriented marital therapy: A 4-year follow-up study. *Journal of Consulting and Clinical Psychology. 59*(1): 138–141.

Snyder, J. J., & Patterson, G. R. (1995). Individual differences in social aggression: A test of a reinforcement model of socialization in the natural environment. *Behavior Therapy. 26*(2): 371–391.

Spoth, R., & Redmond, C. (1995). Parent motivation to enroll in parenting skills programs: A model of family context and health belief predictors. *Journal of Family Psychology. 9*(3): 294–310.

Stanton, M. D. (1985). The family and drug abuse. In *Alcoholism and substance abuse: Strategies for clinical intervention* (pp. 398–430), T. Bratter & G. Forrest, eds. New York: Free Press.

Stanton, M. D., & Shadish, W. R. (1997). Outcome, attrition, and family-couples treatment for drug abuse: A meta-analysis and review of the controlled, comparative studies. *Psychological Bulletin. 122*(2): 170–191.

Stanton, M. D., & Todd, T. C. (1982). *Family therapy for drug abuse and addiction.* New York: Guilford Press.

Stark, K. D. (1990). *Childhood depression school-based intervention.* New York: Guilford Press.

Stark, K. D., Humphrey, L. L., Laurent, J., Livingston, R., & Christopher, J. (1993). Cognitive, behavioral, and family factors in the differentiation of depressive and anxiety disorders during childhood. *Journal of Consulting and Clinical Psychology. 61*(5): 878–886.

Steiner, H., & the Work Group on Quality Issues. (1997). Practice parameters for the assessment and treatment of children and adolescents with conduct disorder. *Journal of the American Academy of Child and Adolescent Psychiatry. 36*(10 Supplement): 122S–139S.

Stoolmiller, M., Duncan, T., Bank, L., & Patterson, G. R. (1993). Some problems and solutions in the study of change: Significant patterns in client resistance. *Journal of Consulting and Clinical Psychology. 61*(6): 920–928.

Substance Abuse and Mental Health Services Administration (SAMHSA). (2001). *Summary of findings from the 2000 National Household Survey on Drug Abuse.* Rockville, MD: Author.

Szapocznik, J., Perez-Vidal, A., Brickman, A., Foote, F. H., Santisteban, D. A., Hervis, O., & Kurtines, W. M. (1988). Engaging adolescent drug abusers and their families in treatment: A strategic structural systems approach. *Journal of Consulting and Clinical Psychology. 56*(4): 552–557.

Szapocznik, J., Rio, A., Murray, E., Cohen, R., Scopetta, M., Rivas-Vazquez, A., Hervis, O., Posada, V., & Kurtines, W. M. (1989). Structural family versus psychodynamic child therapy for problematic Hispanic boys. *Journal of Consulting and Clinical Psychology. 57*(5): 571–578.

Szapocznik, J., & Williams, R. A. (2000). Brief strategic family therapy: Twenty-five years of interplay among theory, research and practice in adolescent behavior problems and drug abuse. *Clinical Child and Family Psychology Review. 3*(2): 117–134.

Tarrier, N., Barrowclough, C., Vaughn, C., Bamrah, J., Porceddu, K., Watts, S., & Freeman, H. (1989). Community management of schizophrenia: A two-year follow-up of a behavioral intervention with families. *British Journal of Psychiatry. 154:* 625–628.

van Furth, E. F., van Strien, D. C., Martina, L. M. L., van Son, M. J. M., Hendrickx, J. J. P., van Engeland, H. (1996). Expressed emotion and the prediction of outcome in adolescent eating disorders. *International Journal of Eating Disorders. 20*(1): 19–31.

Vaughn, C. E., & Leff, J. P. (1976). The influence of family and social factors on the course of psychiatric illness. *British Journal of Psychiatry. 129:* 125–137.

Vuchinich, S., Bank, L., & Patterson, G. R. (1992). Parenting, peers, and the stability of antisocial behavior in preadolescent boys. *Developmental Psychology. 28*(3): 510–521.

Wade, T. D., Treloar, S. A., & Martin, N. G. (2001). A comparison of family functioning, temperament, and childhood conditions in monozygotic twin pairs discordant for lifetime bulimia nervosa. *American Journal of Psychiatry. 158*(7): 1155–1157.

Waldron, H. B. (1997). Adolescent substance abuse and family therapy outcome: A review of randomized trials. In *Advances in clinical child psychology* (Vol. 19, pp. 199–234), T. H. Ollendick & R. J. Prinz, eds. New York: Plenum Press.

Waldron, H. B., Slesnick, N., Brody, J. L., Turner, C. W., & Peterson, T. R. (2001). Treatment outcomes for adolescent substance abuse at 4- and 7-month assessments. *Journal of Consulting and Clinical Psychology. 69*(5): 802–813.

Walker, J. G., Johnson, S., Manion, I., & Cloutier, P. (1996). Emotionally focused marital intervention for couples with chronically ill children. *Journal of Consulting and Clinical Psychology. 64*(5): 1029–1036.

Webster-Stratton, C. (1994). Advancing videotape parent training: A comparison study. *Journal of Consulting and Clinical Psychology. 62*(3): 583–593.

Webster-Stratton, C., & Hammond, M. (1997). Treating children with early-onset conduct problems: A comparison of child and parent training interventions. *Journal of Consulting and Clinical Psychology. 65*(1): 93–109.

Webster-Stratton, C., Hollinsworth, T., & Kolpacoff, M. (1989). The long-term effectiveness and clinical significance of three cost-effective training programs for families with conduct-problem children. *Journal of Consulting and Clinical Psychology. 57*(4): 550–553.

Wells, K. (1995). Family preservation services in context: Origins, practices, and current issues. In *Home-based services for troubled children* (pp. 1–28), I. M. Schwartz & P. AuClair, eds. Lincoln: University of Nebraska Press.

Werner-Wilson, R. J., Price, S. J., Zimmerman, T. S., & Murphy, M. J. (1997). Client gender as a process variable in marriage and family therapy: Are women clients interrupted more than men clients? *Journal of Family Psychology, 11*(3), 373–377.

Whaley, S. E., Pinto, A., & Sigman, M. (1999). Characterizing interactions between anxious mothers and their children. *Journal of Consulting and Clinical Psychology. 67:* 826–836.

Whitbeck, L. B., Hoyt, D. R., Simons, R. L., Conger, R. D., Elder, G. H., Lorenz, F. O., & Huck, S. (1992). Intergenerational continuity of parental rejection and depressed affect. *Journal of Personality and Social Psychology. 63*(6): 1036–1045.

Wierson, M., & Forehand, R. (1994). Parent behavioral training for child noncompliance: rationale, concepts, and effectiveness. *Current Directions in Psychological Science. 3*(5): 146–150.

Willett, J. B., Ayoub, C. C., & Robinson, D. (1991). Using growth modeling to examine systematic differences in growth: An example of change in the functioning of families at risk of maladaptive parenting, child abuse, or neglect. *Journal of Consulting and Clinical Psychology. 59*(1): 38–47.

Williams, R. J., & Chang, S. Y. (2000). A comprehensive and comparative review of adolescent substance abuse treatment outcome. *Clinical Psychology: Science and Practice. 7:* 138–166.

Winters, J., Fals-Stewart, W., O'Farrell, T. J., Birchler, G. R., & Kelley, M. L. (2002). Behavioral couples therapy for female substance-abusing patients: Effects on substance use and relationship adjustment. *Journal of Consulting and Clinical Psychology. 70*(2): 344–355.

Winters, K., Latimer, W., & Stinchfield, R. (1999). Adolescent treatment. In *Sourcebook on substance abuse: Etiology, epidemiology, assessment, and treatment* (pp. 350–361), P. J. Ott, R. E. Tarter, & R. T. Ammerman, eds. Boston: Allyn & Bacon.

Recommended Readings

General Principles of Family Systems

Carter, B., and McGoldrick, M. 1988. *The changing family lifecycle: A framework for family therapy*, 3rd ed. Boston: Allyn & Bacon.

Guerin, P. J., Fogarty, T. F., Fay, L. F., and Kautto, J. G. 1996. *Working with relationship triangles: The one-two-three of psychotherapy.* New York: Guilford Press.

Hoffman, L. 1981. *The foundations of family therapy.* New York: Basic Books.

Imber-Black, E., ed. 1993. *Secrets in families and family therapy.* New York: Norton.

Kerr, M. E., and Bowen, M. 1988. *Family evaluation.* New York: Norton.

Minuchin, S. 1974. *Families and family therapy.* Cambridge, MA: Harvard University Press.

Nichols, M. P. 1999. *Inside family therapy.* Boston: Allyn & Bacon.

Paolino, T. J., and McCrady, B. S., eds. 1978. *Marriage and marital therapy.* New York: Brunner/Mazel.

Watzlawick, P., Beavin, J., and Jackson, D. 1967. *Pragmatics of human communication.* New York: Norton.

Culture and Family Therapy

Boyd-Franklin, N. 1989. *Black families in therapy: A multisystems approach.* New York: Guilford Press.

Davis, L., and Proctor, E. 1989. *Race, gender, and class: Guidelines for practice with individuals, families and groups.* Englewood Cliffs, NJ: Prentice-Hall.

Pedersen, P. 1987. The frequent assumptions of cultural bias in counseling. *Journal of Multicultural Counseling and Development.* 15:16–24.

Pinderhughes, E. 1989. *Understanding race, ethnicity, power: The key to efficacy in clinical practice.* New York: Free Press.

Sue, D. W., and Sue, D. 1990. *Counseling the culturally different: Theory and practice,* 2nd ed. New York: Wiley.

Walsh, F. 1998. *Re-visioning family therapy.* New York: Guilford Press.

Marriage

Dicks, H. V. 1967. *Marital tensions.* New York: Basic Books.

Guerin, P. J., Fay, L., Burden, S., and Kautto, J. 1987. *The evaluation and treatment of marital conflict: A four-stage approach.* New York: Basic Books.

Lederer, W., and Jackson, D. 1968. *The mirages of marriage.* New York: Norton.

Lerner, H. G. 1985. *The dance of anger: A woman's guide to changing patterns of intimate relationships.* New York: Harper & Row.

Scarf, M. 1987. *Intimate partners: Patterns in love and marriage.* New York: Random House.

In-Laws and the Extended Family

Guerin, P. J., ed. 1976. *Family therapy: Theory and practice.* New York: Gardner Press.

Lerner, H. G. 1989. *The dance of intimacy: A woman's guide to courageous acts of change in key relationships.* New York: Harper & Row.

McGoldrick, M., and Gerson, R. 1985. *Genograms in family assessment.* New York: Norton.

Families with Babies and Small Children

Brazelton, T. B. 1983. *Infants and mothers: Differences in development,* rev. ed. New York: Dell.

Combrinck-Graham, L., ed. 1988. *Children in family contexts: Perspectives on treatment.* New York: Guilford Press.

Faber, A., and Mazlish, E. 1974. *Liberated parents, liberated children.* New York: Grosset & Dunlap.

Ginott, H. 1969. *Between parent and child.* New York: Macmillan.

Patterson, G. 1975. *Families: Application of social learning theory to family life.* Champaign, IL: Research Press.

Families with Older Children

Bank, S., and Kahn, M. 1982. *The sibling bond.* New York: Basic Books.

Blos, P. 1979. *The adolescent passage: Developmental issues.* New York: International Universities Press.

Faber, A., and Mazlish, E. 1987. *Siblings without rivalry.* New York: Norton.

Fishel, E. 1979. *Sisters: Love and rivalry inside the family and beyond.* New York: Quill/William Morrow.

Micucci, J. 1998. *The adolescent in family therapy.* New York: Guilford Press.

Schlaadt, R., and Shannon, P. 1986. *Drugs of choice,* 2nd ed. Englewood Cliffs, NJ: Prentice-Hall.

Sells, S. 1998. *Treating the tough adolescent.* New York: Guilford Press.

Divorce, Remarriage, and Stepparenting

Ahrons, C., and Rodgers, R. 1987. *Divorced families: A multidisciplinary developmental view.* New York: Norton.

Isaacs, M. B., Montalvo, B., and Abelsohn, D. 1986. *The difficult divorce.* New York: Basic Books.

Vaughan, D. 1986. *Uncoupling: Turning points in intimate relationships.* New York: Oxford University Press.

Visher, E., and Visher, J. 1988. *Old loyalties, new ties: Therapeutic strategies with stepfamilies.* New York: Brunner/Mazel.

Leaving Home and the Postchildrearing Years

Levinson, D. 1978. *The seasons of a man's life.* New York: Ballantine.

Nichols, M. P. 1987. *Turning forty in the eighties.* New York: Fireside/Simon & Schuster.

Viorst, J. 1986. *Necessary losses.* New York: Simon & Schuster.

Family Therapy Technique

Anderson, C., and Stewart, S. 1983. *Mastering resistance: A practical guide to family therapy.* New York: Guilford Press.

Dattilio, F., ed. 1998. *Case studies in couple and family therapy: Systemic and cognitive perspectives.* New York: Guilford Press.

Donovan, J. M. 1999. *Short-term couple therapy.* New York: Guilford Press.

Gerson, M-J. 1996. *The embedded self: A psychoanalytic guide to family therapy.* New York: Analytic Press.

Guerin, P. J., Fay, L., Burden, S., and Kautto, J. 1987. *The evaluation and treatment of marital conflict: A four-stage approach.* New York: Basic Books.

Isaacs, M. B., Montalvo, B., and Abelsohn, D. 1986. *The difficult divorce: Therapy for children and families.* New York: Basic Books.

Minuchin, S., and Fishman, H. C. 1981. *Family therapy techniques.* Cambridge, MA: Harvard University Press.

Minuchin, S., and Nichols, M. P. 1993. *Family healing: Tales of hope and renewal from family therapy.* New York: Free Press.

Taibbi, R. 1996. *Doing family therapy: Craft and creativity in clinical practice.* New York: Guilford Press.

White, M., and Epston, D. 1990. *Narrative means to therapeutic ends.* New York: Norton.

APPENDIX B

Glossary

accommodation Elements of a system automatically adjust to coordinate their functioning; people may have to work at it.

anorexia nervosa Self-starvation leading to loss of 25 percent or more of body weight, hyperactivity, hypothermia, and amenorrhea (in females).

aversive control Using punishment and criticism to eliminate undesirable responses; commonly used in dysfunctional families.

basic assumption theory Bion's concept that group members become diverted from the group task to pursue unconscious patterns of *fight–flight, dependency,* or *pairing.*

behavior exchange theory Explanation of behavior in relationships as maintained by a ratio of costs to benefits.

black box metaphor The idea that because the mind is so complex, it's better to study people's input and output (behavior, communication) than to speculate about what goes on in their minds.

blended families Separate families united by marriage; stepfamilies.

boundary Emotional and physical barriers that protect and enhance the integrity of individuals, subsystems, and families.

bulimia An eating disorder characterized by bouts of excessive eating followed by self-induced vomiting, purging with laxatives, strenuous exercise, or fasting.

circular causality The idea that actions are related through a series of recursive loops or repeating cycles.

circular questioning A method of interviewing developed by the Milan Associates in which questions are asked that highlight differences among family members.

classical conditioning A form of respondent learning in which an unconditioned stimulus (UCS), such as food, which leads to an unconditioned response (UCR), such as salivation, is paired with a conditioned stimulus (CS), such as a bell, the result of which is that the CS begins to evoke the same response; used in the behavioral treatment of anxiety disorders.

coalition An alliance between two persons or social units against a third.

cognitive-behavior therapy Treatment that emphasizes attitude change as well as reinforcement of behavior.

collaborative model A more egalitarian view of the therapist's role; advocated by critics of what is viewed as authoritarian-

438

ism in traditional approaches to family therapy.

communications theory   The study of relationships in terms of the exchange of verbal and nonverbal messages.

complementary   Relationship based on differences that fit together, where qualities of one make up for lacks in the other; one is one-up while the other is one-down.

complainant   De Shazer's term for a relationship with a client who describes a complaint but is at present unwilling to work on solving it.

concurrent therapy   Treatment of two or more persons, seen separately, usually by different therapists.

conjoint therapy   Treatment of two or more persons in sessions together.

constructivism   A relativistic point of view that emphasizes the subjective construction of reality. Implies that what we see in families may be based as much on our preconceptions as on what's actually going on.

contextual therapy   Boszormenyi-Nagy's model that includes relational ethics.

contingency contracting   A behavior therapy technique whereby agreements are made between family members to exchange rewards for desired behavior.

countertransference   Emotional reactivity on the part of the therapist.

cross-generational coalition   An inappropriate alliance between a parent and child, who side together against a third member of the family.

culture   Common patterns of behavior and experience derived from settings in which people live.

customer   De Shazer's term for a client who not only complains about a problem ("complainant") but is motivated to resolve it.

cybernetics   The study of control processes in systems, especially the analysis of positive and negative feedback loops.

deconstruction   A postmodern approach to exploring meaning by taking apart and examining taken-for-granted categories and assumptions, making possible newer and sounder constructions of meaning.

detriangling   The process by which individuals remove themselves from the emotional field of two others.

differentiation of self   Psychological separation of intellect and emotions, and independence of self from others; opposite of fusion.

directives   Homework assignments designed to help families interrupt homeostatic patterns of problem-maintaining behavior.

disengagement   Psychological isolation that results from overly rigid boundaries around individuals and subsystems in a family.

double bind   A conflict created when a person receives contradictory messages on different levels of abstraction in an important relationship, and cannot leave or comment.

dyadic model   Explanations based on the interactions between two persons or objects: Johnny shoplifts to get his mother's attention.

emotional cutoff   Bowen's term for flight from an unresolved emotional attachment.

emotional reactivity   The tendency to respond in a knee-jerk emotional fashion, rather than calmly and objectively.

emotionally focused couples therapy   A model of therapy based on attachment theory, in which the emotional longings beneath a couple's defensive reactions are uncovered as they are taught to see the reactive nature of their struggles with each other, developed by Leslie Greenberg and Susan Johnson.

enactment   An interaction stimulated in structural family therapy in order to observe and then change transactions that make up family structure.

enmeshment   Loss of autonomy due to a blurring of psychological boundaries.

entitlement   Boszormenyi-Nagy's term for the amount of merit a person accrues for behaving in an ethical manner toward others.

epistemology   The branch of philosophy concerned with the study of knowledge. Used by Bateson to mean worldview or belief system.

equifinality   The ability of complex systems to reach a given final goal in a variety of different ways.

ethnicity   The common ancestry through which groups of people evolve shared values and customs.

exception   De Shazer's term for times when clients are temporarily free of their problems. Solution-focused therapists focus on exceptions to help clients build on successful problem-solving skills.

expressive role   Serving social and emotional functions; in traditional families, the wife's role.

extended family   The network of kin relationships across several generations.

externalization   Michael White's technique of personifying problems as external to persons.

extinction   Eliminating behavior by not reinforcing it.

family drawing   An experiential therapy technique where family members are asked to draw their ideas about how the family is organized.

family group therapy   Family treatment based on the group therapy model.

family homeostasis   Tendency of families to resist change in order to maintain a steady state.

family life cycle   Stages of family life from separation from one's parents to marriage, having children, growing older, retirement, and finally death.

family myths   A set of beliefs based on a distortion of historical reality and shared by all family members that help shape the rules governing family functioning.

family of origin   A person's parents and siblings; usually refers to the original nuclear family of an adult.

family projection process   In Bowenian theory, the mechanism by which parental conflicts are projected onto the children or a spouse.

family ritual   Technique used by Selvini Palazzoli and her Milan Associates that prescribes a specific act for family members to perform, which is designed to change the family system's rules.

family rules   A descriptive term for redundant behavioral patterns.

family structure   The functional organization of families that determines how family members interact.

family system   The family conceived as a collective whole entity made up of individual parts plus the way they function together.

feedback   The return of a portion of the output of a system, especially when used to maintain the output within predetermined limits (negative feedback), or to signal a need to modify the system (positive feedback).

first-order change   Superficial change in a system that itself stays invariant.

first-order cybernetics   The idea that an outside observer can study and make changes in a system while remaining separate and independent of that system.

fixation   Partial arrest of attachment or mode of behavior from an early stage of development.

formula first-session task   Solution-focused therapists routinely ask clients at the end of the first session to think about what they *do not* want to change as a result of therapy. This focuses them on strengths in their lives and begins the solution-generating process.

functional analysis of behavior   In operant behavior therapy, a study of a particular behavior, what elicits it, and what reinforces it.

function of the symptom   The idea that symptoms are often ways to distract or otherwise protect family members from threatening conflicts.

fusion   A blurring of psychological boundaries between self and others, and a contamination of emotional and intellectual functioning; opposite of differentiation.

general systems theory   A biological model of living systems as whole entities that maintain themselves through continuous input and output from the environment; developed by Ludwig von Bertalanffy.

genogram   A schematic diagram of the family system, using squares to represent males, circles to indicate females, horizontal lines for marriages, and vertical lines to indicate children.

group dynamics   Interactions among group members that emerge as a result of properties of the group rather than merely their individual personalities.

hermeneutics   The art of analyzing literary texts or human experience, understood as fundamentally ambiguous, by interpreting levels of meaning.

hierarchical structure   Family functioning based on clear generational boundaries, where the parents maintain control and authority.

homeostasis   A balanced steady state of equilibrium.

idealization   A tendency to exaggerate the virtues of someone, part of the normal developmental process in children's relationships to their parents and in intimate partnerships.

identification   From psychoanalytic theory, not merely imitation, but appropriation of traits of an admired other.

identified patient   The symptom-bearer or official patient as identified by the family.

instrumental role   Decision-making and task functions; in traditional families, the husband's role.

intensity   Minuchin's term for changing maladaptive transactions by using strong affect, repeated intervention, or prolonged pressure.

internal family systems therapy   A model of the mind that uses systemic principles and techniques to understand and change intrapsychic processes, developed by Richard Schwartz.

internal objects   Mental images and fantasies of oneself and others, formed by early interactions with caregivers.

introjection   A primitive form of identification; taking in aspects of other people, which then become part of the self-image.

invariant prescription   A technique developed by Mara Selvini Palazzoli in which parents are directed to mysteriously sneak away together.

invisible loyalties   Boszormenyi-Nagy's term for unconscious commitments that children take on to help their families.

joining   A structural family therapy term for accepting and accommodating to families to win their confidence and circumvent resistance.

linear causality   The idea that one event is the cause and another is the effect; in behavior, the idea that one behavior is a stimulus, the other a response.

live supervision   Technique of teaching therapy whereby the supervisor observes sessions in progress and contacts the therapist to suggest different strategies and techniques.

managed care   A system in which third-party companies manage insurance costs by regulating the terms of treatment. Managed care companies select providers, set fees, and control who receives treatment and how many sessions they are entitled to.

marital schism Lidz's term for pathological overt marital conflict.

marital skew Lidz's term for a pathological marriage in which one spouse dominates the other.

metacommunication Every message has two levels: report and command; metacommunication is the implied command or qualifying message.

miracle question Asking clients to imagine how things would be if they woke up tomorrow and their problem was solved. Solution-focused therapists use the miracle question to help clients identify goals and potential solutions.

mirroring Expression of understanding and acceptance of another's feelings.

modeling Observational learning.

monadic model Explanations based on properties of a single person or object: Johnny shoplifts because he is rebellious.

morphogenesis The process by which a system changes its structure to adapt to new contexts.

multigenerational transmission process Murray Bowen's concept for the projection of varying degrees of immaturity to different children in the same family; the child who is most involved in the family emotional process emerges with the lowest level of differentiation, and passes problems on to succeeding generations.

multiple family therapy Treatment of several families at once in a group therapy format; pioneered by Peter Laqueur and Murray Bowen.

multiple impact therapy An intensive, crisis-oriented form of family therapy developed by Robert MacGregor in which family members are treated in various subgroups by a team of therapists.

mystery questions Questions designed to get clients wondering how their problems got the best of them, which helps to externalize the problems.

mystification Laing's concept that many families distort their children's experience by denying or relabeling it.

narcissism Self-regard. The exaggerated self-regard most people equate with narcissism is pathological narcissism.

narrative therapy An approach to treatment that emphasizes the role of the stories people construct about their experience.

network therapy A treatment devised by Ross Speck in which a large number of family and friends are assembled to help resolve a patient's problems.

neutrality Selvini Palazzoli's term for balanced acceptance of family members.

nuclear family Parents and their children.

object relations Internalized images of self and others based on early parent–child interactions that determine a person's mode of relationship to other people.

object relations theory Psychoanalytic theory derived from Melanie Klein and developed by the British School (Bion, Fairbairn, Guntrip, Winnicott) that emphasizes relationships and attachment, rather than libidinal and aggressive drives, as the key issues of human concern.

operant conditioning A form of learning whereby a person or animal is rewarded for performing certain behaviors; the major approach in most forms of behavior therapy.

ordeals A type of paradoxical intervention in which the client is directed to do something that is more of a hardship than the symptom.

paradox A self-contradictory statement based on a valid deduction from acceptable premises.

paradoxical injunction A technique used in strategic therapy whereby the therapist directs family members to continue their symptomatic behavior. If they conform, they admit control and expose secondary gain; if they rebel, they give up their symptoms.

parental child A child who has been allocated power to take care of younger siblings; adaptive when done deliberately in large or single-parent families, maladaptive when it results from unplanned abdication of parental responsibility.

positive connotation Selvini Palazzoli's technique of ascribing positive motives to family behavior in order to promote family cohesion and avoid resistance to therapy.

postmodern Contemporary antipositivism, viewing knowledge as relative and context-dependent; questions assumptions of objectivity that characterize modern science. In family therapy, challenging the idea of scientific certainty, and linked to the method of deconstruction.

preferred view Eron and Lund's term for the way people would like to think of themselves and be seen by others.

Premack principle Using high-probability behavior (preferred activities) to reinforce low-probability behavior (nonpreferred activities).

prescribing the symptom A paradoxical technique that forces a patient to either give up a symptom or admit that it is under voluntary control.

pretend techniques Madanes's playful paradoxical intervention in which family members are asked to pretend to engage in symptomatic behavior. The paradox is if they are pretending to have a symptom, the symptom cannot be real.

problem-saturated stories The usual pessimistic and blaming accounts that clients bring to therapy, which are seen as helping keep them stuck.

process/content Distinction between how members of a family or group relate and what they talk about.

projective identification A defense mechanism that operates unconsciously, whereby unwanted aspects of the self are attributed to another person and that person is in-

duced to behave in accordance with these projected attitudes and feelings.

pseudohostility Wynne's term for superficial bickering that masks pathological alignments in schizophrenic families.

pseudomutuality Wynne's term for the facade of family harmony that characterizes many schizophrenic families.

psychoeducational family therapy A type of therapy developed in work with schizophrenics, which emphasizes educating family members to help them understand and cope with a seriously disturbed family member.

quid pro quo Literally, "something for something," an equal exchange or substitution.

reflecting team Tom Andersen's technique of having the observing team share their reactions with the family following a session.

reframing Relabeling a family's description of behavior to make it more amenable to therapeutic change; for example, describing someone as "lazy" rather than "depressed."

regression Return to a less mature level of functioning in the face of stress.

reinforcement An event, behavior, or object that increases the rate of a particular response. A positive reinforcer is an event whose contingent presentation increases the rate of responding; a negative reinforcer is an event whose contingent withdrawal increases the rate of responding.

reinforcement reciprocity Exchanging rewarding behaviors between family members.

relative influence questions Questions designed to explore the extent to which the problem has dominated the client versus how much he or she has been able to control it.

resistance Anything that patients or families do to oppose or retard the progress of therapy.

restraining A strategic technique for overcoming resistance by suggesting that a family not change.

role-playing   Acting out the parts of important characters to dramatize feelings and practice new ways of relating.

rubber fence   Wynne's term for the rigid boundary surrounding many schizophrenic families, which allows only minimal contact with the surrounding community.

scaling questions   Solution-focused clients are asked to rate on a 10-point scale how much they want to resolve their problems, how bad the problem is, how much better it is than the last time, and so on. Designed to break change up into small steps.

scapegoat   A member of the family, usually the identified patient, who is the object of displaced conflict or criticism.

schemas   Cognitive constructions, or core beliefs, through which people filter their perceptions and structure their experience.

schizophrenogenic mother   Frieda Fromm-Reichmann's term for aggressive, domineering mothers thought to precipitate schizophrenia in their offspring.

sculpting, family   A nonverbal experiential technique in which family members position themselves in a tableau that reveals significant aspects of their perceptions and feelings.

second-order change   Basic change in the structure and functioning of a system.

second-order cybernetics   The idea that anyone attempting to observe and change a system is therefore part of that system.

selfobject   Kohut's term for a person related to not as a separate individual, but as an extension of the self.

self psychology   Heinz Kohut's version of psychoanalysis that emphasizes the need for attachment and appreciation rather than sex and aggression.

separation-individuation   Process whereby the infant begins, at about two months, to draw apart from the symbiotic bond with mother and develop his or her autonomous functioning.

shaping   Reinforcing change in small steps.

social constructionism   Like constructivism, challenges the notion of an objective basis for knowledge. Knowledge and meaning are shaped by culturally shared assumptions.

social learning theory   Understanding and treating behavior using principles from social and developmental psychology as well as from learning theory.

solution-focused therapy   Steve de Shazer's term for a style of therapy that emphasizes the solutions that families have already developed for their problems.

structure   Recurrent patterns of interaction that define and stabilize the shape of relationships.

subsystem   Smaller units in families, determined by generation, sex, or function.

symmetrical relationship   In relationships, equality or parallel form.

system   A group of interrelated elements *plus* the way they function together.

system, closed   A functionally related group of elements regarded as forming a collective entity that does not interact with the surrounding environment.

system, open   A set of interrelated elements that exchange information, energy, and material with the surrounding environment.

systems theory   A generic term for studying a group of related elements that interact as a whole entity; encompasses general systems theory and cybernetics.

theory of social exchange   Thibaut and Kelley's theory according to which people strive to maximize rewards and minimize costs in a relationship.

three-generational hypothesis of schizophrenia   Bowen's concept that schizophrenia is the end result of low levels of differentiation passed on and amplified across three succeeding generations.

time-out   A behavioral technique for extinguishing undesirable behavior by removing the reinforcing consequences of that behavior. Typically, making the child sit in a corner or go to his or her room.

token economy A system of rewards using points, which can be accumulated and exchanged for reinforcing items or behaviors.

transference Distorted emotional reactions to present relationships based on unresolved, early family relations.

triadic model Explanations based on the interactions among three people or objects; Johnny shoplifts because his father covertly encourages him to defy his mother.

triangle A three-person system; according to Bowen, the smallest stable unit of human relations.

triangulation Detouring conflict between two people by involving a third person, sta-

bilizing the relationship between the original pair.

unconscious Memories, feelings, and impulses of which a person is unaware. Often used as a noun, but more appropriately limited to use as an adjective.

undifferentiated family ego mass Bowen's early term for emotional "stuck-togetherness" or fusion in the family, especially prominent in schizophrenic families.

unique outcome Michael White's term for times when clients acted free of their problems, even if they were unaware of doing so. Narrative therapists identify unique outcomes as a way to help clients challenge negative views of themselves.

visitor De Shazer's term for a client who does not wish to be part of therapy, does not have a complaint, and does not wish to work on anything.

Careers and Training

Becoming a Family Therapist

There are many paths to becoming a family therapist. Not all of them involve going through an academic program in marital and family therapy, although that's the most direct path. Many people who have a state marital and family therapy (MFT) license or certificate graduated with a more traditional degree— master's or Ph.D. in clinical psychology, an MSW from a social work program, or a master's in counseling or nursing. Depending on their state's requirements, these therapists, after completing their non-MFT degree, have to take some additional MFT course work and receive extensive supervision in order to be able to call themselves marital and family therapists (see the section on licensing that follows).

Which path you choose should depend on what you want to do in your career. For example, if you hope to teach or do research in family therapy, you would do well to go through a Ph.D. program. If, on the other hand, you primarily want to do clinical practice, either in an agency or in private practice, you may not need a Ph.D. and could go to one of the many master's programs in MFT (for a list of approved MFT academic programs, contact the American Association for Marriage and Family Therapy, described later).

If you're interested in studying an aspect of mental health not thoroughly covered in MFT programs, for example, psychological testing, social policy, individual psychotherapy, or psychopharmacology, you could get a non-MFT degree and then pick up the required courses and supervision from one of the many nonacademic family therapy institutes described in the last section of this appendix.

Professional Organizations

The *American Association for Marriage and Family Therapy* (AAMFT), located in Washington, DC, was organized in 1942 by Lester Dearborn and Ernest Graves as a professional organization to set standards for marriage counselors. In 1970 it was expanded to include family therapists and has become the major credentialing body for the field. Through its requirements for membership, standards have been set for becoming a family therapist that are used by the various states that regulate the profession. AAMFT also lobbies state and federal governments for the interests of family therapists, such as state licensing.

AAMFT's membership has grown enormously, reflecting the growth of the field. The organization has more than doubled since 1982 and now represents 23,000 marital and family therapists. This kind of membership and the money generated from it has made AAMFT a powerful player in mental health politics and has aided in public and governmental recognition of family therapy as a distinct field.

AAMFT has a code of ethics that covers the following issues: responsibility to clients; confidentiality; professional competence and integrity; responsibility to students, employees, supervisees, and research subjects; financial arrangements; and advertising. AAMFT is located at 1133 15th Street NW, Suite 300, Washington, DC 20005-2710; telephone: 202-452-0109; Web site: http://www.aamft.org.

Although the AAMFT has a presence in California, the dominant organization for MFTs there is the California Association of Marriage and Family Therapists (CAMFT). With twenty-nine regional chapters and 25,000 members, CAMFT's size has given it a strong voice in the state legislature. CAMFT sponsors an annual conference and publishes the *California Therapist*. For further information, contact CAMFT, 7901 Raytheon Road, San Diego, CA 92111; telephone: 619-292-2638; Web site: http://www.camft.org.

The *American Family Therapy Academy* (AFTA) was organized in 1977 to serve the needs of the field's senior researchers, clinicians, and trainers who wanted a smaller, more intimate context for sharing ideas and developing common interests. Despite high standards for membership regarding years of teaching and clinical experience, and an interest in remaining small, AFTA's membership has doubled since 1983, from 500 to over 1,000. AFTA is a high-level think tank focused around its annual conference, described below, and its newsletter. For more information, contact AFTA, 2020 Pennsylvania Avenue NW, #273, Washington, DC 20006; telephone: 202-994-2776.

The *International Family Therapy Association* (IFTA) was begun in 1986 as a way for family therapists around the globe to connect. Each year IFTA sponsors the World Family Therapy Congress in a different country. So far the countries that have hosted the congress include Finland, Greece, Holland, Ireland, Israel, Hungary, Mexico, and Poland. In addition, IFTA biannually publishes a newsletter, *The International Connection*. IFTA can be reached at the Akron Child Guidance Center, 312 Locust Street, Akron, OH 44302.

Conferences

Besides the multitude of workshops or conferences privately sponsored or put on by local chapters of AAMFT, there are four main national meetings. The largest is AAMFT's annual conference each October. With over 200 presentations on various family therapy topics to select from, there is usually something for everyone.

The second largest (over 2,000) is the Family Therapy Network Symposium held each March in Washington, DC. Sponsored by the *Family Therapy Networker* magazine (described later), all presenters are invited so that quality throughout the eighty workshops is ensured. Each year the symposium has a theme, and invited plenary speakers are often famous for work done outside the field of family therapy. For information, telephone: 202-829-2452.

AFTA's annual meeting deliberately has a flavor different from that of other conferences. Because of its small size (usually around 300—it's not open to nonmembers), it's the one place where leaders of the field can gather in a relatively informal setting to discuss ideas. Rather than workshops, the meeting is organized around interest groups and brief presentations designed to promote dialogue and debate.

The other conference where many family therapists can be found isn't devoted exclusively to family therapy. The American

Orthopsychiatric Association is a multidisciplinary organization whose annual conference usually contains a sizable percentage of presentations devoted to family therapy and issues of interest to systems-oriented clinicians.

Publications

The first book devoted entirely to the diagnosis and treatment of families was Nathan Ackerman's the *Psychodynamics of Family Life*, published in 1958. The field's first journal, *Family Process*, was founded in 1961. Since these early publications, the family therapy literature has proliferated to the point where it is virtually impossible to stay on top of it. We count over twenty journals or newsletters devoted to some aspect of family therapy published in the United States, with many other countries publishing their own journals. The number of books is equally overwhelming, so we refer the reader to Appendix A, *Recommended Readings* for a selective guide to some of the most useful books and articles in the field. We describe some of the major periodicals in the following discussion.

Family Process continues to exert a powerful influence on the field. Many of the debates and developments described in earlier chapters of this book appeared first in its pages. Founded in 1961 by Don Jackson and Nathan Ackerman, its editors have included Jay Haley, Don Bloch, Carlos Sluzki, Peter Steinglass, and Carol Anderson. The *Journal of Marital and Family Therapy* is also quite influential and, as the official journal of AAMFT, has a large readership. Under the editorship of Alan Gurman during the 1980s and Douglas Sprenkle and Froma Walsh in the 1990s, it increased its focus on research and improved its standards. Current editor, Karen Wampler, is balancing the research and clinical foci.

The *Psychotherapy Networker*, a magazine devoted to issues related to family therapy and psychotherapy in general, also has a strong influence. Its large readership (over 70,000) has

been won through tackling provocative issues with high-quality writing. Rich Simon has turned what began as a small newsletter into the most widely read publication on psychotherapy and, in so doing, has introduced many of family therapy's ideas to therapists throughout the country. In 1993, the *Networker* won the American Magazine Award for feature writing, the highest honor possible for a magazine.

There are a number of other well-established journals that, like *Family Process* and *Journal of Marital and Family Therapy*, are devoted to general issues in the field. These include the *American Journal of Family Therapy, Journal of Family Psychotherapy, International Journal of Family Therapy, Contemporary Family Therapy*, and *Family Therapy Collections*. In addition, a number of specialized journals have emerged. For example, the *Journal of Systemic Therapies* (formerly the *Journal of Strategic and Systemic Therapies*) is widely read by therapists who use those adjectives to describe themselves, while Bowen systems therapists read *Family Systems* and those interested in Michael White's work subscribe to the *Dulwich Centre Review* and *Family Therapy Case Studies*.

The cross-fertilization of family therapy with other fields is represented by *Family Systems Medicine*, a journal devoted to the collaboration between medicine and family therapy; by the *Journal of Family Psychology*, published by a division of the American Psychological Association; and by *Feminism and Family Therapy*, which reflects the growing influence of feminist thought on the field.

News within the field and digests of important developments are conveyed through AAMFT's newsletter, *Family Therapy News*, and through the *Marriage and Family Review* and the *Brown University Family Therapy Newsletter*. Those interested in the branch of sociology called family studies have much in common with family therapists and read *Family Relations* and the *Journal of Marriage and the Family*.

Licensing

Thirty-seven states currently regulate MFTs, and several other states are currently considering licensing bills. The number of states licensing or certifying MFTs has more than tripled in the past decade. Most state requirements for licensure are comparable to the standards for Clinical Membership in AAMFT. Common requirements include graduation from an accredited marital and family therapy program, two years of post-degree supervised clinical experience, and passing the state exam (eighteen states require this) or the national exam for MFTs, which is conducted by the Association of Marital and Family Therapy Regulatory Board and used by the remaining nineteen states.

Training Centers

As discussed earlier, family therapy developed primarily outside academia. There are, however, a handful of doctoral programs and a larger number of master's degree programs specializing in marital and family therapy in universities around the country. The American Association for Marriage and Family Therapy accredits twenty-nine master's programs and ten doctoral programs and can provide a list of them. Because we are aware of no comparable list of the major nonacademic training centers we will describe some of the best-known centers in the United States here. Although other major centers exist throughout the world, our space is too limited to list them here. The reader may notice that the majority of the centers described are clustered in the Northeast where family therapy is most strongly rooted. We will begin there and move west.

The *Family Institute of Cambridge* in Massachusetts was founded in 1976. Now located in Watertown, it is a nonprofit center of training and research in applied systems theory. Faculty members include such notable therapists as Michele Bograd, Laura Chasin, Richard Chasin,

Terry Real, Kathy Weingarten, and Sallyann Roth. The institute offers four training sequences: (1) narrative approaches, (2) family systems theory, (3) couples therapy, and (4) women's group process. The institute also offers a wide variety of long- and short-term courses, group supervision, and conferences; it has some research stipends for its students. For more information, contact Suzanne Bourque, 51 Kondazian Street, Watertown, MA 02172.

The *Kantor Family Institute*, in Somerville, Massachusetts, was founded by David Kantor after he left the Family Institute of Cambridge in 1980, and is informed by his structural/analytic model of therapy, as well as by psychodynamic and other family therapy influences. This institute offers a sequence of three one-year training programs that build on each other but can be taken independently. They also offer a specialized program in couples treatment and in organizational consultation, as well as a variety of apprenticeships, internships, and courses. For more information, contact Ulrike Dettling, Kantor Family Institute, 7 Sheppard Street, Cambridge, MA 02138.

The *Minuchin Center for the Family* is a small, private training institution in New York City, founded in 1981 by Salvador Minuchin. The faculty also includes David Greenan, Richard Holm, and Wai-Yung Lee. Special programs are designed for on-site training and consultation with agencies that work with poor families, foster care, substance abuse, the homeless, and children in psychiatric facilities. The year-long extern training program is at three levels: beginning family therapists, more experienced therapists, and administrators and supervisors. The orientation emphasizes structural family therapy but has been influenced by feminism and multiculturalism. Inquiries may be directed to David Greenan, 114 East 32nd Street, 4th Floor, New York, NY 10016.

The *Ackerman Institute for the Family* in New York City was founded as the Family Institute by Nathan Ackerman in 1960. Following

Ackerman's death in 1971, the center was renamed in his honor and the directorship was assumed by Donald Bloch, who passed the baton to Peter Steinglass. In addition to Bloch and Steinglass, the institute has such noted family therapists and theorists as Peggy Penn, Peggy Papp, Jorge Colapinto, Olga Silverstein, Marcia Sheinberg, Virginia Goldner, Peter Fraenkel, and Gillian Walker. The institute offers training in systemic family therapy. It offers a two-year clinical externship program for more experienced family therapists and workshops throughout the year. For further information contact Marcia Sheinberg, Director of Training, 149 East 78th Street, New York, NY 10021.

The *Family Institute of Westchester* is directed by Elliott Rosen. The institute teaches the multicontextual approach, which includes aspects of structural and strategic techniques, and is based on the Bowenian model. The institute has been in operation since 1977 and is primarily known for its training program, which usually takes two years to complete. There is also a two-year advanced program that meets weekly. Specialized training programs are offered in multicultural family therapy and therapy with gay and lesbian couples and families. Additional information is available from Pat Colluci, Director of Training, Family Institute of Westchester, 7-11 South Broadway, Suite 400, White Plains, NY 10601.

The *Center for Family Learning* in Rye Brook, New York, was founded in 1973 by Philip Guerin, who was trained by Murray Bowen. The center provides a three-year training program in family systems therapy, which includes a clinical externship year for experienced clinicians, followed by a fellowship year with center faculty working on the Child and Adolescents Project. The third year is another fellowship, studying marital conflict. The center also offers a variety of seminars and workshops and a Community Education Program, which is taped for cable television. For additional information, contact Eileen Guerin Pendagast, Director of Post Graduate and Community Education, 16 Rye Ridge Plaza, Rye Brook, NY 10573.

The *Family Therapy Training Program at the University of Rochester* was established in 1983 by Judith Landau-Stanton and M. Duncan Stanton. This program teaches the Rochester Model, an integration of structural, strategic, transgenerational, experiential, and ecosystemic approaches in a series of externships and seminars. Special areas of interest are cultural transition and medical family therapy. Cases are provided for trainees. The faculty includes Lyman Wynne, Susan McDaniel, David Seaburn, and the founders. For more information, contact David Seaburn, Family Therapy Training Program, Department of Psychiatry, University of Rochester, 300 Crittenden Boulevard, Rochester, NY 14642–8409.

The *Family Institute of New Jersey* was founded in 1991 by its director, Monica McGoldrick. It is committed to training, research, and service in support of cultural diversity and the empowerment of those voices our society silences. In addition to a three-year certificate program, the institute offers a variety of workshops, lectures to the community, and consultation to schools and other organizations. Minority scholarships are available. Faculty includes notable therapists such as Nydia Garcia Preto, Rhea Almeida, Paulette Moore Hines, Eliana Gil and Charlesetta Hutton. For further information, contact Monica McGoldrick, 312 Amboy Avenue, Metuchen, NJ 08840.

The *Family Therapy Institute of Washington, DC*, is the training center and clinic codirected by Jay Haley and Cloe Madanes, until recently when Haley retired. Faculty members teach, supervise, and conduct therapy emphasizing the strategic, problem-focused approach. The institute clinic offers treatment by a multidisciplinary staff, all of whom have previously trained with Haley and Madanes. Inquiries may be made to James Keim, Family Therapy

Institute of Washington, DC, 5850 Hubbard Drive, Rockville, MD 20852.

The *Georgetown Family Center*, located in Washington, DC, exists to refine, test, extend, and define Bowen systems theory. Murray Bowen founded and directed this center until his death in 1990. The current director is Michael Kerr. Training programs include a weekly postgraduate program and a special program for out-of-towners that meets for three consecutive days, four times a year. Other learning opportunities include the monthly Clinical Conference Series and the annual Main Symposium. Descriptions of these programs are available from Georgetown Family Center, 4400 MacArthur Boulevard NW, Suite 103, Washington, DC 20007.

The *Family Therapy Practice Center of Washington, DC,* was founded in 1980 by Marianne Walters, after she left the Philadelphia Child Guidance Clinic. The center has a structural family therapy base and offers a postgraduate externship. In addition, the center develops programs for dealing with at-risk populations and changing family structures such as their adolescent foster care project, family violence assistance project, and runaway youth/multiple family group project. For more information, contact Director of Training, 2153 Newport Place NW, Washington, DC 20037.

The *Philadelphia Child and Family Guidance Training Center, Inc.,* was created in the late 1990s after the training programs at the famous Philadelphia Child Guidance Center were discontinued. Most of the new center's faculty taught at the old center and worked there with Salvador Minuchin as he developed structural family therapy. That faculty includes notable structural therapists: Marion Lindblad-Goldberg, Charles Fishman, Gordon Hodas, and Ruth Sefarbi. The center runs a two-year postgraduate program, three-week summer practica, and a supervision-of-supervision course. For more information contact Marion Lindblad-Goldberg, Director, Philadelphia Child and Family Guid-

ance Training Center, Inc. P. O. Box 4092, Philadelphia, PA 19118–8092.

The *Brief Family Therapy Center* (BFTC) of Milwaukee is known for its specialization in the research, training, and clinical practice of brief, solution-focused therapy. BFTC provides short- and long-term training in solution-focused therapy that attracts practitioners from across North America, Europe, and Asia. The staff includes Steve de Shazer and Insoo Kim Berg, who have presented workshops and seminars in more than thirty countries and have written extensively on solution-focused therapy. For further information, contact Brief Family Therapy Center, P. O. Box 13736, Milwaukee, WI 53213.

The *Family Institute* (formerly of Chicago) was founded in 1968 by Charles Kramer to provide training, research, and clinical services. William Pinsof is the president of the institute, which probably has the largest full-time faculty in the country, including notable family therapists Douglas Breunlin, Cheryl Rampage, Jay Lebow, and Richard Schwartz. They offer a variety of training programs grounded in a multilevel, integrative approach. Elements of the approach include integrative problem-centered therapy, the metaframeworks perspective, the internal family systems model, feminism, and multiculturalism. They offer a master's program in family therapy in affiliation with Northwestern University, and a one-year clinical training practicum, a postdoctoral fellowship, and training programs in internal family systems therapy. In 1994 the institute opened a spacious new facility in Evanston, Illinois. For more information, contact Jenn Pilewski, 618 Library Place, Evanston, IL 60201.

The *Chicago Center for Family Health* (CCFH) was begun in 1991 by codirectors John Rolland and Froma Walsh. Affiliated with the University of Chicago, the center's orientation integrates systems theory with a multigenerational family life-cycle framework. In addition to general training in family therapy, CCFH offers specialized training in couples therapy, divorce mediation, and medical family therapy. Training programs include a two-year certificate program, workshops, courses, and consultation groups. Faculty also include other notable family therapists such as Gene Combs, Jill Freedman, and Tom Todd. For more information, contact John Rolland, CCFH, North Pier, Suite 651, 445 E. Illinois Street, Chicago, IL 60611.

The *Houston Galveston Institute,* a private, nonprofit organization, was founded in 1977 by Harlene Anderson and the late Harry Goolishian. The orientation of the institute is a "collaborative language systems approach" that emphasizes openness, sharing of clinical experiences, live consultation, and observation of faculty work. Programs include (1) residential (fellowships, internships, and apprenticeships); (2) external programs (externships, seminars, supervision, and workshops); and (3) international visitor study programs. For more information, contact Susan Levin, 3316 Mount Vernon, Houston, TX 77006.

The *Mental Research Institute* (MRI) in Palo Alto, California, was founded in 1969 by the late Don Jackson and is considered one of the birthplaces of family therapy. The MRI is best known for its brief therapy approach to families. Its faculty includes such notable names as Paul Watzlawick, Richard Fisch, and Arthur Bodin. The MRI offers a wide variety of training programs, including workshops, continuing seminars, four- or six-week residency programs, and programs in brief therapy or in Michael White's approach. A program for onsite training has also begun recently. For further information, contact Karin Schlanger, Director of Training, 555 Middlefield Road, Palo Alto, CA 94301.

Credits

Page 5, National Library of Medicine; Page 12, Michael Newman/PhotoEdit; Page 23, Photo courtesy of Lyman Wynne and used with his permission; Page 28, Photo courtesy of Wendel Ray. Used by permission of the Jackson Estate and the Don D. Jackson Archive, MRI; Page 66, Laura Dwight/PhotoEdit; Page 68, David Kelly Crow/PhotoEdit; Page 82, Zefa-UK/Corbis Stock Market; Page 111, Photo courtesy of the Psychotherapy Networker. Used by permission of Monica Mc-Goldrick; Page 115, Jose Luis Pelaez/Corbis Stock Market; Page 120 (left), Photo courtesy of the Psychotherapy Networker and Andrea Maloney Schara. Used by permission of Andrea Maloney Schara; Page 120 (right), Photo courtesy of the Psychotherapy Networker. Used by permission of Philip J. Guerin; Page 125, Photo courtesy of Betty Carter and used with her permission; Page 136, Stephen Simpson/Getty Images; Page 150, Photo provided courtesy of the Erickson Fdtn., Inc. and reprinted with their permission; Page 164, Photo courtesy of the Erickson Fdtn., Inc. Used by permission of Jay Haley; Page 165, Photo courtesy of Cloe Madanes and used with her permission; Page 177, Photo courtesy of the Psychotherapy Networker. Used by permission of Salvador Minuchin; Page 187, Frank Pedrick/The Image Works; Page 205, Photo courtesy of the Psychotherapy Networker. Used by permission of Muriel V. Whitaker; Page 213, Photo courtesy of the Psychotherapy Networker. Used by permission of Avanta, The Virginia Satir Network; Page 217, Greg Ceo/Getty Images; Page 219, Photo courtesy of the Psychotherapy Networker. Used by permission of Susan Johnson; Page 232, Myrleen Ferguson Cate/PhotoEdit; Page 242, Photo courtesy of the Psychotherapy Networker. Used by permission of Jill and David Scharff; Page 256, Bob Daemmrich/The Image Works; Page 261, Amy C. Etra/PhotoEdit; Page 265, Laurie Rubin/Getty Images; Page 291, Photo courtesy of the Psychotherapy Networker. Used by permission of Peggy Papp, Olga Silverstein, Marianne Walters, and Betty Carter; Page 295 (top), Photo courtesy of the Psychotherapy Networker. Used by permission of Nancy Boyd-Franklin; Page 295 (bottom), Photo courtesy of the Psychotherapy Networker. Used by permission of Ken Hardy; Page 296, Michael Newman/PhotoEdit; Page 313 (top), Photo courtesy of Steve de Shazer and used with his permission; Page 313 (bottom), Photo courtesy of Insoo Kim Berg and used with her permission; Page 330, Photo courtesy of Michael White and used with his permission; Page 334, Robert Clay; Page 353 (left), Photo courtesy of the Psychotherapy Networker. Used by permission of Joe Eron; Page 353 (right), Photo courtesy of the Psychotherapy Networker. Used by permission of Tom Lund; Page 362 (top), Photo courtesy of

453

the Psychotherapy Networker. Used by permission of Virginia Goldner; Page 362 (bottom), Esbin-Anderson/The Image Works; Page 373, Richard Lord/The Image Works; Page 404, Photo courtesy of Jose Szaponcznik and used with his permission.

Name Index

Subject Index

in Bowen family systems therapy, 386
in comparative analysis, 385–387
in solution-focused therapy, 386
in strategic family therapy, 386
Family therapy, 27, 63
  behavior disorders and, 55–56
  child guidance movement and, 15–17
  circular causality in, 106
  complementarity in, 105–106
  conditions for behavior change, 56–57
  critical change events in, 415–416
  culture in, 114–116
  for depression and anxiety
    family-based treatment, 401–404
    family risk and protective factors for, 401
  for eating disorders, 410–411, 411
    family-based interventions for, 411
    family risk and protective factors, 410–411
  evolution of, 10–44
  family life cycle in, 109–112
  family narratives in, 113
  family structure in, 107–108
  foundations of, 1–9
  fundamental concepts of, 91–116
  gender in, 113–114, 416–417
  golden age of, 41–44
  group dynamics and, 11–15
  identifying mechanisms of therapeutic change in, 414–415
  importance of roles in, 61–62
  individual therapy versus, 6–7
  influence of social work on, 17–18
  major events in history of, xi–xv
  marital violence and, 81–84
  marriage counseling and, 25–27
  meaning (function) of symptoms, 109
  multiple, 58, 62–63
  parent-centered stage in, 58
  pioneers of, 27–41
  positive control in, 389–390
  power of, 7–8
  process/content in, 108–109
  process investigations in, 62, 417–418

process of therapeutic alliance formulation in, 414
psychology and social context of, 7
resistance in, 112–113
for schizophrenia
  family-based interventions for, 409–410
  family risk and protection factors, 408–409
sexual abuse of children, 84–86
stages of
  early phase of treatment, 70–71
  first interview, 67–70
  initial telephone call, 66–67
  middle phase of treatment, 71–72
  termination, 72–73
for substance use disorders
  family-based interventions, 406–407
  family risk and protective factors, 404–406
techniques of, 58–59
theoretical formulations in, 52–53
triangles in, 106–107
in the twenty-first century, 288–307
  constructivism, 292
  erosion of boundaries, 288–289
  family violence, 294
  feminism, 290–292
  gay and lesbian rights, 298
  hermeneutics, 292–293
  home-based services, 300–302
  managed care, 305
  medical family therapy, 304
  multiculturalism, 294–295
  narrative therapy, 293
  postmodernism, 289–290
  poverty and social class, 297
  psychoeducation, 302–304
  race, 295–297
  social constructionism, 293
  solution-focused therapy, 293–294
  spirituality, 298–299
  tailoring treatment to populations and problems, 299–300
working concepts of, 105–116
Family Therapy Case Studies, 448

Family Therapy Collections, 448
Family Therapy Institute of Washington, DC,
    151, 450–451
Family Therapy Networker, 447
Family Therapy News, 448
Family Therapy Practice Center of
    Washington, DC, 451
Family therapy research, advances in,
    395–420
  for childhood and adolescent behavior
    disorders, 397–400
  for depression and anxiety, 401–404
  for eating disorders, 410–411
  for marital and couples therapy, 411–414
  for schizophrenia, 408–410
  for substance use disorders, 404–408
Family Therapy Training Program at the
    University of Rochester, 450
Family violence, 294, 361–363
Feedback, 63
  in communications family therapy, 63
  in cybernetics, 92, 93–94
  negative, 63, 153, 154
  positive, 55, 154, 156
  in strategic family therapy, 153, 154, 156
Feedback loops, 153
  positive, 153
Feminism, 289, 290–292, 306
  on enmeshment, 183
  in family therapy, 121
  gender inequality and, 373–374
Feminism and Family Therapy, 448
Field theory, 12, 52–53
Fight-flight, 12
First-order change, 153
First-order cybernetics, 306, 385–386
Fixation, in psychoanalytic family therapy,
    237
Focusing, 391
Formula tasks in solution-focused therapy,
    318
Freudian drive psychology, 230
Friendly visitor movement, 17, 300
Functional analysis of behavior, 253, 389

Functional family therapy, 169–170, 260,
    399–400
Fused relationships, 120
Fusion, 374–375

Gay and lesbian rights, 298
Gender
  in family assessment, 76–77
  in family therapy, 113–114,
    416–417
  feminism and, 290–292, 373–374
General systems theory, 53, 55, 64, 65,
    96–97
  closed systems in, 96
  equifinality in, 96
  morphogenesis in, 96
  on normal family development, 154
  open systems in, 96
Genograms, 67, 73
  in Bowen family systems therapy, 132–134,
    145
Georgetown Family Center, 121, 451
Gestalt therapy, 14
Good-enough mothering, 232
Good faith contract, in cognitive-behavioral
    family therapy, 271–272
Group dynamics, 55, 61
Group for the Advancement of Psychiatry
    (GAP), 24
Group process, 14

Haley and Madanes approach, to strategic
    family therapy, 163–167
Here-and-now experience, 204
Hermeneutics, 292–293
Hero, myth of, 3–4
Hierarchy in family, in strategic family
    therapy, 154
Home-based services, 300–302
  case management in, 300
  case study in, 301
  crisis intervention in, 300
  family support services in, 300
  therapeutic intervention in, 300